Spencer Bower and Handley: Res Judicata

'What I have written I have written.' John 19:22

BUTTERWORTHS COMMON LAW SERIES

Spencer Bower and Handley

Res Judicata

Fourth Edition

The Honourable Mr Justice KR Handley
Officer of the Order of Australia,
BA, LLB, LLD (Honoris Causa) (Sydney),
Honorary Bencher of Lincoln's Inn,
Visiting Fellow, Wolfson College, Cambridge
A Judge of the Court of Appeal of New South Wales

Series editor
Andrew Grubb MA (Cantab), LLD (Lond), FMedSci
Senior Immigration Judge, Asylum and Immigration Tribunal; Visiting
Professor of Law, Cardiff Law School, Cardiff University

LexisNexis®

Members of the LexisNexis Group worldwide

United Kingdom	LexisNexis, a Division of Reed Elsevier (UK) Ltd, Halsbury House, 35 Chancery Lane, London, WC2A 1EL, and London House, 20–22 East London Street, Edinburgh EH7 4BQ
Australia	LexisNexis Butterworths, Chatswood, New South Wales
Austria	LexisNexis Verlag ARD Orac GmbH & Co KG, Vienna
Benelux	LexisNexis Benelux, Amsterdam
Canada	LexisNexis Canada, Markham, Ontario
China	LexisNexis China, Beijing and Shanghai
France	LexisNexis SA, Paris
Germany	LexisNexis Deutschland GmbH, Munster
Hong Kong	LexisNexis Hong Kong, Hong Kong
India	LexisNexis India, New Delhi
Italy	Giuffrè Editore, Milan
Japan	LexisNexis Japan, Tokyo
Malaysia	Malayan Law Journal Sdn Bhd, Kuala Lumpur
New Zealand	LexisNexis NZ Ltd, Wellington
Poland	Wydawnictwo Prawnicze LexisNexis Sp, Warsaw
Singapore	LexisNexis Singapore, Singapore
South Africa	LexisNexis Butterworths, Durban
USA	LexisNexis, Dayton, Ohio

© Reed Elsevier (UK) Ltd 2009

Reprinted 2013

Published by LexisNexis

This is a Butterworths title

A CIP Catalogue record for this book is available from the British Library.

ISBN 978 1 4057 2673 3

ISBN 978-1-4057-2673-3

9 781405 726733

Typeset by Letterpart Ltd, Reigate, Surrey

Printed in the UK by CPI Group (UK) Ltd, Croydon, CR0 4YY

Visit LexisNexis at www.lexisnexis.co.uk

Preface

It is thirteen years since the last edition, and it was time for a new one. Significant developments in the interval justified this but there also were other reasons. The cases on which I sat, other reported cases, and further reflection made me aware of gaps in the coverage of the subject. There was the need, pointed out by Sir Andrew Longmore in his review of the last edition ((1999) 115 LQR 150), for an introduction 'which deals with the terminology and treatment of the subject.' There was also the need for separate chapters for cause of action and issue estoppel.

The significant developments included *Aegis Ltd v European Re* [2003] 1 WLR 1041 where the Privy Council held that a *res judicata* estoppel is a substantive right; *Pinochet (No2)* [2000] 1 AC 119 and *Taylor v Lawrence* [2003] QB 528 CA which dealt with the power of a court to recall its orders before and after their formal entry, a topic not covered in previous editions; *R v Beedie* [1998] QB 356 CA which simplified the law relating to *autrefois acquit* and *convict*; *R v Z* [2000] 2 AC 483 which significantly narrowed the principle in *Sambasivam v Public Prosecutor* [1950] AC 458 that the prosecution may not lead evidence which challenges an acquittal; *Johnson v Gore Wood & Co* [2002] 2 AC 1 which brought the extended *res judicata* doctrine within proper limits after *Yat Tung* [1975] AC 581; and *Pattni v Ali* [2007] 2 AC 85 dealing with judgments *in personam* and *in rem*.

In *Cambridge Gas* [2007] 1 AC 508 the Privy Council added a new category of decisions on the collective enforcement of the rights of creditors to the established categories of decisions *in personam* and *in rem*. This is criticised as contrary to a decision of the House of Lords and unnecessary because the appellant was a privy who had stood by and allowed its battle in New York to be fought by others in the same interest. The controversial decision in *The Indian Endurance* [1998] AC 878 abolished the rule that Admiralty actions *in rem* and *in personam* were cumulative remedies against different defendants. *Powell v Wiltshire* [2005] QB 117 CA established that the purchaser of personal property *pendente lite* was not bound by the later judgment, and *Unilin Beheer BV v Berry Floor BV* [2008] 1 All ER 156 CA clarified the scope of cause of action estoppels in a patent infringement case.

Legislation in 1996 and 2003 significantly eroded the common law principle that an acquittal on the merits could not be challenged or reopened and cases on the 2003 Act have now been reported. There has also been substantial legislation from the Council of Europe. Regulation 1346/2000 dealt with jurisdiction and the recognition of judgments in insolvency proceedings. Regulation 44/2001 dealt with jurisdiction and the recognition of other civil judgments, displacing the Brussels Convention and much of the Civil Jurisdiction and Judgments Act 1982. Regulation 2201/2003 dealt with jurisdiction and the recognition of judgments in matrimonial proceedings. The High Court of Ireland has held in *Re Cedarlease Ltd* [2005] 1 IR 470 that Art 39 of Council Regulation 1346/2000 abolished within Europe the rule denying recognition and enforcement to foreign revenue debts applied in *Government of India v Taylor* [1955] AC 491.

In *Drouot Assurances SA v Consolidated Metallurgical Industries* [1999] QB 497 the European Court of Justice held that an insurer exercising rights of subrogation in the name of the insured and the latter are different parties if their interests conflict. This should encourage a re-examination of English authority to the contrary. Decisions culminating in *Watt v Ahsan* [2008] 1 AC 696 have confirmed the narrowness of the special circumstances exception for issue estoppel.

Previous criticisms have been maintained for decisions recognising a wide scope for issue estoppels in road accident cases and no scope for them in judicial review. *Taylor v Lawrence* [2003] QB 528 CA is criticised because the perfected orders from the first decision created a cause of action estoppel, and *Arnold v National Westminster Bank plc* [1991] 2 AC established that this bar is absolute.

The text has been thoroughly revised and where necessary rewritten in the interests of brevity, clarity and accuracy. The Introduction in Chapter 1 is new, as are Chapters 7 and 8 dealing with Cause of Action Estoppel and Issue Estoppel. Chapters 5 (Finality), 9 (Parties to decisions *in personam*), 11 (Judgments as evidence), 12 (Road traffic cases), 14 (*Autrefois acquit*), 23 (*Autrefois convict*) and 26 (The extended *res judicata* doctrine) have been substantially rewritten and incorporate much new material. Unlike my pre-decessors I have had the opportunity in a second edition to rectify errors and omissions in the first.

The book attempts to be an accurate statement of the law of England, but as before, cases have been included from elsewhere in the United Kingdom, Ireland, Canada, Australia, New Zealand, the United States, and I have discovered even more Privy Council decisions in Indian appeals. There are also cases from Hong Kong, Malaysia, Singapore and South Africa.

In 1815 Savigny wrote (118 LQR at 151) that the purpose of legal scholarship was the adaptation and rejuvenation of inherited legal materials, creating an indissoluble community with the past, and fostering organic legal development. Those are the aims of this book.

K.R. Handley
Chambers
October 2009

Series Preface

The common law is justifiably seen as a jewel in the crown of English law. The common law has travelled far afield to many other countries where it has been adopted and developed by the local courts. No longer the sole preserve of the judges in London (or Edinburgh and Cardiff), its durability and richness has been due in no small way to the diversity of approach that exists between the common law countries throughout the world. Many of the great judges in England, such as Coke, Mansfield, Blackburn, Atkin, Devlin, Reid and Denning, and those from overseas such as Oliver Wendell Holmes, Benjamin Cardozo and Owen Dixon, have been masters of the common law. As we enter the new Millennium, the common law continues to influence the development of law elsewhere. It will remain a major export, but now also an import, of this country.

Butterworths Common Law Series conceives of the common law in broad terms, providing analyses of the principles informing the frameworks of the law derived from judicial decisions and legislation. The *Series* seeks to provide authoritative accounts of the common law for legal practitioners, judges and academics. While providing a clear and authoritative exposition of the existing law, the Series also aims to identify and examine potential developments in the common law drawing on important and significant jurisprudence from other common law jurisdictions. Judges have increasingly looked to academic works for guidance on the accepted view of the law but also when contemplating a reformulation or change of direction in the law. The *Series* may, it is hoped, provide some assistance such that the law is less likely to be left undeveloped 'marching ... in the rear limping a little', to quote a famous judicial aphorism (*Mount Isa Mines v Pusey* (1970) per Windeyer J).

Andrew Grubb

Contents

Contents

Chapter 3 Proof of the judicial decision

Chapter 4 Jurisdiction

Chapter 5 Finality

Contents

xii

Chapter 9 Parties to decisions in personam

Contents

Chapter 10 Parties II: decisions in rem

Chapter 11 Judgments as evidence

Chapter 12 Road traffic cases

Chapter 13 Taxation and rating

Contents

Chapter 17 Affirmative answers

Chapter 18 Pleading and procedure

Part 2 Merger in judgment

Contents

List of abbreviations

1920 Act	Administration of Justice Act 1920
1933 Act	Foreign Judgments (Reciprocal Enforcement) Act 1933
1935 Act	Law Reform (Married Women and Tortfeasors) Act 1935
1945 Act	Law Reform (Contributory Negligence) Act 1945
1968 Act	Civil Evidence Act 1968
1978 Act	Civil Liability (Contribution) Act 1978
1982 Act	Civil Jurisdiction and Judgments Act 1982
1984 Act	Police and Criminal Evidence Act 1984
1986 Act	Insolvency Act 1986
1996 Act	Arbitration Act 1996
Anshun	*Port of Melbourne Authority v Anshun Pty Ltd* (1981) 147 CLR 589
Daera Guba	*Administration of Papua and New Guinea v Daera Guba* (1972) 130 CLR 353
Duke of Buccleuch	*Duke of Buccleuch v Metropolitan Board of Works* (1870) LR 5 Exch 221
Hope	*Society of Medical Officers v Hope* [1960] AC 551
Personal Representatives of Tang Man Sit	*Personal Representatives of Tang Man Sit v Capacious Investments Ltd* [1996] AC 514
Sneath	*IRC v Sneath* [1932] 2 KB 362
Spring Gardens	*House of Spring Gardens v Waite* [1991] 1 QB 241 CA

Table of Statutes

Table of Statutes

Table of Statutory Instruments

Table of European Legislation

Table of External Cases by Jurisdiction

Table of External Cases by Jurisdiction

Table of External Cases by Jurisdiction

CANADA

Table of External Cases by Jurisdiction

IRELAND

NORTHERN IRELAND

SCOTLAND

SINGAPORE

SOUTH AFRICA

USA

Consolidated Table of Cases

A

l

G

W

X

Y

Decisions of the European Court of Justice are listed below numerically. These decisions are
also included in the preceding alphabetical list.

Chapter 1

INTRODUCTION

1.01 A *res judicata* is a decision pronounced by a judicial or other tribunal with jurisdiction over the cause of action and the parties, which disposes once and for all of the fundamental matters decided, so that, except on appeal, they cannot be re-litigated between persons bound by the judgment. A judgment *in personam* binds the parties and their privies[1], and because this is so basic it will generally be assumed in what follows. A judgment *in rem* is binding on all, party, privy or otherwise[2].

[1] Chapter 9.
[2] Chapter 10.

ELEMENTS OF RES JUDICATA ESTOPPEL[1]

1.02 A party setting up a *res judicata* as an estoppel against his opponent's claim or defence, or as the foundation of his own, must establish its constituent elements[2], namely that:

(i)   the decision, whether domestic or foreign, was judicial in the relevant sense;
(ii) it was in fact pronounced;
(iii) the tribunal had jurisdiction over the parties and the subject matter;
(iv) the decision was –
    (a)   final;
    (b)   on the merits;
(v)   it determined a question raised in the later litigation; and
(vi) the parties are the same or their privies, or the earlier decision was *in rem*[3].

[1] This paragraph from the second edition was cited in *R v Duhamel (No 2)* (1981) 131 DLR (3d), 352–356 Alta CA, affd (1984) 14 DLR (4th) 92 SC and in *Midland Bank Trust Co Ltd v Green* [1980] Ch 590 CA, 607.
[2] *Marginson v Blackburn Borough Council* [1939] 2 KB 426 CA, 438 (*Marginson*); *Leong v Hock Hua Bank Bhd* [2008] 3 MLJ 340, 352–353; *Chong v Leow* [2008] 6 MLJ 781 CA, 787–790.
[3] *Shaw v Sloan* [1982] N1 393 CA, 397 per Lowry CJ: 'The entire corpus of authority on issue estoppel is based on the theory that it is not an abuse of process to relitigate a point where any of the ... requirements of the doctrine is missing.'

PARTIES ESTOPPED FROM DISPUTING DECISION

1.03   A party is estopped, against any other party, from disputing the correctness of the decision, except on appeal, whether it is relied on as a bar to a claim or defence, or in an action on the judgment.

1.04   It is important to distinguish between the effect of a decision as a *res judicata* estoppel, and as a merger of the cause of action. Much confusion has been created by failing to do this[1]. If the action succeeds the cause of action merges in the judgment and is extinguished[2]. A second action cannot be brought on that cause of action, not because there is an estoppel, but because there is no longer a cause of action. Where a judicial decision is relied upon to bar a claim or defence *res judicata* operates as an estoppel in the strict sense[3].

1   In *Greenhalgh v Mallard* [1947] 2 All ER 255 CA, 258 Somervell LJ considered an argument in which the two doctrines were hopelessly confused, counsel having cited *Brunsden v Humphrey* (1884) 14 QBD 141 CA, a case of merger, in support of an issue estoppel. In *Carl Zeiss Stiftung v Rayner and Keeler Ltd (No 2)* [1967] 1 AC 853, 927 (*Carl Zeiss No.2*), Lord Hodson referred to the same confusion.
2   *Blair v Curran* (1939) 62 CLR 464, 532 per Dixon J: 'The very right or cause of action claimed or put in suit has in the first proceedings passed into judgment, so that it merged and has no longer an independent existence'.
3   *Duffield v Scott* (1789) 3 Term Rep 374, 377; *Outram v Morewood* (1803) 3 East 346, 353, 358; *Hannaford v Hunn* (1825) 2 C&P 148, 155; *R v Hutchings* (1881) 6 QBD 300 CA, 304 ('Estoppel *per rem judicatam*'); *Re Surfleet's Estate, Rawlings v Smith* (1911) 105 LT 582, 583 ('Estoppel by *res judicata*'); *New Brunswick Rly Co. v British and French Trust Corpn Ltd* [1939] AC 1 (*New Brunswick*). In *Holland v Clark* (1842) 1 Y & C Ch Cas 151, 171, Knight Bruce VC treats the judgment as conclusive evidence, a synonym of estoppel. In *Morrison, Rose & Partners v Hillman* [1961] 2 QB 266 CA, 277 (*Morrison*) Pearson LJ said: 'The easiest ... approach ... is to regard the previous decision as conclusive evidence.'

1.05   A *res judicata* estoppel may be:

(a)   a cause of action estoppel, or
(b)   an issue estoppel.

1.06   If the earlier action fails on the merits a cause of action estoppel will bar another. Whether it succeeds or fails the decision may also create an issue estoppel on some question of fact or law that was necessarily decided as part of its legal foundation which prevents that question being re-litigated in proceedings on a different cause of action[1].

1   *Blair v Curran* (1939) 62 CLR 464, 531 per Dixon J; *Asia Commercial Finance Bhd v Kawal Teliti Sdn Bhd* [1995] 3 MLJ 189 SC.

RES JUDICATA ESTOPPELS CREATE SUBSTANTIVE RIGHTS

1.07   Estoppel by *res judicata* has sometimes been said to be a rule of evidence[1] and sometimes a rule of public policy[2]. Lord Wright said that estoppel by representation 'is more correctly viewed as a substantive rule of law'[3], and this must also be true of *res judicata* estoppel which applies to questions of law, and can bar a cause of action[4].

1   *Vervaeke v Smith (Messina and A-G intervening)* [1983] 1 AC 145, 162; *Humphries* [1910] 2 KB 531 CA, 536; *Ord* [1923] 2 KB 432, 440 ('The litigant must admit that which has been judicially declared to be the truth with regard to the dispute that he raised'). *Marginson* [1939] 2 KB 426 CA, 437 ('The broader rule of evidence which prohibits the reassertion of a cause of action'); *Morrison* [1961] 2 QB 266 CA, 277. n 3 at para 1.04.
2   In *Mills v Cooper* [1967] 2 QB 459, 469 per Diplock LJ: 'Whatever may be said of other rules of law to which the label of "estoppel" is attached "issue estoppel" is not a rule of evidence. ... It has the effect of preventing the party "estopped" from calling evidence to show that the assertion which is the subject of the issue estoppel is incorrect ... because ... there is no issue ... to which such evidence would be relevant. Issue estoppel is a particular application of the general rule of public policy that there should be finality in litigation'; approved *DPP v Humphrys* [1977] AC 1, 27, 48; *Rogers v R* (1994) 181 CLR 251, 274, 277; *Commonwealth of Australia v Sciacca* (1988) 17 FCR 476, 480 but cf *The Indian Grace* [1993] AC 410, 422 ('no more than a rule of evidence').
3   *Canada and Dominion Sugar Co Ltd v Canadian National (West Indies) Steamships Ltd* [1947] AC 46, 56.
4   *Queensland v Commonwealth* (1977) 139 CLR 585, 614–615 per Aickin J.

1.08 The question was settled in *Associated Electric and Gas Insurance Services Ltd v European Reinsurance Co of Zurich*[1]. An arbitral tribunal upheld one construction of a contract of reinsurance. In a later arbitration under the same contract the unsuccessful party pleaded the construction rejected by the first tribunal. When this was met with a plea of issue estoppel it sought to restrain reliance on the earlier award.

1   [2003] 1 WLR 1041 PC (*Aegis*).

1.09 It argued that the award could not create an issue estoppel for another arbitration because the rules of evidence were a matter for the tribunal[1] but the Privy Council held that an issue estoppel was a substantive right. Lord Hobhouse said[2]:

'The ... award has conferred upon [European Re] a right which is enforceable by ... pleading an issue estoppel. It is a species of the ... rights given by the award just as much as ... a cause of action estoppel. It is true that estoppels can be described as rules of evidence or as rules of public policy ... but that is to look at how estoppels are given effect to, not at what is the nature of the private law right which the estoppel recognises and protects.'

The issue estoppel related to a question of construction which, for most purposes, is a question of law.

1   [2003] 1 WLR 1041 PC, 1047.
2   Ibid at 1048; *Johnson v Gore Wood & Co (a firm)* [2002] 2 AC 1, 59 (*Johnson*) per Lord Millett; see paras 9.38 and 17.25; and *Keating v Calas* [1974] VR 381, 384 (legislation had not retrospectively annulled res judicata estoppels because of presumption against interference with vested rights).

RATIONALE OF DOCTRINE

1.10 The principles behind the requirement for finality were lucidly explained by Lord Wilberforce in *The Ampthill Peerage Case*[1]:

'English law, and it is safe to say, all comparable legal systems, place high in the category of essential principles that which requires that limits be placed on the right of citizens to ... reopen disputes. ... Any determination of disputable fact may, the law recognizes, be imperfect: the law aims at providing the best and safest solution compatible with human fallibility and having reached that solution it closes the book. The law knows, and we all know, that sometimes fresh material may be found, which might perhaps lead to a different result, but in the interests of peace, certainty and security it prevents further inquiry. It is said that in doing this, the law is preferring justice to truth. That may be so: these values cannot always coincide. The law does its best to reduce the gap. But there are cases where the certainty of justice prevails over the possibility of truth, ... and these are cases where the law insists on finality. For a policy of closure to be compatible with justice, it must be attended with safeguards: so the law allows appeals [and] ... allows judgments to be attacked on the ground of fraud ...'

Two policies support the doctrine of *res judicata* estoppel: the interest of the community in the termination of disputes and the finality and conclusiveness of judicial decisions; and the interest of an individual in being protected from repeated suits and prosecutions for the same cause[2]. Maugham LC said[3]:

'The doctrine of estoppel is one founded on considerations of justice and good sense. If an issue has been distinctly raised and decided in an action, in which the parties are represented, it is unjust and unreasonable to permit the same issue to be litigated afresh between the same parties or persons claiming under them.'

The High Court of Australia has said[4]:

'A central and pervading tenet of the judicial system is that controversies, once resolved, are not to be reopened except in a few, narrowly defined, circumstances. That tenet finds reflection in the rules concerning the bringing of an action to set aside a final judgment on the ground that it was procured by fraud, and in the doctrines of *res judicata* and issue estoppel. The principal qualification ... is provided by the appellate system. But in Courts other than the Court of final resort, the tenet also finds reflection in the restrictions upon reopening of final orders after they have been formally recorded.'

---

[1]   [1977] AC 547, 569.

[2]   In 2 *Co Litt* 260a, the doctrine is made to rest upon public convenience: 'for otherwise ... there should never be an end of controversies, which would be inconvenient'; and in *Re May* (1885) 28 Ch D 516, CA, 518 Brett MR said: 'It is one of the most fundamental doctrines of all courts, that there must be an end to all litigation'. This was the view of the Roman jurists: Chapter 27. The principle was relied on in *Ferrer v Arden* (1599) 6 Co Rep 7a, where *expedit rei publicae ut sit finis litium* is given as the foundation of the rule, and at 9a 'otherwise great oppression might be done under colour and pretence of law; for if there should not be an end of suits, then a rich and malicious man would infinitely vex him that had right by suits and actions; and in the end (because he cannot come to an end) compel him ... to relinquish his right'. In *Lockyer v Ferryman* (1877) 2 App Cas 519, 530 Lord Blackburn said: 'The object of the rule of *res judicata* is always put upon two grounds – the one public policy, that it is in the interest of the State that there should be an end of litigation, and the other, the hardship on the individual that he should be vexed twice for the same cause'; *Rogers v R* (1994) 181 CLR 251, 265, 273; *Morrison* [1961] 2 QB 266 CA, 276 and *Carl-Zeiss (No 2)* [1967] 1 AC 853, 909, 933; *Green v Weatherill* [1929] 2 Ch 213, 221: 'The plea of *res judicata* is not a technical doctrine, but a fundamental doctrine based on the view that there must be an end to litigation'; *Irish Land Commission v Ryan* [1900] 2 IR 565 CA, 584; *Cox v Dublin City Distillery Co Ltd (No 3)* [1917] 1 IR 203 CA, 230; *Watt (formerly Carter) v Ahsan* [2008] 1 AC 696, 707 (*Watt*) per Lord Hoffmann: 'the policy of avoiding relitigation of the same issues'; *Asia Commercial Finance (M) Bhd v Karwal Teliti Sdn Bhd* [1995] 3 MLJ 189 SC, 197–198.

³ *New Brunswick* [1939] AC 1, 19–20; *Simpang Empot Plantation Sdn Bhd v Ali bin Tan Sri Abdul Kadir* [2006] 1 MLJ 193 CA, 199: 'it is a doctrine of substantial justice.'
⁴ *Burrell v R* (2008) 82 ALJR 1221, 1226 [para 15].

LIMITS OF THE DOCTRINE

1.11 The principles governing *res judicata* estoppel reflect the attempts of courts to achieve finality in litigation on principled and predictable grounds while allowing some flexibility in special cases. The tension between these competing policies continues to be worked out. The effect of default[1], and foreign judgments[2], the scope of issue estoppels in road accident[3], and annual taxation and rating cases[4], and the significance of the inquisitorial function of the court in divorce cases[5], have tested the boundaries of the doctrine. The tension arises because, as Lord Goff said[6] '*res judicata* is founded upon the public interest in the finality of litigation rather than the achievement of justice as between the individual litigants.'

¹ *New Brunswick* [1939] AC 1, 37, 41; *Kok Hoong v Leong Cheong Kweng Mines Ltd* [1964] AC 993, 1010 (*Kok Hoong*); paras 2.24, 2.25.
² *Carl Zeiss (No 2)* [1967] 1 AC 853, 917.
³ Chapter 12.
⁴ Chapter 13.
⁵ Chapter 15.
⁶ *The Indian Grace* [1993] AC 410, 415.

1.12 There have been significant decisions limiting or qualifying the doctrine. *DPP v Humphrys*[1] decided that issue estoppels have no place in the criminal law, and *Arnold v National Westminster Bank plc* (*Arnold*)[2] recognised an exception to the general rule of issue estoppel in special circumstances. In *The Sennar*[3] an issue estoppel from a contested foreign decision and in *Thrasyvoulou v Secretary of State for the Environment*[4] *res judicata* estoppels from administrative decisions in planning cases were enforced. A wide operation was given to the extended doctrine of *res judicata* in *Hunter v Chief Constable of West Midlands Police*[5]. Dicta in *Yat Tung Investment Co Ltd v Dao Heng Bank Ltd*[6] over extended the *Henderson*[7] principle and the extended doctrine, but proper limits were re-established in *Johnson*[8].

¹ [1977] AC 1.
² [1991] 2 AC 93.
³ [1985] 1 WLR 490 HL.
⁴ [1990] 2 AC 273 (*Thrasyvoulou*).
⁵ [1982] AC 529 (*Hunter*).
⁶ [1975] AC 581 (*Yat Tung*).
⁷ (1843) 3 Hare 100; para 7.3.
⁸ [2002] 2 AC 1.

1.13 The *res judicata* doctrine in English law has been influenced by the adversary system. Diplock LJ commented[1]:

'Estoppel really means that, under the rules of the adversary system of procedure upon which the common law of England is based, a party is not allowed in certain circumstances, to prove ... particular facts ... which ... would assist him to succeed as plaintiff or defendant in an action. If the Court is required to exercise an inquisitorial function and may inquire into the facts

5

which the parties do not choose to prove, or would under the rules of the adversary system be prevented from proving, this is a function to which the common law concept of an estoppel is alien.'

1   *Thoday* [1964] P 181 CA, 197.

CORRECTNESS OF THE DECISION NOT RELEVANT

1.14 The decision need not be correct in law or fact. '*Res judicata* ... gives effect to the policy of the law that the parties to a judicial decision should not afterwards be allowed to re-litigate the same question, even though the decision may be wrong'[1]. A competent tribunal has jurisdiction to decide[2], and if it makes a mistake its decision is binding unless corrected on appeal. Error within jurisdiction is a wrong exercise of the jurisdiction the court or tribunal has, and not a usurpation of a jurisdiction which it has not[3]. 'The doctrine [of *res judicata*] comes into its own only when the decision is wrong; if it is right it merely serves to save time and costs'[4].

1   *Crown Estate Comrs v Dorset County Council* [1990] Ch 297, 305 per Millett J cited in *Mulkerrins v Pricewaterhouse Coopers* [2003] 1 WLR 1937 HL, 1941 (*Mulkerrins*).
2   *Philips v Bury* (1694) Skin 447, 485 per Lord Holt CJ: 'His sentence must have some affect to make a vacancy, be it never so wrong'; para 2.02 n 3.
3   *R v Nat Bell Liquors Ltd* [1922] 2 AC 128, 151–152; *Malkarjun bin Shidramappa Pasere v Narhari bin Shivappa* (1900) LR 27 Ind App 216, 235 (*Malkarjun*) per Lord Hobhouse: 'The court was exercising its jurisdiction. It made a sad mistake it is true; but a court has jurisdiction to decide wrong as well as right'; *Meyers v Casey* (1913) 17 CLR 90, 114–115; *Parisienne Basket Shoes Pty Ltd v Whyte* (1938) 59 CLR 369, 374; paras 4.02, 17.21 nn 6 and 7.
4   *Mulkerrins* [2003] 1 WLR at 1941 per Lord Millett; *Watt* [2008] 1 AC 696, 708.

RES JUDICATA AND JUDICIAL PRECEDENT

1.15 There is an essential difference between *res judicata* estoppel and the doctrine of judicial precedent. The latter makes a decision on a question of law binding upon all persons, parties or not, in all courts of inferior, but not in courts of higher, jurisdiction. The difference is illustrated by the *Waring* cases in 1942 and 1948. In the first Farwell J held that s 25 of the Finance Act 1941 did not apply to an annuity[1]; but the Court of Appeal reversed his decision[2]. The effect was two-fold; it decided as *res judicata* between the executors and that annuitant that s 25 applied, and it bound courts up to the Court of Appeal in other cases. In *Berkeley*[3] the House of Lords overruled the Court of Appeal decision and in 1948 the executors sought a decision as between themselves and the other annuitant who had not been a party to the earlier proceedings[4]. The Court held that the earlier decision continued to bind the first annuitant but the second had the benefit of the decision in *Berkeley*[5].

1   *Re Waring, Westminster Bank Ltd v A Wary* [1942] Ch 309.
2   [1942] Ch 426.
3   [1946] AC 555.
4   *Re Waring, Westminster Bank Ltd v Burton-Butler* [1948] Ch 221, 223, 227. It does not matter that a later decision has shown that the earlier was erroneous: *Watt* [2008] 1 AC 696, 708.

⁵ This is why Courts of Equity require all interested parties to be joined or represented: *Duke of Bedford v Ellis* [1901] AC 1, 8. The second annuitant was not bound because she was living in enemy-occupied Europe and the Court refused to make a representative order.

WHERE RES JUDICATA IS THE FOUNDATION OF AN ACTION

1.16 A judicial decision is conclusive and binding upon the parties when made the basis of an action as the result of an estoppel.

TERMINOLOGY

1.17 The term 'estoppel by record', although widely used in the past, is misleading. It is the *res judicata*, not the record, which creates the estoppel, and it is immaterial whether the court or tribunal is required to keep a written record of its decisions or not[1]. In cases of merger in judgment 'estoppel by record' is even more inapt, as the result is not based on an estoppel at all.

¹ In *Carl-Zeiss (No 2)* [1967] 1 AC 853, 933 Lord Guest said: 'As it is now quite immaterial whether the judicial decision was pronounced by a tribunal which is required to keep a written record of its decisions, ... it may be convenient to describe *res judicata* in its true and original form as "cause of action estoppel" '.

TREATMENT OF THE SUBJECT

1.18 Part One deals with *res judicata* estoppel in its three forms: cause of action estoppel, issue estoppel, and the binding force of a judgment when it is the foundation of a new action. The application of these principles in specific areas of the law and the plea of *autrefois acquit* in criminal cases are then considered. A chapter deals with affirmative answers. Part Two deals with merger in judgment including its application in criminal cases under the plea of *autrefois convict*. Each Part concludes with a chapter on procedure. Part Three deals with the extended doctrine of *res judicata* based on abuse of process and the doctrine of *res judicata* in Roman law.

PART 1

RES JUDICATA ESTOPPEL

Chapter 2

WHAT CONSTITUTES A RES JUDICATA

INTRODUCTION

2.01 A *res judicata* is a decision on the merits[1], pronounced by a tribunal which is judicial in the relevant sense.

[1]   This includes final judgments by default or consent but excludes decisions on procedural grounds and decisions which are not final in any sense.

WHAT IS A JUDICIAL TRIBUNAL?

2.02 It is immaterial for present purposes whether the tribunal is a court of record or not[1], or whether it is a superior court or not[2], or whether it is or is known as a court[3]. Nor does it matter whether the tribunal, if English, has civil or criminal jurisdiction[4]; nor (with certain exceptions) whether the tribunal is English or foreign[5]. It does not matter whether the tribunal has permanent jurisdiction or only jurisdiction over a particular dispute or disputes[6].

[1]   *Williams v Jones* (1845) 13 M & W 628, 633–634; *Re May* (1885) 28 Ch D 516 CA, 518 per Brett MR: 'counsel for the petitioner has argued first of all that this is not *res judicata*, because there was no record, and the doctrine of *res judicata* only applies where there is a record. To my mind that argument cannot be sustained. The doctrine of *res judicata* is not a technical doctrine applicable only to records. It is a very substantial doctrine, and it is one of the most fundamental doctrines of all courts, that there must be an end to all litigation, and that the parties have no right of their own accord, having tried a question between them, and obtained a decision of a court, to start that litigation over again on precisely the same question'. The equivalent of paras 2.01–2.02 in the 2nd edn were referred to with approval by Gibbs J in *Administration of the Territory of Papua and New Guinea v Daera Guba* (1972) 130 CLR 353, 453 (*Daera Guba*). This paragraph in the 3rd edn was referred to with approval by Blanshard J in *Arbuthnot v CE of Dept of Work* [2008] 1 NZLR 13 SC, 16.

[2]   *Williams v Jones* ibid; *Marginson* [1939] 2 KB 426 CA, 438: '... a clear decision on the same issue between the same persons litigating in the present case, and establishes conclusively, albeit in the County Court ...'.

[3]   In *Thrasyvoulou* [1990] 2 AC 273, [1990] 1 All ER 65 decisions of planning inspectors created causes of action and issue estoppels. In *Philips v Bury* (1694) Skin 447 HL, 485 which concerned a sentence of deprivation by a college visitor Holt CJ, whose dissenting judgment was upheld, said: 'you will say that this man hath no Court: will you conclude a man by the sentence of one that hath no Court? It is not, I say, at all material whether he

11

hath a Court, or no; all the matter is, whether he hath a jurisdiction: if he hath a jurisdiction, and conusance of the matter and the person, and he gives sentence in the matter, his sentence must have effect to make a vacancy, be it never so wrong'. Decisions, other than those of a court, which have been treated as founding *res judicata* estoppels include those by arbitrators (para 2.05); and statutory tribunals (para 2.03).

4 Para 2.35.
5 Paras 2.36–2.39.
6 Such as the tribunals referred to in paras 2.03 nn 14–17, 2.05.

STATUTORY TRIBUNALS

2.03 Tribunals established by statute may be 'judicial' for present purposes. They include: a court martial[1]; a naval court under the Merchant Shipping Act 1894[2]; a medical tribunal, such as the College of Physicians, or the General Medical Council[3]; judges appointed to try election petitions under the Parliamentary Elections Act 1868, whose 'certificates' and 'reports' were conclusive[4]; compensation tribunals, whether sheriff and jury, or arbitrator, authorised by the Lands Clauses Consolidation Act 1845, or other statutes, whose judgments or awards were conclusive[5]; an arbitrator under the Inclosure Acts[6]; Commissioners under the Metropolitan Commons Act 1866, with power to settle a scheme[7]; an arbitrator under the Workmen's Compensation Acts 1897 and 1906[8]; the Chief Land Registrar in deciding whether an overriding interest should be entered on the register[9]; the Registrar of Trade Marks in proceedings for a declaration of invalidity[10] or revocation of the registration of a trademark[11], a 'superintending architect', and 'tribunal of appeal' established under metropolitan building statutes[12]; a collegiate or scholastic authority exercising jurisdiction under its statute or charter[13]; and tribunals constituted for a temporary purpose, such as the Commissioners established as a court of record to determine disputes arising out of the destruction of property by 'the late dreadful fire' at Blandford[14]; the 'Court of Claims' established by 11 and 12 W 3, sess 2, c 2[15]; Boundary Commissioners[16]; the Lords of the Treasury, invested by 5 and 6 W 4, c 76, with jurisdiction to fix compensation for the holders of offices whose decisions on amount, but not on any question of right, were conclusive[17]; tribunals appointed to determine applications for exemption from military service[18]; decisions of the Chief Commons Commissioner under the Commons Registration Act 1965[19]; decisions of industrial tribunals in Canada[20]; decisions of a Board of Referees under the Employment Insurance Act 1996[21]; other administrative tribunals[22]; and in general any statutory tribunal[23]. As Gibbs J said[24]:

> 'The use of the phrase "judicial tribunal" in this context is convenient as indicating that an estoppel of this kind does not result from a mere administrative decision, but the question whether such an estoppel is raised is not answered by inquiring to what extent the tribunal exercises judicial functions, or whether its status is judicial or administrative … The doctrine of estoppel extends to the decision of any tribunal which has jurisdiction to decide finally a question arising between parties, even if it is not called a court, and its jurisdiction is derived from statute or from the submission of parties.'

In *Pastras v Commonwealth*[25] Lush J stated the test for distinguishing between decisions which are judicial for present purposes and those which are purely administrative[26]:

'The underlying principle of this form of estoppel is that parties who have had a dispute heard by a competent tribunal shall not be allowed to litigate the same issues in other tribunals. When the decision making body is an administrative body not affording the opportunity of presenting evidence and argument ... there is no room for the operation of this principle ... It appears to me that both upon the general language of the authorities ... and upon ... principle ... no estoppel can arise from a decision of an administrative authority which cannot be classed either as "judicial" or as "a tribunal", and that an authority cannot be given either of those classifications if it ... is under no obligation to receive evidence or hear argument'.

Lord Diplock applied similar principles to the determination of claims under the National Insurance legislation[27]:

'Under the statute benefit of any of the three kinds is payable as the result of an "award of benefit" made by a statutory authority ... in respect to a claim for that particular kind of benefit by a claimant ... The submission of a claim does not give rise to any "*lis*". There is no opponent ... and consequently no "issues" in the sense in which that term is used in relation to adversarial litigation ... The general doctrine of *res judicata* which operates *inter partes* is thus inapplicable to claims for benefit. The sole function of the insurance officer ... is to satisfy himself whether or not the claimant is entitled to the kind of benefit he has claimed, and if so the amounts of benefit to which he is entitled. The legal consequences of his decision are those which the statute ... ascribes to it. There can be no question of issue estoppel.'

Competition proceedings before the European Commission have been held to be administrative not judicial[28].

1 *Hannaford v Hunn* (1825) 2 C & P 148; *A-G for Cape of Good Hope v Van Reenen* [1904] AC 114.
2 *Caine v Palace Steam Shipping Co Ltd* [1907] 1 KB 670 CA; *Hutton v Ras Steam Shipping Co Ltd* [1907] 1 KB 834 CA. In the former the estoppel was abandoned for lack of identity of parties; in the latter it was sustained. Both depended upon s 483(2) of the Merchant Shipping Act 1894, which provides that orders by a naval court shall be conclusive as to the rights of the parties. In New South Wales, where the Navigation Act 1901 contained no such provision, the finding of a Marine Court of Inquiry was not conclusive: *Spain v Union Steamship Co of New Zealand Ltd* (1923) 33 CLR 555, 563; *The European Gateway* [1987] QB 206.
3 *Groenvelt v Burwell* (1700) 1 Ld Raym 454 (College of Physicians under patent of Henry VIII); *Hill v Clifford* [1907] 2 Ch 236 CA (General Medical Council under Dentists Act 1878); *Basser v Medical Board of Victoria* [1981] VR 953; and *X v Y* [1996] 2 NZLR 196, 207 (NZ Medical Practitioners Disciplinary Committee).
4 *Waygood v James* (1869) LR 4 CP 361; *Stevens v Tillett* (1870) LR 6 CP 147; Representation of the People Act 1983 ss 144(1), 145(1).
5 *Taylor v Clemson* (1844) 11 Cl & Fin 610; *Mortimer v South Wales Rly Co* (1859) 1 E & E 375.
6 *Jacomb v Turner* [1892] 1 QB 47; *Collis v Amphlett* [1918] 1 Ch 232 CA.
7 *Cook v Mitcham Common Conservators* [1901] 1 Ch 387.
8 *Crossfield & Sons Ltd v Tanian* [1900] 2 QB 629 CA; *Bailey v Plant* [1901] 1 KB 31 CA; *Sharman v Holliday and Greenwood Ltd* [1904] 1 KB 235 CA; *Blake v Midland Rly Co* [1904] 1 KB 503; *Radcliffe v Pacific Steam Navigation Co* [1910] 1 KB 685 CA; *Green v Cammell, Laird & Co Ltd* [1913] 3 KB 665 CA.
9 *Re Dances Way, West Town, Hayling Island* [1962] Ch 490 CA.
10 *Hormel Foods Corpn v Antilles Landscape Investments NV* [2005] RPC 657, 671 (*Hormel Foods*). An appeal was allowed by consent: *Special Effects Ltd v L'Oreal SA* [2007] EWCA Civ 1371, paras [36], [84], (2007) 71 IPR 188, 199, 211 (*Special Effects*).
11 Ibid at 684–685.

[12] *Spackman v Plumstead Board of Works* (1884) 10 App Cas 229; *Lilley v LCC* [1910] AC 1; *LCC v Galsworthy* [1918] AC 851.

[13] *Philips v Bury* (1694) Skin 447 HL (Visitor of Exeter Coll, Oxon); *R v Grundon* (1775) 1 Cowp 315 (Master and Fellows of Queen's Coll, Camb); *Doe d Davy v Haddon* (1783) 3 Doug KB 310 (trustees of school).

[14] *Sollers v Lawrence* (1743) Willes 413.

[15] *Archbishop of Dublin v Coote* (1849) 12 Ir Eq R 251.

[16] *Brisco v Lomax* (1838) 8 Ad & El 198; *Evans v Rees* (1839) 10 Ad & El 151.

[17] *Sandwich Corpn v R* (1847) 10 QB 571 Ex Ch, 579.

[18] *Langdon v Richards* (1917) 33 TLR 325.

[19] *Crown Estate Comrs v Dorset County Council* [1990] Ch 297.

[20] *Green v Hampshire County Council* [1979] ICR 861; *Staffordshire County Council v Barber* [1996] ICR 379 CA, 396–397; *Ako v Rothschild Asset Management* [2002] ICR 899 CA (*Ako*).

[21] *Minott v O'Shanter Development Co* (1999) 168 DLR (4th) 270, 283–284 (*Minott*).

[22] *Danyluk v Ainsworth Technologies Inc* [2001] 2 SCR 460, 468 (*Danyluk*).

[23] *Thrasyvoulou* [1990] 2 AC 273 (planning inspectors); *Astoria Federal SLL Association v Solimino* 501 US 104, 107–108 (1991) (*Astoria*); (administrative agency acting in judicial capacity); *Lambidis v Police Comr* (1995) 37 NSWLR 320 CA, 332; *Daera Guba* (1973) 130 CLR 353, 402, 453 (ad hoc statutory tribunal); *McNair v Press Offshore Ltd* (1997) 17 WAR 191 (Workers Compensation Tribunal); contrast the Waitangi Tribunal which is not 'judicial' for present purposes: *Te Runangao Muriwhenua Inc v A-G* [1990] 2 NZLR 641 CA.

[24] *Daera Guba* (1973) 130 CLR at 453, para 16.03; *Kuligowski v Metrobus* (2004) 220 CLR 363, 373–374.

[25] (1966) 9 FLR 152 (Sup Ct of Victoria); *Rasanen v Rosemount Instruments Ltd* (1994) 112 DLR (4th) 683 Ont CA, 705.

[26] Ibid at 155; *Astoria* 501 US 104, 107 (1991): 'administrative agency … acting in a judicial capacity and resolves disputed issues of fact properly before it which the parties have had an adequate opportunity to litigate'. This passage in the 3rd edn was approved by Blanshard J in *Arbuthnot v CE Dept of Work* [2008] 1 NZLR 13 SC, 26 who added that the administrative body in that case could not be relevantly judicial because 'it did not have sufficient independence'. Different principles apply where a constitutional separation of powers prevents judicial power being conferred on bodies which are not courts: *Miller v University of New South Wales* (2003) 132 FCR 147, 152, 166–169.

[27] *Hudson v Secretary of State for Social Services* [1972] AC 944, 1010; paras 16.02–16.03.

[28] *Iberian UK Ltd v BPB Industries plc* [1997] ICR 164 (*Iberian*), sed quaere.

CRIMINAL COURTS EXERCISING CIVIL JURISDICTION

2.04 Inferior criminal courts with civil jurisdiction are judicial tribunals for present purposes and their orders or decisions, within jurisdiction, are conclusive in all courts. Examples include the legal settlement of a pauper[1], and (incidentally thereto) the validity of a pauper's marriage; or the legitimacy of his children[2]; judicial separation and maintenance under the former Summary Jurisdiction (Married Women) Act 1895[3]; affiliation cases[4]; liability to repair an alleged highway[5]; observance of a prescribed 'building line' under the Public Health (Building in Streets) Act 1888[6]; detention of, but not (except incidentally) title to, goods under section 40 of the Metropolitan Police Act 1839[7]; claims for wages under the Employers and Workmen Act 1875[8]; apportionment of paving expenses under the Metropolis Management Acts[9]; and the refusal by Quarter Sessions of a declaration of the non-existence of a public right of way under the National Parks and Access to the Countryside Act 1949[10].

[1] *R v Hartington Middle Quarter Inhabitants* (1855) 4 E & B 780.
[2] *R v Wye Inhabitants* (1838) 7 Ad & El 761.

14

3   *Pickavance* [1901] P 60; *Stokes* [1911] P 195; *Hopkins* [1914] P 282; *McGregor v Telford* [1915] 3 KB 237; *Molesworth* [1947] 2 All ER 842. *Hopkins* was overruled in part in *Land* [1949] P 405, and the authority of *Pickavance* restricted; but they still support this proposition.
4   *R v Sunderland Justices, ex p Hodgkinson* [1945] KB 502; *Robinson v Williams* [1965] 1 QB 89.
5   *R v Blakemore* (1852) 21 LJMC 60; *R v Haughton Inhabitants* (1853) 1 E & B 501; *R v Hutchings* (1881) 6 QBD 300 CA; *Heath v Weaverham Overseers* [1894] 2 QB 108; *North Eastern Rly Co v Dalton Overseers* [1898] 2 QB 66; *Wakefield Corpn v Cooke* [1904] AC 31.
6   *Kinnis v Graves* (1898) 67 LJQB 583; *Jenkins v Merthyr Tydvil UDC* (1899) 80 LT 600; *Balby-with-Hexthorpe District Council v Millard* (1903) 68 JP 81.
7   *Dover v Child* (1876) 1 Ex D 172.
8   *Hindley v Haslam* (1878) 3 QBD 481.
9   *Scott v Lowe* (1902) 86 LT 421.
10 *Armstrong v Whitfield* [1974] QB 16.

DOMESTIC TRIBUNALS

2.05 Every domestic tribunal, including any arbitrator, or other person or body of persons invested with authority to hear and determine a dispute by consent of the parties, court order, or statute, is a 'judicial tribunal' for present purposes, and its awards and decisions conclusive unless set aside[1].

1   *Doe d Davy v Haddon* (1783) 3 Doug KB 310, 312 per Lord Mansfield: 'the adjudication was in a domestic forum, and the merits of it cannot be entered into'; *Cummings v Heard* (1869) LR 4 QB 669, 673; *The Warwick* (1890) 15 PD 189; *Gueret v Audouy* (1893) 62 LJQB 633; *Re Newey, ex p Whitman* (1912) 107 LT 832. In *Ayscough v Sheed Thomson & Co Ltd* (1923) 129 LT 429 CA Bankes LJ said at 430: 'An award made under such a submission is a bar to the action', and per Scrutton LJ at 431. In *Fidelitas Shipping Co Ltd v V/O Exportchleb* [1966] 1 QB 630 CA, 643 *(Fidelitas)* Diplock LJ said: 'Issue estoppel applies to arbitration as it does to litigation. The parties, having chosen the tribunal to determine the disputes between them as to their legal rights and duties, are bound by the determination of that tribunal on any issue which is relevant to the decision of any dispute referred to that tribunal'; *Aegis* [2003] 1 WLR 1041 PC, 1048; and the domestic tribunals considered in *Meyers v Casey* (1913) 17 CLR 90, 114; and *Calvin v Carr* [1980] AC 574.

JUDGMENT OF A LOWER COURT CONCLUSIVE IN A HIGHER

2.06 The decision of the lowest civil tribunal is conclusive in the very highest except on appeal[1], but if a party fails in an inferior court for want of jurisdiction, there is no estoppel on the merits[2].

1   Para 2.03, particularly *Lilley v LCC* [1910] AC 1 (certificate of superintending architect under the London Building Act 1894 binding on House of Lords), *Galbraith v Neville* (1789) 1 Doug KB 6n, (judgment of foreign inferior court); *Marginson* [1939] 2 KB 426 CA, 438.
2   *London Corpn v Cox* (1867) LR 2 HL 239, 262; para 2.15.

2.07 Cases in which an English civil authority has been held not to be a 'judicial tribunal' include: The Lord Treasurer and others making a 'decree' limiting the rights of the City of Chester against the County Palatine of Chester[1]; justices acting under the Mental Deficiency Act 1913[2]; the Registrar-General re-registering as legitimate a child previously registered as illegitimate, after the marriage of the parents[3]; justices exercising jurisdiction in licensing matters under earlier legislation[4]; but under current legislation they are judicial[5]; and insurance officers under the National Insurance Legislation[6]. The Waitangi Tribunal in New Zealand is not a judicial tribunal for present purposes[7].

[1]   *Rogers v Wood* (1831) 2 B & Ad 245 held that the 'decree' was not made by the Court of Exchequer, but by members of that court, and others. 'It was evidently, therefore', said Lord Tenterden CJ at 256, 'a proceeding before persons not forming any court known to the laws of this country'.

[2]   *Newman v Foster* [1916] WN 369.

[3]   *Jones* (1929) 140 LT 647.

[4]   *Smith v Shann* [1898] 2 QB 347, 350: 'in no sense a decision, or the judgment of a court upon which an estoppel could be founded'. In the following cases it was held that justices, sitting for licensing purposes, were not a judicial tribunal: *Royal Aquarium and Summer and Winter Garden Society v Parkinson* [1892] 1 QB 431 CA; *Boulter v Kent Justices* [1897] AC 556; *Huish v Liverpool Justices* [1914] 1 KB 109; *Attwood v Chapman* [1914] 3 KB 275.

[5]   *R v East Riding of Yorkshire Quarter Sessions, ex p Newton* [1968] 1 QB 32 CA.

[6]   Para 2.03, n 27.

[7]   *Te Runangao Muriwhenua Inc v A-G* [1990] 2 NZLR 641 CA.

WHAT IS A JUDICIAL DECISION?

2.08   There must be both a tribunal of the necessary kind and a decision or adjudication by that tribunal.

DECISIONS AMOUNTING TO RES JUDICATAE

2.09   These include judgments; orders; decrees; decreets (in Scotland); sentences; 'adjudications' (in bankruptcy); judicial declarations, or declarators (in Scotland); and the like, whether the jurisdiction was original or appellate[1]; and a decision resulting from an equal division in the tribunal[2].

[1]   Para 2.33.

[2]   In *Kinnis v Graves* (1898) 67 LJQB 583 justices, being equally divided, instead of adjourning the case to a day when an uneven number could be present, dismissed the information, and this constituted 'a decision' and 'a bar' to a subsequent information for the same offence. If the jurisdiction is appellate and the court is equally divided, the appeal fails. The decision appealed from remains the *res judicata*, and there is no 'decision' of the appellate court which has effect as an estoppel, cf para 2.33 for the effect of an appellate decision.

DECISIONS NOT AMOUNTING TO RES JUDICATAE

2.10   Pronouncements which are not decisions in any sense, or not judicial decisions, include: a so-called 'sentence' which did not purport to be, or to incorporate anything in the nature of, a decision[1]; a report to a Government, without any pretence to a judicial character[2]; the report of a court of formal investigation under the Merchant Shipping Act expressing opinions on issues of civil liability[3]; the discharge of a jury before verdict although the judge may have decided that there had been a mistrial[4]; a verdict not followed by judgment[5]; reasons for making an order for costs because they do not determine issues[6]; a verdict or judgment which has been set aside[7]; a compromise without an order[8]; a licensing or other administrative grant or order of justices under former legislation[9]; the grant or refusal by a judge or magistrate of a search warrant or similar order pursuant to statute[10]; and generally all decisions of an administrative character made without any hearing in the exercise of a statutory or prerogative power[11]; a statutory 'report' not given the effect of a judgment; an order giving leave to a creditor in bankruptcy to withdraw his proof[12]; a file of proceedings in bankruptcy[13]; a certificate of Quarter Sessions as to a pauper's place of settlement[14]; and a formal police caution or warning[15].

1   *Obicini v Bligh* (1832) 8 Bing 335, an action on a so-called 'sentence' of His Majesty's Vice-Admiralty Court at Malta, where the document did not set out the terms of the sentence, or a report of merchants, or award a sum of money.
2   *Fracis Times & Co v Carr* (1900) 82 LT 698 CA, where the defendant set up as an estoppel the report of a commission appointed by the Sultan of Muscat to inquire into the seizure by the defendant, when in command of one of Her Majesty's gunboats, of the plaintiff's guns and ammunition on a British ship.
3   *The European Gateway* [1987] QB 206.
4   *Norburn v Hillian* (1870) LR 5 CP 129; *Thomas v Exeter Flying Post Co.* (1887) 18 QBD 822, 825–826, in criminal cases *R v Charlesworth* (1861) 1 B & S 460, 507.
5   *Re Dingle, ex p Butterfill, ex p Rashleigh* (1811) 1 Rose 192 (verdict which had not led to judgment, which Lord Eldon LC held to be *prima facie* evidence only); *Brisco v Lomax* (1838) 8 Ad & El 198 (verdict of jury under Boundary Commission); *Bancroft* (1864) 3 Sw & Tr 597 (verdict of jury in a suit for judicial separation which had not led to judgment); cf *Butler* [1894] P 25 CA, paras 15.15–15.16. A jury verdict in land compensation cases under former legislation was a judicial decision where the order giving effect thereto was a ministerial formality, para 2.30 n 5.
6   *Clancy v Santoro* [1999] 3 VR 783.
7   *Roe v R A Naylor Ltd* (1918) 87 LJKB 958 CA, para 5.14.
8   *Dattani v Trio Supermarkets Ltd* [1998] ICR 872 CA, 883–884; likewise an order by consent striking proceedings out following a settlement: *Sweeney v Bus Atha Cliath* [2004] 1 IR 576 SC.
9   Para 2.07 nn 4, 5.
10 *Re Racal Communications Ltd* [1981] AC 374, 380 per Lord Diplock: 'The application does not involve and is not made in the course of any *lis inter partes*. It cannot create *res judicata*; if one judge refuses to make the order there is no legal obstacle to the applicant's making the same application to another judge, although in the absence of additional evidence it is unlikely to be successful'; *Grollo v Palmer* (1995) 184 CLR 348, (telephone interception warrant) and *Ousley v The Queen* (1997) 192 CLR 69 (listening device warrant).
11 Para 2.03, nn 24–27.
12 *Re Greaves, ex p Whitton* (1880) 43 LT 480.
13 *Re Bond, ex p Bacon* (1881) 17 Ch D 447 CA, 451.
14 *R v Lubbenham (Inhabitants)* (1791) 4 Term Rep 251.
15 *Abrahams v Metropolitan Police Comr* [2001] 1 WLR 1257 CA (suspect accepting formal caution not estopped from bringing action for false imprisonment); *R (on the application of R) v Durham Constabulary* [2005] 1 WLR 1184 HL (formal warning did not attract Art. 6(1) of the European Convention on Human Rights); although a caution may make a private prosecution an abuse of process: *Jones v Whalley* [2007] 1 AC 63.

TERMINATION BY WITHDRAWAL

2.11 Prior to the Judicature Acts when a plaintiff at law took a nonsuit to avoid judgment and could bring a fresh action there was no decision[1]. But if the parties intended to terminate litigation, a fresh action was barred and the defendant could apply for a stay[2]. Until 2004 the Employment Tribunals Rules did not allow an applicant to discontinue and withdrawal led to an order for dismissal. In *Barber v Staffordshire County Council*[3] where the applicant abandoned a claim she thought could not succeed the dismissal created a cause of action estoppel. Proceedings for racial discrimination were dismissed after a payment and fresh proceedings for negligence based on the same allegations were struck out for abuse of process[4]. The withdrawal, on agreed terms, of an application for equal pay barred a renewed application on the same facts[5]. There was no cause of action estoppel where the applicant expressly reserved his rights to bring an action[6] or when the applicant withdrew, before the respondent had appeared, intending to bring a second application against an additional respondent[7]. Rule 25(1) of the Employment Tribunals Rules of Procedure 2004 now permits a claim to be withdrawn without being dismissed, but difficulties still arise[8]. In the absence of some statutory prohibition, an applicant to a statutory tribunal may withdraw before the decision is given[9].

[1]   *Nesbit v Rishton* (1839) 11 Ad & El 244 Ex Ch, 250–251; cf *Re May* (1885) 28 Ch D 516 CA, 518 (decision not a nonsuit); *Jones v Dunkel* (1959) 101 CLR 298, 322–331 where Windeyer J reviewed the history of the nonsuit, and *Re Orrell Colliery and Fire Brick Co.* (1879) 12 Ch D 681 for the former practice in Chancery to like effect.
[2]   *Gibbs v Ralph* (1845) 14 M & W 804; cf *Massam v Thorley's Cattle Food Co* (1880) 14 Ch D 748 CA, 751, per James LJ: 'the question whether there is anything in the nature of estoppel, or of a bar to the plaintiffs' right to relief by reason of their having discontinued their former action against the company ... That is not a *res judicata* nor can it be pleaded or dealt with as *res judicata*'; *Magnus v National Bank of Scotland* (1888) 57 LJ Ch 902 (dismissal by consent of Chancery action for want of prosecution before cause set down for hearing a discontinuance); *The Ardandhu* (1887) 12 App Cas 256 (discontinuance by consent without costs no bar to fresh proceedings).
[3]   [1996] ICR 379 CA, 396–397; *Ako* [2002] ICR 899 CA, 904.
[4]   *Sheriff v Klyne Tugs (Lowestoft) Ltd* [1999] ICR 1170 CA.
[5]   *Kirklees Metropolitan Borough Council v Farrell* [2000] ICR 1335, 1340–1341.
[6]   *Safid v Sussex Muslim Society* [2002] IRLR 113 CA; *Ako* [2002] ICR 899 CA, 904–905.
[7]   *Ako* [2002] ICR 899 CA, 902, 906.
[8]   *Khan v Heywood & Middleton Primary Care Trust* [2007] ICR 24; *Cockayne v British Association for Shooting and Conservation* [2008] ICR 185.
[9]   *R v Hampstead and St Pancras Rent Tribunal, ex p Goodman* [1951] 1 KB 541, 545; *Boal Quay Wharfingers Ltd v King's Lynn Conservancy Board* [1971] 1 WLR 1558 CA; *Rydqvist v Secretary of State for Work and Pensions* [2002] 1 WLR 3343 CA; *Uniden Australia Pty Ltd v Collector of Customs* (1997) 74 FCR 190; *Christie v Neaves* (2001) 113 FCR 279. Cf *Hanson v London Rent Assessment Committee* [1976] QB 394, 400–401 (no right to withdraw objection to fair rent).

DISCONTINUANCE

2.12 Discontinuance is now the only means by which a claimant can voluntarily withdraw his claim in whole or in part[1]. CPR 38.2(1) permits a claimant to discontinue at any time but CPR 38.2(2) requires the permission of the court where an interim injunction has been granted, an undertaking to the court given, or an interim payment has been made. In the latter case discontinuance is also possible with the written consent of the defendant. A claimant who discontinues after the defendant filed a defence needs the permission of the court to make another claim against the same defendant arising out of substantially the same facts[2].

[1]   The former right of a plaintiff at law to withdraw and bring a second action has been abolished: *Fox v Star Newspaper Co.* [1900] AC 19; *Gilham v Browning* [1998] 1 WLR 682 CA.
[2]   CPR 38.7.

DISMISSAL FOR WANT OF PROSECUTION

2.13 Such a dismissal is an interlocutory order, is not a decision on the merits, and does not create a *res judicata*[1]. A plaintiff whose action has been dismissed for want of prosecution could formerly bring a second action, unless, for exceptional reasons, this was an abuse of process[2]. Since the Woolf Reforms this is no longer the case[3].

[1]   *Pople v Evans* [1969] 2 Ch 255; *Hart v Hall & Pickles Ltd, Geoffrey Reyner & Co Ltd (third parties)* [1969] 1 QB 405 CA, 411; *Birkett v James* [1978] AC 297.
[2]   *Birkett v James* [1978] AC 297, 320–321. In Singapore and Malaysia a second action will be an abuse unless the plaintiff establishes that his earlier default was not contumacious: *Genesis World Sdn Bhd v Mobikom Sdn Bhd* [2003] 4 MLJ 263; *Changi International Investments Pte Ltd v Dexia BIL Asia Singapore Ltd* [2005] 3 SLR 344 CA.
[3]   *Securum Finance Ltd v Ashton* [2001] Ch 291 CA.

WITHDRAWAL IN COURT OF SUMMARY JURISDICTION

2.14 The withdrawal of a summons in a court of summary jurisdiction because the complainant recognises that he has not complied with some statutory condition, or some rule of evidence, is not an adjudication, and *prima facie* does not bar a fresh summons[1]. The same result follows when a summons is withdrawn to allow a graver allegation to be substituted[2]. It was formerly thought that if the withdrawal was intended to put an end to proceedings, it could be set up as a bar; but it is now clear that this is not so[3].

[1]   *R v Tyrone Justices* [1912] 2 IR 44, 48, 52–53; *Davis v Morton* [1913] 2 KB 479, 484–486; *R v Seddon, ex p Hall* (1916) 85 LJKB 806; *R v Phipps ex p Alton* [1964] 2 QB 420; *Lawson v Wallace* [1968] 3 NSWR 82 CA, 86; *Williams v Letheren* [1919] 2 KB 262 (two summonses to be heard the same day, second withdrawn after conviction on first); *R v Dabhade* [1993] QB 329, 341.
[2]   *Molesworth* [1947] 2 All ER 842.
[3]   *Land* [1949] P 405.

DISMISSAL FOR WANT OF JURISDICTION

2.15 A decision by a tribunal that it has no jurisdiction will not support a plea of *res judicata* on any other question[1] for the reasons given by Lord Russell of Killowen in an Indian appeal[2]:

'The *res judicata* here was the lack of jurisdiction ...not the reason for that decision. A Court which declines jurisdiction cannot bind parties by its reasons for declining jurisdiction: such reasons are not decisions, and are certainly not decisions by a court of competent jurisdiction. It would indeed be strange if on a dispute as to the jurisdiction of a Court to try an issue, that Court by its reasons for holding that it had no jurisdiction, could, on the principle of *res judicata* decide and bind the parties upon the very issue it was incompetent to try'.

Where a judge declined to deal with a claim for interest because he had not been the trial judge, there was no *res judicata* because there had been no adjudication[3]. However a decision by a tribunal denying jurisdiction makes that question *res judicata* in that tribunal[4], unless jurisdiction is later conferred by statute[5].

1   *London Corpn v Cox* (1867) LR 2 HL 239, 262; *Pinnock Bros v Lewis & Peat Ltd* [1923] 1 KB 690, 693; Cf *Ayscough v Sheed Thomson & Co Ltd* (1924) 131 LT 610 HL where contracts for the sale of eggs required quality disputes to be referred to arbitration within three days of the goods becoming available to the buyer. The arbitrators did not find they had no jurisdiction as in *Pinnock Bros*, but held that the buyer was out of time. The award was a bar; *Waine v Crocker* (1862) 3 De GF & J 421, 431–432; *Simpson v Crowle* [1921] 3 KB 243; *Patterson v Knapdale Road Board* (1892) 11 NZLR 599 (items outside jurisdiction of Compensation Court, claim for those items in Supreme Court not barred); para 2.33 n 4.
2   *Upendra Nath Bose v Lall* [1940] AIR (PC) 222, 225; para 2.33 n 4.
3   *Tek Ming Co Ltd v Yee Sang Metal Supplies Co* [1973] 1 WLR 300 PC.
4   *R v Middlesex Justices ex p Bond* [1933] 2 KB 1 CA; *The Sennar* [1985] 1 WLR 490 HL.
5   *Hines v Birbeck College (No 2)* [1992] Ch 37 CA (action dismissed because matter within exclusive jurisdiction of visitor, statute later conferred jurisdiction on the High Court); *Minister for Home & Territories v Smith* (1924) 35 CLR 120, 129.

CONSENT JUDGMENTS

2.16 A judgment (or order) by consent is a *res judicata*[1]. The court is discharged from the duty of investigating or further investigating the matter and does not pronounce a judicial opinion[2]; but at the request of the parties it gives judicial sanction and coercive authority to an agreement which, except by statute[3], could not otherwise operate as a bar. Judgments, orders and awards by consent are as efficacious as those pronounced after a contest in creating cause of action estoppels and merging the cause of action sued on[4]. The extent to which a consent judgment may give rise to issue estoppels has not been finally determined. A judgment for damages consented to by the defendant without admission of liability did not preclude him suing the plaintiff on a cause of action inconsistent with his liability to the plaintiff in the original action[5]. 'The fact that a judgment is entered by consent may ... make it hard to say what was necessarily decided ... especially where it is the defendant who wishes to bring an action at a later date ... But the principle of *res judicata* holds good in such a case.'[6] The efficacy of a consent judgment to found a *res judicata* may depend upon the capacity of a party to enter into the underlying transaction or give consent[7], or the power of the court to make the orders[8].

1   *Kinch v Walcott* [1929] AC 482, 493 per Lord Blanesburgh: 'in relation to this plea of estoppel it is of no advantage to the appellant that the order ... was a consent order'. Under Scots law the plea of *res judicata* must be based on a judicial decision: *Margrie Holdings Ltd v City of Edinburgh* [1994] SLT 971, 974.
2   *Gairy v A-G of Grenada* [2002] 1 AC 167, 181.
3   Cf *Manton v Cantwell* [1920] AC 781, a decision under the Workmen's Compensation Act 1906.
4   *Munster v Cox* (1885) 10 App Cas 680; *The Bellcairn* (1885) 10 PD 161 CA (consent judgment could not be set aside by consent to the prejudice of third party); *Hammond v Schofield* [1891] 1 QB 453; *Thompson v Moore* (1889) 23 LR Ir 599 CA; *Re South American and Mexican Co, ex p Bank of England* [1895] 1 Ch 37 CA, 44–46, 50; *River Ribble Joint Committee v Croston UDC* [1897] 1 QB 251; *Haydock v Goodier* [1921] 2 KB 384 CA (consent award); *Hardy Lumber Co v Pickerel River Improvement Co* (1898) 29 SCR 211; *McGucken* [1991] NI LR 1.

5   *Isaacs v Ocean Accident and Guarantee Corpn Ltd* (1957) 58 SRNSW 69; Cf *SCF Finance Co Ltd v Masri (No 3)* [1987] QB 1028 CA.
6   *Chamberlain v Deputy Comr of Taxation* (1988) 164 CLR 502, 508 (*Chamberlain*).
7   *Great North-West Central Rly Co v Charlebois* [1899] AC 114; *Re Jon Beauforte Ltd* [1953] Ch 131 (*ultra vires* contracts); and paras 9.29–9.31 for children and incapable persons.
8   *Thompson Australian Holdings Pty Ltd v Trade Practices Commission* (1981) 148 CLR 150.

2.17 The court will consider the evidence[1] to ascertain the matters in dispute[2]. Evidence of the objective background is admissible but not direct evidence of the parties' subjective intentions[3]. Any issue which was raised in the litigation and was fundamental to the judgment will be conclusively determined[4]. Where there is no background material neither party is estopped from disputing anything but the actual judgment[5]. Lord Herschell LC said[6]:

> ' ... a judgment by consent is intended to put a stop to litigation between the parties, just as much as is a judgment which results from the decision of the court after the matter has been fought out to the end. And I think it would be very mischievous if one were not to give a fair and reasonable interpretation to such judgments and were to allow questions that were really involved in the action to be fought over again in a subsequent action'.

1   *Khan v Goleccha International Ltd* [1980] 1 WLR 1482 CA; *SCF Finance Co Ltd v Masri (No 3)* [1987] QB 1028 CA; para 8.29.
2   *Cloutte v Storey* [1911] 1 Ch 18, 26, 33.
3   *Ako* [2002] ICR 899 CA, 905.
4   *Thompson v Moore* (1889) 23 LR Ir 599 CA (consent order for perpetual injunction, decision on validity and infringement of patent); *Re South American and Mexican Co, ex p Bank of England* [1895] 1 Ch 37 CA (validity of agreement concluded by consent order); *McGucken* [1991] NILR 1 (consent judgment for possession excluded claim by defendant to unpleaded proprietary estoppel). Compare the equitable rules for the construction of general words in a release by reference to matters in the contemplation of the parties: *Grant v John Grant & Sons Pty Ltd* (1954) 91 CLR 112.
5   *Goucher v Clayton* (1865) 13 WR 336, 337 per Wood VC: 'there appear to have been no pleadings in the action. Had there been an assertion of the validity of the patent on one side, and a denial on the other, the court would have held the defendants estopped by their submission. This, however, did not appear by the record'; *Great-North West Central Rly Co v Charlebois* [1899] AC 114 (contract *ultra vires* and consent judgment did not bar the company from asserting its invalidity, this question not having been raised); *Re Jon Beauforte Ltd* [1953] Ch 131 (judgment founded on *ultra vires* contract cannot be sustained unless issue decided or compromised). A contested judgment where the *ultra vires* issue was not raised could not be challenged, but there would be no estoppel on the *ultra vires* question in other cases. The *ultra vires* doctrine has been practically abolished: para 17.21 n 5.
6   *Re South American and Mexican Co, ex p Bank of England* [1895] 1 Ch 37 CA, 50, cited in *Dinch* [1987] 1 WLR 252 HL, 263 where a consent order for financial provision barred a further application by the former wife; *Rick v Brandsema* (2007) 281 DLR (4th) 517 BCCA.

2.18 Where a judgment creating a *res judicata* has been pronounced after a hearing, a compromise on appeal setting it aside is not binding *in rem* because it is not a judicial decision[1]. The situation is otherwise in proceedings *in personam*. An order which records an undertaking by a party to allow judgment to be signed if he fails to comply with certain conditions[2], or is prefaced by a declaration that no judgment on the matters in issue is pronounced or desired[3], does not create a *res judicata*.

[1] *Jenkins v Robertson* (1867) LR 1 Sc & Div 117 HL. The council of a Scottish borough 'for behoof of the inhabitants and the public' raised an action for a declarator as to a public right of way and obtained a verdict. On the defenders obtaining a rule for a new trial, a consent decree was made which assoilzied the defenders. A second action was raised on behalf of the same inhabitants and public for the same declarator to which the defenders pleaded *res judicata* but the House of Lords held that the consent decree did not involve a declaration that no public right of way existed for the court had 'exercised no judicial function'. Under Scots law there can be no *res judicata* unless the decision was pronounced after a contest, para 2.16 n 1; *The Bellcairn* (1885) 10 PD 161 CA; para 2.16 n 4.

[2] *Litchfield v Ready* (1850) 5 Exch 939, 947.

[3] *Bradshaw v McMullan* [1920] 2 IR 412 HL 415, 424–425.

NO RES JUDICATA AGAINST PARTIES NOT CONSENTING

2.19 As a general rule, but subject to statute, a consent judgment only affects a party who consented[1]. In *James Hardie & Coy Pty Ltd v Seltsam Pty Ltd*[2] the High Court of Australia held, by majority, that the equivalent of the 1935 Act[3] produced a different result. The plaintiff sued three defendants as concurrent tortfeasors and consent judgments were entered in his favour against two, but in favour of the third. The latter was then sued for contribution by the others but the majority held that it was not liable[4] because it had been sued and, under the consent judgment, was not liable. Apart from statute a party, who has not appeared, will not be estopped by a judgment given by consent of the other parties[5]. There cannot be a judgment *in rem* by consent, although the parties may be estopped *inter se*[6].

[1] *Goucher v Clayton* (1865) 13 WR 336; *Wytcherley v Andrews* (1871) LR 2 P & D 327, 329; *Munster v Cox* (1885) 10 App Cas 680; *The Bellcairn* (1885) 10 PD 161 CA at 166; *Ritchie v Malcolm* [1902] 2 IR 403, 409–411.

[2] (1998) 196 CLR 53, paras 9.35–9.36.

[3] The Law Reform (Married Women and Tortfeasors) Act 1935.

[4] The minority applied the general principle in the text: (1998) 196 CLR 53, 69, 88.

[5] *Ritchie v Malcolm* [1902] 2 IR 403, 410.

[6] Para 2.18 n 1.

BANKRUPTCY AND INSOLVENCY

2.20 The Bankruptcy Court when deciding whether to make a bankruptcy order[1] can 'go behind' a judgment against the debtor[2] including one obtained after a hearing[3]. The Court has the same power when deciding whether to admit a judgment debt to proof[4]. It cannot set aside the judgment or finally determine that there was no antecedent debt and the judgment remains a *res judicata* for other purposes. Where a Registrar refused to make a receiving order because the judgment debt was not a good petitioning creditor's debt, the creditor could present a second petition and obtain a receiving order[5]. An order dismissing an application to set aside a statutory demand on the ground that the debt was disputed will generally bind the debtor on the hearing not because the question is *res judicata*, but because of the scheme of the 1986 Act and Rules[6]. The Court will entertain an argument that could not have been raised earlier and receive evidence of a change of circumstances[7]. Where no application was made to set aside the statutory demand the Court may entertain arguments that the debtor could have raised earlier[8]. It can also review an order refusing to set aside a statutory demand, and receive evidence that could have been obtained for the earlier application[9]. A liquidator is in the same position as the trustee in bankruptcy when deciding to admit or reject proofs of debt[10]. If a proof of debt is rejected and there is no appeal the decision of the trustee or liquidator becomes binding for all purposes[11]. Under earlier bankruptcy legislation an adjudication in bankruptcy established conclusively against third parties that the debtor was bankrupt[12] and had committed the act of bankruptcy referred to in the order[13].

[1] Insolvency Act 1986 ss 266(3), 271 (the 1986 Act).

[2] *Re Blythe, ex p Banner* (1881) 17 Ch D 480 CA (dishonest compromise and extortion); *Re Hawkins, exp Troup* [1895] 1 QB 404 CA (judgment founded on unfair and unreasonable compromise); *Re Mead* [1916] 2 IR 285 CA (debtor withdrew plea of infancy, debtor's summons properly dismissed). In *Re Lennox, ex p Lennox* (1885) 16 QBD 315 CA, 323 Esher MR held that *prima facie* regard ought to be paid by the Court of Bankruptcy to a consent judgment, and in *Re Flateau, ex p Scotch Whiskey Distillers Ltd* (1888) 22 QBD 83 CA it was held that the Court ought not to review a judgment except in circumstances suggesting fraud, collusion, or a miscarriage of justice; *Corney v Brien* (1951) 84 CLR 343. In *Re A Debtor (No 27 of 1927)* [1929] 1 Ch 125 the Court declined to reopen a consent judgment from a bona fide compromise. Cf *Re Cole, Trustee in Bankruptcy v Public Trustee* [1931] 2 Ch 174.

[3] *Re Flateau, ex p Scotch Whiskey Distillers Ltd* (1888) 22 QBD 83 CA; *Re Newey, ex p Whiteman* (1912) 107 LT 832 (receiving order made on contested judgment based on award for gaming debt); *Re A Debtor* (1915) 113 LT 704; *Wren v Mahony* (1972) 126 CLR 212, 224–225.

[4] *Re Tollemache, ex p Revelle* (1884) 13 QBD 720 CA. The principle was stated in *Re Van Laun, ex p Patullo* [1907] 1 KB 155, 163 by Bigham J and approved on appeal [1907] 2 KB 23 CA ('No judgment recovered against the bankrupt, no covenant given by him or accounts stated with him, can deprive the trustee of this right. He is entitled to go behind such forms to get at the truth, and the estoppel to which the bankrupt may have subjected himself will not prevail against him').

[5] *Re Vitoria, ex p Vitoria* [1894] 2 QB 387 CA.

[6] *Turner v Royal Bank of Scotland* [2000] BPIR 683 CA, 687–678, 694; *Coulter v Chief Constable of Dorset Police (No 2)* [2006] BPIR 10 CA, 17 overruling *Eberhardt & Co Ltd v Mair* [1995] 1 WLR 1180; *Makhoul v Barnes* (1995) 60 FCR 572 (issue on hearing of petition different from that on application to set aside bankruptcy notice).

[7] *Turner v Royal Bank of Scotland* [2000] BPIR 683 CA, 688, 694; *Coulter (No 2)* [2006] BPIR 10 CA, 16–18.

[8] *Coulter (No 2)* [2006] BPIR 10 CA, 16–17. A similar regime applies in Australia to statutory demands which have not been set aside: Corporations Act 2001 s 459S. Prior to this legislation the issue could arise on the hearing of a winding up application if an injunction to restrain its presentation had been refused: *Australian Mid-Eastern Club Ltd v Elbakht* (1988) 13 NSWLR 697 CA; *Yassim v Australian Mid-Eastern Club Ltd* (1989) 15 ACLR 449.

[9] Section 375(1); *Re a Debtor (No 32/SD/1991)* [1993] 1 WLR 314.

[10] *Re Home and Colonial Insurance Co Ltd* [1930] 1 Ch 102; *Re Jon Beauforte Ltd* [1953] Ch 131; *Re Exchange Securities Financial Services Ltd (in liqu)* [1988] Ch 46, 58; *Tanning Research Laboratories Inc v O'Brien* (1990) 169 CLR 332, 339–340; *Re Sullivan* (1904) 7 GLR 376 (NZ).

[11] *Brandon v McHenry* [1891] 1 QB 538 (creditor who did not appeal against rejection of proof could not recover after bankruptcy annulled); *Bank of Credit and Commerce International (Overseas) Ltd (in liq) v Habib Bank Ltd* [1999] 1 WLR 42, 50 (creditor who did not appeal could not rely on debt as set-off).

[12] *Revel v Blake* (1873) LR 8 CP 533 Ex Ch, 544 (the facts appear (1872) LR 7 CP 300); Bankruptcy Act 1914 s 137(2). There is no equivalent in the 1986 Act or Rules cf r 12.20.

[13] *Re Foulds, ex p Learoyd* (1878) 10 Ch D 3 CA; *Bowler v Power* [1910] 2 KB 229 CA; *Yousuf v Official Assignee* (1943) LR 70 Ind App 93, 98. Acts of bankruptcy were abolished in 1986 and the title of the trustee does not relate back but legislation modelled on the Bankruptcy Act 1914 remains in force in many Commonwealth jurisdictions.

COMPANIES COURT

2.21 When a winding-up application is presented based on a judgment which the company wishes to challenge on substantial grounds the proper course, if the company undertakes to apply to have the judgment set aside, is for the Companies Court to adjourn the petition and not attempt to 'go behind' the judgment[1].

---

1   *Bowes v Directors of Hope Life Insurance Guarantee Co* (1865) 11 HLCas 389.

DEFAULT JUDGMENTS

2.22 A judgment (or order) by default is a judicial decision, whether the default was in filing an appearance; in pleading[1]; in appearance at the hearing[2]; or in prosecution of, or resistance to, an appeal[3]. In *Henderson*[4] the *ex parte* hearings which led to the order for the taking of accounts, the Master's certificate, and the decree on further consideration were in a sense default judgments. Where a point is overlooked in contested proceedings and the relevant party is later estopped[5], the judgment on that point is analogous to a default judgment. It may not be easy to identify the issues of fact or law determined by a default judgment. In some cases it may be a form of judgment by consent[6], but in others it may be the result of negligence, ignorance, or other demands on the defendant's time[7]. A judgment by default in any form will, unless and until set aside[8], conclude the matters expressly decided by its operative and declaratory parts.

---

1   *Aslin v Parkin* (1758) 2 Burr 665, 668 per Lord Mansfield: 'there is no distinction between a judgment in ejectment by a verdict, and a judgment by default'; *Wilkinson v Kirby* (1854) 15 CB 430, 443, 448; *Huffer v Allen* (1866) LR 2 Ex Ch 15; *Harris v Mulkern* (1875) 1 Ex D 31 Ex Ch, 35. In *Kok Hoong* [1964] AC 993, 1010 Viscount Radcliffe said: 'There is no doubt ... that ... a default judgment is capable of giving rise to an estoppel *per rem judicatam*. The question is not whether there can be such an estoppel, but rather what the judgment ... shall be treated as concluding'; *Tira Arika v Sidaway* [1923] NZLR 158. Under Scots law a default judgment cannot support a plea of *res judicata*; *Margrie Holdings Ltd v City of Edinburgh* [1994] SLT 971, 974.
2   *Nesbit v Rishton* (1839) 11 Ad & El 244 Ex Ch, 250–251. In *Ker v Williams* (1885) 29 Sol Jo 681 CA, the dismissal of an action on default of appearance at the trial was held to be a 'judgment' which 'operated as an estoppel to the plaintiff'; *Linprint Pty Ltd v Hexham Textiles Pty Ltd* (1991) 23 NSWLR 508 CA (*Linprint*).
3   *Lockyer v Ferryman* (1877) 2 App Cas 519 (appellant failed to prosecute appeal).
4   (1843) 3 Hare 100 (the ex parte judgments were in Newfoundland).
5   *Hoystead v Federal Taxation Comr* [1926] AC 155 (*Hoystead*); *Port of Melbourne Authority v Anshun Pty Ltd* (1981) 147 CLR 589 (*Anshun*).
6   *Kok Hoong* [1964] AC 993, 1010.
7   *New Brunswick* [1939] AC 1, 21, 35; *Hume v Munro* (1942) 42 SRNSW 218, 221, 229–230 (default judgment for rent in 1939 estopped defendant denying liability under lease with 59 years to run).
8   *Linprint* (1991) 23 NSWLR 508 CA, 517–518; para 3.01 n 4.

2.23 An issue estoppel will only be created by a default judgment[1] if an issue was determined in favour of the claimant which can be formulated with complete precision[2].

1   *New Brunswick* [1939] AC 1, 21, 38–39; *Kok Hoong* [1964] AC 993, 1010. *St L Kelly* (1968) 84 LQR 362 contends, on historical grounds, that default judgments should not create issue estoppels unless the defendant defaulted in pleading, which is contrary to existing authority.
2   *Ozer Properties Ltd v Ghaydi* [1988] 1 EGLR 91 CA, 92; *McConnell v Lombard and Ulster Banking Ltd* [1982] NI 203, 208 where an estoppel failed because the statement of claim contained inconsistent allegations.

NEW BRUNSWICK[1]

2.24 An action was brought for principal and interest under a bond with a 'gold clause' and the statement of claim sought a declaration about its construction. The plaintiff obtained an *ex parte* judgment including the declaration on a motion in default of appearance and defence. A second action was brought on 992 bonds from the same issue and the plaintiff relied on an issue estoppel. The House of Lords held that the judgment had not determined the questions in the second action. The questions although *similar*, were not precisely *the same*. Lord Maugham LC said[2]:

'... the judgment in that action, limited in form to a single bond, was pronounced in default of appearance by the defendants. In my view not all estoppels are "odious"; but the adjective might well be applicable if a defendant, particularly if he is sued for a small sum in a country distant from his own, is held to be estopped not merely in respect of the actual judgment obtained against him, but from defending himself against a claim for a much larger sum on the ground that one of the issues in the first action ... had decided as a matter of inference his only defence in the second ... In my opinion we are at least justified in holding that an estoppel based on a default judgment must be very carefully limited. The true principle in such a case would seem to be that the defendant is estopped from setting up in a subsequent action a defence which was necessarily, and with complete precision, decided by the previous judgment; in other words, by the *res judicata* in the accurate sense'.

Lord Thankerton and Lord Russell of Killowen agreed with the Lord Chancellor. Lord Wright and Lord Romer questioned whether what is now known as issue estoppel had any application to default judgments. Lord Wright said[3]:

'No authority has been produced in which a party has been held to be estopped from raising in a litigation an issue which he might have raised in a previous litigation in which he allowed judgment to go by default ... . There are grave reasons of convenience why a party should not be held to be bound by every matter of fact or law fundamental to the default judgment. It is, I think, too artificial to treat the party in default as bound by every such matter as if by admission. All necessary effect is given to the default judgment by treating it as conclusive of what it directly decides. I should regard any further effect in the way of estoppel as an illegitimate extension of the doctrine, which in the absence of express authority I am not prepared to accept'.

1   [1939] AC 1, and para 8.15. The dispute related to the effect of currency devaluations and the abandonment of the gold standard during the Great Depression.
2   Ibid at 21; *Kok Hoong* [1964] AC 993, 1012; *Carl Zeiss (No.2)* [1967] 1 AC 853, 946.
3   [1939] AC 1, 37.

KOK HOONG[1]

2.25 The plaintiff who sued for instalments under a loan agreement was met with defences based on money-lending and bills of sale legislation. He set up an estoppel based on a default judgment for a previous instalment. If the statutory defences were good, and had been pleaded in the earlier action, the plaintiff could not have recovered. The estoppel failed because the defences raised new issues by way of confession and avoidance[2], and it could not be said that the first judgment 'had necessarily and with complete precision concluded the issue in the second'[3].

[1]   *Kok Hoong* [1964] AC 993; para 8.15.
[2]   Ibid at 1014.
[3]   *New Brunswick* [1939] AC 1, 21.

DEFAULT JUDGMENTS AS TO THE CONSTRUCTION OF DOCUMENTS

2.26 Default judgments should not include a declaration as to the construction of a document[1].

[1]   *Wallersteiner v Moir* [1974] 1 WLR 991 CA, 1029–1030. Such a declaration was made in *Patten v Burke Publishing Co Ltd* [1991] 2 All ER 821.

THE EFFECT OF BANKRUPTCY ON DEFAULT JUDGMENTS

2.27 The principles which apply in bankruptcy to consent judgments also apply to default judgments[1].

[1]   Para 2.20; *Re Onslow, ex p Kibble* (1875) 10 Ch App 373 (infancy); *Re Tollemache, ex p Revell* (1884) 13 QBD 720 CA, 724 (judgment entitled to respect, only questioned when circumstances are suspicious or special); *Re Tollemache, ex p Anderson* (1885) 14 QBD 606 CA, 609–610, *Re Deerhurst, ex p Seaton* (1891) 64 LT 273 CA, 274; *Re Fraser, ex p Central Bank of London* [1892] 2 QB 633 CA (jurisdiction not affected although judgment entered under O 14 and debtor had unsuccessfully appealed); *Re Debtor (No 229 of 1927)* [1927] 2 Ch 367 CA (default judgment by money-lender not good petitioning creditor's debt where contract vitiated by secret commission); *Re Davenport, ex p Bankrupt v Eric Street Properties Ltd* [1963] 1 WLR 817 CA (default judgment against infant for unenforceable debt: adjudication set aside). The power to go behind a judgment is also exercisable where statute provides a discretionary remedy for the enforcement of a judgment eg in applications for a charging order under the Judgments Act 1838: *Re Onslow's Trusts* (1875) LR 20 Eq 677, 680–681; *Re Leavesley* [1891] 2 Ch 1 CA.

DISMISSALS AFTER A HEARING

2.28 The issue estoppel created by a dismissal is limited to 'the actual ground upon which the existence of the right was negatived.'[1] If this cannot be determined the dismissal will only decide that relief was refused. The availability of the court's reasons[2] and the diminished role of the civil jury make it possible in most cases to determine the actual basis of a dismissal. An important question is involved. As Lord Cranworth LC explained[3], it was necessary:

> '... to show that the question raised in the second suit had been adjudicated upon in the first ... this is not ... a technical rule at all, but is one of substance, and unless it is strictly adhered to plaintiffs who have a clear title to relief on account of the breach of an agreement may, by failing to prove a breach, lose all right to complain of future breaches'.

A dismissal is not a decision on title[4] unless that question was finally determined[5]. The discharge of a rule to set aside a bond and warrant of attorney for non-compliance with statutory requirements was a decision that these had been complied with[6]. The dismissal of a petition under the National Debt Act 1870 because the petitioner failed to prove that the testator was the owner of the stock was a decision on title and not a nonsuit[7]. Dismissal of an action for criminal conversation because the cause of action was not known to the law of Hong Kong barred an action after the law was retrospectively changed[8]. A refusal of a certificate of exemption from military service was conclusive of the applicant's liability to serve[9].

[1] *Blair v Curran* (1939) 62 CLR 464, 532; paras 8.02, 8.26.
[2] Para 8.29.
[3] *Moss v Anglo-Egyptian Navigation Co* (1865) 1 Ch App 108, 115; paras 8.17, 8.26.
[4] *Brandlyn v Ord* (1738) 1 Atk 571; *Bainbrigge v Baddeley* (1847) 2 Ph 705, 710.
[5] *Jones v Nixon* (1831) You 359.
[6] *Greathead v Bromley* (1798) 7 Term Rep 455.
[7] *Re May* (1885) 28 Ch D 516 CA, 518, 522.
[8] *Lemm v Mitchell* [1912] AC 400, 405; *Anshun* (1981) 147 CLR 589, 611.
[9] *Langdon v Richards* (1917) 33 TLR 325.

2.29 A decision of arbitrators that a claim was brought out of time barred an action because the claim had been dealt with[1]. On a husband's petition for divorce, the judge found adultery proved, made no finding on desertion, declined to exercise his discretion in the petitioner's favour, and dismissed the petition. This did not stop the husband repeating the charge of adultery since he had succeeded on that issue, nor from repeating the charge of desertion, since there had been no finding upon it; and the wife was not estopped from denying desertion either[2]. The dismissal of an action requiring proof of x or y is a decision negativing both[3], but if the action is founded on x plus y, its dismissal is not a decision on either, since the action may have failed because x was not established, though y was, or *vice versa*, or because neither had been established[4]. A bare dismissal in such a case does not stop the claimant suing on a cause of action for which proof of only x or y is sufficient[5]. These questions are not likely to arise today except in jury cases where there has been a general verdict for the defendant. Where a proceeding has been dismissed, no finding of fact will create an estoppel unless it was necessary to the dismissal. So where the court assumed that a resolution of a municipal council was valid, but refused relief, its validity was not *res judicata*[6]. On the other hand the dismissal of an application which is not pursued will create issue estoppels despite any unilateral reservation of rights or denial of admissions[7].

[1] *Ayscough v Sheed Thomson & Co Ltd* (1924) 131 LT 610 HL, para 2.15 n 1.

[2] *Bernard* [1958] 3 All ER 475.
[3] *Lockyer v Ferryman* (1877) 2 App Cas 519. A Scottish action for a declarator of marriage, on the ground of (i) a contract *per verba de praesenti*, or, (ii) a promise *subsequente copula*, failed, and was a decision that neither existed.
[4] *Re Allsop and Joy's Contract* (1889) 61 LT 213, 215; *Shoe Machinery Co Ltd v Cutlan* [1896] 1 Ch 667. The court's reasons will disclose the basis for its decision: *ACCC v Australian Safeway Stores Pty Ltd* (2001) 119 FCR 1, 266–268.
[5] *Putt v Rawstern* (1681) T Raym 472.
[6] *Vitosh v Brisbane CC* (1955) 93 CLR 622.
[7] *SCF Finance Co Ltd v Masri (No 3)* [1987] QB 1028 CA. Cf *Isaacs v Ocean Accident and Guarantee Corpn Ltd* (1957) 58 SRNSW 69.

REFUSALS OF WRITS OF HABEAS CORPUS

2.30 It was formerly thought[1] that, although an order granting *habeas corpus* was a decision *in rem*[2], a refusal was not a decision, and the applicant could make fresh applications to any court of competent jurisdiction[3]. This was rejected in a series of decisions in 1958–1959[4]. The matter was then dealt with by statute and a second application on the same grounds cannot be made now without fresh evidence[5].

[1] 1st edn, para 42.
[2] Paras 10.07, 16.08.
[3] *Ex p Partington* (1845) 13 M & W 679; *Cox v Hakes* (1890) 15 App Cas 506; *Secretary of State for Home Affairs v O'Brien* [1923] AC 603; *Eshugbayi Eleko v Officer Administering the Government of Nigeria* [1928] AC 459. In New Zealand it was held in *Ex p Bouvy (No 2)* (1900) 18 NZLR 601 that a judge in refusing the writ exercises the whole jurisdiction of the Supreme Court, and a refusal operates as an estoppel; *Wall v R* (1927) 39 CLR 245; *Wall v R (No 2)* (1927) 39 CLR 266.
[4] *Re Hastings (No 2)* [1959] 1 QB 358; *Re Hastings (No 3)* [1959] Ch 368; affd [1959] 1 WLR 807 CA; and *Manoharan v Menteri Dalam Negeri* [2009] 2 MLJ 660 CA.
[5] Administration of Justice Act 1960 s 14(2); *R v Governor of Pentonville Prison ex parte Tarling* [1979] 1 WLR 1417, 1422–1423; paras 10.07, 16.08.

DISMISSALS BY COURTS OF SUMMARY JURISDICTION (CIVIL)

2.31 These principles apply to proceedings before courts of summary jurisdiction in their civil or quasi-civil jurisdiction. Thus the dismissal of an affiliation summons against the alleged father is not a decision that he is not the father[1]. The justices can only make or refuse an order for the maintenance of the child and, although an order cannot be made without deciding that the defendant is the father, it can be refused without a decision on paternity, with the effect of a nonsuit[2]. An unsuccessful applicant can make a fresh application[3], on different evidence[4] which need not be technically fresh[5]. The dismissal on the merits of a summons for a matrimonial offence under the Summary Jurisdiction (Married Women) Act 1895[6] estopped the complainant[7], but a finding that desertion was not proved did not bar such a finding at a later date[8].

[1] *McGregor v Telford* [1915] 3 KB 237; *R v Sunderland Justices, ex p Hodgkinson* [1945] KB 502, 503; *Robinson v Williams* [1965] 1 QB 89, 97.
[2] *McGregor v Telford* [1915] 3 KB 237, 240–242; *R v Sunderland Justices, ex p Hodgkinson* [1945] KB 502, 503.
[3] *Robinson v Williams* [1965] 1 QB 89, 97 per Lord Parker CJ: 'All the cases show that there is no question of *res judicata* in such a case'.

⁴ *R v Sunderland Justices, ex p Hodgkinson* [1945] KB 502, 506–509; *Robinson v Williams* [1965] 1 QB 89, 100; *Re F (W) (an infant)* [1969] 2 Ch 269.
⁵ *Robinson v Williams* [1965] 1 QB 89, 98–100.
⁶ Now the Domestic Proceedings and Magistrates' Courts Act 1978.
⁷ *Stokes* [1911] P 195, 198–200.
⁸ *Froud* (1920) 123 LT 176.

DISMISSALS BY COURTS OF SUMMARY JURISDICTION (CRIMINAL)

2.32 This is considered in paras 14.05 & foll.

APPELLATE DECISIONS

2.33 When an appellate court reverses the judgment below, the former decision, until then conclusive, is avoided *ab initio*[1] and replaced by the appellate decision, which becomes the *res judicata* between the parties. Even if the appeal fails, the decision of the appellate court becomes the source of any estoppels[2]. An issue not dealt with below which the appellate court treats as material when dismissing the appeal is also *res judicata*[3]. Where the appellate tribunal reverses a judgment for lack of jurisdiction, that judgment is a nullity, and the reversal does not decide any question on the merits[4].

¹ *P & O Nedlloyd BV v Arab Metals Co (No 2)* [2007] 1 WLR 2288 CA, 2300–2301; *Railway Comr (NSW) v Cavanough* (1935) 53 CLR 220; D M Gordon 'Effect of reversal of judgment' (1958) 74 LQR 517, 518–521; *The People v Quilligan (No 3)* [1993] 2 IR 305 SC, 328; cf *The People v O'Callaghan* [2001] 1 IR 584, 596–597. For the effect of order for a new trial: para 5.14.
² *Shedden v Patrick* (1854) 1 Macq 535 HL, 590, 599; *Wishart v Fraser* (1941) 64 CLR 470; *R v Marks* (1981) 147 CLR 471, 476.
³ *Midnapur Zamindary Co Ltd v Roy* (1924) LR 51 Ind App 293.
⁴ *Cross v Salter* (1790) 3 TR 639 (reversal for lack of jurisdiction); *R v Drury* (1848) 3 Car & Kir 190, 199, 200; *Conlin v Patterson* [1915] 2 IR 169 (order quashing conviction could not support plea of *autrefois acquit*); *R v Marsham, ex p Phethick Lawrence* [1912] 2 KB 362. For settlement cases *R v St Andrew, Holborn* (1796) 6 Term Rep 613 (quashing of order of removal no adjudication); *R v Wick St Lawrence Inhabitants* (1833) 5 B & Ad 526 (quashing order *prima facie* not a 'decision' on any other question); *Singh v Assets Recovery Agency* [2005] 1 WLR 3747 CA, 3751 (statutory bar to double recovery not attracted where decision quashed for lack of jurisdiction); para 2.15.

2.34 Where an appellate tribunal records a compromise without exercising any judicial function, there is no *res judicata*[1]. However, if it enters a judgment or order *in personam* by consent, the ordinary consequences follow[2].

¹ Para 2.18.
² Paras 2.16–2.19; *Khan v Goleccha International Ltd* [1980] 1 WLR 1482 CA.

CRIMINAL DECISIONS

2.35 These are considered in Chs 14 and 23.

FOREIGN DECISIONS

2.36 With certain exceptions[1] a foreign judicial decision is conclusive and impeachable only on the same grounds as an English decision[2]. Decisions of superior courts in England are presumed, until the contrary is shown, to be within jurisdiction, and as a general rule fraud as an answer to an English judgment must be established in a substantive action. In the case of a foreign decision the onus as to jurisdiction lies upon the party setting it up as a *res judicata*, and answers such as fraud or public policy may be raised in the action in which the judgment is set up. Thus English and foreign judgments still have different consequences[3].

[1] Paras 2.57 *et seq*. An English court will not recognise a foreign judgment which is inconsistent with an earlier decision of a competent English court: *Showlag v Mansour* [1995] 1 AC 431; *E.D. & F. Man (Sugar) Ltd v Yani Haryanto (No 2)* [1991] 1 Lloyd's Rep 429 CA.

[2] *Godard v Gray* (1870) LR 6 QB 139, 150; *Ellis v M'Henry* (1871) LR 6 CP 228, 238; *Grant v Easton* (1883) 13 QBD 302 CA; *Pemberton v Hughes* [1899] 1 Ch 781 CA, 793–794; *Carl-Zeiss (No 2)* [1967] 1 AC 853, 917–918, 925 per Lord Reid: 'At one time foreign judgments were regarded as being only evidence and not conclusive. But at least since the decision in *Godard v Gray* they have been regarded as equally conclusive with English judgments ... The same pleas, e.g. fraud or lack of jurisdiction, are good against both'. The Foreign Judgments (Reciprocal Enforcement) Act 1933 s 8 (the 1933 Act) provides that a judgment to which the Act applies shall be conclusive between the parties in all proceedings founded on the same cause of action, and may be relied upon by way of defence or counterclaim in such proceedings: *Black-Clawson International Ltd v Papierwerke Waldhof-Aschaffenburg AG* [1975] AC 591.

[3] *Carl-Zeiss (No 2)* [1967] 1 AC 853, 917, 966.

2.37 Considerations of convenience encouraged the recognition of the validity of annulments and divorces pronounced by courts in other countries. In 1678, on an appeal to the House of Lords from a decision that the petitioner was precluded by a sentence of the Archbishop of Turin, from asserting that his wife had another husband, Nottingham LC said that 'it is against the law of nations not to give credit to the judgment and sentences of foreign countries, till they be reversed by the law, and according to the form, of those countries wherein they were given. For what right hath one kingdom to reverse the judgment of another? And how can we refuse to let a sentence take place until it be reversed? And *what confusion would follow in Christendom, if they should serve us so abroad, and give no credit to our sentences?*'[1] Decrees by the court of the domicile of the parties have long been recognised; and in more recent times so have decrees by foreign courts in circumstances in which an English court would assume jurisdiction[2].

[1] *Cottington's Case* (1678) 2 Swan 326n.
[2] *Travers v Holley* [1953] P 246 CA; *Indyka* [1969] 1 AC 33; Ch 15.

2.38 A 'foreign' decision for present purposes is any decision of a judicial tribunal outside English jurisdiction in its strict sense[1], including a consular or other court or tribunal exercising jurisdiction in a foreign state pursuant to a treaty or other arrangements between states[2], and an award of a foreign domestic tribunal enforceable according to the law of the state where it was made[3]. The judgment may be that of a court of a member of a federation – eg a court of one of the States of the United States[4], or Australia[5].

¹   Ireland: *Houlditch v Marquess of Donegal* (1834) 2 Cl & Fin 470 HL; Scotland: *Harvey v Farnie* (1881) 8 App Cas 43, 50; *Re Low, Bland v Low* [1894] 1 Ch 147 CA; *Marchioness Huntly v Gaskell* [1905] 2 Ch 656 CA; *Re A Bankruptcy Notice* [1898] 1 QB 383 CA; the Isle of Man: *Harris v Quine* (1869) LR 4 QB 653; *Harris v Taylor* [1915] 2 KB 580 CA. Decisions of courts in the Commonwealth outside the British Isles and in the remaining colonies are foreign for present purposes.

²   *Dent v Smith* (1869) LR 4 QB 414 (Russian Consular Court at Constantinople); *Messina v Petrococchino* (1872) LR 4 PC 144 (Greek Consular Court at Constantinople); *Dallal v Bank Mellat* [1986] QB 441 (international arbitral tribunal established by treaty between USA and Iran operating in Holland); *R v Aughet* (1918) 13 Cr App Rep 101, 109 (foreign court martial exercising jurisdiction by treaty over foreign national charged with crime in England).

³   *Merrifield, Ziegler & Co v Liverpool Cotton Association Ltd* (1911) 105 LT 97, 103–105, (award of Bremen Cotton Association binding though not final).

⁴   *Colt Industries Inc v Sarlie (No 2)* [1966] 1 WLR 1287 CA, 1291 per Lord Denning MR 'The relevant territory is the State of New York'.

⁵   *Travers v Holley* [1953] P 246 CA (New South Wales).

2.39 The elements of a *res judicata* estoppel for a foreign judgment are the same[1].

¹   Para 1.02; *Price v Dewhurst* (1838) 4 My & Cr 76; *Fracis, Times & Co v Carr* (1900) 82 LT 698 CA, 701–702; *Carl-Zeiss (No 2)* [1967] 1 AC 853 (parties not the same, and judgment not final).

PENAL JUDGMENTS

2.40 The courts of this country will not enforce the penal and other public laws which protect the interests of another state[1]. An English court will determine the substance of the right and the fact that the relevant statute imposes criminal sanctions does not necessarily make the right penal[2]. Proceedings by a public body or official of a foreign state, to enforce a statutory remedy for the recovery of the proceeds of consumer frauds, were not penal in substance where recoveries would be held for the defrauded consumers. As the Privy Council said, following judgments of Marshall CJ in the Supreme Court of the United States:

> '... the rule has its foundation in the well-recognised principle that crimes, including in that term all breaches of public law punishable by pecuniary mulct or otherwise, at the instance of the state government, or of someone representing the public, are local in this sense, that they are only cognisable and punishable in the country where they were committed. Accordingly, no proceeding, even in the shape of a civil suit, which has for its object the enforcement by the state, whether directly or indirectly, of punishment imposed for such breaches by the lex fori, ought to be admitted in the courts of any other country.'[3]

¹   *Government of Iran v Barakat Galleries Ltd* [2009] QB 1 CA, 57–58; *Robb Evans v European Bank Ltd* (2004) 61 NSWLR 75 CA.

²   *Government of Iran v Barakat Galleries Ltd* [2009] QB 1 CA, 54.

³   *Huntington v Attrill* [1893] AC 150, 156–157.

2.41 It follows that a foreign decision enforcing a penal law, including one imposing a disqualification or diminution of status, does not create an estoppel in this country[1]. 'Penal' in this connection has a wider meaning than 'punitive'[2]. A judgment which alters the status of a party so as to 'deprive him of a very valuable right' is 'penal' for this purpose. The Privy Council continued[3]:

> 'A proceeding, in order to come within the scope of the rule 'as to the local effect of penal decisions' must be in the nature of a suit in favour of the state whose law has been infringed. All the provisions of municipal statutes for the regulation of trade and trading companies are presumably enacted in the interest and for the benefit of the community at large; and persons who violate these provisions are, in a certain sense, offenders against the state law, as well as against individuals who may be injured by their misconduct. But foreign tribunals do not regard these violations of statute law as offences against the state, unless their vindication rests with the state itself, or with the community which it represents. Penalties may be attached to them, but that circumstance will not bring them within the rules, except in cases where these penalties are recoverable at the instance of the state, or of an official duly authorised to prosecute on its behalf, or of a member of the public in the character of a common informer. An action by the latter is regarded as an actio popularis pursued, not in his individual interest, but in the interest of the whole community'.

If the foreign decision is partly 'penal', but severable, the residue will be recognised as a *res judicata*[4]. The English court determines whether the foreign decision is penal or not and whether any civil residue is severable[5]. The principle is now embodied in s 14(3)(a) of the Private International Law (Miscellaneous Provisions) Act 1995.

[1]   *Worms v De Valdor* (1880) 49 LJ Ch 261; *Re Selot's Trust* [1902] 1 Ch 488 (per Farwell LJ at 492: 'where the disability or the disqualification ... arises from the principles or customs or positive law of a foreign country, especially of a penal nature, it is not regarded by this court'). Both cases related to the status of a 'prodigue' under adjudications of French courts. They were followed in *Re Langley's Settlement Trusts.Lloyds Bank Ltd v Langley* [1962] Ch 541 CA where the order of the Superior Court of California, which the Court refused to recognise, deprived someone with multiple sclerosis of contractual capacity.
[2]   *Re Langley's Settlement Trusts* [1962] Ch 541 CA, 557.
[3]   *Huntington v Attrill* [1893] AC 150,157–158, para 9.13.
[4]   *Raulin v Fischer* [1911] 2 KB 93. This was an action on a French judgment in a proceeding of a criminal nature ('action publique') for reckless riding. French law allowed the person injured to intervene as a 'tiers partie', and to institute a claim for relief ('action civile') against the wrongdoer. The plaintiff intervened, recovered damages and sued on the judgment. Hamilton J held that such a decision was severable, and the civil component could be sued on in this country; *Black v Yates* [1992] QB 526 (Spanish judgment to like effect).
[5]   *Huntington v Attrill* [1893] AC 150, 155; *Raulin v Fischer* [1911] 2 KB 93, 97.

2.42   At common law a claim by or for the benefit of[1] a foreign government for a revenue debt was not entertained[2] and a foreign judgment for a revenue debt was not recognised[3]. The principle is embodied in s 14(3)(a) of the Private International Law (Miscellaneous Provisions) Act 1995, but has been abrogated for Member States by Council Regulation 1346/2000. Article 39 provides that any creditor in a Member State 'including the tax authorities ... of Member States shall have the right to lodge claims in the insolvency proceedings.'[4]

1   *In Peter Buchanan Ltd and Macharg v McVey* [1955] AC 516n the Irish Courts refused to
     entertain a claim by the liquidator of a Scots company brought for the sole benefit of the
     UK Revenue.
2   'No country ever takes notice of the revenue laws of another', per Lord Mansfield in
     Holman v Johnson (1775) 1 Cowp 341, 343; *Planche v Fletcher* (1779) 1 Doug KB 251,
     253; *James v Catherwood* (1823) 3 Dow & Ry KB 190, 191; *Re Visser, Queen of Holland
     v Drukker* [1928] Ch 877, 883; *Sydney Municipal Council v Bull* [1909] 1 KB 7;
     Government of India, Ministry of Finance (Revenue Division) v Taylor [1955] AC 491.
3   *Government of India, Ministry of Finance (Revenue Division) v Taylor* [1955] AC 491,
     506 per Lord Simonds: 'the courts of one country do not regard the revenue laws of
     another, and therefore will not allow judgments for foreign taxes to be enforced'. In
     Regazzoni v K C Sethia (1944) Ltd [1958] AC 301, 318 he said that it is 'beyond all doubt
     that an English court will not enforce the penal or revenue laws of another country at the
     suit of that country'. However English courts can make orders for obtaining evidence in
     connection with revenue litigation abroad: *Re State of Norway's Application* [1990] 1 AC
     723. Orders may also be made under bankruptcy legislation in aid of a foreign trustee to
     reach local assets although the bulk of the proved debts are for foreign taxes: *Re Ayres*
     (1981) 51 FLR 395, *Re Ayres* (1981) 56 FLR 235. Cf the provisions of the 1933 Act
     s 2(1)(b), the Civil Jurisdiction and Judgments Act 1982 (the 1982 Act), and now Council
     Regulation 44/2001, para 2.60.
4   A taxation authority of a Member State can bring winding up proceedings in another
     Member State: *Re Cedarlease Ltd* [2005] 1 IR 470, 476–477. Laffoy J held that since
     Art 39 (mistakenly referring to Council Regulation 1436/2000) permitted the taxation
     authority of a Member State to prove its debt in a winding up, it could initiate insolvency
     proceedings although the Regulation did not expressly provide for this.

CAUSES OF ACTION CONTRARY TO PUBLIC POLICY

2.43 Section 9(2)(f) of the Administration of Justice Act 1920 (the 1920 Act)
provides that a judgment may not be registered 'if the judgment was in respect
of a cause of action which, for reasons of public policy, or for some other
similar reason, could not have been entertained by the registering court'[1].
Section 4(1)(a)(v) of the 1933 Act, article 27(1) of the Brussels Convention
and article 34 of Council Regulation 44/2001 are to the same effect.

1   Cf *Vervaeke v Smith (Messina and A-G intervening)* [1983] 1 AC 145 (recognition denied
     for Belgian nullity decree for English marriage based on different public policy); para 15.03
     nn 18–20.

FOREIGN LAW QUESTION OF FACT

2.44 Foreign law is a question of fact, but in cases tried by a jury, it is decided
by the judge[1]. Any question as to a foreign *res judicata* is one of fact, including
whether the foreign decision is judicial; jurisdiction under the *lex fori*[2];
whether the foreign judgment is *in rem* or *in personam*[3]; final or interlocutory[4]; civil or criminal[5]; the effect of an adjudication of personal disability[6];
whether the judgment operates against the person or only the property of the
judgment debtor[7]; whether the decision of one state in a federation is
recognised in another[8]; the effect of a foreign decision on domicile[9]; the
prerequisites for a divorce[10]; any question as to the practice and procedure of
the foreign tribunal[11]; and any question as to the grounds on which the
foreign decision was based[12]. Such issues must be established by evidence,
which should be from experts in actual practice, not the treatises of jurists,
except as expounded by such experts[13].

¹ Supreme Court Act 1981 s 69(5); County Courts Act 1984 s 68.
² *Price v Dewhurst* (1837) 8 Sim 279, 305; affd (1838) 4 My & Cr 76, 85; *Fracis Times & Co v Carr* (1900) 82 LT 698 CA, 701–702 (whether 'inquiry' and 'report' were of a judicial nature); *R v Aughet* (1918) 13 Cr App Rep 101, 107 (jurisdiction of Belgian court martial to convict for lesser offence).
³ *Castrique v Imrie* (1870) LR 4 HL 414, 427, 429, 430, 443 (French judgment); *Re Macartney, Macfarlane v Macartney* [1921] 1 Ch 522 (Maltese affiliation order).
⁴ *Obicini v Bligh* (1832) 8 Bing 335 (without evidence court could only draw inferences from the document). In *Carl-Zeiss (No 2)* [1967] 1 AC 853 the onus of proof was considered: at 919, 927, 969–970.
⁵ *Raulin v Fischer* [1911] 2 KB 93, 97–99 (whether foreign decision was civil or criminal, and severable, were questions for the English court).
⁶ *Worms v De Valdor* (1880) 49 LJ Ch 261, 262; *Re Selot's Trust* [1902] 1 Ch 488, 492.
⁷ *Re Low, Bland v Low* [1894] 1 Ch 147 CA.
⁸ *Armitage v A-G* [1906] P 135, 140–141; *Cass* (1910) 102 LT 397, 398.
⁹ *Bater* [1906] P 209, CA.
¹⁰ *Harris v Taylor* (1914) 111 LT 564, 568; on appeal [1915] 2 KB 580 CA.
¹¹ *Buchanan v Rucker* (1808) 9 East 192; *Douglas v Forrest* (1828) 4 Bing 686; *Schibsby v Westenholz* (1870) LR 6 QB 155, 157; *Bergerem v Marsh* (1921) 125 LT 630; *Scarpetta v Lowenfeld* (1911) 27 TLR 509 (rule of Italian courts excluding evidence from parties); *Harris v Taylor* (1914) 111 LT 564 (above).
¹² *Harris v Quine* (1869) LR 4 QB 653.
¹³ *Re Selot's Trust* [1902] 1 Ch 488, 492; but in *Brailey v Rhodesia Consolidated Ltd* [1910] 2 Ch 95 Warrington J admitted the evidence of the Reader in Roman-Dutch Law for the Council of Legal Education, to prove Rhodesian law; c f *Jabbour v Custodian of Absentee's Property of State of Israel* [1954] 1 WLR 139, 147; *Perlak Petroleum Maatschappij v Deen* [1924] 1 KB 111 CA, 116.

2.45 Any mistake of English law by the foreign court is an error of fact that cannot be impeached¹.

¹ *Godard v Gray* (1870) LR 6 QB 139, 151.

ACTIONS ON JUDICIAL DECISIONS

2.46 The conclusiveness of a judgment, English or foreign, when sued upon is the result of *res judicata* estoppel. In the case of English but not all foreign judgments it is also a consequence of the principle of merger. The original cause of action having merged in the judgment, no question of merits is left for inquiry. Not every judicial decision can be sued upon. It is necessary, therefore, to consider the common law and statutory rules as they affect: (a) judgments of English superior courts; (b) judgments of English inferior courts; (c) orders of English superior courts; (d) orders of English inferior courts; (e) decisions of English domestic tribunals; and (f) foreign decisions.

ACTIONS ON JUDGMENTS OF ENGLISH SUPERIOR COURTS

2.47 The general rule is that an action will lie in an English superior court on a judgment of any such court, and the burden is on the defendant to establish abuse of process¹.

¹ *Berkeley v Elderkin* (1853) 1 E & B 805, 807 per Lord Campbell CJ: '*prima facie*, an action lies on the judgment of any court of competent jurisdiction'; *Hutchinson v Gillespie* (1856) 11 Exch 798, 815 per Bramwell B: 'I am not aware of any cases, except those of decrees in equity and judgments in County Courts, in which it has been held that no action

will lie upon the final order or judgment of a court for payment of a sum of money';
Hebblethwaite v Peever [1892] 1 QB 124; *Jay v Johnstone* [1893] 1 QB 189 CA; *Taylor v Hollard* [1902] 1 KB 676; *Shaw v Allen* (1914) 30 TLR 631.

2.48 A party who unnecessarily sues on a judgment of an English superior court may be denied costs[1]. The Limitation Act 1980 reduced the limitation period for such actions from 12 years to six[2], and judgment creditors who have not obtained satisfaction should bring an action on their judgment to keep their rights alive[3]. Under O 46 r 2, continued by CPR 70.1, execution may not issue to enforce a judgment after six years without the leave of the Court[4]. Leave was granted after 11½ years where the judgment debtor had been abroad[5].

[1]   The plaintiff was deprived of costs in *Mason v Nicholls* (1845) 14 M & W 118. In *Pritchett v English and Colonial Syndicate* [1899] 2 QB 428 CA, 435 Lindley MR said: 'If a person who has obtained a garnishee order brings an action upon it without any necessity he will run the risk of having it stayed as an abuse of the process of the court, and probably have to pay the costs'; *Furber v Taylor* [1900] 2 QB 719 CA, 721. The rules now enable the court to order the claimant to pay the defendant's costs.
[2]   Section 24.
[3]   An action may be brought on a judgment based on a judgment, and this will be necessary if the limitation period in respect of the second judgment is about to expire: *ED & F Man (Sugar) Ltd v Haryanto (No 3)* (1996) Times, 9 August CA.
[4]   An application for leave is not within Limitation Act s 24: *Lowsley v Forbes (t/a LE Design Services)* [1999] 1 AC 329; nor is a winding up petition: *Ridgeway Motors (Isleworth) Ltd v ALTS Ltd* [2005] 1 WLR 2871 CA; nor an application to enforce a charging order: *Ezekiel v Orakpo* [1997] 1 WLR 340 CA.
[5]   *Lowsley v Forbes* [1999] 1 AC 329. For the principles on which the discretion should be exercised: *Duer v Frazer* [2001] 1 WLR 919.

2.49 At common law an action lies in an inferior court on a superior court judgment on the same conditions, but the County Courts Act 1984 prohibits an action on a judgment of the High Court[1].

[1]   County Courts Act 1984 s 36. A High Court judgment may be enforced in the County Court: County Courts Act 1984 s 105.

ACTIONS ON JUDGMENTS OF ENGLISH INFERIOR COURTS

2.50 At common law there is no distinction for present purposes between judgments of an English superior court and of an English inferior court[1], but the County Courts Act 1846 impliedly prohibited actions on County Court judgments[2]. The decision is still the law, but such a judgment may be removed for execution to the High Court[3].

[1]   *Williams v Jones* (1845) 13 M & W 628, 633–634; *Berkeley v Elderkin* (1853) 1 E & B 805, 807; *Hutchinson v Gillespie* (1856) 11 Exch 798, 815.
[2]   *Berkeley v Elderkin* (1853) 1 E & B 805, 807–809; criticised in *Austin v Mills* (1853) 9 Exch 288; but followed in *Savill v Dalton* [1915] 3 KB 174 CA, 181.
[3]   County Courts Act 1984 s 106.

ACTIONS ON ORDERS OF ENGLISH SUPERIOR COURTS

2.51 At common law an action did not lie on an order of an English superior court[1], except possibly a final order equivalent to a judgment[2]. Under the rules an order, including an order of the Divorce Court[3], is now enforceable as a judgment, and can be sued on subject to the inherent jurisdiction to prevent abuse of process[4]. There is no abuse if satisfaction can only be obtained on a judgment, for instance when an order could not found proceedings in bankruptcy[5], or for winding up[6]. However an action may not be brought on an order in a criminal or quasi criminal case unless authorised by statute[7].

1   *Patrick v Shedden* (1853) 2 E & B 14, 21–22; *Hookpayton v Bussell* (1854) 10 Exch 24, 27; *Furber v Taylor* [1900] 2 QB 719 CA, 720–721.
2   *Ivimey* [1908] 2 KB 260 CA, 263: ('there may be a difference between an interlocutory order and a final order'); *Hutchinson v Gillespie* (1856) 11 Exch 798, 814–816.
3   *W v W* [1961] P 113 CA; *K v K* [1977] Fam 39 CA.
4   *Pritchett v English and Colonial Syndicate* [1899] 2 QB 428 CA, 435; *Furber v Taylor* [1900] 2 QB 719 CA, 721.
5   *Re Boyd, ex p McDermott* [1895] 1 QB 611 CA; *Godfrey v George* [1896] 1 QB 48 CA; *Seldon v Wilde* [1911] 1 KB 701 CA.
6   In *Pritchett v English and Colonial Syndicate* [1899] 2 QB 428 CA, 433–434, an action on a garnishee order against a company, Lindley MR said: 'the avowed object of the plaintiffs was to put themselves in a position to wind up the company" which "had no assets in this country which could be reached by execution … but had property abroad which could be made available in the winding up, *and in no other way*'.
7   *Godfrey v George* [1896] 1 QB 48 CA; *Seldon v Wilde* [1911] 1 KB 701 CA.

ACTIONS ON ORDERS OF ENGLISH INFERIOR COURTS

2.52 At common law an action would not lie on an order of an English inferior court[1], but orders of the County Court are enforceable as judgments[2]. One can only sue on a County Court order[3] in a County Court, but such an order made in bankruptcy is enforceable as an order of the High Court[4].

1   *Patrick v Shedden* (1853) 2 E & B 14, 21–22; *Furber v Taylor* [1900] 2 QB 719 CA, 721–722.
2   County Courts Act 1984 s 85(1).
3   *Savill v Dalton* [1915] 3 KB 174 CA, 180–181, 186–188.
4   1986 Act s 373(2); *Savill v Dalton* [1915] 3 KB 174 CA.

ACTIONS ON ENGLISH AWARDS

2.53 An award is 'the decision of one having a limited authority to determine … matters submitted to him by the parties, or … by a statute'[1]. It is a 'decision' on which an action always lay, and originally this was the only means of enforcement. An action on an award[2] can be for debt or specific performance[3].

1   *Duke of Buccleuch v Metropolitan Board of Works* (1870) LR 5 Exch 221, 29 (*Buccleuch*).
2   *King v Bowen* (1841) 8 M & W 625 (submission) and *Metropolitan District Rly Co v Sharpe* (1880) 5 App Cas 425 (statute).
3   *Eads v Williams* (1854) 4 De GM & G 674; *Blackett v Bates* (1865) 1 Ch App 117.

2.54 The Arbitration Act 1996 (the 1996 Act) confirms the common law rule that awards are conclusive and unimpeachable on their merits[1]. Section 66 authorises a summary application to the High Court for leave to enforce an award. The right to sue remains unaffected[2], but is subject to the inherent jurisdiction to prevent abuse of process. Actions have been allowed to proceed where this was the necessary foundation for bankruptcy proceedings[3]; where an application for leave to enforce could not be served out of the jurisdiction[4]; or where complicated questions arose affecting the validity of the award[5]. Where there are no special circumstances the action may be dismissed[6]. On an application for leave to enforce the court can order judgment on the award[7].

[1] Section 58.
[2] *UK Mutual SS Assurance Association v Houston* [1896] 1 QB 567; *Davis v Witney UDC* (1898) 14 TLR 433.
[3] *China Steam Navigation Co Ltd v Van Laun* (1905) 22 TLR 26; *Re Newey, ex p Whiteman* (1912) 107 LT 832.
[4] *Rasch & Co v Wulfert* [1904] 1 KB 118 CA.
[5] *Re Boks & Co and Peters, Rushton & Co* [1919] 1 KB 491 CA.
[6] *Pedler v Hardy* (1902) 18 TLR 591; *May v Mills* (1914) 30 TLR 287.
[7] *Re Bankruptcy Notice* [1907] 1 KB 478 CA.

2.55 The 1996 Act applies to statutory arbitrations unless the statute discloses a contrary intention[1]. An award under s 150 of the Public Health Act 1875 was only enforceable under that section[2].

[1] Section 94; *Tabernacle Permanent Building Society v Knight* [1892] AC 298; *Potato Marketing Board v Merricks* [1958] 2 QB 316.
[2] *Re Willesden Local Board and Wright* [1896] 2 QB 412 CA.

ENFORCEMENT OF FOREIGN AWARDS

2.56 Under s 36(1) of the Arbitration Act 1950 (the1950 Act)[1] a foreign award to which the New York Convention 1958 does not apply is enforceable by action or application for leave to enforce under s 66 of the 1996 Act. The conditions for enforceability in s 37 of the 1950 Act generally accord with the common law. Foreign awards to which the New York Convention applies are enforceable by leave of the court, but actions on such awards are not expressly authorised[2]. A foreign award enforceable under the 1950 or 1996 Acts is binding on the parties for all purposes and may be relied on by way of defence, set off or otherwise[3]. An award, whether domestic or foreign, will not be enforced if this would be contrary to the public policy of this country[4]. The court refused to enforce an award founded on a contract to commit acts which were illegal under the law of Iran[5]. Where a Swiss tribunal rejected the defendant's claim that the commission contract sued on was illegal under Swiss law because the plaintiff had procured the relevant orders by bribery, the court refused to allow the defendant to lead evidence previously available to it to prove a different case of bribery, and that the award had been procured by perjured evidence[6].

[1] Continued by 1996 Act s 99.
[2] 1996 Act s 101(2).
[3] 1950 Act s 36(2), 1996 Act s 101(1).
[4] *Soleimany* [1999] QB 785 CA, 799.

5   Ibid at 799.
6   *Westacre Investments Inc v Jugoimport – SPDR Holding Co Ltd* [2000] QB 288 CA (*Westacre*).

ENFORCEMENT OF FOREIGN JUDGMENTS

2.57   At common law a foreign money judgment could only be enforced by an action on the judgment[1]. A number of statutes and now Council Regulation 44/2001 provide for the registration of foreign money judgments which then become enforceable in the same manner as English judgments. In an action on a foreign judgment the claimant must prove the judgment and show that: (a) the foreign court had jurisdiction; (b) the judgment is final on the merits; and (c) was given between the same parties. The relevant Acts are those of 1920, 1933, and 1982. Some foreign judgments can be enforced in other ways. A judgment in Kenya for specific performance of a contract for the sale of shares was enforceable in the Isle of Man on an application for rectification of the company's share register, although it was not a party to the proceedings in Kenya[2]. Foreign judgments varying trusts, which are valid under their governing law, may be enforced against the trustees. Foreign judgments are also enforced when the *res judicata* estoppels they established are enforced in other proceedings.

[1]   Para 2.36.
[2]   *Ali v Pattni* [2007] 2 AC 85; *Cambridge Gas Transport Corpn v Official Committee of Unsecured Creditors of Navigator Holdings plc* [2007] 1 AC 508 (*Cambridge Gas*), paras 9.02–9.04.

THE ADMINISTRATION OF JUSTICE ACT 1920

2.58   Part II enabled judgments of superior courts in other parts of His Majesty's Dominions to be enforced in England through certification and registration. Any person who obtained a judgment (or by succession or assignment became entitled to one) in any part of His Majesty's Dominions to which the Act applies may apply to the High Court within 12 months of the judgment, or such further time as may be allowed, to have the judgment registered (s 9). Registration is discretionary, and if granted the judgment has the same force and effect as a judgment obtained in the High Court on the day of registration[1].

[1]   For a list of the countries and colonies to which this Act does or may still apply, 22 *Halsbury's Statutes* 'Judgments' (2006) p 186. When Orders-in-Council are made under the 1933 Act in relation to any such country, Part II of the 1920 Act ceases to apply to it: 1933 Act s 7.

THE FOREIGN JUDGMENTS (RECIPROCAL ENFORCEMENT) ACT 1933

2.59   The Act originally covered both 'foreign' countries (s 1) and His Majesty's Dominions outside the United Kingdom (s 7) and it is based on reciprocity. When reciprocal arrangements have been made between the

Government of the United Kingdom and the Government of a foreign State, an Order-in-Council may extend Part I to specified superior courts of that country. Orders-in-Council may also make the Act applicable to courts of Commonwealth jurisdictions and if this is done the 1920 Act ceases to apply (s 7(2)). The procedure involves an application by the judgment creditor to the High Court. The Court must order registration upon proof of the required matters (s 2(1)). A judgment within the Act can only be enforced by registration. Applications for registration may be made within six years from the date of the judgment or the date of the last judgment on appeal (s 2(1))[1]. Section 1(2A) prohibits the registration of a judgment based on the registration or enforcement of a foreign judgment. A judgment based on a foreign judgment is not enforceable in a third jurisdiction because it is not a judgment on the merits[2].

[1]   A general Order-in-Council was made in 1933 extending this Act to many parts of His Majesty's Dominions outside the United Kingdom. The Act was also extended to various European countries. Countries within the EU to which this Act formerly applied were covered by the 1982 Act and are now covered by Council Regulation 44/ 2001. For details of the countries to which the 1933 Act still applies see 22 *Halsbury's Statutes* 'Judgments' (2006) p 190.

[2]   *Owen v Rocketinfo Inc* (2008) 305 DLR (4th) 320 BCCA; 'Conflict of laws: enforcing a judgment on a judgment' Smart (2007) 81 ALJ 349; 'Registering a registered foreign judgment' Molloy (2007) 81 ALJ 760; cf *Morgan Stanley & Co International Ltd v Pilot Lead Investments Ltd* [2006] 2 HKLRD 731.

CIVIL JURISDICTION AND JUDGMENTS ACT 1982 AND COUNCIL REGULATION 44/2001

2.60 This Act as amended, which gave effect to the 1968 Brussels and 1988 Lugano Conventions and their protocols, enabled judgments given in a Contracting State[1] that were enforceable in that State to be enforced in the United Kingdom (s 4). The Act and the Conventions applied to judgments in any court in civil and commercial matters, except judgments in revenue, customs, or administrative matters, those relating to bankruptcy and insolvency, the status of natural persons, and rights of property arising from a matrimonial relationship or succession (Art 1). Applications for registration were made to the High Court. Article 27 defined the judgments, otherwise eligible, which were not entitled to recognition and registration. Part II enables judgments given or entered in any part of the United Kingdom to be enforced in any other part, including awards which have become enforceable as judgments, and orders of any tribunal enforceable without an order of a court (s 18). Part II does not apply to judgments registered under the 1920 and 1933 Acts or under Part I of the 1982 Act (s 18(7)). A judgment within s 18 may only be enforced by registration (s 18(8)). The Act does not apply to judgments in a contracting state based on a judgment of a non-contracting state[2]. The Brussels Convention and Part 1 of the 1982 Act have been superseded by Council Regulation 44/2001 as from 1 March 2002, except in respect of Denmark. Article 1 of the Regulation continues to exclude revenue, customs, and administrative matters and Article 2 excludes matters relating to the status of natural persons, rights of property arising from a matrimonial relationship or succession, bankruptcy and insolvency, social security and arbitration. The Regulation provides for the recognition and enforcement of other civil and commercial judgments of the courts of a Member State in all other Member States.

1   The member countries of the EU.
2   *Owens Bank Ltd v Bracco (No 2)* [1994] QB 509 ECJ, 544.

Chapter 3
PROOF OF THE JUDICIAL DECISION

INTRODUCTION

3.01 Anyone setting up a *res judicata* as a bar to a claim or defence must establish that the decision was pronounced and remains in force. It is not enough that other proceedings are pending[1]. The material date is when the second proceedings are heard. The decision in the first proceeding is treated as conclusive evidence in the second[2]. A judgment given before the second proceedings are heard may be relied upon[3], unless it has been set aside[4].

[1] *The Delta* (1876) 1 PD 393; *Houstoun v Marquis of Sligo* (1885) 29 Ch D 448, 454–455.
[2] *Morrison* [1961] 2 QB 266 CA, 277.
[3] *Re Defries, Norton v Levy* (1883) 48 LT 703; *Morrison* (ibid) at 276–277; *Bell v Holmes* [1956] 1 WLR 1359, 1365–1366; *Maynard* [1951] SCR 346, 360.
[4] *Noell v Wells and Page* (1668) 1 Lev 235. A default judgment will support an estoppel unless and until set aside: paras 2.22–2.25.

EVIDENCE BY WHICH THE DECISION, AND ITS TERMS, MUST BE ESTABLISHED

3.02 The official 'record' is the best evidence and, subject to statute, the only evidence by which the decision can be established[1], unless its effect may be inferred from the pleadings[2].

[1] *Dyson v Wood* (1824) 3 B & C 449, 451; *The Annie Johnson* (1921) 126 LT 614 PC, 614 ('the plea of *res judicata* cannot be entertained unless the record of the act of the court on which it was founded is forthcoming, or some valid reason is given why it cannot be produced').
[2] *Bell v Holmes* [1956] 1 WLR 1359, 1367.

3.03 The record is conclusive as to the fact of adjudication, the matters adjudicated, and the terms of the decision, and to this extent it operates *in rem*[1]. The other party may plead that the record has been superseded by another, or is a forgery[2].

[1] *Macgrath v Hardy* (1838) 4 Bing NC 782, 796 per Tindal CJ 'as a general rule ... no man can take any averment contrary to a record ... not only parties and privies, but even strangers ... are estopped to aver anything to the contrary'.

[2] *Noell v Wells and Page* (1668) 1 Lev 235. In an action of debt by an executrix 'the defendant pleaded never executrix; and on a trial the plaintiff produced the probate ... in evidence. The defendant said that the will was not a true, but a forged will. And the Chief Justice, before whom it was tried, was of opinion that he could not give such evidence directly contrary to the seal of the Ordinary [judge of ecclesiastical court] in a matter within his jurisdiction, whereupon a case was made for the opinion of the Court, ... and ... the whole Court held that it could not be given. But evidence may be given that the seal was forged, or was repealed ...; for these confess and avoid the seal. But he cannot give in evidence that another was executor; or that the testator was *non compos mentis*, for these falsify the proceedings of the Ordinary in cases of which he is judge'.

3.04 The record is conclusive (except on appeal) not only as to the decision it purports to record, but also as to any other judicial act recited therein[1], including the names, number, capacity, or qualification, of the jurors[2], or the justices[3]; the matters taken into consideration[4]; the appearance of any of the parties[5]; the date of the decision[6]; compliance, or otherwise with any statutory requirement of notice[7]; the findings of the jury[8]; the capacity in which the plaintiff sued[9]; or, in a criminal case, the place where the offence was committed[10]. The Supreme Court of Ireland has held that where the defendant is charged with a continuing offence, the prosecution cannot establish an essential ingredient by tendering a prior conviction which recites the fact[11].

[1] *Ramsbottom v Buckhurst* (1814) 2 M & S 565, 567.
[2] *Irwin v Grey* (1867) LR 2 HL 20, 23–24.
[3] *R v Carlile* (1831) 2 B & Ad 362, 367–369; *R (Carl) v Tyrone Justices* [1917] 2 IR 437, 441.
[4] *Corrigal v London and Blackwall Rly Co* (1843) 5 Man & G 219, 248; *Mortimer v South Wales Rly Co* (1859) 1 E & E 375.
[5] *Russell v Smyth* (1842) 9 M & W 810.
[6] *Trevivan v Lawrance* (1704) 1 Salk 276, 2 Ld Raym 1036, 1048.
[7] *R v Liverpool Corpn* (1768) 4 Burr 2244, 2245 per Willes J: 'if it had been properly set out that 20 days' notice was given pursuant to the Act, ... the inquisition and judgment had been conclusive against the owner of the lands'.
[8] *Keane v O'Brien* (1871) IR 5 CL 531.
[9] *Henderson* (1844) 6 QB 288, 298.
[10] *Re Newton* (1855) 16 CB 97.
[11] *Dublin Corpn v Flynn* [1980] IR 357 SC.

3.05 If the tribunal is not required to keep, and does not keep, an official record of its decisions, the *res judicata* may be proved by the next best evidence. It is the decision not the record which creates the estoppel[1]. The record may also be proved in the manner authorised by statute or statutory rules.

[1] *Dyson v Wood* (1824) 3 B & C 449, 451; *Re May* (1885) 28 Ch D 516 CA, 518.

RECORDS OF ENGLISH DECISIONS

3.06 Records of the superior courts are proved by production of office copies of the judgment or order[1], and orders in bankruptcy as authorised by the rules[2]. Records of judgments and orders of county courts can be proved in accordance with the Act[3].

[1] Supreme Court Act 1981 s 132; CPR 2.6(3).

2   1986 Rules r 7.51, r 12.20.
3   County Courts Act 1984 s 12(2).

3.07 Judgments and orders of the superior criminal courts are proved by production of copies of, or extracts from, the record, certified by the officer having the custody thereof, and otherwise in accordance with statute[1]. Convictions, orders, or dismissals in a court of summary jurisdiction are proved by production of the register, or a certified extract therefrom, or, in the case of a dismissal, by a certificate thereof, and otherwise as prescribed by statutory rules, or the practice of the court[2].

1   Police and Criminal Evidence Act 1984 s 73.
2   Ibid s 73, Magistrates' Courts Act 1980 s 102.

3.08 Orders, and directions of the Court of Protection are proved by office copies and are conclusive in favour of purchasers[1].

1   Mental Capacity Act 2005 s 47(2), (3).

3.09 Awards are proved by producing the original, and the submission is often produced as well. Awards in statutory arbitrations may be proved in accordance with the statute or the 1996 Act.

RECORDS OF FOREIGN DECISIONS

3.10 The record of a foreign judgment may be proved in the manner prescribed by s 7 of the Evidence Act 1851.

Chapter 4

JURISDICTION

4.01 A judicial decision binds the parties, or (in the case of *in rem* decisions) the so called world, if the tribunal had jurisdiction over the cause and the parties[1]. 'The prior decision judicial, arbitral, or administrative must have been made within jurisdiction before it can give rise to *res judicata* estoppels.'[2] A tribunal may exceed its jurisdiction by embarking upon an inquiry outside its province or by making an order in excess of its powers. In either case the decision cannot establish a *res judicata*[3].

[1] '[T]he decision must have been given by a competent tribunal' – per Roche J in *Eastwood and Holt v Studer* (1926) 31 Com Cas 251, 256–257; *O'Keefe v Williams* (1907) 5 CLR 217, 227 per Griffith CJ '... the foundation of that plea of *res judicata* is that the Land Court had jurisdiction to determine whether the ... land was Crown land. There is no provision ... that in any way supports that contention'.
[2] *Danyluk* [2001] 2 SCR 460, 482 per Binnie J.
[3] *R v Willesden Justices, ex p Utley* [1948] 1 KB 397 (fine in excess of jurisdiction); *R v LCC, ex p Entertainments Protection Association Ltd* [1931] 2 KB 215 (licence granted without jurisdiction); *Hereaka v Prichard* [1967] NZLR 18 CA. In *Maharajah of Jeypore v Patnaick* (1904) LR 32 Ind App 45, 51–52 Earl Halsbury LC said: '... the former decision of a Court adjudged by the High Court to be without jurisdiction cannot be treated as *res judicata*.'

MEANING OF JURISDICTION

4.02 Jurisdiction in this context means authority to decide[1]. As Latham CJ said[2], citing *inter alia* Lord Sumner in *R v Nat Bell Liquors Ltd*[3]:

'When jurisdiction is given to decide a question there is power to decide it, rightly or wrongly, and not only power to decide it rightly.'

Lord Sumner had said:

'... his subsequent error, however grave, is a wrong exercise of a jurisdiction which he has, and not a usurpation of a jurisdiction which he has not.'

[1] *Minister for Immigration v B* (2004) 219 CLR 365, 377.
[2] *Parissienne Basket Shoes Pty Ltd v Whyte* (1938) 59 CLR 369, 374.
[3] [1922] 2 AC 128, 151–152: paras 1.14, 17.26.

45

JURISDICTION OF SUPERIOR COURTS OF RECORD

4.03 There is a distinction between judgments and orders of superior courts and those of other courts and tribunals. A superior court of general jurisdiction is presumed to have jurisdiction[1] and its decisions beyond power are not void. As Martin B said[2]:

'It was said by the learned counsel that there was no jurisdiction to make this [order]. That is entirely a mistake. The Court of Common Pleas is one of the superior Courts of Record. It may be that the Act of Parliament did not justify it, but nevertheless the judges had perfect jurisdiction to make it; and the [order] being made by them, it is binding and conclusive ... unless it can be altered by appeal or error'[3].

The jurisdiction of superior courts can be taken away by statute but clear and positive language is required[4]. Even then a decision within the forbidden field is not void but merely wrong, and appeal is the only remedy. The decision could not be ignored or treated as a nullity[5]. Orders of a superior court pursuant to jurisdiction purportedly conferred by invalid legislation are not nullities, but are final and binding unless and until set aside on appeal or constitutional review[6].

[1]   *London Corpn v Cox* (1867) LR 2 HL 239, 259; *Scott v Bennett* (1871) LR 5 HL 234, 248.
[2]   *Scott v Bennett* (1871) LR 5 HL 234, 245.
[3]   To the same effect *Isaacs v Robertson* [1985] AC 97, 102–103 quoted para 4.06 n 6; *Scotch Leasing Sdn Bhd v Chee* [1997] 2 MLJ 105 SC, 110–111; *Badiaddin bin Mahidin v Arab-Malaysian Finance Bhd* [1998] 1 MLJ 393 FC, 409, 425–426; *Cohen v Jonesco* [1926] 2 KB 1 CA (High Court Judge reopened money lending transactions on which the lender had recovered judgment. After the account was taken he held that the order was beyond jurisdiction and disregarded it. The Court of Appeal reversed because the order, right or wrong, bound the Judge); *Brennan* (1953) 89 CLR 129, 134; *Warramunda Village Inc v Pryde* (2002) 116 FCR 58, 78.
[4]   *Balfour v Malcolm* (1842) 8 Cl & Fin 485, 500; *Webster v Bread Carters Union of NSW* (1930) 30 SRNSW 267, 275 and the English cases there cited; *Pyx Granite Co Ltd v Ministry of Housing and Local Government* [1960] AC 260, 286; *Anisminic Ltd v Foreign Compensation Commission* [1969] 2 AC 147, 208–209; *Chee v Scotch Leasing Sdn Bhd* [2001] 4 MLJ 346 CA, 356.
[5]   *Re Racial Communications Ltd* [1981] AC 374, 384 per Lord Diplock: 'There is simply no room for error going to ... jurisdiction'.
[6]   *Re Macks ex parte Sant* (2000) 204 CLR 158.

PROBATE AND ADMINISTRATION

4.04 Before the Judicature Acts grants of probate or administration were not made by a superior court of general jurisdiction. Where probate of a forged will was revoked and administration granted, an action by the administrators to recover a debt due to the testator failed because the debtor had paid the executor while the probate was in force, but there were dicta on the effect of a grant for the estate of a living person. Ashurst J said[1]:

'... every person is bound to pay deference to a judicial act of a Court having competent jurisdiction. Here the Spiritual Court had jurisdiction over the subject matter; and every person was bound to give credit to the probate until it was vacated. The case of a probate of a supposed will during the life of the party may be distinguished ... because during his life the Ecclesiastical Court has no jurisdiction ... but when the party is dead, it is within their jurisdiction.'

Buller J said[2]

'... this case was compared to a probate of a supposed will of a living person; but in such a case the Ecclesiastical Court have no jurisdiction, and the probate can have no effect. Their jurisdiction is only to grant probates of the wills of dead persons.'

The Ecclesiastical Courts and the Court of Probate to which their probate jurisdiction was transferred in 1857 were subject to the supervision of the Court of Kings Bench by the writ of prohibition[3]. The Judicature Acts vested the jurisdiction in the High Court, and a grant for the estate of a living person, or of a forged will or to an imposter are now orders of a superior court of general jurisdiction and valid until set aside[4]. Acts of the executor or administrator, while grants are in force, remain valid after they are revoked[5], but otherwise the former grants become nullities *ab initio*. Where probate of a forged will was revoked more than six years after the death causes of action which arose on death were not statute barred because time only ran from the appointment of the administrator[6]. Grants of probate[7] and administration[8] are not, as against a purchaser, invalid for want of jurisdiction whether the purchaser has notice or not[9].

[1]   *Allen v Dundas* (1789) 3 Term Rep 125, 129; *Chettiar v Low* [1998] 2 SLR 289 CA, 297–298.
[2]   Ibid at 130. In *M'Dougal v O'Shaughnessy* (1868) IR CL 157 the court held that letters of administration de bonis non granted by the Court of Probate of Ireland during the lifetime of an executor by representation were void . In *Monckton v Braddell* (1872) IR Eq 30 CA the court held that letters of administration for the estate of a living person were void.
[3]   *R v St. Edmundsbury & Ipswich Diocese Chancellor, ex p White* [1948] 1 KB 195 CA, 206; para 4.08 n 1.
[4]   *Hewson v Shelley* [1914] 2 Ch 13 CA, 29, 36, 40, 45; *Chettiar v Low* [1998] 2 SLR 289 CA, 297–298. The dicta in *Allen v Dundas* (1789) 3 TR 125 were followed in *Calaway v Primrose* (1900) 17 WN(NSW) 46. The plaintiff, who left New South Wales in 1857 and did not return until 1899, had been presumed dead. Administrators of his estate had sold land to which he became entitled on the death of his mother. He brought ejectment against the purchaser and recovered. Stephen J said: 'The plaintiff is not dead and therefore the land did not pass to his representative. The defendant contends that the letters of administration are valid, but whatever validity they have they do not give the defendant a title to the land'. In *Ex parte Keegan* (1907) 7 SR NSW 565 where compensation had been paid to an administrator of the owner's estate, the Minister was ordered to pay a second time to the owner. Darley CJ said at 566: 'The cases show that the grant of administration in such a case is a nullity.' These decisions are contrary to *Hewson v Shelley* [1914] 2 Ch 13 CA and cannot be supported because the court which made the grants was a superior court of general jurisdiction.
[5]   *Hewson v Shelley* [1914] 2 Ch 13 CA, 29, 35–36, 44–45; *Debendra Nath Dutt v Administrator General of Bengal* (1908) LR 35 Ind App 109, 116–117 per Lord Macnaghten: 'The case of the appellant ... was that the letters of administration granted to Cowie, having been annulled by the Court on the ground of fraud, must be regarded as a mere nullity from the beginning; that Cowie therefore never was administrator, and that the bond, so far as the sureties were concerned was void and of no affect ... [T]here is ... no substance in the appellant's contention. So long as the letters of administration ... remained unrevoked Cowie, although a rogue and an imposter, was to all intents and purposes administrator ... For his acts and defaults as administrator the appellant and his co-surety became and must remain responsible.'
[6]   *Chan Kit San v Ho Fung Hang* [1902] AC 257, 260–261 (the executor had not acted on the faith of the probate).

[7] *Re Bridgett & Hayes' Contract* [1928] Ch 163.
[8] *Hewson v Shelley* [1914] 2 Ch 13 CA, 30, 33.
[9] Law of Property Act 1925 s 204(1); *Hewson v Shelley* [1914] 2 Ch 13 CA, 29–30, 33 on the effect of the equivalent section in the Conveyancing Act 1881; paras 9.35 n 4, 10.15 n 3.

DIVORCE DECREES

4.05 An apparent exception to the general rule was recognised in *Re Seaford, Seaford v Seifert*[1], probably *per incuriam*. A District Registrar of the High Court made absolute a decree nisi for divorce after the husband had died. The Court of Appeal held that the marriage was dissolved by death and the decree absolute was a nullity because the court had no jurisdiction to dissolve a marriage dissolved by death[2]. The decree should be construed as subject to an implied condition precedent that both spouses are still alive so that if one of them has died it would be ineffective but not a nullity.

[1] [1968] P 53 CA.
[2] [1968] P 53 CA, 70, 72, 73.

OTHER APPARENT EXCEPTIONS

4.06 There are other apparent exceptions. In *Craig v Kanssen*[1] an order was made by the High Court although the defendant had not been served and was not aware of the proceedings. Lord Greene MR said that the order was a nullity and must be set aside[2]. Similarly in *Lazard Bros & Co v Midland Bank Ltd*[3] Lord Wright held that a judgment against a Russian Bank which had ceased to exist must be set aside and declared a nullity[4]. A judgment of a superior court in proceedings in the name of or against a deceased person is fundamentally flawed and liable to be summarily set aside but has also been said to be a nullity[5]. Despite the eminence of the judges involved the relevant principles are those stated by Lord Diplock[6]:

> '... in relation to orders of a court of unlimited jurisdiction it is misleading to seek to draw a distinction between orders that are "void" in a sense that they can be ignored with impunity by those persons to whom they are addressed, and orders that are "voidable" and may be enforced unless and until they are set aside. Dicta that refer to the possibility of there being such a distinction between orders to which the descriptions "void" and "voidable" respectively have been applied can be found in ... opinions given by the Judicial Committee of the Privy Council ... but in neither of those appeals nor in any other case to which counsel has been able to refer their Lordships has any order of a court of unlimited jurisdiction been held to fall into a category ... that can simply be ignored because they are void ipso facto without there being any need for proceedings to have them set aside. The cases ... referred to in these dicta ... support ... the quite different proposition that there is a category of orders of such a court which a person affected ... is entitled to apply to have set aside ex debito justitiae in the exercise of the inherent jurisdiction of the Court ... The contrasting legal concepts of voidness and voidability form part of the English law of contract. They are inapplicable to orders made by a court of unlimited jurisdiction in the course of contentious litigation. Such an order is either

irregular or regular. If it is irregular it can be set aside by the Court that made it upon application to that court; if it is regular it can only be set aside by an appellate court.'

Where a superior court has inadvertently exercised jurisdiction that has been taken away by a substantive statutory prohibition and invested elsewhere it has inherent jurisdiction to set aside its order, even after it has been perfected[7].

[1] [1943] KB 256 CA.
[2] Ibid at 262, 263.
[3] [1933] AC 289.
[4] Ibid at 296–297, 306.
[5] *Lazard Bros & Co. v Banque Industrielle de Moscou* [1932] 1 KB 617 CA, 624 per Scrutton LJ; *MacCarthy v Agard* [1933] 2 KB 417 CA, 427 per Romer LJ: 'Where one of the parties was non-existent ... there was no judgment before the Court at all. The Court did not set aside the judgment; it disregarded it because there was no party in existence'; *Dawson (Bradford) Ltd v Dove* [1971] 1 QB 330; *Piggott v Aulton* [2003] RTR 540 CA. *Deveigne v Askar* (2007) 69 NSWLR 327 CA, where the cases are collected, involved a judgment of an inferior court.
[6] *Isaacs v Robertson* [1985] AC 97, 102–103; *Cameron v Cole* (1944) 68 CLR 571, 589, 590–591 per Rich J. Cf *Strachan v Gleaner Co Ltd* [2005] 1 WLR 3204 PC, 3211–3214 per Lord Millett.
[7] *Kofi Forfie Chief v Barima Kwabena Seifah* [1958] AC 59, 67; *Maharajah of Jeypore v Patnaick* (1904) LR 32 Ind App 45, 51; *Badiaddin bin Mahidin v Arab Malaysian Finance Bhd* [1998] 1 MLJ 393 FC, 409–410, 426, 429; *Chee v Scotch Leasing Sdn Bhd* [2001] 4 MLJ 346 CA, 358.

INFERIOR COURTS

4.07 There is a presumption in favour of the jurisdiction of any English court which is not an inferior court[1]. With inferior courts the presumption is the other way. 'The rule for jurisdiction' is that 'nothing shall be intended to be out of the jurisdiction of a superior court but that which specially appears to be so; and ... nothing shall be intended to be within the jurisdiction of an inferior court but that which is ... expressly alleged'[2]. No tribunal of limited jurisdiction can determine conclusively the limits of its own jurisdiction[3]. The estoppels created by decisions of inferior courts are limited to the matters directly in issue, and their opinions on collateral or incidental questions are not *res judicata* in other proceedings. The principles were summarised by Jordan CJ in *Ex p Amalgamated Engineering Union*[4]:

'... in order that a judicial decision may involve an estoppel as to the matter decided it is necessary that the tribunal should possess jurisdiction to decide the matter conclusively and for all purposes between the parties and not merely incidentally and for a limited purpose ... difficulties do occur in the case of subordinate tribunals. Where they have been invested with a general though limited jurisdiction matters incidentally decided are res judicata if they are ...within the limits of the general jurisdiction ... Where however a special jurisdiction is conferred upon a subordinate tribunal to decide some one particular class of matter, the conferring of jurisdiction, although it authorises the tribunal to decide any other matters so far as may be necessary for the exercise of the jurisdiction so conferred, is not regarded as investing it with jurisdiction to decide those matters between the parties conclusively for all purposes. Such matters are collateral to the matter as to which jurisdiction is conferred'.

Averments of jurisdiction in the original action, or in an action on the judgment of an inferior court[5], may be made in general terms. Where a court or tribunal finds it has no jurisdiction, its decision, for that reason, cannot create an issue estoppel on any other question in that tribunal[6].

[1]   In *Sollers v Lawrence* (1743) Willes 413 a party sued on a decision of commissioners appointed by statute to determine disputes arising out of the destruction of house property by 'the late dreadful fire' at Blandford who were constituted a court of record. It was held by the Court of Common Pleas, at 416–418, that a declaration alleging that the tribunal had jurisdiction was well pleaded, for it will be intended, in the case of a statutory court of record, as in the case of a superior court, that the court acted within their jurisdiction unless the record states to the contrary.

[2]   *London Corpn v Cox* (1867) LR 2 HL 239, 259; *Scott v Bennett* (1871) LR 5 HL 234, 248.

[3]   *Crown Estate Comrs v Dorset County Council* [1990] Ch 297, 308–309. However the statute creating the tribunal may give it jurisdiction to decide questions on which its jurisdiction depends, especially where there is a right of appeal. It is a question of construction whether this exception or the general rule applies, para 4.09.

[4]   (1937) 38 SRNSW 13, 19–20.

[5]   *London Corpn v Cox* (1867) LR 2 HL 239, 263.

[6]   Para 2.15.

DECISIONS ON INCIDENTAL OR COLLATERAL QUESTIONS

4.08   If a tribunal cannot finally determine a question its opinion is not *res judicata*. Examples include a decision on the testator's domicile by the Court of Probate because it had no jurisdiction to conclusively determine that[1]; decisions as to title by tribunals with limited jurisdiction[2]; decisions by tribunals under the Inclosure Act 1845 as to the boundaries of, and titles to, lands, their functions being limited to their allotment, exchange, and partition[3]; a decision of justices that frontagers need not contribute to the expense of sewering a street was not a decision that it was a public highway, because the status of the street was only 'incidentally cognisable'[4]; and for the same reason an acquittal on a charge of criminal trespass was not a decision on title[5]. A decision that the judgment on which a bankruptcy petition is based is or is not good for that purpose, is not *res judicata* because the Registrar could only make or refuse a receiving order[6]. Orders of a Master in Chancery declaring the rights of parties in administration proceedings are not *res judicata*, because he can only make orders for the convenience of administration[7]. A Registrar could not determine paternity by making an order for the maintenance of the child[8]. It has been held in Canada that the Exchequer Court had no jurisdiction in an income tax appeal to determine the ownership of an asset where title was only collaterally in question[9]. On the other hand, the Chief Commons Commissioner had jurisdiction to determine whether road verges should be registered as common land, and therefore to determine whether they were part of the highway because his jurisdiction did not depend on a correct answer[10].

[1]   *Concha* (1886) 11 App Cas 541, 565 per Lord Blackburn: 'the judge of the Court of Probate had no jurisdiction to decide what was to be done with the residuary sum of the testator's property ... This being so, ... this is not a decision *in rem* which would bind anyone'; and per Lord Fitzgerald at 568.

2 *Cross v Salter* (1790) 3 TR 639 (decision of ecclesiastical court as to property in pew not
   an estoppel because its only jurisdiction was to deal with disturbance of possessory rights);
   Sandwich Corpn v R (1847) 10 QB 571 Ex Ch (determination by Treasury of office-
   holder's right to compensation not an estoppel, its jurisdiction being limited to amount);
   Archbishop of Dublin v Coote (1849) 12 I Eq R 251, 267–268 (Court of Claims
   established to deal with forfeited lands had no jurisdiction to determine whether land had
   been forfeited); *R v London and North Western Rly Co* (1854) 3 E & B 443 (tribunal to
   assess compensation for land compulsorily taken had no jurisdiction to determine
   questions of title); *Buccleuch* (1870) LR 5 Ex 221, 227 (the like); *Dover v Child* (1876) 1
   Ex D 172, 175–176 (dismissal of summons under s 40 of Metropolitan Police Act 1839,
   did not estop the party from asserting title in action for conversion).
3 *Jacomb v Turner* [1892] 1 QB 47, 51–52; *Collis v Amphlett* [1918] 1 Ch 232 CA, 242:
   ('the valuer had no jurisdiction to settle any question of title or boundaries').
4 *R v Hutchings* (1881) 6 QBD 300 CA, 305; the position was otherwise where the statute
   empowered the court to determine the status of roads: *Wakefield Corpn v Cooke* [1904]
   AC 31.
5 *A-G for Trinidad and Tobago v Eriché* [1893] AC 518.
6 *Re Vitoria, ex p Vitoria* [1894] 2 QB 387 CA. Receiving orders were abolished by the 1986
   Act and a single bankruptcy order is now made under s 271. In *King v Henderson* [1898]
   AC 720, 729–730, a bankruptcy court dismissed a creditor's petition, and the views of the
   judge on other questions were not *res judicata*; *Re Debtor, ex p Petitioning Creditor* [1917]
   2 KB 60 CA, 69–71.
7 *Thompson* [1923] 2 Ch 205, 215–216.
8 *Nokes* [1957] P 213 CA.
9 *Angle v Minister of National Revenue* (1974) 47 DLR (3d) 544, 557 SC; para 13.10.
10 *Crown Estate Comrs v Dorset County Council* [1990] Ch 297, 312.

FINDINGS OF JURISDICTIONAL FACTS BY INFERIOR COURT OR TRIBUNAL

4.09 If the existence of facts collateral to the merits is a condition precedent
to the jurisdiction of an inferior court or tribunal its decision will only be
binding and conclusive if those facts existed. If this is not shown, jurisdiction
will not exist and the decision will not be *res judicata*[1]. An erroneous decision
on jurisdictional facts cannot confer a jurisdiction which the statute never
gave; and a superior court may consider the facts on judicial review or in
collateral proceedings. So where a Rent Tribunal assumed jurisdiction on
finding that the premises had been separately let since 1 September 1939, the
county court could determine whether this finding was erroneous[2]. On the
other hand the statute may constitute the tribunal the judge of the existence or
otherwise of the condition precedent; and if so the decision of the tribunal on
such a point is *res judicata*. The relevant principles were stated by
Lord Esher MR[3]:

'When an inferior court or tribunal ... which has to exercise the power of
deciding facts is first established by Act of Parliament the legislature has to
consider what powers it will give that tribunal ... It may in effect say that, if a
certain state of facts exists and is shown to such tribunal ... before it proceeds
to do certain things, it shall have jurisdiction to do such things, but not
otherwise. There, it is not for them conclusively to decide whether that state of
facts exists, and if they exercise the jurisdiction without its existence, what they
do may be questioned, and it will be held that they have acted without
jurisdiction. But there is another state of things which may exist. The legislature
may entrust the tribunal ... with ... jurisdiction to determine whether the
preliminary state of facts exists as well as jurisdiction on finding that it does
exist, to proceed further'.[4]

4.09   Jurisdiction

Employment tribunals have jurisdiction, subject to appeal on questions of law, to decide jurisdictional facts. In *Watt* Lord Hoffmann said[5]:

> '... when the tribunal has decided that it does have jurisdiction, the question of whether this decision is binding at a later stage of the same litigation, or in subsequent litigation involves ... issues about fairness and economy in the administration of justice ... The jurisdiction of an employment tribunal depends upon whether the facts fall within certain statutory concepts ... The decision as to whether the facts found by the tribunal answer to the statutory description is sometimes treated as a question of fact ... and sometimes as a question of law ... In either case ... the tribunal has jurisdiction to decide the question. I see no basis for distinguishing between questions which 'go to its jurisdiction' and those which do not'.

1   *Bunbury v Fuller* (1853) 9 Exch 111, 140 per Coleridge J: 'Now it is a general rule that no court of limited jurisdiction can give itself jurisdiction by a wrong decision on a point collateral to the merits of the case upon which the limit of its jurisdiction depends'; *R v Shoreditch Assessment Committee, ex p Morgan* [1910] 2 KB 859 CA, 880; *R v Lincolnshire Justices, ex p Brett* [1926] 2 KB 192 CA, 202 per Atkin LJ – 'Here is a collateral issue independent of the merits; no doubt the inferior court must give a decision upon it, but this decision being upon a point collateral to the main matter of complaint is open to review by the superior courts, and if a superior court decides that the matter of complaint arose outside the territorial limits, the result is that the inferior court had no jurisdiction'; *R v City of London etc Rent Tribunal, ex p Honig* [1951] 1 KB 641, 645 per Lord Goddard CJ: 'I have no doubt that we can review the collateral matter which the tribunal have decided, namely, the existence of a tenancy, as it is upon the existence of a tenancy that their jurisdiction depends'.

2   *R v Judge Pugh, ex p Graham* [1951] 2 KB 623, 629 per Lord Goddard CJ: 'If the decision of an inferior court is pleaded as estopping a plaintiff from proceeding, the defendant must first adduce by his plea facts which will show that the inferior tribunal had jurisdiction, and the plaintiff can reply that there was no jurisdiction'; *Bethune v Bydder* [1938] NZLR 1 CA.

3   *R v Income Tax Special Purposes Comrs* (1888) 21 QBD 313 CA, 319.

4   The requirement that the relevant fact be 'proved to the satisfaction of the Commissioners' prevented review; *Spackman v Plumstead Board of Works* (1884) 10 App Cas 229; *R v Bloomsbury Income Tax Comrs, ex p Hooper* [1915] 3 KB 768 ('if the surveyor discovers'); *LCC v Galsworthy* [1917] 1 KB 85; *R v Ludlow, ex p Barnsley Corpn* [1947] KB 634, 640 per Lord Goddard CJ: 'Parliament may entrust the tribunal with the power of deciding whether or not they have jurisdiction, because they are empowered to decide the preliminary facts which alone will give it to them'.

5   [2008] 1 AC 696, 707. The questions Lord Hoffmann was referring to were not 'collateral to the merits' (n 1 above). It is a question of construction whether the tribunal has been given power to decide whether a matter is within its jurisdiction. The Information Tribunal established by the Freedom of Information Act 2000 does not have this power: *BBC v Sugar* [2009] 1 WLR 430 HL, 444, 453–454.

4.10   It was once thought that if the tribunal had jurisdiction to enter on an inquiry, errors of law in the course of that inquiry would not deprive it of jurisdiction. In *Anismimic Ltd v Foreign Compensation Commission*[1] the House of Lords held that such errors could deprive the tribunal of jurisdiction and render its decision liable to judicial review[2]. The tribunal was in no sense a court. Then in *Re Racial Communications Ltd* Lord Diplock said[3]:

> 'The breakthrough made by *Anisminic* ... was that, as respects administrative tribunals and authorities, the old distinction between errors of law that went to jurisdiction and errors of law that did not, was for practical purposes abolished ... But there is no similar presumption that where a decision-making power is conferred by statute upon a court of law Parliament did not intend to

confer upon it power to decide questions of law as well as questions of fact. Whether it did or not ... depends upon the construction of the statute unencumbered by any such presumption ... [U]pon any application for judicial review ... the superior court ... should not be astute to hold that Parliament did not intend the inferior court to have jurisdiction to decide for itself the meaning of ordinary words used in the statute to define the [merits] question which it has to decide'.[4]

The Privy Council[5] and the High Court of Australia[6] have maintained the distinction between jurisdictional and non-jurisdictional error. The distinction analysed by Lord Esher[7] and developed by Lord Diplock in relation to the jurisdiction conferred by statute on courts of law was considered by Dixon J[8]:

'It cannot be denied that if the legislature see fit to do it, any event or fact or circumstance whatever may be made a condition upon the occurrence or existence of which the jurisdiction of a court shall depend ... [C]onceding the abstract possibility of the legislature adopting such a course, nevertheless it produces so inconvenient a result that no enactment dealing with proceedings in any of the ordinary courts of justice should receive such a construction unless the intent is clearly expressed'.[9]

It is submitted that neither Lord Diplock nor Dixon J intended to qualify the well-established principles which govern the conditions in which an inferior court has jurisdiction to enter upon an inquiry. No such question arose in those cases and a preliminary finding by an inferior court that it has jurisdiction to enter upon an inquiry is *prima facie* subject to judicial review which can only be excluded by clear language. Parliament must use language showing that it intended the court or tribunal to determine the limits of its own jurisdiction. As Millett J said, with reference to such preliminary questions[10]:

'The resolution of a jurisdictional issue by a tribunal of limited jurisdiction can never be conclusive or found an issue estoppel. Where such an issue is raised, the tribunal may find it necessary to decide it but its decision must be open to challenge. No tribunal of limited jurisdiction can be permitted conclusively to determine the limits of its own jurisdiction. It can neither confer on itself a jurisdiction which it does not truly possess nor deprive itself of a jurisdiction which it does'.

If the court or tribunal finds that the relevant jurisdictional facts exist that finding will create an issue estoppel in that court or tribunal but not elsewhere and the jurisdictional facts must be proved again if its jurisdiction is challenged directly by judicial review or collaterally.

1   [1969] 2 AC 147.
2   Ibid at 171, 174, 195, 207.
3   [1981] AC 374, 383; *Peters v Davison* [1999] 2 NZLR 164 CA, 181; para 4.09 n 4.
4   *O'Reilly v Mackman* [1983] 2 AC 237, 278, 283; *Boddington v British Transport Police* [1999] 2 AC 143, 154.
5   *South East Asia Fire Bricks Sdn Bhd v Non-Metallic Mineral Products Manufacturing Employees Union* [1981] AC 363.
6   *Public Service Association v Federated Clerks' Union* (1991) 173 CLR 132, 141; *Craig v South Australia* (1995) 184 CLR 163.
7   Para 4.09 n 3.

[8] *Parisienne Basket Shoes Pty Ltd v Whyte* (1938) 59 CLR 369, 391; *Posner v Collector for Interstate Destitute Persons* (1946) 74 CLR 461, 483 per Dixon J 'Modern legislation does not favour the invalidation of orders of magistrates or other inferior judicial tribunals and the tendency is rather to sustain the authority of orders until they are set aside and not to construe statutory provisions as meaning that orders can be attacked collaterally or ignored as ineffectual, if the directions of the statute have not been pursued with exaction'.
[9] *Roos v DPP* (1994) 34 NSWLR 254 CA, 262–263.
[10] *Crown Estate Comrs v Dorset County Council* [1990] Ch 297, 308–309. Parliament may provide otherwise; para 4.09 nn 3–5.

4.11 At common law where a party alleges that the judgment of an inferior court has been unlawfully executed against him, the defendant must prove that the judgment was within the jurisdiction of the court, or be answerable in damages[1]. But a judicial or executive officer of the inferior court is protected if the pleadings, judgment, and other documents of record purport to show jurisdiction on their face[2], unless he knew of its absence[3]. A decision that at common law a magistrate who acted outside his jurisdiction had no protection is of doubtful authority[4].

[1] *London Corpn v Cox* (1867) LR 2 HL 239, 263 per Willes J: 'the Plaintiff is liable to an action for executing the process of an inferior court in a matter beyond its jurisdiction, and cannot justify under such process; whether he knows of the defect or not'; *Posner v Collector for Interstate Destitute Persons* (1946) 74 CLR 461, 476.
[2] *O'Connor v Isaacs* [1956] 2 QB 288, 304.
[3] *London Corpn v Cox* (1867) LR 2 HL 239, 263: 'the judge and officer are liable to a civil action if they knew of the defect of jurisdiction'; *Posner v Collector for Interstate Destitute Persons* (1946) 74 CLR 461, 476, 482–483.
[4] *O'Connor v Isaacs* [1956] 2 QB 288, 308, 312; *Sirros v Moore* [1975] QB 118 CA.

JURISDICTION OF ARBITRAL TRIBUNALS

4.12 An award is only *res judicata* if the tribunal had jurisdiction[1]. Authority may be conferred by agreement, court order, or statute, but in every case the members act as unofficial judges appointed *ad hoc*. If the submission requires arbitrators to have certain qualifications, unqualified arbitrators have no jurisdiction and a party who was not aware of the facts will not be bound[2]. A party who knowingly nominated an unqualified arbitrator was estopped from denying his qualifications, and bound by the award[3]. A claimant suing on an award must allege that it was within the jurisdiction of the tribunal[4], and if it exceeds its jurisdiction the award is a nullity in whole or in part. Blackburn J said that an award[5]:

> 'is the decision of one having a limited authority to determine those matters submitted to him by the parties, or ... by a statute, and no other. And from this it follows that, if that limited authority has not been pursued, and the arbitrator has awarded something beyond his authority, the award is pro tanto void, and, if the void part is so mixed up with the rest that it cannot be rejected, the award is void altogether, ... And I think, both on authority and principle, this is a matter that may be pleaded as a defence to an action'.

[1] *Eastwood v Studer* (1926) 31 Com Cas 251, 256–257.
[2] *Jungheim Hopkins & Co v Foukelmann* [1909] 2 KB 948. Where arbitrators empowered to appoint an umpire with certain qualifications appointed an unqualified umpire, his award was void: *Rahcassi Shipping Co SA v Blue Star Line Ltd* [1969] 1 QB 173.
[3] *Oakland Metal Co Ltd v D Benaim & Co Ltd* [1953] 2 QB 261.

4   *Buccleuch* (1870) LR 5 Exch 221, 231 per Blackburn J: 'this is exactly for the same reason that jurisdiction must be averred in an action on the judgment of an inferior court'.
5   Ibid at 229.

4.13 Absence or excess of jurisdiction is a ground for setting aside or remitting an award, and defeats any reliance on it for a *res judicata* estoppel. The cases in which awards by qualified arbitrators have been impeached for want of jurisdiction fall into three categories. The first is where the tribunal determined issues outside the submission[1], order, or statute[2], from which it derived its jurisdiction. The second is where the tribunal made orders outside its powers[3]; delegated its judicial functions (as distinct from functions of investigation, and obtaining evidence, information, and expert assistance) to an unauthorised person; disregarded the requirements for making an award[4]; or otherwise conduced the arbitration in an unauthorised manner[5]. The third is where jurisdiction depends upon a condition precedent which has not been satisfied. Such an award is not *res judicata*[6], even if it states that the condition has been satisfied[7]; for the tribunal could not give itself jurisdiction by a finding contrary to the fact[8]. Devlin J summarised the principles[9]:

'... at the beginning of any arbitration one side or the other may challenge the jurisdiction of the arbitrator. It is not the law that arbitrators, if their jurisdiction is challenged or questioned, are bound immediately to refuse to act until their jurisdiction has been determined by some court which has power to determine it finally. Nor is it the law that they are bound to go on without investigating the merits of the challenge and to determine the matter in dispute, leaving the question of their jurisdiction to be held over until it is determined by some court which had power to determine it. ... They are entitled to inquire into ... whether they have jurisdiction or not, not for the purpose of reaching any conclusion which will be binding upon the parties – because that they cannot do – but for the purpose of satisfying themselves as a preliminary matter whether they ought to go on with the arbitration or not. ... They are entitled ... to determine their own course of action, and the result of that inquiry has no effect ... upon the rights of the parties. ... The principle *omnia praesumuntur rite esse acta* does not apply to proceedings of arbitration tribunals or, indeed, to the proceedings of inferior tribunals of any sort. There is no presumption that merely because an award has been made it is a valid award. It has to be proved by the party who sues upon it that it was made by the arbitrators within the terms of their authority, that is, with jurisdiction. Jurisdiction has to be proved affirmatively. ... any view which is expressed by the arbitrators expressly or impliedly in the award, any finding ... that they had jurisdiction does not make the award any better, ... [or] any worse'.

If jurisdiction existed, it is immaterial that nothing is said about it in the award[10]. The 1996 Act now authorises the tribunal to determine its jurisdiction, unless the parties have otherwise agreed, subject to appeal in the ordinary way[11] Any objection must be taken promptly[12] and the court can be asked to determine the jurisdiction of the tribunal as a preliminary point[13].

1   *Fisher v Pimbley* (1809) 11 East 188, 192–193 (absence of jurisdiction supports plea of 'no award'); *Bowes v Fernie* (1838) 4 My & Cr 150, 158–162; *Jones v Corry* (1839) 5 Bing NC 187.
2   *Beckett v Midland Rly Co* (1866) LR 1 CP 241; *Re Dare Valley Rly Co* (1868) LR 6 Eq 429; *Davis v Witney UDC* (1899) 15 TLR 275 CA.

3   *Tomlin v Fordwich Corpn* (1836) 5 Ad & El 147 (directing repairs to be executed to satisfaction of third person); *Turner v Swainson* (1836) 1 M & W 572 (ordering works on a third person's land); *Price v Popkin* (1839) 10 Ad & El 139 (ordering works); *Re Green & Co and Balfour, Williamson & Co* (1890) 63 LT 325 CA (directions for payments and allowances when issue was whether goods answered warranty); *Pedler v Hardy* (1902) 18 TLR 591; *Re Stone and Hastie* [1903] 2 KB 463 (orders outside jurisdiction); *Leadbetter v Marylebone Corpn* [1904] 2 KB 893 CA (the same). Orders as to costs may be bad without affecting the residue: *Cockburn v Newton* (1841) 2 Man & G 899.

4   *Tomlin v Fordwich Corpn* (1836) 5 Ad & El 147; *Little v Newton* (1841) 2 Man & G 351 (arbitrators delegated their authority); *Re Templeman and Reed* (1841) 9 Dowl 962 (two arbitrators left decision to the third); *Eads v Williams* (1854) 4 De GM & G 674 (arbitrator delegated his functions to expert); *Whitmore v Smith* (1861) 7 H & N 509 Ex Ch (arbitrators delegated to third person, not as umpire); *UK Mutual SS Assurance Association v Houston* [1896] 1 QB 567 (award by two of three arbitrators void); *Hiscox v Outhwaite* [1992] 1 AC 562 (arbitration in London).

5   Allowing a party to discharge himself by affidavit: *Pedley v Goddard* (1796) 7 Term Rep 73; taking evidence by affidavit when the submission required it to be taken orally: *Banks v Banks* (1835) 1 Gale 46; allowing umpire to decide without having heard the evidence: *Re Salkeld and Slater and Harrison* (1840) 12 Ad & El 767.

6   *The Warwick* (1890) 15 PD 189: (rules of association provided for arbitration in collision cases, but there was no collision); *May v Mills* (1914) 30 TLR 287 (requirement for relationship of landlord and tenant not satisfied).

7   *Samuel v Cooper* (1835) 2 Ad & El 752, 757.

8   *Faviell v Eastern Counties Rly Co* (1848) 2 Exch 344, 350; *A-G for Manitoba v Kelly* [1922] 1 AC 268, 276.

9   *Christopher Brown Ltd v Genossenschaft Osterreichischer Waldbesitzer Holzwirtschafts-bertriebe Registrierte GmbH* [1954] 1 QB 8, 12–13.

10   *Davies v Pratt* (1855) 17 CB 183.

11   Section 30. The appeal may be to the court, or to an arbitral tribunal with appellate jurisdiction.

12   Section 31.

13   Section 32.

4.14 The jurisdiction of the tribunal may depend on its finding that certain facts exist, and in that respect it may be made the final judge of its own jurisdiction[1]. Thus where 'the claims of the plaintiff in the action' were referred by a judge's order the arbitrator had jurisdiction to determine what was a claim in the action, and his decision could not be challenged[2]. A tribunal had jurisdiction to decide that the contract should be construed in the light of a trade custom[3].

1   *Buccleuch* (1870) LR 5 Exch 221, 232. The distinction between a matter going to jurisdiction and one within jurisdiction is illustrated by comparing *Ayscough v Sheed Thomson & Co* (1924) 131 LT 610 HL, with *Pinnock Bros v Lewis & Peat Ltd* [1923] 1 KB 690; para 2.15 n 1.

2   *Faviell v Eastern Counties Rly Co* (1848) 2 Exch 344.

3   *Produce Brokers Co Ltd v Olympia Oil and Cake Co Ltd* [1916] 1 AC 314, 327.

4.15 Where the tribunal dealt separately with matters within and outside its jurisdiction, so much of the award as dealt with the former was conclusive, but the residue was a nullity. Evidence is admissible that the tribunal, in awarding a lump sum, included matters outside its jurisdiction[1], and if this is shown, the whole award is bad[2]. The onus is not discharged by proof that the tribunal heard evidence on the matters in question, because it may have done so to ascertain whether they were within its jurisdiction[3]. It is immaterial that the award does not state whether the tribunal did or did not take those matters into consideration[4].

1   *Buccleuch (1870) LR 5 Exch 221*, 229–230; *Falkingham v Victoria Rly Comr* [1900] AC
    452 (*Falkingham*); *A-G for Manitoba v Kelly* [1922] 1 AC 268.
2   *Tomlin v Fordwich Corpn* (1836) 5 Ad & El 147; *Price v Popkin* (1839) 10 Ad & El 139;
    Beckett v Midland Rly Co (1866) LR 1 CP 241, 246–247. In *Re Penny and South Eastern
    Rly Co* (1857) 7 E & B 660, 668–669 a sheriff's jury, on the direction of the under-sheriff,
    took into consideration the fact that the claimant's premises would be 'overlooked' by the
    railway, which was beyond their jurisdiction, and the verdict was bad.
3   *Falkingham* [1900] AC 452; para 4.13.
4   In *Buccleuch* the umpire gave evidence of the matters he had included.

4.16 Where the tribunal is not shown to have acted in excess of its
jurisdiction, and the other conditions of a valid *res judicata* are established,
the award binds the parties and cannot be impeached for error of law or fact[1].
Under the 1996 Act an award may be set aside or remitted where a serious
irregularity[2] or error of law has been established[3]. In addition an arbitrator or
umpire can 'correct any clerical mistake, or error arising from any accidental
slip or omission'[4]. Unless and until these powers are exercised an award
within jurisdiction, however wrong in law or mistaken in fact, is *res judicata*.

1   1996 Act s 58(1); *Champsey Bhara & Co v Jivraj Balloo Spinning and Weaving Co* [1923]
    AC 480, 486.
2   Ibid s 68(3).
3   Ibid s 69(7). This is the court's only power to correct errors of law, s 1(c).
4   Ibid s 57(3).

JURISDICTION OF CRIMINAL TRIBUNALS

4.17 The same principles apply to decisions of English criminal tribunals.
Thus, a judgment of acquittal pronounced by a criminal court which had no
jurisdiction to convict is a nullity, and cannot support a plea of *autrefois
acquit*, or bar fresh proceedings for the same offence[1].

1   *Crane v DPP* [1921] 2 AC 299.

RECOGNITION OF FOREIGN JUDGMENTS

4.18 England has three regimes for the recognition of foreign judgments:
under the 1982 Act for judgments from elsewhere in the UK, under Council
Regulation 44/2001 for judgments from elsewhere in the EU, and under the
common law for all others.

JURISDICTION OF FOREIGN JUDICIAL TRIBUNALS (COMMON LAW)

4.19 The foreign tribunal must have had internationally recognised jurisdiction whether the decision is set up as a bar[1], or an action is brought on it[2].
Jurisdiction under the law of the foreign forum is not sufficient[3], and its
judgment is conclusive on that question.

1   *General Steam Navigation Co v Guillou* (1843) 11 M & W 877, 894 (plea of estoppel
    based on French judgment had to allege that plaintiff was subject to that jurisdiction).
2   *Adams v Cape Industries plc* [1990] Ch 433 CA, 550 (*Adams*).
3   Ibid.

JURISDICTION OF THE FOREIGN TRIBUNAL OVER THE PARTIES: JUDGMENTS IN REM

4.20 Whether a foreign judgment is *in rem* or *in personam* is a question of fact[1]. A judgment *in rem* deals with the status of persons or things, or effects a disposition of movable or immovable property. Judgments *in rem*[2] derive their validity from the situation of the person or property within the jurisdiction. Judgments dealing with status, to be effective, must bind the so called world because status must be generally accepted[3]. If the action is in *rem* service on or notice to the defendant must still be proved[4].

[1]   Para 2.44 n 1.
[2]   Chapter 10.
[3]   *Pemberton v Hughes* [1899] 1 Ch 781 CA, 793–794.
[4]   Para 10.3.

JURISDICTION OF THE FOREIGN TRIBUNAL OVER THE CAUSE: ACTIONS IN PERSONAM

4.21 Under the common law a foreign tribunal has jurisdiction to render a judgment *in personam* if, at the commencement of the proceedings, the defendant owed allegiance, permanent or temporary, to the state where the tribunal exercised judicial functions. The defendant must also be served with process to bring him before that tribunal. If he was not brought before the foreign tribunal by the prescribed process, it does not matter that he was amenable to its jurisdiction[1]. If he was not subject to its jurisdiction, it does not matter that its process was served on him[2].

[1]   As to substituted service: para 4.24.
[2]   *Schibsby v Westenholz* (1870) LR 6 QB 155, 160; *Turnbull v Walker* (1892) 67 LT 767, 769; *Sirdar Gurdyal Singh v Rajah of Faridkote* [1894] AC 670, 683 (*Sirdar Singh*): 'He was under no obligation to [appear] by reason of the notice of the suits which he thus received, or otherwise, unless that Court had lawful jurisdiction over him'.

ROUSILLON

4.22 In this case Fry J said that a party was amenable to foreign jurisdiction *in personam* on any of five grounds[1]:

> 'Where he [the defendant] is a subject of the foreign country in which the judgment has been obtained; where he was resident in the foreign country when the action began; where the defendant, in the character of plaintiff, has selected the forum in which he is afterwards sued; where he has voluntarily appeared; and where he has contracted to submit himself to the forum in which the judgment was obtained'.

The last three are based on conduct of the defendant and the second enables an unwilling defendant to be sued where he is physically present and can be served with process.

[1]   *Rousillon v Rousillon* (1880) 14 Ch D 351, 371; followed in *Emanuel v Symon* [1908] 1 KB 302 CA, 309, 312; *Phillips v Batho* [1913] 3 KB 25, 29; *Gavin Gibson & Co Ltd v Gibson* [1913] 3 KB 379, 387–388. The Supreme Court of Canada refused to follow those

decisions in *Morguard Investments Ltd v De Savoye* (1990) 76 DLR (4th) 256 in relation to interprovincial judgments, and this decision was extended to US judgments in *Beals v Saldanha* [2003] 3 SCR 416.

NATIONALS OF JURISDICTION

4.23 The first ground assumes that a subject of a foreign state owes permanent allegiance to it in all its functions[1]. However in *Gavin Gibson & Co Ltd v Gibson*[2] Atkin J said, of the cases cited to support this ground, that:

'... in none ... was the defendant in fact a subject of a country where the judgment sued on was pronounced, nor was it claimed that he was, and the judicial expressions are ... obiter dicta. They are, however, of so great weight that I should probably feel compelled to follow them ...'.

In *British Nylon Spinners Ltd v ICI Ltd*[3] Evershed MR said:

'... it is competent for the court of a particular country, in a suit between persons who are either nationals or subjects of that country or are otherwise subject to its jurisdiction, to make orders in personam against one such party – directing it, for example, to do something or to refrain from doing something in another country affecting the other party to the action'.

These statements are *obiter* and it is doubtful whether nationality gives a foreign court jurisdiction in actions *in personam*[4] which will be recognised[5].

[1]   *Schibsby v Westenholz* (1870) LR 6 QB 155; *Rousillon* (1880) 14 Ch D 351; *Emanuel v Symon* [1908] 1 KB 302 CA, 309, cf 313 per Kennedy LJ.
[2]   [1913] 3 KB 379, 388.
[3]   [1953] Ch 19 CA, 25.
[4]   Nationality confers jurisdiction in divorce: *Indyka* [1969] 1 AC 33.
[5]   *Blohn v Desser* [1962] 2 QB 116; *Rossano v Manufacturers Life Insurance Co Ltd* [1963] 2 QB 352; *Vogel v R and A Kohnstamm Ltd* [1973] QB 133; *Rainford v Newell Roberts* [1962] IR 95.

DEFENDANT WITHIN JURISDICTION

4.24 A defendant within the territory of a foreign state is amenable to its jurisdiction[1]. He need not be 'ordinarily resident' or even 'resident' if he was physically present when served with process, and it is immaterial when he arrived or left[2]. It may be sufficient that he held public office in the foreign state on the theory of constructive residence[3]. Substituted service may be ordered if the defendant was within the jurisdiction when the proceedings were commenced, even if he left afterwards[4]. Substituted service will not be recognised if the defendant left the foreign jurisdiction before the issue of process[5].

[1]   *Rousillon* (1880) 14 Ch D 351, 371. The requirement in s 9(2)(b) of the 1920 Act is that the defendant was 'carrying on business or ordinarily resident' within the jurisdiction. In the 1933 Act the requirement in s 4 is 'if the judgment debtor, being the defendant, was at the date of the institution of the proceedings resident in the foreign country, or being a corporation, had its principal place of business in that country'. Another section applies

where the defendant had an office or place of business in the foreign country, and the action was brought in respect of a transaction effected through that office or place.

[2]   *Carrick v Hancock* (1895) 12 TLR 59, 60; *Gaekwar of Baroda v Wildenstein* [1972] 2 QB 283 CA as to English jurisdiction, and *Adams* [1990] Ch 433 CA, 517–518, as to foreign jurisdiction.

[3]   It was said in *Don v Lippmann* (1837) 5 Cl & Fin 1, 21; and *Emanuel v Symon* [1908] 1 KB 302 CA, 310–311 that *Becquet v MacCarthy* (1831) 2 B & Ad 951 could only be supported on this basis.

[4]   *Porter v Freudenberg* [1915] 1 KB 857 CA.

[5]   *Laurie v Carroll* (1958) 98 CLR 310; *Myerson v Martin* [1979] 1 WLR 1390 CA; cases on local rules, but the same principles apply to the recognition of foreign judgments.

4.25 If the defendant was not within the foreign jurisdiction at the material date, it does not matter that he entered into the relevant contract or committed the relevant wrong there[1], nor that the dispute arose when he was within the jurisdiction[2].

[1]   *Turnbull v Walker* (1892) 67 LT 767, 769; *Sirdar Singh* [1894] AC 670, 683; *Emanuel v Symon* [1908] 1 KB 302 CA, 314 (partnership).

[2]   *Don v Lippmann* (1837) 5 Cl & Fin 1, 23; *De Cosse Brissac v Rathbone* (1861) 6 H & N 301, 308; *Sirdar Singh* [1894] AC 670, 685–686; *Emanuel v Symon* [1908] 1 KB 302 CA, 310–311.

DOMICILE

4.26 Domicile without physical presence is not a basis for jurisdiction over parties[1]. It is a foundation of jurisdiction in divorce which is governed by the rules relating to judgments *in rem*[2].

[1]   *Jaffer v Williams* (1908) 25 TLR 12, 13.

[2]   Chapter 15.

CORPORATIONS

4.27 A corporation is present in the country of incorporation[1] and subject to its jurisdiction. It is also present where it has a place of business; but the presence of a salesman or representative is not sufficient[2]. A member as such is not subject to the jurisdiction of the country of incorporation, but the corporation's constitution may contain a submission to its jurisdiction[3].

[1]   *Janson v Driefontein Consolidated Mines Ltd* [1902] AC 484, 505; *A-G v Jewish Colonisation Association* [1901] 1 KB 123 CA, 135; *Gasque v IRC* [1940] 2 KB 80, 84.

[2]   *Adams* [1990] Ch 433 CA, 530–531; 1920 and 1933 Acts; para 4.24 n 1; Brussels Convention Art 5.5, Council Regulation 44/2001.

[3]   Para 4.31.

CLAIMANT IN FOREIGN COURT

4.28 The third ground is the commencement of proceedings in the foreign court. If the claimant is counter-attacked he cannot complain that the court lacks jurisdiction[1]. This is a form of voluntary submission.

[1]   Brussels Convention Art 6.3, Council Regulation 44/2001.

VOLUNTARY SUBMISSION

4.29 The fourth ground is voluntary submission to the foreign court's jurisdiction[1]. If he 'takes the chance of judgment in his favour, he is bound'[2]. Where the defendant has taken a step in the proceedings, which is only necessary or useful if any objection to jurisdiction has been waived[3], the foreign court has jurisdiction unless the appearance was not voluntary[4]. An appearance to protect existing property is not voluntary[5]; but is to protect future property, or general business interests[6].

[1] Included in the 1920 and 1933 Acts, the Brussels Convention, and Council Regulation 44/2001.
[2] *Schibsby v Westenholz* (1870) LR 6 QB 155, 162. A defendant submits by appealing: *SA Consortium General Textiles v Sun and Sand Agencies Ltd* [1978] QB 279 CA; even from an *ex parte* judgment: *Bergerem v Marsh* (1921) 125 LT 630.
[3] *Williams & Glyn's Bank v Astro Dinamico Cia Naviera SA* [1984] 1 WLR 438 HL, 444 (*William & Glyn's*); a case on English jurisdiction but the same principles apply.
[4] *Rousillon* (1880) 14 Ch D 351; *Turnbull v Walker* (1892) 67 LT 767, 769.
[5] *Simpson v Fogo* (1860) 1 John & H 18, 27; *Schibsby v Westenholz* (1870) LR 6 QB 155, 162; *The Challenge and Duc d'Aumale* [1904] P 41.
[6] *Voinet v Barrett* (1885) 55 LJQB 39 CA.

APPEARANCE TO OBJECT TO JURISDICTION

4.30 A defendant who appears to dispute jurisdiction does not submit. In *Re Dulles' Settlement (No 2), Dulles v Vidler* Denning LJ said[1]:

'I cannot see how anyone can fairly say that a man has voluntarily submitted to the jurisdiction of a court, when he has all the time been vigorously protesting that it has no jurisdiction. If he does nothing and lets judgment go against him in default of appearance, he clearly does not submit to the jurisdiction. What difference in principle does it make, if he ... goes to the court and protests that it has no jurisdiction? I can see no distinction at all ... if he fights the case, not only on the jurisdiction, but also on the merits, he must then be taken to have submitted to the jurisdiction, because he is then inviting the court to decide in his favour on the merits; and he cannot be allowed ... to say that he will accept the decision on the merits if it is favourable to him and will not submit to it if it is unfavourable. But when he ...appears with the sole object of protesting against the jurisdiction, I do not think that he can be said to submit to the jurisdiction'.

[1] [1951] Ch 842 CA, 850; *Williams & Glyn's* [1984] 1 WLR 438 HL, 444; Brussels Convention Art 18; Council Regulation 44/2001.

CONTRACT TO SUBMIT TO JURISDICTION

4.31 Such a contract[1] may take many forms, but is not implied from membership of a foreign corporation or partnership[2]. An agreement to submit to the jurisdiction must be express[3], or necessarily arise from the express or implied terms of a contract[4]. An express choice of law clause is not an implied submission[5].

[1] *Feyerick v Hubbard* (1902) 71 LJKB 509, 510–512; *Jeannot v Fuerst* (1909) 100 LT 816; 1920 Act s 9(2)(c), 1933 Act s 4(2)(a), Brussels Convention Art 17, Council Regulation 44/2001.

2   *Copin v Adamson* (1875) 1 Ex D 17 CA. The first replication, which alleged an express
    agreement to submit, in the constitution of the corporation, was upheld on demurrer. The
    second replication which only alleged that the defendant was a member of the corporation
    was held bad on demurrer in the court below, (1874) LR 9 Exch 345, 355–356, and there
    was no cross-appeal; *Emanuel v Symon* [1908] 1 KB 302 CA (partnership).
3   *SA Consortium General Textiles v Sun and Sand Agencies Ltd* [1978] QB 279 CA.
4   *Vogel v R and A Kohnstann Ltd* [1973] QB 133.
5   *Dunbee Ltd v Gilman & Co (Australia) Pty Ltd* [1968] 2 Lloyd's Rep 394, 70 SRNSW
    219 CA.

NOTICE TO DEFENDANT ESSENTIAL

4.32 Natural justice requires that the proceedings be brought to the actual
notice of the defendant, who must have a fair opportunity of presenting his
case[1]. This is reflected in the 1920 Act which prescribes, as a ground for
refusing registration, that 'the judgment debtor was not served and did not
appear in the original proceedings'. Nothing is said about substituted service,
and it is submitted that this is not allowed. The 1933 Act provides that
registration must be set aside 'if the judgment debtor, being the defendant in
the original proceedings, did not receive notice of the proceedings in sufficient
time to enable him to defend them, and did not appear'. See also Brussels
Convention Article 27.2 and Council Regulation 44/2001[2] which appear to
require personal service. These principles do not apply to decisions of an
international tribunal[3]. A foreign decision *in personam* will not be recognised
if aspects of the procedures offend English views of substantial justice[4]. Thus
in *Adams*[5] an arbitrary assessment of the damages awarded to 206 plaintiffs
by a US Federal District Court, not based on evidence or the individual
entitlements of the plaintiffs, was not recognised[6].

1   *Rousillon* (1880) 14 Ch D 351; *Bergerem v Marsh* (1921) 125 LT 630; *Jacobson v Frachon*
    (1927) 138 LT 386 CA, 392; *Jet Holdings Inc v Patel* [1990] 1 QB 335 CA, 345.
2   Para 4.33.
3   *Lenzing AG's European Patent* [1997] RPC 245.
4   *Pemberton v Hughes* [1899] 1 Ch 781 CA, 790–791; *Jet Holdings Inc v Patel* [1990] 1 QB
    335 CA, 345; *Adams* [1990] Ch 433 CA, 497–498, 563–564.
5   [1990] Ch 433 CA.
6   Ibid at 493, 494–495, 500, 564–568; and 'The *Res Judicata* effect in England of a US class
    action settlement' (1997) 46 Int & Comp. LQ 134.

1982 ACT

4.33 This gave effect in the United Kingdom to the 1968 Brussels and 1988
Lugano Conventions and their protocols which were binding on members of
the EU. Title II dealt with jurisdiction, and Title III with recognition and
enforcement of judgments. Title II established a regime under which the courts
of a contracting state had exclusive jurisdiction in certain cases (Art 16), or
acquired such jurisdiction by contract (Art 17), or by becoming first seised
(Arts 18, 21, 22, 23). Article 26 provided simply 'A judgment given in a
Contracting State shall be recognised in the other Contracting States ...', but
Article 27 contained a list of exceptions which broadly reflected the common
law. It provided:

'A judgment shall not be recognised:

(1)   if such recognition is contrary to public policy in the State in which recognition is sought,

(2)   where it was given in default of appearance, if the defendant was not duly served with the document which instituted the proceedings or with an equivalent document in sufficient time to enable him to arrange for his defence[1],

(3)   if the judgment is irreconcilable with a judgment given in a dispute between the same parties in the State in which recognition is sought,

(4)   if the court of the State in which the judgment was given has decided a preliminary question concerning the status or legal capacity of natural persons, rights in property arising out of a matrimonial relationship, wills or succession in a way that conflicts with a rule of the private international law of the State in which recognition is sought, unless the same result would have been reached by the application of the rules of private international law of that State,

(5)   if the judgment is irreconcilable with an earlier judgment given in a non-Contracting State involving the same cause of action and between the same parties, provided that this latter judgment fulfils the conditions necessary for its recognition in the State addressed'.

Under Article 28 recognition was to be refused for judgments which conflict with the provisions of sections 3 (insurance), 4 (consumer contracts) and 5 (exclusive jurisdiction) of Title II. Section 2 of Title III dealt with the enforcement of judgments and Article 31 provided that a judgment given in a contracting state and enforceable in that state shall be enforced in another contracting state when an order for its enforcement has been issued there. Under Article 34 enforcement could only be refused if the judgment was not entitled to recognition. The Convention was superseded, except with respect to Denmark, by Council Regulation 44/2001 with effect from 1 March 2002.

[1]   In *Maronier v Larmer* [2003] 1 All ER (Comm) 225 CA registration of a foreign judgment under the 1982 Act was set aside where the defendant was not given an effective opportunity to defend the claim.

COUNCIL REGULATION 44/2001

4.34 The Regulation has a wider operation than the Brussels Convention. Article 5(1)(a) enables a person 'domiciled' (ie resident) in a Member State to be sued in matters relating to a contract in the courts of the place of performance. Article 5(3) enables such a person to be sued in matters relating to tort in the courts of the place where the harmful event occurred. Article 5(4) enables a settlor, trustee, or beneficiary of a trust to be sued in the courts of the Member State where the trust is domiciled. The Regulation also includes extensive provisions relating to insurance matters, consumer contracts and individual contracts of employment. The Regulation provides for contractual submissions to jurisdiction (Art 23), and submission by voluntary appearance except where this is to contest jurisdiction (Art 24). It provides for a defendant to receive the originating process 'in sufficient time to enable him to arrange for his defence or that all necessary steps have been taken to that end' (Art 26(2)). Article 33(1) requires a judgment given in a Member State to be recognised without any special procedure being required and Article 34 continues the exceptions in Art 27(1), (2), (3) and (5) of the Brussels Convention[1]. The former exception in Article 27(2)[2] has been qualified by a proviso:

> 'unless the defendant failed to commence proceedings to challenge the judgment when it was possible for him to do so.'

[1]   Para 4.33.
[2]   Para 4.33.

Chapter 5

FINALITY

5.01 A judicial decision English or foreign[1] is only a *res judicata* if it is final[2]. The burden of establishing this rests on the party who relies on the decision[3].

[1] Para 2.38.
[2] *Eastwood and Holt v Studer* (1926) 31 Com Cas 251, 256–257 per Roche J: 'where a decision of a competent tribunal is relied on as creating an estoppel and preventing a subsequent review of the matter, it is necessary that the matter should have been raised and controverted before the earlier tribunal and shall have been clearly, and finally, decided by it'.
[3] *Nouvion v Freeman* (1889) 15 App Cas 1, 9; *Carl-Zeiss (No 2)* [1967] 1 AC 853, 919, 936, 949, 971.

MEANING OF FINALITY

5.02 A judicial decision may be final for one purpose but not another. Decisions on finality for purposes of appeal are not always relevant. Some decisions which are final for appeal are not final for *res judicata*[1], and some which are interlocutory for appeal are final for *res judicata*[2]. A more stringent test of finality applies when the decision is the foundation for an action. The decision must then finally determine the defendant's liability[3] leaving nothing to be judicially determined to fix the amount recoverable and render the judgment effective and capable of execution[4]. Many decisions which are not final for this purpose finally declare or determine some right or obligation and can be set up as an estoppel in other proceedings. Declaratory orders[5] and Chancery decrees[6] which have to be worked out by accounts and inquiries are final for *res judicata* and final for appeal. A further class of decisions which are final for present purposes, although interlocutory for appeal, decide some question although the proceedings continue on other issues, or for the purpose of working out the rights of the parties, or execution[7]. Some interlocutory decisions are not final for any purpose, and do not create a *res judicata* even in the same proceedings. Interlocutory orders in matters of practice and procedure remain under the control of the court and subject to review and in such matters a dismissal is not a bar to another application[8]. An action cannot be brought on an interlocutory order for an ascertained amount, e g an interlocutory order for costs which have been taxed[9].

5.02 *Finality*

1 A nonsuit which the plaintiff elected to argue was final for purposes of appeal because it disposed of principal proceedings: *Coroneo v Kurri Kurri and South Maitland Amusement Co Ltd* (1934) 51 CLR 328, 334. It was not a *res judicata* because the plaintiff could bring fresh proceedings.
2 Para 5.31.
3 *Henderson* (1844) 6 QB 288 (unconditional order of Colonial Court of Equity for payment of ascertained balance); *Hutchinson v Gillespie* (1856) 11 Exch 798, 815–816 (order of Privy Council for payment of amount for costs).
4 Matters such as post-judgment interest do not require 'judicial determination'. Judgment for an ascertained sum for debt or damages plus costs is final, although the costs have not been taxed, and may be enforced but it is not final and enforceable as to costs until they have been ascertained.
5 *Becker v City of Marion Corpn* [1977] AC 271.
6 Paras 5.21–5.27.
7 Para 5.31.
8 Para 5.32.
9 Para 5.13 n 5.

FINALITY DEPENDS ON FORMAL ENTRY

5.03 A final judgment perfected by formal entry becomes *res judicata* in the proceedings. An oral judgment is provisionally effective, but until formally entered it can be withdrawn, altered, or modified by the court or judge which pronounced it[1]. As the High Court of Australia said[2]:

> 'Identifying the formal recording of the order of a superior Court of record as the point at which that Court's power to reconsider the matter is at an end provides a readily ascertainable and easily applied criterion. But more than that, identifying the formal recording of the order as the watershed both marks the end of the litigation in that Court, and provides conclusive certainty about … the end result in that Court.'

A judgment that has been formally entered can only be altered by the court or judge which pronounced it within the narrow limits of the slip rule and the inherent jurisdiction. These powers are exercisable to ensure that the judgment gives effect to the court's manifest intention and, in incidental matters such as costs and interest, to relieve against omissions ('slips') by a party or his legal advisers[3]. They do not enable the court to review its decision on the merits, that is, its decision on issues presented to it for decision which it intended to decide[4]. A final judgment can be set aside after formal entry on proof of fraud or collusion[5]. Where through no fault of his own a party has not been heard the court has inherent power to set aside its ex parte order to allow a hearing on the merits[6] and proof of fraud or misconduct by the successful party is not required. The power is also exercisable where the party's absence was due to the fraud of the third party[7].

1 *Re Harrison's Share Under a Settlement, Harrison v Harrison* [1955] Ch 260 CA, 276 (*Harrison*); *Scotch Leasing Sdn Bhd v Chee* [1997] 2 MLJ 105 SC, 110.
2 *Burrell v R* (2008) 82 ALJR 1221, 1227 para [20]; and see para 1.10 n 4.
3 *Re (Earl) Inchcape, Craigmyle v Inchcape* [1942] Ch 394.
4 Ibid at 397; *Burrell v R* (2008) 82 ALJR 1221, 1227 para [21].
5 Paras 17.04–17.06.
6 *Craig v Kanssen* [1943] KB 256 CA; *Grimshaw v Dunbar* [1953] 1 QB 408 CA, 416; *Taylor* (1979) 143 CLR 1.

7   In *Ram Narayan Singh v Adhindra Nath Mukerji* [1917] AC 100 (*Ram Narayan*) the
    respondent arranged with a third party in India, who falsely claimed to be the agent for
    London solicitors, for the latter to act in a Privy Council appeal and paid him money for
    that purpose which he misappropriated. The appeal was heard ex parte and allowed, but
    on proof of the facts in India the order was set aside and the appeal restored. A decision of
    a body amenable to certiorari can be quashed on proof that it was procured by fraud,
    including the fraud of a third party: *R (Burns) v County Court Judge of Tyrone* [1961] NI
    167; *SZFDE v Minister for Immigration and Citizenship* (2007) 232 CLR 189, 197–198,
    206 (rogue fraudulently advised applicant for refugee status not to appear in Review
    Tribunal).

RECALL OF UNPERFECTED JUDGMENT

5.04 The court should only recall its unperfected judgment in exceptional
circumstances[1]. Jenkins LJ said in *Harrison*[2]:

> '... the recall of an unperfected order results in a rehearing at which all parties
> can present such further arguments as they may be advised having regard to the
> matter, whatever it may be, which is sought to cast doubt on the correctness of
> the order as orally pronounced.'

The power to re-open is available in appellate courts and has been invoked in
the High Court of Australia. The existence of the power and the occasions for
its exercise were considered by the Privy Council[3]. The power is to be
exercised with great caution, and the principles were summarised in *Smith v
New South Wales Bar Association*[4]:

> 'The power is discretionary and, although it exists up until the entry of
> judgment, it is one that is exercised having regard to the public interest in
> maintaining the finality of litigation. Thus, if reasons for judgment have been
> given, the power is only exercised if there is some matter calling for review. And
> there may be more or less reluctance to exercise the power depending on
> whether there is an avenue of appeal. It is important that it be understood that
> these considerations may tend against the re-opening of a case, but they are not
> matters which bear on the nature of the review ... once the case is re-opened ...
> the power to review a judgment ... where the order has not been entered will
> not ordinarily be exercised to permit a general re-opening ... but once a matter
> has been re-opened, the nature and extent of the review must depend on the
> error or omission which has led to that step being taken. Very little will be
> required in a case where, for example, all that is involved is a mathematical
> error in the calculation of some particular item of loss or damage. And, in the
> case of a factual error, the extent of the review will vary depending on whether
> the error goes to the heart of the matter or whether its significance is confined
> to some discreet subsidiary issue.'

These principles apply to the Court of Appeal in criminal cases[5].

1   In *Re Barrell Enterprises* [1973] 1 WLR 19 CA, 23–24.
2   [1955] Ch 260 CA,283.
3   In *re Transferred Civil Servants (Ireland) Compensation* [1929] AC 242, 248–252; and its
    decisions reviewed in *State Rail Authority of New South Wales v Codelfa Construction Pty
    Ltd* (1982) 150 CLR 29, 38–39, 45–46.
4   (1992) 176 CLR 256, 265.
5   *R v Cross* [1973] QB 937 CA, 941.

POSITION OF TRIAL COURTS AFTER JUDGMENT ENTERED

5.05 The Court of Chancery could rehear a case after the decree was enrolled by a bill of review[1] for error apparent, that is, error of law on the face of the decree, for new matter since the decree, and by leave on the discovery of fresh evidence in the technical sense[2]. Originally such a bill could be filed at any time, then the period was reduced to 20 years, and by the time of the Judicature Acts it was five years[3]. The Acts and rules reduced the time for an appeal to one year[4]. The Privy Council held that the bill of review procedure was available in respect of the decree of a Colonial court which had been affirmed by the Privy Council and said that a decree in Chancery affirmed by the House of Lords could be reviewed in this way[5]. A decree could be reviewed, on the original materials, on a petition filed before it was enrolled[6]. The framers of the Judicature Acts evidently considered that the quest for perfect justice over such a lengthy period involving the possibility of a rehearing on the original materials, on questions of law, or on fresh evidence with the lack of finality, and the opportunities for vexation and oppression this created, came at too high a price[7]. The Acts transferred the appellate jurisdiction and powers of the Lord Chancellor and the Court of Appeal in Chancery to the new Court of Appeal[8]. Appeals to that Court were by way of rehearing and it had the power to receive additional evidence[9]. The powers of the Court of Chancery to rehear the case on the existing materials, or as supplemented by fresh evidence, were now exercisable only by the Court of Appeal. Thus the former bill of review procedure at first instance was abolished and once the judgment has been entered the High Court has no power to rehear or review the case[10].

1   *Harrison v Schipp* (2002) 54 NSWLR 612 CA, 617 where the historical material is collected.
2   *Ladd v Marshall* [1954] 1 WLR 1489 CA; *Wollongong Corpn v Cowan* (1955) 93 CLR 435.
3   *Re St Nazaire Co* (1879) 12 Ch D 88 CA, 97, 98.
4   Ibid at 97, 98.
5   *Hosking v Terry* (1862) 15 Moo PC NS 493, 510–1 per Lord Kingsdown.
6   *Harrison v Schipp* (2002) 54 NSWLR 612 CA, 616–617.
7   *Re St Nazaire Co* (1879) 12 Ch D 88 CA, 100.
8   Section 18.
9   *Re St Nazaire Co* (1879) 6 Ch D 88 CA, 99–100, 100–101; *DJL v Central Authority* (2000) 201 CLR 226, 244.
10   *Re Suffield and Watts, ex p Brown* (1888) 20 QBD 693 CA, 696–697, 698; *Preston Banking Co v William Allsup & Sons* [1895] 1 Ch 141 CA, 143, 144–145; *Harrison* [1955] Ch 260 CA 276, 282; *Harrison v Schipp* (2002) 54 NSWLR 612 CA, where the post Judicature Act decisions were considered. The Court of Appeal has held that the bill of review procedure no longer exists: *Cinpres Gas Injection Ltd v Melea Ltd* [2008] Bus L R 1157 CA, 1178–1183 (*Cinpres*).

POSITION IN APPELLATE COURTS

5.06 Until *Taylor v Lawrence*[1] the position in appellate courts was the same[2]. Thus only one application could be made to the High Court under s 1(7) of the Arbitration Act 1979[3] for a certificate that a question of law should be considered by the Court of Appeal[4]. The principles which should guide an appellate court in considering whether to allow its final orders, which have not been entered, to be reopened were summarised by Mason CJ in *Autodesk Inc v Dyason (No 2)*[5]:

> 'What must emerge, in order to enliven the exercise of the jurisdiction, is that the Court has apparently proceeded according to some misapprehension of the facts or the relevant law and ... this ... cannot be attributed solely to the neglect of the party seeking the rehearing. The purpose of the jurisdiction is not to provide a backdoor method by which unsuccessful litigants can seek to reargue their cases.'

These principles also apply to criminal appeals. In *Grierson v R*[6] Dixon J said:

> '... a second appeal from a conviction could not be entertained after the dismissal, on the merits, of an appeal or application for leave to appeal and ... the first appeal could not be reopened after a final determination.'

This is the established position in criminal cases in England, even where the second application is based on the discovery of fresh evidence[7]. The position is otherwise where a notice of abandonment was a nullity, or through administrative error the prisoner has not been heard[8]. *Taylor v Lawrence*[9] departed from these long established principles and, despite the eminence of the judges, it is submitted that the decision was clearly wrong. In January 2001 the Court of Appeal dismissed an appeal from the decision of the county court in favour of the claimants in an action for trespass to land and the order was formally entered[10]. The application to reopen in November 2001 was based on the discovery of fresh evidence of alleged ostensible bias by the trial judge. The Court of Appeal held that it had power to entertain the application but dismissed it on the merits. Since an appellate decision which affirms the judgment below replaces it as the source of any estoppels, the first decision of the Court of Appeal created a cause of action estoppel[11]. *Arnold*[12] established that the bar in such a case is absolute and the discovery of fresh evidence did not enable the case to be reopened[13]. This decision was neither cited by counsel nor referred to by the Court. *Taylor v Lawrence* was followed in *R (on the application of Am (Cameroon)) v Asylum and Immigration Tribunal*[14] where the claimant, through no fault of hers or her legal advisers[15], was denied an oral hearing of her application to proceed with judicial review[16]. The Court of Appeal set aside a decision of the High Court in its appellate jurisdiction which the statute made final[17]. There was no need to invoke *Taylor v Lawrence* because a court has inherent jurisdiction to set aside its ex parte orders where a party, though no fault of his own, has not been heard[18], particularly where this is due to an administrative error of the court[19]. Unsurprisingly *Taylor v Lawrence* unleashed a flood of unmeritorious applications that threatened to overwhelm the court, and CPR 52.17 was introduced to deal with the situation[20]. The subsequent case law and the principles which guide the court in the exercise of this newly recognised jurisdiction were reviewed in *Re Uddin*[21] and *Jeffrey v Society of Lloyds*[22]. The pressing claims of finality in litigation remain a highly relevant consideration[23], and the issue is whether the judicial process has been corrupted in some way eg by bias.

[1]   [2003] QB 528 CA.
[2]   *MacCarthy v Agard* [1933] 2 KB 417 CA; *Pearlman (Veneers) SA Pty Ltd v Bartels* [1954] 1 WLR 1457 CA; *Thynne* [1955] P 272 CA, 295–296, 307–308, 314; *Grierson v R* (1938) 60 CLR 431, 436 per Dixon J; *Bailey v Marinoff* (1971) 125 CLR 529; *Gamser v Nominal*

Defendant (1977) 136 CLR 145, 154: *DJL v Central Authority* (2000) 201 CLR 226, 225; *Burrell v R* (2008) 82 ALJR 1221, 1226–1227.

3   Now ss 32(6), 68(4), and 69(8) of the 1996 Act which require the leave of the High Court for an appeal to the Court of Appeal.

4   *National Westminster Bank Plc v Arthur Young McClelland Moores & Co (a firm) (No 2)* [1991] 1 WLR 1256 (second application for certificate in respect of decision of Walton J on the first rent review considered in *Arnold* [1991] 2 AC 93).

5   (1993) 176 CLR 300, 303.

6   (1938) 60 CLR 431, 435; *Elliott v R* (2007) 234 CLR 38, 42, 47–48.

7   *R v Grantham* [1969] 2 QB 574; *R v Pinfold* [1988] QB 462 CA.

8   *DPP v Majewski* [1977] AC 443 CA, 449–451; *R v Daniel* [1977] QB 364 CA; para 5.03 n 6.

9   [2003] QB 528 CA; *Jeffrey v Society of Lloyds* [2008] 1 WLR 75 CA (application to reopen concluded appeal on ground of fraud dismissed).

10 Ibid at 533.

11 *Shedden v Patrick* (1854) 1 Macq 535 HL, 590, 599; *Wishart v Fraser* (1941) 64 CLR 470; *R v Marks* (1981) 147 CLR 471, 476.

12 [1991] 2 AC 93.

13 Ibid at 104.

14 [2008] 1 WLR 2062 CA.

15 Ibid at 2069.

16 Ibid at 2069.

17 Ibid at 2069, 2070–2071, 2073.

18 Para 5.03 n 6.

19 *Grimshaw v Dunbar* [1953] 1 QB 408 CA, 415.

20 Buxton (2009) 125 LQR 78.

21 [2005] 1 WLR 2398 CA.

22 [2008] 1 WLR 75 CA.

23 *Re Uddin (a child) (serious injury standard of proof)* [2005] 1 WLR 2404.

POWER OF FINAL APPELLATE COURT

5.07 The power of a final appellate court to review its judgment before entry was exercised in *R v Bow Street Metropolitan Stipendiary Magistrate ex p Pinochet Ugarte (No 2)*[1] where a differently constituted Appellate Committee set aside the decision of the previous Appellate Committee because of the ostensible bias of one of its members. The House held that a final appellate court could set aside its own orders which had been improperly made[2]. The Privy Council has held that it has power in truly exceptional circumstances to recall its orders even after they have been entered in order to avoid irremediable injustice[3].

1   [2000] 1 AC 119.

2   Ibid at 132. The application was made before formal entry of the orders pronounced on 25 November 1998. The petition was filed on 10 December (ibid at 129) and the speeches do not refer to the entry of the orders.

3   *Maharajah Pertab Narain Singh v Maharanee Subhao Koer ex p Trilokinath* (1878) LR 5 Ind App 171, 173; *Venkata Narasimha Appa Row v The Court of Wards* (1886) 11 App Cas 660; and the cases cited in *State Rail Authority of New South Wales v Codelfa Construction Pty Ltd* (1982) 150 CLR 29, 38–39, 45–46. In *DJL v Central Authority* (2000) 201 CLR 226, 247 the High Court said that there had been no decision dealing with the position after entry of its final orders.

FINALITY FOR ACTION ON JUDGMENT

5.08 An action cannot be based on a judgment for payment of an amount to be judicially determined by the tribunal or some person acting with its authority such as an interlocutory judgment for damages to be assessed[1], a foreign judgment for an amount to be ascertained on a report of merchants[2], or a judgment or order for assessment by an officer of the court[3]. Such judgments will only support an action when the amount has been ascertained[4].

[1]   *Thomas v Bunn* [1991] 1 AC 362; *Electricity Commission of New South Wales v Lapthorne* (1971) 124 CLR 177, 184.
[2]   *Obicini v Bligh* (1832) 8 Bing 335.
[3]   *Carpenter v Thornton* (1819) 3 B & Ald 52, 55, 62; *Sadler v Robins* (1808) 1 Camp 253 (action on decree of Colonial Court of Equity for a payment after deducting defendant's taxed costs).
[4]   *Henley v Soper* (1828) 8 B & C 16 (action on judgment of Colonial Court for balance of a partnership account ascertained by arbitrator).

5.09 Decisions subject to a condition, such as proof of title[1], an award directing a party to pay a sum of money unless he discharges himself by affidavit[2], or to execute works to the satisfaction of a third person[3], are not final.

[1]   *Re Mountcashell's Estate* [1920] 1 IR 1.
[2]   *Pedley v Goddard* (1796) 7 Term Rep 73.
[3]   *Tomlin v Fordwich Corpn* (1836) 5 Ad & El 147.

DEFECTIVE AWARDS

5.10 An award which does not deal with all the matters submitted is not final[1].

[1]   *Re O'Conor and Whitlaw's Arbitration* (1919) 88 LJKB 1242 CA, 1246, 1248.

AMBIGUITY AND UNCERTAINTY

5.11 A decision is not final which leaves the parties in doubt as to their rights and liabilities, such as a verdict in an action of ejectment in respect of freehold and copyhold lands, finding that so many acres were freehold, and so many copyhold, without determining who had title to which[1]; an award directing an act to be performed by A or B[2]; an award that a party had been guilty of fraud, though he had no intention to mislead[3]; an award which did not refer to an admitted item, making it uncertain whether it had been taken into account[4]; where a verdict had been taken for the plaintiff for £3,000 subject to a reference to a barrister, who was empowered to determine other matters in dispute and enter a verdict for either party, an award directing a verdict for the plaintiff for £260.12.6d. leaving it uncertain whether it was intended to reduce the verdict to £260.12.6d., or increase it by that amount[5]; an award directing payment of alternative sums without indicating how the choice would be made[6]; and an award for payment of differences which did not specify the quantities[7].

[1]   *Hardcastle v Shafto* (1974) 1 Anst 184.
[2]   *Lawrence v Hodgson* (1826) 1 Y & J 16, 18.
[3]   *Ames v Milward* (1818) 8 Taunt 637, 641–642.
[4]   *Re Robson and Railston* (1831) 1 B & Ad 723, 726 (it would invite 'no end of disputes').

[5]   *Mortin v Burge* (1836) 4 Ad & El 973, 975.
[6]   *Murray v Dalton* (1920) 65 Sol Jo 55.
[7]   *Margulies Bros Ltd v Dafnis* [1958] 1 WLR 398. The award was remitted.

DECLARATORY JUDGMENTS

5.12 A bare declaration does not lack finality. 'The court may make binding declarations of right whether or not any consequential relief is or could be claimed'[1]. Such an order which disposes of the proceedings is final for purposes of appeal[2], and creates a *res judicata*[3]. A declaration at the end of the first stage of a split trial when quantum remains to be determined is also final and *res judicata*[4]. Although liberty to apply for substantive relief may be implied in an order granting a bare declaration[5] this does not deny finality. Many orders in the Chancery Division have to be worked out by accounts and inquiries. For purposes of appeal and *res judicata* the final order is that which declares the rights of the parties, although further orders will be made as those rights are worked out[6]. The judgment can only be sued on after the rights of the parties have been worked out[7]. Incompleteness due to the objecting party's conduct may not negative finality[8].

[1]   CPR 40.20.
[2]   *Becker v City of Marion Corpn* [1977] AC 271.
[3]   *International General Electric Co of New York Ltd v Customs and Excise Comrs* [1962] Ch 784 CA, 789; *R v IRC, ex p Rossminster Ltd* [1980] AC 952, 1014, 1027.
[4]   *Warramunda Village Inc. v Pryde* (2002) 116 FCR 58, 76–77.
[5]   *Fisher v Secretary of State for India* (1898) LR 26 Ind App 16, 29. Consequential relief should be sought if possible because s 49(2) of the Supreme Court Act 1981 requires the court to 'so exercise its jurisdiction ... as to secure that, as far as possible, all matters in dispute between the parties are completely and finally determined, and all multiplicity of legal proceedings ... is avoided': *Neeta (Epping) Pty Ltd v Phillips* (1974) 131 CLR 286, 307. Where a bare declaration was made against a Government on the supposition that it would act accordingly, a later claim for coercive relief under the Constitution was not barred: *Gairy v A-G for Grenada* [2002] 1 AC 167, 181.
[6]   *Smith v Davies* (1886) 31 Ch D 595 CA (order nisi for foreclosure final); *Blakey v Latham* (1889) 43 Ch D 23 CA, 25–26 (order for costs to be set off interlocutory); *Re Herbert Reeves & Co* [1902] 1 Ch 29 CA (order dismissing summons for delivery of bill of costs final); *Re Jerome* [1907] 2 Ch 145 CA (dismissal of summons for review of taxation interlocutory); *Norton v Norton* (1908) 99 LT 709 CA (interlocutory order working out order for partition).
[7]   *Henley v Soper* (1828) 8 B & C 16.
[8]   See the following cases on awards – *Cockburn v Newton* (1841) 2 Man & G 899 (omitted matters treated as no longer in dispute); *Rees v Waters* (1847) 16 M & W 263 (the party complaining failed to prove omitted matters).

WANT OF FINALITY ON THE FACE OF THE RECORD

5.13 These include decisions which are temporary, provisional, or preliminary such as an interlocutory injunction or an interim order for the preservation of property[1], an order summoning meetings to consider a scheme of arrangement[2], an order directing a preliminary enquiry before a Master[3], an order *pendente lite*, such as for alimony, a decree nisi for divorce[4]; or an interlocutory order for costs[5]. An order for costs in a final judgment[6] and other orders for costs which are final will support an action[7]. An order for costs in civil proceedings bars any claim to recover additional costs as part of the claimant's damages on another cause of action but costs can be recovered as damages in an action for malicious prosecution because an order for costs cannot be made in criminal proceedings[8]. The position is otherwise where the successful party has a pre-existing contractual or equitable right to costs[9]. Separate reasons given for an order for costs do not create issue estoppels[10].

1   *Pim v Curell* (1840) 6 M & W 234, 267.
2   *Australian Securities Commission v Marlborough Gold Mines Ltd* (1993) 177 CLR 485, 503–506.
3   *Re Wright* [1954] Ch 347 CA.
4   Contrast *Butler* [1894] P 25 CA, criticised paras 15.15–15.16.
5   *Patrick v Shedden* (1853) 2 E & B 14 (action on Scottish interim decreet for 'expenses'); *Sheehy v Professional Life Assurance Co* (1857) 2 CBNS 211 (interlocutory order for costs of resisting appeal); *Hutchinson v Gillespie* (1856) 11 Exch 798, 815–816; *Stephenson v Garnett* [1898] 1 QB 677 CA.
6   *Russell v Smyth* (1842) 9 M & W 810 (action on Scottish divorce decree which provided for plaintiff's costs); *Forbes-Smith* [1901] P 258 CA (order for costs in final decree final).
7   *Hutchinson v Gillespie* (1856) 11 Exch 798 (Privy Council order for payment of amount for costs final and action lay thereon). On the Court's reasoning, it is difficult to understand why the orders in *Patrick v Shedden* (1853) 2 E & B 14 and *Sheehy v Professional Life Assurance Co* (1857) 2 CBNS 211 were not final. The order of the Privy Council was not liable to set-offs from further orders in the same proceedings.
8   *Berry v British Transport Commission* [1962] 1 QB 306 CA, 319–320, 322; *Avenhouse v Hornsby SC* (1998) 44 NSWLR 1 CA.
9   *Gomba Holdings (UK) Ltd v Minories Finance Ltd (No 2)* [1993] Ch 171 CA (*Gomba*).
10   *Clancy v Santoro* [1999] 2 VR 783.

NO ESTOPPEL FROM ABORTIVE TRIAL[1]

5.14 A finding at an abortive trial cannot support a *res judicata* estoppel[2], nor will an order for a general new trial[3]. An order for a new trial on limited issues will be interlocutory as to those but final as to all others[4]. Where an appellate court, in granting a new trial, decides a substantive issue in the proceedings, that part of the decision is capable of creating a *res judicata*[5]. Otherwise the reasons for ordering a new trial are only binding as a judicial precedent[6].

1   This paragraph from the 2nd edn was cited in *Duhamel v R (No 2)* (1981) 131 DLR (3d) 352, 357, Alta CA; affd (1984) 14 DLR (4th) 92 SC.
2   *Roe v R A Naylor Ltd* (1918) 87 LJKB 958 CA, 963 per Swinfen Eady LJ 'This action was sent for a new trial, and the second trial superseded the first, and any finding in the first action was got rid of when the action was sent for a new trial'; *Bobolas v Economist Newspaper Ltd* [1987] 1 WLR 1101 CA; *O'Connor v Malone* (1839) 6 Cl & Fin 572; *Butler* [1894] P 25 CA; para 14.02; *Lynch v Moran* [2006] 3 IR 389 SC. The effect of reversal by an appellate court is considered para 2.33.
3   *Gray v Dalgety & Co Ltd* (1916) 21 CLR 509, 520 per Griffith CJ: 'I never before heard it suggested that a grant of a new trial was a final decision upon any point except that the matter should be further investigated'; *Lyons v Nicholls (No 3)* [1958] NZLR 755 CA; *Zatorski v South Australian Rlys Comr* (1982) 68 FLR 450; *Rainbow Industrial Caterers Ltd v Canadian National Railway* [1991] 3 SCR 3; contrast *Butler* [1894] P 25 CA; criticised paras 15.15–15.16.
4   *Forge v ASIC (No 2)* (2007) 69 NSWLR 575 CA.
5   *Western Canada Power Co v Bergklint* (1916) 34 DLR 467 SC, 477 per Duff J; *MacKinnon v National Money Mart Co* (2009) 304 DLR (4th) 331 BCCA, 373–374.
6   Para 1.15.

DECISION SUBJECT TO REVISION BY TRIBUNAL

5.15 A judgment capable of rescission or modification by the tribunal which pronounced it such as an affiliation order for the maintenance of a child is *prima facie* not final. Such orders are not final because the court has continuing authority to extinguish, reduce, or increase the sums to be paid[1]. Orders of the Divorce Court for permanent maintenance or alimony can now be enforced as a judgment and are therefore final[2]. Some orders under the general law are final, although subject to recall by the court which pronounced them. Grants of probate and administration in common form are final[3], although subject to recall[4]. Orders for specific performance are also final although they can be rescinded if performance becomes impossible[5].; or the contract is frustrated[6]. Where a statute empowers the tribunal to rescind or vary its decision, but indicates that it is final in the meantime, it creates a *res judicata*[7]. The principles were stated by Isaacs J[8]:

> 'The true rule is to see whether or not the Legislature has by its enactment left the order entirely floating, so as to speak, as a determination enforceable only as expressly provided and in the course of that enforcement subject to revision, or whether the order has been given the effect of finality unless subsequently altered'.

Orders, other than interim orders[9], for periodical payments under the Inheritance (Provision for Family and Dependants) Act 1975 are final for appeal purposes and for *res judicata*[10], although they may be varied or discharged[11]. Bankruptcy orders are final although there is power to review and rescind them[12]. A decision of the Chief Land Registrar directing cancellation of a note on the register but declining to direct an entry that the land was free from the alleged encumbrance was final[13]. A decision in opposition proceedings that a patent or trademark should proceed to grant does not finally determine its validity and is not *res judicata*[14] because the court may later revoke the patent or rectify the register[15].

[1] *Re Macartney* [1921] 1 Ch 522, 531–532: (order that estate pay allowance not final because court could terminate it).
[2] *W v W* [1961] P 113 CA; *K v K* [1977] Fam 39 CA; overruling *Re Woolgar* [1942] Ch 318 and earlier cases.
[3] *Cf Migneault v Malo* (1872) LR 4 PC 123, 135, 139 as to grants in solemn form.
[4] *Poulton v Adjustable Cover and Boiler Block Co* [1908] 2 Ch 430, 433 (*Poulton*).
[5] *Johnson v Agnew* [1980] AC 367.
[6] *Hasham v Zenab* [1960] AC 316, 330.
[7] *Austin v Mills* (1853) 9 Exch 288.
[8] *Ainslie* (1927) 39 CLR 381, 390 (judicial separation subject to variation final in the meantime); *Somodaj v Australian Iron and Steel Ltd* (1963) 109 CLR 285, 297–298 (workers' compensation award final although subject to rescission or amendment), *Kiligowski v Metrobus* (2004) 220 CLR 363, 374–375.
[9] Section 5.
[10] Section 19.
[11] Section 6.
[12] 1986 Act s 375(1); *Re a (No 32/50/1991) Debtor* [1993] 1 WLR 314. The power may extend to decisions of the Court of Appeal in bankruptcy: *Ex p Banco de Portugal in re Hooper* (1880) 14 Ch D 1 CA.
[13] *Re Dances Way, West Town, Hayling Island* [1962] Ch 490 CA.
[14] *Unilin Beheer* [2008] 1 All ER 156 CA, 174–175; Patents Act 1977 s 72(5); *Buehler AG v Chronos Richardson Ltd* [1998] 2 All ER 960 CA.
[15] *Special Effects* [2007] EWCA Civ 1371 para [71], (2007) 71 IPR 188, 207.

JUDGMENTS BY DEFAULT

5.16 A judgment by default is final[1] although either party[2] may apply to have it set aside.

1 Paras 2.22–2.25.
2 Para 22.05 nn 7–9.

DISMISSALS FOR WANT OF PROSECUTION

5.17 A dismissal for want of prosecution is not final[1].

1 Para 2.13.

JUDGMENTS BY CONSENT

5.18 A judgment by consent is final[1].

1 Paras 2.16–2.19.

FINALITY NOT AFFECTED BY APPEAL

5.19 A judgment can be final[1], although it may be reversed or varied by an appellate court[2], and is under appeal when set up as a *res judicata*[3]. Although only part of a judgment is challenged on appeal, there is no estoppel for the rest because the appeal trumps any estoppel[4]. The 1920 Act cannot be invoked if an appeal is pending or intended[5], but the 1933 and 1982 Acts and Council Regulation 44/2001 are different in this respect[6]. Finality is not affected although execution has been stayed[7] or levied[8].

1 The possibility of revision under the slip rule is ignored for this purpose.
2 *Nouvion v Freeman* (1889) 15 App Cas 1, 10–11, 15; *Wakefield Corpn v Cooke* [1904] AC 31, 36; *Colt Industries Inc v Sarlie (No 2)* [1966] 1 WLR 1287 CA; *Minott* (1999) 168 DLR (4th) 270 Ont CA, 282. The finality of a judgment is often a condition for an appeal as of right.
3 *Scott v Pilkington* (1862) 2 B & S 11, 41; *Marchioness of Huntley v Gaskell* [1905] 2 Ch 656 CA, 667.
4 *Unilin Beheer* [2008] 1 All ER 156 CA, 174
5 Section 9(2)(e).
6 The 1933 Act s 1 (3) provides that a judgment shall be deemed final and conclusive notwithstanding that an appeal may be pending or that it may be subject to appeal. The fact that an appeal is pending or the judgment debtor intends to appeal is a ground for an application to set aside registration on such terms as may be thought just; s 5(1). Article 30 of the Brussels Convention provides that a court in which recognition of a judgment is sought may stay the proceedings if an appeal has been lodged, and Art 37(1) of the Regulation is to the same effect.
7 *Hall v Odber* (1809) 11 East 118.
8 *R v Haughton Inhabitants* (1853) 1 E & B 501, 515.

FOREIGN JUDGMENTS

5.20 A foreign judgment capable of being reopened by the tribunal which pronounced it is not a *res judicata* while this remains possible. Spanish law provided for two types of judgment in civil cases, one 'remate' or 'executive', the other 'plenary' or 'declaratory'. A 'remate' judgment was not final and a plaintiff could not sue on it in England while the defendants could start plenary proceedings[1]. In *Colt Industries Inc v Sarlie (No 2)*[2] a New York judgment which was final there but not elsewhere in the USA, was treated as final. The party with the onus must adduce evidence that the decision is final in its country of origin. In *Carl-Zeiss (No 2)*[3] Lord Reid said:

> '... it seems ... to verge on absurdity that we should regard as conclusive something in a German judgment which the German court ... would not regard as conclusive. It is quite true that estoppel is a matter for the lex fori, but the lex fori ought to be developed in a manner consistent with good sense. The need to prove whether West German law would permit these issues to be re-opened there appears to have escaped the notice of the appellant's advisers'.

The majority held that the decision was not shown to be final and did not create a *res judicata*[4]. Preliminary decisions of a foreign court on procedural issues such as jurisdiction, personal service, or voluntary submission, although final[5] are not decisions on the merits and are not *res judicata*[6]. The party setting up the foreign decision cannot rely on the presumption that foreign law is the same, because there is no English law as to the finality of a foreign judgment in its country of origin. A foreign arbitral award is not final if, under the relevant law, the foreign court must make an enforcement order[7].

1   *Nouvion v Freeman* (1889) 15 App Cas 1.
2   [1966] 1 WLR 1287 CA.
3   [1967] 1 AC 853, 919.
4   Ibid at 936, 949, 971, contra 927. In *Blohn v Desser* [1962] 2 QB 116 a cause of action estoppel against a partner based on an Austrian judgment against the firm failed for lack of finality because additional proceedings were necessary in which the partners might raise personal defences which could not be raised earlier.
5   *Vitkovice Horni a Hutni Tezirstvo v Korner* [1951] AC 869, 887, 889; *Desert Sun Loan Corpn v Hill* [1996] 2 All ER 847 CA, 858, 863; *The Jarguh Sawit* [1998] 1 SLR 648 CA.
6   Chapter 6.
7   *Merrifield, Ziegler & Co v Liverpool Cotton Association Ltd* (1911) 105 LT 97, 105 106.

EFFECT OF FINAL JUDGMENTS IN CHANCERY ON LATER PROCEEDINGS IN THE ACTION

5.21 Judgments in the Chancery Division such as those for foreclosure, redemption, specific performance or general administration, declare the rights of the parties, but have to be worked out[1]. Such a judgment creates a *res judicata* binding in later proceedings in the action, and the relevant issues must be decided at the trial. It will be too late to raise them in the course of accounts and inquiries directed by the judgment based on the rights declared at the trial[2]. This reflects the practice of the Court of Chancery described by Lord Cottenham LC[3]:

> '... the enquiry is merely whether the party was in occupation ... and whether he was liable for rent; the latter being a mere roving enquiry ... leaving it open to the Defendant to make any possible case that might turn up. I do not apprehend that to be a proper course in directing enquiries ... when an enquiry is ... directed, it should be very strictly confined ... and should not leave it open to the party to make an entirely new case before the Master.'

Any special matter affecting the account should be brought forward at the trial, and cannot be raised 'during the mechanical operation of taking an ordinary account'[4]. Where a co-owner in possession was ordered to account for the rents and profits the order should have defined the receipts and outgoings to be included and allowed, and those matters should not have been left to be resolved on the taking of the account or on further consideration[5].

[1]   Para 5.12 n 6.
[2]   An order reopening transactions under the Money-lenders Act 1900 was binding in later proceedings in the action although arguably beyond power: *Cohen v Jonesco* [1926] 2 KB 1 CA; para 4.03 n 3.
[3]   *M'Mahon v Burchell* (1846) 2 Ph 127, 136–137.
[4]   *Sanguineti v Stuckey's Banking Co (No 2)* [1896] 1 Ch 502.
[5]   *Squire v Rogers* (1979) 39 FLR 106, 123 (Federal Court of Australia).

ORDERS FOR GENERAL ADMINISTRATION

5.22   The common decree for general administration of an estate or trust fund can be made without proof of a breach of trust or wilful default, but in taking common accounts the trustee cannot be charged with a breach of trust or wilful default. Under such a decree the trustee is charged with his actual receipts, but devastavits arising on the accounts can be considered, improper payments disallowed, and he can be charged with interest on uninvested balances[1]. He can be charged with 'a passive breach of trust, an omission by a trustee to do something which as a prudent trustee, he ought to have done – as distinct from an active breach of trust ... doing something which the trustee ought not to have done'[2]. If the claimant wishes to obtain a special account on the basis of wilful default, at least one act of wilful default must be charged in the pleadings and established[3]. This requires proof that an asset has not been received because of the defendant's wilful default[4]. Active breaches of trust[5] and failure to maintain proper records and accounts are not acts of wilful default[6].

The trial is the time to decide such questions, and to make any order for a special account[7], although in a proper case the order can be made later[8]. Liberty may be reserved to apply for an account on the basis of wilful default which can be availed of before final judgment if the necessary evidence emerges while taking common accounts[9]. Consent orders for common accounts and payment of the amount found to be due were final and once entered the court had no power to order special accounts[10]. For this reason an order for payment should not be made when accounts are ordered but further consideration should be reserved[11]. If an act of wilful default is established the court can order a general account on the basis of wilful default or limit that account to the proved default and otherwise order common accounts. The court will order a general account on the basis of wilful default if there is a prima facie inference that other acts of wilful default have occurred[12]. If a common decree for administration has been made, the claimant cannot maintain another action charging the defendant with wilful default without proof that fresh evidence has since been discovered which entitles him to such relief[13]. The question of charging interest on uninvested balances at simple or compound rates may be raised on further consideration[14]. A defendant may plead a settled account as a defence in whole or in part, and in taking common accounts settled accounts are not disturbed[15]. A claimant wishing to disturb a settled account must plead and prove at least one important error before the account will be reopened[16].

[1]   *Re Stevens* [1898] 1 Ch 162 CA, 170, 172, 176; *Meehan v Glazier Holdings Pty Ltd* (2002) 54 NSWLR 146 CA, 149 (*Meehan*).
[2]   *Bartlett v Barclays Bank Trust Co. Ltd (No.2)* [1980] Ch 515, 546 (*Bartlett*).
[3]   *Dowse v Gorton* [1891] AC 190, 202–203; *Re Wells* [1962] 1 WLR 874.
[4]   *Partington v Reynolds* (1858) 4 Drew 253; *Re Wood* [1961] Qd R 375.
[5]   *Russell* (1891) 17 VLR 729, 732. A trustee living in trust property who is chargeable with an occupation rent, and a trustee who 'lends' trust money to himself or a co-trustee commit active breaches of trust not acts of wilful neglect and default.
[6]   *Meehan* (2002) 54 NSWLR 146 CA, 163.
[7]   *Re Armitage* (1883) 24 Ch D 727.
[8]   *Job* (1877) 6 Ch D 562, 564; *Barber v Mackrell* (1879) 12 Ch D 534 CA, 538–539; *Re Symons* (1882) 21 Ch D 757; *Re Youngs* (1885) 30 Ch D 421 CA, 431–432.
[9]   *Re Tebbs* [1976] 1 WLR 924, 931.
[10] *Meehan* (2002) 54 NSWLR 146 CA, 153.
[11] Ibid at 153.
[12] *Re Tebbs* [1976] 1 WLR 924, 928, 930 (sale at undervalue, but this was an active breach of trust); *Bartlett* [1980] Ch 515, 546 (letting company property to directors at an undervalue an act of wilful default and not an active breach of trust because the trustees who owned 99% of the shares had no representation on the board, did not exercise any control, and had not required proper information and accounts). Letting property vested in the trustee at an undervalue would be an active breach of trust.
[13] *Laming v Gee* (1878) 10 Ch D 715. Quaere whether this power survived the Judicature Acts: para 5.05.
[14] *Re Barclay* [1899] 1 Ch 674, 684.
[15] *Holgate v Shutt* (1884) 27 Ch D 111 CA; 28 Ch D 111 CA.
[16] *Parkinson v Hanbury* (1867) LR 2 HL 1, 11, 12, 19; *Whyte v Ahrens* (1884) 26 Ch D 717 CA.

ACTIVE BREACH OF TRUST

5.23 Charges of active breach of trust must be pleaded and proved at the trial. It is not the practice of the court, where one breach has been proved, to direct a roving inquiry to ascertain whether there have been others[1].

[1]   *Re Wrightson* [1908] 1 Ch 789, 798–800; *Bartlett* [1980] Ch 515, 546; see para 5.21 n 4.

SPECIFIC PERFORMANCE

5.24 The claimant in a suit of specific performance must establish the contract at the trial. This only creates a difficulty where the existence or terms of the contract are in dispute or rectification is sought. When a decree was made for specific performance of an open contract and an inquiry as to title was directed, the vendor could not contend that its implied obligation to show a good title was modified by the purchaser's knowledge before contract of irremovable defects. Viscount Haldane said[1]:

> 'The terms of the decree have, in the eye of the law, superseded and excluded all other evidence, and it is too late, if the decree remains unaltered, to try to import new terms in the course of inquiries which follow merely consequentially'[2].

¹ *McGrory v Alderdale Estate Co Ltd* [1918] AC 503, 511. In *Caird v Moss* (1886) 33 Ch D 22 CA it was too late to seek rectification after the court had construed the contract, and the fund had been distributed. Rectification was barred by a cause of action estoppel; paras 7.14, 26.14 n 10.
² A decree for specific performance may be rescinded, and damages awarded if performance becomes impossible: *Johnson v Agnew* [1980] AC 367; or just rescinded if the contract is frustrated: *Hasham v Zenab* [1960] AC 316, 330.

MORTGAGES

5.25 In an action for redemption or account against a mortgagee who has been in possession, the mortgagor is entitled to an account on the basis of wilful default without charging and proving any breach of duty at the trial[1]. This is an exception to the general rule in relation to an order for such an account[2]. A simple order for an account against a mortgagee who has sold the security does not entitle the mortgagor to impeach the sale when taking the account[3]. The following matters must be established at the trial, and unless expressly reserved, cannot be raised on taking the accounts:

(a)   charging a mortgagee in possession with an occupation rent[4];
(b)   allowing a mortgagee the cost of improvements or the enhancement in value which resulted[5];
(c)   charging a mortgagee with loss from a sale at an undervalue[6];
(d)   charging a mortgagee in possession with loss or damage to the security[7];
(e)   whether the account against a mortgagee in possession should be taken with rests[8];
(f)   any other special circumstance affecting the mortgage debt[9].

¹ *Mayer v Murray* (1878) 8 Ch D 424. Since a valid exercise of the power of sale bars the mortgagor's equity of redemption actions for an account are now almost always brought against the mortgagee unless there is a deficiency.
² Ibid at 427. The other exception is an account against a bailiff: *Parkinson v Hanbury* (1867) LR 2 HL 1, 15.
³ Ibid at 429.
⁴ *Shepard v Jones* (1882) 21 Ch D 469 CA, 475.
⁵ Ibid at 476–479, 480–481; *Henderson v Astwood* [1894] AC 150, 163; *Southwell v Roberts* (1940) 63 CLR 581, 589–598 where Dixon J collected the authorities.
⁶ *Mayer v Murray* (1878) 8 Ch D 424, 429; para 7.15.
⁷ *Taylor v Mostyn* (1886) 33 Ch D 226 CA (improper working of mines).
⁸ *Webber v Hunt* (1815) 1 Madd 13; *Neesom v Clarkson* (1845) 4 Hare 97. The question of rests may be reserved until further consideration: *Wrigley v Gill* [1905] 1 Ch 241, 253.
⁹ *Sanguinetti v Stuckey's Banking Co (No 2)* [1896] 1 Ch 502.

PARTNERSHIP SUITS

5.26 Similar rules apply in partnership suits[1]. Issues relating to the existence and continuance of the partnership, the identity of the partners, the terms of the partnership agreement, any mortgage or sale of a share, trading with the assets of a deceased partner, a claim to property acquired by a partner, reopening settled accounts, setting aside a release, any fraudulent abstraction, and similar issues, must be raised and dealt with at the trial[2]. Charging a partner with interest on partnership balances requires proof of fraud, and, except in special circumstances, at least one fraudulent withdrawal must be pleaded and proved at the trial to entitle the claimant to a general inquiry as to sums improperly withdrawn[3]. The court deals at the trial with every claim and cross claim which must be investigated to adjust and settle the account[4]. It is not the practice of the court to order accounts and inquiries without resolving all substantive issues which would affect the content of the account[5]. Ordinary partnership accounts are taken in accordance with the principles stated by Lord Hardwicke LC in *West v Skip*[6].

> '... each is entitled to be allowed against the other everything he has advanced or brought in as a partnership transaction, and to charge the other in the account with what the other has not brought in or has taken out more than he ought'.

A dispute as to a partner's liability to account to the firm for a profit or asset which it is claimed should have been acquired for the firm should be resolved at the trial[7].

[1]   *Barber v Mackrell* (1879) 12 Ch D 534 CA.
[2]   Lindley & Banks on Partnership 18th edn (2002), para 23–79.
[3]   *Barber v Mackrell* (1879) 12 Ch D 534 CA, 544, 551–552.
[4]   Op cit para 23–79.
[5]   Op cit para 23–81.
[6]   (1749) 1 Ves Sen 239, 242.
[7]   *Pathirana* [1967] 1 AC 233 (partner obtaining renewal for himself of licence to operate service station); *Thompson's Trustee in Bankruptcy v Heaton* [1974] 1 WLR 605 (former partner in possession under lease which was partnership property accountable for profit from purchase of freehold reversion).

INTELLECTUAL PROPERTY CASES

5.27   It is the same in patent infringement actions[1]. Issues of infringement and validity should be decided at the trial. As Fletcher Moulton LJ said in *Poulton* where a patent held valid and infringed was revoked in later proceedings[2]:

> '... the inquiry as to damages ... must ... proceed on the basis of the judgment already given upon the issues as to the validity of the patent and its infringement by the defendants, a judgment which binds the parties and ... is not affected by the subsequent proceedings for revocation'.

In *Coflexip (No 2)*[3] the majority followed *Poulton*, but Neuberger LJ held that the special circumstances exception in *Arnold*[4] applied and the infringer should be allowed to rely in the inquiry on the subsequent revocation of the patent by Laddie J. The question was not tested in the House of Lords, despite the amount at stake, because a few weeks later a differently constituted Court of Appeal reversed the decision of Laddie J[5] and the House of Lords refused leave to appeal[6]. Parties may agree to defer some infringement issues to the inquiry[7]. Where infringement was established in respect of one contract, but the inquiry as to damages extended to another 14 in the same situation there was a cause of action estoppel for all contracts[8]. Ordinarily, an inquiry is limited to the infringements established at the trial[9], but a direction should be sought for the assessment to include all damages or profits accruing to the date of the inquiry[10]. A defendant who secretly changes its process or product from that referred to in the particulars of infringement and fails on those issues is likely to be estopped[11] at the inquiry from relying on the secret alteration to limit its liability. The change would be a matter arising after the commencement of the proceedings[12], which the defendant should have raised by amendment to limit its liability to the earlier period[13], leaving the claimant to amend its particulars of infringement if so advised, or start fresh proceedings. The position in trademark, passing off and confidential information cases is somewhat different as the Court of Appeal explained[14] in a breach of confidence case. The plaintiff pleaded and proved over 100 instances of wrongful use of its confidential information by its former licensee. Cross J restrained the defendant from using any of the plaintiff's confidential information but limited the inquiry to the damages suffered from the misuse of the drawings identified in the further and better particulars. The Court of Appeal removed this restriction. Willmer LJ said[15]:

> 'Cross J thought that the inquiry should be limited to breaches of confidence that had already been proved and admitted, and that it would be wrong to direct a roving inquiry to ascertain whether the defendants had committed any further breaches ... In my judgment ... this case is more analogous to a passing off action. In such cases the settled practice[16] is to direct an inquiry covering the same field as the injunction.'

1   *Hormel Foods* [2005] RPC 657, 683; an appeal was allowed by consent. *Special Effects* [2007] EWCA Civ 1371 paras [36], [84], (2007) 71 IPR 188, 199, 207.
2   [1908] 2 Ch 430 CA, 439.
3   *Coflexip SA v Stolt Offshore MS Ltd (No 2)* [2004] FSR 708 CA (*Coflexip No 2*).
4   Ibid at 728–735.
5   *Rockwater Technip France SA* [2004] RPC 919 CA.
6   11 October 2004.
7   *General Tire and Rubber Co v Firestone Tyre and Rubber Co Ltd* [1975] RPC 203 CA, 207, 241, 259; *Harrison v Project and Design (Redcar) Ltd* [1987] RPC 151 CA, 157; *Unilever plc v Chefaro Proprietaries Ltd* [1994] RPC 567, 593–595; *Gerber Garment Technology Inc v Lectra Systems Ltd* [1995] RPC 383, 411; *Unilin Beheer* [2008] 1 All ER 156 CA, 168–169; para 17.18.
8   *Unilin Beheer* [2008] 1 All ER 156 CA, 168–169 disapproving dicta in *Coflexip (No 2)* [2004] FSR 708 CA, 728, 747–748 that there were only issue estoppels.
9   *Colbeam Palmer Ltd v Stock Affiliates Pty Ltd* (1968) 122 CLR 25, 35–39 (trademark infringement, assignment, equitable relief, account of profits, period of account).
10   Cf RSC O 37 r 6. There appears to be no equivalent in the CPR or Practice Directions, but this was probably unnecessary.
11   On the *Henderson* principle (1843) 3 Hare 100; para 7.03.
12   Cf RSC O 18 r 9. There appears to be no equivalent in the CPR or Practice Directions, but this was probably unnecessary.
13   Cf *Unilever plc v Chefaro Proprietaries Ltd* [1994] RPC 567, 593–595 where the defendant gave notice shortly before trial of its intention to introduce a new product it claimed did not infringe.
14   *National Broach and Machine Co v Churchill Gear Machines Ltd* [1965] 1 WLR 1199 CA.
15   Ibid at 1202–1203.
16   Willmer LJ referred to *A G Spalding & Brothers v A W Gamage Ltd and Benetfink & Co Ltd* (1915) 32 RPC 273 where in a passing off case, the House of Lords restored the order of Sargent J for an inquiry 'what damages the plaintiffs had sustained by reason of the acts the repetition of which was restrained by the judgment.' A similar order was made in *Aktiebolaget Manus v R J Fullwood & Bland Ltd* (1949) 66 RPC 285, 286, a trademark infringement and passing off case.

SEPARATE DECISIONS

5.28 Issue estoppels operate in later stages of the same suit[1], whenever the trial is split[2]. Where questions of liability in common law proceedings are separately determined and the claimant succeeds, the court enters interlocutory judgment for damages to be assessed[3]. The judgment is final for purposes of *res judicata*, and binding on the parties in the assessment[4], but would not support an action until the assessment was completed[5]. The position where issues are separately determined was stated by Diplock LJ[6]:

'Where the issue separately determined is not decisive of the suit the judgment upon that issue is interlocutory ... and the suit continues. Yet I take it to be too clear to need citation of authority that the parties to the suit are bound by the determination of the issue. They cannot subsequently in the same suit advance an argument or adduce further evidence directed to showing that the issue was wrongly determined'.

This reasoning applies where a case is stated to an appellate court for the decision of preliminary questions[7]. Subordinate legislation now provides that a separate decision is final for appeal purposes[8]. A decision dismissing one of several defendants from the proceedings is final and *res judicata* for that defendant although the proceedings continue against others[9]. In these cases the so-called interlocutory decision is really part of a composite final decision. Where there was no order for the determination of separate questions and the judge published findings of fact and law without making any orders there was no appealable decision and no *res judicata*[10].

[1] *Fidelitas* [1966] 1 QB 630 CA, 642; *O'Toole v Charles David Pty Ltd* (1990) 171 CLR 232, 245, 260, 298; *Lalwani v Vickerama* [2001] 1 SLR 90, 101; *Abric Project Management v Palmshine Plaza Sdn Bhd* [2007] 5 MLJ 685, 694–695.
[2] *Johnson v Felton* [2006] 3 NZLR 475 CA, 486–488 (actions by Official Assignee and creditors to set aside pre-bankruptcy transaction. The claim by the Official Assignee was heard first, and issue estoppels from that trial bound the parties and privies in the second trial).
[3] *Thomas v Bunn* [1991] 1 AC 362; *Electricity Commission of New South Wales v Lapthorne* (1971) 124 CLR 177, 184.
[4] *Strachan v The Gleaner Co Ltd* [2005] 1 WLR 3204 PC, 3209. (Interlocutory judgment for damages to be assessed set aside on terms after assessment and final judgment).
[5] Para 5.08 n 4.
[6] *Fidelitas* [1966] 1 QB 630 CA, 642; *Bass v Permanent Trustee Co. Ltd.* (1999) 198 CLR 334, 360. The res judicata may be affected if the pleadings are later amended: *Bobolas v Economist Newspaper Ltd* [1987] 1 WLR 1101 CA; *Hockin v Bank of British Columbia* (1993) 123 DLR (4th) 538 BCCA, 551–552.
[7] *O'Toole v Charles David Pty Ltd* (1990) 171 CLR 232, 244–245, 259–260.
[8] Access to Justice Act 1999 (Destination of Appeals) Order 2000 incorporated in Part 52 Practice Direction para 2A.2, 2A.3, 2A.4; *Roerig v Valiant Trawlers Ltd* [2002] 1 WLR 2304 CA, 2319–2321.
[9] *Dundas v Waddell* (1880) 5 App Cas 249.
[10] *Landsal Pty Ltd v REI Building Society* (1993) 41 FCR 421. Because there was no judgment or order there was no cause of action estoppel, merger, or issue estoppel which only applies to matters 'necessarily decided by the judgment decree or order': *Blair v Curran* (1939) 62 CLR 464, 532–533 per Dixon J.

THE FINALITY OF FINAL RELIEF

5.29 A final judgment or order for coercive relief fixes the relief to which the claimant is entitled[1]. This may be the result of the cause of action merging in the judgment. A claimant who has recovered damages in tort cannot bring a second action to recover additional damages if the original award proves too low, even for losses not known or foreseen at that time[2], and the defendant cannot recover the excess if the award proves too high[3]. The principle extends to claims for contribution or indemnity[4] and other cases. Final relief enforcing the planning laws included an order for the demolition of a contravening building. This was *res judicata* and there could be no stay pending an application to the planning authority for *ex post facto* approval[5]. All matters relevant to the court's discretion to order demolition had to be brought forward in the trial.

[1]   Orders for specific performance are an exception because they may be rescinded and damages awarded if performance becomes impossible, e g because the vendor does not have a good title or the purchaser cannot complete: *Johnson v Agnew* [1980] AC 367; *Hasham v Zenab* [1960] AC 316, 330.
[2]   *Fetter v Beale* (1697) 1 Ld Raym 339; *Rothwell v Chemical and Insulating Co Ltd* [2008] AC 281, 291.
[3]   *Corpn of Dublin v Building and Allied Trade Union* [1996] 1 IR 468 SC (award of compensation excessive in light of later events, but excess not recoverable); para 8.32 n 3.
[4]   *Anshun* (1981) 147 CLR 589.
[5]   *Tynan v Meharg* (1998) 102 LGERA 119 (NSWCA).

INTERLOCUTORY DECISIONS REVIEWABLE ON APPEAL FROM FINAL ORDER

5.30 A litigant will not be prejudiced by not immediately appealing an adverse interlocutory decision because on an appeal from the final order the appellate court can correct any interlocutory order which affected the final result[1]. This principle was established by the Privy Council[2]. Dr Lushington explained[3]:

'We are not aware of any law ... which renders it imperative upon the suitor to appeal from every interlocutory order by which he may conceive himself aggrieved, under the penalty, if he does not do so, of forfeiting forever the benefit of the consideration of the appellate court. No authority ... has been cited in support of such a proposition and we cannot conceive that anything would be more detrimental to the expeditious administration of justice than the establishment of a rule which would impose upon the suitor the necessity of so appealing ... We believe there have been very many cases before this Tribunal in which their Lordships have deemed it to be their duty to correct erroneous interlocutory orders, though not brought under their consideration until the whole cause had been decided, and brought hither by appeal for adjudication'[4].

It was once thought that there could only be one final judgment or order in an action for purposes of appeal, and all others were interlocutory[5], but decisions on separate questions were held to be final for appeal purposes[6], contrary to the opinion of Diplock LJ[7]. The question was settled for the Court of Appeal by a rule of court[8]. CPR 52.3(1) now requires permission to appeal to the Court of Appeal in practically all cases. The appropriate appellate court may depend on whether the decision was final, as defined by a regulation[9] incorporated in Part 52 Practice Direction para 2A.2, 2A.3 and 2A.4. Judgments at each stage of a split trail and on any preliminary question are now final for appeal purposes[10].

1   *Gerlach v Clifton Bricks Ltd* (2002) 209 CLR 478.
2   *Jones v Gough* (1865) 3 Moo PCCNS 1, 12; *Forbes v Ameeroonissa Begum* (1865) 10 Moo Ind App 340, 359–360; *Sheonath v Ramnath* (1865) 10 Moo Ind App 413, 423.
3   *Maharajah Moheshur Sing v Bengal Government* (1859) 7 Moo Ind App 283, 302.
4   *Crowley v Glissan* (1905) 2 CLR 402; *Grigson v Ministry of Fisheries* [1998] 3 NZLR 202, 223.
5   *Smith v Cowell* (1880) 6 QBD 75 CA, 78.
6   *White v Brunton* [1984] QB 570 CA, *Radke v JS* (2006) 262 DLR (4th) 681 BCCA; *Charlebois v Les Enterprises Normand Ltee* (2006) 266 DLR (4th) 732 Ont CA.
7   Para 5.28 n 6.
8   RSC O 59 r 1A which came into effect in 1988. In *Strathmore Group Ltd v Fraser* [1992] 2 AC 172 the Privy Council held that a separate decision was final for appeal purposes, but the decision of the NZ Court of Appeal for dismissal of the proceedings was final because there was no suggestion that the proceedings were frivolous or vexatious. A dismissal on the latter ground is interlocutory for appeal purposes: *Tampion v Anderson* (1974) 48 ALJR 11 PC; *Hunt v Allied Bakeries Ltd* [1956] 1 WLR 1326 CA; *Re Luck* (2003) 78 ALJR 177.
9   Para 5.28 n 8.
10 *Roerig v Valiant Trawlers Ltd* [2002] 1 WLR 2304 CA, 2319–2321.

OTHER INTERLOCUTORY DECISIONS FINAL FOR RES JUDICATA

5.31 Other interlocutory decisions before or after the final decree may determine some question so that it becomes *res judicata*[1]. An interesting example occurred in an Indian appeal[2]. During execution proceedings a judge determined that the decree awarded future *mesne* profits to the judgment creditor. Some years later this interpretation was challenged and an appellate court held otherwise. This decision was set aside by the Privy Council which said[3]:

> 'The matter … was not decided in a former suit, but in a proceeding of which the application in which the orders reversed by the High Court were made was merely a continuation. It was as binding between the parties and those claiming under them as an interlocutory judgment in a suit is binding upon the parties in every proceeding in the suit, or as a final judgment in a suit is binding upon them in carrying the judgment into execution. The binding force of such a judgment depends … upon general principles of law. If it were not binding, there would be no end to litigation'.

Orders in proceedings for the administration of an estate may finally determine the rights of the parties on some question and create a *res judicata*. In *Peareth v Marriott*[4] the suit was commenced in 1856 and a decree for general administration was made in 1857. In 1861 an order was made until further order for payment of an annuity to the widow free of all deductions except income tax and directions were given for the manner of payment. Further orders were made in 1862 and 1866 pursuant to liberty to apply. In 1882 the widow sought to enforce payment of the annuity clear of income tax, contending that the 1861 order was interlocutory, and the question was not *res judicata*. Jessel MR[5] said: 'It is clear that it was meant to be a declaration of right. It was a decision between the parties as to the proper amount to be paid to the annuitant'. Cotton LJ said[6]: 'The order was only temporary as to the mode in which the payment was to be made and the funds out of which it was to come. It was final as to the rights of the parties'. This decision was applied in the Indian appeal referred to and in later cases[7]. An order for a new trial is generally interlocutory, but if the court limits the issues by finally deciding any question, it will, to that extent, create a *res judicata*[8].

An interlocutory order in an administration suit does not necessarily create a *res judicata*. In *Re Wright*[9] an originating summons asked the court to determine the validity of a charitable trust. The court directed an inquiry as to whether 'it is now or will at any future time be possible to carry into execution the charitable trust' and ordered the summons to stand over. On completion of the inquiry, the Attorney General argued that the relevant date was the death of the testatrix. The argument of the next of kin that the question was *res judicata* failed because the order had simply directed the inquiry as a preliminary step[10]. Other interlocutory decisions, which are final for *res judicata*, although not part of a composite final decision, include the dismissal of an application by a third party to have property excluded from a *Mareva* injunction because it did not belong to the defendant[11]; and a decision refusing to dismiss proceedings as an abuse of process which was a final decision that the plaintiffs had standing[12]. An order refusing an interlocutory injunction would not ordinarily be a final decision on any question but could be in special circumstances[13]. A decision that a cross claim did not warrant setting aside a default judgment did not create an issue estoppel barring fresh proceedings[14].

[1]   *Carl Zeiss (No 3)* [1970] Ch 506, 539; *Desert Sun Loan Corpn v Hill* [1996] 2 All ER 847 CA, 863. An example, although not recognised, was *Stephenson v Garnett* [1898] 1 QB 677 CA where the plaintiff was given leave to tax costs and enforce his judgment despite a release obtained by fraud; *Renaissance Leisure Group Inc v Frazer* (2001) 197 DLR (4th) 336 (order dismissing motion for summary dismissal for abuse of process barred relitigation of that issue at trial).

[2]   *Ram Kirpal Shukul v Mussumat Rup Kuari* (1883) LR 11 Ind App 37.

[3]   Ibid at 41; *Rajah of Ramnad v Velusami Tevar* (1920) LR 48 Ind App 45 (interlocutory decision that execution not barred by limitation *res judicata*; *Diamond v Western Realty Co* [1924] 2 DLR 922 SC, 929.

[4]   (1882) 22 Ch D 182 CA; *Arnold* [1990] Ch 573 CA, 588; *Kanawagi v Penang Port Commission* [2001] 5 MLJ 433, 450–451; *Abric Project Management v Palmshine Plaza Sdn Bhd* [2007] 5 MLJ 685, 695.

[5]   Ibid at 191.

[6]   Ibid at 193.

[7]   *Gopal Lal Sett v Purna Chandra Basak* (1921) LR 49 Ind App 100, 106 per Lord Buckmaster: 'A direction given in an administration suit has the effect of an order binding all parties and determines the construction to which it gives effect so that after the lapse of time necessary for appeal it becomes final and conclusive'; *Hook v Administrator-General of Bengal* (1921) LR 48 Ind App 187; *Ramachandra Rao* (1922) LR 49 Ind App 129.

[8]   Para 5.14.

[9]   [1954] Ch 347 CA.

[10]   Cf *Hook v Administrator-General of Bengal* (1921) LR 48 Ind App 187.

[11]   *SCF Finance Co Ltd v Masri (No 3)* [1987] QB 1028 CA. Such a decision will not be final if the court maintains the injunction until trial.

[12]   *Chambers v An Bord Pleanala* [1992] IR 134 SC. The court may decide to determine this question at trial.

[13]   *Joseph Lynch Land Co Ltd v Lynch* [1995] NZLR 37 CA (order removing a caveat not final for *res judicata*).

[14]   *Mullen v Conoco Ltd* [1998] QB 382 CA, 391.

INTERLOCUTORY ORDERS NOT FINAL FOR ANY PURPOSE

5.32 The dismissal of an interlocutory application on procedural grounds or on the merits is not final and does not bar a further application[1], although that is not likely to succeed unless supported by additional evidence or a different argument. Courts have sometimes enforced a requirement for the additional evidence to be 'fresh'[2], but in other cases a second application has been granted on evidence that should have been before the court on the first[3]. The *Henderson*[4] principle is applied less strictly, at least where the earlier application was unsuccessful[5]. Where permission to apply for judicial review was refused on one ground but granted on another the former could be argued at the final hearing although there had been no change of circumstances[6]. The dismissal of an application to set aside a default judgment to allow a counterclaim will not ordinarily create a *res judicata* against proceedings by the defendant on the same cause of action[7].

Interlocutory orders in matters of practice and procedure, such as an interlocutory injunction, remain under the control of the court, and subject to review[8]. Such orders do not decide any question finally, not even whether there should be an interlocutory injunction, or its terms[9]. *Buttes Gas and Oil Co v Hammer (No 3)*[10] is a graphic illustration. In November 1980 an appellate committee granted leave to appeal from a 1974 decision of the Court of Appeal, discharging an earlier order of another committee which had refused leave[11]. This was regular because orders granting or refusing leave to appeal are interlocutory[12]. These principles do not apply to applications for leave to appeal to the House of Lords under s 33 of the Criminal Appeal Act 1968 and semble to applications for a certificate under s 1(2) of the Administration of Justice Act 1960 that a point of law of general public importance was involved[13].

In *Midland Bank Trust Co Ltd v Green*[14] Oliver J said that a decision striking out a pleading was final for *res judicata*. It was suggested in the previous edition that this was not correct, although the decision would ordinarily be followed in the same proceedings. However if an appellate decision changed the law in the meantime, or further evidence became available, it may be appropriate for the struck out material to be restored. The plea of *res judicata*, if valid, would be inconvenient because the original decision may have been correct when given. If the application to amend arises from a change in the law, the difficulty could be overcome by extending the time for an application for leave to appeal, but if it arises from the discovery of further evidence, the Court of Appeal would have to grant leave to adduce it, which would be inconvenient and artificial. Principle and convenience support the view that such decisions are not *res judicata*, and this has now been established[15]. The decision in *R v Governor of Brixton Prison ex p Osman*[16], that the order refusing discovery on the ground of public interest privilege, was *res judicata* was also wrong because privilege could later be waived or lost[17]. Dicta in the Court of Appeal suggest that summary dismissal for failure to disclose a cause of action created a cause of action estoppel[18], but the decision was interlocutory[19], and there was no *res judicata* although fresh proceedings could be an abuse unless the law has changed[20], or additional evidence became available[21].

---

[1] *Atwood v Chichester* (1878) 3 QBD 722 CA (second application to set aside default judgment, point not argued); *Dombey & Son Ltd v Playfair Bros* [1897] 1 QB 368 (second application for summary judgment after first failed on technicality); *W T Lamb & Sons v Rider* [1948] 2 KB 331 CA, 334 (second application for leave to issue execution); *Hall v Nominal Defendant* (1966) 117 CLR 423, 429, 440–441, 444; *Nominal Defendant v*

Manning (2000) 50 NSWLR 139 CA (second application for extension of limitation period); *Carr v Finance Corpn of Australia Ltd* (1981) 147 CLR 246, 248, 253–254 (second application to set aside default judgment); *Kinex Exploration Pty Ltd v Tasco Pty Ltd* [1995] 2 VR 318 (second application to set aside ex parte judgment); *El Capistrano SA v ATO Marketing Ltd* [1989] 1 WLR 471 CA (second motion for civil contempt); *Techmex Far East Pte Ltd v Logicraft Products Manufacturing Pte Ltd* [1998] 1 SLR 483 (second application for summary judgment).

2   *Chanel Ltd v FW Woolworth & Co Ltd* [1981] 1 WLR 485 CA, 492–493 per Buckley LJ: 'Even in interlocutory matters a party cannot fight over again a battle which has already been fought unless there has been some significant change of circumstances, or the party has become aware of facts which he could not reasonably have known, or found out in time.'

3   *Woodhouse v Consignia plc* [2002] 1 WLR 2558 CA, 2575; *Nominal Defendant v Manning* (2000) 50 NSWLR 139 CA.

4   (1843) 3 Hare 100; para 7.03.

5   *Woodhouse* [2002] 1 WLR 2558 CA, 2575.

6   *R (on the application of Smith) v Parole Board* [2003] 1 WLR 2548 CA, 2552; citing this passage in the previous edition.

7   *Mullen v Conoco Ltd* [1998] QB 382 CA.

8   *Pocklington Foods Inc v R* (1995) 123 DLR (4th) 141, 144–145 Alta CA.

9   Para 5.13.

10   [1982] AC 888.

11   Ibid at 922; *Khawaja v Secretary of State for the Home Department* [1984] AC 74, 79.

12   *Parke Davis & Co v Sanofi* (1982) 149 CLR 147.

13   *R v Ashdown* [1974] 1 WLR 270 CA; *Sweet v Parsley* [1968] 2 QB 418 CA, 426.

14   [1980] Ch 590, 594, 594, 607.

15   *R (on the application of Smith) v Parole Board* [2003] 1 WLR 2548 CA, 2552.

16   [1991] 1 WLR 281, 291.

17   *Sankey v Whitlam* (1978) 142 CLR 1; *Pocklington Foods Inc v R* (1995) 123 DLR (4th) 141, 145 Alta CA.

18   *Electra Private Equity Partners v KPMG Peat Marwick* [2001] 1 BCLC 589 CA, 625 (*Electra*). The court accepted a concession from leading counsel.

19   Para 5.30 n 8, and n 15 above.

20   An action may have been struck out before *Hedley Byrne & Co. Ltd v Heller & Partners Ltd* [1964] AC 465 which would not have been struck out afterwards.

21   *Electra* [2001] 1 BCLC 589 CA, 629–630.

Chapter 6

DECISION ON THE MERITS

6.01 A judicial decision must be 'on the merits' before it can constitute a *res judicata*. This is mentioned in other contexts but is a separate requirement.

6.02 The question has commonly arisen in relation to foreign judgments. In *Carl-Zeiss (No 2)* the majority held that a foreign judgment can only create a *res judicata* if it is a final judgment on the merits[1] of the issue. In that case this was the capacity of the Stiftung to function and instruct solicitors to commence proceedings on its behalf. In *Black-Clawson International Ltd v Papierwerke Waldhof-Aschaffenburg AG*[2] a German judgment upholding a time bar was not final on the merits and proceedings in England, where a longer limitation period applied, were not barred[3]. These decisions were followed in *Tracomin SA v Sudan Oil Seeds Co Ltd*[4] where Staughton J held a Swiss judgment final on the merits where the question was whether an arbitration clause had been incorporated in a contract of sale, although recognition was denied on other grounds. In *The Sennar (No 2)*[5] the decision that an exclusive jurisdiction clause in bills of lading barred the consignee's action in tort against the shipowners in Holland was on the merits and barred its action in tort against the shipowners in England. Lord Brandon said[6]:

'... a decision on procedure alone is not a decision on the merits. Looking at the matter positively a decision on the merits is a decision which establishes certain facts as proved or not in dispute, states what are the relevant principles of law applicable to such facts, and expresses a conclusion with regard to the effect of applying those principles to the factual situation concerned'.

Lord Diplock said[7]:

'What it means in the context of judgments delivered by courts of justice is that the court has held that it has jurisdiction to adjudicate upon an issue raised in the cause of action to which the particular set of facts give rise'.

Accordingly a decision which determines an issue otherwise than on purely procedural grounds is a decision on the merits although it may not determine all the issues in controversy[8]. Dismissal of an action for criminal conversation because the cause of action was not known to the law of Hong Kong was a decision on the merits[9]. The decision may be that of a court or arbitral tribunal, but it must have jurisdiction to determine the issue.

[1]   [1967] 1 AC 853, 918, 927, 933, 935, 948 and 969.
[2]   [1975] AC 591.
[3]   Ibid at 615, 618, 626, 631–632, 642. The Foreign Limitation Periods Act 1984 now provides that a foreign judgment based on a limitation provision is on the merits.
[4]   [1983] 1 WLR 662.
[5]   [1985] 1 WLR 490 HL.
[6]   Ibid at 499.
[7]   Ibid at 494.
[8]   Cf *Westfal-Larsen & Co A S v Ikerigi Compania Naviera SA, The Messiniaki Bergen* [1983] 1 All ER 382, 390 (doubtful whether foreign decision on the merits where issue was timely demand for arbitration).
[9]   *Lemm v Mitchell* [1912] AC 400, 405; para 2.28 n 8.

6.03 The Court of Appeal has considered[1] whether a decision of a foreign court that a defendant had submitted to its jurisdiction was a decision on the merits. Summary judgment was refused because it was not clear that the foreign court had decided the issue which was relevant under English law[2]. Evans LJ considered that the issue was procedural and doubted whether a decision on it could be on the merits[3], but held that it could give rise to an issue estoppel[4]. This was unsound because jurisdiction of the relevant kind is an essential condition for the recognition of any foreign judgment, and until this is established the judgment cannot create a *res judicata* estoppel. If jurisdiction is in issue it cannot be proved by estoppels based on the foreign judgment itself.

Should an exception be recognised where the validity of service was litigated in the foreign court? Should this be treated as the submission of that issue to the foreign jurisdiction? If so a defendant who loses on that issue in the foreign court will have submitted to its jurisdiction on the merits. His unsuccessful challenge to its jurisdiction would be treated as a general submission. This is similar to the view rejected in *Re Dulles' Settlement (No.2)*[5] and is contrary to the position where fraud in the foreign proceedings is alleged[6]. The better view is that service is a matter of procedure and, as Lord Brandon said in *The Sennar (No.2)*[7], a decision on procedure is not one on the merits. In the language of Lord Diplock[8] the question of service, submission to the jurisdiction and fraud in the proceedings are not 'issue[s] raised in the cause of action' in the foreign court. Decisions on such matters are not on the merits.

[1]   *Desert Sun Loan Corpn v Hill* [1996] 2 All ER 847 CA.
[2]   Ibid at 860, 862, 863.
[3]   Ibid at 856.
[4]   Ibid at 858, 863.
[5]   [1951] Ch 842 CA; para 4.30.
[6]   *Owens Bank Ltd v Bracco* [1992] 2 AC 443.
[7]   Para 6.02 n 6.
[8]   Para 6.02 n 7.

6.04 A dismissal for want of prosecution is not on the merits[1], nor is a dismissal for want of necessary parties[2]. Dismissals for want of jurisdiction are not on the merits[3], except on the issue of jurisdiction[4] The Privy Council twice held that a default judgment was not a decision on the merits for the purposes of an Indian statute providing for the registration and enforcement of foreign judgments[5], but these decisions are inconsistent with later authority[6], and would not be followed. A judgment obtained by the registration of a foreign judgment is not on the merits[7].

1   Para 2.13. Dismissal for failure to comply with an order for discovery is not on the merits: *Baines v State Bank* (1985) 2 NSWLR 729; nor is an order for summary dismissal for failure to disclose a cause of action: *Rogers v Legal Services Commission of South Australia* (1995) 64 SASR 572.
2   *Sheosayer Singh v Sitaram Singh* (1897) LR 24 Ind App 50.
3   *The Sennar (No 2)* [1985] 1 WLR 490 HL; *R v Middlesex Justices, ex p Bond* [1933] 2 KB 1 CA.
4   Para 2.15.
5   *Keymer v P Viswanath Reddi* (1916) LR 44 Ind App 6; *L Oppenheim & Co v Mahomed Haneef* [1922] 1 AC 482.
6   *New Brunswick* [1939] AC 1; *Kok Hoong* [1964] AC 993.
7   Para 2.59 n 2.

Chapter 7

CAUSE OF ACTION ESTOPPEL

UNDERLYING PRINCIPLES

7.01 The maxim *transit in rem judicatam* prevents a successful plaintiff re-asserting a cause of action on which he recovered judgment. This is the doctrine of merger considered in Part 2. One of its most common manifestations is the finality of damages awards. A plaintiff cannot recover more if the award proves too low, and a defendant cannot recover the excess if it proves too high[1]. There is no true estoppel because the cause of action has merged in the judgment and ceased to exist. On the other hand the maxim *interest rei publicae ut sit finis litium* denies an unsuccessful plaintiff the chance of re-litigating a case he lost and is the basis of cause of action estoppel[2].

[1] Para 5.29. The principle applies to a detailed assessment of costs. All relevant items must be included in the bill and after a final certificate further items cannot be included in another bill: *Harris v Moat Housing Group–South Ltd* [2008] 1 WLR 1578.
[2] *Dacosta v Villa Real* (1734) 2 Stra 961.

7.02 The term 'cause of action estoppel' was coined by Diplock LJ in *Thoday*. He distinguished it from merger saying[1]:

> '... cause of action estoppel ... prevents a party from asserting or denying as against the other party, the existence of a particular cause of action, the existence or non–existence of which has been determined by a court of competent jurisdiction in previous litigation between the same parties. If the cause of action was determined to exist ie judgment was given upon it, it is ... merged in the judgment. If it is determined not to exist, the unsuccessful plaintiff can no longer assert that it does; he is estopped per rem judicatam.'

[1] [1964] P 181 CA, 197–198; *Town of Grandview v Doering* [1976] 2 SCR 621. In *Workington Harbour and Dock Board v Trade Indemnity Co Ltd (No 2)* [1938] 2 All ER 101 HL where a cause of action estoppel was upheld Lord Atkin said at 106: 'The result is that the plaintiffs, who appear to have a good cause of action for a considerable sum of money, failed to obtain it, and on what may appear to be technical grounds. Reluctant however as a judge may be to fail to give effect to substantial merits, he has to keep in mind principles established for the protection of litigants from oppressive proceedings. There are solid merits behind the maxim *nemo bis vexari debet pro eadem causa*'. The requirements for cause of action estoppel in Singapore were reviewed in *Goh v Goh* [2007] 1 SLR 453.

THE SCOPE OF CAUSE OF ACTION ESTOPPEL

7.03 A cause of action estoppel bars relitigation of the cause of action by either party on grounds, other than fraud or collusion, that were not raised in the earlier proceedings. The leading authority is *Henderson* where Wigram VC said[1]:

> ' … where a given matter becomes the subject of litigation in, and of adjudication by, a court of competent jurisdiction, the court requires the parties to that litigation to bring forward their whole case, and will not (except under special circumstances) permit the same parties to open the same subject of litigation in respect of matter which might have been brought forward as part of the subject in contest, but which was not brought forward, only because they have, from negligence, inadvertence, or even accident, omitted part of their case. The plea of *res judicata* applies, except in special cases, not only to points upon which the court was actually required by the parties to form an opinion and pronounce a judgment, but to every point which properly belonged to the subject of litigation, and which the parties, exercising reasonable diligence, might have brought forward at the time.'

Binnie J said in the Supreme Court of Canada[2]:

> 'The law rightly seeks a finality to litigation … it requires litigants to put their best foot forward … when first called upon to do so. A litigant … is only entitled to one bite of the cherry.'

Cause of action estoppels can arise whenever a substantive claim is granted or refused even if the claimant has no cause of action in the traditional sense. Thus a decision that a lane was a public highway created a cause of action estoppel. Proceedings by the plaintiff's predecessor in title before Quarter Sessions in 1958 determined the status of the lane. The effect of a barrier to vehicular traffic in limiting the dedication was not then in issue, but the question was clearly relevant when the status of the lane was being determined *in rem*, and it 'properly belonged' to the litigation. The plaintiff was therefore barred from raising that question in the High Court in 1975[3]. If a defendant succeeds on an extraneous defence, unrelated to the elements of the cause of action, such as bankruptcy, there will only be an issue estoppel[4]. Where A and B are jointly liable in contract to X, who unsuccessfully sued A alone, the judgment creates a cause of action estoppel for the benefit of B only if it was based on a ground common to A and B, and not one personal to A such as bankruptcy or infancy[5]. A cause of action estoppel from a judgment for the defendant will be no answer to an action on a cause of action which accrued after that previously sued on because, for example, the period of credit has expired in the meantime, a later breach is relied on, or the contract has been rescinded.

---

[1] (1843) 3 Hare 100, 114–115; the facts appear in para 26.03; 'A closer look at *Henderson v Henderson*' Handley (2002) 118 LQR 397. The decision involved a judicial account. For the effect of an account as a cause of action estoppel paras 7.14, 26.03; *Town of Grandview v Doering* [1976] 2 SCR 621, 637–638; *AA v The Medical Council* [2003] 4 IR 302 SC, 316.

[2] *Danyluk* [2001] 2 SCR 460, 473.

[3] *L E Walwin & Partners Ltd v West Sussex County Council* [1975] 3 All ER 604.

[4] Para 8.02.

[5] *Phillips v Ward* (1863) 2 H & C 717, 720–721.

BAR IS ABSOLUTE

7.04 The bar created by a cause of action estoppel is absolute with no exception for special circumstances. In *Arnold*[1] Lord Keith said:

'Cause of action estoppel arises where the cause of action in the later proceedings is identical to that in the earlier proceedings, the latter having been between the same parties or their privies and having involved the same subject matter. In such a case the bar is absolute ... unless fraud or collusion is alleged, such as to justify setting aside the earlier judgment. The discovery of new factual matter which could not have been found out by reasonable diligence for use in the earlier proceedings does not, according to the law of England, permit the latter to be reopened ... The principles upon which cause of action estoppel is based are expressed in the maxims *nemo debet bis vexari pro una et eadem causa* and *interest rei publicae ut finis sit litium*. Cause of action estoppel extends also to points which might have been but were not raised and decided in the earlier proceedings for the purpose of establishing or negativing the existence of a cause of action.'

Arnold made it important to distinguish between cause of action and issue estoppels because the latter are subject to a special circumstances exception.

[1]   [1991] 2 AC 93, 104.

IDENTITY OF CAUSES OF ACTION[1] (TORT)

7.05 The identity of causes of action is determined as a matter of substance[2]. This is particularly important where the first action was brought in a foreign forum. A passenger with causes of action for personal injuries against a carrier who failed in an action in tort could not bring an action in contract and *vice versa*. An employee with causes of action against his employer in tort and contract[3] is in the same position. The principle was stated by Maugham J[4]:

'... the cause of action in the two cases is strictly speaking not the same. On the other hand the plea of res judicata is not a technical doctrine, but a fundamental doctrine based on the view that there must be an end to litigation.'

In *Macdougall v Knight*[5] a plaintiff, who failed in an action for libel based on parts of a pamphlet, brought a second action based on other parts which was dismissed for what we now recognise was a cause of action estoppel. However publications of the same libel on different dates creates separate causes of action[6]. In *Greenhalgh v Mallard*[7] the plaintiff, who failed in an action for conspiracy to effect an unlawful purpose, brought an action on the same facts for conspiracy to injure by unlawful means. This was dismissed for *res judicata* because a given set of facts gives rise to only one cause of action for conspiracy. In *Wright v Bennett*[8] after an action for fraud failed, the plaintiff brought an action for fraudulent conspiracy based on the same facts. It was dismissed for abuse of process but Cohen LJ held that there was a cause of action estoppel, and since identity is a question of substance this must be correct.

[1]   Chapter 21 also deals with the identity of causes of action.
[2]   *Trawl Industries of Australia Pty Ltd v Effem Foods Pty Ltd* (1992) 36 FCR 406, 418–419, 422 (*Effem Foods*).

3   *Matthews v Kuwait Bechtel Corpn* [1959] 2 QB 57 CA.
4   *Green v Weatherill* [1929] 2 Ch 213, 221. The case concerned alternative remedies but the
    principle is not affected: para 21.03 n 2.
5   (1890) 25 QBD 1 CA; *Lee v Kim* (2006) 68 NSWLR 433 CA, 436–437.
6   *Dingle v Associated Newspapers Ltd* [1961] 2 QB 162 CA,186; *Harris v 718932 Pty Ltd*
    (2003) 56 NSWLR 276 CA, 280, 282 (*Harris*).
7   [1947] 2 All ER 255 CA, 257–259.
8   [1948] 1 All ER 227 CA, 230.

7.06 In an Australian case[1] the dismissal of an action for damages for innocent misrepresentation under the Trade Practices Act in a State court barred an action for negligent misrepresentation based on substantially the same facts in the Federal Court. Gummow J said[2]:

> '... Trawl seeks to recover a loss measured in the same way and in the same quantum as it did on the Trade Practices claim it propounded in the Supreme Court proceeding. Not all of the misrepresentations alleged in this Court are found in the pleading in the Supreme Court, but some are ... each set of claims in this Court is particularised by reference to statements which were in evidence in the Supreme Court. Thus, this is a case where it can be said that the same evidence would be led to prove the case Trawl propounded in its pleadings in both actions. The one factual matrix has generated the controversy which is given legal form in the two pleadings. As a matter of substance in this Court Trawl seeks to attack Effem again upon a corresponding cause of action. In my view Effem has made out its case of cause of action estoppel against Trawl. This is so, even though no claim previously was made in negligence. The substance of the controversy embraces such a claim. The gist of the recovery both in negligence and for contravention of the [Trade Practices Act] is the same.'

1   *Effem Foods* (1992) 36 FCR 406, 422; not challenged on appeal (1993) 43 FCR 510, 520.
2   Ibid at 422.

7.07 The dismissal of an action for damages under the Misrepresentation Act 1967 or the Companies Act 1985 would bar actions for negligent misrepresentation or fraud based on the same facts and *vice versa*. Judgment for rescission and restitution did not bar a claim for damages for deceit, fraud not being necessary for rescission[1]. Defendants did not plead to an action for a declaration that a contract of sale had been rescinded, and judgment was given against them by default. They were estopped from denying that they had been in breach of contract, but not from alleging fraud[2]. A plaintiff who lost an action for rescission based on an innocent oral misrepresentation could sue for breach of a written[3], but not an oral warranty, to the same effect[4]. The claim on the written warranty was not barred because of the differences between the causes of action. An action for flooding caused by a dam failed. A second action for later floods alleging a different causal link between the dam and the flooding was dismissed because the issue of causation was *res judicata*, in other words there was a cause of action estoppel[5].

1   *Goldrei Foucard & Son v Sinclair and Russian Chamber of Commerce in London* [1918]
    1 KB 180 CA (*Goldrei*); paras 21.10 n 5, 21.12 n 12.
2   *Tira Arika v Sidaway* [1923] NZLR 158.
3   *Thompson and Taylor v Ross* [1943] NZLR 712, 718–719.
4   Ibid at 719.
5   *Town of Grandview v Doering* [1976] 2 SCR 621.

7.08 In *Hitchin v Campbell* the plaintiff who had lost an action for conversion sued the same defendant for money had and received in respect of the same goods. A plea of *res judicata* which alleged that the goods were the same was held bad on demurrer[1]. A case was then stated for the court which held[2]: 'In this second action ... there arises the same question of property. The first action has determined the goods not to be the [plaintiff's]. He shall not now try whether the money produced by those goods is his or not.' The demurrer decision was explained by Jervis CJ in *Buckland v Johnson*[3]:

> '... the verdict for the defendants in the action of trover might have gone upon the ground that the sale of the goods took place with the plaintiff's authority, – which, though it would negative the alleged conversion, would be no answer whatever to an action for money had and received ...'

Where a building contract was not enforceable because the builder was not licensed, but an action in restitution could be brought, the dismissal of a claim under the contract barred an action in restitution[4]. Judgment for the defendant in an action for conversion did not bar an action in trespass[5] but there could be an issue estoppel if the claimant attempted to re–litigate an issue he had lost. The dismissal of summary proceedings to enforce a solicitor's undertaking did not bar proceedings for breach of contract and negligence based on the same facts. The causes of action and remedies were different[6].

[1] (1771) 2 Wn Bl 779 (The reasons were cryptic).
[2] (1772) 2 Wm Bl 827, 832.
[3] (1854) 15 CB 145, 162.
[4] *Zavodnyik v Alex Constructions Pty Ltd* (2005) 67 NSWLR 457 CA.
[5] *Lacon v Barnard* (1626) Cro Car 35; *Put v Rawsterne* (1681) Temp Raym 472.
[6] *Ulster Bank Ltd v Fisher & Fisher (a firm)* [1999] NI 68, 80.

OTHER CAUSES OF ACTION

7.09 Where an action on promissory notes failed because of material alterations, an action to recover the consideration was not barred. The claims arose out of the same transaction but the causes of action were different[1]. Where a plaintiff sued for interference with his prescriptive right over both banks of a river, dismissal of the action established that he had no right over either bank[2]. An action for a declaration of marriage was brought on two grounds, but, although only one was pressed, judgment for the defendant negatived both[3]. A local authority which consented to a conviction for pollution of a river could not later set up excuses it could have raised earlier[4]. An order for costs in civil proceedings bars any claim to recover additional costs from the same party as part of the claimant's damages on another cause of action[5]. The position is otherwise when the successful party has a pre–existing contractual or equitable right to costs[6]. A plaintiff with separate causes of action arising out of the same transaction, as distinct from several remedies for one cause of action[7], is not bound to join all of them in the one action[8]. This distinction has been litigated in employment cases. Dismissal by an employment tribunal of a claim for unfair dismissal barred actions for wrongful dismissal[9] and racial discrimination based on the same facts[10] and dismissal on agreed terms of a claim for equal pay in February 1999 barred a renewed claim in May[11]. Dismissal of a claim for unfair dismissal based on procedural unfairness did not bar an action for breach of contract based on orders for the performance of unlawful work[12]. In Canada dismissal of a claim for termination pay under a statute did not bar an action for wrongful dismissal[13] but the second action might be an abuse of process.

[1]   *Saminathan v Palaniappa* [1914] AC 618.
[2]   *Long v Gowlett* [1923] 2 Ch 177, 193–194. There would be no estoppel if the case failed because there had been no interference .
[3]   *Lockyer v Ferryman* (1877) 2 App Cas 519.
[4]   *River Ribble Joint Committee v Croston UDC* [1897] 1 QB 251.
[5]   Para 5.13 n 8.
[6]   Para 5.13 n 9.
[7]   *United Australia Ltd v Barclays Bank Ltd* [1941] AC 1, 27–28 (*United Australia*); *Saminathan v Palaniappa* [1914] AC 618.
[8]   *Duedu v Yiboe* [1961] 1 WLR 1040 PC (defendant who succeeded when sued for trespass not barred from suing for declaration of title).
[9]   *Green v Hampshire County Council* [1979] ICR 861.
[10]   *Divine–Bortey v Brent London Borough Council* [1998] ICR 886 CA.
[11]   *Kirklees Metropolitan Borough Council v Farrell* [2000] ICR 1335, 1340–1341.
[12]   *Friend v Civil Aviation Authority* [2002] ICR 525 CA.
[13]   *Heynen v Frito–Lay Canada Ltd* (1999) 179 DLR (4th) 317 Ont CA (*Heynen*).

7.10 An unsuccessful attack on the validity of a trademark does not bar an application for revocation which did not attack the original registration[1] but the second application might be an abuse of process[2]. Where a patent has been held valid and infringed, the decision creates cause of action estoppels on validity and the proved infringements[3]. In an action for infringement of a patent the defendant denied infringement and alleged anticipation by various specifications. The patent was held valid but infringement was not proved. In an action for later infringements the defendant raised validity based on other specifications but the issue was *res judicata*[4].

[1]   *Hormel Foods* [2005] RPC 657, 683. An appeal was allowed by consent: *Special Effects* [2007] EWCA Civ 1371 paras [36], [84], (2007) 71 IPR 188, 199, 207.
[2]   Ibid at 685–686. In view of the provisions for opposition and rectification of the register 'the circumstances would need to be unusual to justify holding that a party who did take advantage of the second opportunity provided by the legislation is abusing the process of the court': *Special Effects* [2007] EWCA Civ 1371 para [77], (2007) 71 IPR 188, 209, per Lloyd LJ.
[3]   *Unilin Beheer* [2008] 1 All ER 156 CA, 168–169.
[4]   *Shoe Machinery Co Ltd v Cutlan* [1896] 1 Ch 667. The proceedings related to the third patent in suit in earlier proceedings between the same parties (*Shoe Machinery Co Ltd v Cutlan* [1896] 1 Ch 667) when the other two patents were held valid and infringed. *Shoe Machinery v Cutlan* [1896] 1 Ch 108 CA related to the defendant's appeal from the decision that those patents were valid and infringed. The former was applied in *Chiron Corpn v Organon Tecknika Ltd (No 6)* [1994] FSR 448, 455; and on appeal: (*No 14*) [1994] FSR 448 CA 701; *Old Digger Pty Ltd v Azuko Pty Ltd* (2002) 123 FCR 1, 16–20; *Coflexip (No 2)* [2004] FSR 708 CA.

7.11 A claimant who challenges an administrative decision must put his whole case before the court. If he fails he will be barred by a cause of action estoppel from bringing a second challenge on other grounds. The principle extends to judicial review proceedings following an unsuccessful appeal from an administrative decision if the grounds for review could have been raised in the appeal[1]. A solicitor could be examined under the Bankruptcy Act although before the client became bankrupt he brought proceedings against the solicitor for a cash account in the same transactions[2]. In *Re Hilton*[3] an action by a trustee in bankruptcy alleging that a deed of assignment was invalid failed, and this barred a second action alleging invalidity on another ground. A claimant's cause of action in ejectment to recover a property covered other property that could be claimed from the same defendant under the same title[4]. The principle applies to personal property.

[1]   *Asher v Secretary of State for the Environment* [1974] Ch 208 CA (*Asher*). The Secretary of State directed the district auditor to audit a local authority. The auditor surcharged the councillors who appealed unsuccessfully to the Divisional Court. They then challenged the direction in judicial review proceedings against the Secretary of State which were dismissed for abuse of process. Lord Denning MR held that the direction could have been attacked on the appeal but the matter was not strictly *res judicata* but Lawton LJ applied *Henderson* and held that it was. Since the Minister was not a party to the appeal he was neither bound by, nor entitled to the benefit of any cause of action estoppel. However, as Lord Denning MR held, abuse of process is available in such a case; paras 8.36 n 4, 26.04 nn 8–10.
[2]   *Re (No 472 of 1950) Debtor* [1958] 1 All ER 581 CA.
[3]   *Re Hilton, ex p March* (1892) 67 LT 594.
[4]   *Mohammed Khan v Mahbub Ali Mian* [1948] AIR (PC) 78, 84–86.

IDENTIFY OF CAUSES OF ACTION (CONTRACT)

7.12 Where an action for breach of contract failed because the plaintiff did not prove a breach, an action for a later breach was not barred. Lord Cranworth LC said that it was necessary[1]:

> '... to show that the question raised in the second suit had been adjudicated upon in the first ... this is not ... a technical rule ... but is one of substance, and unless it is strictly adhered to plaintiffs who have a clear title to relief on account of the breach of an agreement may, by failing to prove a breach, lose all right to complain of future breaches.'

When the same facts give rise to more than one breach of a single contract there is a composite breach and only one cause of action. In *The Indian Grace*[2] lack of care for cargo resulted in short delivery and delivery of damaged cargo, but there was only one cause of action. When the plaintiff obtained damages for failure to build a house in a good and workmanlike manner he could not bring a further action for failure to build with proper materials. The damage was different but there was a single obligation to complete the building, and only one cause of action[3]. This principle bars a second action for latent defects discovered since the first judgment[4].

[1]   *Moss v Anglo–Egyptian Navigation Co* (1865) 1 Ch App 108, 115.
[2]   [1993] AC 410.
[3]   *Conquer v Boot* [1928] 2 KB 336.
[4]   *Honeywood v Munnings* (2006) 67 NSWLR 466 CA.

7.13 A financier's claims against solicitors for failing to register assignments of life policies, and for failing to arrange valid guarantees and third party mortgages, were different causes of action[1]. The breaches were different, they occurred at different times, and the losses were different.

[1]   *Macquarie Bank Ltd v National Mutual Life Association of Australia Ltd* (1996) 40 NSWLR 543 CA, 559, 561.

ACCOUNT AS CAUSE OF ACTION ESTOPPEL

7.14 A judicial account establishes a cause of action estoppel. As Buckley J said in *Public Trustee v Kenward*[1]:

> '... the object of the account ... was to arrive at finality ...'

A judicial account requires the netting off of all relevant claims and cross claims. There was a cause of action estoppel in *Henderson*[2] because the Newfoundland court found that Jordan's Estate was not indebted to Bethel, and this was recognised in *Carl Zeiss (No 2)*[3], *Arnold*[4] and *Johnson*[5]. Cause of action estoppels were not recognised in *Yat Tung*[6] and *Yorkshire Bank Plc v Hall*[7] where money judgments in favour of mortgagees based on accounts taken summarily at the trial[8] barred proceedings against them for wilful default in the exercise of the power of sale[9]. *Caird v Moss*[10] is another case where a cause of action estoppel was not recognised. The plaintiff claimed on the taking of accounts that his specialty debt had priority over the defendant's debt. The claim failed and a fund in court was distributed. The plaintiff then commenced proceedings for rectification of the agreement. The Court of Appeal rejected a defence of *res judicata* but held that it was too late to seek rectification because the judgments would be inconsistent. In fact the *Henderson* principle applied and there was a cause of action estoppel.

1 [1967] 1 WLR 1062, 1067.
2 (1843) 3 Hare 100; paras 7.03, 26.03.
3 [1967] 1 AC 853, 916, 946, 966.
4 [1991] 2 AC 93, 107.
5 [2002] 1 AC 1, 30–31.
6 [1975] AC 581, para 26.05 has a summary of the facts.
7 [1999] 1 WLR 1713 CA; para 7.15 nn 3–5.
8 Simple accounts may be taken at the trial: *House of Spring Gardens Ltd v Point Bland Ltd* [1985] FSR 327 (SCIr), 339, 346.
9 (2002) 118 LQR at 400–402; cited *Hormel Foods* [2005] RPC 657, 680.
10 (1886) 33 Ch D 22 CA; paras 5.24, 26.14 n 10.

7.15 Equity required a mortgagee to account, but as a general rule only once[1] and the mortgagor and all puisne mortgagees were necessary parties. If a puisne mortgagee sued the rule was redeem up and foreclose down. Prior mortgages had to be redeemed, and later mortgagees and the mortgagor had to be foreclosed. The result was either redemption of all mortgages or a foreclosure. Accounts in such proceedings bound all parties. A mortgage can be paid off without redemption by an exercise of the power of sale, but the mortgagee is still liable to account. Because a proper exercise of the power bars the equity of redemption[2] the mortgagee's duty is equitable[3]. The mortgagee can be charged on such an account with 'wilful default if he does not receive what might have been received with due diligence'[4]. The propriety of the sale and the adequacy of the price can only be investigated if wilful default is charged in the pleadings and proved at the trial[5]. Thus a money judgment in favour of the mortgagee following an exercise of its power of sale creates a cause of action estoppel which bars a later claim by the mortgagor that the sale was at an undervalue[6]. In the words of Hutley JA in the New South Wales Court of Appeal[7]: '... a party cannot ... have little bits of accounts. There is one account and one account only and the issue is what is owed and what is not owed.' Judgment for possession in favour of the mortgagee, without judgment for the mortgage debt, does not bar an action by the mortgagee for the debt or an action by the mortgagor for an account[8].

1   An account can be reopened for fraud, and a supplementary account might be required.
2   *In Re Harwood* (1887) 35 Ch D 470 CA, 472; *Coroneo v Australian Provincial Assurance Association Ltd* (1935) 35 SR (NSW) 391, 394.
3   *Downsview Nominees Ltd v First City Corpn Ltd* [1993] AC 295.
4   *Mayer v Murray* (1878) 8 Ch D 424, 426.
5   Ibid at 429, *Tomlin v Luce* (1889) 43 Ch D 1 CA; para 5.25.
6   Para 7.14 nn 6–8.
7   *Adams v Bank of New South Wales* [1984] 1 NSWLR 285, 296.
8   *Murphy v Abi–Saab* (1995) 37 NSWLR 280 CA; *Ulster Bank Ltd v Lyons* [2000] 3 IR 337; para 2.17 n 4.

WHAT MATERIALS MAY BE CONSIDERED

7.16 It was formerly thought that the subject matter of a judicial decision must be ascertained from the pleadings and the formal judgment and the court's reasons could not be considered. This view has been rejected in issue estoppel cases, and the wider view should apply in all cases[1]. The particulars of claim under the CPR, and the Statement of Claim before it, need only plead the material facts on which the claimant relies without identifying or pleading a cause of action[2]. A cause of action is disclosed if it could be established by evidence admissible under the pleading[3]. Evidence may be admitted without objection which is outside the pleadings and the parties are entitled to a judgment based on the whole of the evidence[4]. The pleadings should be amended[5], but failure to do this does not prevent the court giving the appropriate judgment, but this will only be apparent from the reasons for judgment. Thus the cause of action on which the claimant succeeded may not be apparent from the particulars of claim and the formal judgment. Cause of action estoppels may be based on foreign judgments, and an English court must be able to consider all relevant materials to determine whether the cause of action in the domestic proceedings is the same.

1   Para 8.29.
2   This was well established prior to the CPR: *Konskier v B Goodman Ltd* [1928] 1 KB 421 CA, 427; *Phillip Morris Inc v Adam P Brown Male Fashions Pty Ltd* (1981) 148 CLR 457, 473.
3   *Mutual Life and Citizens Assurance Co. Ltd v Evatt* [1971] AC 793, 801.
4   *Neville v Fine Arts and General Insurance Co* [1897] AC 68, 76; *Browne v Dunn* (1893) 6 R 67 HL, 75–76; *Gould v Mt Oxide Mines Ltd* (1916) 22 CLR 490, 517; *Sri Mahant Govind Rao v Sita Ram Kesho* (1898) LR 25 Ind App 195, 207; *Banque Commerciale SA v Akhil Holdings Ltd* (1990) 169 CLR 279, 286–287; *Boustead Trading (1985) Sdn Bhd v Arab–Malaysian Merchant Bank Bhd* [1995] 3 MLJ 331 CA, 341.
5   *Clough v London and North Western Railway Co* (1871) LR 7 Ex 26 Ex Ch, 30; *Keith v R Gancia & Co Ltd* [1904] Ch 774 CA, 789.

Chapter 8

ISSUE ESTOPPEL

GENERAL

8.01 A decision will create an issue estoppel if it determined an issue in a cause of action as an essential step in its reasoning. Issue estoppel applies to fundamental issues determined in an earlier proceeding which formed the basis of the judgment[1]. There is nothing new about issue estoppel[2] which was recognised in the advice of the judges to the House of Lords in the *Duchess of Kingston's* case[3]. The term was coined by Higgins J in 1921 in his (dissenting) judgment in *Hoystead v Federal Taxation Comr* which was upheld by the Privy Council[4]. It was taken up by Dixon J nearly 20 years later[5] and then by Fullagar J[6], and then by the House of Lords.[7] Diplock LJ defined it in *Thoday*[8]:

'... "issue estoppel" is an extension of the same rule of public policy. There are many causes of action which can only be established by proving that two or more different conditions are fulfilled. Such causes of action involve as many separate issues between the parties as there are conditions to be fulfilled by the plaintiff to ... establish his causes of action; and there may be cases where the fulfilment of an identical condition is a requirement common to two or more different cause of action. If in litigation upon one such cause of action any of such separate issues as to whether a particular condition has been fulfilled is determined by a court of competent jurisdiction, either upon evidence or upon admission ... neither party can, in subsequent litigation between one another upon any cause of action which depends upon the fulfilment of the identical condition, assert that the condition was fulfilled if the court has in the first litigation determined that it was not, or deny that it was fulfilled if the court in the first litigation determined that it was'.

[1] The requirements for issue estoppel in Singapore were reviewed in *Goh v Goh* [2007] 1 SLR 453.
[2] *Carl-Zeiss (No 2)* [1967] 1 AC 853, 913.
[3] (1776) 2 Smith's LC (13th edn) 644, 645; para 8.22 n 1.
[4] (1921) 29 CLR 537, 561; [1926] AC 155 (*Hoystead*).
[5] *Blair v Curran* (1939) 62 CLR 464, 531.
[6] *Jackson v Goldsmith* (1950) 81 CLR 446, 466.
[7] *Carl-Zeiss (No 2)* [1967] 1 AC 853, 913, 926, 934, 946, 964.
[8] [1964] P 181 CA, 198; cited *Thrasyvoulou* [1990] 2 AC 273, 295–296.

8.02   A fuller statement in the judgment of Dixon J in *Blair v Curran*[1] merits quotation:

> 'A judicial determination directly involving an issue of fact or of law disposes once for all of the issue, so that it cannot afterwards be raised between the same parties or their privies. The estoppel covers only those matters which the prior judgment, decree or order necessarily established as the legal foundation or justification of its conclusion ... the distinction between *res judicata* and issue-estoppel is that in the first the very right or cause of action claimed or put in suit has in the former proceedings passed into judgment, so that it is merged and has no longer an independent existence, while in the second, for the purpose of some other claim or cause of action, a state of fact or law is alleged or denied the existence of which is ... necessarily decided by the prior judgment, decree or order.
>
> Nothing but what is legally indispensable to the conclusion is thus finally ... precluded. In matters of fact the issue-estoppel is confined to those ultimate facts which form the ingredients in the cause of action, that is, the title to the right ... Where the conclusion is against the existence of a right or claim which in point of law depends upon a number of ingredients or ultimate facts the absence of any one of which would be enough to defeat the claim, the estoppel covers only the actual ground upon which the existence of the right was negatived. But in neither case is the estoppel confined to the final legal conclusion expressed in the judgment, decree or order ... the judicial determination concludes, not merely as to the point actually decided, but as to a matter which it was necessary to decide and which was actually decided as the groundwork of the decision itself, though not then directly the point at issue. Matters cardinal to the latter claim or contention cannot be raised if to raise them is necessarily to assert that the former decision was erroneous.
>
> In the phraseology of Lord Shaw "a fact fundamental to the decision arrived at" in the former proceedings and 'the legal quality of the fact' must be taken as finally and conclusively established[2]. But matters of law or fact which are subsidiary or collateral are not covered by the estoppel. Findings, however deliberate and formal, which concern only evidentiary facts and not ultimate facts forming the very title to rights give rise to no preclusion. Decisions upon matters of law which amount to no more than steps in a process of reasoning tending to establish or support the proposition upon which the rights depend do not estop the parties if the same matters of law arise in subsequent litigation.
>
> The difficulty in the actual application of these conceptions is to distinguish the matters fundamental or cardinal to the prior decision or judgment, decree, or order or necessarily involved in it as its legal justification or foundation from matters which even though actually raised and decided as being in the circumstances of the case the determining considerations, yet are not in point of law the essential foundation or groundwork of the judgment, decree or order.'

Two matters emerge from this statement which merit further mention. The first is the importance of the formal order of the court. An issue estoppel is limited to 'a state of fact or law which is necessarily decided by the prior judgment, decree or order.' The second is that the issue estoppel created by a dismissal is limited to 'the actual ground upon which the existence of the right was negatived.'[3]

---

[1]   (1939) 62 CLR 464, 531–533; cited *Belton v Carlow County Council* [1997] IR 172 SC 180; *Leong v Hock Hua Bank* Bhd [2008] 3 MLJ 340, 360. Issue estoppel is recognised in the Roman-Dutch law of South Africa and is discussed, although not by name, by the leading Dutch jurists Voet and Vinnius. The principles are similar to our own; paras 27.12–27.13.

2   *Hoystead* [1926] AC 155, 165.
3   Para 2.28.

ESTOPPEL WHERE ONUS OF PROOF NOT DISCHARGED

8.03 In civil proceedings the court decides questions of past fact on the balance of probabilities. 'Anything that is more probable than not it treats as certain'[1]. Lord Hoffmann recently said[2]:

> 'The law operates a binary system in which the only values are zero and one. The fact either happened or it did not ... If the party who bears the burden of proof fails to discharge it, a value of zero is returned and the fact is treated as not having happened. If he does discharge it, a value of one is returned and the fact is treated as having happened.'

The High Court of Australia made the same point[3]:

> 'A Common Law Court determines on the balance of probabilities whether an event has occurred. If the probability of the event having occurred is greater than it not having occurred, the occurrence ... is treated as certain; if the probability of it having occurred is less than it not having occurred, it is treated as not having occurred.'

It should therefore follow, as the New South Wales Court of Appeal has held[4], that a finding that an ultimate fact was not established creates an issue estoppel that it does not exist. The High Court of Australia has questioned whether the rejection of the case of the party with the onus of proof will establish an issue estoppel to the opposite effect[5], and referred to the principle that disbelief in the evidence of a witness does not establish the contrary[6], and *The Popi M*[7]. The tribunal of fact is not bound to make positive findings but may decide that the party with the onus has failed to discharge it.

1   *Mallett v McMonagle* [1970] AC 166, 176 per Lord Diplock.
2   *In Re B (children) (sexual abuse: standard of proof)* [2009] AC 11, 17.
3   *Malec v J.C. Hutton Pty Ltd* (1990) 169 CLR 638, 642–643.
4   *Egri v DRG Australia Ltd* (1988) 19 NSWLR 600 CA.
5   *Kuligowski v Metrobus* (2004) 220 CLR 363, 385–386.
6   *Hobbs v CT Tinling & Co Ltd* [1929] 2 KB 1 CA, 21.
7   [1985] 1 WLR 948 HL, 955.

THE DETERMINATIONS MAY BE OF FACT OR LAW

8.04 The determinations which will found an issue estoppel may be of law, fact, or mixed fact and law[1]. Examples of the first include cases where the issue is one of construction. In *Hoystead*[2] this was the application of a revenue statute to a will, and in *Blair v Curran*[3] and *Re Waring*[4] the construction of wills. In road traffic cases[5] the issues have generally been of fact or mixed fact and law.

1   *Jones v Lewis* [1919] 1 KB 328 CA, 344–345.
2   [1926] AC 155.
3   (1939) 62 CLR 464.
4   [1948] Ch 221.
5   Chapter 12.

IDENTITY OF SUBJECT MATTER ESSENTIAL

8.05 Estoppels require a court invited to apply contradictory statements to take the earlier as the truth. There can be no issue estoppel unless there is a substantial discrepancy between the *res judicata* and an issue in the later proceedings. Both must relate to the same subject matter[1], and the party setting up the estoppel must establish this[2].

[1] This paragraph in the 3rd edn was cited in *Ulster Bank Ltd v Fisher & Fisher (a firm)* [1999] NI 68.

[2] As to onus see *Behrens v Sieveking* (1837) 2 My & Cr 602 (plea not alleging identity of subject matter bad); *Moss v Anglo Egyptian Navigation Co* (1865) 1 Ch App 108, 114–116 quoted at para 2.28; *Robinson* (1877) 2 PD 75 (wife, petitioning for divorce, moved to strike out the answer which alleged her adultery with Furber and unknown persons, on the ground that a former suit by the husband, alleging adultery by her with Furber and Petro Cocchino, had been dismissed; but the motion failed because it did not appear that the conduct relied on was the same); *Ripley v Arthur & Co.* (1902) 86 LT 735 CA (in contempt proceedings for breach of an injunction restraining dealing in colourable imitations of the plaintiff's goods, the evidence did not allege that the articles were the same as those prohibited, and *res judicata* was not established).

MEANING OF DECISION

8.06 The term decision, depending on the context, may mean either the act, or the opinion of the tribunal – either the grant or refusal of relief, or the determination of a question of law or issue of fact. The former is relevant for cause of action estoppel and former recovery or merger, the latter for issue estoppel[1].

[1] *Outram v Morewood* (1803) 3 East 346, 354 per Lord Ellenborough CJ: 'It is not the recovery, but the matter alleged by the party and upon which the recovery proceeds, which creates the estoppel. The recovery itself ... is only a bar to the future recovery of damages for the same injury, but the estoppel precludes parties and privies from contending to the contrary of that point or matter of fact, which having been once distinctly put in issue ... has been ... solemnly decided against them.'

EXPRESS JUDICIAL DECLARATIONS

8.07 If the formal record contains the opinion of the court on any issue of law or fact the subject matter will be disclosed[1] unless the record is ambiguous[2].

[1] *Shedden v A-G* (1860) 30 LJPM & A 217 (declaration of legitimacy); *MackIntosh v Smith and Lowe* (1865) 4 Macq 913 HL (declaration of sanity); *Dundas v Waddell* (1880) 5 App Cas 249 (separate decision); *Shoe Machinery Co Ltd v Cutlan* [1896] 1 Ch 667 (separate declarations of validity of patent and non infringement); *River Ribble Joint Committee v Croston UDC* [1897] 1 QB 251 (declaration that offence had been committed); *Badar Bee* [1909] AC 615 (construction of will).

[2] *Bernardi v Motteux* (1781) 2 Doug KB 575 (equivocal foreign prize sentence); *Dalgleish v Hodgson* (1831) 7 Bing 495 (the same); *Hobbs v Henning* (1865) 17 CBNS 791, 822–825 (the same); *Harris v Taylor* [1915] 2 KB 580 CA (contradictory statements as to whether defendant had appeared).

INFERRED JUDICIAL DETERMINATIONS

8.08 A finding may also be inferred from the judicial act, but this can be difficult if there are no pleadings[1]. It was decided as long ago as 1747[2] that an issue necessarily decided in an earlier case, although not in express terms, could not be raised again between the parties[3]. However the inferred determination must be reasonably clear. As Lane LJ said[4]:

'... a case of issue estoppel cannot begin to be established unless it can be ascertained with some degree of precision what ... the dominant judgment decided.'

In that case the issue estoppel failed because 'the findings of the Industrial Tribunal were not sufficiently clear and precise'[5]. Browne LJ said[6]:

'The essential foundation of a plea of issue estoppel must be that the issue or issues raised in the first proceedings, and the issue or issues raised in the second proceedings are identical. It is for the party who seeks to rely on the estoppel to establish this.'

The judgment of Coleridge J in *R v Hartington Middle Quarter Inhabitants*[7] contains the classic statement of principle. 'The judgment' relied upon as a *res judicata* 'concludes, not merely as to the point actually decided, but as to a matter which it was necessary to decide, and which was actually decided, as the groundwork of the decision itself, though not then directly the point in issue.'[8] It is 'conclusive evidence, not merely of the fact directly decided, but of those facts also which are ... necessary steps to the decision[9], ... [and] so cardinal to it that without them it cannot stand. Unless they are necessary steps, the rule fails and they are collateral facts only.'[10] He rejected the proposition that 'the judgment can only be evidence of the very fact actually decided.'[11] Where the decision necessarily involves a judicial determination of some issue of law or fact, because it could not have been legitimately or rationally pronounced without determining or assuming a particular answer[12], that determination, though not expressed, is an integral part of the decision. There is otherwise no such thing as an issue estoppel by implication.

[1] *Re Koenigsberg* [1949] Ch 348 CA, 363.
[2] *Gregory v Molesworth* (1747) 3 Atk 626.
[3] *Shoe Machinery Co Ltd v Cutlan* [1896] 1 Ch 667, 670–671 per Romer J : 'It is not necessary ... that there should be an express finding in terms'; *Duedu v Yiboe* [1961] 1 WLR 1040 PC (judgment for defendant in action for trespass to land made title *res judicata* in his action for declaration); *Chambers v An Bord Pleanala* [1992] IR 134 SC (decision that proceedings not an abuse of process inferentially decided plaintiffs had standing).
[4] *Turner v London Transport Executive* [1977] ICR 952 CA, 966.
[5] Ibid at 963.
[6] Ibid at 964.
[7] (1855) 4 E & B 780.
[8] Ibid at 794.
[9] Ibid at 797.
[10] Ibid at 794.
[11] Ibid at 797.
[12] *Hoystead* [1926] AC 155. Although not authoritative in annual tax cases since *Caffoor* (*Trustees of the Abdul Caffoor Trust*) *v Income Tax Comr* [1961] AC 584 (*Caffoor*), it contains a valuable exposition of the general principles. At 170 Lord Shaw said 'If in any

Court of competent jurisdiction a decision is reached, a party is estopped from questioning it in a new legal proceeding. But the principle ... extends to any point, whether of assumption or admission, which was in substance the ratio of and fundamental to the decision.'

INFERRED JUDICIAL DETERMINATIONS: EXAMPLES

8.09 The condemnation of goods for offences against the revenue estopped the offender disputing the necessary facts in later civil proceedings[1]. Affiliation orders presuppose a finding of paternity, but a dismissal does not negative paternity[2]. An order for the removal of a pauper was conclusive as to the 'necessary steps' to the order[3]. In an action by a company for calls, where a verdict was taken for the plaintiff, subject to a special case on whether the defendant was a shareholder, judgment for the defendant was a decision that he was not[4], though it may have been otherwise 'if the special case had left it open to the court to decide in favour of the defendant upon several grounds.'[5] A declaration that the plaintiff had a lien on debentures was a decision that they were valid[6]. A conviction for non-repair of a road determined that it was a highway, but an acquittal would not determine that it was not, because it may have been based on other grounds[7]. A decision that a frontager did not have to contribute to the repair of the road did not establish that it was a highway because this was not a 'necessary step' to the decision[8].

[1] *Scott v Sherman* (1775) 2 Wm Bl 977 (condemnation of goods in the Court of Exchequer for breach of the Customs laws conclusive *in rem* that goods forfeited to the Crown, and conclusive *in personam* in an action for trespass or trover against the customs officers for seizing the goods); *R v Matthews* (1797) 5 Price 202n (condemnation of boat for having smuggled goods on board conclusive evidence of smuggling and ownership in proceedings to enforce bond); para 10.27 n 6.
[2] Para 2.31.
[3] *R v Hartington Middle Quarter Inhabitants* (1855) 4 E&B 780; para 8.08 n 4.
[4] *Re Bank of Hindustan, China, and India* (1873) 9 Ch App 1, 25–26.
[5] Ibid at 26. The court's reasons normally disclose this.
[6] *Cox v Dublin City Distillery Co Ltd (No 3)* [1917] 1 IR 203 CA, 224–229.
[7] *R v Houghton Inhabitants* (1853) 1 E & B 501, 514.
[8] *R v Hutchings* (1881) 6 QBD 300 CA, 305; *North Eastern Rly Co v Dalton Overseers* [1898] 2 QB 66, 73–74; para 4.08.

8.10 Judgment for damages in an action for trespass to land establishes the claimant's right to possession, but not necessarily his title[1]. A judgment for the plaintiff in ejectment determines the claimant's right to possession on the relevant date, but not issues such as length of occupation or the value of the premises[2]. Judgment in a probate suit did not determine the domicile of the testator which was not an essential issue[3]. Judgment against the will in a probate suit did not determine that the defendant was the widow of the testator[4]. An order by a Master in an administration action for the transfer of funds to a particular account was not a declaration of right[5]. An agreement to pay compensation registered under the Workmen's Compensation Act estopped the employer from disputing liability for the accident; but not the cause of the worker's later death[6]. Reasons for an order for costs do not create issue estoppels[7]. A certificate by a court officer which was not necessary for the ultimate decision is not part of it[8]. Authorities on decisions of the former ecclesiastical courts illustrate these principles[9]. An order approving a property settlement on divorce did not bar an action by the former wife against her former husband for damages for fraud during the negotiations, no such question having been raised in the earlier proceedings[10].

1   *Outram v Morewood* (1803) 3 East 346, 357, 366; para 8.06 n 5.
2   *Aslin v Parkin* (1758) 2 Burr 665, 668; *Burnham v Carroll Musgrove Theatres Ltd* (1928) 41 CLR 540.
3   *Concha* (1886) 11 App Cas 541, 552.
4   *Re Park's Estate* [1954] P 89, 94–95 (affirmed on appeal but estoppel not raised).
5   *Thompson* [1923] 2 Ch 205, 213–215.
6   *Cleverley v Gas Light and Coke Co.* (1907) 24 TLR 93; *O'Donel v Comr for Road Transport and Tramways (NSW)* (1938) 59 CLR 744, 76.3 (*O'Donel*).
7   *Clancy v Santoro* [1999] 3 VR 783.
8   *Re Mountcashel's Estate* [1920] 1 IR 1, 5–6.
9   In *Blackham's Case* (1709) 1 Salk 290 the defendant having proved that the goods belonged to Jane B, and that he had taken out letters of administration to her estate, the plaintiff set up a marriage between himself and Jane (which would have given him title to her goods), and the defendant replied estoppel in that the Spiritual Court could not have made the grant except upon the supposition that there had been no such marriage; but it was held that this was a 'collateral matter'. Holt CJ said at 290–291: 'a matter which has directly been determined by their sentence cannot be gainsaid: their sentence is conclusive in such cases ... but that is ... only in the point directly tried; otherwise it is if a collateral matter be collected or inferred from the sentence, as in this case'. It was followed by the House of Lords in 1776 in *Bouchier v Taylor*, fully reported only in Hargrave's Law Tracts 472, but sufficiently summarised in *Barrs v Jackson* (1845) 1 Ph 582; paras 8.23, 10.26. Jackson sued for administration in the Ecclesiastical Court claiming as next of kin of the intestate joining Mrs Barr as defendant. The Court awarded him administration but Mrs Barr brought a suit in Chancery claiming the residuary estate as niece of the intestate. Lord Lyndhurst LC followed *Bouchier v Taylor* and held (at 585) that the decision of the Ecclesiastical Court 'was conclusive notwithstanding the differences ... between the two suits and ... the Court of Chancery ... was concluded by sentences of the Spiritual Court in granting administration and not at liberty to re-examine the point decided.' He distinguished (at 588–589) *Blackham's Case* (1709) 1 Salk 290 where the marriage had not been in issue in the Ecclesiastical Court.
10 *Gipps* [1974] 1 NSWLR 259 CA. Compare *de Lasala* [1980] AC 546, 561 (proceedings based on fraud to set aside consent order approving financial provision); *Worman* (1889) 43 Ch D 296 (approval of compromise on behalf of infant no decision on breach of trust, which had not been raised).

ISSUES NOT RAISED IN EARLIER PROCEEDINGS

8.11 In *Hoystead*[1] the Privy Council extended the *Henderson* principle[2] to issue estoppel. In the earlier proceedings the trustees were held entitled to six deductions in their land tax assessment because the six life tenants were joint owners. The Commissioner decided this was incorrect and in assessing for a later year allowed only one deduction[3]. The High Court of Australia held by majority that the earlier decision did not estop the Commissioner assessing on a different basis, but the Privy Council held that he was bound by an issue estoppel to allow six deductions. Lord Shaw said[4]:

'... the admission of a fact fundamental to the decision ... cannot be withdrawn and a fresh litigation started, with a view to obtaining another judgment upon a different assumption of fact; ... the same principle applies not only to an erroneous admission of a fundamental fact, but to an erroneous assumption as to the legal quality of that fact. Parties are not permitted to begin fresh litigations because of new views they may entertain on the law of the case, or new versions ... as to ... the legal result either of the construction of the documents or the weight of certain circumstances[5]. If this were permitted litigation would have no end except when legal ingenuity is exhausted. It is a principle of law that this cannot be permitted ... the same principle – namely, that of setting to rest rights of litigants, applies to the case where a point, fundamental to the decision, taken or assumed by the plaintiff and traversable by the defendant, has not been traversed. In that case also a defendant is bound by the judgment, although ... subsequent light or ingenuity might suggest some traverse which had not been taken. The same principle of setting parties' rights to rest applies and estoppel occurs ... [I]f in any Court of competent jurisdiction a decision is reached, a party is estopped from questioning it in a new legal proceeding. But the principle also extends to any point, whether or assumption or admission, which was in substance the ratio of and fundamental to the decision.'[6]

A medical practitioner who had been acquitted on charges of sexual assault attempted, unsuccessfully, to restrain an enquiry into his fitness to practise on constitutional grounds. A second challenge, on different constitutional grounds, was dismissed by the Supreme Court of Ireland for breach of the *Henderson* principle[7].

[1]   [1926] AC 155; para 8.21.
[2]   Para 7.03.
[3]   The authority of *Hoystead* in annual tax cases was destroyed in *Caffoor* [1961] AC 584 which established that there is no issue estoppel from one year to another. It remains an authority on the general principles.
[4]   [1926] AC 155, 165–166, 170.
[5]   *Greathead v Bromley* (1798) 7 Term Rep 455.
[6]   An omission founded an estoppel in *Fidelitas* [1966] 1 QB 630 CA, 649 but in *Vitosh v Brisbane County Council* (1955) 93 CLR 622, 628 an assumption did not. An application for mandamus to compel the Council to exercise its discretion under a resolution failed and an action for a declaration that the resolution was invalid succeeded because the estoppel from the earlier proceedings was limited to the actual ground for dismissal; *Maynard* [1951] SCR 346; *Town of Grandview v Doering* [1976] 2 SCR 621; *Lim v Lim* (1999) 180 DLR (4th) 87 BCCA.
[7]   *AA v The Medical Council* [2003] 4 IR 302 SC. The principle applies to repeated challenges on other grounds: *Carroll v Ryan* [2003] IR 309 SC; *Akram v Minister for Justice* [2004] 1 IR 452.

8.12   A general decision in favour of the claimant extends to any fundamental allegation by him, express or implied, which his opponent failed to challenge. In an action on an agreement for lease the plaintiff necessarily alleged that it was valid and when this was not put in issue, judgment for the plaintiff precluded the defendant[1] setting up the Statute of Frauds[2] in a later action on the same agreement. Where the plaintiff recovered under a contract the defendant, who had not pleaded absence of consideration, could not do so in a later action on the same contract[3]. Judgment for the insured in an action on the policy barred an action by the underwriters to enforce its avoidance[4]. If the defendant succeeds any admissions on the pleadings have no effect in another case[5].

[1]   *Humphries* [1910] 2 KB 531 CA, 534–537.
[2]   Now Law of Property (Miscellaneous Provisions) Act 1989.
[3]   *Cooke v Rickman* [1911] 2 KB 1125.
[4]   *ICCI v Royal Hotel Ltd* [1998] Lloyds Ins & Reins 151.
[5]   *Boileau v Rutlin* (1848) 2 Ex ch 665, 681; 'The facts actually decided by an issue in any suit cannot be again litigated between the same parties and are evidence between them, and that conclusive ... and so are the material facts alleged by one party which are directly

admitted by the opposite party, or indirectly admitted by taking a traverse on some other facts, but only if the traverse is found against the party making it'; *Hutt v Morell* (1849) 3 Exch 240, 241: 'if the issue be found for him the admission avails nothing.'

PLENE ADMINISTRAVIT

8.13 Where an executor or administrator who is sued for a debt of the deceased, fails to plead *plene administravit*, an adverse judgment covers the point he failed to raise[1]. Thus, as Dixon and Evatt JJ held in *Levy v Kum Chah*[2] the judgment establishes that the executor has been in possession of sufficient assets of the testator to satisfy the debt and he is personally liable.

[1]   *Erving v Peters* (1790) 3 Term Rep 685, 693 ('if an executor may plead *plene administravit*, and neglect to do so, I see no difference between such a case and one where ... the plea is found against him'); *Palmer v Waller* (1836) 1 M&W 689. In *Jewsbury v Mummery* (1872) LR 10 CP 56 Ex Ch the plaintiff recovered against an executor for a debt of the testator after *plene administravit* had been found for the plaintiff. The plaintiff then sued for a *devastavit*. The defendant pleaded that the acts complained of had been done with the plaintiff's leave. The plaintiff relied upon the earlier judgment as an estoppel and it was held (at 60) that 'if the defendant could have shown ... that though assets had come to his hands, he had parted with them under circumstances which precluded the plaintiff from alleging that they had not been duly administered ... that would have been a defence under the plea of *plene administravit*' and the defendant was estopped (at 61–62).
[2]   (1936) 56 CLR 159, 168–169.

UNDEFENDED DIVORCES

8.14 This topic is considered in Chapter 15.

JUDGMENTS BY CONSENT OR BY DEFAULT

8.15 There is an obvious difference between a default judgment and one where the unsuccessful party contested the case but made some admission or failed to take some point[1]. Lord Maugham LC said[2]:

> 'The true principle with a default judgment would seem to be that the defendant is estopped from setting up in a subsequent action a defence which was necessarily, and with complete precision, decided by the previous judgment; in other words, by the *res judicata* in the accurate sense. If that be the principle, the appellants are not in the present case estopped from raising any contention they think fit in an action on the 992 bonds.'

It has been said that the scope of issue estoppels created by default judgments, or judgments where the point went by default, should not be governed by whether, under the rules of common law pleading, the issue could have been raised by a traverse, the general issue, or a plea in confession and avoidance[3]. The latter[4] does not depend on technicalities and Lord Hailsham LC had no difficulty with the concept[5]. The principles were[6]:

> 'Pleas in confession and avoidance confess the truth of the facts alleged in the declaration to which they are pleaded, and state new facts which avoid their legal effect. They have been naturally divided into two classes ... : pleas in justification or excuse, stating facts which show that the plaintiff never had any

cause of action; ... and pleas in discharge, stating facts which show a subsequent discharge of a cause of action once subsisting; ... The distinction depends upon whether the defence existed before the alleged breach or arose after it.'

A judgment in favour of the plaintiff, by default or otherwise, establishes that he had a cause of action and each essential element of it, but will not negative any matter extraneous to that cause of action which had to be raised by a plea in confession and avoidance, requiring proof by the defendant of additional facts.

1   *New Brunswick* [1939] AC 1, 28, 38; *Kok Hoong* [1964] AC 993, 1012. The judgments in
    Henderson (1843) 3 Hare 100 were *ex parte* and the new points in *Hoystead* [1926] AC
    155; *Humphries* [1910] 2 KB 531 CA; and *Cooke v Rickman* [1911] 2 KB 1125 had gone
    by default earlier.
2   Ibid at 21 (the first action was on a single bond); para 2.24.
3   *Kok Hoong* [1964] AC 993, 1011–1012, para 2.25; *Anshun* (1981) 147 CLR 589, 601.
4   Such as the statutory defences in *Kok Hoong*.
5   *Benning v Wright* [1972] 1 WLR 972 HL, 979.
6   Bullen & Leake, Precedents of Pleadings, 3rd edn 1868, p 437.

NO ISSUE ESTOPPEL WHERE DEFENDANT NOT BOUND TO RAISE ISSUE

8.16 Where there was no duty to raise an issue, or raising it attracted some disadvantage, an adverse decision does not cover it. Judgment in an action for the price of goods or work, to which the defendant was not bound to plead a breach of warranty in reduction of the price, does not negative such a breach[1]. An employer sued in the county court for wages did not set up a claim for damaging materials, preferring his statutory remedy in a court of summary jurisdiction, and was not estopped[2]. An issue estoppel was rejected in a will construction case where related issues had been raised on an earlier summons[3]. The court will be reluctant to find an issue estoppel in such a case[4] unless the point was actually decided[5] or there was a duty to raise it[6].

1   *Davis v Hedges* (1871) LR 6 QB 687, 691, where the court distinguished 'the general rule
    that, where a party has the opportunity to raise some question and does not avail himself
    of it, he is in no better position than if he had raised it,' now Sale of Goods Act 1979, s 53.
    Where the defendant sued for fees alleged lack of diligence and a failure to exercise due
    care on the part by the plaintiff, and paid a lesser amount into court, acceptance of the
    payment in did not bar an action by the defendant for professional negligence: *Hoppe v
    Titman* [1996] 1 WLR 841 CA.
2   *Hindley v Haslan* (1878) 3 QBD 481.
3   *Kennedy* [1914] AC 215, 220 (decision that clause not void for uncertainty did not bar
    contention that it was void for perpetuity); *Re Koenigsberg* [1949] Ch 348 CA, 362.
4   *Re Koenigsberg* [1949] Ch 348 CA, 365.
5   *Re Waring* [1948] Ch 221.
6   *Re Koenigsberg* [1949] Ch 348 CA, 363; *Re Westlake* [1940] NZLR 887 (declaration as to
    vesting did not bar question as to different contingency).

PROCEEDINGS BASED ON CHANGED CIRCUMSTANCES

8.17 If an action is brought prematurely, for example, before a period of credit has expired or a contract has been rescinded, an action after those events have occurred will not be barred[1]. If an action fails because a composition with creditors remains in force, an action after the composition has become void is not barred[2]. An application which failed because it was not made to the trial judge could be renewed before him[3]. A prosecution which failed because notice was not given did not bar a prosecution after it was[4]. These cases illustrate the principle that a decision in favour of a defendant does not bar proceedings 'founded on any new or altered state of circumstances'[5], and the statement by Dixon J[6] that an issue estoppel created by a dismissal is limited to 'the actual ground upon which the existence of the right was negatived.'

1 *Palmer v Temple* (1839) Ad & El 508, 521; *Lordsvale Finance Plc v Bank of Zambia* [1996] QB 752, 759 (claim for penalty interest not barred because cause of action had not accrued at date of earlier proceedings).
2 *Hall v Levy* (1875) LR 10 CP 154.
3 *Tek Ming Co v Yee Sang Metal Supplies Co* [1973] 1 WLR 300 PC.
4 *Jenkins v Merthyr Tydvil UDC* (1899) 80 LT 600.
5 *Liverpool Corpn v Chorley Waterworks Co* (1852) 2 De GM & G 852, 866; *Moss v Anglo-Egyptian Navigation Co* (1865) 1 Ch App 108, 115 quoted para 2.28 n 3; *Re Anglo-French Co-Operative Society* (1880) 14 Ch D 533, 536; *Richards* [1953] P 36.
6 *Blair v Curran* (1939) 62 CLR 464, 532 quoted paras 8.02, 2.28, 8.26.

NO ISSUE ESTOPPEL IN CHANGING SITUATION

8.18 This topic is considered in para 17.30.

THE ISSUE MUST BE THE SAME

8.19 An issue estoppel only applies if an issue in the second proceedings is the same as one decided in or covered by the first. The difficulty in determining this in some cases is demonstrated by the conflicting judgments in *Blair v Curran*[1]. The court construed a clause in a will which governed the destination of particular property. The later proceedings concerned the destination of other property under the same clause. Rich J upheld a *res judicata* estoppel in spite of 'the difference in subject matter'[2]. Dixon J[3] did so because the issues were the same. Starke J, on the other hand, could not 'assent to the applicability of these principles [of estoppel] in cases in which the subject matter of the litigation was not the same'[4]. The proper inquiry, as Dixon J held, was whether the same issue arose. This is supported by a Privy Council decision that a finding that the plaintiff had not been adopted was binding in a later suit over different property[5]. A decision of Walton J[6] that the construction of a clause dealing with the destination of the share of one deceased daughter did not create an issue estoppel for the share of another is contrary to principle[7].

1 (1939) 62 CLR 464.
2 Ibid at 502.
3 Ibid at 531–533.
4 Ibid at 510.
5 *Rajah of Pittapur v Sri Rajah Garu* (1884) LR 12 Ind App 16, 18–19; *Re Westlake* [1940] NZLR 887; para 8.16 n 6.
6 *Re Manly's Will Trusts (No 2)* [1976] 1 All ER 673. It is also contrary to *Bader Bee* [1909] AC 615; *Re Lart* [1896] 2 Ch 788.

7   Walton J's decision that the parties were different was also wrong because the trustees had
     represented the class of future great grandchildren, no member being in existence: *Re
     Whiting's Settlement* [1905] 1 Ch 96.

WHERE ISSUE NOT THE SAME

8.20 Where the issue in the second proceedings is not the same as that
decided in, or covered by the first, there is no estoppel. A decision which did
not determine the validity of a will did not bar a challenge in later
proceedings[1]. A declaration that a person was *compos mentis* did not estop a
defendant sued for his illegal detention from asserting statutory authority[2]. A
decision that royalties were the bankrupt's personal earnings did not estop the
trustee claiming the surplus after the maintenance of the bankrupt and his
family[3]. A judgment that an underlessee was liable for failure to repair during
the term did not bar a claim for failure to deliver up in good repair[4]. A
judgment in an ecclesiastical court repelling the husband's suit for judicial
separation for his wife's adultery did not estop him setting up the same
adultery in a suit by his wife for restitution of conjugal rights because of the
lower standard of proof[5]. When the wife sued for maintenance under a deed
of separation the husband unsuccessfully sought to have it set aside for fraud.
When sued for further instalments he could rely on conduct not known to him
earlier[6]. Judgment for possession against a mortgagor does not bar proceedings against the mortgagee for an account[7].

1   *Bainbrigge v Baddeley* (1847) 2 Ph 705, 709; cf *Beardsley* [1899] 1 QB 746, 749: 'The
     question decided was the validity of the will; the issue of fact is the same whether the will
     relates to real or to personal property.'
2   *Mackintosh v Smith and Lowe* (1865) 4 Macq 913 HL (if the defendants acted with
     statutory authority it did not matter how sane the plaintiff was, while if they did not, it did
     not matter how insane).
3   *Re Graydon, ex p Official Receiver* [1896] 1 QB 417.
4   *Ebbetts v Conquest* (1900) 82 LT 560, 572.
5   *Moore* (1840) 3 Moo PCC 84, 86–87.
6   *Ord* [1923] 2 KB 432, 440 per Lush J: 'One has always to see what was the precise
     question, the precise point, that has been decided.'
7   *Murphy v Abi-Saab* (1995) 37 NSWLR 280 CA.

8.21 The decisions in *Hoystead*[1] and *New Brunswick*[2] make an interesting
contrast. *Hoystead* concerned the construction of a revenue statute and a will
and the estoppel was sustained, but there was no estoppel in *New Brunswick*
because bonds in the same terms did not necessarily have the same construction. Lord Maugham LC said[3]:

> 'If an issue has been distinctly raised and decided in an action, in which both
> parties are represented, it is unjust and unreasonable to permit the same issue to
> be litigated afresh between the same parties or persons claiming under them;
> but ... the doctrine cannot ... extend to presumptions or probabilities as to
> issues in a second action which cannot be asserted beyond all possible doubt to
> be identical with those raised in the previous action ... The issue of construction
> in the second action could ... be similar to that decided in the first; but it related
> to a different cause of action based on other bonds and could not be asserted to
> be the same issue ... such bonds are often issued at different dates and in
> different countries, matters which might well have a possible bearing on their
> true construction.'

Shiels v Blakeley is another illustration[4]. The same challenge to identical amendments to a superannuation trust deed made on different dates only confronted an issue estoppel, because the causes of action arose on different dates.

[1] [1926] AC 155; para 8.11.
[2] [1939] AC 1; para 8.15.
[3] Ibid at 20. In *Co-Ownership Land Development Pty Ltd v Queensland Estates Pty Ltd* (1973) 47 ALJR 519, 522 Walsh J said: 'In order that the principle of issue estoppel may apply it ... must be possible to assert without doubt that the issues are identical.' An attempt to re-run the construction question in the absence of additional evidence or a new argument might be an abuse of process, but in *New Brunswick* the first judgment was ex parte.
[4] [1986] 2 NZLR 262 CA (The first amendment was invalid because a condition precedent had not been satisfied, but a different challenge in other proceedings failed. After the condition had been satisfied the deed was again amended and the plaintiff was estopped from renewing the challenge that failed).

ISSUE ESTOPPEL CANNOT BE ENLARGED

8.22 It follows from the reasoning of Lord Maugham LC in para 8.21 that an issue estoppel cannot be enlarged by evidence, inference or argument. In the *Duchess of Kingston's Case*[1] the judges advised the House of Lords that 'the judgment of a court of concurrent or exclusive jurisdiction is [not] evidence ... of any matter to be inferred by argument from the judgment.' As Evatt J said[2]:

' ... when a distinct and separate issue arises subsequently [the unsuccessful party] is not bound to submit to the second issue being established by the combination of a former issue with additional evidence, no matter how strong that evidence may be.'

[1] (1776) quoted *R v Hutchings* (1881) 6 QBD 300 CA, 304; para 8.23 n 4; *Grdic v R* [1985] 1 SCR 810, 816.
[2] *O'Donel* (1938) 59 CLR 744, 763. A decision awarding worker's compensation for a period of incapacity caused by blindness did not estop the employer alleging that later blindness arose from a different cause.

THE DETERMINATION MUST BE FUNDAMENTAL, NOT COLLATERAL[1]

8.23 An express decision will not necessarily create an issue estoppel. Only determinations which are necessary for the decision, and fundamental to it, will do so[2]. Other determinations, however positive, do not[3]. Authority for this may be traced to the judgment of Lord Holt CJ in *Blackham's Case*[4] and the judgment of Knight Bruce VC in *Bars v Jackson*[5] who said:

'... the rule against re-agitating matter adjudicated is subject generally to this restriction, that, however essential the establishment of particular facts may be to the soundness of a judicial decision, however it may proceed on them as established, and however binding and conclusive the decision may as to its immediate and direct object be, those facts are not all necessarily established conclusively between the parties, and ... either may again litigate them for any other purpose as to which they may come in question, provided the immediate subject of the decision be not attempted to be withdrawn from its operation so as to defeat its direct object.'

8.23 *Issue estoppel*

In *Hoystead*[6] Lord Shaw said:

> 'It was not merely incidental or collateral to the question so decided, that the appellants were joint owners. It was fundamental to it. Unless it had been decided that ... Mr Campbell's children had a beneficiary interest in land or income "in such a way as they are taxable as joint owners" they could not have been taxed at all.'

In *Blair v Curran*[7] Dixon J said:

> 'In the phraseology of Lord Shaw 'a fact fundamental to the decision arrived at' in the former proceedings and "the legal quality of that fact" must be taken as finally and conclusively established ... but matters of law or fact which are subsidiary or collateral are not covered by the estoppel. Findings, however deliberate and formal, which concern only evidentiary facts and not ultimate facts forming the very title to rights give rise to no preclusion. Decisions upon matters of law which amount to no more than steps in a process of reasoning tending to establish or support the proposition upon which the rights depend do not estop the parties if the same matters of law arise in subsequent litigation.'

Fullagar J may be permitted a postscript[8]:

> 'Issue estoppel only applies to issues. There is no estoppel as to evidentiary facts found in the course of determining the affirmative or negative of an issue.'

The principle that a collateral finding cannot create an issue estoppel flows from the requirements stated by Dixon J in *Blair v Curran*[9], that the 'state of fact or law' must have been necessarily decided by the prior judgment, decree or order. An issue not dealt with in the lower court which the appellate court treats as material when dismissing the appeal is *res judicata*[10].

[1] The corresponding passage in the 2nd edn was cited in *Duhamel v R* (*No 2*) (1981) 131 DLR (3rd ed) 352, 358 Alta CA, affd (1984) 14 DLR (4th) 92 SC; and in *Re State of Norway's Application* (*No 2*) [1990] 1 AC 723 CA, 743, 751.

[2] *Danyluk* [2001] 2 SCR 460, 476.

[3] The corresponding passage in the 3rd edn was cited in *Sun Life Assurance Co of Canada v Lincoln National Life Insurance Co* [2005] 1 Lloyds Rep 606 CA, 621 (*Sun Life*); and *Meretz Investments NV v ACP Ltd* [2007] Ch 197, 253 (*Meretz*), not affected on appeal [2008] Ch 244 CA.

[4] (1709) 1 Salk 290; para 8.10 n 9. The opinion of De Grey CJ on behalf of the judges in the *Duchess of Kingston's* case in the House of Lords was quoted by Selborne LC in *R v Hutchings* (1881) 6 QBD 300 CA, 304: 'The judgment ... of a court of concurrent (or of exclusive) jurisdiction, directly upon the point, is conclusive upon the same matter between the same parties coming incidentally in question in another court for a different purpose. But neither the judgment of a concurrent or exclusive jurisdiction is [conclusive] evidence ... of any matter which came collaterally in question, though within their jurisdiction; nor of any matter incidentally cognisable, nor of any matter to be inferred by argument from the judgment.'

[5] (1842) Y & C Ch Cas 585, 595, 597–598; rev (1845) 1 Ph 582 on other grounds.

[6] [1926] AC 155, 171.

[7] (1939) 62 CLR 464, 532.

[8] *Brewer* (1953) 88 CLR 1, 15.

[9] (1939) 62 CLR 564, 532–533, quoted para 8.02; *Re Hawksley's Settlement* [1934] Ch 384, 397 (opinion of Probate Division Judge on construction of will not necessary for decision, and not binding in construction summons in the Chancery Division).

[10] *Midnapur Zamindary Co Ltd v Roy* (1924) LR 51 Ind App 293, 303.

116

IDENTIFYING THE FUNDAMENTAL[1]

8.24 The difficulty said Dixon J[2] 'is to distinguish the matters fundamental or cardinal to the prior decision or judgment, or necessarily involved in it as its legal justification or foundation, from matters which, even though actually raised and decided as being in the circumstances of the case the determining considerations, yet are not in point of law the essential foundation or groundwork of the judgment.' The question is whether the determination was so fundamental that the decision cannot stand without it[3]. Dixon J says that there is a further test viz: Whether the determination is the 'immediate foundation' of the decision or 'no more than part of the reasoning supporting the conclusion'.

[1] This paragraph in the 2nd edn was cited in *Spens v IRC* [1970] 1 WLR 1173, 1184, *Duhamel v R (No 2)* (1981) 131 DLR (3d) 352, 358 Alta CA; affd (1984) 14 DLR (4th) 92 SC; *Angle v Minister of National Revenue* (1974) 47 DLR (3d) 544, 556 SC; *Re State of Norway's Application (No 2)* [1990] 1 AC 723 CA, 752; *P & O Nedlloyd BV v Arab Metals Co* [2007] 1 WLR 2288 CA, 2299.
[2] *Blair v Curran* (1939) 62 CLR 464, 533.
[3] *Re Allsop and Joy's Contract* (1889) 61 LT 213. This may explain *Rowling vTakaro Properties Ltd* [1988] AC 473, 504 where the Board held that, although a decision in judicial review proceedings that a particular fact was an irrelevant consideration 'may' have been res judicata, the construction of the legislation was not; *Johnson v Felton* [2006] 3 NZLR 475 CA, 486–487. *Duedu v Yiboe* [1961] 1 WLR 1040 PC does not appear relevant in this context. This passage in the 3rd edn was cited in *Meretz* [2007] Ch 197, 253.

NO ESTOPPEL AGAINST SUCCESSFUL PARTY ON ISSUE HE LOST

8.25 Another useful test is whether, given a right of appeal, the losing party could effectively appeal against the determination. If there can be no effective appeal against a determination this normally indicates that it was not fundamental. The test is not universally valid because decisions of a court of final appeal and of lower courts from which there is no right of appeal create issue estoppels in the normal way. The ultimate test is whether the determination is such that without it the judgment cannot stand. A decision of fact or law against the party who succeeded[1] or one which was not necessary to the decision will not found an estoppel because it cannot be fundamental to the decision. It would be unjust for such a decision to create an estoppel because the person who failed on that issue cannot effectively appeal against it[2]. An application for production of documents was refused although the court held it had power to make the order. There was no estoppel on this issue because a ruling against the defendant could not be essential to the decision in its favour[3]. Where a claim that a statute was *ultra vires* was rejected, but the plaintiff won on another ground he was not estopped on the constitutional issue because the adverse decision was not necessary to the judgment in his favour[4]. The same principle applies where the court finds alternative grounds in favour of the successful party. Those findings do not create issue estoppels because the defendant could not effectively appeal against any of them separately[5], and if one was upheld the appeal would fail[6]. There is a cause of action estoppel but no issue estoppel because no single finding could be 'legally indispensable to the conclusion' or the 'essential foundation or groundwork of the judgment, decree, or order' as Dixon J said in *Blair v Curran*[7].

[1] This passage in the 3rd edn was cited in *Sun Life* [2005] 1 Lloyds Rep 606 CA, 621–622, and is supported by *Midnapur Zamindari Co Ltd v Roy* (1920) LR 48 Ind App 49, 55 per Lord Dunedin.

[2] *Concha* (1886) 11 App Cas 541, 552 per Lord Herschell LC: '… it would be very strange, if although the finding in the decree as to the testator's domicil could not be appealed from because it was not essential to the decision, nevertheless it conclusively determined that fact against all the world', 554, and per Lord Bramwell at 567.

[3] *Penn-Texas Corpn v Murat Anstalt (No 2)* [1964] 2 QB 647 CA, 660 per Lord Denning MR: 'One of the tests in seeing whether a matter was necessary to the decision, or only incidental to it, is to ask: Could the party have appealed from it? If he could have appealed, and did not he is bound by it … if he could not have appealed from it (because it did not affect the order made) then it is only an incidental matter, not essential to the decision, and he is not bound'; *Re State of Norway's Application (No. 2)* [1990] 1 AC 723 CA, 743, 752, 772; *Arbuthnot v CE Dept of Work* [2008] 1 NZLR 13 SC, 27.

[4] *James v Commonwealth* (1935) 52 CLR 570, 584 per Rich J: 'Although the Court ruled that he was wrong upon his first ground, he is not estopped, because the decision passed in his favour. He could not appeal from the Court's ruling', and at 590–591 per Dixon J: ' … it is true that the question was decided against him. He submitted the contention to the Court which announced an opinion that he was wrong; but that … was not translated into a decree or order, because upon an independent contention he succeeded. There was no judgment from which he could … appeal, none which estopped him.'

[5] In *The Good Challenger* [2004] 1 Lloyds Rep 67 CA the court left open the correctness of this proposition; *Meretz* [2007] Ch 197, 253.

[6] *Lake* [1955] P 336 CA (finding of adultery against wife but petition dismissed because of condonation, wife having succeeded could not appeal against finding of adultery); *Cie Noga D'Importation Et D'Exportation SA v Australia and New Zealand Banking Group Ltd (No 3)* [2003] 1 WLR 307 CA, 321–322, 328; *Talyancich v Index Developments Ltd* [1992] 3 NZLR 28 CA; *Johnson v Felton* [2006] 3 NZLR 475 CA, 487; *Murphy v Abi-Saab* (1995) 37 NSWLR 280 CA, 288; *Arbuthnot v CE Dept of Work* [2008] 1 NZLR 13 SC, 25–27; *Lee v Tang* [1997] 3 SLR 489 CA, 498.

[7] *Blair v Curran* (1939) 62 CLR 464, 532, 533; *Re Hawksley's Settlement* [1934] Ch 384, 397 (opinion on incidental question not mentioned in order, and therefore no right of appeal); *R v Sillim, The Alexandra* (1864) 10 HL cas 704, 724 per Lord Westbury 'An appeal is a right of entering a superior Court and invoking its aid and interposition to redress the error of the Court below'; *Commonwealth of Australia v Bank of New South Wales* [1950] AC 235, 294: 'An appeal is the formal proceeding by which an unsuccessful party seeks to have the formal order of a court set aside or varied in his favour by an appellate court'; *Driclad Pty Ltd v Federal Comr of Taxation* (1968) 121 CLR 45, 64.

ISSUE ESTOPPELS CREATED BY DISMISSALS

8.26 As Dixon J explained in *Blair v Curran* the issue estoppel created by a dismissal is limited to the actual ground on which the claimant failed[1]. If A and B are jointly liable in contract to X, and X unsuccessfully sued A, the judgment creates an issue estoppel for the benefit of B if it was based on a ground common to A and B, but not if it was based on a ground personal to A such as infancy or bankruptcy[2].

[1] (1939) 62 CLR 464, 532 quoted paras 8.02, 2.28, 8.17.

[2] *Phillips v Ward* (1863) 2 H & C 717, 720–721. At common law a judgment against one joint tortfeasor or joint contractor released the others but these rules have been abrogated by statute: paras 9.48, 22.02.

ARBITRATION

8.27 An award in arbitration proceedings can create an issue estoppel[1]. The parties having chosen the tribunal, or been compelled by statute to resort to it, are bound by its determinations on any issue fundamental to the award.

[1]   *Fidelitas* [1966] 1 QB 630 CA, 643; *Aegis* [2003] 1 WLR 1041 PC, 1048.

FOREIGN JUDGMENTS

8.28 *The Sennar* established that foreign judgments can create issue estoppels and the same principles apply. Lord Diplock said[1]:

> 'It is far too late ... to question that issue estoppel can be created by the judgment of a foreign court if that court is recognised in English private international law as being a court of competent jurisdiction.'

Issue estoppels created by foreign judgments extend to questions that a party should have raised but did not[2]. It is not clear whether these principles apply to the full extent to foreign default judgments[3].

[1]   [1985] 1 WLR 490 HL, 493; *Carl-Zeiss (No 3)* [1970] Ch 506. *The Irina A (No 2)* [1999] 1 Lloyds Rep 189 (judgment of Togo Court).
[2]   *Henderson* (1843) 3 Hare 100; *Godard v Gray* (1870) LR 6 QB 139; *Ellis v M'Henry* (1871) LR 6 CP 228; *Re Trufort* (1887) 36 Ch D 600.
[3]   A foreign judgment created a cause of action estoppel in *Henderson* (1843) 3 Hare 100 although the defendant did not appear at the trial, on the taking of the accounts, or on further consideration; paras 7.03, 7.14; *Carl-Zeiss (No 2)* [1967] 1 AC 853, 918, 925–926, 948–949.

WHAT MATERIALS MAY BE CONSIDERED

8.29 The court can consider for this purpose any relevant material including the court's reasons[1]. In *DPP v Humphrys*[2] Lord Hailsham said: 'The court will inquire into realities, and not mere technicalities', and in *Rogers v R*[3] Brennan J said that the court could look at 'any material that shows what issues were raised and decided.' The point is now assumed. In *Thrasyvoulou*[4] the House of Lords considered the reports of planning inspectors. Since an issue estoppel can be excluded in special circumstances the Court must be able to consider all relevant material.

[1]   *Carl-Zeiss (No 2)* [1967] 1 AC 853, 946, 965; *Tagore v Secretary of State for India* (1888) LR 15 Ind App 186, 192–193; *Sri Raja Rao v Sri Raja Inuganti* (1898) LR 25 Ind App 102, 108: 'In order to see what was in issue in the suit, or what has been heard and decided the [reasons for] judgment must be looked at'; *Hook v Administrator-General of Bengal* (1921) LR 48 Ind App 187; *Ord* [1923] 2 KB 432 CA; *Diamond v Western Realty Co* [1924] 2 DLR 922 SC, 929; *Blueberry River Indian Band v Canada* (2001) 201 DLR (4th) 35, 51 FCA; *O'Donel* (1938) 59 CLR 744, 758; *Marginson* [1939] 2 KB 426 CA, 437; *Jackson v Goldsmith* (1950) 81 CLR 446, 467; *Somodaj v Australian Iron and Steel Ltd* (1963) 109 CLR 285, 299; *Jenkins v Tileman (Overseas) Ltd* [1967] NZLR 484; *Nesbitt Thompson Deacon Inc v Everett* (1989) 37 BCLR 2d 341 CA, 347–349.
[2]   [1977] AC 1, 41.
[3]   (1994) 181 CLR 251, 263.
[4]   [1990] 2 AC 273.
[5]   *Arnold* [1991] 2 AC 93; *Watt* [2008] 1 AC 696, 708.

QUESTIONS OF LAW AND FACT

8.30 Whether a question determined by or necessarily involved in a judicial decision is the same as one raised in subsequent proceedings is a question of law[1]. Questions as to physical identity and as to what was actually decided in former proceedings, where this depends on oral evidence, are questions of fact[2].

---

[1] It could be determined on demurrer: *Howlett v Tarte* (1861) 10 CBNS 813; *Jackson v Goldsmith* (1950) 81 CLR 446; *Ramsay v Pigram* (1967) 118 CLR 271 and can now be decided as a preliminary question: para 12.10. The decision of arbitrators on such a question can be reviewed by the court: *Fidelitas* [1966] 1 QB 630 CA.

[2] Such questions were left to the jury in *R v Sheen* (1827) 2 C&P 634, 639–640; *R v Tancock* (1876) 13 Cox CC 217; *Overton v Harvey* (1850) 9 CB 324, 331; and *Ripley v Arthur and Co* (1902) 86 LT 735 CA, 736 (non-jury case).

EXCEPTION FOR SPECIAL CIRCUMSTANCES

8.31 An exception for special circumstances was established in *Arnold*[1]. The parties entered into a 32 year lease which provided for periodic rent reviews. On the first review the arbitrator assumed that the rent could be reviewed at the next review date. Walton J reversed this decision, holding that the hypothetical lease for the balance of the term contained no provision for any further review. A certificate under s 1(7)(b) of the Arbitration Act 1979[2] was refused and the Court of Appeal held that it had no power to grant leave to appeal. The tenant challenged this interpretation at the next review but was met with an issue estoppel. This failed in all courts because of the special circumstances. These included the bizarre construction adopted by Walton J which had been rejected in later cases, and the absence of any right of appeal. The refusal of a certificate had been wrong, if not perverse[3], having regard to the amounts involved, the continuing importance of the question in that and other cases, and the debatable nature of the decision. Lord Keith, who gave the principal speech, held that while the bar created by merger and cause of action estoppel was absolute[4], it was not for issue estoppel[5]. He said[6]:

> '... there may be an exception to issue estoppel in the special circumstance that there has become available to a party further material relevant to the correct determination of a point involved in the earlier proceedings, whether or not that point was specifically raised and decided, being material which could not by reasonable diligence have been adduced in those proceedings. One of the purposes of estoppel being to work justice between the parties, it is open to courts to recognise that in special circumstances inflexible application of it may have the opposite result.'

---

[1] [1991] 2 AC 93; *Watt* [2008] 1 AC 696, 708.

[2] Now s 69(8) of the 1996 Act.

[3] [1991] 2 AC 93, 110.

[4] Ibid at 104; *Chamberlain* (1988) 164 CLR 502.

[5] Ibid at 106–107.

[6] Ibid at 109.

8.32 The issue estoppel stands if there was no newly discovered fact, or the party had only just realised its importance[1], where it was discoverable with reasonable diligence[2] or was not sufficiently material. The exception must be kept within narrow limits to avoid undermining the general rule and provoking increased litigation and uncertainty[3]. Although the House relied upon several matters the absence of an effective right of appeal was critical[4], because otherwise the case would have been within the principle stated by Lord Macnaghten[5]:

> 'If the decision was wrong, it ought to have been appealed from in due time nor can the [interested parties] be heard to say that the value of the subject matter on which the former decision was pronounced was comparatively so trifling that it was not worth their while to appeal from it. If such a plea were admissible there would be no finality in litigation. The importance of a judicial decision is not to be measured by the pecuniary value of the particular item in dispute.'

There is no appeal from a court of final appeal but its decisions still create issue estoppels. This exception was doubted by one member of the High Court of Australia[6], but the question has not been squarely raised there. The exception has been applied by the Supreme Court of Canada[7].

1   *Boswell v Coaks (No 2)* (1894) 86 LT 365n HL; *Greathead v Bromley* (1798) 7 Term Rep 455; *Lockyer v Ferryman* (1877) 2 App Cas 519; *Phosphate Sewage Co Ltd v Molleson* (1879) 4 App Cas 801.
2   *Shoe Machinery Co Ltd v Cutlan* [1896] 1 Ch 667, 672.
3   As Staughton LJ said in *Arnold* [1990] Ch 573 CA, 598: 'It cannot by itself be enough that the previous decision was arguably wrong in law; nor, in my judgment, is it by itself enough that the previous decision was plainly wrong in law. The remedy for such errors is ... provided by the appellate process.' In *Corpn of Dublin v Building and Allied Trade Union* [1996] IR 468 the Supreme Court rejected a claim that, in special circumstances, a resuming authority could recover an overpayment of compensaton under what had proved, in hindsight, to be an excessive award; para 5.29.
4   This statement in the 3rd edn was approved in *Coflexip SA* [2004] FSR 708 CA, 731, 749 where Peter Gibson LJ and Sir Martin Nourse said *Arnold* was decided on 'exceptional facts'.
5   *Badar Bee* [1909] AC 615, 623; *Re Waring* [1948] Ch 221 (issue estoppel enforced although decision overruled in other proceedings); and the principle that there is no issue estoppel for findings against the successful party; para 8.25.
6   *O'Toole v Charles David Pty Ltd* (1991) 171 CLR 232, 258.
7   *Danyluk* [2001] 2 SCR 460, 492–493, 498–499.

8.33 There have been very few cases where special circumstances have been established[1]. The fact that the earlier proceedings were in an industrial tribunal was not sufficient[2]. In *Westacre*[3] the majority held that the illegality of a contract induced by bribery was not a special circumstance where that defence had been rejected by a foreign arbitral tribunal. An illegality will generally trump a *res judicata* estoppel unless the question was litigated in the earlier proceedings[4]. In *Coflexip (No 2)*[5], Neuberger LJ, in dissent, held that the revocation of the patent was a special circumstance which defeated issue estoppels that it was valid and infringed, but it is now clear that they were cause of action estoppels[6], which could not be displaced in this way.

1   Claims of special circumstances failed in *Talbot v Berkshire County Council* [1994] QB 290 CA (*Talbot*) and *The Indian Endurance* [1998] AC 878 CA, 897–898; affirmed [1998] AC 878, 916. In Malaysia the test seems to be whether the new proceedings are an abuse of process: *Simpang Empat Plantation Sdn Bhd v Ali bin Tan Sri Abdul Kadir* [2006] 1 MLJ 193 CA, 201.
2   *Divine Bortey v Brent London Borough Council* [1998] ICR 886 CA.

8.33   *Issue estoppel*

[3]   [2000] QB 288 CA.
[4]   Para 17.21.
[5]   [2004] FSR 708 CA.
[6]   *Unilin Beheer* [2008] 1 All ER 156 CA, 168–169.

8.34 In *Watt*[1] the House of Lords declined to apply the exception to a decision later shown to be wrong. An objection to jurisdiction in a racial discrimination case was overruled and an appeal to the Employment Appeal Tribunal failed. The claims were then heard on the merits and succeeded. Meanwhile the respondent took the jurisdiction point to the House of Lords in another case and won. The employment tribunal held that it was bound by the unappealed decision of the Appeal Tribunal and the House of Lords agreed. Lord Hoffmann said[2]:

> 'It does not matter that a later decision, now approved by this House, had shown that it was erroneous in law ... The whole point of an issue estoppel on a question of law is that the parties remain bound by an erroneous decision.'

[1]   [2008] 1 AC 696. Intermediate appellate courts in Canada have reached the same result: *Smith Estate v National Money Mart Co* (2008) 303 DLR (4th) 175 CA Ont; *MacKinnon v National Money Mart Co* (2009) 304 DLR (4th) 331 BCCA.
[2]   Ibid at 708.

8.35 The exception was applied in *Electra*[1]. The plaintiff's action against auditors for negligence causing it economic loss in a takeover had been struck out. The plaintiff later obtained highly relevant documents on discovery by the remaining defendant and applied for leave to rejoin the auditors. Leave was refused at first instance because of an issue estoppel, but the Court of Appeal held that the auditors' failure to discover those documents displaced the estoppel[2]. There was no estoppel because the strike out decision was interlocutory[3]. A claim of special circumstances succeeded where the Supreme Court of Canada in another case had disapproved a separate decision in the subject proceedings[4]. This was correct because the separate decision could be challenged on appeal from the final judgment[5], and the Supreme Court could grant special leave to challenge the separate decision out of time. Either way the result was a foregone conclusion. The Supreme Court of Canada has held that a denial of procedural fairness by an administrative tribunal was a special circumstance that displaced any issue estoppel[6].

[1]   [2001] 1 BCLC 589 CA.
[2]   Ibid at 628, 630, 634, 642; *Arnold* [1991] 2 AC 93, 108–109; *Commonwealth Bank v Quade* (1991) 178 CLR 134.
[3]   Para 5.32 nn 14–21.
[4]   *Hockin v Bank of British Columbia* (1995) 123 DLR (4th) 538 BCCA, 552.
[5]   Para 5.30.
[6]   *Danyluk* [2001] 2 SCR 460, 492–493, 498–499.

THE EFFECT OF REFUSAL OF LEAVE TO AMEND

8.36 The *Henderson* principle[1] applies although leave to raise the omitted matter was refused. If that matter properly belonged to the earlier litigation, its omission, for whatever reason, until it was too late to obtain leave to amend, bars its assertion in later proceedings. This was decided for cause of action estoppel in an Indian appeal, where Sir Madhavan Nair said[2]:

'It was next argued that having regard to the fact that the plaintiffs made an attempt – though unsuccessful it proved to be – to get the Shahjahanpur property included in suit no 8 by their application for amendment ... it cannot be said that they 'omitted to sue in respect of any portion of their claim' ... it is impossible to accept this argument. The fact cannot be denied that the Shahjahanpur property was not included in the plaint ... and it was because it was omitted ... that the application for amendment was made ... their Lord-ships are unable to hold that, because the plaintiffs attempted to get it included ... but were not allowed to do so ... they did not 'omit to sue' in respect of it. No authority was cited in support of this contention.'[3]

This must also apply for issue estoppel, and an unsuccessful application in the earlier proceedings for leave to amend should not be a special circumstance which displaces the estoppel. Where a party failed to take a point which properly belonged to the subject matter of the litigation that would have required the joinder of an additional party there is no *res judicata* estoppel in favour of that party because there is no mutuality, but proceedings against that party may be an abuse of process[4].

[1]   (1843) 3 Hare 100, 114–115; paras 7.03, 8.11.
[2]   *Mohammed Khan v Mahbub Ali Mian* [1948] AIR (PC) 78, 84–86. The Board included Lord Simonds and Lord Morton.
[3]   The contrary view of Powell JA in *Macquarie Bank Ltd v National Mutual Life Association of Australia Ltd* (1996) 40 NSWLR 543 CA, 619 cannot be accepted.
[4]   *Asher* [1974] Ch 208 CA; paras 7.11 n 1, 26.04 nn 8–10.

TAXATION AND RATING CASES

8.37 Decisions in annual taxation cases do not create issue estoppels for other years[1].

[1]   *Caffoor* [1961] AC 584; Chapter 13.

CRIMINAL CASES

8.38 Issue estoppels are not recognised in criminal cases[1], and an acquittal will not bar civil proceedings based on the same facts. The parties will generally be different and the onus of proof is different[2].

[1]   *DPP v Humphrys* [1977] AC 1; para 14.04.
[2]   *Maxwell v IRC* [1962] NZLR 687 CA.

DIVORCE

8.39 Issue estoppels have limited application in divorce and custody cases because of the court's statutory duties to investigate the facts and treat the welfare of the child as paramount[1].

[1]   Para 15.05.

Chapter 9

PARTIES TO DECISIONS IN PERSONAM

ESTABLISHED CATEGORIES OF JUDICIAL DECISIONS

9.01 It was long thought that there were only two categories of judicial decisions, those *in personam* which determine the rights and liabilities of parties, and those *in rem* which determine the status of a person or thing which bind strangers, loosely referred to as the world. The latter are considered in the next chapter.

NEW CATEGORY – INSOLVENCY DECISIONS

9.02 In *Cambridge Gas*[1] the Privy Council recognised a third category, judgments in bankruptcy and insolvency proceedings. Although the result was undoubtedly correct the recognition of this novel category was unnecessary and unsound. The debtor, Navigator Holdings, was incorporated in the Isle of Man and owned shares in another Manx company which owned the shares in five single vessel Manx companies. The appellant, incorporated in the Cayman Islands, owned at least 70% of the shares in the debtor. The debtor applied to the Bankruptcy Court of the Southern District of New York for a Chapter 11 reorganisation. The court approved the creditors' plan which would vest the shares in the debtor, and not its assets, in their committee. The New York court sent a letter of request to the Manx court seeking its assistance in vesting the shares in the committee. The appellant argued that the judgment was not *in rem* because the shares were not situated in New York, and it was not bound *in personam* because it had not submitted to the jurisdiction.

[1]   [2007] 1 AC 508.

9.03 Lord Hoffmann sidestepped this argument by recognising the new category[1]:

> 'If the New York order ... had to be classified as falling within one category or the other, the appeal would have to be allowed. But their Lordships consider that bankruptcy proceedings do not fall into either category. Judgments *in rem* and *in personam* are judicial determinations of the existence of rights ... The purpose of bankruptcy proceedings, on the other hand, is not to determine or

125

establish the existence of rights, but to provide a … collective execution against the property of the debtor by creditors whose rights are admitted or established. … The important point is that bankruptcy, whether personal or corporate, is a collective proceeding to enforce rights and not to establish them.'

1   [2007] 1 AC 508, 516.

9.04 He held that bankruptcy and corporate insolvency proceedings are universal in their operation and the Manx court had jurisdiction to enforce the Chapter 11 plan[1]. The fact that proceedings enforce the collective rights of creditors is an inadequate reason for holding that a judgment is not *in personam*. The claimant enforces the rights of a class, and all creditors are bound by, and entitled to the benefit of the judgment. Nor is it apparent why proceedings to enforce a collective execution against the property of a debtor are not proceedings to establish rights merely because the debts do not merge in the order for bankruptcy or winding up[2]. An execution for the benefit of the claimant appears to be *in personam*. Lord Hoffmann relied on[3] *Solomons v Ross*[4] to support the universal operation of such orders without noticing that it had been overruled in *Galbraith v Grimshaw and Baxter*[5]. There were at least two grounds for holding that the New York judgment was binding on Cambridge *in personam*. Although there were concurrent findings that it had not submitted to the jurisdiction[6] it was aware, through its parent and directors, of the proceedings and could have intervened, but allowed the proceedings to be conducted by its parent in the same interest[7], and was therefore a deemed party[8]. As a 70% owner of the debtor it was also bound as a privy of its subsidiary and its own parent[9] which participated in the Chapter 11 proceedings[10].

1   [2007] 1 AC 508, 518.
2   *Wight v Eckhardt Marine GmbH* [2004] 1 AC 147, 155–156.
3   [2007] 1 AC 508, 517.
4   (1764) 1 Hy Bl 131n.
5   [1910] AC 508, 511, followed in *Anantapadmanabhaswami v Official Receiver of Secunderabad* [1933] AC 394.
6   [2007] 1 AC 508, 515.
7   Ibid at 520.
8   Para 9.12.
9   Para 9.47.
10   [2007] 1 AC 508, 514–515; para [8].

MUTUALITY

9.05 A decision *in personam* only operates as an estoppel in favour of, and against, parties and privies, not strangers[1]. Thus, as *Petrie v Nuttall* decided[2], *res judicata* estoppels in civil cases must be 'mutual'. This was rejected by Lord Denning MR and Sir George Baker in *McIlkenny v Chief Constable of West Midlands Police Force*[3] who followed the US Supreme Court[4] and would have overruled *Petrie v Nuttall*, but Reginald Goff LJ held that mutuality was basic to *res judicata*[5], and his judgment was approved by the House of Lords[6]. This is important when determining whether a person is a privy[7]. The position of the parties on the record in the two cases is irrelevant[8].

126

1   *Duchess of Kingston's Case* (1776) quoted *R v Hutchings* (1881) 6 QBD 300 CA, 304;
    para 8.23 n 4; *Gray v Lewis* (1873) 8 Ch App 1035, 1059–1060 per Mellish LJ: 'It
    unquestionably is not the general rule of law that a judgment obtained by A against B is
    conclusive in an action by B against C. On the contrary, the rule of law is otherwise ... a
    judgment *inter partes* is conclusive only between the parties and those claiming under
    them.'
2   (1856) 11 Exch 569, 575 per Alderson B: 'It is essential to a *[res judicata]* estoppel that it
    be mutual, so that the same parties or privies may both be bound and take advantage of it.'
3   [1980] QB 283 CA, 321.
4   *Blonder-Tongue Laboratories Inc v University of Illinois Foundation* 402 US 313 (1971).
    Saffron v Federal Comr of Taxation (No 2) (1991) 30 FCR 578 contains a discussion of
    the US doctrine of collateral estoppel that a party who litigated an issue and lost is bound
    against a non-party.
5   *McIllkenny* [1980] QB 283 CA, 329.
6   *Hunter* [1982] AC 529; *Concha* (1886) 11 App Cas 541, 553, 554; *Carl-Zeiss (No 2)*
    [1967] 1 AC 853, 909–910, 928, 935, 942–943, 968–969; *Blathwayt v Baron Cawley*
    [1976] AC 397, 419, 430; *DPP v Humphrys* [1977] AC 1, 20, 33, 51; *Sun Life* [2005] 1
    Lloyds Rep 606 CA, 627, 630; *Ramsay v Pigram* (1967) 118 CLR 271, 276, 282; *Rogers
    v R* (1994) 181 CLR 251, 267; *Effem Foods* (1993) 43 FCR 510, 526, 528, 543; *Danyluk*
    [2001] 2 SCR 460, 491.
7   *Spencer v Williams* (1871) LR 2 P&D 230, 237; *Concha* (1886) 11 App Cas 541, 553;
    Ramsay v Pigram (1867) 118 CLR 271, 276; *Carl-Zeiss (No 3)* [1970] Ch 506, 541; *Effem
    Foods* (1993) 43 FCR 510, 542.
8   *Kinsey* (1754) 2 Ves Sen 577; *Eastmure v Laws* (1839) 5 Bing NC 444; *Geils* (1852) 1
    Macq 255 HL; *Webster v Armstrong* (1885) 54 LJQB 236; *Marginson* [1939] 2 KB 426
    CA.

BURDEN OF PROOF

9.06   The person asserting the estoppel must establish identity or privity[1]. Any
question of physical identity is one of fact[2].

1   *Carl-Zeiss (No 2)* [1967] 1 AC 853; *O'Keefe v Williams* (1907) 5 CLR 217, 228.
2   *Russell v Smyth* (1842) 9 M & W 810.

FOREIGN DECISIONS

9.07   The rules as to parties and privies apply to foreign decisions *in
personam*[1].

1   *Carl-Zeiss (No 2)* [1967] 1 AC 853, 910, 919, 928–929, 936–937, 945–946, 968–969
    where the estoppel failed *inter alia* for lack of privity; *Blohn v Desser* [1962] 2 QB 116,
    124.

ESTOPPELS BETWEEN DEFENDANTS

9.08   *Res judicata* estoppels may operate between defendants. The principles
were developed by the Privy Council in Indian appeals. In *Munni Bibi v
Tirloki Nath*[1] Sir George Lowndes said:

> ' ... three conditions are requisite: (1) there must be a conflict of interest
> between the defendants ...; (2) it must be necessary to decide the conflict ... to
> give the plaintiff the relief he claims and (3) the question between the
> defendants must have been judicially decided.'

The principles apply where the plaintiff failed[2]. In a later case Lord Simonds said[3]:

> '... the doctrine may apply even though the party, against whom it is sought to enforce it, did not in the previous suit ... enter an appearance and contest the question. But ... if such a party is to be bound ..., it must be proved clearly that he had, or must be deemed to have had, notice that the relevant question was in issue and would have to be decided.'

A defendant prejudiced by a judgment for or against a co-defendant on liability or quantum can appeal from it[4]. The decision to the contrary in *The Millwall*[5] must be treated as overruled. In *North Wales Water Ltd v Binnie & Partners*[6] Drake J, who was not referred to the Privy Council decisions, held that it was an abuse of process for consulting engineers, held liable with their client to third parties, to attempt to relitigate their negligence in proceedings brought by their client. The existence of an issue estoppel in such a case continues to be overlooked[7]. The Privy Council cases illustrate a wider principle formulated by Fisher J in *Taylor v Ansett Transport Ltd*[8]:

> '... issue estoppel can only be raised by or applied against parties who were in "controversy" ... when the issue was first determined, either in their favour or adversely to them. If a party was not involved in the litigation of that issue, either because it was not an issue between him and another party in the proceedings, or because he was not a party at all ... he is not affected by nor can he raise an estoppel. Likewise his presence initially or subsequently cannot affect the right of other parties to raise or rely upon issue estoppel as between themselves.'

[1] (1931) 58 LR Ind App 158, 165–166 (the Board included Lord Tomlin) (dispute as to title between co-defendants); *Cottingham v Earl of Shrewsbury* (1843) 3 Hare 627, 638 (dispute between mortgagees).
[2] *Maung Sein Done v Ma Pan Nyun* (1932) LR 59 Ind App 247, 256 (administration suit by daughter against sons, other daughter joined as defendant, decision that plaintiff not entitled binding in suit by other daughter against sons).
[3] *Chandu Lal Agarwalla v Khalilur Rahaman* (1949) LR 77 Ind App 27, 30.
[4] *Moy v Pettman Smith* [2005] 1 WLR 581 HL, 602–604; *Insurance Exchange of Australasia v Dooley* (2000) 50 NSWLR 222 CA, 228.
[5] [1905] P 155 CA.
[6] [1990] 3 All ER 547.
[7] *Secretary of State for Trade and Industry v Bairstow* [2004] Ch 1 CA, 14; *Conlon v Simms* [2008] 1 WLR 484 CA, 521, 523.
[8] (1987) 18 FCR 342, 358; para 16.07 n 24.

SUBMITTING DEFENDANTS

9.09 A party who submits to the judgment of the court is bound by any *res judicata* estoppels. A magistrate who submitted in proceedings in which a warrant of commitment was held void for lack of jurisdiction, was bound in proceedings against him for false imprisonment[1].

[1] *Spautz v Butterworth* (1996) 41 NSWLR 1 CA, 19–20.

INTERPLEADER

9.10 This remedy is available to a stakeholder, bailee or the like faced with conflicting claims to the same property in which he claims no personal interest[1]. The court tries the issue between the claimants and the interpleading party submits to its judgment. This equitable remedy has been available at law since the Interpleader Act 1831. Greene LJ summarised the principles[2]:

> 'It is a method to enable the court to decide the claims ... so that the person interpleading will get the relief to which he is entitled ... The object ... is to enable a person who is harassed by claims made by two or more persons to be quieted.'

This will only occur if the decision binds all parties. The procedure would be pointless if the unsuccessful party could still sue the interpleading party. The judgment of Robert Walker LJ, dissenting on this point, in *Gribbon v Lutton*[3] was correct.

[1]   *De la Rue v Hernu Peron & Stockwell Ltd* [1936] 2 KB 164 CA, 170–172; *ANZ Banking Group Ltd v Ding* [2004] 3 SLR 489.
[2]   Ibid at 173, 175.
[3]   [2002] QB 902 CA.

THIRD AND SUBSEQUENT PARTIES (PT 20 PARTIES)

9.11   A third or subsequent party, subject to any order of the court, becomes a party to the proceedings between the prior parties and bound by issue estoppels created by the judgment or judgments between them. The position was explained by Scrutton LJ[1]:

> '... it is important to keep clearly in mind what the third party procedure is. A plaintiff has a claim against the defendant. The defendant thinks if he is liable he has a claim over against the third party. With that matter between the defendant and the third party the plaintiff has obviously nothing to do. He is not concerned with the question whether the defendant has a remedy against somebody else. His remedy is against the defendant. But the defendant is much interested in getting the third party bound by the result of the trial between the plaintiff and himself, for otherwise he might be at a great disadvantage if, having fought the case against the plaintiff and lost, he had then to fight the case against the third party possibly on different materials, with the risk that a different result might be arrived at. The object of the third party procedure is ... to get the third party bound by the decision between the plaintiff and the defendant.'

A third or subsequent party bound by a judgment between prior parties can appeal from that judgment[2]. The decisions to the contrary in *The Millwall*[3] and *Ashphalt and Public Works Ltd v Indemnity Guarantee Trust Ltd*[4] must be treated as overruled.

[1]   *Barclays Bank v Tom* [1923] 1 KB 221 CA, 223–224; *Sandtara Pty Ltd v Abigroup Ltd* (1997) 42 NSWLR 5 CA; *Financial Wisdom Ltd v Newman* (2005) 12 VR 74 CA, 90–92.
[2]   *Borealis AB v Stargas Ltd, The Berge Sisar* [2002] 2 AC 205, 217–218 paras [15]–[16]; *Helicopter Sales Pty Ltd v Rotor-Work Pty Limited* (1974) 132 CLR 1; *Insurance Exchange of Australasia v Dooley* (2000) 50 NSWLR 222 CA, 228–233.
[3]   [1905] P 155 CA.
[4]   [1969] 1 QB 465 CA.

PARTIES WHO INTERVENE OR COULD

9.12 The parties to proceedings *in personam* include a person who intervenes and takes an active part[1]. A public authority, notified pursuant to statute, which appears and merely announces its attitude does not become a party[2]. Whether an intervener becomes a party depends on the extent to which it participates[3]. Under a rule which originated in the probate jurisdiction any person claiming an interest in the estate could intervene and if he stood by and allowed the litigation to be conducted by others in the same interest he was bound by the result[4]. The Privy Council applied this principle to a land dispute[5] and it was then applied to joint tortfeasors. Stuart–Smith LJ said that although the rule may have originated in the probate jurisdiction 'justice and common sense [did not] require it to be so confined'[6]. The cases considered in para 9.14 support this view. In Canada a party who could have intervened, but chose to stand by has been treated as a privy of the litigant in the same interest by a form of estoppel by conduct[7]. Someone who ought to have been a party, but elects not to be joined, will not be bound where there was no contradictor in the same interest[8]. An employer who could have actively participated before a board of reference under unemployment insurance legislation, but did not, was not a party. Laskin JA said[9]:

> 'A person must actively participate ... to meet the same parties' requirement of issue estoppel.'

The ability of an interested person to make itself a party by intervening has sometimes been overlooked in clear cases. In competition proceedings the European Court upheld findings that the defendants had abused their dominant position in the market. In civil proceedings against them for damages Laddie J held[10] that the plaintiff was not a party to the competition proceedings and could not rely on any issue estoppels but the defendants' challenge to those findings was an abuse of process. He said[11] 'it was not possible for the plaintiff to be more fully involved in the competition proceedings. It initiated the procedure, it formulated the allegations ... it presented written submission, answered the defendants' responses and played a full part in the oral hearing ... it played an equally full part before the Court of First Instance and the Court of Justice.' The plaintiff had made itself a party but the point went begging. In Canada an intervener which identified itself with and actively supported one of the parties was held to be its privy[12]. Where a party failed to take a point which would have required the joinder of another the latter will not be entitled to the benefit of any *res judicata* estoppel[13] but an action by the unsuccessful claimant against the absent party is likely to be an abuse of process.

[1] *Tebbutt v Haynes* [1981] 2 All ER 238 CA; *Cheesman v Waters* (1997) 77 FCR 221, 227. This was overlooked in *Iberian UK ltd v BPB Industries plc* [1997] ICR 164 (*Iberian*).
[2] *Australian Securities Commission v Marlborough Gold Mines Ltd* (1993) 177 CLR 485, 505.
[3] *Minott* (1999) 168 DLR (4th) 270, 284–287 Ont CA.
[4] *Re Langton* [1964] P 163 CA, 169; *Osborne v Smith* (1960) 105 CLR 153.
[5] *Nana Ofori Atta II, Oman hereof Akyem Abuakwa v Nana Abu Bonsra II as Adansehene and Representing state of Adanse* [1958] AC 95 (*Nana Ofori*); *Daera Guba* (1973) 130 CLR 353, 403, 456.

6   *House of Spring Gardens Ltd v Waite* [1991] 1 QB 241 CA, 253 (*Spring Gardens*); *Powell v Wiltshire* [2005] QB 117 CA, 126; *Thomas & Agnes Carvel Foundation v Carvel* [2008] Ch 395, 407 (*Carvel*). See also *Re Lart* [1896] 2 Ch 788, 794–795 where the rule was applied to a beneficiary who should have been joined in a construction summons, and was aware of the proceedings, but was 'content to stand by and see his battle fought by someone else.'
7   *Bank of Montreal v Mitchell* (1997) 143 DLR (4th) 697, 732–738, 739; affirmed sub nom *Timmins v Toronto Dominion Bank* (1997) 151 DLR (4th) 574 Ont CA.
8   *Tedeschi v Legal Services Comr* (1997) 43 NSWLR 20.
9   *Minott* (1999) 168 DLR (4th) 270, Ont CA, 285–286.
10 *Iberian* [1997] ICR 164.
11 Ibid at 179.
12 *BNP Canada v Canadian Imperial Bank of Commerce* (2001) 195 DLR (4th) 308 Ont CA.
13 *Asher* [1974] Ch 208 CA; paras 7.11 n 1; 8.36 n 4; 26.04 nn 8–10.

PARTY ENFORCING PUBLIC RIGHT

9.13 Where a party invokes the right of the public or a class, the latter are parties and will be bound. When a common informer sues to enforce a penal law the action is brought in the interest of the community[1]. Where the Attorney-General brings proceedings *ex officio*, or by a relator, to enforce a public right, the public are parties and will be bound. As Aickin J said[2]:

> 'Generally speaking when an Attorney-General sues to enforce a public right or liberty he does so as representing Her Majesty's subjects, and not the body politic of the government unit in which he holds office.'

In *Brisbane County Council v A-G for Queensland*[3] Lord Wilberforce doubted whether the Attorney-General suing at the relation of a ratepayer to restrain *ultra vires* acts by a Council was the same person for *res judicata* when suing by a relator to enforce a charitable trust. An invalid patent interferes with the right of the public to trade and prior to the *Patents Act* 1949 revocation proceedings could only be brought by the Attorney-General or with his permission. A defendant sued for infringement had a personal right to raise validity in his defence but the decision could not revoke the patent. Before the 1949 Act a defendant sued for infringement and the same individual suing for revocation with the permission of the Attorney-General were different persons[4]. The Attorney-General suing in respect of a different interest is a different party.

1   *Girdlestone* (1879) 4 Ex D 107 CA; *Huntington v Attrill* [1893] AC 150, 158; quoted para 2.41.
2   *Queensland v Commonwealth* (1977) 139 CLR 585, 615; cf *Re a Medical Practitioner* [1959] NZLR 784 CA (Solicitor General applying ex officio for removal of practitioner from roll not the Crown which had unsuccessfully prosecuted for the same matter).
3   [1979] AC 411, 426; para 9.24.
4   *Re Deeley's Patent* [1895] 1 Ch 687 CA (successful defendant in patent infringement proceedings suing for revocation not entitled to benefit of estoppel because he was suing on behalf of the public); *Shoe Machinery Co Ltd v Cutlan* [1896] 1 Ch 108 CA, 113 (unsuccessful defendant in patent action not bound by estoppel when suing for revocation because he was suing on behalf of the public), *Hormel Foods* [2005] RPC 657, 671–679. The Patents Act 1949 s 32(1) enabled any interested person to petition for revocation.

IDENTITY OF PARTIES: FORM AND SUBSTANCE

9.14 Where a party on the record is suing or defending 'on account of or for the benefit of another'[1] and relying on that person's right or title, the court can look behind the record to identify the 'real' party. As Lord Wilberforce said[2]: 'One must look to see who in reality is behind the action' [or defence]. In *Re Walton*[3] the plaintiff's predecessor in title recovered in an action for trespass in 1738 against a servant of the Corporation of Ipswich who claimed to have been on its land. This decision was binding on the Corporation in favour of the plaintiff because, as Wickens VC held[4] 'the same titles ... came into direct collision' . The rationale was articulated by Megarry VC[5]:

> '... a [party] ought to be able to put his own [case] in his own way and ... call his own evidence. He ought not to be concluded by the failure of the [case] and evidence adduced by another ... in other proceedings unless ... a decision ... in them ... [was] in substance a decision against him.'

Before the procedural reforms in the 19th century, ejectment proceedings were brought by a fictional lessee (John Doe etc), holding under a fictional lease from the real plaintiff, against a fictional casual ouster as sole defendant. The writ was served on the person in possession and if he did not appear[6] judgment by default against the casual ouster could be executed against him. The judgment bound the person in possession because, as Lord Mansfield CJ said on behalf of the judges[7]:

> '... the lessor of the plaintiff, and the tenant in possession, are, substantially, and in truth ... the only parties to the suit ... an action for the mesne profits is consequential to the recovery in ejectment. It may be brought by the lessor of the plaintiff in his own name, or in the name of the nominal lessee; and in either shape it is equally his action. The tenant is concluded by the judgment, and cannot controvert the title. Consequently, he cannot controvert the plaintiff's possession; because his possession is part of his title.'

[1] *Carl-Zeiss (No 2)* [1967] 1 AC 853, 911–912 per Lord Reid, 969 per Lord Wilberforce; *MCC Proceeds Inc v Lehman Bros International (Europe)* [1998] 4 All ER 675 CA, 695, 698 (*MCC Proceeds*).
[2] Ibid at 968.
[3] (1873) 28 LT 12.
[4] Ibid at 16.
[5] *Gleeson v J Wippell & Co Ltd* [1977] 1 WLR 510, 516 (*Gleeson*); *Re Norris* [2001] 1 WLR 1388 HL, 1400–1401.
[6] That is intervene.
[7] *Aslin v Parkin* (1758) 2 Burr 665, 668.

9.15 An interested party who employs a servant or agent to test the right as in *Re Walton*[1] will be bound. He cannot avoid a *res judicata* estoppel by employing a different servant or agent and *Kinnersley v Orpe*[2] does not decide otherwise. The plaintiff successfully sued a servant of C for trespass to his fishery. C gave notice that he would raise the question again by directing another servant to fish. The plaintiff sued this servant for a penalty under a statute which allowed a defence of claim of right. Perryn B held that the judgment in the first case was conclusive[3], both servants 'having acted under the authority of C who was the real defendant in both cases.' The court in banc ordered a new trial because a claim of right was a defence. The decision would have been different if the second action had been for trespass and does not affect the principle that the real parties are bound although the nominal parties change[4].

1   Para 9.14 n 3.
2   (1780) 2 Doug KB 517.
3   Ibid at 517.
4   *Doe d Foster v Earl of Derby* (1834) 1 Ad & El 783, 787, 790, 791; para 9.39. The dictum of Lord Ellenborough CJ in *Outram v Morewood* (1803) 3 East 346, 366 was brushed aside by Lord Reid in *Carl-Zeiss (No 2)* [1967] 1 AC 853, 912.

9.16   A landlord is not a party to proceedings commenced or defended by his tenant without his authority[1]. Lord Denning said[2]:

'English law recognises that the conduct of a person may be such that he is estopped from litigating the issue all over again. This conduct sometimes consists of active participation in the previous proceedings, as, for instance, when a tenant is sued for trespassing on his neighbour's land and he defends on the strength of the landlord's title and does so by the direction and authority of the landlord. If a tenant loses the action, the landlord would not be allowed to litigate the title all over again by bringing an action in his own name.'

1   *Lady Wenman v MacKenzie* (1855) 5 E & B 447, 458–459.
2   *Nana Ofori* [1958] AC 95, 101–102; para 9.43.

BANKRUPTCY AND INSOLVENCY

9.17   Proceedings by a member of a class, such as creditors, shareholders, or next of kin, may invoke a class right and the members will be bound without a representative order. Bankruptcy and insolvency proceedings are collective in nature, brought to enforce a compulsory administration of the debtor's assets for the benefit of those with claims on them[1]. The right of an unpaid creditor to a winding up order is a right to equitable execution[2], and Buckley J said[3]:

'... the petitioning creditor has, as between himself and his debtor, a ... right *ex debito justitiae* to seize his debtor's assets by the hand of a liquidator and administer them for the benefit of his class ... the order which the petitioner seeks is not an order for his benefit, but an order for a class of which he is a member. The right *ex debito justitiae* is not his individual right but his representative right. If a majority of the class are opposed to his view ... the Court gives effect to such right as the majority of the class desire to exercise. This ... affirms that it is the right not of the individual, but of the class ...'

The Bankruptcy Act 1914, repealed by the 1986 Act, made the equivalent of a bankruptcy order binding and conclusive on the debtor, the creditors, and third persons[4]. The section was not re-enacted presumably because it was thought to be unnecessary. In *Mulkerrins*[5] Lord Millett held that an order declaring that a chose in action had not vested in the trustee in bankruptcy but remained with the bankrupt bound the trustee 'and through him the creditors'. A winding up order is binding on the members and those claiming under the company, but not on a stranger such as a purchaser[6].

1   *Re Lines Bros Ltd* [1983] Ch 1, 20; *Cambridge Gas* [2007] 1 AC 508, 516.
2   *Re Crigglestone Coal Co Ltd* [1906] 2 Ch 327, 331.

3   Ibid at 331–332. In *Re J D Swain Ltd* [1965] 1 WLR 909 CA, 915 Diplock LJ described a
     winding up order obtained on the application of a creditor as 'a class remedy'.
4   Section 137(2); *Boaler v Power* [1910] 2 KB 229 CA, 232; *Heath v Tang* [1993] 1 WLR
     1421 CA; *Cummings v Claremont Petroleum NL* (1996) 185 CLR 124, 133–136. For the
     effect on third persons: *Re Foulds, ex p Learoyd* (1878) 10 Ch D 3 CA; *Yousuf v Official
     Assignee* (1943) LR 70 Ind App 93.
5   [2003] 1 WLR 1937 HL, 1941, 1942.
6   *Re Bowling and Welby's Contract* [1895] 1 Ch 663 CA, 667–668, 671, 673; para 10.15.

9.18 Bankruptcy[1] and winding up[2] orders operate for the benefit of all
creditors whose debts are not time barred when the order is made. *Re General
Rolling Stock Co*[3] decided that a debt which was not time barred when the
winding up order was made could be proved. The High Court of Australia
held that time ceases to run against the petitioning creditor when winding up
proceedings are commenced[4] and refused to apply *Re General Rolling
Stock Co* where it was alleged that the petitioning creditor's debt had become
statute barred while the petition was pending. Time should cease to run
against all creditors when bankruptcy or winding up proceedings are commenced[5] because they invoke a class right. Otherwise creditors whose debts
could become statute barred would have to commence proceedings to stop
time running[6]. The position in proceedings, now obsolete, for the administration of an estate or trust fund is instructive. A creditor could sue for
administration on his own behalf[7] but, without a representative order[8], he
could also sue on behalf of all creditors[9]. Actions by a beneficiary, executor, or
creditor in his own right did not stop time running against other creditors
before the order but proceedings by a creditor on behalf of the class did[10].

1   *Re Coles, ex p Ross* (1827) 2 Gl & J 330; *Re Westby, ex p Lancaster Banking Corpn*
     (1879) 10 Ch D 776, 784; *Re Cullwick, ex p London Official Receiver* [1918] 1 KB 646,
     653.
2   *Re General Rolling Stock Co, Joint Stock Discount Co's Claim* (1872) LR 7 Ch App 646.
3   Ibid.
4   *Motor Terms Co Pty Ltd v Liberty Insurance Ltd* (1967) 116 CLR 177, 190–191 (*Motor
     Terms*).
5   This does not limit the provable debts to those in existence when winding up proceedings
     were commenced: *Day & Dent Constructions Pty Ltd v North Australian Properties Pty
     Ltd* (1982) 150 CLR 85. The fact that the class does not close until the order is made is not
     inconsistent with time ceasing to run against other creditors when proceedings are
     commenced.
6   *Motor Terms* (1967) 116 CLR 177, 190–191.
7   *Re Greaves* (1881) 18 Ch D 551, 554; *Re James* [1911] 2 Ch 348.
8   *May v Newton* (1887) 34 Ch D 347, 349.
9   *Re Richardson* (1880) 14 Ch D 611, 613; *Re McRea* (1886) 32 Ch D 613, 615. This had
     to be disclosed on the face of proceedings: *Re Tottenham* [1896] 1 Ch 628.
10 *Re Greaves* (1881) 18 Ch D 551, 552–553.

9.19 In *John v Mendoza*[1] the bankruptcy was annulled on the ground that
creditors had been paid in full. The debtor induced the plaintiff not to prove
by promising to pay in full after the annulment and the question was whether
the plaintiff was bound by the order. Du Parcq LJ said[2]:

> '... one must treat the plaintiff ... as having been a party ... to the bankruptcy
> proceedings. ... he knew that a receiving order had been made. He knew that it
> was his duty under the Act, if he desired to claim that he was a creditor, to
> lodge a proof ... It was open to him by proving to prevent any annulment of the
> receiving order ... ... [O]n the general principles of estoppel by record he is just

as much estopped after that order of annulment ... as if there had been a judgment to the opposite effect to that for which he now contends ...'

The plaintiff was bound while the adjudication was in force but was not an actual party to the annulment proceedings. Once the adjudication was annulled prima facie there was no answer to his claim. Would a creditor with no knowledge of the bankruptcy be bound? In *More*[3] an unproved creditor succeeded in similar circumstances. Cross J doubted *John v Mendoza* and distinguished it on flimsy grounds. It is unlikely to be followed.

1   [1939] 1 KB 141.
2   Ibid at 147.
3   [1962] Ch 424.

REPRESENTATIVE ACTION AUTHORISED BY COURT

9.20 The court may authorise a member of a numerous class to sue or defend in the interest of the class. Lord Macnaghten explained[1]:

'The old rule in the Court of Chancery was very simple ... the Court required the presence of all parties interested in the matters in suit, in order that a final end might be made of the controversy. But when the parties were so numerous that you could never "come at justice" ... the rule was not allowed to stand in the way ... Given a common interest and a common grievance, a representative suit was in order if the relief sought was in its nature beneficial to all whom the plaintiff proposed to represent.'

The order could be made in respect of a class of claimants or defendants and 'absent parties would be bound as though they had been present throughout'[2]. An unnamed represented party is a party for present purposes[3]. A member who believes that a different substantive order would be more beneficial cannot appeal from an order obtained 'on his behalf'[4], but must apply to be added as a defendant and, in that capacity, appeal from the order or seek its discharge. The absent members are only bound if their representative conducts the proceedings in good faith in the interests of the class[5]. However as Lord Blanesburgh said[6]:

'... in a representative action the class of persons on behalf of whom relief is sought should be clearly defined ... the gist of the requirement is that as the judgment in such an action is binding on all members of the class represented it is of the essence that the range of the estoppel be defined somewhere on the face of the proceedings.'

1   *Duke of Bedford v Ellis* [1901] AC 1, 8.
2   *May v Newton* (1887) 34 Ch D 347, 349, 350; *Cox v Dublin City Distillery Co Ltd (No 3)* [1917] 1 IR 203 CA (second debenture holders estopped by *Dublin City Distillery Ltd v Doherty* [1914] AC 823 from disputing that D was entitled to a lien on his debentures, the class having been represented by the trustees (at 224–224, 234–236) who requested the liquidator and receiver to fight the second debenture holders' battle (at 217–218)). An order made on an application on behalf of a group with their consent bound every member: *Cornell v Inspector General in Bankruptcy* (2000) 105 FCR 146, 148–149.
3   *Moon v Atherton* [1972] 2 QB 435 CA.
4   *Watson v Cave* (1881) 17 Ch D 19 CA, 21; *Fraser v Cooper Hall & Co* (1882) 18 Ch D 718; *James v British Columbia* (2007) 288 DLR (4th) 380, 396 BCCA.
5   *Wytcherley v Andrews* (1871) LR 2 P & D 327, 328.
6   *Kumaravelu Chettiar v Ramaswami Ayya* (1933) LR 60 Ind App 278, 285.

9.21 The difficulties of bringing a class action under such rules in a product liability case are illustrated by *Naken v General Motors of Canada Ltd*[1]. In *Carnie v Esanda Finance Corpn Ltd*[2] a representative action on behalf of parties to a type of credit contract was allowed[3]. In the United States *res judicata* will only bind absent class members where there was adequate representation throughout the litigation, reasonable notice to absent members and an opportunity to opt out.[4] The class certified must be homogeneous, without diverse interests[5]. Hence a single class comprising current sufferers from asbestos diseases and those who had only been exposed to asbestos could not properly be certified as a single class. In *Irish Shipping Ltd v Commercial Union Assurance Co plc, The Irish Ravan*[6] the plaintiff was permitted to sue the lead underwriter and another on their own behalf and on behalf of the other 75 underwriters who had subscribed the policy, although many could not have been served within the jurisdiction. Purchas LJ held[5] that any judgment would be binding upon the other underwriters.

1 (1983) 144 DLR (3d) 385 SC.
2 (1995) 182 CLR 398, 423–424 (effect of judgment in such action as a *res judicata*); *Campbells Cash and Carry Pty Ltd v Fostif Pty Ltd* (2006) 229 CLR 386 (class to be identified by opt in procedure).
3 Cf 'The Res Judicata effect in England of a US class action settlement' (1997) 46 Int & Comp LQ 134.
4 *Stephenson v Dow Chemical Co* 273 F 3rd 249 (2nd cir) 2001, 260; varied on appeal 539 US 111 (2003) on different grounds.
5 Ibid at 259–261.
6 [1991] 2 QB 206 CA.

PARTY LITIGATING IN DIFFERENT CAPACITIES

9.22 A party who litigates in different capacities is a different party in each capacity. *Res judicata* estoppels binding a person in an official capacity bind his successors as privies[1], but do not bind him personally or in another capacity and *vice versa*. A decision for or against a party in one capacity is not binding on him personally or in a different capacity[2]. However a legal personal representative or trustee litigating for his personal benefit and litigating in his own right are the same party[3]. This only applies where the legal personal representative or trustee would personally benefit from the litigation, eg as the specific devisee of the property or a residuary beneficiary. The principle applies to trustees and the like suing or defending for the benefit of others[4].

1 *Dundas v Waddell* (1880) 5 App Cas 249; *Jones v Lewis* [1919] 1 KB 328 CA, 345; *Asher* [1974] Ch 208 CA, 210, 225; cf *Society of Medical Officers of Health v Hope* [1960] AC 551, 568 (*Hope*).
2 *Bainbrigge v Baddeley* (1847) 2 Ph 705, 709–710; *Overton v Harvey* (1859) 9 CB 324, 336 (Counsel: 'Suppose a first action brought by a person as executor, but … he now claimed by letters of administration'; and Cresswell J replied: 'In that case he would be a different person'); *Blake v O'Kelly* (1874) IR 9 Eq 54, 57–58 (defendant sued as executor de son tort, later held as fraudulent donee); *Leggott v Great Northern Rly Co* (1876) 1 QBD 599 (plaintiff sued as administratrix for damages sustained by deceased and later as administratrix under *Lord Campbell's Act*); *Manton v Cantwell* [1920] AC 781, 788, 791 (widow claiming compensation for herself and children under the Workmen's Compensation Act 1906 could not rely on an estoppel between employer and deceased because she had an independent right); *Harper v Burton's Haulage Co Pty Ltd* (1954) 55 SRNSW 236

(the same); *Marginson* [1939] 2 KB 426 CA (estoppel against M not binding on him as administrator of wife's estate). A party suing in right of the public was a different person when suing in his own right: para 9.13.

³ *Carvel* [2008] Ch 395, 406–407; para 9.44.

⁴ Cf the requirement for mutuality in set-off: *N W Robbie & Co Ltd v Witney Ware-house Ltd* [1963] 1 WLR 1324 CA; *Rother Iron Works Ltd v Canterbury Precision Engineers Ltd* [1974] QB 1 CA (equitable assignment); *Sankey Brook Coal Co Ltd v Marsh* (1871) LR 6 Exch 185 (no set-off of pre and post liquidation debts); *Churchill and Sim v Goddard* [1937] 1 KB 92 CA, 103–104 (trustee liable to set-off available against beneficiary); *Secretary of State for Trade and Industry v Frid* [2004] 2 AC 506, 515 (*Frid*); para 9.26.

INSURER AND INSURED

9.23 This principle should also apply to insurers exercising rights of subrogation in proceedings in which their insured has a conflicting interest. An insurer subrogated to a cause of action of the insured has control of any litigation, an equitable lien over any recovery[1], and probably over the cause of action[2]. An underwriter claims through the insured and is bound as a privy where the estoppel arose before the right of subrogation accrued. Courts have sometimes refused to distinguish between a nominal party litigating in the interests of his insurer and litigating in his own interest[3]. Since identity of parties is a matter of substance an insured with a conflicting interest should not be bound by *res judicata* estoppels from proceedings in which the real party was his insurer[4]. This is the position in a number of common law jurisdictions[5]. Under the Brussels Convention identity of parties is a matter of substance. After a barge sank in the Netherlands the cargo owner and its insurer sued the owner and master there and the hull insurer sued the cargo owner and its insurer in France. If the barge owner and the hull insurer were the same party Article 21 required the French proceedings to be stayed. In *Drouot*[6] the European Court said[7]:

'... there may be such a degree of identity between the interests of an insurer and those of its insured that a judgment delivered against one of them would have the force of *res judicata* as against the other. That would be the case ... where an insurer, by virtue of its right of subrogation, brings or defends an action in the name of its insured without the latter being in a position to influence the proceedings. In such a situation insurer and insured must be considered to be one and the same party for the purposes of ... Article 21 ... On the other hand ... Article 21 cannot have the effect of precluding the insurer and its insured, where their interests diverge, from asserting their respective interests before the courts as against the other parties concerned ... article 21 ... is not applicable ... unless it is established that, with regard to the subject matter of the two disputes, the interests of the insurer of the hull of the vessel are identical to and indissociable from those of its insured, the owner and the charterer of that vessel.'

A collision between two motor vehicles could injure both drivers, one more seriously than the other. If the same insurer was on risk, its interest and that of the more seriously injured driver would conflict because the insurer would benefit from maximising his fault. If the other claim was a modest one the insurer may not devote adequate resources to its defence. The decision of the European Court is only persuasive in domestic cases, but it is consistent with the principle that identity of parties is a matter of substance[8]. The Court of Appeal should be free to depart from *Talbot* on this question[9].

[1]   *Lord Napier and Ettrick v Hunter* [1993] AC 713, noted 109 LQR 159; *Lonrho Exports Ltd v Export Credits Guarantee Department* [1999] Ch 158, 181–182.
[2]   Ibid at 740, 745, 752.
[3]   *Wall v Radford* [1991] 2 All ER 741, 750; *Talbot* [1994] QB 290 CA, 298–299 (overruled on another ground in *Johnson* [2002] 2 AC 1); *Craddock's Transport Ltd v Stuart* [1970] NZLR 499 CA, 524 (*Craddock*).
[4]   Paras 9.14, 9.16, 12.03–12.04.
[5]   *Shaw v Sloan* [1982] NI 393 CA, 397, 410–411; *Lawless v Bus Eireann* [1994] 1 IR 474 SC; *Linsley v Petrie* [1998] 1 VR 427 CA, 445–446, 450–451.
[6]   *Drout Assurances SA v Consolidated Metallurgical Industries (CMI Industrial Sites)* [1999] QB 497 ECJ; 'Res Judicata in the European Court' Handley (2000) 116 LQR 191; *Kolden Holdings Ltd v Rodette Commerce Ltd* [2008] Bus LR 1051 CA, 1072.
[7]   Ibid at 514.
[8]   Para 9.14. In *The Indian Endurance* [1998] AC 878, 910 decisions of the European Court were treated as persuasive.
[9]   [1994] QB 290 CA, overruled on another ground: para 9.23 n 3.

DEPARTMENTS OF STATE

9.24 The Executive administers the affairs of Government on behalf of the Crown through the departments of State. Is the Executive Government one party, the Crown, for present purposes? Is the Attorney-General joined in relation to the functions of one department bound by a decision in relation to the functions of another? The question was posed in an income tax appeal[1] where the issue was whether a trust was charitable. The trustees argued that the Revenue were estopped by the decision sanctioning the scheme. The first question was whether the Attorney-General, as a party to the charity proceedings, was estopped from denying that the scheme provided for a charitable trust, and the second was whether that bound the Revenue. The estoppel failed on the facts but in charity cases the Attorney-General represents the public and not the Executive government[2]. The activities of the departments of State, with separate functions and budgets, suggests that it may not be enough to simply ask whether the Crown is estopped. Some support for this view can be derived from an Australian case where it was held that the Crown in right of the Commonwealth as criminal prosecutor was not the same party as the Commonwealth Commissioner of Taxation[3]. Another aspect of the Crown may also be relevant. In 1919 Viscount Haldane was able to say[4]: 'The Crown is one and indivisible throughout the Empire' but this has long been 'remote from practical realities'[5]. The Crown in right of a dependent territory such as South Georgia and the South Sandwich Islands acting through a Secretary of State is not the same person for legal purposes as the Crown in right of the United Kingdom represented by the same Secretary of State[6].

[1]   *Vernon (Trustees of Employees Fund of William Vernon & Sons Ltd) v IRC* [1956] 1 WLR 1169.
[2]   Para 9.13.
[3]   *Saffron v FCT (No 2)* (1991) 30 FCR 578, 581 (no estoppel in any event because the issues in civil and criminal proceedings are not the same).
[4]   *Theodore v Duncan* [1919] AC 696, 706; Cf *A-G v Great Southern and Western Rly Co of Ireland* [1925] AC 754.

5   *Bradken Consolidated Ltd v Broken Hill Pty Co Ltd* (1979) 145 CLR 107, 122; *R v Secretary of State for Foreign and Commonwealth Affairs, ex p Indian Association of Alberta* [1982] QB 892 CA.
6   *R (on the application of Quark Fishing Ltd) v Secretary of State for Foreign and Commonwealth Affairs* [2006] 1 AC 529.

9.25 *Dyson v A-G*[1] established that proceedings could be brought against the Attorney-General representing the Crown for a declaration of right which would be binding on the Executive[2]. Although only the Revenue were concerned, the implication seemed to be that the Crown would be bound in all capacities. In *Robertson v Minister of Pensions*[3] Denning J held that the Ministry of Pensions was estopped by a letter written by the War Office. Recent authority has confirmed the indivisibility of the Crown in right of the central Government of the United Kingdom. In *Town Investments Ltd v Department of the Environment*[4] the Crown, was held to be the tenant under a lease granted to 'the Minister for Works ... for and on behalf of Her Majesty'. Lord Diplock said[5]:

> ' ... instead of speaking of "the Crown" we [should] speak of "the government" – a term appropriate to embrace both collectively and individually all of the ministers of the Crown and Parliamentary Secretaries under whose direction the administrative work of government is carried on by the civil servants employed in the various government departments. It is through them that the executive powers of Her Majesty's government in the United Kingdom are exercised ... Executive acts of government that are done by any of them are acts done by "the Crown" in the fictional sense in which that expression is now used in English public law ... The leases were executed under his official designation by the Minister of the Crown in charge of the government department ... In my opinion the tenant was the government acting through its appropriate member or, expressed in the term of art in public law, the tenant was the Crown.'

1   [1911] 1 KB 410 CA; [1912] 1 Ch 158 CA.
2   Ibid at 417, 421.
3   [1949] 1 KB 227 CA.
4   [1978] AC 359.
5   Ibid at 381.

9.26 In *Frid*[1] the Crown was held entitled to set-off debts owed by a company to the Secretary of State for Trade and Industry, the Inland Revenue, and the Department of Social Security against a debt owed by the Department of Customs and Excise for overpayment of VAT. Lord Hoffmann said[2]:

> 'The final question is whether there is mutuality between a claim against Customs and Excise and a claim by the Secretary of State on behalf of the National Insurance Fund. Mutuality requires that each party should be debtor and creditor in the same capacity. ... the Crown through its various emanations is the beneficial owner of all central funds. ... It follows that in my opinion the set-off due to the Secretary of State ... should have been allowed ...'

A *res judicata* estoppel against the Crown in right of one department should therefore bind the Crown generally.

1   [2004] 2 AC 506.
2   Ibid at 515.

SURETYSHIP AND INDEMNITY

9.27 Apart from statute a defendant who has suffered judgment and sues another for indemnity or contribution cannot rely on the judgment as *res judicata* because that other was neither party nor privy[1]. Where the principal contract contains an arbitration clause a surety is not bound by an award against the principal debtor[2]. The position is different where there is an express contract of indemnity as Mellish LJ explained[3]:

> ' … the law with reference to express contracts of indemnity is, that if a person has agreed to indemnify another against a particular claim or a particular demand, and an action is brought on that demand, he may then give notice to the person who has agreed to indemnify him to come in and defend the action, and if he does not come in, and refuses to come in, he may then compromise at once on the best terms he can, and … bring an action on the contract of indemnity. On the other hand, if he does not choose to trust the other person with the defence of the action, he may, if he pleases, go on and defend it, and then, if a verdict is obtained against him, and judgment signed upon it, … that judgment, in the case of [an] express contract of indemnity is conclusive. But … it is conclusive on account of what the law considers the true meaning of such a contract of indemnity to be.'

Mellish LJ said that in the absence of an express contract the requirements for mutuality would apply[4]. This exception only applies as between the parties to such a contract[5]. A debenture holder sued an assignee of the company's property[6] to enforce the debentures and relied on a *res judicata* estoppel against the company said to be binding on the assignee because it had agreed to indemnify the company. Romer J said[7]:

> ' … it was said that in as much as the [company] defended with the knowledge and approval of the [defendant] the latter would be estopped under their covenant of indemnity from disputing the judgment as against the [company] suing them on the express covenant of indemnity. That is quite true. But this is not an action on the covenant of indemnity. The estoppel last referred to is only between the party indemnifying and the party indemnified … In the present case not only are the [company] not suing, but they are not even parties to the action. The plaintiffs are suing the [assignee] on grounds which, the plaintiffs maintain, make the [assignee] directly liable to them, and not merely to the [company]. In such an action I can find no grounds for estoppel merely because the [assignee] may be estopped as against the [company] if and when the latter sue on their covenant of indemnity'.

A principal creditor who has failed on the merits in an action against the principal debtor, except on a ground such as bankruptcy or limitation, cannot recover against the surety. This flows from the contract, and not from a *res judicata* estoppel, because the liability of the surety is secondary and collateral to that of the principal debtor.

[1]   *Pritchard v Hitchcock* (1843) 6 Man & G 151 (payment by debtor set aside as fraudulent preference, judgment not conclusive against surety); *King v Norman* (1847) 4 CB 884; *Parker v Lewis* (1873) 8 Ch App 1035, 1059–1060; *Gracechurch Holdings Pty Ltd v Breeze* (1992) 7 WAR 518; *Lloyds Bank plc v Independent Insurance Co. Ltd* [2000] QB 110 CA, 126. A debtor company owned and controlled by sureties may be their privy: para 9.47.

2   *Re Kitchen, ex p Young* (1881) 17 Ch D 668; *The Vasso* [1979] 2 Lloyd's Rep 412; *Sun Life* [2005] 1 Lloyds Rep 606 CA, 624, 629; *Sabah Shipyard (Pakistan) Ltd v Islamic Republic of Pakistan* [2008] 1 Lloyds Rep 210.

3   *Parker v Lewis* (1873) 8 Ch App 1035, 1059; *Duffield v Scott* (1789) 3 TR 374, 377; *Smith v Compton* (1832) 3 B & Ad 407; *Jones v Williams* (1841) 7 M & W 493; *Ben Shipping Co. (Pte) Ltd v An Bord Bainne, The C Joyce* [1986] 2 All ER 177, 185–187; *London Guarantee and Accident Co v Davidson* [1926] 1 DLR 66, 70.

4   *Parker v Lewis* (1873) 8 Ch App 1035, 1059.

5   *Mercantile Investment and General Trust Co. v River Plate Trust, Loan and Agency Co* [1894] 1 Ch 578 (*Mercantile Investment*).

6   There was no privity because the assignment predated the judgment: para 9.41.

7   Ibid at 595–596.

LIABILITY INSURANCE AND REINSURANCE

9.28 Policies of insurance against liability to third parties commonly provide that the insurer will indemnify the insured against all sums which he becomes legally liable to pay[1]. Under such policies the obligation to indemnify arises when the insured's liability has been established by judgment or award[2]. The insurer promises to pay in that event, and the insured only has to prove the judgment or award. This flows from the contract and not from a *res judicata* estoppel[3]. These principles do not apply to contracts of reinsurance strictly so called, which insure the risk originally insured, not the interest of the reinsured under the original insurance[4]. The reinsured must prove that it was liable to the insured and all defences available to the former are available to the reinsurer[5]. Such policies are not liability policies[6] and the reinsured cannot prove its case against the reinsurer by simply proving the judgment or award in favour of the insured. 'Follow the settlements'[7] or 'follow the fortunes' clauses[8] change the nature of the reinsurer's obligation. Nevertheless, with some qualifications, a judgment or award against the reinsured is strong *prima facie* evidence against the reinsurer[9]. An insured who relies on a judgment or award must take it as a whole and is not free to relitigate against the insurer adverse findings fundamental to the judgment or award. Where the reckless conduct of the insured attracted an award of exemplary damages, and the material findings established a breach of a condition in the policy[10], the insured could not challenge those findings[11].

1   *Post Office v Norwich Union Fire Insurance Society Ltd* [1967] 2 QB 363 CA; *Bradley v Eagle Star Insurance Co. Ltd* [1989] AC 957, 966; *Cacciola v Fire and All Risks Insurance Ltd* (1971) 1 NSWLR 691 CA; *CE Heath Casualty and General Insurance Ltd v Pyramid Building Society* [1997] 2 VR 256 CA, 273, 294.

2   *Post Office v Norwich Union Fire Insurance Society Ltd* [1967] 2 QB 363 CA, 373–374, 375; *Brice v JH Wackerbarth (Australasia) Pty Ltd* [1974] 2 Lloyds Rep 274 CA, 275–276; *Cacciola v Fire and All Risks Insurance Ltd* [1971] 1 NSWLR 691 CA, 695. Subject to the terms of the policy and the conduct of the insurer it may be possible for legal liability to be established by a settlement.

3   *Parker v Lewis* (1873) 8 Ch App 1056, 1059. Just as an insurer may contract itself out of the benefit of an estoppel from a decision in rem (para 10.31 n 3), an insurer may contract to accept a decision to which it was not a party: *Aetna Insurance Co. v Canadian Surety Co.* (1994) 19 Alb LR (3d) 317 CA, 336.

4   *Commercial Union Assurance Co plc v NRG Victory Reinsurance Ltd* [1998] 2 All ER 434 CA, 444, 446 (*Commercial Union*).

5   Ibid at 441–442.

6   *Wasa International Insurance Co Ltd v Lexington Insurance Co* [2009] 3 WLR 575 paras [32], [33] (*Wasa*).

7   *Commercial Union* [1998] 2 All ER 434 CA, 44; *Wasa* [2009] 3 WLR 575 HL para [37].
8   *Hayter v Nelson and Home Insurance Co* [1970] 2 Lloyds Rep 265, 271–272.
9   *Commercial Union* [1998] 2 All ER 434 CA, 448–449. The court must be a court of competent jurisdiction, there must be no breach of a jurisdiction clause in the original policy, all proper defences must be taken, and in the case of a foreign judgment it must not be manifestly perverse. In *Wasa* [2009] 3 WLR 575 para [37] Lord Mance expressed reservations about this part of that decision
10 The insured 'shall take all reasonable precautions to prevent bodily injury ... and shall take reasonable measures to maintain all premises ... appliances and plant in a sound condition ...'.
11 *VACC Insurance Ltd v BP Australia Ltd* (1999) 47 NSWLR 716 CA, 724–725.

CHILDREN

9.29 An infant who sued or defended by his litigation friend can take the benefit, and must bear the burden, of an estoppel[1] both before and after his majority[2]. There is no estoppel unless the infant was represented by a litigation friend[3]. The objection that an infant, approaching his majority, purported to act without a litigation friend may be capable of being waived by a defendant[4] but this has been doubted[5] Proof that the infant was not represented by a litigation friend in the earlier proceedings should defeat any issue estoppels but there would be a cause of action estoppel unless the judgment could be set aside.

1   *Gregory v Molesworth* (1747) 3 Atk 626; *Don v Lippman* (1837) 5 Cl & Fin 1; *Shedden v Patrick* (1854) 1 Macq 535 HL, 588; *Vaughton v Bradshaw* (1869) 9 CBNS 103.
2   *Venkata Narasimha Appa Row v The Court of Wards* (1886) 11 App Cas 660.
3   *Rhodes v Swithenbank* (1889) 22 QBD 577 CA; *Arabian v Tuffmall & Taylor Ltd* [1944] KB 685; *C v Hackney London Borough Council* [1996] 1 WLR 789 CA; *Dey v Victorian Rly Comrs* (1949) 78 CLR 62, 82–84, 85, 100, 112–115; cf *John* [1965] P 289 (infant co-respondent did not appear, decree voidable). The procedure is governed by UCPR Part 21.
4   *Re Brocklebank, ex p Brocklebank* (1877) 6 Ch D 358 CA.
5   *Dey v Victorian Rly Comrs* (1949) 78 CLR 62, 114–115.

PROTECTED (INCAPABLE) PERSONS

9.30 An adult unable to make decisions for himself[1] (incapable person) lacks the capacity to retain a solicitor if he cannot understand the nature of the acts he would be authorising[2]. Attempts by an incapable person to conduct proceedings in person are liable to be set aside as fundamentally irregular. When a deputy is appointed under s 16 of the Mental Capacity Act 2005 or its equivalent, the incapable person is deprived of the legal capacity to instruct a solicitor while the order remains in force[3]. Any existing retainer is automatically revoked, whether the solicitor knows of the order or not[4]. An incapable person must conduct legal proceedings through a litigation friend even if an order is not in force[5]. The position where an incapable person retains a solicitor, appears in person, or fails to appear and the matter proceeds to judgment is not clear. The question arose in *Balloqui*[6]. The wife, although duly served, did not appear and a decree absolute was pronounced. She applied by her next friend to have the decrees set aside. She was an incapable person at the relevant time but under the rules had the onus of showing that the husband or his solicitors knew or had reasonable grounds for believing this[7]. She failed to discharge that onus but the court suggested that if she had done so it would have had power to set aside the proceedings as irregular[8].

1   Mental Capacity Act 2005 s 3.
2   *Murphy v Doman* (2003) 58 NSWLR 51 CA, 58.
3   Para 10.12.
4   *Yonge v Toynbee* [1910] 1 KB 215 CA, 216, 229, 231, 235. An order operates in rem: para 10.12.
5   *Richmond v Branson & Son* [1914] 1 Ch 968.
6   [1964] 1 WLR 82 CA.
7   Ibid at 89, 90, 91; cf as to contracts in such circumstances: *Hart v O'Connor* [1985] AC 1000.
8   Ord 70 r 1. There is no corresponding rule in the CPR, but the previous rule was probably declaratory.

9.31 If an order is not in force and a person known to be incapable commences proceedings without a litigation friend the claimant is not before the court. If the claimant's solicitors and the defendant and his solicitors have no reason to suspect that the claimant is an incapable person was treated as capable, and as a result the proceedings should be valid in accordance with *Hart v O'Connor*[1]. In *Murphy v Doman*[2] the incapable person had been denied a proper hearing and since the defendant and his solicitors suspected the truth a rehearing was ordered. Proof that an incapable person was not represented by a litigation friend should defeat any issue estoppels but there would be a cause of action estoppel unless the judgment could be set aside.

1   [1985] AC 1000.
2   (2003) 58 NSWLR 51 CA.

NON-PARTIES AFFECTED BY JUDGMENTS

9.32 A person who is neither a party nor a privy may find his rights affected by litigation between others, not because of an estoppel, but because he must accept facts created by the judgment. Where the court determined the rights of beneficiaries in an estate the Revenue, although not a party, was bound to assess in accordance with those rights[1]. In *Green v New River Co*[2]. the court held that a judgment against an employer based on his vicarious liability was admissible against the negligent servant in an action for breach of contract but only to prove the employer's loss. An award in favour of sub-charterers against charterers was admissible against the disponent owners to quantify the damages suffered by the charterers as a result of the owner's breach of contract[3].

1   *Executor Trustee and Agency Co. v DCT* (1939) 62 CLR 545, 562–3, 570; para 13.09.
2   (1792) 4 Term Rep 589; approved in *Hollington v F Hewthorn & Co. Ltd* [1943] KB 587 CA, 597 (*Hollington*); *Lister v Romford Ice and Cold Storage Co. Ltd* [1957] AC 555, 573, 597.
3   *Sun Life* [2005] 1 Lloyds Rep 606 CA, 625.

9.33 The effect of judgments on strangers in the context of double insurance was considered in *Drake Insurance plc v Provident Insurance plc*[1]. Mrs K, when driving her husband's car, injured a motorcyclist, and was sued for damages. She was covered by a policy with Drake and by her husband's policy with Provident but both contained rateable contribution clauses[2]. An arbitrator held that Provident had avoided its policy for non–disclosure. Drake settled and sought contribution. It argued that it could ignore the award to establish that Provident was a co-insurer, but rely on it to show why it had to pay the claim in full. Clarke LJ said that this apparent contradiction did not matter. As between Mrs K and Drake there was 'no other existing insurance' because of the award[3]. Mance LJ has approved[4] the decision of Clarke LJ that under such a clause what mattered 'was the position as it actually existed'.

1   [2004] QB 601 CA (*Drake*).
2   Ibid at 643. The clause in Drake's policy read: 'If at any time ... there is any other existing insurance covering the same loss ...'. The clause in the Provident policy was similar.
3   Ibid at 644. Rix LJ was inclined to agree (at 638) but preferred to decide the case on another ground.
4   *Sun Life* [2005] 1 Lloyds Rep 606 CA, 626, 631.

9.34 In *Sun Life*[1] the Court of Appeal held that an award between Sun Life and Cigna a reinsurer, which established that certain risks were covered by the latter, was neither binding nor admissible against Sun Life in an arbitration against Lincoln, another reinsurer, to establish that those risks were excluded from Lincoln's cover by a net retained lines clause[2]. Mance LJ held[3] that the clause did not make the award a relevant fact. However a judgment or award in favour of Sun Life against Cigna would have established as a fact that the subject risks had not been retained. *Mulkerrins* is another example[4]. The claimant alleged that the negligence of her accountants caused her bankruptcy. The bankruptcy court held that her cause of action had not vested in her trustee for the benefit of her creditors but the accountants had not been parties. Lord Millett said[5]:

> '[The defendants] are not ... bound by the order ... But this does not mean that they can simply ignore it or that they are unaffected by it ... [R]ight or wrong ... the order bound the trustee and through him the creditors. Ms Mulkerrins' claim must be taken to form no part of the bankrupt estate available to her creditors, and she is at liberty to pursue it in her own name and for her own benefit.'

Lord Walker said[6]:

> 'If the trustee in bankruptcy, as the only possible rival claimant, was bound by the order, its practical effect was not open to challenge.'

Another recent example is *Ali v Pattnii*[7] where a judgment in Kenya against a vendor for specific performance of a contract for the sale of shares in a Manx company was enforceable against the company on an application for rectification of its share register although it had not been a party. In actions for malicious prosecution, malicious arrest and false imprisonment a judgment in favour of the claimant in the original proceedings is an essential element of the cause of action, but the defendant need not be a party to those proceedings. In *Gilding v Eyre* the court said[8]:

> 'It is a rule of law, that no one shall be allowed to allege of a still depending suit that it is unjust. This can only be decided by a judicial determination, or other final event of the suit in the regular course of it. That is the reason given in the

cases which established the doctrine that in actions for a malicious arrest or prosecution, or the like, it is requisite to state in the declaration the determination of the former suit in favour of the plaintiff, because the want of probable cause cannot otherwise be properly alleged.'

In *Castrique v Behrens* Crompton J said[9]:

'... in such an action it is essential to shew that the proceeding alleged to be instituted maliciously and without probable cause has terminated in favour of the plaintiff ... The reason seems to be that, if in the proceeding complained of the decision was against the plaintiff, and was still unreversed, it would not be consistent with the principles on which the law is administered for another court, not being a court of appeal, to hold that the decision was come to without reasonable and probable cause.'

Actions for negligence against lawyers for the accused are *prima facie* abusive unless the conviction has been set aside[10]. This depends on the prohibition against collateral attacks and the futility of attempting to recover damages for being properly convicted and sentenced for a crime. Detention authorised by law can affect the damages recoverable by the detainee for a prior tort, especially if he has been sentenced for a criminal offence[11]. The deprivation is a fact, but its legal consequences depends on the order which authorised it[12].

1 *Sun Life* [2005] 1 Lloyds Rep 606 CA.
2 The Cigna policy had been avoided but the risks it 'covered' had not been retained by Sun Life for the purposes of the net retained clause in the Lincoln policy.
3 Ibid at 626 para [62].
4 [2003] 1 WLR 1937 HL.
5 Ibid at 1941, 1942.
6 Ibid at 1951.
7 [2007] 2 AC 85.
8 (1861) 10 CB NS 592, 604.
9 (1861) 3 E & E 709, 721; *Basebe v Matthews* (1867) LR 2 CP 684, 688; *Huffer v Allen* (1866) LR 2 Ex Ch 15. In *Bynoe v Bank of England* [1902] 1 KB 467 CA, 470 Collins MR said: 'that as long as a conviction stands no one against whom it is producible shall be permitted to aver against it;' *Commonwealth Life Assurance Society Ltd v Smith* (1938) 59 CLR 527, 538–540 per Rich, Dixon, Evatt and McTiernan JJ; *Everett v Ribbands* [1952] 2 QB 198 CA, 202; *Van Heeren v Cooper* [1999] 1 NZLR 731 CA, 737–740.
10 *Arthur JS Hall & Co. v Simons* [2002] 1 AC 615, 679, 685, 706, 727, 730, 752 (*Arthur Hall*); paras 11.02 n 6, 26.07–26.08.
11 For example, a hospital order under Mental Health legislation.
12 *Gray v Thames Trains Ltd* [2009] 3 WLR 167 HL established that a civil court will not compensate a claimant for a loss or disadvantage imposed as punishment; para 11.02 n 7.

NON-PARTIES BOUND BY STATUTE

9.35 A statute may make a court order binding on persons who are not parties[1]. Section 425 of the Companies Act 1985 makes a scheme of arrangement sanctioned by the court binding on the company, its shareholders and creditors, and means what it says[2]. Where the scheme included agreements with third parties they could not be challenged as *ultra vires*[3]. Section 204(1) of the Law of Property Act 1925 provides that an order of the court is not invalid as against a purchaser for want of jurisdiction or otherwise, whether the purchaser has notice or not[4]. Another well known example was s 6(1)(c) of the 1935 Act which provided:

'(c)   Any tortfeasor liable in respect of that damage may recover contribution from any other tortfeasor who is, or would if sued have been liable in respect of the same damage …'

The word 'liable' where it first appeared was said by Viscount Simonds and Lord Tucker to include a person held liable by judgment[5] a construction adopted by the High Court of Australia[6]. Proof that a plaintiff had recovered judgment against a tortfeasor entitled the latter, without any other proof of its liability, to claim contribution from a joint or concurrent tortfeasor who was not a party to the original proceedings. A judgment in favour of a defendant on a limitation defence bound other tortfeasors who could not claim contribution from that defendant although it would otherwise have been liable[7]. A consent judgment in favour of a tortfeasor is binding on other joint or concurrent tortfeasors in the same way[8]. Dismissal of an action against a tortfeasor for want of prosecution is not a final judgment and does not bar a contribution claim[9].

[1]   Para 10.09.
[2]   *Nicholl v Eberhardt Co. Ltd* (1888) 59 LT 860 (Ch D); (1889) 1 Meg 402 CA.
[3]   *British and Commonwealth Holdings plc v Barclays Bank plc* [1996] 1 WLR 1 CA.
[4]   Para 10.15. The section does not make an order binding on others, or give it greater effect than it appears to have: *Jones v Barnett* [1900] 1 Ch 370 CA; para 4.04 n 9.
[5]   *George Wimpey & Co. Ltd v British Overseas Airways Corpn* [1955] AC 169, 178, 192 (BOAC).
[6]   *Bitumen and Oil Refineries (Australia) Ltd v Commissioner for Government Transport* (1955) 92 CLR 200, 212; *Brambles Constructions Pty Ltd v Helmers* (1966) 114 CLR 213.
[7]   *BOAC* [1955] AC 169; *County of Parkland No 31 v Stetar* [1975] 2 SCR 884, 896–897.
[8]   *James Hardie & Co. Pty Ltd v Seltsam Pty Ltd* (1998) 196 CLR 53; para 2.19.
[9]   *Hunt v Hall & Pickles Ltd* [1969] 1 QB 405 CA.

9.36 Section 1(1) of the Civil Liability (Contribution) Act 1978 (the 1978 Act), which replaced the 1935 Act, provides:

'… any person liable in respect of any damage suffered by another person may recover contribution from any other person liable in respect of the same damage …'.

There is every reason for giving the word 'liable' where it first appears there the meaning favoured for s 6(1)(c) of the 1935 Act. Section 1(5) is also relevant:

'A judgment given in any action brought in any part of the United Kingdom by or on behalf of the person who suffered the damage in question against any person from whom contribution is sought under this section shall be conclusive in the proceedings for contribution as to any issue determined by that judgment in favour of the person from whom the contribution is sought'.

It applies to an action against a defendant *from* whom contribution is sought, and not to an action against a defendant who later seeks contribution. It only operates *in favour of* the party from whom contribution is sought. Consequently a judgment for that 'tortfeasor' on the merits binds other tortfeasors and bars any claim for contribution. Although a judgment for a defendant on limitation or other procedural grounds is within s 1(5) it would not establish that the defendant was not liable in respect of the same damage within s 1(1).

This is consistent with s 1(3) which provides that a limitation defence which does not extinguish the right does not affect the tortfeasor's liability for contribution under s 1(1). Thus[1] the 1978 Act displaced the result in BOAC[2].

[1]   *Nottingham Health Authority v Nottingham County Council* [1988] 1 WLR 903 CA, 906.
[2]   [1955] AC 169.

9.37 Section 1(1) of the Fatal Accidents Act 1976 provides:

> 'If death is caused by any wrongful act, neglect or default which is such as would (if death had not ensued) have entitled the person injured to maintain an action and recover damages in respect thereof, the person who would have been liable if death had not ensued shall be liable to an action for damages, notwithstanding the death of the person injured.'

The statute confers a new cause of action based on the death which the deceased could never have enforced[1], provided he could have maintained an action if death had not ensued. Judgment recovered by the deceased bars any action by or on behalf of his dependants after his death[2], as does a judgment for the defendant[3] or a release by the victim in his lifetime[4].

[1]   *The Vera Cruz* (1884) 10 App Cas 59, 67, 70.
[2]   *Pickett v British Rail Engineering Ltd* [1980] AC 136, 146, 152.
[3]   *Noall v Middleton* [1961] VR 285, 288; *Scala v Mammolitti* (1965) 114 CLR 153, 161.
[4]   *Cable Estate v Ferguson* (2008) 301 DLR (4th) 746.

PRIVIES (GENERAL)

9.38 *Res judicata* estoppels operate for or against privies of the parties in blood, title or interest[1] for the reasons explained by Cababe[2]:

> '... although the estoppel is only a personal matter between the particular parties yet to really give the parties the benefit of it, and subject them to the burden of it, it is essential that not they only, but those of whom it can be predicted that they are their representatives in interest, should likewise have the benefit of and be subject to the burden of the [estoppel]. Upon any one therefore upon whom all the rights and obligations of any legal entity devolved such as an executor, administrator or trustee in bankruptcy, there will devolve as one of such rights and obligations, the right to exact or the obligation to be subjected to, the [estoppel], and so too upon anyone upon whom the right and obligations arising out of a particular transaction that gave rise to the estoppel devolve, as, for example, a purchaser or assignee, that will also devolve this right and this obligation.'

Privies include any person who succeeds to the rights or liabilities of a party on death[3], insolvency[4], by assignment or by statute, or who is otherwise identified in estate or interest[5]. The party estopped by privity must have some interest, legal or beneficial, in the previous litigation or its subject matter[6], and accordingly assignees are privies of the assignor[7]. Privity was described by the US Supreme Court as a mutual or successive relationship to the same right of property[8], although this cannot be exhaustive. Privity is a matter of substance, not form[9].

[1]   *Carl-Zeiss (No.2)* [1967] 1 AC 853, 909–910.

2 *Cababe 'Principles of Estoppel'* (1888) at 111–113 cited by Starke J in *Partridge v McIntosh & Sons Ltd* (1933) 49 CLR 453–463. This passage in the 3rd edn was cited in *Powell v Wiltshire* [2005] QB 117 CA, 123, 130. A *res judicata* estoppel is a substantive right: paras 1.08–1.09.

3 *Douglas v Forest* (1828) 4 Bing 686; *Don v Lippman* (1837) 5 Cl & Fin 1; *Holland v Clark* (1842) 1 Y & C Ch Cas 151; *Reimers v Druce* (1857) 26 LJ Ch 196; *Innis v Rochford* (1884) 14 LR Ir 285; *Barrs v Jackson* (1845) 1 Ph 582 (residuary legatee); *Whittaker v Jackson* (1864) 2 H & C 926 (devisee).

4 *Douglas v Forest* (1828) 4 Bing 686 (assignees entitled to estoppel); *Re South American and Mexican Co, ex p Bank of England* [1895] 1 Ch 37 CA (liquidator liable to estoppel).

5 *R v Blakemore* (1852) 21 LJMC 60 (privy in estate); *Re Allsop and Joy's Contract* (1889) 61 LT 213 (successor in title); *North Eastern Rly Co. v Dalton Overseers* [1898] 2 QB 66 (successors of highway authority); *O'Connor* [1916] 2 IR 148 (sucessors in title); *Jones v Lewis* [1919] 1 KB 328 CA (successor in office).

6 *Carl-Zeiss* (*No.2*) [1967] 1 AC 853, 910; *Effem Foods* (1992) 43 FCR 510, 540–542.

7 *Kolden Holdings Ltd v Rodette Commerce Ltd)* [2008] Bus LR 1051 CA, 1073 (citing this passage from the 3rd edn).

8 *Bigelow v Old Dominion Copper Mining Co.* 225 US 111 (1912), 128–129.

9 *MCC Proceeds Inc* [1998] 4 All ER 675 CA, 695–696.

PRIVITY OF ESTATE

9.39 Where privity of estate exists, a judgment binding on the assignor is binding on the assignee. There are three possible situations, the judgment may predate the assignment, the assignment may occur while the action is pending or the judgment may postdate the assignment. An assignee who acquired his interest before the proceedings against his assignor were commenced is not bound by the judgment. The question arose in *Doe d Foster v Earl of Derby*[1]. The Earl claimed under a conveyance in 1823 by Henry Foster as heir of Mary Travers. In 1834 in an action of ejectment against Thomas Foster, who also claimed to be the heir of Mary Travers, counsel for the Earl tendered the evidence of a witness, since deceased, given in 1830 in an ejectment action between Henry Foster and Thomas Foster relating to a different estate owned by Mary Travers at the date of her death. The estate acquired by the Earl in 1823 was not, in any sense, 'represented' in the 1830 litigation. The evidence was rejected and Littledale J said[2]:

> 'A passage has been cited from Com. Dig. Evidence … where it is said that "a verdict in another action for the same cause shall be allowed in evidence between the same parties so, it shall be evidence, where the verdict was for one under whom any of the present parties claim." But that must mean a claim acquired through such party subsequently to the verdict: if, as has been now argued, the rule could be extended to parties claiming other lands under the same title previously to the verdict the effect of such verdicts might be carried back for 100 years.'

1 (1834) 1 Ad & El 783.
2 Ibid at 790; *Hodson v Walker* (1872) LR 7 Ex ch 55, 61.

9.40 This was treated as settled law by the Privy Council in 1948[1] where Sir John Beaumont said:

> 'It is contended that appellants 2 and 3 are bound by the decree in the former suit because they claim through Din Mohammad who was a party to that suit. But the answer to this contention is that the alienations under which appellants

2 and 3 claimed were made before the date of the former suit. Those appellants therefore do not claim under a party to the former suit who represented their interests in that suit, but under a person who subsequently became a party, and who at the time of the suit did not represent their interests. Their Lordships think that appellants 2 and 3 ... are not affected by the plea of *res judicata*.'

The position is also clear where the judgment predates the assignment as Madden J said[2]:

'According to the clear principles of the law of estoppel it is necessary, in order to estop the [assignee], to show that he derives title under [the assignor] by act or operation of law subsequent to the recovery of the judgment. If this is shown it is reasonable that he should be estopped, because his estate was represented at the time of the recovery of the judgment, though not in his person.'

This was approved in *Powell v Wiltshire*[3], where the assignment occurred during pending litigation. These decisions are consistent with the principle that an assignor cannot[4] 'by any statement ... after he had parted with his interest, make evidence against the title of the party to whom he had conveyed.' In the same way the admissions of a husband after the marriage that he was already married and his first wife was alive, were not admissible to invalidate the marriage or bastardise the children[5].

[1] *Beli Ram v Chandri Mohammad Afzal* [1948] AIR (PC) 168, 171. The Board included Lord Normand and Lord MacDermott.
[2] *In Re De Burgho's Estate* [1896] 1 IR 274, 280 (real estate); *Re Walton* (1873) 28LT 12, 16; para 9.14 nn 3–4.
[3] [2005] QB 117 CA, 126, 128, 132 (personal property).
[4] *Roe of Lord Trimelstown v Kemmis* (1843) 9 Cl & F 749, 779.
[5] *Dysart Peerage Case* (1881) 6 App Cas 489, 499–500.

LIS PENDENS

9.41 An alienation of real, but not personal property, while litigation is pending, attracts the *lis pendens* principle. Alienations of personal property are governed by the general principle that a judgment against the vendor only binds the purchaser if it predates the assignment[1]. The doctrine of *lis pendens* as it affected real estate or chattels real was summarised by Lord Cranworth LC in *Bellamy v Sabine*[2]:

'Where a litigation is pending ... as to ... a particular estate, the necessities of mankind require that the decision of the Court in the suit shall be binding, not only on the litigant parties, but also on those who derive title under them by alienations pending the suit, whether such alienees had or had not notice of the pending proceedings. If this were not so there could be no certainty that the litigation would ever come to an end. A mortgage or sale made before final decree to a person who had no notice of the pending proceedings would always render a new suit necessary, and ... interminable litigation might be the consequence.'

In the same case Turner LJ said[3]:

'The doctrine of *lis pendens* is not ... founded upon any of the peculiar tenets of a Court of Equity as to implied or constructive notice. It is ... a doctrine common to the Courts both of Law and of Equity, and rests ... upon the foundation that it would plainly be impossible that any action or suit could be brought to a successful termination if alienations *pendente lite* were permitted to prevail. The plaintiff would be liable in every case to be defeated before the judgment or decree, and would be drawn to commence his proceedings *de novo*, subject again to being defeated by the same course of proceeding.'

[1]   *Wigram v Buckley* [1894] 3 Ch 483 CA; *Powell v Wiltshire* [2005] QB 117 CA.
[2]   (1857) 1 De G & J 566, 578. (The alienation pre-dated the Judgments Act 1839); *Damodaran s/o Raman v Choe Kuan Him* [1980] AC 497, 503.
[3]   (1857) 1 De G&J 566, 584.

9.42 The doctrine operated harshly on bona fide purchasers without notice and Parliament intervened in 1839[1]. The Judgments Act s 7 established a system for the registration of pending actions or suits and provided that 'no *lis pendens* shall bind a Purchaser or Mortgagee without express Notice thereof unless and until' a memorandum or minute thereof had been duly recorded in the Court of Common Pleas. The position with land under common law title is now governed by the Land Charges Act 1972. Section 5(1)(a) provides for a register of pending land actions[2], and subs (7) provides that such an action shall not bind the purchaser without express notice unless it is for the time being registered under the section[3]. A pending land action affecting registered land will not prevent its alienation unless the claimant entered notice of his action in the register. If this is done a subsequent registered disposition is postponed to the interest protected by the notice[4]. The Torrens system of title by registration excludes the *lis pendens* doctrine and the claimant in a pending action must lodge a caveat[5].

[1]   2 & 3 Vict c 11.
[2]   The action must be capable of binding the land: *Mercantile Investment* [1894] 1 Ch 578, 595.
[3]   *Perez-Adamson v Perez-Revas* [1987] Fam 89 CA (mortgagee without notice bound by registered pending action).
[4]   Land Registration Act 2002 ss 34(1), (2)(b); 35; 87(1)(c).
[5]   *Damodaran s/o Raman v Choe Kuan Him* [1980] AC 497, 503, 504; *ACC Bank plc v Markham* [2007] 3 IR 533.

PRIVITY IN INTEREST

9.43 A landlord is not the privy of a tenant unless the latter litigates with his authority[1]. A mortgagee who has not adopted a tenancy is not a privy of the mortgagor as landlord[2]. Receivers appointed by mortgagees of a leasehold (and thus agents of the mortgagor) were privies of the mortgagor as lessee[3]. Children, not claiming through their mother as administratrix of their deceased father, but as next of kin to others are not privies of their father and cannot set up a judgment obtained by their mother as administratrix[4]. Children are not privies of parents or grandparents when their claims to share in a gift to issue per capita compete with those of their ancestors[5]. Parties who claim under a common ancestor are not estopped *inter se* by a decision between their ancestor and a stranger[6].

[1]   *Lady Wenman v McKenzie* (1855) 5 E & B 447, 458–459; para 9.16.
[2]   *Clarke v Hall* (1888) 24 LR Ir 316.
[3]   *Official Custodian for Charities v Mackey (No. 2)* [1985] 1 WLR 1308 (judgment for *mesne* profits against lessee barred landlord claiming higher rate from receivers).

4   *Spencer v Williams* (1871) LR 2 P&D 230.
5   *Re Manly's Will Trusts (No. 2)* [1976] 1 All ER 673.
6   *De Mora v Concha* (1885) 29 Ch D 268 CA, 305; *Syed Ashgar Reza Khan v Syed Mohamed Khan* (1903) LR 30 Ind App 71, 75.

9.44 A *res judicata* estoppel against the beneficiary binds the trustee by privity of interest and *vice versa*, and a *res judicata* estoppel binding on former trustees binds the new[1]. Different legal personal representatives for the same estate in different jurisdictions are privies[2]. Privity of interest exists where a party bound by an estoppel employs a servant or agent in an attempt to relitigate the question[3]. It is not enough that a relationship of principal and agent exists between a party to the earlier action, and the party sought to be estopped, if it is not binding on the latter. In *Pople v Evans*[4] C as the undisclosed agent of P entered into a contract for sale and, without disclosing the relationship, brought an action for specific performance against E which was dismissed for want of prosecution. P was not estopped from seeking the same relief[5].

1   *Churchill and Sim v Goddard* [1937] 1 KB 92 CA, 103–104; *Gleeson* [1977] 1 WLR 510, 515; *Cromwell v County of Sac* 94 US 351 (1876); *Young v Murphy* [1996] 1 VR 279 CA, 285–287.
2   *Carvel* [2008] Ch 395, 406–407.
3   Paras 9.14–9.16.
4   [1969] 2 Ch 255.
5   The estoppel also failed because the dismissal was not a final decision on the merits. The decision on the absence of privity is suspect. C held the benefit of the contract in trust for P (at 261) and this should have established privity. P would have been bound if he had allowed C to litigate the claim to a final decision on the merits. The rights of E appear irrelevant. C would hold the contract for the benefit of P even if E elected to hold C personally liable.

9.45 The privy must claim under, through, or on behalf of, the party bound. So it was held by the High Court of Australia that a judgment in favour of the driver did not create an estoppel in favour of his employer who had no interest in that action, and did not claim under or through his employee[1]. In *Reichel v Bishop of Oxford*[2] the House of Lords held that a former incumbent had resigned his parish. The patrons presented and the Bishop appointed a successor, but the former incumbent refused to leave. When the successor brought ejectment the defendant's plea that he was the incumbent was struck out as an abuse of process[3]. While this was clearly correct the question was *res judicata* because the plaintiff claimed under the patrons and the Bishop[4]. The first decision was also *in rem*, because it determined the status of the incumbent[5]. A party suing an agent who challenges his authority to act for a principal, cannot rely on a judgment against the principal which will only bind the agent if he is a privy[6]. Where a trade union secured a judicial interpretation of an industrial award, employees suing in their own right did not claim through or under the union, and were not its privies[7]. Where a trade union brought proceedings against trustees of a superannuation fund on behalf of its members, but not in a representative action, a member was bound as a privy of the union[8].

Privity is not established by proof of curiosity or concern about the litigation, or 'some interest in the outcome'[9]. Megarry VC proposed[10] as the test of privity, in cases outside any recognised category, the existence of 'a sufficient degree of identification between the two parties to make it just to hold that the decision to which one was party should be binding in proceedings to which the other was party'. This is circuitous and does not identify the necessary degree of identification[11] but was approved by Lord Bingham in *Johnson*[12]. A person who has relied on a decision, such as an incumbrancer who obtained stop orders on a fund in court, claims under the assignor and is a privy[13]. A person who has given financial assistance or an indemnity to a party does not become his privy[14]. However the principle in *Spring Gardens*[15] might establish privity if the indemnifier took a more active role. In Canada Lloyds names bound to indemnify banks which had opened letters of credit in favour of Lloyds were privies of the banks 'because they shared an identical interest in substance.'[16]

[1]   *Ramsay v Pigram* (1967) 118 CLR 271, 279–280, 282, 290; nor is the driver of a motor vehicle, without more, the privy of its owner: *Bryan v Kildangan Stud Unlimited* [2005] 1 IR 587. An employer who paid workers' compensation to an injured worker and sued a tortfeasor for indemnity does not claim through the worker and is not bound by a judgment in proceedings brought by the worker: *QBE Workers Compensation (NSW) v Dolan* (2004) 62 NSWLR 42 CA.
[2]   (1889) 14 App Cas 259.
[3]   *Reichel v Magrath* (1889) 14 App Cas 665; para 10.11 nn 3–4.
[4]   The view in the 3rd edn is now supported by *Arthur Hall* [2002] 1 AC 615, 701. In *R v York Corpn* (1792) 5 Term Rep 66, 72 Kenyon CJ said during argument that a judgment of ouster bound a person holding office under the vote of the ousted office holder.
[5]   Para 10.11.
[6]   *Carl-Zeiss* (No. 2) [1967] 1 AC 853. The defendant challenged the retainer of the solicitors, ie asserted in proceedings against them that they had no authority from the plaintiff to commence or carry on the proceedings. Lord Reid was surprised that the defendants thought their case could be assisted by a judgment against the plaintiff which would only bind the solicitors if they were privies (ibid at 910); *Carl-Zeiss (No.3)* [1970] Ch 506, 541.
[7]   *Young v Public Service Board* [1982] 2 NSWLR 456.
[8]   *Shiels v Blakeley* [1986] 2 NZLR 262 CA; *James v British Columbia* (2007) 288 DLR (4th) 380 BCCA.
[9]   *Gleeson* [1977] 1 WLR 510, 515. Plaintiffs in different class actions against the defendant, based on the same conduct, and represented by the same solicitors were not privies: *Currie v McDonald's Restaurants of Canada Ltd* (2005) 250 DLR (4th) 224 Ont. CA.
[10] Ibid at 515; *Sheils v Blackley* [1986] 2 NZLR 262 CA, 268.
[11] *Effem Foods* (1992) 36 FCR 406, 416; (1993) 43 FCR 510, 540–541; *Carl-Zeiss (No.3)* [1970] Ch 506, 541–542.
[12] [2002] 2 AC 1, 32.
[13] *Re Eyton* (1890) 45 Ch D 458.
[14] *Mercantile Investment* [1894] 1 Ch 578, 594–595; *Carl-Zeiss (No.2)* [1967] 1 AC 853, 911; *Gleeson* [1977] 1 WLR 510, 514.
[15] [1991] 1 QB 241 CA, 252–254; para 9.12.
[16] *Bank of Montreal v Mitchell* (1997) 143 DLR (4th) 697, 740; aff sub nom *Timmis v Toronto Dominion Bank* (1997) 151 DLR (4th) 574 CA Ont.

ESTOPPEL BY CONDUCT IN PROCEEDINGS

9.46 A party's conduct in legal proceedings may estop him adopting an inconsistent position in later proceedings. In *Kok Hoong* Viscount Radcliffe said[1] this was the basis of *Roe v Mutual Loan Fund Ltd*[2] and continued:

> '... a litigant may be shown to have acted positively in the face of the Court, making an election and procuring from it an order affecting others apart from

himself in such circumstances that the Court has no option but to hold him to his conduct and refuse to start again on the basis that he has abandoned.'

An estoppel of this kind has been found in a number of cases. In *Re Lart*[3] the beneficiary's husband[4], was aware of proceedings to determine the construction of a will, to which he should have been a party, and he benefited from a distribution of a share following the decision. He was estopped from contending for a different construction of the same language in relation to another share. *Gandy*[5] was a clear case. The husband successfully defended alimony proceedings relying on his obligations under a deed of separation. When the wife sued on the deed the husband relied on a different construction. Cotton LJ said[6]:

'It would be wrong ... to allow him to take advantage of a decision given on one construction ... and to give another decision in his favour on the ground that that was not the true construction'.

Bowen LJ was more forthright[7]:

' ... there would be monstrous injustice if the husband, having suggested one construction of the deed in the old suit and succeeding on that footing, were allowed to turn round and win the new suit upon a diametrically opposed construction of the same deed. It would be playing fast and loose with justice if the Court allowed that'.

The doctrine, known there as judicial estoppel, was applied by the US Supreme Court in *New Hampshire v Maine*[8]. Part of their boundary was fixed by a decree of George II in 1740. Disputes about the marine boundary led to litigation in 1977 which terminated in a consent judgment of the Supreme Court based on a construction of that decree. In 2000 New Hampshire brought proceedings to settle the inland river boundary relying on a different construction. Ginsburg J, writing for a unanimous court, said[9]:

'Where a party assumes a certain position in a legal proceeding, and succeeds in maintaining that position, he may not thereafter, simply because his interests have changed, assume a contrary position, especially if it is to the prejudice of the party who has acquiesced in the position formerly taken by him. ... [The] purpose is to protect the integrity of the judicial process by prohibiting parties from deliberately changing position according to the exigencies of the moment ... Several factors typically inform the decision whether to apply the doctrine ...: First, a party's later position must be "clearly inconsistent" with its earlier position. ... Second, ... whether the party has succeeded in persuading a Court to accept that party's earlier position, so that judicial acceptance of an inconsistent position in a later proceeding would create the perception that either the first or the second court was misled ... Absent success in a prior proceeding, a party's later inconsistent position introduces no risk of inconsistent court determinations ... A third consideration is whether the party ... would derive an unfair advantage or impose an unfair detriment on the opposing party if not estopped'.

This is no reason for thinking the law of England is different.

[1] [1964] AC 993, 1018.

2   (1887) 19 QBD 347 CA. The facts as summarised by Viscount Radcliffe: [1964] AC 993, 1018 were that the debtor gave a bill of sale on his furniture to secure an advance. He was made bankrupt on his own petition which showed the lenders as secured creditors under the bill of sale . They seized and sold the furniture and proved for the balance. A composition with creditors was sanctioned by the Court, and the debtor was released from his debts. He then sued the lenders for trespass alleging that the bill of sale was invalid. The court held that the plaintiff obtained an advantage by treating it as valid, and was not entitled to a further advantage by treating it as invalid.

3   *Re Lart* [1896] 2 Ch 788; *Nana Ofori* [1958] AC 95, 102.

4   The vesting occurred before the Married Women's Property Act.

5   (1885) 30 Ch D 57 CA; *B (MAL) v B (NE)* [1968] 1 WLR 1109, 1123–1124.

6   Ibid at 80. There may have been an issue estoppel, but this does not affect the principle.

7   Ibid at 82. Other cases include *Re Savoy Estate Ltd* [1949] Ch 622 CA, 634, 636; *Meng Leong Development Pty Ltd v Jip Hong Trading Co Pty Ltd* [1985] AC 511, 522, 525 (*Meng Leong*); *Nurcombe* [1985] 1 WLR 370 CA.

8   532 US 742 (2001).

9   Ibid at 749–751.

COMPANIES

9.47 Since privity of interest is a matter of substance, not form[1], courts have been prepared to pierce the corporate veil and recognise the substantial identity between a company and its controlling directors and shareholders. In *Johnson*[2] Lord Bingham held that Johnson and his company were privies: '[It] was the corporate embodiment of Johnson. He made decisions and gave instructions on its behalf.' This also applies to a parent and its subsidiaries[3]. There is no general principle that each company in a group is the privy of all others but privity may exist where two or more subsidiaries have a direct financial or proprietary interest in the litigation, eg where one holds the intellectual property and another uses it[4]. A company may also be the privy of its shareholders[5]. The principle is now widely accepted[6]. Representations to a company were relied on by its directors and associates who lent it money and guaranteed its obligations. They had independent causes of action and were not its privies[7]. The Supreme Court of Ireland has held that shareholder directors were not privies of the company if it had no interest in the proceedings against them[8], but they had been interested in the earlier proceedings against the company. It has been held in Canada that the sole director shareholder could not rely on a judgment in favour of the company because he would not have been personally liable if it had lost[9], but this has not previously been considered a test of privity.

1   Paras 9.14–9.16.

2   [2002] 2 AC 1, 32; *Carvel* [2008] Ch 395, 496–497.

3   *MCC Proceeds* [1998] 4 All ER 675 CA, 695–696.

4   *Special Effects* [2007] EWCA Civ 1371 para [82], (2007) 71 IPR 188, 210.

5   *Wire Supplies Ltd v CIR* [2006] 2 NZLR 384, 395–398; affirmed [2007] 3 NZLR 458 CA, 465.

6   *Effem Foods* (1993) 43 FCR 510, 542; *Shears v Chisholm* [1994] 2 VR 535, 545; *Laughland v Stevenson* [1995] 2 NZLR 474, 478; *420093 BC Ltd v Bank of Montreal* (1995) 128 DLR (4th) 488, 495–6 Alta CA; *Belton v Carlow County Council* [1997] 1 IR 172; *Nike International Ltd v Campomar Sociedad Limitada* [2005] 4 SLR 76.

7   *Effem Foods* (1993) 43 FCR 510, 533–534, 536–537.

8   *Belton v Carlow County Council* [1997] 1 IR 172 SC, 181–182.

9   *Keller v Glenko Enterprises Ltd* (2008) 290 DLR (4th) 712, 728 CA Man.

JOINT TORTFEASORS

9.48 Prior to the 1935 Act, judgment against one joint tortfeasor extinguished the liability of the others as the only cause of action merged in that judgment[1]; and there was no right of contribution[2]. An innocent principal, liable for the torts of his agent or employee, could claim an indemnity from that agent or employee as damages for breach of contract[3]. Similarly an innocent agent was entitled to be indemnified by his principal who, innocently or otherwise, instructed him to perform an unlawful act[4]. In the first situation there was no privity and the agent or employee was not bound by a judgment against the employer except on the quantum of damages[5]. In the second there was also no privity because a principal does not claim through or under his agent[6]. The effect of the judgment in fixing damages in these cases depends on the contract and its breach. At common law where the plaintiff failed against one joint tortfeasor on the merits, and not because of a personal defence, the others could probably rely on a cause of action estoppel because there was only one cause of action[7].

The 1935 and 1978 Acts enable a plaintiff who recovered judgment against one joint tortfeasor to obtain judgments against others in the same or a later action[8], but the first will cap the damages. Joint tortfeasors are not privies[9] without a special relationship[10]. Under the Acts, judgment for or against one joint tortfeasor does not create a cause of action or issue estoppel as between the claimant and others except where one would be vicariously liable for the torts of the first[11]. The Acts, by creating separate causes of action against each joint tortfeasor, have changed the effect at common law of a judgment on the merits in favour of a joint tortfeasor[12] except in cases of vicarious liability[13].

1 *Brinsmead v Harrison* (1872) LR 7 CP 547 Ex Ch.
2 *Merryweather v Nixon* (1799) 8 Term Rep 186.
3 *Green v New River Co* (1792) 4 Term Rep 589; para 9.32 n 2.
4 *Adamson v Jarvis* (1827) 4 Bing 66 (auctioneer sells goods of third party).
5 *Bigelow v Old Dominion Copper Mining and Smelting Co* 225 US 111 (1912), 131 (*Bigelow*): 'There is no privity between joint wrongdoers because all are jointly and severally liable.'
6 *Shaw v Sloan* [1982] NI 393 CA; *Ramsay v Pigram* (1967) 118 CLR 271, 279–280, 282, 290.
7 In *Phillips v Ward* (1863) 2 H & C 717, 720–721, the court held that judgment in favour of one joint contractor establishes a res judicata estoppel for the others if it was based on a ground common to all and not one personal to the defendant. In *Bigelow* (above) the Supreme Court held (at 127–128) that an innocent employer could not be vicariously liable if the agent or employee had been found not liable.
8 Section 6; *Wah Tat Bank Ltd v Chan Cheng Kum* [1975] AC 507 (*Wah Tat*).
9 *Ramsay v Pigram* (1967) 118 CLR 271, 288; *Thompson v Australian Capital Television Pty Ltd* (1996) 186 CLR 574, 584–585 (*Thompson*).
10 *Spring Gardens* [1991] 1 QB 241 CA. However a judgment in favour of a joint tortfeasor on the merits will bind the others in contribution proceedings: para 9.36.
11 Since an employer is not a privy of his employee the estoppel (n 7 above) will depend either on abuse of process, on the first judgment creating a fact which the claimant and the court cannot ignore, or possibly on the fact that the claimant will be claiming against the employer through the servant (paras 9.32–9.34). If an employer could be held liable after there has been a verdict for his employee he would be doubly prejudiced because he would not have a right of indemnity against his employee who has been sued and held not liable: *BOAC* [1955] AC 169. The 1935 Act abolished the common law rule that a cause of action against joint tortfeasors was one and indivisible: *Wah Tat* [1975] AC 507; *Thompson* (1996) 186 CLR 574. Accordingly a claimant who has released one joint

tortfeasor can now recover against another: *Thompson* (above) disapproving *Bryanston Finance Ltd v de Vries* [1975] QB 703 CA, 732; and the releasee would be subject to claims for contribution.

12 *Wah Tat* [1975] AC 507; *Thompson* (1996) 186 CLR 574.

13 The effect of a judgment against a tortfeasor suing as claimant, or sued as a defendant in creating issue estoppels in road traffic cases is considered in para 12.14.

IDENTITY OF INTEREST INSUFFICIENT

9.49 Persons with separate but identical interests in the same question are not privies. A trustee may have obligations to a class, but the members have their own interests, and are not privies of each other. Thus an interpretation of the trust instrument in proceedings in which only some members of a class are parties will not bind the others[1].

1 *Re Waring* [1948] Ch 221. The rules as to joinder of parties are intended to prevent such a situation; para 1.15.

Chapter 10

PARTIES II: DECISIONS IN REM

10.01 A decision *in rem* conclusively determines the status of a person or thing; that is its jural relation to persons generally, not just parties and privies[1]. It is sometimes said to be binding on the world, unlike decisions *in personam* which determine the jural relation of persons to each other[2]. References in this connection to the 'the world' cannot always be taken literally. Some decisions *in rem*, such as a grant of probate, only operate within the jurisdiction. Others, such as admiralty orders *in rem* have international effect. In *Ali v Pattni* Lord Mance said[3]: '... in order for a judgment to have *in rem* effect ... the determination must be a determination regarding the status or disposition of property which is to be valid as against the whole world. The fact that a judicial determination determines or relates to the existence of property rights between parties does not ... mean that it is *in rem*[4].' These expressions, taken from Roman law[5], with its distinction between a *jus in rem*, and a *jus in personam*, are not happily chosen. '*In rem*' is inappropriate in its literal sense of 'against a thing', because the *rem* may be a person. It would have been clearer if decisions had been classified *inter omnes*, and *inter partes*[6] – expressions that have been used by high judicial authorities[7].

1 *Minna Craig Steamship Co v Chartered Mercantile Bank of India, London and China* [1897] 1 QB 460 CA.
2 *P E Bakers Pty Ltd v Yehuda* (1988) 15 NSWLR 437 CA, 442.
3 [2007] 2 AC 85, 98.
4 The Singapore Court of Appeal held in *Chettiar v Low* [1998] 2 SLR 289 that a judgment in default of a defence that declared that the plaintiff had a possessory title and the defendant's title had been extinguished was a judgment *in rem*. The point was conceded ([1998] 2 SLR 289, 296). The judgment did not effect a disposition of the property, but merely declared the rights of the parties. The decision is doubtful.
5 Para 27.08.
6 This passage in the 3rd edition was cited in *Ali v Pattni* [2007] 2 AC 85, 98.
7 *Katama Natchier v Rajah of Shivagunga* (1863) 9 Moo Ind App 543, 601; *Castrique v Imrie* (1870) LR 4 HL 414, 435; *Gray v Lewis* (1873) 8 Ch App 1035, 1060; *R v Hutchings* (1881) 6 QBD 300 CA, 304; *Re Allsop and Joy's Contract* (1889) 61 LT 213, 215.

DECISION PARTLY IN REM, PARTLY IN PERSONAM

10.02 As Lord Mance has said[1]:

'There is no reason why an order should be characterised as either wholly in rem or wholly in personam … The extent … to which an order operates in part in rem and in part in personam is a matter of analysis …'

This is well-established in relation to divorce decrees[2].

[1]   *Ali v Pattni* [2007] 2 AC 85, 103.
[2]   *B v A-G (NEB Intervening)* [1965] P 278, 284; para 10.08 n 4.

10.03   Since a decision *in rem* is available for and against persons generally, one is not concerned with parties or privies[1], but all other conditions for a valid *res judicata* estoppel must be satisfied. A judgment *in rem* cannot be obtained by consent and such a judgment only operates *in personam*[2]. The *Henderson* principle was applied in proceedings to determine the status of a lane[3] and applies with added force to all proceedings *in rem*.

[1]   *Bernardi v Motteux* (1781) 2 Doug KB 575, 580 per Lord Mansfield: 'all the world are parties to a sentence of a court of admiralty'.
[2]   *Ali v Pattni* [2007] 2 AC 85, 98, 103, *Ritchie v Malcolm* [1902] 2 IR 403; *Jenkins v Robertson* (1867) LR 1 Sc & Div 117.
[3]   *L E Walwin & Partners Ltd v West Sussex County Council* [1975] 3 All ER 604.

SCOPE OF DECISION IN REM

10.04   A judgment *in rem* is conclusive as to the status of the person or thing but, except in prize cases[1], is not conclusive *in rem* as to the grounds of the decision. In *Castrique v Imrie* Blackburn J said[2]: 'A judgment … is not conclusive as to anything but the point decided.' In *Ballantyne v Mackinnon*[3] a salvage award established a maritime lien *in rem*, but against marine underwriters was not conclusive 'as to the grounds upon which it must have proceeded', that a peril of the sea created the need for the salvage services. In *Harvey v R*[4] the Privy Council held that orders in lunacy appointing a receiver of the income from the patient's property, and authorising her to defend proceedings against him, were evidence that the patient was incapable of managing his affairs but not conclusive because that finding was not about his status. In *Burden v Ainsworth*[5] the grant of the licence was a judgment *in rem* as to the status of the licensee, but the finding that its controlling director was a fit and proper person did not determine his status and was not conclusive[6].

[1]   The condemnation of a vessel as prize is a judgment *in rem*. Ordinarily the ground that the vessel was not a neutral, would not be binding *in rem* but in this situation it is: *Castrique v Imrie* (1870) LR 4 HL 414, 434–435; *Ballantyne v Mackinnon* [1896] 2 QB 455 CA, 467; para 10.22 nn 1 and 2.
[2]   (1870) LR 4 HL 414, 434.
[3]   [1896] 2 QB 455 CA, 461–463.
[4]   [1901] AC 601, 611 (*Harvey*).
[5]   *Burden v Ainsworth* (2004) 59 NSWLR 506 CA, 511–512.
[6]   Ibid at 512.

STATUS OF PERSONS

10.05   Status is 'the legal position of the individual in or with regard to the rest of the community'[1]; 'the condition of belonging to a class in society to which the law ascribes peculiar rights and duties, capacities and incapacities'[2], and 'a condition attached by law to a person which confers or affects or limits a legal capacity of exercising some power that under other circumstances he could not or could exercise without restriction'[3].

[1]   *Niboyet* (1878) LR 4 PD 1 CA, 11.
[2]   *Ampthill Peerage Case* [1977] AC 547, 577.
[3]   *Daniel* (1906) 4 CLR 563, 566.

ENGLISH DECISIONS ON STATUS OF PERSON

10.06   The status of a person, which may be the subject of a decision *in rem*, includes his domestic, matrimonial, corporate, professional, financial, parliamentary, official, or civic status or position. An English criminal decision is conclusive *in rem* as to the conviction, or acquittal; because it determines whether the accused is a convict. Except by statute[1], it is not otherwise conclusive *in rem*[2]. A finding that a person is not a money-lender within s 6 of the Money lenders Act 1900 is not a decision *in rem*[3].

[1]   A conviction is conclusive evidence of guilt in defamation proceedings: Civil Evidence Act 1968 s 13(1).
[2]   Chapter 11.
[3]   *United Dominions Trust Ltd v Kirkwood* [1966] 2 QB 431 CA.

10.07   An order that an applicant for *habeas corpus* be discharged from custody is a determination *in rem* of his right to liberty, and the legality of his discharge[1]. A refusal is not a judgment *in rem*, but has the same effect as any other dismissal[2].

[1]   *Cox v Hakes* (1890) 15 App Cas 506, 514; *Secretary of State for Home Affairs v O'Brien* [1923] AC 603. This was overlooked in *Budd v Anderson* [1943] KB 642, 647 where Asquith J held that an order for the release of the plaintiff on *habeas corpus* did not establish in an action for false imprisonment that his detention had been illegal because the parties were different.
[2]   Paras 2.30, 16.08.

10.08   Decisions as to the existence, validity[1], nullity or dissolution[2], of a marriage determine the domestic status of the parties, and are conclusive *in rem*. This is so, even where there is no specific determination, if this was necessarily involved[3]. A declaration of the legitimacy of named children in a divorce decree is not *in rem*[4]. Jurisdiction to grant declarations *in rem* as to parentage, legitimacy, legitimation, adoption, and marital status is conferred by the Family Law Act 1986 ss 55–60.

[1]   *Brownsword v Edwards* (1751) 2 Ves Sen 243, 245.
[2]   *Bunting v Lepingwell* (1585) 4 Co Rep 29a; *Meddowcroft v Huguenin* (1844) 4 Moo PCC 386.
[3]   *Woodland* [1928] P 169. In *Needham v Bremner* (1866) LR 1 CP 583, in an action for necessaries supplied to the defendant's wife, the defendant set up, as an estoppel, a finding in a divorce suit that his wife had been guilty of adultery. Since the defendant's petition for divorce had been dismissed the plea of estoppel failed. Erle CJ said at 585: 'the judge of the Divorce Court has not altered the status of the parties. The woman still continues the wife of the defendant. The case does not fall within the class of cases ... where the sentence put

an end to the relation of husband and wife. There is nothing here but the mere verdict of a jury, binding as between the parties to the suit, but not as between other parties'; para 15.04.

4 *B v A-G (NEB Intervening)* [1965] P 278, 284 per Willmer LJ: 'it would be absurd to suppose that, because a maintenance order may be embodied in the same document as that which determines the status of the parties it is, therefore, to be regarded as an order binding *in rem*. I do not see why an order for custody should be regarded any differently; that is to say, as anything other than an order binding on the parties to the suit'; para 10.02.

BANKRUPTCY

10.09 A bankruptcy order[1] affects the debtor's status, and is conclusive *in rem* at common law. Such orders were formerly conclusive by statute (repealed in 1986) so as to estop not only the debtor[2], but everyone else from disputing the fact of the order; the date thereof[3]; the petitioning creditor's debt; the act of bankruptcy; and its date to which the title of the trustee related back[4]. Those whose rights were conclusively determined in their absence, and without notice, could appeal against the adjudication. If necessary they could seek an extension of time which was generally granted *ex debito justitiae*[5]. The Privy Council has recently held that a judgment in bankruptcy and insolvency proceedings is neither *in personam* nor *in rem*, but a collective execution[6], but the author has reservations[7].

1 1986 Act s 278.
2 *Boaler v Power* [1910] 2 KB 229 CA, 232. The High Court will not entertain an action by the bankrupt to set aside for fraud the judgment on which he was made bankrupt: *Heath v Tang* [1993] 1 WLR 1421 CA; *Cummings v Claremont Petroleum NL* (1996) 185 CLR 124, 133–136.
3 Bankruptcy Act 1914 s 137(2), repealed by the 1986 Act, partially continued by the 1986 Rules r 12.20.
4 *Re Foulds, ex p Learoyd* (1878) 10 Ch D 3 CA; *Yousuf v Official Assignee* (1943) LR 70 Ind App 93. Acts of bankruptcy have been abolished and the title of the trustee no longer relates back: 1986 Act s 278.
5 *Re Tucker, ex p Tucker* (1879) 12 Ch D 308; *Yousuf v Official Assignee* (1943) LR 70 Ind App 93.
6 *Cambridge Gas* [2007] 1 AC 508, 516.
7 Paras 9.02–9.04.

QUO WARRANTO

10.10 A judgment of ouster on a *quo warranto* affects the corporate or official status of the defendant, and is *in rem*. In one case where the parties were not the same it was held that such a judgment, though evidence, was not conclusive[1]; but in another the judgment was held to be conclusive[2], that is, *in rem*.

1 *R v Hebden* (1738) Andr 388.
2 *R v York Corpn* (1792) 5 Term Rep 66, 76 per Buller J 'Judgment of ouster is conclusive' (the corporation was not a party); *Balmain Association Inc v Planning Administrator for Leichhardt* (1991) 25 NSWLR 615 CA, 640 and the English cases there cited. *R v York Corpn* establishes that a judgment of ouster is conclusive against a privy deriving title under the displaced office holder through his vote; paras 9.45 n 4, 16.08.

10.11 Sentences of deprivation of a collegiate office[1], or of expulsion from a college[2], affect the academic or corporate status of the person, and are *in rem*. The decision in *Reichel v Bishop of Oxford*[3] that the incumbent had resigned his benefice was *in rem* because it determined his status[4]. A decision on an election petition is *in rem* at common law and by statute since it determines the parliamentary status of the candidate[5]. An order for the expulsion or degradation of a member of a profession affects his professional status, and is conclusive *in rem* that the acts proved constitute professional misconduct[6], and prima facie evidence *in rem* that he was guilty of them.

[1]   *Philips v Bury* (1694) Skin 447 (sentence of Visitor of Exeter Coll Oxon). The majority of the KB held that it was not conclusive, but the House of Lords upheld the dissenting judgment of Holt CJ; para 2.02 n 3.
[2]   *R v Grundon* (1775) 1 Cowp 315 (indictment for assault in turning prosecutor out of Queen's Coll Cambridge). The accused justified under a sentence of expulsion by the Master and Fellows. It was held (at 322) that Willes J was 'extremely right' in rejecting evidence impugning the legality of the sentence, because 'this expulsion ... must be taken *by everybody* to be a right sentence until avoided or set aside by the visitor who is the sole judge'.
[3]   (1889) 14 App Cas 259.
[4]   *Bragg v Oceanus Mutual Underwriting Association (Bermuda) Ltd* [1982] 2 Lloyd's Rep 132 CA, 137 (*Bragg*); para 9.45 nn 2–5.
[5]   *Waygood v James* (1869) LR 4 CP 361; *Stevens v Tillett* (1870) LR 6 CP 147. The common law is embodied in s 145(1) of the Representation of the People Act 1983.
[6]   *Hill v Clifford* [1907] 2 Ch 236 CA, 245, 252, 257; affirmed on other grounds [1908] AC 12, 15; para 11.08.

ORDERS IN COURT OF PROTECTION

10.12 Inquisitions of lunacy under the former law, and equivalent orders under modern legislation appointing a deputy, receiver or committee of the property of the protected person, have a double aspect. They alter the status of the protected person[1], and as such are binding and conclusive *in rem*. While in force they are evidence *in rem,* but not conclusive, that the protected person lacks the capacity to make decisions and may be evidence of this during earlier periods[2]. While the order stands the protected person cannot deal with his property and his purported dispositions are void[3], despite any recovery, the fairness of the transaction, or the lack of notice of the disponee[4]. These cases have been applied in Australia[5]. Foreign orders which alter the status of a protected person or patient on a finding of mental incapacity, and vest control of his property in a curator or administrator, are recognised and enforced[6].

[1]   Para 11.08 nn 3–6.
[2]   *Bird v Keep* [1918] 2 KB 692 CA, 700; para 11.08.
[3]   *Re Walker* [1905] 1 Ch 160 CA (deed of lunatic so found void); *Re Marshall* [1920] 1 Ch 284 (order appointing receiver for patient, subsequent disposition by patient void).
[4]   The position is otherwise for persons of unsound mind who are not lunatics so found, or the modern equivalent: *Gibbons v Wright* (1954) 91 CLR 423; *Hart v O'Connor* [1985] AC 1000.
[5]   *Gibbons v Wright* (1954) 91 CLR 423, 439–440; *David* (1993) 30 NSWLR 417 CA.
[6]   *Didisheim v London and Westminster Bank* [1900] 2 Ch 15 CA, 26, 28, 29, 49, 51; *Pélégrin v Coutts & Co* [1915] 1 Ch 696. Cf *Kamouh v Associated Electrical Industries International Ltd* [1980] QB 199.

10.13 A Scottish declarator is a decision *in rem*[1].

[1]   *Shedden v A-G* (1860) 30 LJPM & A 217, 231; *Jenkins v Robertson* (1867) LR 1 Sc & Div 117, 121, 124; cf *Armitage v A-G* [1906] P 135.

DECISIONS NOT IN REM

10.14 There are two classes of such decisions. There are those which are not evidence against strangers of anything, except that the decision was pronounced. Then there is a second class, considered in the next chapter, where the decision is prima facie evidence *in rem*.

THE FIRST CLASS

10.15 A winding-up order is not *in rem*, and although binding on the company and persons claiming under it[1], it is not binding on a stranger. *Bowling's Case*[2] established that the title of a liquidator under an invalid winding-up order could not be forced on a purchaser but the court was not referred to s 70(1) of the Conveyancing Act 1881[3]. 'A judgment is not … *in rem* because in a suit by A for the recovery of an estate from B, it has determined an issue concerning the status of a particular person or family'[4]. The verdict of a jury at an inquest into a person's death is not evidence for or against anyone[5].

[1]   The 1986 Act s 130(4) provides that a winding-up order operates in favour of all creditors and contributories.
[2]   *Re Bowling and Welby's Contract* [1895] 1 Ch 663 CA.
[3]   Section 204(1) of the Law of Property Act 1925 provides that an order of the court is not invalid as against a purchaser on the ground of want of jurisdiction or otherwise, whether the purchaser has notice or not. The section does not validate an order for the sale of the property of B, who was not a party, in the belief that it was the property of A: *Pritchard v Briggs* [1980] Ch 338 CA, 408, 421, 423; *Templeton v Leviathan Pty Ltd* (1921) 30 CLR 34, 58–59, 79; paras 4.04 n 9, 9.35 n 4.
[4]   *Katama Natchier v Rajah of Shivagunga* (1863) 9 Moo Ind App 543, 601.
[5]   *Bird v Keep* [1918] 2 KB 692 CA; *Barnett v Cohen* [1921] 2 KB 461.

FOREIGN DECISIONS ON STATUS OF PERSON

10.16 A foreign decision is only *in rem* in England if it determined the status of a person or thing and is *in rem* in the foreign forum[1]. The most important foreign decisions determining the status of persons *in rem* are those relating to marriage, considered in Chapter 15. Foreign decisions as to the legitimacy or otherwise of a person domiciled in the foreign forum and their rights of inheritance, are conclusive *in rem* in England[2]. So also is a foreign declaration of the paternity of a child domiciled in the foreign forum[3].

[1]   This is a question of fact: *Castrique v Imrie* (1870) LR 4 HL 414, 429–430; para 2.44.
[2]   *Doglioni v Crispin* (1866) LR 1 HL 301, 311, 314, 315; *Re Trufort* (1887) 36 Ch D 600, 609–611.
[3]   *Re Macartney* [1921] 1 Ch 522, 532.

10.17 A foreign decision which does not establish or alter the status of a person is not *in rem* in England. Thus, an adjudication as a 'prodigue' by a French court, which prevents a man dealing with his property and suing without a 'conseil judiciare', is not *in rem*. It does not prevent him suing in England because 'the disability, or the disqualification, arises from the ... positive law' of the foreign state and the person's status is not changed[1]. An order of the Superior Court of California appointing a guardian for a person suffering from multiple sclerosis was not recognised because of its disabling and penal consequences[2].

1   *Worms v De Valdor* (1880) 49 LJ Ch 261; *Re Selot's Trust* [1902] 1 Ch 488.
2   *Re Langley's Settlement Trusts* [1962] Ch 541 CA.

ENGLISH DECISIONS DETERMINING THE STATUS OF A THING[1]

10.18 An English decision which effects a disposition of a thing or determines its status is conclusive *in rem* for, or against, any member of the English public. An order setting aside an alienation of property to defeat creditors or a spouse is *in rem*[2]. A decision can only operate *in rem*[3] if the thing was within the territorial jurisdiction of the court[4]. Lord Hoffmann has said[5]:

> 'When a judgment *in rem* ... is recognized by a foreign court it is accepted as establishing the right ... without further enquiry ... The judgment ... is treated as the source of the right.'

The same principles apply to the domestic effect of such a judgment. A judgment which merely determines existing property rights between the parties is *in personam*. The distinction was explained by Lord Mance[6]:

> 'An order purporting actually to transfer or dispose of property, is however, to be distinguished from a judgment determining the contractual rights of parties to property. Courts frequently adjudicate on the rights to property and otherwise of parties before them arising from contractual transactions relating to movables or intangibles situate in other states; in doing so common law courts apply the governing law of the relevant contract and the lex situs of the relevant movable or intangible to the contractual and proprietary aspects of the transaction as appropriate.'

The former are *in rem*, the latter *in personam*. A judgment in Kenya for specific performance of a contract to sell the shares in a Manx company was *in personam* although the purchaser could apply to the Manx court to rectify the company's share register.

1   This para in the 2nd edn was cited in *McGovern v State of Victoria* [1984] VR 570, 575.
2   *Turner v Official Trustee* (1999) 97 FCR 241, 245–246.
3   *Ballantyne v Mackinnon* [1896] 2 QB 455 CA, 462: 'as to a judgment being only conclusive as to the point decided, there is no distinction between a judgment *in rem*, and a judgment *in personam*, except that, in the one, "the point" adjudicated upon (which in a judgment *in rem* is always as to the status of the *res*) is conclusive against all the world as to that status, whereas, in the other, "the point", whatever it may be which is adjudicated upon, ... is only evidence between parties or privies', and *Wik Peoples v Queensland* (1994) 49 FCR 1, 4–6 (requirements for judgment *in rem* in claim for native title).
4   *Cambridge Gas* [2007] 1 AC 508, 515; *Ali v Pattni* [2007] 2 AC 85, 97, 98–99.
5   Ibid at 516.
6   *Ali v Pattni* [2007] 2 AC 85, 99.

PATENTS

10.19 An order revoking a patent is *in rem*. It extinguishes the patent with retrospective effect[1], but does not avoid estoppels from a decision that the patent was valid and infringed. A decision in favour of validity is *in personam*[2]. A decision upholding the validity of a European patent remains *res judicata* even after the patent is revoked by the European Patent Office[3]. Any injunction to restrain infringement lapses on revocation because there is no longer any patent but a judgment for damages to be assessed, or an account of profits for past infringements is not affected[4]. A patentee who succeeded on validity on one construction of the claims may be issue estopped from relying on a different construction in respect of other infringements[5]. At common law, patents depended on a Crown grant under the prerogative subject to the Statute of Monopolies 1628. *Scire facias* proceedings could be brought to repeal or revoke the patent, but revocation was placed on a statutory basis during the 19th century.

[1] *Unilin Beheer* [2008] 1 All ER 156 CA, 169.
[2] *Poulton* [1908] 2 Ch 430 CA, *Coflexip (No.2)* [2004] FSR 708 CA.
[3] *Unilin Beheer* [2008] 1 All ER 156 CA.
[4] *Coflexip (No.2)* [2004] FSR 708 CA, 720, 743 affirming Jacob J [2004] FSR 118, 125 who cited Parker J in *Poulton* (1908) 25 RPC 529, 532 not reported [1908] 2 Ch 430; *Unilin Beheer* [2008] 1 All ER 156 CA, 166–168.
[5] *Hormel Foods* [2005] RPC 657, 678.

SCIRE FACIAS AND CERTIORARI

10.20 An order of *scire facias* repealing or revoking a Crown grant or charter[1] is *in rem*[2]. An order of *certiorari* quashing a decision of an inferior court or tribunal extinguishes it, and is also *in rem*. The Supreme Court of Canada however has held, by majority, that a decision quashing a warrant on *certiorari* was not *in rem*[3].

[1] Para 16.08 n 15.
[2] The decisions on the revocation of patents apply: para 10.19.
[3] *Sleeth v Hurlbert* (1896) 25 SCR 620. The old cases cited by Sedgewick J (at 631) writing for the majority were not *certiorari* cases and do not support the majority decision.

SUBORDINATE LEGISLATION

10.21 In Canada, decisions invalidating resolutions or by-laws of local councils are *in rem*, but the Supreme Court has not decided whether a declaration that a regulation is *ultra vires* is *in rem*[1]. In *Hoffmann-La Roche*[2], Lord Diplock said that a declaration that a statutory instrument was *ultra vires* was not *in rem*. It does not formally quash the instrument, but declares that it has no legal effect. Despite the eminence of Lord Diplock it is thought that where the Crown is a party his dictum is not correct and the analogy from orders for *scire facias* and *certiorari* applies[3]. A decision that subordinate legislation is valid will be *in personam*.

[1] *Emms v R* (1980) 102 DLR (2d) 193, 199, 201; para 17.31.

²   *Hoffmann-La Roche & Co AG v Secretary of State for Trade and Industry* [1975] AC 295, 365 (*Hoffmann-La Roche*).
³   Para 10.20.

ADMIRALTY DECISIONS

10.22 English Admiralty decisions which make a disposition of the vessel or an interest in her are *in rem*[1], but only as to the point actually determined. Thus a declaration, in a salvage suit, that a maritime lien attached to the vessel for the award, was a decision *in rem* that the lien existed, but not that the vessel was damaged by a peril of the sea so as to bind an insurer[2].

¹   *Duckworth v Tucker* (1809) 2 Taunt 7, 34–36 (sentence of Prize Court, condemning a vessel 'as lawful prize of His Majesty', conclusive *in rem*, so as to estop the world disputing that the vessel was captured by the naval forces of this country); *Ballantyne v Mackinnon* [1896] 2 QB 455 CA, 462.
²   *Ballantyne v Mackinnon* [1896] 2 QB 455 CA, 462; *McGovern v State of Victoria* [1984] VR 570 (forfeiture of vessel for breach of fishing laws *in rem*); *Readhead v Admiralty Marshall* (1998) 87 FCR 229 (sale by Admiralty Marshall). Decisions condemning vessels as lawful prize are an exception: para 10.04 n 1.

ORDERS FOR SALE PENDENTE LITE

10.23 An order for sale *pendente lite* of perishable or other property within the jurisdiction, made in Admiralty or otherwise, is *in rem*[1].

¹   *Ali v Pattni* [2007] 2 AC 85, 97.

ROADS AND OTHER PUBLIC RIGHTS

10.24 A declaration by a competent tribunal that a road is, or is not, repairable by the inhabitants at large, determines its status, and operates *in rem*[1]. A declaration as to the existence or otherwise of a public right of way is also *in rem*[2]. But dismissal of a summons for payment of a rateable share of the expenses of repairing a road is not *in rem* if the tribunal did not have jurisdiction to determine that question conclusively[3]. Decisions under Inclosure Acts were not conclusive *in rem* on questions of title[4]. A decision pursuant to statute, fixing the building line of a road was *in rem*[5]. A decision on the validity of the conditions of a planning consent is *in rem*[6], but an acquittal on a charge of using land in breach of planning control is not[7].

¹   *Wakefield Corpn v Cooke* [1904] AC 31.
²   *Armstrong v Whitfield* [1974] QB 16.
³   *R v Hutchings* (1881) 6 QBD 300 CA, 303; *Heath v Weaverham Overseers* [1894] 2 QB 108; *North Eastern Rly Co v Dalton Overseers* [1898] 2 QB 66.
⁴   *Jacomb v Turner* [1892] 1 QB 47, 51–52; *Collis v Amphlett* [1918] 1 Ch 232 CA, 242, 251.
⁵   *Lilley v LCC* [1910] AC 1; *LCC v Galsworthy* [1917] 1 KB 85.
⁶   *P E Bakers Pty Ltd v Yehuda* (1988) 15 NSWLR 437 CA.
⁷   *El Alam v Northcote County Council* [1996] 2 VR 672, 680.

LICENSING DECISIONS

10.25 The grant of a liquor or similar licence is *in rem*[1].

[1]   *Burden v Ainsworth* (2004) 59 NSWLR 506 CA, 509.

PROBATE DECISIONS

10.26 A probate establishes conclusively in civil proceedings in England that the instrument admitted to probate was a will, validly executed according to the laws of this country, by a testator of sound disposing mind without fraud or coercion, and that the executor named was entitled to that office[1]. Grants of probate or administration do not have extra-territorial effect[2], and an executor or administrator under a foreign grant is not recognised as such[3]. A foreign executor can neither sue to recover an estate asset, nor be sued for an estate liability[4]. However a legal personal representative without a local grant can vindicate his possession of an estate asset because possession is a good title against those who do not have a better one. An unrevoked probate is no bar to a prosecution for forgery of the will[5]. Letters of administration are conclusive *in rem* as to the fact of the grant[6], and that the applicant is entitled to it and, where applicable, is one of the next of kin[7]. Such decisions are not conclusive *in rem*, except as to the point actually decided[8]. They are not conclusive as to the parts of the will which are effectual, or its construction[9], or on any question of administration[10]. A grant to an administrator described as one of the next of kin barred a claim that he was illegitimate unless and until the grant was revoked[11], but a grant which identified the only next of kin did not bar others[12].

[1]   *Noell v Wells* (1668) 1 Lev 235; *Allen v Dundas* (1789) 3 Term Rep 125; *Thornton v Curling* (1824) 8 Sim 310; *Douglas v Cooper* (1834) 3 My & K 378; *Allen v M'Pherson* (1847) 1 HLC 191; *Whicker v Hume* (1858) 7 HLC 124, 143–144; *Meluish v Milton* (1876) 3 Ch D 27 CA, 33; *Birch* [1902] P 130 CA, 137–138. The principle only applies with full rigour to a grant in solemn form: *Migneault v Malo* (1872) LR 4 PC 123, 135.

[2]   *Ewing v Orr Ewing* (1883) 9 App Cas 34, 39 (*Ewing*).

[3]   Ibid; *New York Breweries Co. v A-G* [1899] AC 62; *Finnegan v Cementation Ltd* [1953] 1 QB 688 CA; *McSweeney v Murphy* [1919] 1 IR 16 CA.

[4]   Ibid; *Nagel v Hough* (1927) 27 SR (NSW) 418; *Boyd v Leslie* [1964] VR 728.

[5]   *R v Gibson* (1802) Russ & Ry 343 n; *Buttery's Case* (1818) Russ & Ry 342.

[6]   *Blackham's Case* (1709) 1 Salk 290.

[7]   *Barrs v Jackson* (1845) 1 Ph 582, 587–588; para 8.10 n 6.

[8]   Ibid at 588–589; *Concha* (1886) 11 App Cas 541, 552.

[9]   *Thornton v Curling* (1824) 8 Sim 310, 313–314; *Concha* (1886) 11 App Cas 541; *Re Hawksley's Settlement* [1934] Ch 384; para 8.23 n 9.

[10]   *Whicker v Hume*, (1858) 7 HL Cas, 156–157, 165–166.

[11]   *In Re Ivory* (1878) 10 Ch D 372.

[12]   *In Re Ward* [1971] 1 WLR 1376.

TAX DECISIONS

10.27 The previous authors considered that judgments declaring the legality of a tax were *in rem*, citing *Lord Say's Case*[1], but that can be supported on the doctrine of precedent[2]. The only modern decision, by a single judge of the Supreme Court of British Columbia, rejected the principle[3]. It has not been applied in cases determining the validity of tax legislation under the Canadian and Australian Constitutions[4]. A condemnation of goods for offences against the Revenue is conclusive *in rem* as to the forfeiture, and the facts which constituted the offence[5]. A judgment for penalties under customs legislation does not determine the status of the goods and is not *in rem*[6]. A decision in civil proceedings on the tariff classification is not *in rem* or admissible in criminal proceedings[7].

1   (1639) Cro Car 524.
2   Cf *Hoffmann-La Roche* [1975] AC 295, 365 per Lord Diplock, para 10.21.
3   *Coquitlam City v Construction Aggregates Ltd* (1998) 65 BCLR (3rd) 275.
4   *Hughes & Vale Pty Ltd v State of New South Wales* [1955] AC 241; *Dickenson's Arcade Pty Ltd v Tasmania* (1974) 130 CLR 177, *Ha v New South Wales* (1997) 189 CLR 465. The Supreme Court of Canada treats decisions in constitutional cases as precedents only: *Emms v R* (1980) 102 DLR (2d) 193, 201. The High Court of Australia favours this approach: *Queensland v Commonwealth* (1977) 139 CLR 585, 597, 614–615.
5   Para 8.09 n 1.
6   *Hart v M'Namara* (1817) 4 Price 154n, where, in an action for the price of rum, the defendant relied on its condemnation, and the plaintiff's conviction. Gibbs CJ held that the record of the condemnation was admissible, being *in rem*, but he refused to admit the record of conviction for penalties, as it was *in personam*, and it was not evidence in any case in which the parties were different.
7   *Neil Pearson & Co Pty Ltd v Comptroller-General of Customs* (1996) 38 NSWLR 443 CA.

STATUS OF PROPERTY UNDER THE RENT ACTS

10.28 The Rent Acts operate *in rem*; but judgments on their operation are not *in rem*[1]. A transferee of the reversion claims under an earlier owner, and an assignee of the lease claims under the tenant but a new tenant does not claim under his predecessor. In Australia, judgments fixing the fair rent under equivalent legislation were held to be *in rem*[2].

1   *Lazarus-Barlow v Regent Estates Co Ltd* [1949] 2 KB 465 CA.
2   *Washington H Soul, Pattinson Ltd v Ogilvy* (1955) 55 SR (NSW) 143, 148.

FOREIGN DECISIONS WHICH DETERMINE THE STATUS OF A THING

10.29 A foreign decision which determines the status of a thing is *in rem* in England. '[T]he inquiry is, first, whether the subject-matter was ... within the lawful control of the State under the authority of which the court sits; and, secondly, whether the sovereign authority of that State has conferred on the court jurisdiction to decide as to the disposition of the thing, and the court has acted within its jurisdiction. If these conditions are fulfilled, the adjudication is conclusive against all the world'[1]. In the case of 'proceedings *in rem* as to moveable property, within the jurisdiction of the court pronouncing the judgment, ... whatever it settles as to the right or title, or whatever disposition it makes of the property by sale ... , transfer, or other act, will be held valid in every other country'[2]. The 'thing' adjudicated upon is usually a vessel. Decisions of foreign admiralty courts are conclusive, such courts having 'a rightful jurisdiction' in such proceedings, 'founded on ... actual or constructive possession of the subject-matter'[3].

1   *Castrique v Imrie* (1870) LR 4 HL 414, 429.
2   Ibid at 428.
3   Ibid at 429.

10.30 An order of a foreign court of admiralty for the attachment and sale of a vessel to satisfy a claim for necessaries is 'conclusive everywhere and upon everybody'[1]. It asserts jurisdiction over, and changes the property in the ship[2]. But when the order disposes of a party's interest in a ship by way of execution, or is for the benefit of the general body of creditors, it is not *in rem*[3].

1   *Castrique v Behrens* (1861) 3 E & E 709, 722; *Minna Craig Steamship Co v Chartered Mercantile Bank of India, London and China* [1897] 1 QB 460 CA.
2   *Castrique v Imrie* (1870) LR 4 HL 414, 429–432, 442–445, 447.
3   *Simpson v Fogo* (1863) 1 Hem & M 195, 224, 243.

10.31 The sentences of a foreign court of admiralty condemning a vessel as lawful prize are conclusive *in rem*. The question arose in actions on policies of marine insurance, where the plaintiff alleged loss by capture, and the defendant set up the assured's breach of warranty of neutrality. The decision that the vessel was 'lawful prize'[1] bound the world that it was not a neutral ship[2]. Underwriters could contract out of the benefit of this estoppel by undertaking to pay on the assured proving the vessel's neutrality by special evidence[3].

1   *Bernardi v Motteux* (1781) 2 Doug KB 575, 580 per Lord Mansfield: 'all the world are parties to a sentence of a court of admiralty … which … is conclusive upon all persons'; *Dalgleish v Hodgson* (1831) 7 Bing 495, 504 per Tindal CJ: 'the sentence of a foreign Court of Admiralty is binding upon all parties and in all countries as to the fact upon which the condemnation proceeded, *where such fact appears upon the face of the sentence, free from doubt and ambiguity*'; *Hobbs v Henning* (1864) 17 CBNS 791, 824.
2   *Geyer v Aguilar* (1798) 7 TR 681, 697; *Bolton v Gladstone* (1809) 2 Taunt 85 Ex Ch, 94–95.
3   *Lothian v Henderson* (1803) 3 Bos & P 499 HL, 546–547.

Chapter 11

JUDGMENTS AS EVIDENCE

11.01 A conviction does not estop the accused, as against the so-called world, from denying his guilt[1], but was long thought to be *prima facie* evidence[2]. Thus in *Re Weare*, which concerned a solicitor, Lord Esher MR said[3]:

> 'Where a man has been convicted of a criminal offence, that prima facie at all events does make him a person unfit to be a member of the honourable profession'.

A conviction should not always be conclusive in civil proceedings, but there are good reasons for it being *prima facie* evidence. In *Hollington*[4] Denning KC argued for this but the court held that the opinion of the criminal court was irrelevant and no better than that of an eye witness[5]. *Prima facie* evidence was of little value since, if the conviction was challenged, the court must retry the case[6]. The court asked how the evidence of witnesses could be weighed against a conviction, a matter which did not trouble Parliament in 1968[7] and has not troubled the courts since. The utility of *prima facie* evidence in discouraging vexatious claims or defences and in forcing the accused into evidence and perhaps the witness box was ignored. In *Harvey*[8], which was cited in *Hollington* but not referred to, Lord Lindley said:

> 'Mr Haldane was bold enough to contend that the orders in lunacy were not admissible in evidence ... at all ... Their Lordships are not prepared to accede to this contention. The orders are not conclusive evidence of anything except their own existence; but, being made by a competent tribunal in a matter within its jurisdiction, they cannot be rejected as inadmissible, or as no evidence of the truth of those facts recited in them which are essential to their validity. They are admissible as prima facie evidence, and if uncontradicted they ought to be regarded as sufficient evidence of those facts, not only in this country, but in all His Majesty's dominions.'

In *Hill v Clifford*[9] the Court of Appeal applied this decision to an order of the General Medical Council striking off dentists for professional misconduct, but this case was not referred to in *Hollington*. The orders considered in *Harvey* were *in rem*[10] and the principle only applies to such orders[11], as the majority in *Hill v Clifford* held. Evidence that a party to a joint criminal enterprise had been convicted of manslaughter and acquitted of murder is not admissible in favour of another party to that enterprise on his trial for murder[12].

169

11.01 *Judgments as evidence*

Lord Lowry cited *Hollington* and said that the verdict of the jury at the first trial was '*no more than evidence of the opinion of that jury*'[13]. He then gave a better reason, the irrelevance of the evidence to the guilt of the accused[14]. However in exceptional circumstances, illustrated by *R v Cooke*[15], the acquittal of a third party may be relevant, and therefore admissible in favour of the accused.

[1] *Petrie v Nuttall* (1856) 11 Exch 569, 576; *Castrique v Imrie* (1870) LR 4 HL 414, 434; *Leyman v Latimer* (1878) 3 Ex D 352 CA, 354; *Ballantyne v Mackinnon* [1896] 2 QB 455 CA, 462; *Caine v Palace Steam Shipping Co* [1907] 1 KB 670 CA, 677, 683; *Re Crippen's Estate* [1911] P 108.

[2] *Re Crippen's Estate* [1911] P 108, 115; *Mash v Darley* [1914] 1 KB 1; affd on different ground [1914] 3 KB 1226 CA; *Re Hall's Estate, Hall v Knight and Baxter* [1914] P 1 CA, 7; *Partington* [1925] P 34; *O'Toole* (1926) 42 TLR 245 and *Hill v Clifford* [1907] 2 Ch 236 CA (finding of misconduct by General Medical Council admissible in civil proceedings between partners); affirmed on different grounds [1908] AC 12, 15. See also the argument of counsel for the plaintiff in *Helsham v Blackwood* (1851) 11 CB 111, 121–123, 124 which collected authorities for the proposition that a conviction was evidence against the accused in a civil case, but an acquittal was not evidence in his favour, noted *Helton v Allen* (1940) 63 CLR 691, 710.

[3] [1893] 2 QB 439 CA, 445 (conviction *prima facie* evidence of guilt); *Re A Solicitor* [1993] QB 69, 78; and *Ziems v Prolhonotary of the Supreme Court of New South Wales* (1957) 97 CLR 279, 298–299.

[4] [1943] KB 587 CA.

[5] Ibid at 595, a view rejected by the Law Reform Committee, by commentators and by the New Zealand Court of Appeal: *Jorgensen v News Media (Auckland) Ltd* [1969] NZLR 961, 976–7 (*Jorgensen*).

[6] Ibid at 595.

[7] Civil Evidence Act 1968 s 11(1), (2); para 11.05.

[8] [1901] AC 601, 611 (English order in Ceylon). Lord Lindley did not rely on the interlocutory nature of the proceedings in Ceylon.

[9] [1907] 2 Ch 236 CA; affirmed on different grounds [1908] AC 12, 15.

[10] Para 10.12.

[11] *Quinn v Leathem* [1901] AC 495, 606 per Lord Halsbury LC: 'every judgment must be read as applicable to the particular facts proved,' *Hill v Clifford* [1907] 2 Ch 236 CA, 244–245, 257–258.

[12] *Hui Chi-Ming v R* [1992] 1 AC 34.

[13] Ibid at 42–43.

[14] Ibid at 43.

[15] *R v Cooke* (1986) 84 Cr App Rep 286 approved in *Hui Chi-Ming v The Queen* [1992] 1 AC 34, 44.

11.02 *Hollington* stood until 1968 as authority for the proposition that there was no halfway house between a decision *in rem*, estopping the accused denying his guilt[1], and a decision *in personam*, estopping him only against the Crown. Convictions continued to be admissible as evidence of general reputation where that was relevant eg as proof of a public right. As Lord Abinger CJ said[2]:

> ' ... in the cases where reputation is evidence – that is cases involving a general right in which all the Queen's subjects are concerned – a verdict or a judgment, upon the matter directly in issue between the parties – although between other parties – is also evidence; not ... of any specific fact ... but evidence of the most solemn kind of an adjudication of a competent tribunal upon the state of facts and the question of usage at that time'.

In *Petrie v Nuttall*[3] Alderson B said of a conviction for obstructing a highway:

'... the judgment in the indictment may be given in evidence upon the trial of the issue as to whether the *locus in quo* is a public highway, but it cannot be pleaded as an estoppel.'

Convictions are also evidence of the general reputation of the claimant in a defamation action[4]. There is also a body of authority in the divorce court that convictions are *prima facie* evidence except where the conduct is co-extensive with the matrimonial offence charged, eg rape[5]. An unreversed conviction is admissible against the accused in any proceedings for malicious prosecution, false imprisonment, or negligence in the conduct of his defence[6]. The House of Lords has recently held that damages will not be awarded for a loss or disadvantage which the criminal courts imposed as punishment[7].

[1] In *Arthur Hall* [2002] 1 AC 615, 702 Lord Hoffmann said 'a conviction has some of the quality of a judgment *in rem*.'
[2] *Pim v Curell* (1840) 6 M & W 234, 266.
[3] (1856) 11 Exch 569, 576.
[4] *Goody v Oldhams Press Ltd* [1967] 1 QB 333 CA, 341, 343; *Jorgensen* [1969] NZLR 961 CA, 965.
[5] *Ingram* [1956] P 390, 403–408.
[6] Paras 9.34 n 10, 26.07–26.08.
[7] *Gray v Thames Trains Ltd* [2009] 3 WLR 167 HL.

11.03 *Hollington* has been subjected to persistent criticism. Professor Good-hart[1] wrote 'although experience shows that the law and the ordinary practice of the community are not always in accord, there is at least a presumption against a legal rule which gives rise to a conflict between them'. He pointed out that the court had not referred to the use of convictions on credit. The Criminal Procedure Act 1865 s 6 entitled counsel to ask a witness 'whether he has been convicted of any felony or misdemeanour and upon being so questioned, if he either denies or does not admit the fact, or refuses to answer, it shall be lawful for the cross-examining party to prove such conviction'. The statute, which remains in force, applies in civil proceedings and any conviction can be used[2]. The credit of a witness could be impeached at common law by prior convictions[3], which could be proved if not admitted, but they had to damage the witness' credit.

The right to use convictions in cross-examination was extended by the Criminal Evidence Act 1898. Section 1(f) enabled the accused to be cross-examined about prior convictions, and for them to be proved when '... proof that he has ... been convicted ... is admissible evidence to show that he is guilty of the offence wherewith he is then charged', or when he had put character in issue, or given evidence against a co-accused[4]. All this assumed that the convictions were evidence that he was guilty of the offence[5], because the tribunal of fact could not otherwise find that the witness was discredited, or the accused more likely to be guilty of the offence charged[6]. There was also a rule that on a charge of being an accessory to a felony the prior conviction of the principal offender was *prima facie* evidence against the accessory that the principal offender committed the felony[7]. The decisions are of doubtful validity since *R v Welsh*[8] and are not likely to survive a direct challenge. The most persistent critic was Lord Denning MR who said in *Goody v Oldhams Press Ltd*[9]:

'... there is a strange rule of law ... that a conviction is no evidence of guilt, not even prima facie evidence. That was decided in *Hollington* ... I argued that case myself, and did my best to persuade the court that a conviction was evidence of guilt. But they would not have it. I thought that the decision was wrong at the time. I still think that it was wrong. But in this court we are bound by it. It means that when anyone publishes a story about a crime, he is in peril of being sued for libel ... he cannot rely on the conviction as proof of guilt. He has to prove it all over again, if he can'.

In *Barclays Bank Ltd v Cole*[10] he said:

'He wishes to canvass again his guilt or innocence, but this time before a jury in a civil case. There is too much of this sort of thing going on ... It is made possible by the unfortunate decision of this court in *Hollington* ... that a conviction ... cannot be used as evidence, not even prima facie evidence, in a civil case. I hope it will soon be altered. See what it means here. In order to be able to bring this civil action *Barclays Bank* had first to make sure that [the defendant] was prosecuted in the criminal court ... Now after seeing him duly prosecuted and convicted they are asked to prove his guilt all over again in this civil suit'.

His observations were echoed by other Lords Justices. Legislation followed in 1968.

[1]   59 LQR 299–301.
[2]   *Clifford* [1961] 1 WLR 1274, 1276; *Thomas v Metropolitan Police Comr* [1997] QB 813 CA, 829. In *Ingram* [1956] P 390, 405 Sachs J said it would be strange if a court could draw inferences from a conviction on credit but not on conduct. The section was amended by the Access to Justice Act 1999.
[3]   *Bugg v Day* (1949) 79 CLR 442, 465, 467 per Dixon J.
[4]   The section was amended by the Youth, Justice and Criminal Evidence Act 1999 Sch 4, s 6 and no longer covers the use of prior convictions.
[5]   As a party to any conviction on indictment the Crown could rely on the estoppel, but this cannot explain the use of foreign convictions against the accused, the use of convictions against other witnesses, their use by a co-accused, or their use in civil proceedings.
[6]   In *Ingram* [1956] P at 406 Sachs J said: 'on questions of credit a conviction is *prima facie* assumed to be justified'.
[7]   *Smith's Case* (1783) 1 Leach 288; *Prosser's Case* (1784) 1 Leach 290n; *R v Dawson* [1961] VR 773, 774.
[8]   [1999] 2 VR 62 CA. The judgment of Brooking JA contains a review of the English, Australian, Canadian and United States authorities.
[9]   [1967] 1 QB 333 CA, 339. Salmon LJ said at 342 that the rule was 'strange' and 'wholeheartedly' agreed with Lord Denning. Danckwerts LJ also agreed.
[10] [1967] 2 QB 738 CA, 743. Diplock LJ said at 746 that the rule was 'ripe for re-examination.'

11.04   The Court of Appeal of New Zealand refused to follow *Hollington*[1], to the delight of Lord Denning MR, who said in *McIlkenny*[2] that *Hollington* was decided *per incuriam*. On appeal Lord Diplock said[3] that it 'is generally considered to have been wrongly decided'. In *Arthur Hall*[4] Lord Hoffmann said: 'The Court of Appeal is generally thought to have taken the technicalities of the matter much too far when it decided ... that in civil proceedings a conviction was ... no evidence whatever that the accused had committed the offence.' Then in *R v Hayter* Lord Steyn said[5] that the Acts[6] which abolished the rule 'marked an advance in the rationality of our law' and Lord Carswell[7] referred to 'the much criticized rule in *Hollington*'. The Ontario Court of

Appeal has refused to follow it[8], as has the Full Court of the Supreme Court of Western Australia[9]. It is not likely to be followed elsewhere.

1   *Jorgensen* [1969] NZLR 961. The court preferred *Harvey* [1901] AC 601; *Hill v Clifford* [1907] 2 Ch 236 CA and *Re Estate of Crippen* [1911] P 108.
2   [1980] QB 283 CA, 319, cf per Sir George Baker at 342.
3   *Hunter* [1982] AC 529, 543.
4   [2002] 1 AC 615, 702, cf per Lord Hobhouse at 751.
5   [2005] 1 WLR 605 HL, 613.
6   Paras 11.05–11.10.
7   [2005] 1 WLR 605, 630.
8   *Demeter v British Pacific Life Insurance* (1984) 13 DLR (4th) 318.
9   *Mickelberg v Director of Perth Mint* [1986] WAR 365.

THE CIVIL EVIDENCE ACT 1968

11.05   The Act provides:

(1)   In any civil proceeding the fact that a person has been convicted of an offence before any court in the United Kingdom, or by a court martial is admissible for the purpose of proving that he committed that offence, whether he was convicted on a plea of guilty or after trial, and whether or not he is a party to the later proceedings[1].

(2)   Proof of the conviction is evidence that the person convicted committed the offence unless the contrary is proved[2].

(3)   A similar rule applies to a finding of adultery in matrimonial proceedings, and of paternity in affiliation proceedings. The findings in the first proceeding raise a presumption in the second[3], which can be rebutted.

The 1968 Act applies where the first decision is either (a) a conviction in the United Kingdom; (b) a conviction before a court martial; (c) a finding of adultery or (d) a finding of paternity. The common law applies to other convictions. There has been relatively little case law[4]. In *Hunter*[5] Lord Diplock said that acquittals were not admissible because the result may have been different under the civil standard but convictions were because the result could not have been affected. In *Stupple v Royal Insurance Co Ltd*[6] Lord Denning MR said that a conviction not only activated the presumption under s 11(2)(a), it was a weighty piece of evidence under s 11(1). In *Taylor*[7] Davies LJ said: 'when a man has been convicted ... at a criminal trial, the verdict of the jury is ... entitled to very great weight when the convicted person is seeking, in the words of the statute, to prove the contrary'. In *Hunter*[8] Lord Diplock disapproved the statement of Lord Denning MR in *McIlkenny*[9] that the defendant could only rebut the presumption by proof of fraud, collusion, or 'fresh evidence' but said that a defendant who challenges his conviction has an 'uphill task'. A claimant who pleaded a conviction obtained summary judgment when the defendant sought to relitigate the issues on the same evidence[10], but this decision was disapproved in *McCauley v Vine*[11] where summary judgment based on a conviction for driving without due care was set aside and the action allowed to go to trial. Then *J v Oyston*[12] decided that it was not an abuse of process for a defendant sued for assault, following his conviction for rape, to defend the proceedings and challenge his conviction[13]. In Canada summary judgment for the plaintiff based on the defendant's conviction for sexual assault was upheld where the only evidence in opposition was the defendant's evidence at the trial[14], an insurer could not relitigate the issue of negligence when its insured had been convicted of dangerous driving[15], and a defendant convicted of arson could not relitigate that issue in a civil action[16]. In Canada a civil action which challenges the plaintiff's conviction is treated as an abuse of process[17].

[1]   Section 11(1).
[2]   Section 11(2). Where the conviction and indictment did not disclose the facts on which the conviction was based the summing-up was admissible under s 4(1) and s 11(2)(b): *Brinks Ltd v Abu-Saleh (No 2)* [1995] 1 WLR 1478.
[3]   Section 12 restores the effect of *Partington* [1925] P 34 and *O'Toole* (1926) 42 TLR 245.
[4]   *Re Raphael (Decd)* [1973] 1 WLR 998 (civil court should not act on conviction until appeal determined).
[5]   [1982] AC 529, 543.
[6]   [1971] 1 QB 50 CA, 72.
[7]   [1970] 1 WLR 1148 CA, 1152.
[8]   [1982] AC 529, 544.
[9]   [1980] QB 283 CA, 320.
[10] *Brinks Ltd v Abu-Saleh* [1995] 1 WLR 1478.
[11] [1999] 1 WLR 1977 CA, 1984.
[12] [1999] 1 WLR 694.
[13] Cf *Conlon v Simms* [2008] 1 WLR 484 CA, 517–518, 522–523, 523–524. A defendant is generally entitled to defend himself: para 26.15 n 3.
[14] *F(K) v White* (2001) 198 DLR (4th) 541 CA Ont.
[15] *Economical Mutual Insurance Co v Dorkin* (2008) 303 DLR (4th) 377 Ont CA.
[16] *Ecclesiastical Insurance Office plc v Michaud* (2008) 304 DLR (4th) 245 CA Man.
[17] *F(K) v White* (2001) 198 DLR (4th) at 555 CA Ont; cf *Hunter* [1982] AC 529; para 26.07.

CONVICTIONS AS EVIDENCE AGAINST AN ACCUSED

11.06 Some of the difficulties under the Criminal Procedure Act 1865 and the Criminal Evidence Act 1898 were addressed by the Police and Criminal Evidence Act 1984. The fact that a person *other than the accused* has been convicted of an offence in the UK or in a Service court is admissible for the purpose of proving that that person committed that offence, unless the contrary is proved[1]. Proof of the conviction must be 'relevant to [an] issue in those proceedings'[2]. Where evidence is admissible that *an accused* committed an offence, proof of his conviction by a court in the UK or a Service court establishes that fact 'unless the contrary is proved'[3]. Section 74 makes the conviction of one participant in a joint criminal enterprise evidence of his guilt against the others in a separate trial. It also applies indirectly in joint trials to make the confession of a participant evidence of his guilt against the others[4]. Before admitting the conviction the court is required by s 78 to consider whether its reception would have an adverse effect on the fairness of the proceedings. If so the conviction should be rejected[5]. *R v Robertson*[6] decided that 'any issue' in s 74(1) included evidential issues. The section has been used by the prosecution to prove convictions of a co-accused[7], and that third parties resorted to premises to purchase illicit drugs[8]. The admissibility of prior convictions of the accused as evidence of his bad character is now governed by ss 101–106 of the Criminal Justice Act 2003. Under s 101(1)(d) evidence of the accused's bad character[9] (and hence evidence of his prior convictions) is admissible if it is relevant to an important matter in issue between the accused and the prosecution[10]. Such evidence is also admissible under s 101(1)(e) if it has substantial probative value in relation to an important matter in issue between the accused and a co-accused[11]. Convictions admitted under s 101(1) are relevant both to propensity to offend and credibility[12]. The admissibility of convictions by a court outside the United Kingdom, other than a Service court, continues to be governed by the common law and s 6 of the Criminal Procedure Act 1865.

1   Section 74(2).
2   Section 74(1). 'It ... should be sparingly used': per Lord Lane CJ in *R v Robertson* [1987] QB 920, 928. The section was amended by the Criminal Justice Act 2003.
3   Section 74(3).
4   *R v Hayter* [2005] 1 WLR 605 HL.
5   *R v Mahmood and Manzur* [1997] 1 Cr App Rep 414, 417. The trial judge must consider whether the conviction was clearly relevant to an issue in the trial, and whether its probative value outweighed its prejudicial effect. The court held that a conviction based on a plea of guilty by a co-accused in a mass rape trial should not have been admitted against another co-accused.
6   [1987] QB 920 CA (convictions of co-accused).
7   *R v Robertson (above); R v Kempster* [1989] 1 WLR 1125.
8   *R v Warner* (1992) 96 Cr App Rep 324 CA.
9   Defined in s 98 of the 2003 Act as evidence of misconduct or a disposition to misconduct other than evidence to do with the facts of the offence with which the accused is charged.
10   *R v S* [2007] 1 WLR 63 CA.
11   *R v Lawson* [2007] 1 WLR 1191 CA.
12   *R v Campbell* [2007] 1 WLR 2798 CA.

CONVICTIONS AS EVIDENCE OF THE BAD CHARACTER OF OTHERS

11.07 Convictions are admissible at common law to prove the bad character of persons other than an accused, eg the deceased where self defence is in issue. The matter is now governed by s 100 of the 2003 Act which makes evidence of prior convictions admissible both for this purpose and to damage the credibility of a witness including a complainant[1]. The New Zealand courts have considered whether convictions of the deceased for crimes of violence are admissible where self defence is in issue. This question does not appear to have arisen in England or Australia, but it has arisen in the United States where such convictions are generally admissible for this purpose. In *R v Davis*[2] the question arose on an appeal from a conviction for manslaughter. The trial judge rejected evidence that the deceased had such convictions, and the court held that those which were not known to the accused at the time were properly excluded. Convictions for rape, burglary and theft were not relevant and those for assault and threatening grievous bodily harm did not evidence violence which could lead the accused to stab the deceased in self defence. Cooke J referred to *Wigmore* and the *Corpus Juris Secundum* and said[3]:

> 'We do not ... affirm that convictions of a deceased for crimes of violence, unknown to the accused at the time of the killing, can never be admissible when self defence is in issue ... In commonsense and justice there may be occasions when knowledge of the violent disposition of a deceased should not be withheld from a jury'.

He thought the cases where such evidence was admissible would be rare. The question arose in *R v Wilson*[4] where Fisher J ruled that, where self defence is raised, convictions of the deceased for criminal violence are admissible as evidence that he acted in that way on the occasion in question. He said[5]:

> '... the convictions of the deceased could be accepted as a means of proving that he had in fact committed the crimes'.

He rejected convictions for offensive behaviour, assault on a constable on duty, and resisting police, as not sufficiently relevant.

[1] *R v S* [2007] 1 WLR 63 CA.
[2] [1980] 1 NZLR 257 CA.
[3] Ibid at 261–262.
[4] [1991] 2 NZLR 707.
[5] Ibid at 714.

CIVIL JUDGMENTS AS EVIDENCE

11.08 As a general rule judicial findings in civil proceedings are only admissible in later proceedings, as proof of their truth, against the parties and their privies[1]. To that extent, and subject to limited exceptions, *Hollington* remains good law[2]. The verdict of a jury on an inquisition in lunacy[3], and equivalent orders[4], including an order that a person is a mental defective[5] are judgments *in rem* and evidence *in rem* of the unsoundness of mind of the patient while they remain in force[6]. They may also be evidence *in rem* of the patient's condition at an earlier date[7]. An order of the General Medical Council removing the name of a medical practitioner from the register is a decision *in rem* as to his status and *prima facie* evidence *in rem* that he was guilty of the professional misconduct found[8]. The finding of a jury summoned under a Boundary Commission is evidence *in rem* of the boundary[9]. A decision of a naval court under s 483 of the Merchant Shipping Act is conclusive *in rem* by statute[10], but the findings of a court of formal investigation under that Act are not admissible in civil proceedings[11]. Findings in the principal proceedings may be admitted without further proof in summary proceedings against the solicitor on the record for an order that he pay costs personally, but the findings are not admissible for that purpose against other non-parties[12].

In *Conlon v Simms*[13] the defendant had been struck off by the Solicitors Disciplinary Tribunal, and his appeal to the Divisional Court had been dismissed. His former partners brought proceedings against him for damages and attempted to prove fraud by tendering the decisions of the Tribunal and the Divisional Court as *prima facie* evidence of their truth. Lawrence Collins J held that the findings were not admissible[14] but it was an abuse of process for the defendant to put his former partners to proof of the fraud, which had been investigated by the Tribunal during a 14 day hearing, and found for the claimants[15]. The Court of Appeal ordered a new trial[16]. The orders of the Tribunal, and the Divisional Court altered the status of the solicitor and were judgments *in rem*, and in accordance with *Hill v Clifford*[17] and *Harvey*[18] the findings should have been admitted as *prima facie* evidence. Since *Hill v*

Clifford was not considered in *Hollington* it remains authoritative on the evidentiary effect of judgments *in rem*. The judgment and reasons of a judge of the Family Division in care proceedings finding the father guilty of sexual abuse of his children are admissible on his appeal against conviction where the issues are identical or similar[19]. A tribunal that is not bound by the rules of evidence may treat a conviction or a judgment in civil proceedings as *prima facie* evidence of the facts[20].

[1] *Conlon v Simms* [2006] 2 All ER 1024, 1069 (Ch D); [2008] 1 WLR 484 CA, 521. In *Arthur Hall* [2002] 1 AC 615, 751 Lord Hobhouse said that the principle in Hollington 'applied to any decision of another court which did not come within the principles of res judicata as between the parties to the later action', cf Lord Hoffmann at 702.

[2] *Bairstow* [2004] Ch 1 CA, 12; *Conlon v Simms* [2008] 1 WLR 484, 515–516.

[3] *Sergeson v Sealey* (1742) 2 Atk 412, 412–413 (inquisition of lunacy in 1726 admissible but not conclusive as to mental capacity in 1724); *Faulder v Silk* (1811) 3 Camp 126 (inquisition that deceased insane since February 1808 admissible but not conclusive as to mental capacity in July 1808); *Prinsep and East India Co. v Dyce Sombre, Troup and Solaril* (1856) 10 Moo PCC 232, 236–239, 244–245 (verdict of jury in 1843 finding deceased insane, and decisions of Lord Chancellor in 1844, 1848 and 1849 admissible but not conclusive as to testamentary capacity, which may exist while commission in lunacy in force); *Hill v Clifford* [1907] 2 Ch 236 CA, 244–245 where Cozens-Hardy MR said that in *Van Grutten v Foxwell* [1897] AC 658 the CA held that the invalidity of a deed of 1835 was not established *in rem* by the finding of an inquisition in 1845 that the party had been a lunatic since 1833, but it was evidence for third parties to rebut; *DPP v Head* [1959] AC 83, 107; para 10.12.

[4] *DPP v Head* [1959] AC 83, 107.

[5] *Harvey* [1901] AC 601, 611 (the Board included Lord Macnaghten and Lord Lindley); *Re Marshall* [1920] 1 Ch 284, 288.

[6] *Ex p Holyland* (1805) 11 Ves 10, 11. Such orders are decisions *in rem* and conclusive as to the status of the patient, and of his receiver or committee, while in force.

[7] Para 11.08 n 3.

[8] *Hill v Clifford* [1907] 2 Ch 236, 245, 252.

[9] *Brisco v Lomax* (1838) 8 Ad & El 198, 212, 214–215.

[10] *Hutton v Ras Steam Shipping Co Ltd* [1907] 1 KB 834 CA.

[11] *The European Gateway* [1987] QB 206; *Spain v Union Steamship Co of New Zealand Ltd* (1923) 33 CLR 555.

[12] *Symphony Group plc v Hodgson* [1994] QB 179, 193.

[13] [2006] 2 All ER 1024 (Ch D), [2008] 1 WLR 484 CA.

[14] Ibid at 1074.

[15] Ibid at 1074, 1075.

[16] [2008] 1 WLR 484 CA.

[17] [1907] 2 Ch 236 CA. Although affirmed on different grounds, [1908] AC 12, 15, the reasoning of the majority in the Court of Appeal was not disapproved.

[18] [1901] AC 601.

[19] *R v D* [1996] QB 283 CA, 291; the reasons for judgment would not have been admissible before the jury: ibid at 288.

[20] *General Medical Council v Spackman* [1943] AC 627.

ACQUITTALS

11.09 At common law an acquittal did not establish the innocence of the accused against the world and was not admissible in civil proceedings[1]. There are many reasons for this, not least the different onus of proof[2]. In *Helton v Allen*[3] the High Court of Australia held that an acquittal on a charge of murder did not establish an estoppel in favour of the accused in civil proceedings brought to prevent him deriving a financial benefit from the death.

1   Para 11.05 n 5.
2   *Helsham v Blackwood* (1851) 11 CB 111. Acquittals are not admissible in civil proceedings in Canada: *Rizzo v Hanover Insurance Co* (1993) 103 DLR (4th) 577 Ont CA.
3   (1940) 63 CLR 691, 710 per Dixon, Evatt and McTiernan JJ: 'His acquittal cannot operate as an estoppel. The plaintiff ... is not bound by it as decisive of ... innocence. Nor indeed do we think that it would be admissible against her as an evidentiary fact ... The only ground upon which the acquittal of Helton could exclude the operation of the rule [against deriving a benefit from crime] is that ... it ought not ... to be extended to a case where the claimant has been absolved in the criminal jurisdiction from the material crime. In other words it may be said that to retry as a civil issue the guilt of a man who has been acquitted on a criminal inquest is so against policy that a rule drawn from public policy ought not to authorise it. There is, however, no trace of any such conception in the history of the principle that by committing a crime no man could obtain a lawful benefit to himself'.

Chapter 12

ROAD TRAFFIC CASES

12.01 Issue estoppels in road traffic cases were first considered in England in *Marginson*[1] but the question had arisen earlier in the United States. The cases fall into two broad groups. The English first instance decisions, said to reflect robust commonsense, favour the recognition of issue estoppels. The other view, said to be strict or technical, recognises very few. The problem is complicated by compulsory insurance for personal injuries and widespread, but sometimes separate, insurance for property damage. *Brunsden v Humphrey*[2] established that there are separate causes of action for property damage and personal injuries. The former tend to be modest in amount and the first litigated, generally in the county court or equivalent, frequently by insurers who may not be on risk for personal injury claims. In the latter drivers who are defendants or Part 20 parties represented by insurers, may also be claimants.

1. [1939] 2 KB 426 CA.
2. (1884) 14 QBD 141 CA; para 21.11.

12.02 In *Linsley v Petrie*[1] in a personal injury case the majority rejected an issue estoppel, from a judgment in a property damage case conducted by an insurer, by distinguishing between the standards of care for property and personal safety, but the distinction was rejected in another Australian case[2] based on English, Northern Irish, New Zealand, and other Australian decisions.

1. [1998] 1 VR 427 CA, 435, 450.
2. *Tiufino v Warland* (2000) 50 NSWLR 104 CA, 113.

THE EFFECT OF INSURANCE

12.03 In a number of cases, personal injury claimants have been confronted with issue estoppels from proceedings in the county court or equivalent conducted by property damage insurers. In *Wall v Radford*[1] and *Talbot*[2] a litigant in his own right and in right of his insurer were held to be the same person for *res judicata* purposes. It is suggested that identity does not necessarily exist in such cases[3]. This is not a technical question because a litigant should not be concluded by a decision in proceedings conducted by others[4]. In *Gleeson*[5] Megarry VC said:

> 'Any contention which leads to the conclusion that a person is liable to be condemned unheard is plainly open to the greatest of suspicions. A [party] ought to be able to put his own [case] in his own way, and to call his own evidence. He ought not to be concluded by the failure of the [case] and the evidence adduced by another … in other proceedings unless … a decision … in them ought fairly and truly … to be in substance a decision against him.'

[1]   [1991] 2 All ER 741, 749–750.
[2]   [1994] QB 290 CA.
[3]   Paras 9.14–9.16.
[4]   *Re Norris* [2001] 1 WLR 1388 HL, 1400–1401.
[5]   [1977] 1 WLR 510, 516.

12.04   Lowry CJ said[1]: 'there is … an argument against allowing a party to be prejudiced in later proceedings by the way in which his insurers have in their own interests conducted the earlier proceedings.' This view prevailed in the Supreme Court of Ireland[2]. The plaintiff's husband died of injuries sustained when his vehicle collided with a bus. A passenger in the bus sued the bus company and a nominee of the husband's insurer, and he was held solely to blame. When the widow sued the bus company its plea of issue estoppel failed. O'Flaherty J said[3]:

> '… neither Mrs Lawless, her children or the other dependants were in any sense represented at the [earlier] hearing … I have no doubt that those who represented the insurance company's interests … did their best. But that is not the point. The point is the entitlement of a person to have an opportunity to present his or her case in court, to decide the tempo of the case, decide what witnesses should be called or not called, and so forth. It is impossible to conclude that there was any privity of interest … between … [the] nominee of the insurance company and the plaintiff and the dependants of the deceased.'

There is support for this view in Australia[4]. In *Marginson*[5]; *Jackson v Goldsmith*[6]; *Craddock*[7]; *Shaw v Sloan*[8] and *Sellen v Bailey*[9] the first action was for property damage and the second for personal injuries. In *Bell v Holmes*[10]; *Randolph v Tuck*[11]; *Wood v Luscombe*[12]; and *Wall v Radford*[13] drivers suing in their own interest had earlier been defendants or third parties represented by insurers. There will be many fewer successful pleas of issue estoppel in road accident cases if a party suing or defending in the interest of an insurer is not the same person for *res judicata* when suing or defending in his own interest.

[1]   *Shaw v Sloan* [1982] NI 393 CA, 397.
[2]   *Lawless v Bus Eireann* [1994] 1 IR 474 SC; cf *Sweeney v Bus Atha Cliath* [2004] 1 IR 576 HC, 85–587; 590 SC.
[3]   Ibid at 478.
[4]   *Linsley v Petrie* [1998] 1 VR 427 CA, 447–448, 451–452.
[5]   [1939] 2 KB 426 CA.
[6]   (1950) 81 CLR 446.
[7]   [1970] NZLR 499 CA.
[8]   [1982] NI 393 CA.
[9]   [1999] RTR 63 CA (the same insurer was on risk).
[10]   [1956] 1 WLR 1359.
[11]   [1962] 1 QB 175.

12   [1966] 1 QB 169.
13   [1991] 2 All ER 741.

WALL V RADFORD

12.05 The most recent considered decision in England is *Wall v Radford*[1] where Popplewell J rejected the so-called technical view adopted by Lawton J in *Randolph v Tuck*[2]. The latter was later said in the Court of Appeal[3] to be 'out of line' with other first instance decisions in England which 'understandably' were not challenged, but the point was not argued or further considered. The 'common sense' view[4] can fairly be tested by examining a reasoning in *Wall v Radford*[5]. W was the driver of a vehicle in which V was the passenger. R had abandoned a vehicle which obstructed the road. W swerved to avoid the abandoned vehicle and collided with another. In an action by the passenger V, R and W were held equally to blame. W, who had also been injured, sued R who pleaded that W was issue estopped by the earlier apportionment. The first action had determined the liability of the drivers to a passenger. The second involved an action by one driver against the other. Popplewell J acknowledged the legal distinction but upheld the estoppel[6]:

> '... the contributory negligence of the plaintiff ... is ... the same issue as her negligence in [the earlier action] ... Although a separate duty is owed to another driver from that owed to a passenger that does not mean ... that the duty is in any way different. *The facts giving rise to a breach of that duty are identical and liability for that breach of duty is identical*[7]. ... The duty is to take reasonable care. It is in the absence of special circumstances ... the same care which has to be taken in respect of the passenger, another driver and the driver himself ... It is not a different duty. It is the same duty owed to a different person.'

1   [1991] 2 All ER 741.
2   [1962] 1 QB 175.
3   *Sellen v Bailey* [1999] RTR 63 CA, 68.
4   The other decisions are *Bell v Holmes* [1956] 1 WLR 1359; *Wood v Luscombe* [1966] 1 QB 169; *North West Water Ltd v Binnie & Partners* [1990] 3 All ER 547, 559–561. *Randolph v Tuck* [1962] 1 QB 175, is to the contrary.
5   [1991] 2 All ER 741.
6   Ibid at 750–751.
7   Emphasis supplied.

12.06 The estoppel prevented R contending for a more favourable apportionment. Popplewell J acknowledged[1] that there may be cases where the 'duty' owed by a driver to himself[2] can differ from that owed to another driver eg, the 'duty' to wear a seatbelt, but said that the allegations of negligence and contributory negligence in the driver W's action were the same as those in the passenger V's action and '[t]he issues of fact are identical'. *Nance*[3] established that contributory negligence may involve either a breach of duty owed to the defendant or a failure by the claimant to take reasonable care for his own safety. In the passenger's action the contributory negligence of driver W was irrelevant, but it was relevant in W's action. How could the issues be the same?

1   [1991] 2 All ER 741, 749.

2   There is no such 'duty' in the strict sense. Cf *Nance v British Columbia Electric Railway Co Ltd* [1951] AC 601, 611 (*Nance*).
3   Ibid.

12.07 In *Edwards v Joyce*[1], actions were brought by passengers against both drivers and Sholl J held that the apportionment in the first was not *res judicata* in the second. Popplewell J thought that the apportionment between drivers in claims by passengers could not be different[2], and referred to a hypothetical collision between two buses, each with 50 passengers, to illustrate the absurd results if apportionment could be relitigated. In *Anderson v Wilson*[3] Lord Keith (later Lord Keith of Kinkel) did not find that absurd. The absurdity would flow from the defendants' failure to ensure that liability was determined at a single hearing[4]. Unless this is done the findings of liability to the claimant in one passenger's action will not be binding on any party in any other action. Passengers in the same or different vehicles are not privies of each other. The apportionment between the defendants must be based on the evidence which may differ from case to case. The state of the evidence cannot be known before the end of the trial even if the allegations of negligence are the same. There is no certainty that the factual issues will be the same, or that the second tribunal of fact will take the same view as the first.

The question arose in *Hood v Commonwealth of Australia*[5]: In the first action P, a passenger in Hood's vehicle, recovered against the owners of both with responsibility apportioned 40:60. In the second H, a passenger in the Commonwealth vehicle, recovered against Hood who was held solely responsible, and the court held that the apportionment in the first action was not binding in the second. Gowans J, delivering the judgment of the court said[6]:

'... the contention involves a misconception as to the nature of the issue ... in the contribution proceedings in [P's] action. That ... was as to the contribution between the defendants in respect of the damage suffered by [P] and no one else. A decision ... as to the rights and obligations of defendants to contribution ... in respect of damage suffered by one passenger ... involves a different issue from the question ... of contribution between the same defendants in respect of damage suffered by a different passenger ... in the same collision ... [T]he duties of drivers to passengers in different vehicles or even the same vehicle can be different, depending upon whether, for example, a passenger has voluntarily undertaken a risk. Likewise, whether there has been a breach of duty to different passengers can vary according to whether or not a passenger has for example interfered with the driving ... or has requested the driver to drive in a particular manner ... The duty owed by each driver to each passenger is a different duty from that owed to each other passenger. The issues involved in ... claims by different passengers may often be similar but they are never the same ... [I]t was said that the decision in the contribution proceedings in the [P] action determined as between Hood and the Commonwealth an issue as to whether ... the latter was responsible for the collision ... as to this, two things may be said ... One is that it treats of negligence as being 'in the air' ... whereas there must be a breach of duty owed towards someone in particular. The other is that issue estoppel only operates upon ... ultimate facts ... It does not operate on evidentiary facts ... it would not ... establish by estoppel the Commonwealth's liability as a tortfeasor to [H].'

1   [1954] VLR 216.
2   [1991] 2 All ER 741, 752.

3   [1972] SC 147.
4   By consolidating all actions to determine the question of liability or by the selection of a
    test case by agreement or court order: *Ashmore v British Coal Corpn* [1990] 2 QB 338 CA.
5   [1968] VR 619.
6   Ibid at 625–627.

EACH DUTY IS DISTINCT IN LAW

12.08 Negligence 'must be tested by asking with reference to each of the
several complainants was a duty owed to him or her? It is not enough to say
the cyclist was guilty of negligence to someone'[1]. Since a duty of care is
personal to each claimant the duty to passenger A cannot, as a matter of law,
be the same as the duty to passenger B. B cannot sue for breach of the
defendant's duty to A. They are different duties, even if their practical content
is much the same. There is the same difference between the duties of a driver
to a passenger and to another driver. The statement in *Wall v Radford*[2] that:
'It is the same duty owed to a different person' was flawed.

1   *Bourhill v Young* [1943] AC 92, 117 per Lord Porter,and also at 108 per Lord Wright.
2   Para 12.05 n 6.

THE ISSUES MUST BE IDENTICAL AS A MATTER OF LAW

12.09 The fact that the issues are, for all practical purposes, the same does
not establish the basis for an issue estoppel. This was decided in *New
Brunswick*[1] where Lord Maugham LC said[2]:

> '... the doctrine cannot ... extend to presumptions or probabilities or to issues
> in the second action which may be, but cannot be asserted beyond all possible
> doubt to be, identical with those raised in the previous action ... The issue of
> construction in the second action could indeed be ... similar to that decided in
> the first; but it related to a different cause of action ... on other bonds, and
> could not be asserted to be the same issue.'[3]

Lord Romer said[4]:

> '... whenever a question has in substance been decided ... each party is
> estopped from litigating the same question thereafter. But this is very different
> from saying that he may not thereafter litigate ... a question which is merely
> substantially similar to the one that has already been decided ... he is not
> estopped from subsequently litigating the construction of another document
> even though the second one may be in substantially identical words. The
> documents are two distinct documents, and ... their construction two distinct
> questions.'

1   [1939] AC 1, 14. The *res judicata* estoppel failed for this reason.
2   [1939] AC 1, 20 (the first action was on one bond, and the plaintiff obtained judgment on
    a motion in default of appearance. The second was on 992 bonds in the same issue).
3   Lord Maugham LC said at p 20 there was no allegation in the first action that the other
    bonds were in the same terms, and such an allegation would have been irrelevant and
    improper. He also said that the bonds may have been issued in different countries and at
    different times, which might have 'a possible bearing' on their construction.
4   [1939] AC 1, 43.

12.10 The identity of issues is a question of law for the judge[1], not one of fact for any jury. Before the Judicature Acts it could be determined on demurrer[2] and can now be determined as a preliminary issue[3]. The first instance decisions in England which favour the commonsense approach treat the question as one of fact[4]. *Marginson*[5] does not bind the Court of Appeal or the High Court to adopt the commonsense approach. There were two claims in the first action, one by the owners and tenants of the damaged houses against the owners of both vehicles, and one by the Corporation against Marginson for damage to its bus. The Court of Appeal based its findings of *res judicata* estoppel on the decision in the second claim that Mrs Marginson and the bus driver had been 'equally to blame'[6]. The Corporation's claim for damage to its bus failed because the contributory negligence of its driver was a complete defence. The finding that Mrs Marginson was negligent was not necessary for the decision in her favour and could not create an issue estoppel[7].

[1] *Marginson* [1939] 2 KB 426 CA, 430, 438; *Wall v Radford* [1991] 2 All ER 741, *Craddock* [1970] NZLR 499 CA, *Anderson v Wilson* [1972] SC 147.
[2] Para 8.30.
[3] The question was decided as a preliminary issue in the cases referred to in paras 12.10 n 1, 18.09 n 5.
[4] *Bell v Holmes* [1956] 1 WLR 1359, 1366–1367; *Wall v Radford* [1991] 2 All ER 741, 750–751.
[5] [1939] 2 KB 426 CA.
[6] Ibid at 438–439. This was recognised in *Randolph v Tuck* [1962] 1 QB 175, 187 and *Wall v Radford* [1991] 2 All ER 741, 748.
[7] Para 8.25.

THE OTHER LINE OF CASES

12.11 The reasoning in the other line of cases appears in *Jackson v Goldsmith*[1]. J, the owner and driver of a motorcycle on which W was a pillion passenger, collided with a car owned and driven by G. G sued J for property damage and the court held that the accident was caused by J's negligence and that G was not guilty of contributory negligence. The pillion passenger W sued J the motorcycle rider and J claimed contribution from G the car driver. G pleaded that his liability to J was *res judicata*. The High Court of Australia held that there was no issue estoppel because the issues were different. The issue in the first action was whether G, the driver of the car, was guilty of contributory negligence. This was not the same as the question whether G was in breach of a duty to the pillion passenger. Latham CJ said[2]:

'In the district court the issue was whether Goldsmith had been guilty of contributory negligence, that is, had he contributed to the injury ... by either – (1) carelessness with respect to his own safety; or (2) breach of a duty which he owed to Jackson [the rider of the motorcycle] to take care? What was decided was that Goldsmith was not guilty of contributory negligence. This decision therefore negated the following propositions: (1) that Goldsmith contributed to his own injury by carelessness for his own safety; (2) that he contributed thereto by ... a breach of duty owed by him to Jackson to take care. In the third party proceedings ... the question is whether Goldsmith is liable ... to White [the pillion passenger] by reason of a breach of duty to take care which he owed to White. The proceedings in the district court did not determine whether there was any breach by Goldsmith of a duty which he owed to White. Neither the proposition (1) or proposition (2) is a determination of the issue in the third party proceedings. Therefore the decision in the district court does not estop Jackson from alleging that Goldsmith was guilty of a breach of a duty which he owed to White.'

1 (1950) 81 CLR 446.
2 Ibid at 455.

POSITION IN SCOTLAND

12.12 In *Anderson v Wilson*[1] a passenger in a minibus which collided with a car succeeded against both drivers and liability was apportioned. The question of apportionment arose again in the action by the other passengers and the bus owner's plea that this was *res judicata* was overruled by Lord Keith who said[2]:

'... in a question with the pursuers both the defender [bus owner] and the third party are undoubtedly entitled to maintain ... that the other is wholly to blame for the accident ... and each of them has a plea to that effect. The court or jury would in any event have to hear all the evidence bearing on the question of fault in relation to each of them. Further it is at least conceivable that one or other would escape all liability to the pursuers and in that event there could be no question ... of contribution ... In the event of both ... being found liable ... I cannot see that it would add materially to the length or expense of the ... trial if it were open to apportion liability among them in such proportions as the court or jury "may deem just" ...'

1 [1972] SC 147; para 12.07 n 3; followed in *Clink v Speyside Distillery Ltd* [1995] SLT 1344.
2 Ibid at 153.

THE STATUTES

12.13 The statutes authorising apportionment between defendants and between a claimant and the defendant focus on responsibility for the damage to the claimant and appear to exclude issue estoppels. The 1945 Act[1] authorises an apportionment based on the parties' 'responsibility for the damage'. Claims for property damage and personal injury are separate causes of action[2], and in Australia it has been held that the equivalent of the 1945 Act authorises different apportionments where the damage is different[3]. Under s 1(1) of the 1945 Act the issue is responsibility for the claimant's damage, not that of anyone else, particularly not the defendant's damage. Likewise under s 2(1) of the 1978 Act the contribution recoverable from a co–tortfeasor 'shall be such as may be ... just and equitable having regard to the extent of that person's responsibility for the damage in question.'

1 Law Reform (Contributory Negligence) Act 1945.
2 *Brunsden v Humphrey* (1884) 14 QBD 141 CA.
3 *Azzopardi v Bois* [1968] VR 183, 187–188. Different apportionments could be supported where a seat belt or helmet were not worn.

12.14 The so called technical approach has been accepted by appellate courts in Australia[1], New Zealand[2], New York[3], Ireland[4] and is the law in Scotland[5]. This invites a re-examination of the question in England. The commonsense

185

view does not prevent the relitigation of similar questions. In *Marginson*[6] the wrongful death and estate claims were not barred. Where an owner sued the other driver for property damage and failed because of his employee's contributory negligence, a claim by the employee was not barred[7]. The decision as to liability and contribution in a claim by one passenger will not bind any party in a claim by another[8]. Where employer and employee are sued as joint tortfeasors neither will be estopped unless both are[9]. There will be fewer issue estoppels if an insured in his own right and in right of an insurer are different parties.

[1] *Jackson v Goldsmith* (1950) 81 CLR 446; *Ramsay v Pigram* (1967) 118 CLR 271.
[2] *Craddock* [1970] NZLR 499 CA.
[3] *Neenan v Woodside Astoria Transportation* 256 NYS 38 (1932), cited by Lawton J in *Randolph v Tuck* [1962] 1 QB 175, 185, 188. The Appellate Division of the Supreme Court held that a judgment in proceedings between the owners of the vehicles was not *res judicata* on liability or contribution in proceedings by a passenger.
[4] *Lawless v Bus Eireann* [1994] 1 IR 474 SC.
[5] *Anderson v Wilson* [1972] SC 147.
[6] [1939] 2 KB 426 CA. The decision that M's personal claim was barred (para 12.10 for the facts) depended on the assumption, which was not challenged, that he was vicariously liable for his wife's negligence. Although on that assumption they were joint tortfeasors he was not her privy and should not have been bound: para 9.48.
[7] *Townsend v Bishop* [1939] 1 All ER 805; *Bryan v Kildangan Stud Unlimited* [2005] 1 IR 587.
[8] *Anderson v Wilson* [1972] SC 147 (passengers are not privies).
[9] *Shaw v Sloan* [1982] NI 393 CA; contra *Edwards v Joyce* [1954] VLR 216, and as to joint tortfeasors generally, para 9.48.

12.15 In *Wall v Radford*[1] Popplewell J also held that relitigation of the apportionment was an abuse of process. Recognition that the driver as an insured defendant and a claimant in his own interest are different parties should preclude such a finding[2], and the cases in para 12.07 suggest that there is little scope for that when apportionment depends on the evidence called by each claimant. However, subject to the effect of insurance, if one driver recovers his property damage in full without any deduction for contributory negligence, there will be an issue estoppel in any proceedings for personal injuries[3].

[1] [1991] 2 All ER 741.
[2] Paras 9.14–9.16, 9.23; *Tiufino v Warland* (2000) 50 NSWLR 104 CA, 113–114.
[3] *Tiufino v Warland* (2000) 50 NSWLR 104 CA, 109–110; *Donohoe v Browne* [1986] IR 90.

TALBOT

12.16 In *Talbot*[1] the Court of Appeal applied *Henderson*[2] in a road traffic case. A car struck a pool of water and hit a tree, and the driver and a passenger were badly injured. The passenger sued the driver who, represented by his insurer, sought contribution from the Council which was then joined as second defendant. The passenger succeeded and the driver was held two–thirds and the Council one–third responsible. The driver then sued the Council but was met with defences of limitation and *res judicata*. He was suing on a different cause of action, and the defendant was not relying on an issue estoppel which would have entitled the driver to one third of his damages. The

Court of Appeal held that the claim should have been included in the contribution proceedings, that there were no special circumstances, and the driver's action was barred by the Kilbrandon principle in *Yat Tung*[3]. The driver argued that there were special circumstances because 'his' solicitors in the contribution proceedings were instructed by his insurer. He was advised against applying to have his personal claim joined to the contribution proceedings although, under rules of court, this would have avoided a limitation defence. The court held that the driver was bound by the conduct of the solicitors.

¹ [1994] QB 290 CA.
² (1843) 3 Hare 100; para 7.03 (party must bring forward his whole case).
³ [1975] AC 581, 590 where Lord Kilbrandon held that *Henderson* barred issues which 'could and therefore should' have been litigated, a view rejected in *Johnson* [2002] 2 AC 1.

12.17 The driver brought the contribution proceedings for the benefit of the insurer and should have been treated as a different party when suing in his own right[1]. Stuart Smith LJ applied *Henderson* and the Kilbrandon principle without finding that the second action was an abuse[2]. Mann LJ applied the Kilbrandon principle[3]. *Talbot* was doubted in Northern Ireland[4] and impliedly overruled in *Johnson*[5] when the Kilbrandon principle was rejected. The test is now abuse and the inability of the driver to control the first proceedings should have precluded such a finding.

¹ Paras 9.14–9.16, 9.23.
² [1994] QB 290, 296–297.
³ Ibid at 301. He also held (at 300) that the plaintiff was barred by a cause of action estoppel, which was contrary to *Brunsden v Humphrey* (1884) 14 QBD 141 CA. Stuart Smith LJ recognised that the causes of action were different.
⁴ *Ulster Bank Limited v Fisher & Fisher (a firm)* [1999] NI 68.
⁵ [2002] 2 AC 1.

Chapter 13

TAXATION AND RATING

13.01 Decisions on income tax, rating and other annual taxes are an established exception to the general rules as to *res judicata*. Decisions on one year's tax or rate, or one rating valuation or assessment list, do not create estoppels for another year's tax or rate, or a later valuation or assessment list[1]. 'The assessment seems inherently to be of a passing nature'[2]. While such decisions (subject to appeal) are conclusive for the particular assessment[3], they will not estop either party when the question arises on another year's assessment, or on a new valuation or list.

[1] *Caffoor* [1961] AC 584, 599–600; Andrews 'Estoppels against Statutes' (1966) 29 MLR 1, 13–14.
[2] *IRC v Sneath* [1932] 2 KB 362 CA, 383 (*Sneath*); *Hope* [1960] AC 551, 563.
[3] Ibid at 383–384; *Broken Hill Pty Co Ltd v Broken Hill Municipal Council* [1926] AC 94, 100 (*Broken Hill*) per Lord Carson: 'No doubt as regards that year the decision could not be disputed'.

13.02 The liability of the taxpayer for one year's tax or rate is not the same question as his liability for another year[1], even if the law and the material facts are the same. What might be the same question in other cases is not in taxation and rating cases, which are *sui generis* in this regard[2]. This was long in doubt because of a remarkable conflict between two decisions of the Privy Council in Australian appeals in the same volume of the Appeal Cases. The first allowed relitigation in a later year, the second did not.

[1] *Broken Hill* [1926] AC 94, 100 per Lord Carson: 'The present case relates to a new question – namely the valuation for a different year and the liability for that year. It is not *eadem quaestio*, and ... the principle of *res judicata* cannot apply'; *Spassked Pty ltd v FCT (No. 2)* (2007) 165 FCR 484, 500–501 (*Spassked*).
[2] *Caffoor* [1961] AC 584, 599.

13.03 *Broken Hill* was heard in July 1925 and judgment was delivered on 10 November[1]. The earlier decision on rating value had been given by the High Court of Australia, but it was held that this did not estop the parties relitigating the issue on a subsequent year's assessment. *Hoystead* was heard in October 1925, and judgment was delivered in December[2]. In the earlier case a construction of the will assumed by the parties was an essential basis of the

189

High Court's decision, which estopped the revenue contending for a different construction in a later year's assessment.

1   The Board included Viscount Cave, Lord Carson, Lord Blanesburgh and Duff J.
2   [1926] AC 155. The Board included Lord Sumner, Lord Shaw, Lord Phillimore, Lord Darling and Lord Salvesen.

HOPE

13.04 A local valuation court decided in 1951 that the Society's land was exempt from rates. In 1956 a new valuation list showed its land as rateable. Although there had been no change of circumstances the Lands Tribunal held that there was no *res judicata*. The House of Lords held that 'it is not in the nature of a decision given on one rate or tax that it should settle anything more than the bare issue of that one liability, and that, consequently, it cannot constitute an estoppel when a new issue of liability to a succeeding year's rate or tax comes up for adjudication ... this liability is a "new question".'[1]

1   [1960] AC 551, 562 per Lord Radcliffe.

WHY A 'NEW QUESTION'?

13.05 Lord Radcliffe gave two reasons[1]:

'The reason why, when you are dealing with rates and taxes, the difference of subject-matter is treated as being so important seems to lie in two considerations which, ... are peculiar to their particular field. One consideration is that the jurisdiction of the tribunal to which the decision belongs by the administrative scheme is a limited one. It is limited in the sense that its function begins and ends with that of deciding what is to be the assessment or liability of a person for a defined and terminable period. "The assessment seems inherently to be of a passing nature".[2] For the purpose of arriving at its decision the tribunal may well have to take account of, and form its own opinion on, questions of general law; ... but ... the view adopted ... is incidental to its only direct function, that of fixing the assessment. For that limited purpose it is a court with a jurisdiction competent to produce a final decision between the parties before it: but it is not a court of competent jurisdiction to decide general questions of law with that finality which is needed to set up ... estoppel per rem judicatam.'

His other reason[3] was the special position of the valuation officer or equivalent official. Lord Keith of Avonholm said[4]:

'What we are faced with here is an administrative act of a public official, the valuation officer, against which the party affected has a right of appeal to the local valuation court, with further appeals to higher courts. The valuation officer has a public duty to perform by making ... every five years a valuation list of all hereditaments, with certain exceptions, in his rating area. He must necessarily reconsider and revise the previous valuation list. He has no personal interest in any appeals taken against his valuations, and has a duty to hold the scales as fairly as he can among the ratepayers affected, the occupiers of the various hereditaments. The general body of ratepayers is constantly changing. With each quinquennium the revaluations will affect a new body of ratepayers. I doubt if the valuation officer owing such a duty to an everchanging body of ratepayers can be regarded as always the same party ... for ... res judicata. What if the appellant society ... moves into another rating area with a different valuation officer?

I emphasise these aspects of the functions of a valuation officer ..., for they lead to what I regard as the true answer to the submission for the appellants, which is that a public officer in the position of the respondent cannot be estopped from carrying out his duties under the statute. The case is, I think, a fortiori of ... *Maritime Electric Co Ltd v General Dairies Ltd*'.[5]

1   [1960] AC 551, 563.
2   *Sneath* [1932] 2 KB 362, CA 383 per Hanworth MR. In *Montreal v Sun Life Assurance Co of Canada* [1952] 2 DLR 81 PC, 98 which dealt with valuations for municipal rating Lord Porter said: '... each new assessment constitutes a fresh start and the former has very little value'.
3   [1960] AC 551, 565.
4   Ibid at 568.
5   [1937] AC 610 (estoppel by representation).

CAFFOOR

13.06 In *Caffoor*[1] the Privy Council had to choose between its former decisions, and held that taxation and rating decisions were *sui generis*, adopting the principle in *Broken Hill*. Lord Radcliffe said[2]:

'It may be that the principles applied in these cases form a somewhat anomalous branch of the general law of estoppel per rem judicatam, and are not easily derived from or transferred to other branches of litigation in which such estoppels have to be considered; but in their Lordships' opinion they are well established in their own field, and it is not ... to be assumed that the result ... should be regretted in the public interest'.

Recently Lord Hope said[3]:

'The purpose of an appeal under s 31 of the 1970 Act is to challenge the amount charged to tax by an assessment ... The question as to the amount of any relief carried forward to subsequent periods remains open for examination as the assessment of each subsequent period is issued. This is because the Taxes Act do not provide any means by which that amount can be determined conclusively ... for any period other than that to which the assessment relates.'

Hope and *Caffoor* were followed in Ireland where the Supreme Court held that an action to recover council rates was not barred by a decision in prior years[4]. *Caffoor* remains good law despite subsequent legislative changes[5]. There is some uncertainty in Canada about possible exceptions to the general rule that there is no issue estoppel from one rating valuation to another[6].

1   [1961] AC 584; *Comr v Sunnen* 333 US 591 (1948), 599: estoppel by *res judicata* 'is not meant to create vested rights in decisions that have become obsolete or erroneous with time thereby causing inequities among taxpayers'. The Appellate Division of the Supreme Court of South Africa, applying Roman-Dutch law, rejected an issue estoppel in an income tax case without deciding whether *Caffoor* should be followed: *KVBI v ABSA Bank Bok* [1995] (1) SA 653 [1995] SALR Translations 52 (*Absa Bank*).
2   [1961] AC 584, 599–600; *Chamberlain* (1988) 164 CLR 502, 510; *Spassked* (2007) 165 FCR 484. *Douglas v CIR* [2006] 1 NZLR 513 appears inconsistent with *Caffoor* which was not referred to.

3 *MacNiven v Westmoreland Investments Ltd* [2003] 1 AC 311, 340, 343. The same point was made in *Absa Bank* (para 13.06 n 1) at 57, 69 where it was argued that the court hearing an appeal from the assessment for the 1981 year could not determine the liability of the taxpayer for the 1978 year. In *Spassked* (2007) 165 FCR 484, 507–508 Edmonds J held that a decision on the 1992 tax year could not determine any question for the 1991, 1993 and later years because the Commissioner had not yet determined the taxpayer's objections to those assessments which was a pre-condition for any appeal.
4 *Kildare County Council v Keogh* [1971] IR 330.
5 *King v Walden* (2001) 74 TC 45, 105; *Stow* [2008] Ch 461, 478; para 13.06 n 3.
6 *New Brunswick v Ganong Bros Ltd* (2004) 240 DLR (4th) 687, 704–706, NBCA.

RATIONALE FOR EXCEPTION

13.07 Another rationale for these decisions is that each year every taxpayer should be correctly assessed for the tax properly due under the statute. Past errors in the construction or application of the statute are not carried forward indefinitely but, subject to the doctrine of precedent, each year begins, as it were, with a clean slate. The principle is not confined to the construction of the statute but extends to decisions about private rights which would normally attract an issue estoppel. The rationale is that given by Lord Selborne LC in an analogous situation[1]:

'To hold the Crown or the urban authority estopped for ever … would be to deprive the other adjoining landowners, who were not parties or privies to the proceeding, of their statutable right to have a just rateable contribution from the defendant and his successors in estate … There would therefore be, within the same district, two laws operating simultaneously in opposite directions as against different persons in exactly the same circumstances, under the same words of taxation, in the same public Act of Parliament; and either imposing upon some of those individuals and their privies in estate a liability which the statute had not in fact imposed, or exonerating others, and their privies in estate (to the prejudice of the rest) from the share of a common burden which the statute had imposed equally upon all.'

1 *R v Hutchings* (1881) 6 QBD 300 CA, 305–306; para 13.06 n 1.

OTHER TAXES

13.08 Warren J has recently questioned whether *Cafoor* applies to decisions on taxes, such as inheritance tax, which do not attract an annual assessment[1]. Although decisions on an annual assessment create no estoppel for another year, where the same transaction is assessable at different dates for stamp duty and death duty a decision as to its effect for one tax will estop the parties contending for a different effect for the other[2]. The US Supreme Court has held that *res judicata* has a restricted application to decisions on customs duty[3], which are only *res judicata* for the subject importation. The court said[4]:

' … circumstances justify limiting the finality of the conclusion in customs controversies to the identical importation. The business of importing is carried on by large houses between whom and the Government there are innumerable transactions … and there are constant differences as to proper classifications of similar importations. The evidence which may be presented in one case may be much varied in the next. The importance of a classification and its far-reaching effect may not have been clearly understood … when the first litigation was carried through. One large importing house may secure a judgment in its favour ... If that house can rely upon a conclusion in early litigation as one which is to remain final as to it ... while a similar importation made by another ... may be tried ... and a different conclusion reached, a most embarrassing situation is presented. The importing house which has ... obtained a favourable decision permanently binding on the Government will be able to import the goods at a much better rate than ... its competitors. Such a result would lead to inequality in the administration of the customs law, to discrimination and to great injustice and confusion. In the same way if the first decision were against a large importing house, and its competitors ... succeeded in securing a different conclusion, the first litigant, bound by the judgment against it ... must permanently do business ... at great and inequitable disadvantage with its competitors'.

This reasoning applies to all taxes on recurring business transactions such as excise duties, value added tax, sales tax and stamp duty on common form business instruments. The principle is derived from the statute which discloses an intention to impose a tax which operates uniformly. The point was made by Lord Selborne LC in *R v Hutchings*[5].

1   *Stow* [2008] Ch 461, 478.
2   *Queensland Trustees Ltd v Comr of Stamp Duties* (1956) 96 CLR 131. In 1942 the Commissioner assessed an instrument to *ad valorem* stamp duty as a resettlement by the executors and the assessment was upheld. In 1954 the Commissioner assessed the settled property to succession duty on the basis that the settlement was created by the will but was issue estopped by the first decision; *Spassked* (2007) 165 FCR 484, 505.
3   *United States of America v Stone & Downer Co* 274 US 225 (1927).
4   Ibid at 235–236; para 10.27.
5   (1881) 6 QBD 300 CA, 305–306 quoted para 13.07.

EFFECT OF DECISIONS INTER PARTES ON THE REVENUE

13.09 Many civil decisions have direct or indirect consequences for the Revenue. Where a company recovers damages for breach of a trading contract the proceeds will be taxable income. A claimant who recovers a large verdict can more readily pay outstanding tax assessments, and his taxable income and taxable estate may increase. Everyday experience confirms that the Revenue are not necessary parties to such proceedings, but there are exceptions. In *Re Sassoon*[1] the interest of Ronald in an estate did not pass on his death if it had been forfeited. The question of forfeiture was litigated in the absence of the Crown and Luxmoore J held that there had been a forfeiture. The Crown refused to refund the excess duty and the trustees and Ronald's executors sued. Farwell J held that the rights of the beneficiaries had been settled by the decision of Luxmoore J and the Crown could not tax on any other basis but two members of the Court of Appeal[2] disagreed[3]. Romer LJ said[4]:

'Whenever ... after the death of a person a question arises whether certain property does or does not pass ... the Crown is directly interested in that question and cannot be deprived of any rights it may have ... by the decision of the court given in its absence. Where, however, any question as to a person's interest in any property falls to be dealt with by the courts in that person's lifetime, no claim of the Crown in respect of estate duty payable upon his death has come into existence, and the Crown is in no way interested ... in the question ... On the person's death, therefore, the Crown could not question a decision given in his lifetime as to his interest in the property ... its interest would only have come into being after the decision has been given'.

The question considered by Romer LJ arose in the High Court of Australia soon afterwards[5]. A trustee was assessed for land tax in accordance with the rights of the beneficiaries declared by the court. The trustee appealed, contending that the beneficiaries' rights were different and the Commissioner, who had not been a party, could not rely on any issue estoppel. The court held there was no issue estoppel but the Commissioner could only tax on the interests declared by the court[6]. In *Vandervell Trustees Ltd v White*[7], the Revenue claimed that the deceased retained an interest in shares he had settled and assessed him to surtax. The assessments were challenged. His executors claimed that the shares were held on a resulting trust, and sought to join the Crown to obtain a decision that would be binding in the tax appeals. The House of Lords held that the Crown could not be joined. Most of the issues fall outside the scope of this book, but differing views were expressed about the effect on the tax appeals of a decision in the High Court to which the Crown was a party. Lord Reid said[8]:

> 'I have ... no hesitation in holding that the Commissioners are bound to treat as res judicata any decision of a competent court to which the Revenue were parties on any issue which may come before them'.

Lord Diplock[9] however considered that the Special Commissioners were not bound by issue estoppels in such circumstances. The question was considered again in *Stow*[10] where disputes about beneficial ownership arose between trustees of settlements, the widow and the Revenue. The trustees had appealed against assessments of capital transfer tax and inheritance tax, and the same questions could arise in income tax appeals. They sought declaratory relief and joined the Revenue who applied to strike out the action against them because the Special Commissioners had exclusive jurisdiction. Warren J dismissed the application, saying[11]:

> 'If a dispute ... arises between a person and HMRC which is independent of the tax appeal ... the exclusive jurisdiction principle does not render that dispute ... non-justiciable in the High Court simply because the same, or a very similar, issue will be relevant to, or perhaps even determinative of, both that dispute and the tax appeal.'

This assumes that a judgment of the High Court to which HMRC is a party will create issue estoppels for tax appeals.

[1] [1933] Ch 858 CA.
[2] Ibid per Lawrence LJ at 881, Romer LJ at 893.
[3] The decision of Luxmoore J was upheld: *IRC v Raphael* [1935] AC 96.
[4] Ibid at 893. Where a deceased's property rights are judicially determined in his lifetime, the Crown when taxing his estate on death claims through him. When it taxes his income it also claims through him.
[5] *Executor Trustee and Agency Co v DCT* (1939) 62 CLR 545.
[6] Ibid at 562–563, 570. In *Spens v IRC* [1970] 1 WLR 1173 the taxpayer's attempt to defeat surtax assessments by an issue estoppel from an order under the Variation of Trusts Act 1958 failed on the facts, cf *Vernon v IRC* [1956] 1 WLR 1169; para 9.24 n 1.
[7] [1971] AC 912. The decision on RSC O 15 r 6(2)(b) was effectively reversed by r 6(2)(b)(ii). CPR Pt 19.1 and 19.2 authorise the joinder of the HMRC in appropriate cases.

8   [1971] AC 912, 929.
9   Ibid at 943.
10   [2008] Ch 461. In Ireland the High Court does not have original jurisdiction to determine an individual's tax liability, which can only be determined on an appeal from an assessment: *Criminal Assets Bureau v Hunt* [2003] 2 IR 168 SC, 185. Query whether this bars proceedings to determine an isolated issue as in *Stow*.
11   Ibid at 475.

EFFECT OF TAX DECISION IN OTHER PROCEEDINGS

13.10 The converse situation arose in the Supreme Court of Canada[1]. The Exchequer Court confirmed an income tax assessment which included the value of improvements to the taxpayer's land paid for by a company despite her claim she owed it the money. When the Revenue sought to attach this debt for taxes due from the company, she set up an estoppel. The majority, in a judgment delivered by Dickson J, held that the questions in the two proceedings were not the same and a finding that the taxpayer had no liability to the company 'was not legally indispensable to the judgment in the income tax appeal or a necessary finding to support that judgment.'[2] The Exchequer Court had no jurisdiction to make a binding decision on the existence of the debt which only came into question collaterally in the tax appeal[3].

1   *Angle v Minister of National Revenue* (1974) 47 DLR (3d) 544; paras 4.07 n 4, 4.08 n 9. An estoppel by conduct in court proceedings was not argued; para 9.46.
2   Ibid at 556.
3   Ibid at 557, citing *A-G for Trinidad and Tobago v Eriché* [1893] AC 518. The company was not a party to the tax appeal, and was not bound in any event.

RECOVERY PROCEEDINGS

13.11 The operation of the merger principle in the recovery of assessed tax arose in unusual circumstances in the High Court of Australia[1]. The Deputy Commissioner sued for outstanding tax but, through a typing error, the writ claimed $25,557.92 instead of $255,579.20. Consent judgment was entered and the debt was paid. The Deputy Commissioner sued for the balance, but the court held that he was not in a special position and the cause of action had merged in the judgment[2].

1   *Chamberlain* (1988) 164 CLR 502.
2   The Deputy Commissioner then had the consent judgment set aside for unilateral mistake: *Chamberlain (No 2)* (1990) 26 FCR 221 but this was reversed because the claim was *res judicata* as the result of the High Court decision: *Chamberlain (No 2)* (1991) 28 FCR 21; criticised para 26.14.

EFFECT OF CRIMINAL PROCEEDINGS

13.12 Cases in Australia and New Zealand illustrate some of the problems which can arise in tax appeals as a result of criminal proceedings. The Australian case concerned a conviction and the New Zealand cases concerned acquittals. In *Saffron v Federal Comr of Taxation (No 2)*[1] the taxpayer had been convicted of conspiracy to defraud the Commonwealth through fraudulent income tax returns. His appeals against assessments based on the Crown case in the criminal proceedings raised the same issues. The Federal Court held by majority that the taxpayer could challenge the facts in the Crown case which the jury must have accepted[2]. In *Maxwell v IRC*[3] the acquittal of the taxpayer on charges of wilfully making false returns did not bar civil claims by the Commissioner that they were fraudulent or wilfully misleading because the issues were not identical. In *Gregoriadis v Comr of Inland Revenue*[4] the taxpayer's acquittal on charges of wilfully making false tax returns did not support a defence of *autrefois acquit*[5] against assessments for penal tax but they were set aside because the Commissioner who unusually, had the onus of proof, could only support the assessments by challenging the acquittals. The standard of proof was held to so 'closely' approximate the criminal standard[6] that the issues were identical[7]. One member of the court considered that the civil proceedings were an abuse of process[8]. In Australia repeated appeals in different tax years involving the same transaction may be an abuse of process[9].

[1]   (1991) 30 FCR 578. Canadian decisions are to the same effect; *Rans Construction (1966) Ltd v R* (1987) 87 DTC 5415; *Minister of National Revenue v Van Rooy* (1988) 88 DTC 6323.

[2]   The majority held that the appeals were not an abuse of process, applied *General Medical Council v Spackman* [1943] AC 627, and rejected the US doctrine of collateral estoppel. The admissibility of the convictions was not in issue, but there was no equivalent of the 1968 Act; para 11.05.

[3]   [1962] NZLR 683 CA.

[4]   [1986] 1 NZLR 110 CA.

[5]   [1986] 1 NZLR 110 CA, 112, 114.

[6]   Ibid at 116.

[7]   Ibid at 117.

[8]   Ibid at 118. The commissioner was only defending his assessments in the appeals by the taxpayer. The decision is doubtful. The standard of proof of a crime in civil proceedings is not 'the very high standard required by the criminal law' (*Hornal v Neuberger Products Ltd* [1957] 1 QB 247 CA, 258, *Nishiwa Trading Co Ltd v Chiyoda Fire and Marine Insurance Co Ltd* [1969] 2 QB 449 CA) and the issue estoppel should have failed because the questions were not the same: *Craddock* [1970] NZLR 499 CA, 515, 520.

[9]   *Spassked* (2007) 165 FCR 484, 499; *Wire Supplies Ltd v CIR* [2007] 3 NZLR 458 CA, 467.

Chapter 14

AUTREFOIS ACQUIT

INTRODUCTION

14.01 *Autrefois acquit* is the plea which enforces a *res judicata* estoppel in the criminal law[1]. It bars a second prosecution of the accused for the same crime after an acquittal[2]. In *Coke's Institutes*[3] the plea is said to be a defence to a further charge 'of the same felony', and *Blackstone*[4] states:

> 'The plea of *autrefois acquit,* or a former acquittal, is founded on this universal maxim of the Common Law of England, that no man is to be brought into jeopardy of his life, more than once, for the same offence'.

The plea has also been said to reflect the maxim *nemo debet bis vexari pro eadem causa:* that no man ought to be vexed twice for the same offence[5]; but this obscures its limits and the principle on which it is based. There must, in substance, have been an acquittal on the merits. The emphasis on vexation is not adequate because, if it were, the plea would be good even if the acquittal was a nullity for want of jurisdiction, or had been quashed[6], or a *nolle prosequi* had been entered. It is the acquittal, not the harassment, which creates the bar[7]. Lord Devlin summarised the doctrine[8]:

> 'For the doctrine of *autrefois* to apply it is necessary that the accused should have been put in peril of conviction for the same offence as that with which he is then charged. The word "offence" embraces both the facts which constitute the crime and the legal characteristics which make it an offence. For the doctrine to apply it must be the same offence both in fact and in law.'

The plea rests on the rule against double jeopardy[9].

[1] *Connelly* [1964] AC 1254, 1356; *R v Wilkes* (1948) 77 CLR 511, 519 where Dixon J referred to the rules of *res judicata* 'which in criminal proceedings are expressed in the plea of *autrefois acquit* and *autrefois convict*'; *Re a Medical Practitioner* [1959] NZLR 784 CA, 806 where Gresson P said: 'The principle of *res judicata* is applicable both in criminal law and in civil law; indeed the doctrine of *autrefois acquit* or *autrefois convict* in criminal law is but an expression of *res judicata*'.

[2] In some jurisdictions the plea is governed by statute.

[3] Part III 213.

[4] *Commentaries* (1769) Book IV 329; *Hale's Pleas of the Crown* (1778) Vol II 240; *Hawkins' Pleas of the Crown* 8th ed (1824) 515.

[5] *R v Haughton Inhabitants* (1853) 1 E & B 501, 506; *R v Ollis* [1900] 2 QB 758, 771.

6   *R v Drury* (1848) 3 Car & Kir 190 (judgment reversed on writ of error could not support plea of *autrefois convict*, and judgment of reversal could not support plea of *autrefois acquit*). In Ireland the quashing of a conviction for non jurisdictional error supports a plea of *autrefois acquit*, but not where the error went to jurisdiction: *Stephens v Connellan* [2002] 4 IR 321, 344–345; *Whelan v Kirby* [2005] 2 IR 30 SC, 51.

7   *Pearce v R* (1998) 194 CLR 610, 627.

8   *Connelly* [1964] AC 1254, 1339–1340; *Broome v Chenoweth* (1946) 73 CLR 583, 599 per Dixon J; *Yeung v Secretary for Justice* [2008] 3 HK LRD 1 CA.

9   *Island Maritime Ltd v Filipowski* (2006) 226 CLR 328, 336, 343 (*Island Maritime*).

STATUTORY EXCEPTIONS

14.02 At common law a valid plea operated as a complete bar to a second prosecution, but in recent years Parliament has created exceptions which permit a second trial for the same offence following an acquittal on the merits in the first. Sections 54 and 55 of the Criminal Procedure and Investigation Act 1996 enable a 'tainted acquittal' to be quashed and the accused can then be prosecuted again for the offence for which he was acquitted. Section 54 applies where a person has been convicted of interference with or intimidation of a juror, a witness or a potential witness in any proceedings which led to the acquittal[1]. If the court in which that person was convicted of the administration of justice offence finds that there is a real possibility that, but for the interference or intimidation, the accused would not have been acquitted and s 54(5) does not apply[2] it shall so certify[3]. The prosecution can then apply to the High Court for an order quashing the acquittal which that court 'shall' make if the conditions in s 55 are satisfied[4]. Sections 75 to 79 of the Criminal Justice Act 2003 enable the prosecution to apply to the Court of Appeal for orders quashing a person's acquittal of a qualifying offence[5] and for a new trial for that offence. The Court of Appeal may make such orders if the prosecution has new and compelling evidence[6] and the interests of justice so require[7]. In *R v Dunlop*[8] the new and compelling evidence which justified the quashing of the acquittal was a detailed and apparently truthful confession. In *R v Andrews*[9] where an acquittal on charges of indecent assault and rape of a teenage girl were quashed, the new and compelling evidence was similar fact and propensity evidence of indecent assaults on seven other young victims over an extended period before and after the events involving the first victim. Lord Judge CJ[10] rejected a defence submission that the new evidence 'in relation to the qualifying offence'[11] must be direct evidence that the victim had been raped and held that 'any admissible evidence in relation to the qualifying offence related to it for the purposes of s 78(1)'.

1   Section 54(1)(b).
2   Subsection (5) applies if, because of lapse of time or for any other reason, it would be contrary to the interests of justice to take proceedings against the acquitted person for the offence of which he was acquitted.
3   Section 54(2).
4   The conditions include a finding by the High Court that it is likely that, but for the interference or intimidation, the acquitted person would not have been acquitted, and it must not appear that, because of lapse of time or for other reason it would be contrary to the interests of justice to take proceedings against the acquitted person for the same offence.
5   Widely defined in Pt 1 of Sch 5.
6   Section 78.

⁷   Section 79. The relevant considerations for this purpose do not include the need for finality
     in litigation: *R v Andrews* [2009] 1 WLR 1947, 1958.
⁸   [2007] 1 WLR 1657.
⁹   [2009] 1 WLR 1947.
¹⁰ Ibid at 1956–1957.
¹¹ Section 78(1).

COMPARISON WITH AUTREFOIS CONVICT

14.03 Although the two pleas are often associated there is an important distinction between the principles on which they rest[1]. *Autrefois acquit* is a form of estoppel which precludes the Crown from reasserting guilt once that question has been determined against it. *Autrefois convict* is based on the principle of merger[2] and reflects the application in the criminal law of the maxim *transit in rem judicatam*. It precludes the Crown reasserting guilt after a conviction in which its rights had merged. It is considered in Chapter 23, which should also be consulted.

¹   This passage in the previous edition was cited in *Pearce v R* (1998) 194 CLR 610, 626, and
     R v Carroll (2002) 213 CLR 635, 646.
²   *Island Maritime* (2006) CLR 328, 343.

NO ISSUE ESTOPPEL IN CRIMINAL LAW

14.04 The doctrine of *res judicata* is narrower in the criminal law because, as *DPP v Humphrys*[1] established, there are no issue estoppels. That decision has been followed in Australia[2], despite earlier High Court authority to the contrary. Moreover the parties need not be the same. Summary criminal proceedings are between subjects[3], but the plea or its equivalent is available whether the acquittal occurred in summary proceedings or on a trial by indictment, and whether the later charge is to be heard summarily or on indictment. The accused must be the same, but *autrefois convict* is available although the prosecutors on behalf of the Crown are different[4], and the position with this plea must be the same[5]. There is no reported case where an acquittal on a private prosecution barred the Crown or a different private prosecutor, but the plea should be available in such cases[6].

¹   [1977] AC 1. It has been followed in Ireland: *Dublin Corpn v Flynn* [1980] IR 357 SC;
     Lynch v Moran [2006] 3 IR 389 SC, 401, 410; and in New Zealand: *R v Davis* [1982] 1
     NZLR 584 CA; *Bryant v Collector of Customs* [1984] 1 NZLR 280 CA (*Bryant*), but not
     in Canada: *Gushoe v R* (1979) 106 DLR (3rd) 152 SC; *Duhamel v R* (*No 2*) (1984) 14
     DLR (4th) 92 SC; *Grdic v R* [1985] 1 SCR 810, 822. In *R v Mahalingan* [2008] 3 SCR 316,
     335 McLachlin CJ said: 'issue estoppel in Canadian law operates to prevent the Crown
     relitigating an issue that has been determined in the accused's favour in a prior criminal
     proceeding, whether on the basis of a positive finding or reasonable doubt'.
²   *Rogers v R* (1994) 181 CLR 251.
³   *Munday v Gill* (1930) 44 CLR 38, 86 per Dixon J; *R v Tween* [1965] VR 687 (police
     informant in summary proceedings did not represent the Crown).
⁴   *R v Walker* (1843) 2 Mood & R 446; *Wemyss v Hopkins* (1875) LR 10 QB 378; *R v Miles*
     (1890) 24 QBD 423.
⁵   *Re a Medical Practitioner* [1959] NZLR 784 CA, 806 per Gresson P 'the plea of *autrefois
     acquit* can operate where there are different prosecutors', and at 813 per North and
     Cleary JJ.

⁶   Common informers, who represent the public, are the same party for legal purposes: *Girdlestone* (1879) 4 Ex D 107 CA, *Huntington v Attrill* [1893] AC 150, 158 cited para 9.13 n 1.

THE NATURE OF THE ACQUITTAL

14.05   The first proceeding must have been a prosecution on a criminal charge which terminated in favour of the accused, and that termination must have been on the merits[1]. The dismissal on the merits of a summons, complaint, or charge by a court of summary jurisdiction is a decision that the defendant is not guilty even if the case is dismissed for insufficient evidence[2] or procedural reasons[3]. The accused must have been in jeopardy in the earlier prosecution. This involves a time element and a qualitative one.

¹   *Haynes v Davis* [1915] 1 KB 332, 338; *R v Dabhade* [1993] QB 329 CA, 337–338, 342.
²   *Kinnis v Graves* (1898) 78 LT 502 (dismissal, after hearing of information for building beyond the building line decision that it did not project); *Bailey v McCree & Son* [1937] NZLR 508.
³   *R v Brakenridge* (1884) 48 JP 293 (charge of night poaching dismissed because accused arrested without jurisdiction).

THE TIME ELEMENT

14.06   The proceedings must have reached the stage where the accused was in peril of conviction[1]. The court presumes that the earlier case would have been decided on correct legal principles[2]. This element is satisfied if the dismissal occurred after the final hearing commenced, that is after plea in summary proceedings, or after the accused has been put in charge of the jury in a trial on indictment[3]. The dismissal of a summary prosecution after the trial has commenced, without a decision on the merits because, for example, the informant cannot proceed, will support the plea, or at least attract the court's power to stay a second prosecution for abuse[4]. The Supreme Court of Canada has held that a stay for abuse of process is an acquittal[5]. A discharge at committal will not support the plea[6], nor will the discharge of a jury before verdict[7]. The withdrawal of a summons before the hearing, the dismissal of a charge before trial because the prosecution wish to proceed on a different charge[8], or a discharge for any reason prior to trial[9] will not support the plea. Where the complainant did not appear on the hearing of a summons for assault, having given notice of his intention to sue in the county court, the dismissal was not on the merits[10]. Where the prosecution offered no evidence on a lesser charge prior to the trial, and a verdict of not guilty was entered, the plea was available at the trial on an aggravated charge[11]. The prosecution should have filed a *nolle prosequi*.

¹   *R v Dabhade* [1993] QB 329, 340.
²   *DPP v Williams* [1991] 1 WLR 1160, 1170
³   *R v Dabhade* [1993] QB 329, 340, 341.
⁴   Ibid at 341; *R v Riddle* (1979) 100 DLR (3rd) 577 SC (dismissal of information for assault after plea because the prosecution could not proceed an acquittal on the merits).
⁵   *R v Jewitt* (1985) 20 DLR (4th) 651; *Anshun* (1980) 147 CLR 35; *Walton v Gardiner* (1993) 177 CLR 379, 396–398.
⁶   *R (on the application of Redgrave) v Metropolitan Police Comr* [2003] 1 WLR 1136 CA, 1143.

7   *R v Charlesworth* (1861) 1 B & S 460, 507; *DS v Judges of the Cork Circuit Court* [2008] 4 IR 379 SC, 388–389.
8   *R v Dabhade* [1993] QB 329, 341.
9   *R v Taylor* [2009] 1 NZLR 654 CA.
10 *Reed v Nutt* (1890) 24 QBD 669.
11 *R v G* (*Autrefois Acquit*) [2001] 1 WLR 1727.

THE QUALITATIVE ELEMENT

14.07 The qualitative element is not satisfied where there has been a summary dismissal of a charge or a count in an indictment because it did not disclose an offence[1], or was otherwise defective. As Dixon J said in *Broome v Chenoweth* where the first information did not allege two elements of the offence[2]: 'if a conviction in that proceeding could not have been effective the defendant never did stand in jeopardy upon the earlier charge.' The defendant will not have been in jeopardy merely because the charge might have been amended[3]. The dismissal of a prosecution commenced without the approval required by statute cannot support the plea[4], nor will a dismissal because a condition precedent to jurisdiction was not satisfied[5]. A dismissal because, as a matter of law, the evidence available to the prosecution could not support a conviction, will not support the plea, but this must not be misunderstood because a dismissal on a submission of no case will support the plea.

1   *Jenkins v Merthyr Tydvil UDC* (1899) 80 LT 600;*Broome v Chenoweth* (1946) 73 CLR 583, 598–601 per Dixon J; *Island Maritime* (2006) 226 CLR 328, 335–336, 341–342. In *R v Moore* [1998] 1 SCR 1097 the court by a 4:3 majority upheld the plea based on the quashing of defective counts which lacked an essential averment. The majority relied on special provisions in the Canadian statute. The decision could not be supported at common law.
2   (1946) 73 CLR 583, 99.
3   *R v Green* (1856) Dears & B 113; *Broome v Chenoweth* (1946) 73 CLR 583, 601.
4   *R v Bates* [1911] 1 KB 964; *Yusofali v The King* [1949] AIR (PC) 264.
5   *R v Bitton* (1833) 6 C & P 92; *R v Marsham,ex p Petwick Lawrence* [1912] 2 KB 362; *Williams v Letheren* [1919] 2 KB 262.

14.08 The principle that the plea is not available where the evidence could not support a conviction is illustrated by *Williams v DPP*[1], *R v Dabhade*[2] and *Island Maritime*[3]. In each case the charges were good on their face, but the available evidence could not support a conviction. In *Williams* the first charge was for driving with excess blood alcohol ascertained by a specimen of breath, but the defendant had also given a sample of blood, and in such a case the statute required the analysis of the specimen of breath to be disregarded. The first prosecution had been brought under the wrong section, and the evidence could not support the charge. This was also the position in *Island Maritime* where a submission of no case was upheld. The defendants had been charged under the wrong section, and could never have been convicted, although this did not become clear until the close of the prosecution case. In *Dabhade* the charge that the accused had falsely represented that he was the payee of a cheque payable to cash was bound to fail. In each of these cases there was a fundamental defect in the charge and the deficiency in the evidence was due to the defect. In *Gilham v R*[4] the accused raised provocation in answer to a charge of murdering his brother. The Crown, which could not call rebutting evidence, accepted a plea of guilty to manslaughter. When the question arose later the majority held that the accused had been in jeopardy[5] because the evidence available to the prosecution could support a conviction for murder.

[1] [1991] 1 WLR 1160.
[2] [1993] QB 329.
[3] (2006) 226 CLR 328, 337–338, 341.
[4] *Gilham v R* (2007) 178 Aust Crim R 72, 110–111, 112–113, 114–117. The decision is further considered and the facts given in para 14.22.
[5] Ibid at 118–119.

ACQUITTAL BY APPELLATE COURT

14.09 An acquittal by an appellate court does not bar a trial on a lesser charge in another indictment[1], or a new trial on another charge in the same indictment[2].

[1] *Connelly* [1964] AC 1254 (quashing by Court of Criminal Appeal of conviction of accused for murder did not bar charge of aggravated robbery in alternative indictment based on the same events).
[2] *DPP v Nasralla* [1967] 2 AC 238 (quashing of conviction of murder did not bar new trial for manslaughter when the jury could not agree on the alternative verdict); *AJS v R* (2007) 235 CLR 505 (acquittal by Court of Criminal Appeal did not preclude new trial on alternative charge in the same indictment).

ACQUITTAL IN FOREIGN PROCEEDINGS

14.10 The plea may be supported by an acquittal in a foreign court with jurisdiction to try the charge[1], but offences under different legal systems may not be 'the same'[2].

[1] *Treacy v DPP* [1971] AC 537, 562.
[2] In *Bartkus v Illinois* 359 US 121 (1959) the court held that an accused acquitted of the federal offence of bank robbery could be convicted of robbery under state law based on the same facts. In *Van Rassell v R* [1990] 1 SCR 225 acquittal of federal offences in the USA did not support plea against Canadian charges based on the same facts.

DECISION IN CIVIL PROCEEDINGS CANNOT SUPPORT PLEA

14.11 A decision in civil proceedings will not support the plea. A declaration by a civil court that past conduct did not constitute a criminal offence does not bar a prosecution, and cannot support a plea of *autrefois acquit*[1]. The inability of the judge hearing care proceedings to determine which parent was responsible for the death of a child could not support the plea or a stay for abuse when the father was charged with manslaughter. Judge P said[2]:

> '... the decision in the care proceedings was not, and could not be, a final determination of the criminal proceedings. Moreover, no question of *autrefois acquit* ... or double jeopardy could arise ... [In] the care proceedings the appellant was not being prosecuted, ... he was never at risk of conviction, and ... the Judge who decided those proceedings lacked jurisdiction finally to exonerate or condemn.'

The decision of the Special Immigration Appeals Committee to set aside a certificate by the Secretary of State authorising the detention and deportation of a suspected terrorist did not attract the double jeopardy principle when the suspect was charged with terrorist offences. Judge P said[3]:

'... as a matter of principle double jeopardy is not available as a plea in bar unless both sets of proceedings ... are criminal proceedings. Given the developing jurisprudence in relation to abuse of process, there is no realistic scope for, nor any purpose in, developing the concept of double jeopardy beyond its established limits. Anything falling outside those limits which savours of abuse of process, or unfairness, or oppression, can be addressed and decided on now well established principles.'

A renewed application for extradition following the failure of the first is not barred for abuse of process or otherwise[4], but repeated applications may be abusive.

[1] *Imperial Tobacco Ltd v A-G* [1981] AC 718, 741, 752.
[2] *R v L* [2006] 1 WLR 3092 CA, 3106–3107.
[3] *R v K* [2007] 2 Cr App Rep 187, 206.
[4] *In re Rees* [1986] AC 937, 961–962; *Dutton v Republic of South Africa* (1999) 84 FCR 291, 295–298.

SCOPE OF THE PLEA

14.12 Although it is now established[1] that the plea is only available where the offences are the same in fact and in law, it was long thought that the ratio in *Connelly*[2] included the third and fourth propositions of Lord Morris which extended the plea to offences which were substantially the same as those for which the accused had been expressly or impliedly acquitted. He said[3]:

'In my view, both principle and authority establish: ...; (3) that the ... rule [that a man cannot be tried for a crime in respect of which he could on some previous indictment have been convicted] applies if the crime in respect of which he is being charged is in effect the same, or is substantially the same, as either the principal or a different crime in respect of which he has been acquitted or could have been convicted or has been convicted; (4) that one test as to whether the rule applies is whether the evidence which is necessary to support the second indictment, or whether the facts which constitutes the second offence, would have been sufficient to procure a legal conviction upon the first indictment either as to the offence charged or as to an offence of which, on the indictment, the accused could have been found guilty.'

Lord Devlin said[4] in *Connelly* that Lord Morris:

'... extends the doctrine to cover offences which are in effect the same or substantially the same ... I have no difficulty about the idea that one set of facts may be substantially but not exactly the same as another. I have more difficulty with the idea that an offence may be substantially the same as another in its legal characteristics; legal characteristics are precise things and are either the same or not ... I am inclined to favour keeping it within limits that are precise.'

Then in *R v Beedie* Rose LJ held that the third and fourth propositions were not part of the ratio in *Connelly*[5]:

' ... the majority ... identified a narrow principle of *autrefois*, applicable only where the same offence is alleged in the second indictment. Lord Devlin said at 1339–40 "For the doctrine to apply it must be the same offence both in fact and in law", and he went on, having rejected the idea that an offence [for this purpose] may be substantially, rather than precisely, the same as another in its legal characteristics, to reject the idea that *autrefois* applies in favour of an accused who has been prosecuted on substantially the same facts. Lord Pearce at 1368 agreed with the opinion of Lord Devlin. Lord Reid said at 1295 "Many generations of judges have seen nothing unfair in holding that the plea of *autrefois acquit* must be given a limited scope ... I cannot disregard the fact that, with certain exceptions it has been held proper ... to try a man a second time on the same criminal conduct where the offence charged is different from that charged at the first trial." '

R v Beedie was cited with approval by Lord Hutton in *R v Z*[6]. It is necessary to focus on the elements of the two offences[7]. Other propositions of Lord Morris have not been challenged. The accused is not restricted to a comparison of the indictments but may prove the identity of persons and transactions to support the plea[8]. Identity is not established by proof that the events and witnesses will be the same[9]. The decision in *Beedie* has simplified the law, and increased the importance of the power to stay a prosecution for abuse of process.

[1]   *Connelly* [1964] AC 1254, 1339–1340 per Lord Devlin; para 14.01 n 8.
[2]   In successive editions of *Archbold* up to that for 1997, and in the last two editions of this work.
[3]   Ibid at 1305.
[4]   Ibid at 1340, and 1339–1340 cited para 14.01 n 8; *Pearce v R* (1998) 194 CLR 610, 617, 620; *R v Brightwell* [1995] 2 NZLR 435 CA, 438–439.
[5]   [1998] QB 356, 360–361. Rose LJ (at 366) accepted the analysis by Clarke J (as he then was) of the ratio in *Connelly* and added 'which, if we may say so, was no mean feat'; *DPP v Humphrys* [1977] AC 1, 55. Breach of an enforcement notice under planning legislation is a continuing offence, but a different offence each day and a plea of *autrefois acquit* is not available: *Clare CC v Floyd* [2007] 2 IR 671.
[6]   [2000] 2 AC 483, 505.
[7]   *Connelly* [1964] AC 1254, 1306, 1309, 1324, 1325, 1327, 1332, 1332–1333, 1333, 1340, 1341 (in most instances the facts referred to are the ultimate facts which constitute the offence); *R v Beedie* [1998] QB at 360; *Island Maritime* (2006) 226 CLR 328, 338–340, 345–346; *Pearce v R* (1998) 194 CLR 610, 617, 620.
[8]   Ibid at 1307–1308.
[9]   Ibid at 1309–1310, 1323, 1325.

IMPLIED ACQUITTAL WHERE ALTERNATIVE VERDICT OPEN

14.13   Lord Morris's second proposition[1] was:

'that a man cannot be tried for a crime in respect of which he could on some previous indictment have been convicted.'

It was well established before *Connelly* that an implied acquittal could support the plea. In *R v Barron* Lord Reading CJ said[2]:

'... the law does not permit a man to be twice in peril of being convicted of the same offence. If ... he has been acquitted ... such acquittal is a bar to a second indictment for the same offence. This rule applies not only to the offence actually charged ... but to any offence of which he could have been properly convicted on the trial of the first indictment. Thus an acquittal on a charge of murder is a bar to a subsequent indictment for manslaughter as the jury could have convicted of manslaughter ... The question is whether the appellant has been acquitted of an offence which is the same offence as "gross indecency" ie whether the acquittal on the charge of sodomy necessarily involves an acquittal on a charge of gross indecency. It is quite clear that the jury could not have convicted the appellant of gross indecency at the first trial.'

Lord Morris made other references to this principle[3] as did Lord Devlin[4]. Four of the speeches referred to *R v Barron* without any suggestion of disapproval[5]. The second proposition was not relevant in *R v Beedie*[6] and was not mentioned, and there is no reason for thinking that it is not the law. At common law a jury which acquitted the accused of the offence charged could sometimes find him guilty of another offence and alternative verdicts may be authorised by statute. An acquittal for a completed offence bars a later charge of attempt because a conviction for that had been open[7]. Details of the alternative verdicts open to a jury at common law or by statute are outside the scope of this work.

1   [1964] AC 1254, 1305.
2   [1914] 2 KB 570, 574, 576 (*autrefois acquit* not available for charge of gross indecency).
3   [1964] AC 1254, 1306, 1307, 1310–1311, 1322–1323, 1324, 1325, 1327.
4   Ibid at 1340, 1342–1343.
5   Ibid at 1322–1323, 1333, 1335, 1338, 1352, 1364, 1365.
6   [1998] QB 356.
7   Criminal Law Act 1967 s 6(3), (4); replacing earlier legislation.

PLEA OTHERWISE NOT AVAILABLE FOR LESSER CHARGE

14.14 In principle the plea should apply where all elements of the first charge are included in the second. A conviction on the second, which would require proof of all its elements, would be inconsistent with an acquittal on the first when at least one of the common elements was not established. The position is the same with *autrefois convict*, but while the converse also applies with that plea it does not with *autrefois acquit*. An acquittal on a charge with six elements would not bar a charge for an offence with only four. The first charge may have failed because the jury were not satisfied about one or both of the additional elements. This is also the position where the charges have common elements but neither is wholly included in the other. If the two charges, each with six elements, had four in common an acquittal on either would not be inconsistent with a conviction on the other. The first charge may have failed because one or both of the disparate elements was not established. On the other hand a conviction on either would only support a plea of *autrefois convict* on the other if the four common elements constituted a separate offence. The plea in bar is not available where the second prosecution is for a lesser offence following an acquittal for the greater. In *R v Barron* Lord Reading CJ said[1]:

'... the acquittal on the graver charge did not necessarily involve an acquittal of the minor offence. The graver charge of sodomy involves gross indecency and something else, and ... an acquittal of the whole of an offence does not involve an acquittal of every part of it.'

14.14 *Autrefois acquit*

In *Connelly* Lord Pearce[2] referred with approval to the cases where second prosecutions 'in a descending scale of charges had been allowed.'

1 [1914] 2 KB 570, 576; cited with approval in *Connelly* [1964] AC 1254, 1322–1323, 1333, 1335, 1338, 1352, 1364, 1365.
2 [1964] AC 1254, 1325.

AVAILABLE FOR AGGRAVATED CHARGE

14.15 In *R v Miles*[1] the plea was not available because, as Lord Morris said[2]: 'On the second indictment the necessary proof did not involve guilt of the first offence', that is, the first charge was not included in the second. The plea is available where the first offence is included in the second, which will generally be an aggravated version of the first. In *Connelly* Lord Morris referred[3] to *R v Salvi* where the accused who had been acquitted of wounding with intent to murder, was indicted for murder after the victim died. A plea *autrefois acquit* was disallowed because murder could be committed without an intention to commit it, and the first offence was not wholly included in the second. Pollock CB said[4]:

'The acquittal of the whole offence is not an acquittal of every part of it, it is only an acquittal of the whole.'

Lord Hodson said[5]:

'… where there is acquittal of a lesser offence which is in law an essential ingredient in a greater it is plainly not possible to convict on the greater without in effect reversing the acquittal on the … lesser.'

He later referred[6] to that part of the principle of *autrefois acquit* which applies where:

'… his previous acquittal necessarily involves a finding on one of the essential elements of the present offence so that he could not be convicted of the present offence without involving a contrary finding on that essential element.'

He cited *R v Barron*[7] where the plea was not available for a lesser offence, and *R v Kupferberg* where A T Lawrence J said[8]:

'For a plea of *autrefois acquit* to be maintainable, the offence of which the accused has been acquitted and that with which he is charged must be the same … each must have the same essential ingredients. The facts which constitute the one must be sufficient to justify a conviction for the other.'

This only applies where the first offence is the same as or is wholly included in the second, because *R v Barron* decided that the plea of *autrefois acquit* is not available where the second offence is wholly included in the first. Lord Devlin referred[9] with apparent approval to:

'… the proposition … that the plea can arise whenever, in order to prove the offence alleged in the second indictment, the prosecution is obliged to prove that the accused has committed an offence on which he has previously been either convicted or acquitted.'

A conviction for simple or aggravated assault will not support a plea of *autrefois convict* to a charge of murder or manslaughter if the victim dies later because the second offence was not complete until the victim died[10]. There is no decision that a plea of *autrefois acquit* is not available if the first prosecution ended in an acquittal but there is a dictum of Williams J to that effect in *R v Friel*[11]. The decision, that *autrefois convict* was not available, was approved by Lord Morris in *Connelly*[12], but the passage he quoted from the judgment of Williams J did not include the dictum. There is also a dictum of Lord Hodson to the same effect which he acknowledged was contrary to principle[13]:

'... the defence of *autrefois* is not available where the subsequent charge is murder or manslaughter. See *R v Morris* [LR 1 CCR 90] ... *R v Salvi* [10 Cox CC 481 n], *R v Thomas* [[1950] 1 KB 26]. It makes no difference whether there has been a previous acquittal or a previous conviction, although where there has been a previous acquittal of the lesser charge the rule of autrefois if logically followed would be expected to apply.'

In the first and third of the cases he cited the accused had been convicted of the lesser offence while the victim was alive. In *R v Salvi* the plea of *autrefois acquit* failed because the specific intent in the first charge was not an ingredient of the charge of murder[14]. *Salvi* is not authority for a general proposition about *autrefois acquit*. The point is clear in principle and the contrary *dicta* should not be followed. In *R v Elrington* the accused was acquitted of common assault, and then indicted for assault causing grievous bodily harm and assault causing actual bodily harm. A plea of *autrefois acquit* was upheld. Cockburn CJ said[15]:

'[W]e must bear in mind the well-established principle of our criminal law that a series of charges shall not be preferred, and whether a party accused of a minor offence is acquitted or convicted, he shall not be charged again on the same facts in a more aggravated form.'

In *Connelly* the Law Lords, other than Lord Reid, held that a plea in bar could be available in an *Elrington*[16] case, but Lord Devlin[17] and Lord Pearce[18] held that the principle could also apply where the plea was not available[19].

1   (1909) 3 Cr App Rep 13.
2   [1964] AC 1254, 1368.
3   Ibid at 1319.
4   (1857) 10 Cox CC 481n.
5   [1964] AC 1254, 1332.
6   Ibid at 1332.
7   [1914] 2 KB 570.
8   (1918) 13 Cr App Rep 166, 168.
9   [1964] AC 1254, 1341.
10 *R v Thomas* [1950] 1 KB 26, 30, 32, 35.
11 (1890) 17 Cox CC 325.
12 [1964] AC 1254, 1319.
13 Ibid at 1332. Earlier he had recognised (para 14.15 nn 5, 6) how the matter stood in principle.
14 Para 14.15 nn 3–4.
15 (1861) 1 B & S 688, 696.
16 [1964] AC 1254, 1315, 1332, 1341, 1367.
17 Ibid at 1358.
18 Ibid at 1363.

THE POSITION IN AUSTRALIA

14.16 The position in Australia, established by early decisions of the High Court, was once quite clear, as Griffith CJ said[1]:

> 'The true test whether such a plea [of *autrefois acquit*] is a sufficient bar in any particular case is, whether the evidence necessary to support the second charge would have been sufficient to procure a legal conviction upon the first.'

He was referring to the facts constituting the essential elements of the charge[2]. Thus an acquittal on a more serious charge would not support the plea to a lesser charge, as in *R v Barron*[3], but an acquittal on a lesser included charge would support the plea to an aggravated charge. This was the view of Gleeson CJ, Heydon and Crennan JJ in *dicta* in *Island Maritime*[4], where the plea of *autrefois acquit* failed because the accused had not been in jeopardy on the earlier charge. However Gummow and Hayne JJ said[5]: that the order in which charges are preferred does not affect the availability of the plea or its equivalent, although they also said[6] that the plea 'prevents the relitigation of matters already determined in favour of the accused. Like the plea of *autrefois convict* the plea of *autrefois acquit* prevents inconsistent decisions.' Their later reasons were directed to establishing that the plea of *autrefois acquit* is not 'confined' to situations where the elements of the offences are the same, or all elements of the first are included in the second[7]. They concluded[8]:

> '... the plea of *autrefois acquit*, and the analogous principle applied in summary jurisdiction [are] available whenever all the elements of one offence ... are included in the other offence ... and [are] available ... no matter the order in which the offences are charged.'

This is contrary to the cases approved in *Connelly*[9], where an acquittal did not bar a prosecution for a lesser included offence. Callinan J agreed[10] with Gummow and Hayne JJ, but Kirby J declined to express a view[11]. The *dicta* are evenly balanced and the question awaits resolution.

[1] *Li Wan Quai v Christie* (1906) 3 CLR 1125, 1131; *Ex p Spencer* (1905) 2 CLR 250, 251; *Chia Gee v Martine* (1905) 3 CLR 649, 653.
[2] *Island Maritime* (2006) 226 CLR 328, 339–340, *Pearce v R* (1998) 194 CLR 610, 617.
[3] [1914] 2 KB 570.
[4] *Island Maritime* (2006) 226 CLR 328, 338–340.
[5] Ibid at 343.
[6] Ibid at 343–344.
[7] Ibid at 346, 347, 348.
[8] Ibid at 350.
[9] [1964] AC 1254.
[10] (2006) 226 CLR 328, 360.
[11] Ibid at 357.

WHEN AND HOW THE PLEA SHOULD BE RAISED

14.17 *Autrefois acquit* is an alternative to a plea of not guilty on arraignment. The Crown must either admit it, in which event the accused will be discharged, or file a notice denying the plea. The validity of the plea is tried by a jury, but if there is no question of fact for their determination the judge may direct the jury to find the appropriate verdict[1]. The plea cannot be considered with a plea of not guilty[2]. The accused has the onus of proof to the civil standard, and if the issue is found against him he is called on to plead generally to the charge. The plea, or its equivalent in summary proceedings, may be raised later should its availability emerge during the trial[3]. In *Flatman v Light* Lord Goddard CJ referred to the procedure[4]:

> '... if during the course of the case it turned out that the man had been previously convicted or acquitted of the same offence with which he was then charged the court would, of course, allow him to plead it and would give effect to that plea. When a case is before justices I doubt very much whether it is right to say that a plea that a man has been already acquitted or convicted ... is in any strictness a plea of *autrefois acquit* or *autrefois convict*, because those pleas ... have to be pleaded formally because they form part of the record of the court. They ought to be pleaded in writing and then a replication is pleaded by the prosecution. When the case is being dealt with by a court of summary jurisdiction ... what the court must do is to give effect to the maxim *Nemo debet bis vexari pro una et eadem causa*. I do not think it is technically *autrefois acquit*, but that does not matter.'

1 *Connelly* [1964] AC 1254, 1298, 1339; *R v Tonks* [1916] 1 KB 443, 448.
2 *R v Banks* [1911] 2 KB 1095; *R v Kent Newbold* (1940) 62 CLR 398; *R v Stone* (2005) 64 NSWLR 413, 418.
3 *Connelly* [1964] AC 1254, 1331.
4 [1946] KB 414, 419.

DUTY TO INCLUDE ALL CHARGES IN THE INDICTMENT

14.18 In the absence of special circumstances the prosecution must include in the indictment[1] all the charges on which they intend to proceed[2]. Independently of this duty 'prosecuting authorities have sought to frame charges ... that ... reflect all of [the] accused's criminal conduct and thus enable the imposition of punishment that will truly reflect the criminality of that conduct.'[3] In *Connelly* Lord Devlin said[4] 'it is absolutely necessary that issues of fact that are substantially the same should, whenever practicable, be tried by the same tribunal and at the same time.' Fresh charges should only be preferred after an acquittal if their omission was consented to or was consistent with proper practice[5]. The court can order separate trials in the interests of justice, and, as Lord Devlin explained[6]:

> 'If the prosecution considers that there ought to be two or more trials, it can make its choice plain by preferring two or more indictments. In many cases this may be to the advantage of the defence. If the defence accepts the choice without complaint and avails itself of any advantage that may flow from it, I should regard that as a special circumstance; for where the defence considers that a single trial of two indictments is desirable it can apply to the judge.'

1 *Connelly* [1964] AC 1254, 1296, 1313, 1350, 1367; *R v Beedie* [1998] QB 356, 361; *Pearce v R* (1998) 194 CLR 610, 620–621; *R v Arnold* [2008] 1 WLR 2881, 2892.
2 Ibid at 1296 per Lord Reid, and at 1347 per Lord Devlin.
3 *Pearce v R* (1998) 194 CLR 610, 615
4 *Connelly* [1964] AC 1254, 1353.

5   Ibid at 1296, 1352.
6   Ibid at 1360.

THE SECOND PROCEEDING

14.19 The plea is only available if the second proceedings are criminal. Subject to statute an acquittal does not bar a civil action based on the same facts[1]. Neither a conviction nor an acquittal will bar disciplinary proceedings to enforce proper standards in a profession, the public service, a disciplined force, and the like[2]. The armed services legislation provides that where a person subject to military law has been tried for an offence by a court-martial, he cannot be tried by a civil court for substantially the same offence, and the reverse also applies[3].

1   *Helton v Allen* (1940) 63 CLR 691 (acquittal on charge of murder did not bar civil proceedings to prevent accused deriving financial benefit from the death).
2   *Re Weare* [1893] 2 QB 439 CA; *Ziems v Prothonotary of the Supreme Court of New South Wales* (1957) 97 CLR 279; *Re a Medical Practitioner* [1959] NZLR 784 CA, 800, 814; *Health Care Complaints Commission v Litchfield* (1997) 41 NSWLR 630 CA; *Re Barings plc (No 2), Secretary of State for Trade v Baker* [1999] 1 WLR 1985 CA (unsuccessful proceedings against company director for removal from register of the Securities and Futures Authority followed by proceedings to disqualify him as a company director); *AA v The Medical Council* [2002] 2 IR I; *Z v Dental Complaints Assessment Committee* [2009] 1 NZLR 1 SC.
3   Army Act 1955 (as amended) ss 133, 134; Air Force Act 1955 (as amended) ss 133, 134; Naval Discipline Act 1957 s 129; Armed Forces Act (1966) (as amended) s 26.

ABUSE OF PROCESS

14.20 The discretion to stay a second prosecution for abuse of process after an acquittal in the first, where the plea in bar is not available, was considered in *Connelly*. Lord Devlin said[1]:

'As a general rule a judge should stay an indictment ... when he is satisfied that the charges ... are founded on the same facts as the charges in a previous indictment on which the accused has been tried ... he will do this because it is as a general rule oppressive to an accused ... But a second trial on the same or similar facts is not always and necessarily oppressive. ... The judge must then ... exercise his discretion.'

Lord Pearce said[2]:

'A man ought not to be tried for a second offence, which is manifestly inconsistent on the facts with either a previous conviction or a previous acquittal. And it is clear that the formal pleas which a defendant can claim as of right will not cover all such cases. Instead of attempting to enlarge the pleas beyond their proper scope, it is better that the courts should apply ... an avowed judicial discretion based on the broader principles which underly the pleas.'

Lord Reid, who agreed generally with Lord Devlin and Lord Pearce, said[3]:

'... there must always be a residual discretion to prevent anything which savours of abuse of process.'

The principle stated by Lord Pearce (above) is illustrated by *R v King* where the accused who had been convicted of obtaining goods by false pretences (when the property passed) was later convicted of larceny of the same goods (when the property did not pass). The second conviction was quashed because[4] 'the second trial ought not to have taken place.' Lord Reading CJ referred to this case in *R v Barron*[5] and said that 'the judge should not, as a matter of fairness and in the exercise of a proper judicial discretion, have allowed the second trial to take place.' Lord Morris said in *Connelly*[6] that *King* was a case of *res judicata* because 'the adjudication at the first trial was conclusive and precluded a contrary adjudication' but a plea of *autrefois convict* was not available. Lord Pearce said[7] *King* established that the pleas in bar do 'not comprehend the whole of the power on which the court acts in considering whether a second trial can properly follow an acquittal or conviction.'

[1]   [1964] AC 1254, 1359–1360.
[2]   Ibid at 1364, cited *R v Carroll* (2002) 213 CLR 635, 648–649.
[3]   Ibid at 1296.
[4]   [1897] 1 QB 214, 218 per Hawkins J.
[5]   [1914] 2 KB 570, 575.
[6]   [1964] AC 1254, 1321.
[7]   Ibid at 1364, approved by Lord Hutton in *R v Z* [2000] 2 AC 483, 504 quoted para 14.27 n 9; *Gilham v R* (2007) 178 Aust Crim Rep 72, 121.

14.21 In *Connelly* the accused was convicted of aggravated robbery at a second trial following his acquittal by the Court of Criminal Appeal of murder during the robbery. The House of Lords unanimously upheld the second conviction and rejected the plea of *autrefois acquit*. The majority, who held that a second prosecution could be stayed for abuse of process, considered that there was nothing unfair in the second trial when the acquittal was due to an error in the summing up. *R v Riebold*[1] is a clear example of an abuse. The accused had been indicted on charges of conspiracy and 27 substantive offences. The prosecution elected to proceed on conspiracy and the accused were convicted. After they were acquitted on appeal the prosecution sought to proceed on the substantive charges based on the overt acts relied on to support the conspiracy. Barry J was satisfied that the proposed trial would be 'a complete reproduction of the previous trial,' and refused leave. This decision was cited with approval by Lord Hutton in *R v Z*[2]. In *Bryant*[3] a conviction for smuggling, supported only by a confession which had been ruled inadmissible in an unsuccessful prosecution for theft of the same goods, was quashed. In *Hui Chi-Ming v R*[4] it was held not to be abusive for the Crown to charge an accessory with murder although the principal had only been convicted of manslaughter, and evidence was not admissible of the result of that trial[5]. In *R v Beedie* the accused, a landlord, had been convicted of regulatory offences following the death of a tenant from carbon monoxide poisoning due to a defective gas fire. He was later charged with manslaughter based on the same facts. *Autrefois convict* was not available but Rose LJ said[6]:

'A stay should have been ordered because the manslaughter allegation was based on substantially the same facts ... and gave rise to a prosecution for an offence of greater gravity, no new facts having occurred, in breach of the principle in *R v Elrington*'[7]

14.21 *Autrefois acquit*

The discretion will be exercised to prevent unfair oppression of the accused from repeated prosecutions after an acquittal or conviction[8].

1 [1967] 1 WLR 674.
2 [2000] 2 AC 483, 497, 505.
3 [1984] 1 NZLR 280 CA.
4 [1992] 1 AC 34, 57.
5 Ibid at 42–43.
6 [1998] QB 356, 366.
7 (1861) 1 B & S 688.
8 *Yeung v Secretary of Justice* [2008] HK LRD 1 CA.

14.22 A recent case in New South Wales raised the discretion in unusual circumstances. When charged with the murder of his brother the accused raised provocation based on the discovery that his brother had murdered their parents. The Crown, which could not negative this defence, accepted his plea of guilty to manslaughter. Evidence later emerged which led the Crown to charge him with the murder of his parents. His application for a stay was refused and his interlocutory appeal was dismissed by a court of five judges[1]. The accused argued that the prosecution controverted both his acquittal for the murder of his brother[2], and his conviction for manslaughter[3]. The majority accepted this and held that he had been in jeopardy for murder but a stay was refused because there had been no hearing on the merits, and the prosecution was for an entirely separate offence. The public interest in the prosecution of the offender for murder trumped any concerns about potential inconsistencies between verdicts[4].

1 *Gilham v R* (2007) 178 Aust Crim Rep 72. The Court was unanimous but the reasoning of
   Spigelman CJ differed.
2 Ibid at 75.
3 Ibid at 95.
4 Ibid at 122.

THE DISCRETION

14.23 Although the power to stay a second prosecution for abuse of process has been said to involve a judicial discretion this is not its true character. In *Hunter*[1] Lord Diplock said that in a proper case the court has a duty, not a discretion, to exercise this power. The court will consider all relevant factors and make a value judgment, but once that is made there is no discretion to stay a prosecution which is not an abuse, or to allow one to proceed which is[2]. This reflects the distinction drawn in *Evans v Bartlam* by Lord Wright[3]:

> 'A discretion necessarily involves a latitude of individual choice according to particular circumstances and differs from a case where the decision follows *ex debito justitiae* once the facts are ascertained.'

1 [1982] AC 529, 536; applied in *Bryant* [1984] 1 NZLR 280 CA, 283.
2 *R v Carroll* (2002) 213 CLR 635, 657 per Gaudron and Gummow JJ; *Batistatos v RTA*
   (2006) 226 CLR 256, 264 per Gleeson CJ, Gummow, Hayne and Crennan JJ.
3 [1937] AC 473, 489; *DPP v Humphrys* [1977] AC 1, 40 'not as a matter of discretion but
   as a matter of law.'

PROSECUTION FOR PERJURY AFTER ACQUITTAL (HUMPHRYS)

14.24 The discretion to stay a prosecution of the accused for perjury at a trial in which he was acquitted was considered in *DPP v Humphrys*[1]. The accused, who had been charged with driving while disqualified, denied on oath that he was the driver, and said that he had not driven all year. The only issue was his identification by a police officer and he was acquitted. He was then charged with perjury. *Autrefois acquit* was not available because the offences were different. The Crown called the police officer and witnesses who had not been called at the first trial. The accused was convicted, and the House of Lords held that there was no abuse of process. Lord Hailsham said[2]:

'The doctrine in criminal proceedings is aimed at the need to prevent double jeopardy and not at the need to effect finality in litigation. It is thus aimed at verdicts rather than issues and ... where there is no such double jeopardy ... the prosecution is not prohibited from adducing evidence or making assertions the incidental effect of which is to cast doubt on a previous verdict ... In an indictment for perjury ... it is the duty of the court to apply the double jeopardy rule against the Crown not as a matter of discretion but as a matter of law where ... in substance ... the prosecution is trying to get behind the original verdict by re-trying the same evidence. But where the prosecution, by calling additional evidence which it could not have had available using reasonable diligence at the time of the first trial, is in substance, as well as in form, putting the accused in jeopardy ... for his crime against justice ... there is no double jeopardy[3].'

As Gaudron and Gummow JJ said in *R v Carroll*[4]: 'Proof of the falsity of that general denial did not directly controvert the earlier acquittal on the specific charge of driving while disqualified on a particular day.'

[1]   [1977] AC 1.
[2]   Ibid at 40.
[3]   Lord Salmon (at 47) and Lord Edmund-Davies (at 48, 57) agreed. Viscount Dilhorne thought (at 22, 26) that a prosecution for perjury did not place the accused in double jeopardy and was not an abuse of process.
[4]   (2002) 213 CLR 635, 667.

PROSECUTION FOR PERJURY AFTER ACQUITTAL (CARROLL)

14.25 The question was considered by the High Court of Australia in *R v Carroll*[1]. The accused had been acquitted of murder following a trial in which he had denied his guilt on oath. Fourteen years later he was indicted for perjury based on that denial. The court held that this involved a retrial of the charge for murder[2], and set aside the conviction because of 'a manifest inconsistency between the [new] charge ... and the acquittal'[3]. The charge 'solely on the basis of the respondent's sworn denial of guilt, for the evident purpose of establishing his guilt of murder' was an abuse regardless of the cogency of the further evidence[4]. The underlying principle was the need for court decisions to be accepted as incontrovertibly correct[5]. Gleeson CJ and Hayne J said[6]:

'... where it is said that the abuse lies in seeking to controvert an earlier verdict of acquittal, there appears much to be said for the view that it is necessary to direct attention to the elements of the [two offences] ... Seldom, if ever, will considering whether the later charge controverts an earlier acquittal require attention to whether evidence which would be led at a second trial is new or persuasive.'

Gaudron and Gummow JJ distinguished between a charge of perjury relating to an ultimate issue and one which would not 'directly impeach the prior acquittal'[7]. They gave as examples a false alibi, and the false evidence in *Humphrys*[8] that the accused had not driven the previous year[9].

[1]   (2002) 213 CLR 635.
[2]   Ibid at 645, 649.
[3]   Ibid at 649.
[4]   Ibid at 650.
[5]   Ibid at 648, 650, 663, 672, 675, 676.
[6]   Ibid at 651.
[7]   Ibid at 666.
[8]   [1977] AC 1.
[9]   (2002) 213 CLR 635, 667.

POSITION IN CANADA

14.26   Issue estoppels are part of the criminal law of Canada[1], and estoppels from an acquittal prevent the Crown charging the accused with perjury unless that charge is supported by evidence that was not called at the trial and could not have been discovered by the exercise of reasonable diligence[2]. The accused cannot be tried for perjury on the evidence given when he was acquitted[3].

[1]   Para 14.04 n 1.
[2]   *Grdic v R* [1985] 1 SCR 810, 829 (the majority); *R v Arp* [1998] 3 SCR 339.
[3]   Ibid at 819 (the minority), 827 (the majority). It does not appear that these requirements depend on issue estoppels from the acquittal.

EFFECT OF ACQUITTAL ON EVIDENCE AT A LATER TRIAL

14.27   The effect of an acquittal on the admissibility of evidence on other charges not covered by the plea in bar is now governed by *R v Z*[1]. The earlier position is illustrated by *R v Ollis*[2] and *Sambasivam v Malaya Federation Public Prosecutor*[3]. In *R v Ollis* the accused had been acquitted of obtaining a cheque on 5 July 1899 by falsely pretending that his own cheque was a good and valid order for the payment of money. He was then tried for similar offences committed on 24 and 25 June, and 6 July 1899 involving other victims, and the first victim was recalled to give the same evidence. The evidence was admissible to prove that the acts of the accused were not inadvertent or accidental but part of a systematic fraud. Lord Russell of Killowen CJ said[4]:

'The evidence was not less admissible because it tended to shew that the accused was in fact guilty of the former charge. The point is, was it relevant in support of the three subsequent charges?'

Wright J said[5]:

'... the use at the subsequent trial of Ramsey's evidence was not an attempt to reopen the question of the prisoner's innocence on the charge on which he had been acquitted, or to defeat ... the former acquittal ...'

In *Sambasivam* the accused was charged with possession of a firearm and ammunition. He was acquitted on the ammunition charge but the trial judge ordered a retrial on the firearms charge. On the retrial the prosecution produced for the first time an unsigned confession to possession of both. The Board's reasons for setting aside the conviction were delivered by Lord Mac-Dermott who said[6]:

'the effect of the verdict of acquittal pronounced by a competent court on a lawful charge and after a lawful trial is not completely stated by saying that the person acquitted cannot be tried again for the same offence. To that it must be added that the verdict is binding and conclusive in all subsequent proceedings between the parties to the adjudication. ... the appellant having been acquitted ... on the charge of having ammunition in his possession, the prosecution was bound to accept the correctness of that verdict and was precluded from taking any steps to challenge it at the second trial. And the appellant was no less entitled to rely on his acquittal in so far as it might be relevant in his defence ... [T]he statement was left to the assessors ... without any intimation that the prosecution could not assert, or ask the Court to accept, a substantial and important part of what it said ... the second trial ended without anything having been said or done to inform the assessors that the appellant had been found not guilty of being in possession of the ammunition and was to be taken as entirely innocent of that offence.'

In *R v Z*[7] the defendant was charged with rape. The Crown wished to call four previous complainants to give similar fact evidence of the conduct of the accused to negative defences of consent or reasonable belief of consent. In three of the earlier cases the accused had been acquitted. The House of Lords held that the evidence of the three complainants was admissible subject to exclusion on discretionary grounds. Lord Hutton, who delivered the principal speech, said[8]:

'(1) The principle of double jeopardy operates to cause a criminal court in the exercise of its discretion, and subject to the qualification as to special circumstances stated by Lord Devlin in *Connelly* ... to stop a prosecution where the defendant is being prosecuted on the same facts or substantially the same facts as gave rise to an earlier prosecution which resulted in his acquittal (or conviction). (2) Provided that the defendant is not placed in double jeopardy as described in (1) above evidence which is relevant on a subsequent prosecution is not inadmissible because it shows or tends to show that the defendant was, in fact, guilty of an offence of which he had earlier been acquitted. (3) It follows from (2) above that a distinction should not be drawn between evidence which shows guilt of an earlier offence of which the defendant has been acquitted and evidence which tends to show guilt of such an offence or which appears to relate to one distinct issue rather than to the issue of guilt for such an offence.'

He explained *Sambasivam*[9]:

'it was right to set aside the conviction ... for the reason given by Lord Pearce in *Connelly* ... namely, that a man should not be prosecuted a second time where the two offences were in fact founded on one and the same incident and that a man ought not to be tried for a second offence which was manifestly inconsistent on the facts with a previous acquittal. The carrying of the revolver and the carrying of the ammunition constituted one and the same incident, and the appellant having been acquitted of having possession of the ammunition, the allegation of carrying the revolver (in which some of the ammunition was loaded) was manifestly inconsistent with the previous acquittal. But ... provided that a defendant is not placed in double jeopardy in a way described by Lord Pearce, evidence which is relevant on a subsequent prosecution is not inadmissible because it shows or tends to show that the defendant was, in fact, guilty of an offence of which he had earlier been acquitted.'

1   [2000] 2 AC 483.
2   [1900] 2 QB 758.
3   [1950] AC 458.
4   [1900] 2 QB 758, 764.
5   Ibid at 771.
6   [1950] AC 458, 479–480.
7   [2000] 2 AC 483.
8   Ibid at 505.
9   Ibid at 504.

14.28 In *R v Hay*[1] the accused signed a confession to arson and burglary. At his trial for arson he disputed its truth and was acquitted. He was entitled at his trial for burglary to require the whole confession to be tendered and could rely on his acquittal to establish that part of it was false. Lord Hutton referred to this case and said[2] that the issue did not arise in *R v Z* and without intending to cast any doubt on the decision he expressed no opinion about it. In *R v Davis*[3] the accused had been acquitted on a charge of importing cannabis in January 1982. He was then tried for importing other cannabis in December 1981. The method on both occasions was distinctive and the Crown proposed to call evidence of the later importation. The Court of Appeal excluded it in the exercise of its discretion because it could not be satisfactorily edited and an appropriate direction was not likely to overcome its prejudicial effect. In *R v Moore*[4] the appellant had been charged in 1998 with conspiracy to pervert the course of justice in a murder trial in 1992 in which he and another were acquitted. The Crown was permitted to lead evidence which had not been available at the earlier trial, together with evidence which had been called before, despite its tendency to implicate the appellant in the murder[5]. In *R v Degnan* the court held that similar fact evidence of prior indecent assaults on males could be called although the accused had been acquitted of those assaults[6]. In *The People v Matthews*[7] evidence of possession of explosives was admitted on a charge of membership of an unlawful association although the accused had been acquitted on a charge of possessing explosives.

1   (1983) 77 Cr App Rep 70.
2   [2000] 2 AC 483, 505.
3   [1982] 1 NZLR 584 CA.
4   [1999] 3 NZLR 385.
5   Ibid at 390–391, approved on appeal at 397 para [22].
6   [2001] 1 NZLR 280 CA.
7   [2007] 2 IR 169.

ACQUITTAL NOT CONCLUSIVE OF INNOCENCE

14.29 *R v Z*[1] was considered in *R v Terry* where Auld LJ held[2] that an acquittal was not conclusive evidence of innocence, and did not establish that all relevant issues were resolved in favour of the accused. He also held that *R v Z* applied to evidence generally, and not just similar fact evidence[3]. The trial judge declined to tell the jury that directed acquittals on four counts, where voice identification was the only evidence against the accused, were conclusive evidence that he had not been present when the conversations were recorded by listening devices and someone else had uttered the incriminating words. The jury were directed that the acquittals were conclusive on those charges, but had no impact on the rest, and the rulings and directions were upheld[4]. The Supreme Court of Canada has taken the other view. In *R v Arp* Cory J, writing for the court, cited with approval[5] the statement of Lamer J writing for the majority in *Grdic v R*[6]:

'... there are not different kinds of acquittals ... an acquittal is the equivalent to a finding of innocence ... this does not mean that, for the purposes of the application of the doctrine of *res judicata*, the Crown is estopped from re-litigating all or any of the issues raised in the first trial. But it does mean that any issue, the resolution of which had to be in favour of the accused as a prerequisite to the acquittal, is irrevocably deemed to have been found conclusively in favour of the accused'.

This view has not been accepted in New Zealand or Australia. *R v Z* was followed in *R v Degnan*[7] where Tipping J, giving the judgment of the court, said[8]:

'The accused has the benefit of the earlier acquittal or acquittals in that he can never again be tried for the offences involved. But he should not have the further benefit of being immunized from the relevant evidence when facing a similar charge in the future. ... We find it difficult to endorse the approach taken in some of the Canadian cases that a verdict of not guilty is the equivalent of a declaration of innocence. That approach risks elevating perceived theory over the realities of criminal practice.'

In *R v Carroll* Gleeson CJ and Hayne J said[9]:

'... a jury's finding of guilt depends upon the jury being satisfied beyond reasonable doubt that all elements of the charged offence had been proved, whereas the jury that entertains a reasonable doubt about any one of the elements of the offence is bound to acquit. Seldom, if ever, therefore, can a verdict of acquittal be understood as some positive finding by the jury in favour of the accused about any of the issues that may have been contested at the trial ... in most cases of trial by jury, it will not be known why the accused was acquitted, and in many cases the reason may simply be that the jury had a doubt about whether the prosecution had established some element of the offence ...'

Then in *Island Maritime*[10] Gummow and Hayne JJ said:

'... a conviction or acquittal in a court of summary jurisdiction will be explained and supported by reasons. The bases on which a court of summary jurisdiction has acquitted or convicted of a charge are thus ascertainable. That is not always so when there has been trial by jury. No doubt a jury's verdict of guilt is to be understood as expressing the jury's satisfaction, beyond reasonable doubt, of all the elements of charge. But the jury's verdict of not guilty is entirely unrevealing. The most that it can be taken as showing is that the jury was not satisfied beyond reasonable doubt that all the elements of the relevant charge had been established. It will not reveal which element or elements were not established or why that was so.'

Lord Mance may be permitted the last word[11]:

'In some contexts (eg the use of similar fact evidence in "brides in the bath" type cases: see R v Z ...) great injustice would be done if courts were bound to treat acquittals as positive proof of innocence.'

1   [2000] 2 AC 483.
2   [2005] QB 996, 1009.
3   Ibid at 1009.
4   Ibid at 1012.
5   [1998] 3 SCR 339, 382. The appellant who was convicted of the murder of two women had previously been charged with the murder of the first but was discharged at the preliminary enquiry some years before the second murder.
6   [1985] 1 SCR 810, 825. The first trial was by a judge alone who had given reasons.
7   [2001] 1 NZLR 280 CA.
8   Ibid at291.
9   (2002) 213 CLR 635, 646, 649.
10 (2006) 226 CLR 328, 344; and at 347.
11 *R v Briggs-Price* [2009] 2 WLR 1101 HL, 1139.

POSITION IN AUSTRALIA

14.30 The High Court applied the *Sambasivan* principle in *Garrett v R*[1], and *R v Storey*[2] before the principle was restated and narrowed in *R v Z*[3]. In the first of those cases the accused, who had lived with the prosecutrix, and was charged with raping her after they had separated, had been acquitted of raping her on an earlier occasion. The Crown were held entitled to lead evidence that she had informed against the accused and willingly given evidence for the Crown at his earlier trial at which he had been acquitted[4] but were not entitled to assert or lead evidence that she had been raped on that occasion. It was therefore a misdirection to tell the jury that the acquittal was a neutral fact. In *R v Storey*[5] the accused were charged at the first trial with the abduction and rape of the prosecutrix. They were acquitted of abduction but the jury could not agree on the rape charge and they were tried again and convicted of rape. The court held that evidence of the earlier events was admissible on the second trial but the majority held that the jury had not been properly directed on its use, and ordered a new trial. Mason J, part of the majority said[6]:

'Compliance with the principle of *res judicata* does not ... necessarily entail the exclusion at a subsequent trial of relevant evidence which might on its face, if unexplained, tend to suggest that the accused was guilty of an offence of which he has already been acquitted ... There are some cases ... in which the exclusion of a part of the testimony of a material witness in deference to the principle of *res judicata* would render the balance of the witness' testimony so incomplete and artificial as to provoke a dangerous speculation on the part of the jury. In such circumstances, provided that it works no injustice to the accused, it is preferable that the evidence of the witness should be led and precise instructions should be given to the jury as to the use to which that evidence can be put ... Fairness to the Crown and to the accused therefore suggests that the totality of the prosecutrix's testimony as to the events occurring at the railway station should have been led at the second trial and that it should have been accompanied by a direction that the respondents' acquittal on the charge of abduction could not be challenged and that the evidence must be understood in this light.'

Gibbs J, part of the minority, said[7]:

'... evidence otherwise relevant is not rendered inadmissible by the fact that it may tend to show that the accused was guilty of an offence of which he has been acquitted. Where such evidence is admitted it will sometimes be necessary to warn the jury that the accused having been acquitted in the previous proceedings is to be taken as entirely innocent of the offence with which he was then charged. ... It was immaterial to the Crown's case whether or not the jury concluded that the prosecutrix was taken from the railway station by force ... The evidence was relevant to the question whether the prosecutrix had consented to have intercourse with the appellants even if the jury concluded (as they were bound to do if they adverted to the question) that the prosecutrix had not been abducted. The Crown, by leading the evidence, did not challenge or call in question the verdict of not guilty of abduction. In my opinion the evidence was admissible and it was unnecessary to exclude any part of it.'

The High Court has referred to those decisions, *R v Z*[8], and *R v Degnan*[9], without indicating whether it would be prepared to reconsider its decisions[10]. However in *R v Carroll* Gleeson CJ and Hayne J said[11]:

'Finality of a verdict of acquittal does not necessarily prevent the institution of proceedings, or the tender of evidence, which might have the incidental effect of casting doubt upon, or even demonstrating the error of, an earlier decision. There may be cases where, at a later trial of other allegedly similar conduct of the accused, evidence of conduct may be adduced even though the accused had earlier been ... acquitted of an offence said to be constituted by that conduct ... In such cases, the earlier acquittal would not be controverted by a guilty verdict at the second trial.'

1   (1977) 139 CLR 437.
2   (1978) 140 CLR 364.
3   [2000] 2 AC 483.
4   *Garrett v R* (1977) 139 CLR 437, 444, 447.
5   (1978) 140 CLR 364.
6   Ibid at 397–398.
7   Ibid at 387–390.
8   [2000] 2 AC 483.
9   [2001] 1 NZLR 280 CA.
10 *Pearce v R* (1998) 194 CLR 610, 628; *R v Carroll* (2002) 213 CLR 635, 645, 648, 650, 651, 660, 663, 663–664, 674, 675, 676, 679; *Island Maritime* (2006) 226 CLR 328, 343; *Washer v Western Australia* (2007) 234 CLR 492, 508.
11 (2002) 213 CLR 635, 651.

ROGERS V R

14.31 *Rogers v R*[1] merits separate treatment. The accused, while in police custody, signed four records of interview admitting participation in a number of armed robberies. In 1989 at his trial on four charges of armed robbery on different days the trial judge, following a *voir dire*, rejected the three records of interview then tendered. The accused was acquitted on the first two charges but convicted on the others. In 1992 he was indicted on eight further charges of armed robbery. The prosecution proposed to rely on the relevant part of the fourth record of interview previously rejected and the third taken about the same time which had not been tendered at the first trial. In respect of four counts, the records of interview were the only evidence available to the prosecution. The accused applied for a declaration that the proposed use of the records of interview would be an abuse of process. The court upheld this claim by majority, but there are difficulties as the judgments of Brennan J and McHugh J demonstrate. The majority held that the proposed tender was oppressive and unfair to the accused because it exposed him to relitigation of the admissibility issue previously determined in his favour[2], and was a direct challenge[3] to the earlier decision on their admissibility. Since the Crown did not allege fraud or have new evidence, the challenge involved the potential scandal of conflicting decisions which would jeopardise public confidence in the administration of justice[4]. Brennan J held that the proposed tender would not be an abuse of process[5]:

> 'There is nothing to suggest that the tender was for any purpose other than proof of the issues in the second trial. The [earlier] ruling ... would be left untouched if the Crown succeeded in having the relevant, and different, parts of the records of interview admitted in evidence at the second trial.'

McHugh J held that rulings on the admissibility of evidence were not final or fundamental and did not determine ultimate issues[6], except possibly in cases such as *Hunter*[7] and *Bryant*[8]. Since it would not be an abuse for an accused to relitigate the admissibility issue if the earlier ruling had been adverse and he had been convicted[9], McHugh J could see no reason why it would be an abuse for the Crown to do so where he had been acquitted. A ruling on admissibility at a trial which terminates without verdict, or results in a conviction which is set aside, is not binding at a new trial[10]. The majority acknowledged that the ruling was subject to review by the trial judge, and only became final with the jury's verdict. If it was reviewable by the first trial judge, why not by the second? McHugh J said[11]:

> '... the prospect of inconsistency between a ruling and a prior ruling is not enough to constitute an abuse of process. Even the fact that a ruling or decision in one case may inferentially lead to a conclusion that a ruling or decision in an earlier case was wrong does not mean that it is an abuse of process to ask a court to make the ruling or give the decision. In the light of ... *R v Darby*[12] ... it could not be ... an abuse to indict a conspirator simply because a co-conspirator was acquitted in an earlier trial.'

He commented that[13] it would follow from the majority decision that '... if an accused person obtains a favourable ruling in a criminal trial, it is an abuse of process for the Crown to lead any evidence in another trial to challenge that finding, even if, despite the ruling, the accused was convicted at the original trial. That proposition goes beyond anything that has hitherto been regarded as an abuse of process'. In *Duhamel v R (No 2)*[14] the Supreme Court of Canada held that rulings on the admissibility of confessions were interlocutory and did not determine ultimate issues or create issue estoppels[15]. In that case an accused was tried successively for two robberies. The first trial judge rejected his confession and the accused was acquitted. The second trial judge admitted the confession, the accused was convicted, and the Supreme Court upheld the conviction. *Rogers* has been treated as finally establishing that issue estoppels have no place in the criminal law in Australia, and statements of principle in the majority judgments have been cited[16], but the High Court has yet to consider this 3:2 decision in the context of rulings on evidence.

1   (1994) 181 CLR 251.
2   Ibid at 256, 278.
3   The challenge was not direct but collateral as counsel argued (at 252), because it was brought in separate proceedings and could not affect the earlier ruling: *Hunter* [1982] AC 529, 540, 541, 542, 545; *Bryant* [1984] 1 NZLR 280 CA, 282, 283; *Rogers* (1994) 181 CLR 251, 270.
4   (1994) 181 CLR 251, 255, 267, 280.
5   Ibid at 270.
6   Ibid at 290, 293.
7   [1982] AC 529. McHugh J said (at 289) that *Hunter* was best explained as based on improper purpose.
8   [1984] 1 NZLR 280, CA. This was certainly so in *Bryant* where the confession was ruled inadmissible at the first trial and there was no other evidence to support a conviction in the second, but not in *Hunter* where the decision to admit the confession, while fundamental to the verdict of guilty, did not ensure it because the jury could have acquitted.
9   (1994) 181 CLR 251, 292, and per Deane and Gaudron JJ at 280.
10 *R v Blair* (1985) 1 NSWLR 584. (No 'estoppel' from ruling at abortive trial. This accords with the principle in civil cases where a new trial is ordered: para 5.14; followed *Lynch v Moran* [2006] 3 IR 389 SC, 409).
11 (1994) 181 CLR 251, 290–291.
12 (1982) 148 CLR 668; to the same effect *DPP v Shannon* [1975] AC 717 and *Hui Chi-Ming v R* [1992] 1 AC 34, 57; para 14.21 n 4.
13 (1994) 181 CLR 251, 294.
14 (1984) 14 DLR (4th) 92. In *Lynch v Moran* [2006] 3 IR 389 SC the Supreme Court held that rulings on evidence at a criminal trial which was aborted, where the jury failed to agree, or where the conviction was set aside and a new trial ordered, were not binding in a later trial.
15 The Supreme Court has recognised issue estoppels in criminal cases: para 14.04 n 1.
16 *Pearce v R* (1998) 194 CLR 610, 620, 625, 628; *R v Carroll* (2002) 213 CLR 635, 647–648, 650, 662, 663, 678; *Island Maritime* (2006) 226 CLR 328, 343, 354.

Chapter 15

MATRIMONIAL PROCEEDINGS

SECTION 7: FOREIGN DECREES

Jurisdiction of foreign courts in matrimonial cases

15.01 A foreign decree will only be recognised if it was pronounced by a court of competent jurisdiction. Decrees of nullity and divorce are judgments *in rem*[1] and jurisdiction cannot depend on consent or contract.

[1]   As to decrees of divorce *Pemberton v Hughes* [1899] 1 Ch 781 CA, 793; *Bater* [1906] P 209 CA, 228. As to decrees of nullity *Salvesen v Austrian Property Administrator* [1927] AC 641, 655, 663.

Jurisdiction in divorce: historical

15.02 It was for long an inflexible rule that a divorce decree pronounced in a foreign jurisdiction would only be recognised if the parties were domiciled there when the proceedings were commenced[1]. Divorce proceedings had to be brought where the husband was domiciled, because until 1973 a wife acquired and retained her husband's domicile[2]. This worked much injustice which was progressively remedied by judicial decision and legislation here and in most Commonwealth jurisdictions.

[1]   *Leon* [1967] P 275, 284 'once competent always competent'; *Indyka* [1969] 1 AC 33, 55.
[2]   *A-G for Alberta v Cook* [1926] AC 444, 465; *Indyka* [1969] 1 AC 33, 55, 74, 81.

Jurisdiction in divorce: current position

15.03 The Domicile and Matrimonial Proceedings Act 1973[1] abolished the rule that a wife acquired the domicile of her husband and provided that her domicile should be ascertained independently. The court[2] now has jurisdiction in divorce judicial separation and nullity if it has jurisdiction under Council Regulation 2201/2003, and no other court in a Member State has jurisdiction. It has jurisdiction under the Regulation if either party was habitually resident

223

in England and Wales when the proceedings were begun, was habitually resident for six months and domiciled there, or both parties were domiciled there[3].

In 1971, following the decision in *Indyka*[4] which broadened but unsettled the rules for recognition of foreign decrees, Parliament passed the Recognition of Divorces and Legal Separations Act. Part II of the Family Law Act 1986 now contains substantially the same code for the recognition of divorce, legal separation and nullity decrees pronounced by courts elsewhere in the United Kingdom, or outside the EU[5]. The validity of a divorce, annulment or legal separation obtained outside the United Kingdom and the EU (an overseas decree) may be recognised by virtue of that or some other Act[6]. An overseas decree will be recognised if it is effective under the law of the country in which it was pronounced, and if at the relevant date either party was habitually resident or domiciled in, or a national of, that country[7]. The relevant date is the date of commencement of proceedings and in cases of annulment it includes the date of the death of either party[8]. Domicile may be determined either by the law of the foreign forum or by the law of the United Kingdom forum in which the question of recognition arises[9]. Findings of jurisdictional fact in foreign proceedings are conclusive if both parties took part in the proceedings and in other cases are sufficient proof unless the contrary is shown[10]. A party who has appeared in proceedings is treated as having taken part[11]. Council Regulation 2201/2003[12] requires a judgment in a Member State on matrimonial matters and matters of parental authority to be recognised in other Member States without any special procedure being required. Recognition is not to be granted if this would contravene the public policy of the Member State in which recognition is sought, if there has been a denial of natural justice, or if the judgment is irreconcilable with an earlier judgment between the same parties[13].

Recognition of an overseas decree may be refused if it is irreconcilable with a decision determining the subsistence or validity of the marriage previously given by a court in the United Kingdom entitled to recognition[14]. Recognition may be refused if the divorce or separation was granted when, according to the law of that part of the United Kingdom in which the question arises (including its rules of private international law and the provisions of Part V), there was no subsisting marriage between the parties[15]. Recognition may also be refused if the decree was obtained without reasonable steps being taken to give notice of the proceedings to a party or without that party having a reasonable opportunity to take part[16]. These provisions enact the previous law[17]. Section 51(3)(c) further provides that recognition may also be refused where this would be manifestly contrary to public policy. This reflects the decision in *Vervaeke v Smith*[18], where recognition was refused for a Belgian nullity decree based on a different public policy of marriage. Recognition of a Bolivian decree obtained by deceiving the Court was refused[19]. However the discretion to withhold recognition on this ground should be exercised sparingly and a Turkish decree was recognised where both parties deceived the Court to shorten the husband's national service[20]. Recognition is not required for any finding of fault or any maintenance, custody or other ancillary order. Part II applies to a divorce, annulment, or legal separation granted by a court in the British Islands before the Act and to overseas decrees obtained before or after the Act[21]. Overseas decrees granted before the Act may also be recognised if they were entitled to recognition under repealed legislation.

[1] Section 1.
[2] The Family Division and a County Court exercising jurisdiction under Part V of the Matrimonial and Family Proceedings Act 1984.
[3] Article 3.
[4] [1969] 1 AC 33.
[5] The provisions of the 1986 Act dealing with the recognition of non-judicial divorces and the earlier common law rules are outside the scope of this work.
[6] Section 45.
[7] Section 46(1).
[8] Section 46(3)(a), (4).
[9] Section 46(5).
[10] Section 48(1)(a), (b).
[11] Section 48(3). Section 47 contains corresponding provisions for the recognition of overseas decrees granted in cross proceedings. Section 49 contains corresponding provisions with respect to countries with territories having different systems of law.
[12] Council Regulation 2201/2003 art 21.
[13] Ibid art 22.
[14] Section 51(1). This was one of the grounds for refusing recognition of the Belgian nullity decree in *Vervaecke v Smith* [1983] 1 AC 145.
[15] Section 51(2).
[16] Section 51(3).
[17] As to divorce decrees, *Macalpine* [1958] P 35; *Middleton* [1967] P 62; and *Indyka* [1969] 1 AC 33. As to nullity decrees *Gray v Formosa* [1963] P 259 CA, 270 and *Lepre* [1965] P 52 (Maltese decrees based on requirement for religious ceremony not recognised for civil marriages in England).
[18] *Vervaecke v Smith* [1983] 1 AC 145.
[19] *Kendall* [1977] Fam 208.
[20] *Eroglu* [1994] 2 FLR 287.
[21] Section 52(1)(a), (b).

SECTION 2: ISSUE ESTOPPEL IN MATRIMONIAL LITIGATION

Introduction

15.04 A decision in the divorce jurisdiction may be *in personam*[1], or partly *in rem* and partly *in personam*[2]. The rules of issue estoppel applicable to decisions, or parts of decisions which are *in personam*, will now be considered.

[1] Para 12.17. *Needham v Bremner* (1866) LR 1 CP 583; *Conradi* (1868) LR 1 P & D 514, 518–519.
[2] *B v A-G (NEB Intervening)* [1965] P 278.

Issue estoppels of limited application

15.05 Issue estoppels are now rarely litigated in divorce proceedings as few divorces are contested, and those cases are normally tried in the County Court. Issue estoppels have limited application in divorce because the court by statute is 'under a duty to inquire into the facts' as a condition of granting relief and must find 'proved', or 'be satisfied' that the marriage has broken down irretrievably[1] for one or more of the grounds specified in s 1(2) of the

1973 Act. The court is also enjoined to 'inquire into' facts alleged by the respondent[2]. A finding in earlier proceedings cannot bind the court which must be free to investigate the facts itself[3]. In *Laws*[4] a wife obtained a restitution decree on the ground of desertion; and on the husband's failure to comply petitioned for judicial separation. The husband alleged cruelty. There was no estoppel because the court had a duty to enquire into any counter charge; and could dismiss the petition if the petitioner had been guilty of cruelty.

[1] 1973 Act s 1(2), (3).
[2] Section 1(3) of the 1973 Act provides that '... it shall be the duty of the court to inquire, so far as it reasonably can, into the facts alleged by the petitioner and into any facts alleged by the respondent'. Section 20 provides that a respondent who proves any of the facts in s 1(2) is entitled to the same relief as if he were a petitioner.
[3] *Harriman* [1909] P 123 CA, 142, 144; *Hudson* [1948] P 292; *Thompson* [1957] P 19 CA, 29, 36, 42; *Keast* [1934] NZLR 316 CA.
[4] [1963] 1 WLR 1133.

Estoppels do not bind the divorce court

15.06 The statement that the parties are estopped but 'the court is not'[1]. was discussed by Denning LJ in *Thompson*[2]:

> 'The question ... is ... whether those ordinary principles [of issue estoppel] ... apply to the Divorce Division (sic). The answer is, I think, that they do apply, but subject to the important qualification that it is the statutory duty of the Divorce Court to inquire into the truth of a petition – and of any counter-charge – which is properly before it, and no doctrine of estoppel by res judicata can abrogate that duty ... The situation has been neatly summarised by saying that in the Divorce Court "estoppels bind the parties but do not bind the court": but this is perhaps a little too abbreviated. The full proposition is that, once an issue of a matrimonial offence has been litigated between the parties and decided by a competent court, neither party can claim as of right to re-open the issue and litigate it all over again if the other party objects ... but the Divorce Court has the right, and indeed the duty in a proper case, to re-open the issue, or to allow either party to re-open it, despite the objection of the other ... . Whether the Divorce Court should re-open the issue depends on the circumstances. If the Court is satisfied that there has already been a full and proper inquiry in the previous litigation, it will often hold that it is not necessary to hold another ... . But if the court is not so satisfied, it has a right and a duty to inquire into it afresh. If the court does decide to re-open the matter, then there is no longer any estoppel on either party. Each can go into the matter afresh'.

Prior to the Matrimonial Causes Act 1973[3], the court, treated its orders[4] and orders of courts of summary jurisdiction[5] as evidence in later proceedings between the same parties, though not conclusive.

[1] *Harriman* [1909] P 123, 131–132. In *Conradi* (1868) LR 1 P & D 514, 520–521 the court held that it could act on a finding of adultery in a previous decree as *res judicata*.
[2] [1957] P 19 CA, 29.
[3] Section 6, now 1973 Act s 4(2), *Kara* [1948] P 287 CA, and *Turner* [1962] P 283 CA.
[4] *Bland* (1866) LR 1 P & D 237.
[5] *Harriman* [1909] P 123 CA, 132–133, 142, 144–145.

Where no inquisitorial function involved

15.07 Where the court has no inquisitorial function, the ordinary rules apply[1]. Where the earlier proceedings were in the High Court[2], and the determination was a negative one, the result may found an estoppel; for to estop the party who failed does not offend against the duty to be satisfied of the ground before granting relief. In *Finney*[3] a wife's petition for judicial separation for cruelty was dismissed on the merits. She petitioned for divorce on the ground of adultery and cruelty but failed because the cruelty was the same. In *Hopkins*[4] the husband had been granted a divorce for his wife's adultery with a named co-respondent. When sued for damages the co-respondent raised defences of connivance and conduct inducing. Since the decree rested on an implied finding of no connivance, the co-respondent was estopped from raising this defence[5], but not the discretionary bar of conduct inducing which was not implicitly denied by the decree[6]. In *James*[7] a husband's petition for his wife's adultery with a named co-respondent was dismissed on the merits. In proceedings for maintenance before justices the husband was precluded from repeating the charges because the matter was *res judicata*. In *Field*[8] a husband sued for divorce on the ground of adultery and the wife cross-petitioned on the same ground. The wife denied adultery on oath and the husband did not proceed and she obtained a decree on her cross-petition. Six years later the husband applied to vary the maintenance order but was estopped from raising his wife's adultery because the court had no inquisitorial duty in maintenance matters.

[1] *Conradi* (1868) LR 1 P & D 514. Where the second proceedings are not in the High Court or County Court the ordinary rules as to issue estoppel apply.
[2] Cf para 15.10.
[3] (1868) LR 1 P & D 483; *Bright* [1954] P 270.
[4] (1933) 50 TLR 99.
[5] Connivance being an absolute bar.
[6] Absolute and discretionary bars no longer exist under the 1973 Act. See also *Brewer* (1953) 88 CLR 1.
[7] [1948] 1 All ER 214.
[8] [1964] P 336.

15.08 The parties will be estopped by a finding that their marriage is valid and subsisting. In *Wilkins*[1] a husband who unsuccessfully claimed that his marriage was bigamous was estopped in later proceedings, even after the former husband turned up, until he obtained an order for a new trial of the first proceedings[2]. In *Woodland*[3] a restitution decree was made against a husband who had no ground for thinking that his marriage was bigamous. He was estopped, after he learned the truth, while the decree stood. In *Hull*[4] the earlier finding was affirmative in form but negative in substance. The wife having been granted a divorce for desertion, the husband's plea in custody proceedings that she had deserted him was rejected as *res judicata*. He also alleged that she had committed adultery which had not been disclosed in her discretion statement[5], but there was no estoppel because that allegation had not been before the court[6].

[1] [1896] P 108 CA.
[2] The application was three years out of time.
[3] [1928] P 169.

⁴   [1960] P 118.
⁵   Discretion statements have been abolished.
⁶   In *Warren* [1962] 3 All ER 1031 the wife was estopped from setting up in support of a charge of desertion the same facts she had set up to support a charge of cruelty which had failed. She was not estopped from proceeding for desertion on different evidence: *Hill* [1954] P 291 and *Holland* [1961] 1 All ER 226 CA.

Omissions may found an issue estoppel

15.09   The principles governing issue estoppel require each party to bring forward his whole case. A party is not permitted to raise a matter later which properly belonged to the earlier case but was not brought forward unless he can establish special circumstances[1]. The principle applies whether the matter was omitted through the negligence or inadvertence of the party or his advisers, or even by accident[2]. However the point must be one which if determined in the successful party's favour would have been fundamental to the judgment and if determined the other way would have changed the result[3]. This rule applies in matrimonial causes[4], subject to the court's inquisitorial function[5], which excludes any estoppel from omissions in summary proceedings.

¹   Paras 8.31–8.35.
²   *Henderson* (1843) 3 Hare 100, 115; para 7.03.
³   In *Lake* [1955] P 336 CA the husband's petition for adultery was dismissed on findings of adultery and condonation. The wife had no right of appeal since she had succeeded and the finding of adultery was not *res judicata*: *Cie Noga D'Importation Et D'Exportation SA v Australia and New Zealand Banking Group Ltd (No 3)* [2003] 1 WLR 307 CA, 321–322, 328; para 8.25.
⁴   *Lindsay* [1934] P 162, 167 overruled, but not on this point, in *Rowe* [1980] Fam 47 CA.
⁵   In *Winnan* [1949] P 174 CA the estoppel was rejected because the earlier proceedings were before justices, but in *Bright* [1954] P 270 the court applied *Hoystead* [1926] AC 155.

Where first proceedings before justices

15.10   Where the first proceedings were before justices and failed the ordinary rules would require the unsuccessful party to be estopped in other courts, for it cannot be said that the inquisitorial duty must lead to a different result. But in practice the divorce court generally investigates the charges afresh[1], as Denning LJ explained in *Thompson*[2]:

> 'The reason is because it is known that magistrates are inclined to concentrate more on the question: ought this husband to pay maintenance to the wife, and less on the other issues, however relevant they may be. At any rate the Divorce Court does not consider it satisfactory to allow the matter to be conclusively determined by the magistrates. The Divorce Court regards their finding as evidence, but not as conclusive, on the issue'.

¹   *Hayward* [1961] P 152, 161 per Phillimore J: 'In so far as there is any question of estoppel *per rem judicatam* it can only arise from the decision of the justices, which is not binding upon this court'.
²   [1957] P 19 CA, 31–32; *Harriman* [1909] P 123 CA, 142, 144–145, *Winnan* [1949] P 174 CA, 183; *Turner* [1962] P 283 CA.

Estoppel in summary proceedings

15.11 When the second proceeding is before justices the parties will be estopped by a finding in the High Court[1], County Court[2], or before justices[3] which was fundamental to the judgment. The estoppel will arise whether the finding was affirmative or negative for justices have no inquisitorial duty. In *Whittaker*[4] the husband covenanted in a separation deed to pay maintenance *dum casta*. The wife sued in the County Court for arrears but the husband pleaded adultery and succeeded. The wife then brought proceedings before justices alleging wilful failure to maintain but was estopped from denying adultery.

[1] *Sternberg* [1963] 3 All ER 319.
[2] *Stokes* [1911] P 195.
[3] *Whittaker* [1939] 3 All ER 833.
[4] Ibid.

Decree refused

15.12 1f a decree is refused in a defended suit the result is *res judicata*[1]. The dismissal of an undefended petition is not a judgment *in rem*[2] and if a second suit is brought and the respondent does not raise the estoppel no one else can[3]. It is not clear that there is an estoppel in such a case. In some jurisdictions the dismissal of an undefended petition is regarded as a nonsuit[4] allowing a second petition on fuller evidence. There appears to be no decision in this country on the point[5].

[1] Para 15.07.
[2] Chapter 10.
[3] Counsel would disclose the position to the court.
[4] *Hung* [1956] NZLR 203 doubted in *Campbell* [1957] NZLR 1123, 1127. Such a dismissal was held to be in the nature of a nonsuit in *Gainsford* (1899) 25 VLR 176.
[5] The better course is to stand the petition over: *Dean* (1879) 5 VLR (IP & M) 116.

The issues must be identical

15.13 In divorce, as elsewhere, an issue estoppel must relate to an issue[1]. A complainant estopped from relitigating an issue of cruelty can retender the evidence in a later proceeding on a different issue[2]. In *Cooper (No 2)*[3] a court of summary jurisdiction dismissed a wife's charge of persistent cruelty, but she could present the same evidence in proceedings for desertion and wilful failure to maintain. In *Bohnel (No 2)*[4] the wife's petition for cruelty failed but when the husband petitioned for desertion she could rely on the same evidence to establish just cause[5].

[1] *Brewer* (1953) 88 CLR 1,15 per Fullagar J.
[2] *Foster* [1954] P 67.
[3] [1955] P 168.
[4] [1963] 2 All ER 325.
[5] In *Cooper (No 2)* [1955] P 168, 172 Lord Merriman P said there was 'unquestionably an overlap' between those issues. See also *Thompson* [1957] P 19 CA; *Fisher* [1960] P 36, CA.

Issue estoppel in maintenance proceedings

15.14 The conduct of the parties is relevant in maintenance proceedings[1]. *Res judicata* estoppel prevents a party challenging the ground on which the decree was pronounced or the ultimate findings on which it was based but otherwise there is no estoppel[2]. There is no rule of public policy which prevents conduct being raised that could have been raised in the divorce proceedings but was not[3]. A custody order in a decree nisi in an undefended suit does not create a *res judicata* estoppel[4]. A wife who did not seek maintenance for a child about to be born (where paternity was denied) when consenting to a decree which contained no order for maintenance for herself or the other children (custody being given to the husband) was precluded from applying to a magistrate for maintenance for that child, although she could have applied to the Supreme Court for a variation of the original order[5].

1   *Restall* [1930] P 189; 1973 Act s 25(1), (2)(g).
2   *Tumath* [1970] P 78 CA, 85, 91–92; *Porter* [1971] P 282, 284–285.
3   *Tumath* [1970] P 78 CA. In *Brewer* (1953) 88 CLR 1 the High Court of Australia refused to follow *Duchesne* [1951] P 101, later overruled in *Tumath* (above).
4   *Rowe* [1980] Fam 47 CA.
5   *Brown* (1905) 3 CLR 373.

Where decree nisi rescinded

15.15 If a decree nisi is rescinded can any issue estoppel continue to bind ? In principle the answer must be 'No'. When a judgment is set aside any estoppel is extinguished. This admittedly occurs when a decree is rescinded on a ground which challenges it on the merits – for instance fraud or fresh evidence[1]. Where a decree was rescinded on the application of the Queen's Proctor for other reasons it was held in *Butler*[2] that the estoppels continued. AL Smith LJ said[3]:

> ' … the decree nisi granted in the former suit has been rescinded, and it is said that as a verdict not followed by judgment is no evidence at all, as no judgment is now extant it is the same thing as if there had been no judgment at all. We think Mr Channell was well founded when he said that in ordinary actions at law … a verdict given therein and not followed by a judgment is no evidence at all. … in ordinary cases if a verdict be followed by a verdict, and such judgment is afterwards set aside, the verdict falls with the judgment, and, as was held in *O'Connor v Malone* (1839), 6 Cl & Fin 572, neither party can give such verdict in evidence upon the second trial. But why is this? A judgment in such cases is set aside upon the ground that the verdict upon which it is founded was obtained either by fraud or by misdirection of the judge, or against evidence, or by surprise, or by some other means, which shewed that the verdict itself could not be supported, and consequently a judgment founded thereon was erroneous. In such cases the setting aside of the judgment vacates not only the judgment but the erroneous verdict, and places the parties in the same position as if no verdict had been given. But how does this apply to a case like the present? The verdict was followed by a judgment, and no fraud or error existed in the obtaining of that verdict, which stands unimpeached and upon which the decree nisi was founded. As regards the issues adjudicated upon between the parties, all was in order, and the judgment given thereon (i.e. the decree nisi) was perfectly valid and would have remained in force, and in due

course would have become a decree absolute, had it not been that, dehors the verdict and wholly unconnected therewith, it was subsequently ascertained that the husband and wife had been guilty of conduct which disentitled them from reaping the benefit of the decree which both ... so much desired. The material facts suppressed related to the conduct of the wife (petitioner), not to the conduct of the husband'.

1   Cf *Wilkins* [1896] P 108 CA; *Woodland* [1928] P 169.
2   [1894] P 25 CA.
3   Ibid at 29.

15.16 Although *Butler* has been accepted in leading textbooks it is wrong in principle because a plea of *res judicata* cannot be supported by a judgment which has been set aside[1]. A decree nisi is not even a final judgment and on this ground alone the issue estoppel should have failed[2]. This point was glossed over by A L Smith LJ who said[3]:

'It cannot, we think, be doubted, if in the present suit the decree nisi had remained unrescinded or had ripened into a decree absolute, that then the verdict and decree in the former suit would have been conclusive evidence in the present suit of the husband's adultery and cruelty, and that it would not have been open to the husband in the present suit to controvert the fact of such adultery and cruelty having been committed by him'.

There is a significant difference between a decree nisi '*remaining unrescinded*' and '*ripening into a decree absolute*'. Only in the latter case does it become a final judgment. The same question arises when a spouse dies before the decree nisi is made absolute. The suit abates, there is no final judgment and the findings cannot support an issue estoppel[4]. The position would be otherwise where claims for a property adjustment order or maintenance survived for or against the estate of a deceased spouse[5].

1   Paras 2.33, 5.14.
2   *Kemp v Pearce* [1972] VR 805 where the court declined to follow *Butler*.
3   [1894] P 25 CA, 29.
4   *Kemp v Pearce* [1972] VR 805.
5   *D'Este* [1973] Fam 55.

Discharge of decree absolute

15.17 A decree absolute binds the world, and continues to bind until set aside. Applications can be made to set it aside for fraud[1], or for a new trial with an enlargement of time if necessary[2]. The decree is only voidable[3], and an appellate court may decline to intervene after the time for appeal has expired, particularly if either party has remarried[4]. Decrees nisi and absolute pronounced on a petition which had not been served were said to be void[5] but this is not correct.

1   Paras 17.02 and foll.
2   *Wilkins* [1896] P 108 CA; *Woodland* [1928] P 169; para 15.08; *Edwards* [1951] P 228, 234–235.
3   *Marsh* [1945] AC 271.
4   *McPherson* [1936] AC 177, 205; *Wiseman* [1953] P 79 CA.
5   *Ali Ebrahim* [1983] 1 WLR 1336. An order of the High Court, however fundamentally irregular, is never void: *Isaacs v Robertson* [1985] AC 97, 102–103; paras 4.03, 4.05, 4.06.

Legitimacy

15.18 Questions of paternity may arise in divorce proceedings. *Rowe*[1] decided that a decree nisi for divorce in undefended proceedings, with an order for custody of named children of the marriage, did not estop a party claiming that one was not a child of the marriage. The question was whether children of another had been accepted by the husband as children of the family. A decree absolute for divorce, though a judgment *in rem* as regards the parents, is not as regards the children. They are not parties and are not bound on questions of each other's legitimacy[2].

[1]   [1980] Fam 47 CA.
[2]   *B v A-G* [1965] P 278, *Nokes* [1957] P 213. For the difficulties attending declarations of legitimacy where persons have not been made parties: *Aldrich v A-G* [1968] 1 All ER 345.

Orders for custody and welfare of children

15.19 Issue estoppels are not binding in proceedings for the care or custody of children because the court's overriding duty is to have regard to the welfare of the child[1], and there is no issue estoppel in a changing situation[2]. However the court may enforce an issue estoppel in such cases, even where the parties are not the same[3].

[1]   *In Re B* [1997] Fam 117, 123, 124, 127; approved *In Re B* [2000] 1 WLR 790 CA, 796.
[2]   Para 17.30.
[3]   *In re B* [1997] Fam 117, 128; *JEN v MEN* [2007] 3 IR 517.

Property adjustment orders

15.20 If in making a property adjustment order[1] the Family Division determines property rights between a third party and either or both spouses, that is *res judicata* in other Divisions of the High Court and elsewhere[2]. The effect of a consent order for financial provision on divorce in barring a further application by the wife was considered in *Dinch*[3]. In Australia, court approval of a property settlement on divorce was no bar to an action by the wife for damages for fraud against her former husband, as no such question had been litigated[4].

[1]   1973 Act s 24.
[2]   *Tebbutt v Haynes* [1981] 2 All ER 238 CA.
[3]   [1987] 1 WLR 252 HL, 263; para 2.17 n 6.
[4]   *Gipps* [1974] 1 NSWLR 259 CA; para 8.10 n 10, compare *de Lasala* [1980] AC 546 (fraud as ground for setting aside order approving deed of arrangement on divorce).

Withdrawal of summary application

15.21 The withdrawal before adjudication of a summons under the Domestic Proceedings and Magistrates' Courts Act 1978 does not create an issue estoppel[1].

[1]   *Land* [1949] P 405; *Molesworth* [1947] 2 All ER 842.

Chapter 16

ADMINISTRATIVE LAW AND JUDICIAL REVIEW

TRANSFORMATION OF ADMINISTRATIVE LAW

16.01 English administrative law has undergone a revolution in the last 50 years[1]. In 1977 its procedural basis was rationalised and reformed by Order 53[2] and it was placed on a statutory basis by s 31 of the Supreme Court Act 1981. These reforms did not alter the substantive law which had governed the availability of the prerogative writs[3].

[1]   The history is traced by Lord Diplock in *O'Reilly v Mackman* [1983] 2 AC 237, 277–284.
[2]   Now CPR Pt 54.
[3]   *R v IRC, ex p National Federation of Self Employed and Small Businesses* [1980] QB 407 CA, 429; *O'Reilly v Mackman* [1983] 2 AC 237, 279–285.

STATUTORY POWERS

16.02 The validity of administrative action depends on the scope of the power and the manner of its exercise. Wade and Forsyth commented[1]:

> 'The numerous cases which hold that a decision within jurisdiction is unchallengeable have ... no necessary connection with *Res judicata*. *Res judicata* does nothing to make the initial decision binding: it is only because the decision is ... binding that it may operate as *res judicata*..'

However, as Lord Diplock held[2] valid administrative decisions, such as those made by insurance officers under the National Insurance legislation, do not give rise to issue estoppels.

[1]   Wade and Forsyth 'Administrative Law' (9th edn 2004) at 244.
[2]   *Hudson v Secretary of State for Social Services* [1972] AC 944, 1010; para 2.03 n 27.

RES JUDICATA AND ADMINISTRATIVE DECISIONS

16.03 Decision-makers other than courts may have powers of adjudication which attract the *res judicata* doctrine[1]. Decisions in annual taxation, rating and valuation cases stand outside the doctrine for other reasons, but *Thrasyvoulou*[2] established that decisions of planning inspectors are within it. In the

233

first case the council had served enforcement notices in October 1981 alleging a material change of use. On appeal to the Secretary of State the inspector found that there had been no change of use since 1964. In 1985 the council served further enforcement notices alleging the same breach of planning control. It was common ground that there had been no change of use since the 1981 notices. The second inspector upheld the notices, but the House of Lords held that the issue was *res judicata*. The Environment Secretary argued that the inspector could not be fettered by any estoppel in the exercise of his powers or the performance of his duties. Lord Bridge, who delivered the principal speech, said[3]:

> ' ... the rationale which underlies the doctrine of *res judicata* is so different from that which underlies the doctrine of estoppel by representation that I do not think these authorities have any relevance for present purposes[4]. The doctrine of *res judicata* rests on the twin principles which cannot be better expressed than in terms of the two Latin maxims *interest reipublicae ut sit finis litium* and *nemo debet bis vexari pro una et eadem causa.*. These principles are of such fundamental importance that they cannot be confined ... to litigation in the private law field. They certainly have their place in criminal law. In principle they must apply equally to adjudications in the field of public law. In relation to adjudications subject to a comprehensive self-contained statutory code the presumption, ... must be that where the statute has created a specific jurisdiction for the determination of any issue which establishes the existence of a legal right, the principle of *res judicata* applies to give finality to that determination unless an intention to exclude that principle can properly be inferred as a matter of construction ...'[5]

In the first appeal the enforcement notices were in the same terms in respect of the same development, and a cause of action estoppel was upheld[6]. The second notice was in different terms and an issue estoppel was upheld[7]. Lord Bridge concluded[8]:

> '... it follows ... that the local planning authority are now estopped from asserting that there was a material change of use between 1963 and 1982 which expressly contradicts a finding made by the first inspector, which was not merely incidental or ancillary to his decision but was the essential foundation for his conclusion that no breach of planning control was involved ...'.

The High Court has held[9] that an issue estoppel can only arise from a decision of a planning inspector on a mixed question of fact and law where the question had been fully addressed and unequivocally decided, and this was 'clear on the face of the decision'. These requirements are not relevant where an inspector resolved 'clear issues of fact'.

[1]   *Daera Guba* (1972) 130 CLR 353, 453; para 2.03 n 24. The decision-maker must be bound to receive evidence and argument, and have power to make a binding decision: para 2.03 n 26.
[2]   [1990] 2 AC 273; *Danyluk* [2001] 2 SCR 460, 475.
[3]   Ibid at 289.
[4]   *Watt* [2008] 1 AC 696, 707 per Lord Hoffmann: 'Although estoppel in pais and estoppel *per rem judicatam* share the word estoppel, they share very little else.'
[5]   The US Supreme Court applied similar principles in *Astoria* 501 US 104 (1991), 107–108 where 'an administrative agency is acting in a judicial capacity and resolves disputed issues of fact properly before it which the parties have had an adequate opportunity to litigate'.
[6]   *Thrasyvoulou* [1990] 2 AC 273, 296.
[7]   Ibid at 296–297.

8   Ibid at 297; distinguished in *Porter v Secretary of State for Transport* [1996] 3 All ER 693
     CA where a certificate under s 17 of the Land Compensation Act 1961 and the decision of
     a planning inspector on which it was based did not create an issue estoppel in the owner's
     claim for compensation.
9   *Watts v Secretary of State for the Environment and South Oxfordshire District Council*
     [1991] JPL 718, 726.

DEFENCE OF THRASYVOULOU

16.04 The decision has been criticised[1] on the ground that it complicates
planning appeals and hampers councils, with their limited resources, in the
enforcement of planning controls. It could not be suggested that the pleas of
autrefois acquit and *autrefois convict* are affected by the funding of the DPP.
Councils with access to public funds should not be able to harass land owners
with successive enforcement notices based on the same breach of planning
control. The established exceptions for special circumstances[2], and fraud[3]
provide substantial protection for councils. The procedures considered in
Thrasyvoulou provide for the determination in civil proceedings of claims of
right by land owners threatened with criminal prosecution for an unlawful use
or change of use. Such claims would otherwise be determined in criminal
proceedings where the plea of *autrefois acquit* might be available[4]. A land
owner could also invoke the inherent jurisdiction of the criminal court to
prevent abuse of its process if the plea was strictly not available. There seems
no reason why he should lose similar safeguards merely because the issues
have been split between jurisdictions.

1   (1990) 53 MLR 814.
2   *Arnold* [1991] 2 AC 93; paras 8.31–8.35.
3   Paras 17.02 & foll.
4   *Hailsham RDC v Moran* (1966) 18 P & CR 428, 433–434.

16.05 It has been suggested that the real question in *Thrasyvoulou* concerned
the scope of the power to issue an enforcement notice. Section 12(1) of the
Interpretation Act 1978 provides:

> 'Where an Act confers a power or imposes a duty it is implied, unless the
> contrary intention appears, that the power may be exercised, or the duty is to
> be performed, from time to time as occasion requires'.

An Australian commentator has written[1]:

> 'If, on the proper construction of the Act the council was empowered, in the
> public interest, to serve a further enforcement notice, notwithstanding that
> there had been no change of circumstances since the prior decision of a delegate
> of the Minister, there is surely no warrant for invoking *res judicata* to prevent
> the lawful discharge by the council of its statutory power or duty. On the other
> hand if, as would seem to follow from their Lordships' reasoning, there was no
> proper "occasion" for the service of a further notice, absent a relevant change
> of circumstances, the second enforcement notice lacked statutory authority. On
> that analysis the council having once exercised its powers in respect of the
> alleged breach of town planning controls, was *functus officio* unless and until
> there was a change of circumstances. No question of *res judicata* would then

arise, nor would there be any question of the council being prevented from performing its statutory function. Its powers would be exhausted, at least for the time being'.

The House of Lords decided the case on the construction of the appeal provisions[2] and this was correct. The scope of the power read with s 12(1) had to be determined in the light of the Act as a whole. The provisions which authorised appeals indicated the nature of the power. Different considerations may apply in countries where the Constitution provides for the separation of powers and judicial power can only be exercised by courts[3].

[1]   Hall 'Res Judicata and the Administrative Appeals Tribunal' (1994) 2 Australian Journal of Administrative Law 22, 29–30. As to whether a decision-maker can resile from an exercise of statutory power, and whether the power is spent: *Minister for Immigration v Kurtovic* (1990) 21 FCR 193, 211–213.
[2]   [1990] 2 AC 273, 289, quoted para 16.03 n 3.
[3]   *Miller v University of New South Wales* (2003) 132 FCR 147, 166–173.

PLANNING ENFORCEMENT DECISIONS

16.06 An owner who uses his land, or causes or permits its use, in contravention of a subsisting enforcement notice, is guilty of an offence, and if the use continues after conviction he will be liable to a daily penalty. He cannot challenge the enforcement notice in the criminal proceedings, but the prosecution must prove that the use on the date charged contravened the notice. Unlawful use on different days involves separate offences and an acquittal on a charge for one day will not support a plea of *autrefois acquit* on a charge for another[1]. Nor will a conviction for an offence on one day establish an offence on another because there are no issue estoppels in criminal proceedings. If the defendant is flouting planning control, the Attorney-General *ex officio*, or in relator proceedings, or the local authority may seek an injunction in the High Court. An issue estoppel as at one date for a state of affairs which can alter is not binding for a different date[2]. An acquittal on a charge of breaching planning control did not prevent the council seeking an injunction to restrain similar conduct at a later date[3]. The defendant could not extend the estoppel by evidence[4], and the court referred to the fallacy:

'... that, where an issue between A and B relates to a state of things which is capable of subsequent alteration, the conclusive determination in A's favour of that state of things as at one date plus conclusive proof that up to a later date there had been no alteration of such state of things establishes in A's favour as against B an estoppel as to the state of things existing at the later day'[5].

[1]   In *Mills v Cooper* [1967] 2 QB 459 a finding that the defendant was not a gipsy on one date did not bar that assertion at a later date since 'being a gipsy is not an unalterable status but depends upon the way of life which a person is leading at any particular time' per Diplock LJ at 470.
[2]   Para 17.30.
[3]   *Ryde Municipal Council v Lizzio* (1982) 46 LGRA 431 (NSWCA); reversed on other grounds (1983) 155 CLR 211, but at 232 Deane J in dissent applied this principle; *El Alam v Northcote County Council* [1996] 2 VR 672, 684.
[4]   Para 8.22.
[5]   *O'Donel* (1938) 59 CLR 744, 763; *New Brunswick* [1939] AC 1, 20 to the same effect.

ISSUE ESTOPPELS IN JUDICIAL REVIEW

16.07 In *R v Secretary of State for the Environment, ex p Hackney London Borough Council*[1] the Divisional Court rejected an issue estoppel on the facts, but doubted whether one was available in judicial review proceedings. May LJ noted that they were not available in criminal proceedings and said[2]:

'... similar considerations apply to proceedings for judicial review. ... there are no formal pleadings and it will frequently be difficult if not impossible to identify a particular issue which the "first" application will have decided. Moreover we do not think that there is in proceedings brought under Order 53 any true *lis* between the Crown, in whose name the proceedings are brought (and we venture a reservation about whether or not issue estoppel could operate against the Crown) and the respondent or between the *ex parte* applicant and the respondent. Further we doubt whether a decision in such proceedings, in the sense necessary for issue estoppel to operate, is a final decision; the nature of the relief, in many cases, leaves open reconsideration by the statutory or other tribunal of the matter in dispute'.

He favoured the views of Professor Wade[3]:

'... the Court "is not finally determining the validity of the tribunal's order as between the parties themselves" but "is merely deciding whether there has been a plain excess of jurisdiction or not". They are a special class of remedies designed to maintain due order in the legal system, nominally at the suit of the Crown, and they may well fall outside the ambit of the ordinary doctrine of *res judicata*'.

An applicant under Order 53 needs leave, relief is discretionary, and May LJ said that these discretions enabled the court to achieve finality in litigation. The issue estoppel failed again in the Court of Appeal[4] where Dunn LJ[5] and Donaldson MR[6] were also inclined to the view that such estoppels could not arise. Browne-Wilkinson LJ made no comment. The view that there was no *res judicata* in prerogative writs because there was no judgment was explained on historical grounds by Lord Goddard[7]. Cause of action estoppels have long ceased to depend on the existence of a 'strict formal judgment'[8], and issue estoppels may be established from other materials[9]. Decisions in prerogative writ cases must be *res judicata* in contempt proceedings[10]. The other reasons given by May LJ[11] are not persuasive. The Crown is bound by *res judicta* estoppels in the criminal law and is otherwise bound by and entitled to the benefit of such estoppels in the civil law[12]. *Thrasyvoulou*[13] is tacit authority for this and the absence of pleadings cannot be a ground for holding that judicial review proceedings do not create *res judicata* estoppels[14]. The objection that it may be impossible to identify the basis of the decision is no reason for rejecting *res judicata* estoppels where this can be done and the court's reasons and orders will normally disclose this[15]. *R (on the application of Munjaz) v Mersey Care NHS Trust*[16] contains further dicta. Hale LJ giving the judgment of the court said[17]:

'... issue estoppel is a doctrine appropriate to proceedings in private law ... But in judicial review ... there is always a third party who is not present: the wider public ... We therefore share the doubts expressed by this Court in [*Hackney*] as to whether the doctrine ... is applicable at all in judicial review proceedings. But even if it may be, it would not ... prevent the hospital defending its new policy.'

It is not clear whether the court considered that the estoppel failed because there could be no estoppel in a changing situation[18], or because of the special circumstances exception. None of this matters because these *dicta* are contrary to *Thrasyvoulou*. The statement of principle of Lord Bridge[19] is worth repeating[20]:

'The doctrine of *res judicata* rests on ... principles ... of such fundamental importance that they cannot be confined in their application to litigation in the private law field ... In principle they must apply equally to adjudication in the field of public law.'

The House upheld a cause of action estoppel in the first appeal[21] and an issue estoppel in the second[22]. *Rowling v Takaro Properties Ltd*[23] illustrates the utility of such estoppels. A Minister's decision was quashed, and he was sued for damages for negligence and misfeasance in public office. The action failed in the Privy Council, and the point was never taken, but it would be strange if the judicial review decision was not binding in the later proceedings. Austral-ian authority supports the existence of *res judicata* estoppels in this field[24]. A warrant for arrest was quashed and its invalidity was *res judicata* in proceedings for false imprisonment[25]. The extended doctrine based on abuse of process applies to *habeas corpus*[26], and in Australia applies in judicial review generally[27]. In Canada issue estoppels from judicial review proceedings can bar or limit the issues in an action in tort or for breach of contract[28].

1   [1983] 1 WLR 524.
2   Ibid at 538–539.
3   Now Wade and Forsyth 'Administrative Law' (9th edn, 2004) at p 249.
4   [1984] 1 WLR 592 (*Hackney*).
5   Ibid at 602.
6   Ibid at 606; *R v Secretary of State for the Home Department, ex p Momin Ali* [1984] 1 WLR 663 CA, 669–670.
7   'A note on *habeas corpus*' (1949) 65 LQR 30, 34–35.
8   Ibid at 35; *Thrasyvoulou* [1990] 2 AC 273; para 16.02.
9   Para 8.29.
10   Borrie & Lowe 'Law of Contempt' (3rd edn, 1996) pp 589–590.
11   Para 16.07 n 2.
12   *Brisbane County Council v A-G for Queensland* [1979] AC 411; *Hoystead* [1926] AC 155; *Chamberlain* (1988) 164 CLR 502 (Crown bound by merger of cause of action in judgment); the *habeas corpus* cases, *Hoffmann-La Roche* [1975] AC 295, 365 and *Crown Estate Comrs v Dorset County Council* [1990] Ch 297. In *Robertson v Minister of Pensions* [1949] 1 KB 227, 231 Denning J said that the doctrine that estoppels do not bind the Crown 'has long been exploded'.
13   [1990] 2 AC 273.
14   The owners appealed to the High Court from the enforcement notices. Decisions in proceedings commenced by summons and petition, and decisions of inferior courts and tribunals give rise to *res judicata* estoppels; paras 2.06, 8.29.
15   The views to this effect in the 3rd edn were adopted in *Wire Supplies Ltd v CIR* [2006] 2 NZLR 384, 399–400.
16   [2004] QB 395 CA; reversed on other grounds [2006] 2 AC 148.
17   Ibid at 437.
18   Paras 16.06, 17.30.
19   Para 16.02.

20 [1990] 2 AC 273, 289. They were not judicial review proceedings but this should not matter. In *Hoffmann-La Roche* [1975] AC 295, 365 Lord Diplock said that a decision that a statutory instrument was ultra vires created a *res judicata* estoppel. In *Asher* [1974] Ch 208 CA judicial review proceedings which propounded a second challenge to the decision of the auditor after an unsuccessful appeal were dismissed for abuse of process: paras 7.11, 8.36 n 4, 26.04 nn 8–10.

21 Ibid at 296.

22 Ibid at 296–297.

23 [1988] AC 473.

24 *Taylor v Ansett Transport Industries Ltd* (1987) 18 FCR 342; para 17.29 nn 3–7; *Vitosh v Brisbane City Council* (1955) 93 CLR 622; para 8.11 n3 (action not barred on the facts by decision refusing mandamus, but no suggestion that refusal was not *res judicata*); *Re Wakim* (1999) 198 CLR 511, 632.

25 *Spautz v Butterworth* (1996) 41 NSWLR 1 CA.

26 *Re Hastings* (No. 2) [1959] 1 QB 358, 371; *R v Governor of Pentonville Prison ex p Tarling* [1979] 1 WLR 1417, 1422–1423.

27 *Stuart v Sanderson* (2000) 100 FCR 150, 156–157.

28 *Hughes Land Co v Manitoba* (1998) 167 DLR (4th) 652 CA Man; *Mohl v University of BC* (2006) 265 DLR (4th) 109 BCCA.

PREROGATIVE WRITS

16.08 Since the 1977 reforms were procedural, the earlier case law on *res judicata* in prerogative writ proceedings remains relevant. Most of the decisions concerned second applications on different evidence. In *R v Bodmin Corpn*[1], the court discharged a rule *nisi* for *mandamus* because there had been no demand for performance of the duty. A demand was then made and refused and a second rule *nisi* was discharged, Day J saying[2]:

> '… no second application for a prerogative writ will be granted when the first application has been discharged'.

This principle has been applied to applications for *quo warranto*[3], *certiorari*[4] and semble prohibition[5]. The rule appears to be one of practice[6], and the Court of Appeal for Ontario has held that a second application for *mandamus* may be granted where the applicant would otherwise suffer a serious injustice without legal remedy[7]. There is no suggestion in the pre–1977 case law that the discharge of a rule *nisi* on the merits or an order absolute would not estop the parties in later litigation. After much uncertainty it was decided in *Re Hastings (No 2)* that although 'the decision whether or not to issue a writ of *habeas corpus* is not a judgment so that there is no *res judicata*,' since 'the decision … involves the exercise of a judicial discretion, the court must have an inherent jurisdiction to refuse, … to hear the same matter argued again'[8]. Before the Judicature Acts the practice in *habeas corpus* and the other prerogative writs was the same, but an unsuccessful applicant for *habeas corpus* could apply once to each of the common law courts in banc and to the Court of Chancery without being faced with a plea of *res judicata* based on other refusals[9], but could not apply to the same court again on the same facts[10]. *Re Hastings (No 2)* decided that the Divisional Court would not entertain a second application, and in 1960 legislation provided that a second application cannot be made on the same grounds without fresh evidence[11]. An order for *habeas corpus* setting the applicant at liberty is binding on the Crown and a judgment *in rem*. In *Cox v Hakes*[12] Lord Halsbury LC said:

'If discharge followed the legality of that discharge could never be brought in question'.

The effect of an order for discharge is dealt with in s 5 of the Habeas Corpus Act 1679 which provides:

'... no person ... which shall be delivered or set at large upon any *habeas corpus* shall at any time thereafter be again imprisoned or committed for the same offence ... other than by the legal order and process of such court wherein he ... shall be bound to appear'

In *A-G for Colony of Hong Kong v Kwok-a-Sing*[13] Mellish LJ said:

'... [the section] can only apply when the second arrest is substantially for the same cause as the first, so that the return to the second writ of *habeas corpus* raises for the opinion of the Court the same question with reference to the validity of the grounds of detention as the first.'

An order for ouster on a *quo warranto* is a judgment *in rem*[14], as are orders for *certiorari* and *scire facias*[15].

1   [1892] 2 QB 21.
2   Ibid at 23.
3   *R v Orde* (1830) 8 Ad & El 420n.
4   *R v Manchester and Leeds Rly Co* (1838) 8 Ad & El 413, 427 per Denman CJ: '... the rule of practice, if not altogether universal and [in]flexible, is as nearly so as possible, that the court will not allow a party to succeed on a second application, who has previously applied for the very same thing without coming properly prepared. We are constantly acting on that principle ...'; Second applications for prohibition were refused in *Bodenham v Ricketts* (1836) 6 Nev & MKB 537 and *Ex Parte Sherry* (1909) 9 SR (NSW) 461.
5   *R v Kensington Income Tax General Comrs, ex p Princess De Polignac* [1917] 1 KB 486 CA, 519.
6   Para 16.08 n 4.
7   *Re Permanent Investment Corpn Ltd* (1967) 62 DLR (2d) 258, 266–268. In Canada mandamus may be refused without prejudice to a further application.
8   *Re Hastings (No 2)* [1959] 1 QB 358, 371.
9   'A note on *habeas corpus*' (1949) 65 LQR 30, 34.
10 *Re Hastings (No.2)* [1959] 1 QB 358, 371.
11 Paras 2.30, 10.07. An applicant for *habeas corpus* must bring forward his whole case, and the extended doctrine applies: *Reg v Governor of Pentonville Prison ex parte Tarling* [1979] 1 WLR 1417, 1422–1423. In Hong Kong the refusal of *habeas corpus* creates *res judicata* estoppels in the broad sense involving abuse of process which bar a second application on new grounds: *Lam v HKSAR* [2004] 3 HKLRD 458 CA.
12 (1890) 15 App Cas 506, 514; *Secretary of State for Home Affairs v O'Brien* [1923] AC 603, 610, 622; and *Wall v R (No 2)* (1927) 39 CLR 266, 291 per Isaacs J: 'it is a judgment *in rem* and conclusive on all the world'.
13 (1873) LR 5 PC 179, 202; *R v Governor of Brixton Prison, ex p Stallman* [1912] 3 KB 424.
14 Para 10.10.
15 *R v Hughes* (1865) LR 1 PC 81, 87–88; *A-G (at the relation of Allen) v Colchester Corpn* [1955] 2 QB 207, 215; paras 10.19–10.20.

WHETHER REFUSAL OF RELIEF FINAL

16.09 Devlin J said that an order refusing judicial review is not necessarily final[1]:

'Orders of certiorari and prohibition are concerned principally with public order, it being part of the duty of the High Court to see that inferior courts confine themselves to their own limited sphere. They also afford speedy and effective remedy to a person aggrieved by a clear excess of jurisdiction by an inferior tribunal. But they are not designed to raise issues of fact for the High Court to determine de novo. Accordingly it has never been the practice to put the party who asserts that the inferior court has jurisdiction to proof of the facts upon which he relies[2]... the court is not, as I conceive it, finally determining the validity of the tribunal's order as between the parties ... but is merely deciding whether there has been a plain excess of jurisdiction or not ... where the dispute turns on a question of fact, about which there is a conflict of evidence, the court will generally decline to interfere'.

When judicial review is refused because the claimant has not discharged the onus of proof the decision may be in the nature of a nonsuit , leaving the claimant free to raise a collateral challenge if this is possible. However unless the court makes this clear a finding in judicial review proceedings that an ultimate fact has not been established would create an issue estoppel that it does not exist[3]. Where judicial review is granted the court may quash the decision and remit the matter for redetermination according to law. Such decisions are final because they determine the scope of the power and whether it was lawfully exercised.

[1] *R v Fulham, Hammersmith and Kensington Rent Tribunal, ex p Zerek* [1951] 2 KB 1, 11; contra *R v Alley, ex p NSW Plumbers and Gasfitters Union* (1981) 153 CLR 376, 382, 390, 392–394, 395.
[2] This is contrary to the established principles governing the jurisdiction of inferior courts: paras 4.07, 4.09, and is not the law in Australia; para 16.09 n 1.
[3] Paras 8.03, 8.26.

PARTIES IN JUDICIAL REVIEW

16.10 The Crown is only a nominal party although its rights are put in suit by the claimant. The real parties are the claimant or prosecutor and the respondents, who can appeal[1] and are entitled or subject to orders for costs[2]. Since the rights and duties enforced in judicial review proceedings are derived from public law[3] the claimant may not be the only person with standing. Where relief is granted, the orders may operate for the benefit of a class, but where it is refused on the merits, others may seek judicial review relying on different arguments or evidence. Assuming no relevant delay it may be difficult as a matter of discretion to refuse leave. However if, like common informers[4], all persons with standing are identical in title and interest, later claimants would be bound by *res judicata* estoppels from the earlier proceedings.

[1] Halsbury's Laws (4th ed) paras 1569–1570; *R v Murray and Cormie, ex p Commonwealth* (1916) 22 CLR 437. The judgments contain a comprehensive review of the English case law and support the proposition that the applicant or prosecutor is a party and the Crown, although nominally on the record, is not.
[2] Halsbury (4th ed) paras 1571–1572.
[3] *O'Reilly v Mackman* [1983] 2 AC 237, 283–285.
[4] Para 9.13 n 1.

Chapter 17

AFFIRMATIVE ANSWERS

INTRODUCTION

17.01 A party may have an affirmative answer to a prima facie case of *res judicata* estoppel.

FRAUD

17.02 'Acts of the highest judicial authority', though 'not to be impeached from within are impeachable from without' for 'although it is not permitted to shew that the court was mistaken, it may be shewn that they were misled. Fraud is an extrinsic collateral act which vitiates the most solemn proceedings of courts of justice. Lord Coke says it avoids all judicial acts, ecclesiastical or temporal'[1]. Proceedings can be brought to rescind a judicial act for fraud or collusion[2], and these are defences to an action on the judgment, and an answer to any estoppel based on it. Lord Brougham said[3], 'you may at all times, … either as actor or defender, object to the validity' of the decision, 'provided that it was pronounced through fraud … of any description, or not in a real suit", and it "shall avail nothing for, or against, the parties affected by it'. Lord Langdale MR said[4], 'if a sentence, decree, or judgment … can be shewn to have been obtained by fraud or collusion, it is not to be used in any court as evidence against the right of the party who might be precluded by a sentence properly obtained'.

[1] *Duchess of Kingston's Case* (1776) 2 Smith LC 13th ed 644, 651; *Barrs v Jackson* (1845) 1 Ph 582, 586; *Lazarus Estates Ltd v Beasley* [1956] 1 QB 702 CA, 712 per Denning LJ: 'fraud unravels everything'; *Chee v Scotch Leasing Sdn Bhd* [2001] 4 MLJ 346 CA, 360.
[2] *Jonesco v Beard* [1930] AC 298.
[3] *Earl Bandon v Becher* (1835) 3 Cl & Fin 479, 510 (bill to redeem mortgage, plea decree for foreclosure, reply of fraudulent collusion good).
[4] *Perry v Meddowcroft* (1846) 10 Beav 122, 136–137.

17.03 The fraud which destroys a *prima facie* case of *res judicata* estoppel includes every variety of *mala fides* and *mala praxis* by a party[1] which deceives the tribunal[2], and certain forms of misconduct by the tribunal[3]. It defeats estoppels *in rem* and *in personam*[4]; and applies with one exception, to

243

all English[5], and without exception, to all foreign, decisions. There must be actual fraud[6], that is conscious and deliberate dishonesty, and the judgment must be obtained by it[7].

[1] Paras 17.12–17.13.
[2] This passage in the 2nd edn was cited in *DPP v Humphrys* [1977] AC 1, 21 by Viscount Dilhorne. In *Dsane v Hagan* [1962] Ch 193 an action to set aside a decree for specific performance in default of appearance, the executor of the defendant in the earlier suit alleged that the other party knew that the deceased was incapable of contracting, or obtained the contract by undue influence. Buckley J declined to summarily dismiss the suit for *res judicata*, and said, at 200–201: 'it would be ... unfortunate if the court could not under its inherent jurisdiction recall its own judgment and allow the merits of the case to be litigated, if ... the party who has obtained that judgment ought not fairly to be allowed to enforce it. ... I do not disregard the salutary maxim '*interest rei publicae ut sit finis litium*', but the court has never allowed that maxim to prevent [it] ... protecting itself from being deceived, and it seems to me to be at least arguable that if the contract was obtained by fraud or was to the knowledge of the purchasers unenforceable for lack of capacity ... the purchasers were guilty of deceiving the court.'
[3] Para 17.12.
[4] *Moody v Ashton* (2004) 248 DLR (4th) 690, 754, 766–767 (fraud barred debtor and his privies from relying on issue estoppels from dismissal of a bankruptcy petition in proceedings to set aside an alienation of his property in fraud of creditors).
[5] *DPP v Humphrys* [1977] AC 1, 21, 30, 46. (The exception is an acquittal on the merits of a criminal charge which, until recent legislation, could not be reopened for fraud); para 14.02.
[6] *Patch v Ward* (1867) LR 3 Ch App 203, 207.
[7] *The Amphtill Peerage Case* [1977] AC 547, 571, 591.

FRAUD IN RELATION TO ENGLISH JUDGMENTS

17.04 Proof that an English decision was procured by the fraud or collusion of the successful party is an answer to reliance on that judgment as an estoppel or otherwise for any purpose, including an action[1] or other proceeding such as an application for bankruptcy[2]. The principle applies to an ex parte judgment[3], and one entered by consent which can be set aside on any ground, including fraud, on which a court can set aside a contract[4]. An action for rescission of the judgment is the proper procedure because it enables the facts to be properly investigated[5], but other procedures are permissible, particularly if there is no objection[6]. The claimant must provide proper particulars and plead and prove that since the judgment he has discovered fresh facts which alone, or in combination with those previously known, establish that the judgment was obtained by fraud or collusion[7]. The action can be summarily dismissed if it does not disclose a proper case[8]. The claimant must plead and prove that the party seeking to benefit from the judgment[9] was responsible for the fraud. The perjury of a witness is not enough[10]. The fraud of a stranger is only relevant if the judgment was *ex parte*[11]. The action is not a rehearing and fraud is the only proper issue. The claimant is not entitled to a rehearing unless fraud is established[12].

[1] *Lloyd v Mansell* (1722) 2 P Wms 73 (foreclosure obtained by fraud); *Duchess of Kingston's Case* (1776) 2 Smith LC 13th ed 644 (collusive sentence for jactitation of marriage); *Earl Bandon v Becher* (1835) 3 Cl & Fin 479; *Harrison v Southampton Corpn* (1853) 4 De GM & G 137 (fraudulent and collusive nullity decree); *Doe d Davey v Haddon* (1783) 3 Doug KB 310 (dismissal of schoolmaster after hearing procured by fraud); *Pearse v Dobinson* (1865) 35 LJ Ch 110 (consent orders procured by fraud and

collusion); *Weaver v Law Society of New South Wales* (1979) 142 CLR 201 (dismissal of charges of professional misconduct procured by wilfully false evidence).

2   Paras 2.20, 2.27.

3   Para 17.03 n 2.

4   *Kinch v Walcott* [1929] AC 482; *Harvey v Phillips* (1956) 95 CLR 235, 243–244; *Spies v Commonwealth Bank of Australia* (1991) 24 NSWLR 691 CA *(Spies)*.

5   *Jonesco v Beard* [1930] AC 298; *Hip Fong Hong v H. Neotia & Co.* [1918] AC 888, 894, *(Hip Fong)*; *Kuwait Airways Corpn v Iraqi Airways Co (No 2)* [2001] 1 WLR 429 HL; *McDonald* (1965) 113 CLR 529; *Hurlstone v Steadman* [1937] NZLR 708 CA; *Sulco Ltd v E.S. Redit & Co Ltd* [1959] NZLR 45 CA; *Chee v Scotch Leasing Sdn Bhd* [2001] 4 MLJ 346 CA, 366–367; *Su v Wee* [2007] 3 SLR 673 CA.

6   *Ram Narayan* [1917] AC 100 (application to set aside ex parte order); para 5.03 n 7; *Hip Fong* [1918] AC 888 (application for new trial). An application for a new trial on the ground of fraud is an independent proceeding in which the moving party will fail unless the court, as a tribunal of fact, finds fraud proved: *Meek v Fleming* [1961] 2 QB 366 CA; *McDonald* (1965) 113 CLR 529, 535; *Nicholls v Carpenter* [1974] 1 NSWLR 369 CA, 374; *Su v Wee* [2007] 3 SLR 673 CA.

7   *Birch* [1902] P 130 CA; *DPP v Humphrys* [1977] AC 1, 30; *The Amphtill Peerage Case* [1977] AC 547, 591; *McIlkenny* [1980] QB 283 CA, 333; *McHarg v Woods Radio Pty Ltd* [1948] VLR 496, 498 *(McHarg)*; *Spies* (1991) 24 NSWLR 691 CA, 700–701; *Tassan Din v Banco Ambrosiano Spa* [1991] 1 IR 569, 582; *Lim v Lim* (1999) 180 DLR (4th) 87 BCCA.

8   *Birch* [1902] P 130; *McHarg* [1948] VLR 496, 498; *Spies* (1991) 24 NSWLR 691 CA.

9   This may be the defendant whose fraud reduced the judgment recovered by the claimant. An appeal in which the appellant alleged that the respondent's fraud had reduced his damages came before the New South Wales Court of Appeal when the author was a member of the bench. The question of restitution on rescission of the satisfied judgment was raised by the Court and the charge of fraud was dropped.

10   *Shedden v Patrick* (1854) 1 Macq 535 HL, 615, 643; *Birch* [1902] P 130 CA, 137–138; *Cinpress* [2008] Bus LR 1157 CA, 1183–1184; *Spies* (1991) 24 NSWLR 691 CA, 700.

11   *Ram Narayan* [1917] AC 100; para 5.03 n 7.

12   *Flower v Lloyd* (1877) 6 ChD 297 CA, 302.

FRESH FACTS SUFFICIENT WITHOUT PROOF OF DILIGENCE

17.05 Despite dicta from eminent judges, a party who challenges a judgment for fraud need not allege or prove that he used reasonable diligence before the trial to discover and obtain the evidence on which he now relies. Due diligence must be shown where a new trial is sought on the ground of fresh evidence[1],but not where fraud can be established. The dicta are from Parker LJ and Lord Bridge in *Owens Bank Ltd v Bracco* and Lord Templeman in *Owens Bank Ltd v Etoile Commerciale SA*[2]. The latter referred to *Boswell v Coaks (No 2)*[3], which does not support this requirement. Earl Selborne stated[4] 'a double proposition' in a case of this kind 'first, that something has been newly discovered … and … that something is material'. He did not mention any requirement for due diligence. The dicta are contrary to earlier authority[5] and contrary to principle. In *Toubia v Schwenke*[6] Handley JA said:

> 'The assumption is that the Court and the losing party were successfully imposed on by the fraud of the successful party, but relief shall nevertheless be denied and the judgment allowed to stand because the defrauded party was careless or lacked diligence in the preparation of his case. Such a result would be contrary to long established and fundamental principles. Contributory negligence is not a defence to an action for fraud … and a representee has no duty to make enquiries to ascertain the truth.'

¹ *Ladd v Marshall* [1954] 1 WLR 1489 CA, 1491; *Wollongong Corpn v Cowan* (1955) 93 CLR 435.
² *Owens Bank Ltd v Bracco* [1992] 2 AC 443, 459–460 per Parker LJ; 483–484 per Lord Bridge; *Owens Bank Ltd v Etoile Commerciale SA* [1995] 1 WLR 44 PC, 48.
³ (1894) 6 R 167, 86 LT 365 n.
⁴ Ibid at 174.
⁵ *Hip Fong* [1918] AC 888, 894; *Jonesco v Beard* [1930] AC 298, 301–302; *Birch* [1902] P 130 CA, 138; *McDonald* (1965) 113 CLR 529, 532–533, 535, 542.
⁶ *Toubia v Schwenke* (2002) 54 NSWLR 46 CA, 54–55; special leave refused by the High Court (2002) 209 CLR 694. This is also the law in Canada: *Canada v Grantile Inc* (2008) 302 DLR (4ᵗʰ) 40, 106–110.

17.06 There must be actual fraud. Irregularity or insistence on rights which proved to be overstated is not enough¹, nor is evidence which is merely misleading or erroneous². Where the allegation or evidence of fraud is inconclusive, vague, or gives rise to no more than suspicion, the challenge fails³. Grants of probate are implied decisions that fraud was not practised on the testator, but not that it was not practised on the court⁴.

¹ *Patch v Ward* (1867) LR 3 Ch App 203, 207; *Chee v Scotch Leasing Sdn Bhd* [2001] 4 MLJ 346 CA, 367.
² *Giffen v Leggatt* [1902] 2 NZLR 427; *Price v Stone* [1964] VR 106; *Chee* [2001] 4 MLJ 346 CA, 360.
³ *Burke v Crosbie* (1811) 1 Ball & B 489, 505 (faint suggestion of fraud, not substantiated); *Meddowcroft v Huguenin* (1844) 4 Moo PCC 386 (vague allegations bad on demurrer); *Perry v Meddowcroft* (1845) 10 Beav 122, 137 ('surmise and inference ... which do not ... necessarily lead to that conclusion'); *Natal Land and Colonization Co v Good and Barres* (1868) LR 2 PC 121, 133; *Birch* [1902] P 130 CA, 138 (vague allegations). This passage in the 2nd edn was cited with approval in *The Amphtill Peerage Case* [1977] AC at 591.
⁴ *Allen v M'Pherson* (1847) 1 HL Cas 191; *Melhuish v Milton* (1876) 3 Ch D 27 CA, 33 per James LJ: 'a will obtained by fraud is not the will of the testator. A probate which is not recalled is conclusive proof in all other courts that the will is his will ... no other court can listen to the allegation that the will was obtained by fraud'.

FRAUD IN RELATION TO ENGLISH AWARDS

17.07 An award of an English tribunal¹ can only be impeached for fraud or misconduct by a motion to set it aside². Fraud is not a defence to proceedings to enforce a domestic award³, which is *res judicata*, unless and until set aside⁴. The position in a statutory arbitration⁵, where the 1996 Act is excluded, depends on the statute.

¹ Para 2.05.
² *Holland v Brooks* (1795) 6 Term Rep 161; *Braddick v Thompson* (1807) 8 East 344; *Macarthur v Campbell* (1834) 2 Ad & El 52; *Whitmore v Smith* (1861) 7 H & N 509 Ex Ch; *Woollen v Bradford* (1864) 33 LJQB 129; *Thorburn v Barnes* (1867) LR 2 CP 384.
³ *Bache v Billingham* [1894] 1 QB 107 CA; *Oppenheim & Co v Haneef* [1922] 1 AC 482; *Birtley District Co-operative Society Ltd v Windy Nook Co-operative Society* [1959] 1 WLR 142.
⁴ An action for rescission is the proper procedure where a judgment is attacked: *Jonesco v Beard* [1930] AC 298.
⁵ Para 2.55.

FRAUD IN RELATION TO FOREIGN JUDICIAL DECISIONS

17.08 Fraud defeats a *prima facie* case of estoppel based on a foreign judgment¹; which cannot be set aside by an English court². Proof that a foreign judgment *in personam* was obtained by the fraud or collusion of the opponent, or by certain forms of judicial misconduct, defeats any estoppel, or action on the judgment[3]. A foreign judgment *in rem* can only be impeached for fraud by a party to the foreign proceedings[4]. A foreign judgment can be impeached without proof of newly-discovered facts even where fraud was raised as a defence[5], but not where the judgment was unsuccessfully impeached on this ground in the foreign court[6]. The court has inherent jurisdiction to prevent abuse of its process, and a defence of fraud to an action on a foreign judgment can be struck out if the issue of fraud was litigated, and there is no *prima facie* case[7]. The 1920 and 1933 Acts provide that a judgment shall not be or remain registered if it was obtained by fraud[8]. There is no such exception in the 1982 Act or Council Regulation 44/2001 unless recognition of such judgments is contrary to public policy. In *Interdesco SA v Nullifire Ltd*[9] Phillips J held that *Abouloff*[10] did not apply where the foreign judgment is enforced under the 1982 Act.

1 See para 2.36; *Abouloff v Oppenheimer & Co* (1883) 10 QBD 295 CA, 303 per Lord Coleridge CJ 'no action can be maintained on a judgment of a court, either in this country or in any other, which has been obtained by the fraud of the person seeking to enforce it'.
2 *Abouloff* (1883) 10 QBD 295 CA, 305 per Brett LJ; *Jet Holdings Inc v Patel* [1990] 1 QB 335 CA.
3 *Bowles v Orr* (1836) 1 Y & C Ex 464, 473; *Price v Dewhurst* (1837) 8 Sim 279, 305; affd (1838) 4 My & Cr 76, 84–85 (Danish court decided in their own favour); *Gossain* (1860) 8 WR 196 PC (decree embodying compromise induced by fraud); *Abouloff* (1882) 10 QBD 295 CA (defence to action on Russian judgment, alleging that it had been obtained by misrepresentation to, and concealment from, the tribunal); *Manger v Cash* (1889) 5 TLR 271 (the like); *Vadala v Lawes* (1890) 25 QBD 310, CA (Italian judgment procured by fraudulent concealment); *Bonaparte* [1892] P 402 (Scottish divorce obtained by fraud and collusion); *Codd v Delap* (1905) 92 LT 510 HL (allegation that Canadian judgment obtained by fraud entitled defendant to unconditional leave to defend); *Godard v Gray* (1870) LR 6 QB 139, 148–149; *Ellis v M'Henry* (1871) LR 6 CP 228, 239; *Messina v Petrocochino* (1872) LR 4 PC 144, 157; *Ochsenbein v Papelier* (1873) 8 Ch App 695, 698–700, 701; *Macalpine* [1958] P 35 (divorce obtained by fraud); *Middleton* [1967] P 62 (same). If the charge of fraud fails the estoppel stands: *Shedden v Patrick* (1854) 1 Macq 535 HL; *Cammell v Sewell* (1858) 3 H & N 617, 646; *Bater* [1906] P 209 CA, 218–219, 228–229. The onus of proof is heavy: *Blohn v Desser* [1962] 2 QB 116, 122 ('deep suspicion' not enough).
4 *Bater* [1906] P 209 CA 228, 239 (status of persons), following *Castrique v Behrens* (1861) 30 E & E 709 (status of things).
5 *Vadala v Lawes* (1890) 25 QBD 310 CA; *Owens Bank Ltd v Bracco* [1992] 2 AC 443; contra: *Jacobs v Beaver* (1908) 17 OLR 496 CA; *Keele v Findley* (1990) 21 NSWLR 444 not cited in *Owens Bank Ltd v Bracco*.
6 *Spring Gardens* [1991] 1 QB 241 CA, 251.
7 *Owens Bank Ltd v Etoile Commerciale SA* [1995] 1 WLR 44 PC, 50 per Lord Templeman: 'their Lordships do not regard ... *Abouloff's* case [n 1] with enthusiasm'.
8 1920 Act s 9(2)(d); 1933 Act s 4.
9 [1992] 1 Lloyds Rep 180; *Westacre* [2000] QB 288 CA, 307, 316, 317.
10 Para 17.08 n 1.

FRAUD IN RELATION TO FOREIGN AWARDS

17.09 Fraud has the same effect on a foreign award, and the *res judicata* estoppels it created, as it has for a domestic award but an English court cannot set aside a foreign award. There must be new evidence to establish the fraud that was not before the tribunal and the new evidence, if unanswered, must be strong enough to produce the opposite result[1].

[1] *Westacre* [2000] QB 288 CA, 309, 316, 317.

COLLUSION

17.10 Collusion is play-acting by litigants for a common purpose involving the pretence of a contest[1]. The 'play' is generally 'foul play', but need not be[2]. There is a distinction between fraud and collusion[3] although their effect is the same[4].

[1] The argument of Wedderburn SG in the *Duchess of Kingston's Case* (1776) 20 State Tr 355, 478–479 included the following passage cited in *Earl Bandon v Becher* (1845) 3 Cl & Fin 479, 510–511; *Shedden v Patrick* (1854) 1 Macq 535 HL, 608, and *Boswell v Coaks (No 2)* (1894) 6 R 167 HL, 168–169: 'in order to make a sentence, there must be a real interest, a real argument ... a real defence, a real decision. Of all these requisites, not one takes place in case of a fraudulent and collusive suit: there is no judge; but a person, invested with the ensigns of a judicial office, is misemployed in listening to a fictitious cause proposed to him: there is no party litigating ... no real interest brought into question: and, to use the words of a very sensible civilian on this point, *fabula non judicium, hoc est; in scena, non in foro, res agitur*'.
[2] *Bater* [1906] P 209 CA, 227: '... there was no collusion in the sense of the two parties having conspired together to deceive ... the Court'.
[3] *Boswell v Coaks (No 2)* (1894) 6 R 167 HL, 168–169.
[4] Collusion was a good answer in *Brownsword v Edwards* (1750) 2 Ves Sen 243, 245 ('collusion affects everything'); *Earl Bandon v Becher* (1835) 3 Cl & Fin 479, 510; *Re Onslow* (1875) 10 Ch App 373 (collusive judgment by insolvent); *Re Onslow's Trusts* (1875) LR 20 Eq 677 (the like); *Re Blythe* (1881) 17 Ch D 480 CA (the like); *Girdlestone* (1879) 4 Ex D 107 CA; *Re Leavesley* (1891) 64 LT 269.

CONCEALMENT OF MATERIAL FACTS FROM THE TRIBUNAL

17.11 Fraud cannot be established by proof of silence unless the party had a duty to the tribunal to reveal the undisclosed facts. In the absence of such a duty no litigant is bound to divulge evidence against himself[1]. It must be shown that the undisclosed fact existed, was known to the party, but not to the tribunal or his opponent, and was material[2]. It may be the duty of a party seeking judgment to draw the attention of the court to facts within his knowledge which may be fatal to his claim. A claimant who knows or suspects that the defendant lacked capacity to contract, or was the victim of undue influence is guilty of deceiving the court if he obtains an ex parte decree for specific performance without proper disclosure[3].

[1] *Bater* [1906] P 209 CA, 218–219, 228–229.
[2] *Shedden v Patrick* (1854) 1 Macq 535 HL, 622.
[3] *Dsane v Hagan* [1962] Ch 193; para 17.03 n 2.

UPON WHOM, AND BY WHOM, THE FRAUD MUST BE SHOWN TO HAVE BEEN PRACTISED

17.12 The fraud must have misled the tribunal either directly or by misleading the other party. If the tribunal was misled it is immaterial that the opponent was not[1]. Thus the evidence to support a defence of fraud to an action on a foreign judgment can be the same as that led in the foreign proceedings[2]. The fraud may be a breach of the rule that no one shall be judge in their own cause[3]. However the allegation and proof must be specific; a suggestion of inveterate and notorious corruption in all the courts of a foreign state is not sufficient[4].

[1] *Middleton* [1967] P 62.
[2] *Abouloff* (1883) 10 QBD 295 CA; *Vadala v Lawes* (1890) 25 QBD 310 CA.
[3] *Price v Dewhurst* (1837) 8 Sim 279; affd (1838) 4 My & Cr 76; para 17.08 n 3; *Cammell v Sewell* (1858) 3 H & N 617, 646.
[4] *Abouloff* (1883) 10 QBD 295 CA (the original author recorded that an allegation to this effect was struck out).

17.13 Since an English judgment *in rem* binds 'the world', anyone, whether a party or not[1], can bring an action for its rescission[2], even if personally implicated in the fraud, and the person implicated need not have been a party[3]. However a foreign judgment *in rem* can only be impeached by a party to the proceedings[4].

[1] *Birch* [1902] P 130 CA, 137–138 (action to set aside English probate).
[2] *Duchess of Kingston's Case* (1776) 2 Smith LC 644, 652 (Crown could 'avoid the effect of a decision *in rem* by proving that it was obtained by fraud or collusion').
[3] *Re Lennox* (1885) 16 QBD 315 CA (debtor fraudulently consented to judgment but proved the fraud); *Bonaparte* [1892] P 402, 410–411 (party proved fraud and collusion).
[4] *Bater* [1906] P 209 CA, 228, 239.

MISTAKE

17.14 The court can set aside a default judgment for mistake on the application of the claimant[1]. A consent order may also be set aside for mistake in substantive proceedings if a contract could be set aside in the same circumstances[2]. Where the consent order does not embody a compromise[3] the court's power is not so confined[4].

[1] Para 22.05 nn 7–9.
[2] *Huddersfield Banking Co Ltd v Harvey Lister & Son Ltd* [1895] 2 Ch 273 CA, 280; *Kinch v Walcott* [1929] AC 482; *Harvey v Phillips* (1956) 95 CLR 235, 243–244.
[3] *National Benzole Co Ltd v Gooch* [1961] 1 WLR 1489 CA.
[4] *Bullivant v ENZA Ltd* [2001] 1 NZLR 498.

CROSS-ESTOPPEL

17.15 An earlier *res judicata* estoppel prevails over a later, and there is no cross-estoppel. If the decisions relate to the same subject matter, the earlier prevails[1], if not there is no conflict[2].

[1] *Showlag v Mansour* [1995] 1 AC 431. In *Vervaeke v Smith* [1983] 1 AC 145 recognition was denied for a Belgian nullity decree, an English court having earlier held the English marriage valid.
[2] *Poulton* [1908] 2 Ch 430 CA (order *in rem* for revocation of patent did not negate estoppel from decision that patent valid and infringed); para 10.19.

17.16 An estoppel by representation can create a genuine cross-estoppel. A having established a *res judicata* estoppel against B, B confesses and avoids by proving that A has precluded himself from relying on it. B does not deny that he is estopped, but insists that A is estopped from saying so[1], and so in Coke's phrase, he sets the matter at large. 'The result is … that … the general rule of public policy enshrined in the principle of *res judicata* is subject to a particular exception which enables practical justice to be done in rare cases'[2]. A cross-estoppel may arise from failure to plead the *res judicata*[3], or in other ways. In *The Indian Endurance*[4] the defendant was held estopped by convention or representation from relying on a former recovery in India as an answer to a cargo claim in England, but the cross estoppel was rejected on appeal[5].

[1] This passage in the 2nd edn was cited in *The Indian Grace* [1993] AC 410, 422 and *Showlag v Mansour* [1995] 1 AC 431, 441.
[2] *The Indian Grace* [1993] AC 410, 424 per Lord Goff.
[3] Ibid at 423. In *Magrath v Hardy* (1838) 4 Bing NC 782, 797–798, the defendant by not pleading *res judicata*, 'waived any benefit he might have derived from the estoppel'; *Litchfield v Ready* (1850) 5 Exch 939, 945: 'a judgment … is conclusive evidence of the plaintiff's title, unless he waives his right of replying it by way of estoppel'; and *Langdon v Richards* (1917) 33 TLR 325 where the Crown, by not raising any objection was held to have 'waived' its right to rely on the estoppel.
[4] [1994] 2 Lloyd's Rep 331 QBD.
[5] *The Indian Endurance* [1998] AC 878 CA, affirmed [1998] AC 878 HL.

CONTRACT[1]

17.17 Parties can contract out of the burden and benefit of a *res judicata* estoppel[2].

[1] In *The Indian Grace* [1993] AC 410, 422 Lord Goff said of this para in the 2nd edn: 'There is much to be said for the opinion so expressed'.
[2] *Lothian v Henderson* (1803) 3 Bos & P 499 HL, 546–548, (contract that rights of neutral insured not concluded by foreign prize decision); para 10.31. A party can contract out of the right to challenge an award for the fraud or misconduct of the arbitrator: *Tullis v Jacson* [1892] 3 Ch 441; cf Spencer Bower, Turner and Handley 'Actionable Misrepresentation' 4th edn para 375; 'Exclusion Clauses for Fraud' Handley (2003) 119 LQR 537.

CONSENT

17.18 In patent actions and the like where the scope of any inquiry or account is normally determined at the trial, it has been common for the parties to consent to some issues of infringement being reserved to any inquiry. Such consent, at least when acted on, is an affirmative answer to a *prima facie* case of *res judicata*[1].

[1] Para 5.27 n 7.

INFANTS AND INCAPABLE PERSONS

17.19 These are considered paras 9.29–9.31.

PUBLIC POLICY

17.20 The public policy in favour of the finality of judicial decisions reflected in the *res judicita* doctrine may be trumped by the public policy against the enforcement of illegal contracts. Neill LJ said of such a case[1].

> '... a Court would entertain an argument that despite a declaration as to the validity of a contract the Court should go behind the declaration because the contract related, for example, to the import of drugs ... reliance could be placed on principles of public policy which are of the greatest importance and which are almost certainly recognised in most jurisdictions throughout the world.'

1 *ED & F Man (Sugar) Ltd v Haryanto* [1991] 1 Lloyds Rep 429 CA, 436.

17.21 This exception did not apply where breach of foreign import controls was not raised in the original proceedings[1] and where an allegation of bribery had been rejected[2]. Illegality and public policy will prevent a *res judicata* estoppel legalising in the future what a statute prohibits. A public corporation which cannot estop itself by representation or contract from performing a public duty[3] may be bound by a *res judicata* estoppel[4]. A distinction must be drawn between cases where the question of public policy was litigated or compromised and those where the question was not raised. A judgment founded on an *ultra vires* contract only creates a *res judicata* on that issue if it was decided or compromised[5]. Where the Rent Acts or equivalent apply a *res judicata* estoppel cannot require the court to give a judgment it has no jurisdiction to give[6]. As Lord Thankerton said[7]:

> ' ... it is idle to suggest that either estoppel or res judicata can give the court a jurisdiction under the Rent Restriction Acts which the statute says it is not to have'.

1 *ED & F Man (Sugar) Ltd v Haryanto* [1991] 1 Lloyds Rep 429 CA.
2 *Westcare* [2000] QB 288 CA, 316, 317.
3 *Maritime Electric Co Ltd v General Dairies Ltd* [1937] AC 610; *Southend-on-Sea Corpn v Hodson (Wickford) Ltd* [1962] 1 QB 416.
4 *Thrasyvoulou* [1990] 2 AC 273, 289.
5 *Re Jon Beauforte (London) Ltd* [1953] Ch 131; *Great North-West Central Rly Co v Charlebois* [1899] AC 114. The ultra vires doctrine has effectively been abolished: Companies Act 1985 ss 35, 35A; Building Societies Act 1986 s 5(8), Sch 2 Pt 11 cl 16(1); Local Government (Contracts) Act 1996.
6 *Griffiths v Davies* [1943] KB 618 CA; *Langford Property Co Ltd v Goldrich* [1949] 1 KB 511 CA; cf *Newport CC v Charles* (2009) 1 WLR 1884 CA (no estoppel by representation against Housing Act 1985).
7 *J & F Stone Lighting and Radio Ltd v Levitt* [1947] AC 209, 216; *Secretary of State for Employment v Globe Electric Thread Co Ltd* [1980] AC 506, 519. Consent cannot confer jurisdiction: *Essex County Council v Essex Incorporated Congregational Church Union* [1963] AC 808, 820–821, 828; *Watt* [2008] 1 AC 696, 707; *Naidoo v Sastri* (1887) LR 14 Ind App 160, 166–167.

17.22 In *Kok Hoong*[1] the Privy Council held that moneylending and bills of sale legislation supported an affirmative answer of illegality and public policy to *res judicata* estoppels based on a default judgment[2]. Viscount Radcliffe said[3]:

> 'It has been said that the question whether an estoppel is to be allowed or not depends on whether the enactment or rule of law relied on is imposed in the

public interest or "on grounds of general public policy" ... In their Lordships' opinion a more direct test to apply in any case such as the present, where the laws of moneylending or monetary security are involved, is to ask whether the law that confronts the estoppel can be seen to represent a social policy to which the court must give effect in the interests of the public generally or some section of the public, despite any rules of evidence as between themselves that the parties may have created by their conduct or otherwise. Thus the laws of gaming or usury ... overrule an estoppel: so do the provisions of the Rent Restriction Acts with regard to orders for possession of controlled tenancies ... These principles, as their Lordships understand them, would point very directly to the conclusion that there can be no estoppel in face of the Moneylenders Ordinance, since the provisions on which the respondent seeks to rely render him a "protected person" for this purpose, nor any estoppel in the face of the Bills of Sale Ordinance, the provisions of which ... are at least intended for the protection of other creditors who may have dealings with the borrower'.

Moneylending and similar legislation do not override a *res judicata* estoppel based on a contested decision. A judge reopened all moneylending transactions between the parties, including one merged in a judgment, and directed an inquiry. He later held that a transaction could not be reopened after judgment and varied the Master's Certificate[4]. The Court of Appeal[5] held that he was bound by his original order, right or wrong, and entered judgment on the certificate.

[1]   [1964] AC 993.
[2]   Andrews 'Estoppels against Statutes' (1966) 29 MLR 1, 8–15.
[3]   [1964] AC 993, 1016.
[4]   *Cohen v Jonesco* [1926] 1 KB 119 (the doctrine of merger does not operate by estoppel and the bar is absolute: para 19.01 nn 4–5). The Consumer Credit Act 1974 s 139(4) provides that an order reopening a credit bargain 'shall not alter the effect of any judgment.' Mummery LJ said this reflects the 1926 decision: *Rahman v Sterling Credit Ltd* [2001] 1 WLR 496 CA, 503.
[5]   [1926] 2 KB 1 CA.

17.23   Viscount Radcliffe also considered common law rules of public policy, and distinguished cases such as *Humphries*[1], where a *res judicata* estoppel trumped the Statute of Frauds[2]:

'It does not appear to their Lordships that the principle invoked is confined to transactions that have been made the subject of legislation or that, where legislation is in question, the bare prescription that a transaction is to be void or unenforceable is sufficient by itself to justify the principle's application. Thus, on the one hand, the common law may itself prohibit the enforcement of certain contracts, such as those of an infant not for necessaries, and it cannot be supposed that it would any the less refuse to base a judgment on an estoppel against an infant who had so contracted. An infant who has obtained goods from a tradesman by representing himself to be of full age cannot be estopped from setting up his infancy ... . On the other hand, there are statutes which, though declaring transactions to be unenforceable or void, are nevertheless not essentially prohibitory and so do not preclude estoppels'.

[1]   [1910] 2 KB 531 CA; para 8.12; *Bradshaw v M'Mullan* [1920] 2 IR 412 HL, 425–426.
[2]   [1964] AC 993, 1015.

17.24   The inquisitorial duty of the Divorce Court excludes issue estoppels which would inhibit its exercise[1], and there are no *res judicata* estoppels in care proceedings[2]. The court may refuse to recognise an issue estoppel based on a foreign judgment which gives effect to a radically different public policy. A Belgian nullity decree was not recognised where the marriage had taken place in England[3]. The court cannot disable itself from determining a complaint of professional misconduct against one of its officers[4].

[1] Para 15.06.
[2] *Re B* [1997] Fam 117.
[3] *Vervaeke v Smith* [1983] 1 AC 145; para 15.03 nn 18–20. The recognition of EU matrimonial judgments is now governed by Council Regulation 2201/2003, para 15.03.
[4] *Weaver v Law Society of New South Wales* (1979) 142 CLR 201, 207.

RETROSPECTIVE LEGISLATION

17.25 There is a presumption that Parliament does not intend to affect vested rights[1], but it may change the law as at a past date and courts give effect to Parliament's intention if it is sufficiently clear. There is also a presumption that retrospective legislation is not intended to affect pending proceedings[2], and a strong presumption that it is not intended to affect completed proceedings which are *res judicata*. In such a case[3]:

> ' ... the ordinary principle that a man is not to be vexed twice for the same alleged cause of action applies, unless it be excluded by the legislature in explicit and unmistakable terms ... It would require language much more explicit than that which is to be found in the ordinance ... to justify a court of law in holding that a legislative body intended not merely to alter the law, but to alter it so as to deprive a litigant of a judgment rightly given and still subsisting'.

[1] *Yew Bon Tew v Kenderaan Bas Mara* [1983] 1 AC 553.
[2] *Zainal bin Hashim v Government of Malaysia* [1980] AC 734; *Bawn Pty Ltd v Metropolitan Meat Industry Board* (1970) 72 SRNSW 466 CA.
[3] *Lemm v Mitchell* [1912] AC 400, 405–406; *Day v Kelland* [1900] 2 Ch 745 CA; *Grainger v Order of Canadian Home Circles* (1918) 44 OLR 53; *Federated Engine Drivers and Firearms Association of A/Asia v Broken Hill Pty Co Ltd* (1913) 16 CLR 245; *Re a Debtor, ex p Debtor (No 490 of 1935)* [1936] Ch 237 CA, 243; *Jenkins v Tileman (Overseas) Ltd* [1967] NZLR 484; *Keating v Calas* [1974] VR 381, 384; *Hornby Island Trust Committee v Stormwell* (1988) 53 DLR (4th) 435, 441–444 BCCA.

UNCONSTITUTIONAL STATUTES

17.26 A statute beyond the powers of the legislature is void, and cannot confer rights or impose duties. A judgment declaring a statute unconstitutional determines that decisions which enforced it were wrongly decided[1], but does not affect the *res judicata* estoppels they created[2], but the issue estoppels may be within the special circumstances exception. The invalidity of a statute which purported to confer jurisdiction on a court it otherwise did not possess makes prior decisions invalid for want of jurisdiction and nullifies any *res judicata* estoppel[3]. However a decision by the Constitutional Court that the jurisdiction was validly conferred on the relevant court will not be nullified by a later decision of that court that the jurisdiction was not validly conferred[4] because the Constitutional Court has jurisdiction to decide such questions.

The question is whether the court which ruled on the jurisdiction of the other court or tribunal was a court of competent jurisdiction for that purpose[5].

[1]   It does not matter whether the point was conceded or rejected in error: paras 8.11–8.12.
[2]   *Turigan v Alberta* (1988) 53 DLR (4th) 321 (Alta CA). The author prefers the majority decision despite the criticism of *Tur* [2001] 1 Com LJ 123. It is supported by *Poulton* [1908] 2 Ch 430 CA (order for revocation of patent did not override estoppel from earlier decision that patent valid and infringed); para 17.15. The overruling of a decision, although retrospective, does not affect cases in which that decision was applied: *Iarnród Éireann v Ireland* [1996] 3 IR 321, 363.
[3]   Jurisdiction is a fundamental requirement for all *res judicata* estoppels: chapter 4.
[4]   *Re Wakim* (1999) 198 CLR 511 (the actual case was *Re Brown ex parte Amann*) at 564–565, 588–593 esp 591; para 17.21 nn 6–7.
[5]   *Watt* [2008] 1 AC 696, 707.

DENIAL OF NATURAL JUSTICE

17.27 Spencer Bower thought that denial of natural justice was not an answer to an estoppel based on a foreign decision. The courts have taken a different view and held that the defendant must have received actual notice of the foreign proceedings, and been given a reasonable opportunity of presenting his case. The proceedings must not otherwise offend English views of substantial justice[1].

[1]   Para 4.32. The recognition of EU civil and commercial judgments is governed by Council Regulation 44/2001; paras 2.60, 4.34.

SPECIAL CIRCUMSTANCES

17.28 This is considered in paras 8.31–8.35.

ONE OR MORE PARTIES NOT BOUND

17.29 A *res judicata* estoppel is not enforceable where one defendant is bound, and another against whom the same relief is sought, is not. The matter is then at large. The court would be in an invidious position if it had to give conflicting judgments in the same case, one on the merits, and one on the estoppel[1]. A party cannot rely in the same proceedings on an estoppel by representation for one purpose and on the truth for another[2]. In an Australian case[3] an applicant obtained an order, over objection, requiring an administrative decision-maker to give written reasons[4]. These were provided and the applicant sought judicial review. The objection was renewed but rejected as *res judicata*. An additional applicant and respondent were then joined[5]. On appeal the decision maker's argument that the additional parties displaced the estoppel failed[6]. The first decision created a fact which the new parties could not ignore[7].

[1]   *Re Savoy Estates Ltd* [1949] Ch 622 CA, 634, 636; *Shaw v Sloan* [1982] NI 393 CA, 395, 398 (joint tortfeasors sued for contribution, but only one had benefit of estoppel, matter at large); contra *Edwards v Joyce* [1954] VLR 216.

² *Scarf v Jardine* (1882) 7 App Cas 345, 350 per Lord Selborne LC: 'You cannot at once rely upon estoppel and set up the facts'; *Heskell v Continental Express Ltd* [1950] 1 All ER 1033, 1044. A party held liable on the basis of an estoppel in one proceeding may rely on the truth against a different party in another: Cleary v Jeans (2006) 65 NSWLR 355 CA, 359.

³ *Taylor v Ansett Transport Industries Ltd* (1987) 18 FCR 342.

⁴ Under the Administrative Decisions (Judicial Review) Act 1977 (C'wlth) s 13(4A).

⁵ (1987) 18 FCR 342, 358.

⁶ Ibid at 356–357, 358, 365.

⁷ Cf *Mulkerrins* [2003] 1 WLR 1937 HL, 1941, 1942; paras 9.32–9.34.

CHANGING SITUATION

17.30 There can be no effective *res judicata* in a changing situation. A decision on greater hardship under the Rent Acts is not *res judicata* because the facts may alter[1]. A decision that a person was not a gipsy did not bar that allegation at a later date[2] because 'being a gipsy is not an unalterable status but depends on the way of life which a person is leading at any particular time'. A decision that a liquidator had not carried on a trade in one year was not *res judicata* in the next because 'The facts in the latter year may have been … different'[3]. Breach of planning control on one date does not establish a breach at any other[4]. In *Thrasyvoulou*[5] Lord Bridge said:

> '… a decision to withhold planning permission resolves no issue of legal right … It is no more than a decision that in existing circumstances and in the light of existing planning policies the development … is not one which it would be appropriate to permit … such a decision cannot give rise to an estoppel *per rem judicatam.*'

A refusal to find desertion[6] or cruelty[7] will not bar such a finding at a later date. Evidence relied on unsuccessfully before can be called again because the question[8] "can only be judged in the light of the whole course of conduct" and the earlier decision 'does not shut out that evidence forever'. The principle was applied in the High Court of Australia where Evatt J referred to the fallacy[9]:

> ' … that, where an issue between A and B relates to a state of things which is capable of subsequent alteration, the conclusive determination in A's favour of that state of things as at one date plus conclusive proof that up to a later date there had been no alteration of such state of things establishes in A's favour as against B an estoppel as to the state of things existing at the later day'.

Lord Maugham LC made the same point in *New Brunswick*[10]:

> ' … the doctrine cannot be made to extend to presumptions or probabilities as to issues in a second action which may be, and yet cannot be asserted beyond all possible doubt to be, identical with those raised in the previous action'.

The Employment Appeals Tribunal has held that potential for change is not enough, and dismissal of a claim to equal pay created an issue estoppel against a later claim where the facts had not changed[11]. Such cases are better dealt with for abuse of process. A decision in favour of a defendant does not prevent the claimant commencing fresh proceedings 'founded on any new or altered state of circumstances'[12].

1   *Burman v Woods* [1948] 1 KB 111 CA; *Macdonald v Fyson* [1948] NZLR 669; *DCT v Swain* (1988) 20 FCR 507.

2   *Mills v Cooper* [1967] 2 QB 459, 470 per Diplock LJ; *Carl-Zeiss (No 2)* [1967] 1 AC 853, 913 (authority of Council of Gera at one date different question from authority at another).

3   *Edwards v Old Bushmills Distillery Co Ltd* (1926) 10 TC 285 HL, 299.

4   Para 16.06.

5   [1990] 2 AC 273, 290.

6   *Froud* (1920) 123 LT 176.

7   *Richards* [1953] P 36.

8   Ibid at 40: 'The conduct … alleged to amount to persistent cruelty can only be judged in the light of the whole course of conduct and the mere fact that at an earlier stage, when the conduct was only partly completed, a court has adjudged that at that point it does not amount to persistent cruelty does not shut that evidence out forever.'

9   *O'Donel* (1938) 59 CLR 744, 763; para 16.06.

10   [1939] AC 1, 20.

11   *McLoughlin v Gordon (Stockport) Ltd* [1978] ICR 561. The decision is contrary to principle because the facts had to be found at both dates to determine whether there was an issue estoppel; para 17.30 n 3.

12   *Liverpool Corpn v Chorley Waterworks Co* (1852) 2 De GM & G 852, 866; para 8.17; *Moss v Anglo Egyptian Navigation Co* (1865) LR 1 Ch App 108, 114–116 (finding that breach of contract not established no bar to allegation of later breach).

CONSTITUTIONAL QUESTIONS

17.31 A special public policy exception exists for decisions on the construction of a written constitution. The Supreme Court of Canada[1] and the High Court of Australia[2] treat them as precedents only. A Federal Constitution must operate consistently at any one time. Any other result would be unworkable for reasons similar to those given by Lord Selborne LC for deciding that issue estoppels should not be recognised in the construction of statutes authorising local taxation[3]:

> 'There would therefore be, within the same district, two laws operating simultaneously in opposite directions as against different persons in exactly the same circumstances, under the same words of taxation in the same public Act of Parliament; and either imposing on some … a liability which the statute had not in fact imposed … or exonerating others … from the share of a common burden which the statute had imposed equally on all.'

1   *Emms v R* (1979) 102 DLR (3d) 193, 201.

2   *Victoria v Commonwealth* (1957) 99 CLR 575, 654; *Queensland v Commonwealth* (1977) 139 CLR 585, 597, 614–615; *Re Wakim* (1999) 198 CLR 511, 564–565, 633; and the exception for special circumstances paras 8.31–8.35.

3   *R v Hutchings* (1881) 6 QBD 300 CA, 305–306.

SPURIOUS ANSWERS: ERROR IN AN ENGLISH COURT

17.32 It is no answer that the prior judgment was wrong; a competent tribunal has jurisdiction to give a wrong decision and if a mistake is made the judgment is conclusive unless and until corrected on appeal[1].

1   Para 1.14. The point was made in *Meyers v Casey* (1913) 17 CLR 90, 115 by Isaacs J who referred to 'the well known rule that a competent court or other tribunal has jurisdiction to give a wrong judgment, and if there is no appeal in the strict sense then its decision, right or wrong, must stand, and cannot be questioned in any subsequent proceedings elsewhere',

citing *Malkarjun* (1900) LR 27 Ind App 216, 235 where Lord Hobhouse said 'the court was exercising its jurisdiction. It made a sad mistake, it is true; but a court has jurisdiction to decide wrong as well as right. If it decides wrong, the wronged party can only take the course prescribed by law for setting matters right; and if that course is not taken the decision, however wrong, cannot be disturbed'. Similarly in *R v Nat Bell Liquors Ltd* [1922] 2 AC 128, 151–152 Lord Sumner said: ' ... his subsequent error however grave, is a wrong exercise of a jurisdiction which he has and not a usurpation of a jurisdiction which he has not'. As Lord Millett said in *Mulkerrins* [2003] 1 WLR 1937 HL, 1941: 'The doctrine [of issue estoppel] comes into its own only when the decision is wrong; if it is right it merely serves to save time and costs'; *Watt* [2008] 1 AC 696, 708 per Lord Hoffmann; para 8.34 n 2.

SPURIOUS ANSWERS: ERROR IN A FOREIGN COURT

17.33 Estoppels founded on a foreign decision are not defeated by proof that the tribunal misapplied its own law[1], or the law of England[2]. Where the foreign tribunal should have applied English law, but deliberately ignored it for the supposed benefit of the foreign litigant, this defiance of international comity was held to justify the refusal of recognition[3]. In *Carl-Zeiss (No 2)* the House took a guarded view of this decision[4], Lord Reid saying[5]:

'If *Simpson v Fogo* can stand at all it must be limited to cases where the law of the foreign country applied in the foreign judgment is at variance with generally accepted doctrines of private international law'.

[1] *Scott v Pilkington* (1862) 2 B & S 11, 41–42; *Vanquelin v Bouard* (1863) 15 CBNS 341, 368–369, 374; *Messina v Petrocochino* (1872) LR 4 PC 144, 159.

[2] *Dent v Smith* (1869) LR 4 QB 414, 450–451, 454–455; *Castrique v Imrie* (1870) LR 4 HL 414, 432–437, 445–446, 447–448; *Godard v Gray* (1870) LR 6 QB 139; *Re Trufort* (1887) 36 Ch D 600.

[3] *Simpson v Fogo* (1863) 1 Hem & M 195; *Godard v Gray* (1870) LR 6 QB 139, 148–149.

[4] [1967] 1 AC 853, 917–918, 922, 928, 978.

[5] Ibid at 922.

Chapter 18

PLEADING AND PROCEDURE

THE CIVIL PROCEDURE RULES

18.01 Civil procedure in the High Court and County Court is governed by the CPR but in many Commonwealth jurisdictions it continues to be governed by rules derived from the Rules of the Supreme Court 1965 (RSC). Pt 1.1(1) of the CPR states that they have the overriding objective of enabling the court to deal with cases justly. This includes, as far as practicable, ensuring that the parties are on an equal footing, and the case is dealt with 'fairly'[1]. The court is to do this by active case management[2] and identifying the issues at an early stage[3].

[1]   CPR Pt 1.1(2)(a), (d).
[2]   CPR Pt 1.4(1).
[3]   CPR Pt 1.4(2)(b).

PLEADING GENERALLY

18.02 A claimant must file and serve particulars of claim[1] containing a concise statement of the facts on which he relies[2]. If he intends to rely on an estoppel he should plead the facts in accordance with the estoppel but not those which create it, unless he knows that the issue is bound to arise. A defendant who denies an allegation must state his reasons and put forward his version[3]. If he wishes to assert that the claimant is estopped from alleging any of the facts in the particulars of claim he will have to raise that issue and plead the additional facts. The CPR do not, in terms, require a defendant to specially plead a *res judicata* estoppel. Before considering whether the general pleading rules in the CPR require this it will be convenient to consider the position under former procedures. Many of the general principles of pre-Judicature Act pleading remain relevant.

[1]   CPR Pt 7.4.
[2]   CPR Pt 16.4(a).
[3]   CPR Pt 16.5(2)(a), (b).

PLEADING RES JUDICATA UNDER FORMER PROCEDURES

18.03 In the *Duchess of Kingston's Case* the judges advised the House of Lords that estoppel *per rem judicatam* 'is as a plea a bar, or as evidence conclusive'[1]. Before the Judicature Acts a *res judicata* estoppel had to be pleaded, if this was possible, at the earliest opportunity and a party who did not, waived his right to insist on the estoppel[2]. In *The Indian Grace* Lord Goff said[3]:

> '... I think it desirable ... to return to the background ... with the purpose of considering ... how far the principles of waiver or estoppel apply to the common law principle of *res judicata* ... I strongly suspect that, in practice, the point seldom arises, except where ... the principle of estoppel *per rem judicatam* is not invoked and the party who might have taken it but does not do so thereby waives his right to rely upon it.'

He referred, with reservations, to two pre-Judicature Act cases. In *Magrath v Hardy*[4] Tindal CJ said:

> '... the defendant by taking issue on the replication has waived any benefit he might have derived from the estoppel, and has left the matter at large to be decided according to the truth and justice of the case.'

In *Litchfield v Ready*[5] Parke B said:

> '... a judgment ... is conclusive evidence of the plaintiff's title, unless he waives his right of replying it by way of estoppel, when he has an opportunity of placing it on the record, but fails to do so.'

[1] *Duchess of Kingston's Case* (1776) 2 Smith LC 13th ed 644, 645.
[2] Paras 17.15,–17.16.
[3] [1993] AC 410, 421–423.
[4] (1838) 4 Bing NC 782, 798; *Matthew v Osborne* (1853) 13 CB 919, 942–943.
[5] (1850) 5 Exch 939, 945.

18.04 The RSC provided that all matters must be pleaded which made any claim or defence of the opposite party not maintainable, which if not specifically pleaded might take the opposite party by surprise, or which raised issues of fact not arising out of the preceding pleading[1]. Estoppel is one such matter and pleading it was important[2]. One could also plead a pending action, and the judgment could be given in evidence at the trial[3]. If there is no opportunity for pleading the estoppel, eg when it is relevant only to damages, the objection had to be raised as soon as possible.

[1] RSC O 18 r 8.
[2] *Edevain v Cohen* (1889) 43 Ch D 187 CA,189; *New Civilbuild Pty Ltd v Guobena Sdn Bhd* [2000] 2 SLR 378, 400.
[3] *Re Defries* (1883) 48 LT 703, 704; *Spring Gardens* [1991] 1 QB 241 CA, 254.

18.05 As long as the preceding pleading did not contradict the *res judicata* there was no need for a plea of estoppel. Where in an action relating to land the defendant pleaded 'not guilty'[1], or that he 'is in possession by himself or his tenants', there was nothing on the record which attacked the claimant's title as declared by a *res judicata*. But it was otherwise where the defendant pleaded that 'the plaintiff is not possessed of the premises', for this asserted that title was not in the plaintiff, and required the plaintiff to set up as an estoppel any judicial decision on which he intended to rely[2]. Where the decision was *in rem*[3], the old system did not require the estoppel to be pleaded[4]: but an unpleaded decision *in rem* would be 'likely to take the opposite party by surprise', and under the RSC failure to plead it would have waived the estoppel.

[1]   *R v Blakemore* (1852) 21 LJMC 60, 64 (plea of 'not guilty' to indictment for non-repair of highway); *R v Haughton Inhabitants* (1853) 1 E & B 501, 512 (the same).
[2]   *Matthew v Osborne* (1853) 13 CB 919; *Wilkinson v Kirby* (1854) 15 CB 430, 443, 446.
[3]   See Chapter 10.
[4]   *Cammell v Sewell* (1858) 3 II & N 617, 646–647.

18.06 In an action on a judgment, English or foreign, the plaintiff necessarily asserted that the decision is unimpeachable on the merits and he did not have to plead the estoppel. If the defendant pleaded to the merits, the plaintiff had to raise the estoppel in his reply or move to strike out the defence.

POSITION UNDER CPR

18.07 CPR Pt 16.5(2)(b) requires a defendant who relies on a different version of the facts to plead them. If he relies on a *res judicata* estoppel he will have to plead and particularise any additional facts needed to establish it because only in this way can the case be dealt with fairly, with the parties on an equal footing[1]. Thus a defendant seeking to raise a *res judicata* estoppel must plead it in his defence, and a claimant seeking to raise a *res judicata* estoppel must plead it in his reply[2]. This is supported by *McPhilemy v Times Newspapers Ltd* where Lord Woolf MR said[3]:

'Pleadings are still required to mark out the parameters of the case that is being advanced by each party. In particular they are still critical to identify the issues and the extent of the dispute between the parties. What is important is that the pleadings should make clear the general nature of the case of the pleader.'

[1]   CPR Pt 1.1(2)(a), (d), para 18.01, n 1.
[2]   Under CPR Pt 15.8 a claimant need not serve a reply unless he wishes to allege facts not included in his claim.
[3]   [1999] 3 All ER 775 CA, 793.

AMENDMENT

18.08 A party who has served his statement of case may amend it with the written consent of all other parties or the court[1]. The CPR, unlike the RSC, do not define the principles the courts should apply in allowing or refusing amendments. In *Cobbold v Greenwich London Borough Council* Peter Gibson LJ said[2]:

'Amendments in general ought to be allowed so that the real dispute between the parties can be adjudicated upon provided that any prejudice to the other party or parties caused by the amendment can be compensated for in costs, and the public interest in the efficient administration of justice is not significantly harmed.'

These are the principles which previously applied.

1   CPR Pt 17.1(2)(a), (b).
2   (August 1999, unreported), CA. It has frequently been cited.

MODERN PRACTICE

18.09   The strictness of the rule requiring prompt pleading of any *res judicata* estoppel has been relaxed; and the court will consider whether justice requires the unpleaded estoppel to be rejected. In *Winnan*[1] a wife obtained a maintenance order in a court of summary jurisdiction for wilful failure to maintain. Constructive desertion which would have been a defence was not raised. The husband petitioned for divorce, alleging constructive desertion. The wife raised estoppel without having pleaded it, and the Court of Appeal held that she was not too late[2]. In *Re Langton*[3] leave to issue a writ claiming probate of a will in solemn form was refused because the court had considered that will when granting probate of another. The estoppel should be raised in answer to the first pleading which contradicts the *res judicata*. If this is in the points of claim the defendant must plead the estoppel in his defence[4]; if in the defence, the claimant must plead the estoppel in his reply; if in the reply, the defendant must take it up in a rejoinder. The estoppel may be raised before trial by an application to strike out a pleading or as a preliminary point[5]. Applications for leave to amend to plead *res judicata* will be determined in accordance with familiar principles[6]. A late application may be refused[7]. Where the question arises in a court of summary jurisdiction or in proceedings without pleadings the estoppel must be raised at the first convenient opportunity.

1   [1949] P 174 CA.
2   Ibid at 180–181. The point failed for other reasons.
3   [1964] P 163.
4   *Mercantile Investment* [1894] 1 Ch 578; *Beardsley* [1899] 1 QB 746; *Ritchie v Malcolm* [1902] 2 IR 403; *Hill* [1954] P 291.
5   RSC O 18 r 11. *Houston v Marquis of Sligo* (1885) 29 Ch D 457 CA; *Nouvion v Freeman* (1889) 15 App Cas 1, 6; *Ritchie v Malcolm* [1902] 2 IR 403; *R v Brixton Prison Governor, ex p Savarkar* [1910] 2 KB 1056 CA (preliminary objection on hearing of appeal); *Robinson v Fenner* [1913] 3 KB 835 CA (not suitable for preliminary point procedure); *Kok Hoong* [1964] AC 993, 995 per Viscount Radcliffe: 'The issue is one of law. The relevant facts embrace nothing more than the circumstances of the earlier action, in which was given the judgment which is said to have created the estoppel, and the pleadings in the present action'. The procedure is mentioned in the report at [1964] 1 All ER 300 PC, 302. In *Bright* [1954] P 270, 278 the question was argued immediately before trial as a preliminary point. Willmer J said 'The proper way to deal with it would have been to apply in Chambers before trial for an order striking out the offending part or parts of the petition, so as to get these questions decided without waiting for the trial, and without incurring the expense of collecting the witnesses and making all the other preparations for trial'; para 12.10.
6   *Edevain v Cohen* (1889) 43 Ch D 187 CA where North J refused to allow the defendant, at the close of the plaintiff's evidence, to add a plea of *res judicata* and the CA declined to interfere; *Winnan* [1949] P 174 CA, 180–181, n 1 above; *Cooper (No 2)* [1955] P 168, 172.
7   *Ketteman v Hansel Properties Ltd* [1987] AC 189; *Aon Risk Services Australia Ltd v Australian National University* (2009) 83 ALJR 951.

PLEA FIRST RAISED ON APPEAL

18.10   A court of appeal will not entertain a new point of law if it could have been answered by evidence at the trial[1]. A party wishing to rely on *res judicata* estoppel must establish the necessary factual basis, and if this has not been done at the trial, it can seldom be done for the first time on appeal[2].

1   *Re Cowburn, ex p Firth* (1882) 19 Ch D 419 CA, 429; *North Staffordshire Rly Co v Edge* [1920] AC 254, 262–264; *Suttor v Gundowda Pty Ltd* (1950) 81 CLR 418.
2   *Sanders* [1952] 2 All ER 767, 769.

PART 2

MERGER IN JUDGMENT

Chapter 19

MERGER IN JUDGMENT

GENERAL

19.01 *Res judicata* has a twofold operation. It prevents the parties disputing the decision and bars a party who obtained relief from seeking it again. Diplock LJ said in *Thoday*[1]:

> '... cause of action estoppel ... prevents a party to an action from asserting or denying, as against the other party, the existence of a particular cause of action, the non-existence or existence of which has been determined by a court of competent jurisdiction in previous litigation between the same parties. If the cause of action was determined to exist i.e. judgment was given upon it, it is ... merged in the judgment ... If it was determined not to exist, the unsuccessful plaintiff can no longer assert that it does; he is estopped per rem judicatam'.

Any person in whose favour an English judicial tribunal of competent jurisdiction has pronounced a final judgment, is precluded from recovering before any English tribunal a second judgment on the same cause of action[2]. The principle extends to awards by competent tribunals. A plea of former recovery is distinguishable from one of *res judicata* estoppel. The latter prohibits contradiction, the former reassertion. In cases of estoppel what must not be controverted is a proposition of law or finding of fact. In cases of former recovery what is not allowed is a second proceeding for the same relief[3]. *Arnold*[4] established that the merger rule against double recovery is inflexible with no exception for special circumstances and *Chamberlain* is to the same effect[5]. *Chamberlain* was followed where a bank recovered judgment for the personal debt of the chargor and brought a second action under an 'all moneys clause'[6] on a guarantee.

[1]   [1964] P 181 CA, 197–198; *Leong v Hock Hua Bank Bhd* [2008] 3 MLJ 340, 360.
[2]   This passage in the 2nd edn was cited by Lord Goff in *The Indian Grace* [1993] AC 410, 417, and that in the 3rd edn was approved in *Zukowski v Royal Insurance Co of Canada* (2000) 189 DLR (4th) 476, 482.
[3]   *Outram v Morewood* (1803) 3 East 346, 354 per Lord Ellenborough CJ: 'it is not the recovery, but the matter alleged by the party, and upon which the recovery proceeds, which creates the estoppel. The recovery itself ... is only a bar to the taking recovery of damages for the same injury, but the estoppel precludes parties and privies from contending to the contrary of that point, or matter of fact, which, having once been distinctly put in issue by them, ... has been ... solemnly decided against them'; *King v Hoare* (1844) 13 M & W 494, 502; *Buckland v Johnson* (1854) 15 CB 145, 153.

4   *Arnold* [1991] 2 AC 93.
5   *Chamberlain* (1988) 164 CLR 502; para 13.11.
6   *Lloyds Bank plc v Hawkins* [1998] Lloyds Rep Bank 379, [1998] EWCA Civ 1391.

RATIONALE

19.02 The doctrine of former recovery has been justified on three grounds, two of which apply to *res judicata* estoppel. Firstly, the general interest of the community in the termination of disputes between litigants[1]: *interest reipublicae ut sit finis litium*[2]. Second, the interest of the individual litigant in the termination of disputes: *nemo debet bis vexari pro una et eadem causa*[3], regardless of the apparent merits of the second claim[4]. The third, merger, only applies to the doctrine of former recovery. Any cause of action for which judgment is given by an English judicial tribunal merges in that judgment: *transit in rem judicatam*. The cause of action ceases to exist and cannot support a second action[5]. This explains certain features of the doctrine; for instance, the rules, now abolished by statute, that a foreign judgment did not bar recovery on the cause of action[6], and that an English judgment against one or more persons jointly liable in contract or tort barred an action against any others[7]. It also explains the principle that a promise to pay interest on a debt ceases to be effective once judgment is given for the debt. In *Director-General of Fair Trading v First National Bank plc* Lord Bingham adopted[8] this statement of Peter Gibson LJ:

> ' … once a judgment is obtained under a loan agreement for a principal sum … the contract merges in the judgment and the principal becomes owed under the judgment and not under the contract. If under the contract interest on any principal sum is due, absent special provisions the contract is considered ancillary to the covenant to pay the principal, with the result that if judgment is obtained for the principal, the covenant to pay interest merges in the judgment. Parties to a contract may agree that a covenant to pay interest will not merge in any judgment for the principal sum due, and in that event interest may be charged under the contract on the principal sum due even after judgment for that sum.'

1   *Green v Weatherill* [1929] 2 Ch 213, 221.
2   *Ferrer v Arden* (1599) 6 Co Rep 7a, 9a; *Randal v Higgins* (1605) 6 Co Rep 44b; *Stafford v Clark* (1824) 2 Bing 377, 382; *Brinsmead v Harrison* (1872) LR 7 CP 547 Ex Ch, 551–553.
3   *Wemyss v Hopkins* (1875) LR 10 QB 378, 381–382.
4   *Workington Harbour and Dock Board v Trade Indemnity Co Ltd (No 2)* [1938] 2 All ER 101 HL, 106 per Lord Atkin: 'The result is that the plaintiffs, who appear to have had a good cause of action for a considerable sum of money, failed to obtain it, and on what may appear to be technical grounds. Reluctant, however, as a judge may be to fail to give effect to substantial merits, he has to keep in mind principles established for the protection of litigants from oppressive proceedings. There are solid merits behind the maxim *nemo bis vexari debet pro eadem causa*'; *Chamberlain* (1988) 164 CLR 502; para 13.11 and the rule that damages can only be assessed once.
5   *Randal v Higgins* (1605) 6 Co Rep 44b, 44b, 45a; *Drake v Mitchell* (1803) 3 East 251, 258 per Lord Ellenborough CJ: 'I have always understood the principle of *transit in rem judicatam* to relate only to the particular cause of action in which the judgment is recovered operating as a change of remedy from its being of a higher nature than before'; *Bowden v Home* (1831) 7 Bing 716, 723: 'the nature of his original demand is changed, *quia transit in rem judicatam*'; *King v Hoare* (1844) 13 M & W 494, 504 per Parke B: 'the cause of action is changed into matter of record, which is of a higher nature, and the

inferior remedy is merged in the higher'; *Brinsmead v Harrison* (1872) LR 7 CP 547 Ex Ch, 553; *Kendall v Hamilton* (1879) 4 App Cas 504, 526, 542.

[6]   1982 Act s 34; para 20.03.

[7]   1978 Act s 3; para 22.02. The rule for joint tortfeasors was abolished by s 6 of the 1935 Act.

[8]   [2002] 1 AC 481, 487–488.

THE CONSTITUENTS OF A GOOD PLEA OF FORMER RECOVERY

19.03 A party setting up a former recovery must establish that:

  (i)   the former judgment can in law support the plea;
  (ii)   it was in the terms alleged;
  (iii) the tribunal had jurisdiction;
  (iv) the former judgment was final and remains in force;
  (v)   the claimant is suing on the same cause of action; and
  (vi) the parties are the same or their privies.

Chapter 20

WHAT CONSTITUTES A FORMER RECOVERY

JUDGMENT

20.01 For present purposes a *res judicata* means a judicial decision or award[1] granting relief[2] but acceptance of a payment into court in full satisfaction has the same effect[3]. The cause of action may be at common law, equitable, or statutory[4], the decision may be *in rem* or *in personam*[5] and it may have been obtained after a hearing, by default[6] or by consent[7]. The relief may be judgment for debt or damages, or coercive. None of these differences matter. A cause of action for specific performance, including the contract, merges in a decree of specific performance. As Viscount Haldane explained[8]:

> 'The terms of the decree have, in the eye of the law, superseded and excluded all other evidence, and it is too late, if the decree remains unaltered, to try to import new terms in the course of inquiries which follow merely consequentially on the rights which the purchaser has been given as the result of the trial.'

If performance by either party cannot be enforced the decree can be rescinded. The contract will then revive and can be terminated by leave of the court[9]. The following do not qualify as a judgment granting relief for present purposes: a declaration of right; a verdict not followed by judgment[10]; a right to sign judgment on default[11]; a compromise without judgment[12]; and a balance order in the winding up of a company[13].

[1] *Golightly v Jellicoe* (1769) 4 Term Rep 147n; *Ravee v Farmer* (1791) 4 Term Rep 146; *Thorpe v Cooper* (1828) 5 Bing 116 Ex Ch, 129–130. In these cases the defendant failed to establish that the award included the relief sued for, or that the new claim was within the submission.
[2] Para 19.1.
[3] *Reardon Smith Line Ltd v Cayzer Irvine & Co Ltd* (1929) 35 Com Cas 270, 280; *Hills v Co-operative Wholesale Society Ltd* [1940] 2 KB 435 CA.
[4] *Wemyss v Hopkins* (1875) LR 10 QB 378, 381; *Girdlestone* (1879) 4 Ex D 107 CA.
[5] *Nelson v Couch* (1863) 15 CBNS 99, 108–112.
[6] *Bowden v Home* (1831) 7 Bing 716, 723; *Marston v Phillips* (1863) 9 LT 289; *Girdlestone* (1879) 4 Ex D 107 CA.
[7] *Hammond v Schofield* [1891] 1 QB 453 (express consent) and *Wright v London General Omnibus Co* (1877) 2 QBD 271 (implied consent based on acceptance of criminal compensation paid into court), criticised: para 21.12 n 3. This passage in the 2nd edn was cited in *Macquarie Bank Ltd v Beaconsfield* [1992] 2 VR 461, 467.
[8] *McGrory v Alderdale Estate Co Ltd* [1918] AC 503, 511; *Hasham v Zenab* [1960] AC 316, 330.

271

9   *Johnson v Agnew* [1980] AC 367.
10 *Morris v Robinson* (1824) 3 B & C 196, 205, 207.
11 *Goldrei* [1918] 1 KB 180 CA, 191.
12 *Thomas v Exeter Flying Post Co* (1887) 18 QBD 822.
13 *Westmoreland Green and Blue Slate Co v Feilden* [1891] 3 Ch 15 CA.

20.02 Any cause of action successfully taken to arbitration merges in the award[1]. The plea is also substantiated by proof that the claimant recovered against the defendant on the same cause of action in an inferior court.[2]

1   *Moakes v Blackwell Colliery Co* [1917] 1 KB 565 CA (statutory); *Ayscough v Sheed Thomson & Co Ltd* (1923) 129 LT 429 CA (domestic), para 2.05; *H E Daniels Ltd v Carmel Exporters and Importers Ltd* [1953] 2 QB 242, 255.
2   In *Wright v London General Omnibus Co* (1877) 2 QBD 271 and *Sanders v Hamilton* (1907) 96 LT 679 inferior court judgments barred actions in an inferior court; in *Austin v Mills* (1853) 9 Exch 288; *Gibbs v Cruikshank* (1873) LR 8 CP 454; *Clarke v Yorke* (1882) 52 LJ Ch 32; inferior court judgments barred actions in a superior court. In *Birmingham Corpn v S Allsopp & Sons Ltd* (1919) 119 LT 775, the corporation, having been awarded a sum 'by way of compensation' in a criminal proceeding was precluded from bringing a civil action for the rest of its damage.

FOREIGN JUDGMENTS[1]

20.03 At common law an unsatisfied foreign judgment did not bar proceedings on the original cause of action[2], but a satisfied foreign judgment did. As Erle CJ said in *Barber v Lamb*[3]:

> '... here the defence does not rest on merger, but on the principle that the plaintiff has obtained the judgment of a tribunal to which he has resorted for enforcing his debt, and that the judgment so obtained has been satisfied ... it would be manifestly contrary to reason and justice to allow the successful party to endeavour to obtain a better judgment in respect of the same matter from some other tribunal'.

The general rule about foreign judgments was criticised in *Carl-Zeiss (No 2)*[4] but not overruled. Its status in other jurisdictions is unclear[5]. It was abolished by s 34 of the 1982 Act, which provides that no proceeding may be brought on a cause of action in respect of which the plaintiff has obtained a judgment in proceedings between the same parties or their privies in a court in another part of the United Kingdom, or in a court of an overseas country unless the judgment is not enforceable or entitled to recognition. The section was considered in *Black v Yates*[6]. Following a fatal road accident in Spain, criminal proceedings were brought against the driver. The widow intervened, as permitted by Spanish law, and was awarded substantial compensation. She later sued in England under the Fatal Accidents Act 1976, but was met with a defence under s 34 which succeeded because[7] the cause of action was the same despite the differences in procedure. The section was also considered in *The Indian Endurance*[8].

1   This paragraph in the 2nd edn was referred to in *The Indian Grace* [1993] AC 410, 417.
2   *Hall v Odber* (1809) 11 East 118; *Smith v Nicolls* (1839) 5 Bing NC 208; *Bank of Australasia v Harding* (1850) 9 CB 661; *Barber v Lamb* (1860) 8 CBNS 95, 100; *Taylor v Hollard* [1902] 1 KB 676, 681.
3   (1860) 8 CBNS 95, 100; *Kohnke v Karger* [1951] 2 KB 670, 676; *Black v Yates* [1992] QB 526, 550–551.

4   [1967] 1 AC 853, 917, 927, 938, 966.
5   *Tanning Research Laboratories Inc v O'Brien* (1990) 169 CLR 332, 346; Campbell 'Res
    Judicata and Decisions of Foreign Tribunals' (1994) 16 Syd Law Rev 311, 339–341.
6   [1992] QB 526.
7   Ibid at 543–544.
8   [1998] AC; para 21.13 nn 8–16, and earlier in *The Indian Grace* [1993] AC 410.

RECOVERY

20.04 A former recovery is established by proof that the party against whom the plea is set up, obtained as claimant, counterclaimant or the like, a judgment or award on the same cause of action. A plea of payment under a former judgment can be established without proving that the judgment was a bar[1]. Whether there was a former recovery is a question of fact[2].

1   *Barber v Lamb* (1860) 8 CBNS 95, 100 per Erle CJ. A plaintiff who sued one party abroad
    and obtained satisfaction and sued another in England on a different cause of action could
    recover, but had to give credit for the recovery, there being an equity to prevent double
    satisfaction: *Kohnke v Karger* [1951] 2 KB 670, 675; para 21.04 n 2.
2   *Edevain v Cohen* (1889) 43 Ch D 187 CA, 189–190.

20.05 'Recovery' does not mean satisfaction. The plea is good although the judgment is unsatisfied[1], the right to execution under it has been abandoned[2]; or the claimant had abandoned part of his claim to bring it within the jurisdiction of an inferior court[3]. It is no answer that the plaintiff recovered less than he would on another cause of action[4].

1   *Randal v Higgins* (1605) 6 Co Rep 44b (plea of former recovery without execution good
    on demurrer); *King v Hoare* (1844) 13 M & W 494 (immaterial that judgment
    unsatisfied); *Buckland v Johnson* (1854) 15 CB 145; *Kendall v Hamilton* (1879) 4 App Cas
    504; *Re Hodgson* (1885) 31 Ch D 177 CA.
2   In *Bowden v Home* (1831) 7 Bing 716, 723 the plaintiff obtained judgments on a bill of
    exchange, and for the price of goods sold and work and labour. Worried that the two
    claims might drive the defendant into bankruptcy, the claimant entered a *nolle prosequi* as
    to the second. Tindal CJ said that 'after the plaintiff has obtained a judgment ... and has
    given up the damages upon the record ... he has precluded himself from suing again on the
    original cause of action'.
3   *Clarke v Yorke* (1882) 52 LJ Ch 32, 34.
4   *Buckland v Johnson* (1854) 15 CB 145; *Wright v London General Omnibus Co* (1877) 2
    QBD 271; *Banks v Wilson* (1910) 29 NZLR 832.

PROOF

20.06 This is considered in Chapter 3.

JURISDICTION

20.07 A judgment pronounced by an inferior court without jurisdiction is a nullity[1] whether so declared by a court with appellate or supervisory jurisdiction or not. It can neither be enforced in the original court nor be sued on in another. The claimant must sue again on the original cause of action. A party setting up a former recovery in an inferior court must allege and prove its jurisdiction[2]. If the former recovery was in a superior court jurisdiction is presumed. The judgment of an English superior court that is beyond power is wrong, or irregular, but not void[3].

[1] Civil: *Fisher v Lane* (1772) 3 Wils 297; *Smith v Nicolls* (1839) 5 Bing NC 208, 222–223; Criminal: *R v Marsham, ex p Pethick Lawrence* [1912] 2 KB 362; *Conlin v Patterson* [1915] 2 IR 169; *Bannister v Clarke* [1920] 3 KB 598, 605–607; court of summary jurisdiction: *R v Brisby* (1849) 18 LJMC 157; *Midland Rly Co v Martin & Co* [1893] 2 QB 172.
[2] Paras 4.03, 4.07–4.11.
[3] Paras 4.03, 4.06. Parliament could provide otherwise but has not done so.

FINALITY

20.08 The former recovery must be a final judgment capable of supporting an action[1]. Other final judgments which will support a plea of *res judicata* estoppel, such as declaratory judgments, will not support this plea[2]. The party pleading former recovery must prove that the judgment was complete and final and nothing further had to be done judicially to render it effective and enforceable[3]. A judgment for damages to be assessed[4] is not final before the assessment[5]. A judgment which may be rescinded or modified by the court which pronounced it also lacks finality, but a default judgment for a definite sum is final although liable to be set aside[6]. Where a judgment was liable to revision, but statute made it final in the meantime, it had that effect[7].

[1] Paras 5.02 , 5.08.
[2] Para 5.12.
[3] A judgment debt may be enforced before costs are taxed.
[4] Paras 5.02, 5.08 n 1.
[5] *Marston v Phillips* (1863) 9 LT 289; *Goldrei* [1918] 1 KB 180 CA, 191.
[6] Para 22.05 nn 7–9.
[7] *Austin v Mills* (1853) 9 Exch 288, 293; para 5.15.

20.09 The judgment must still be in force. If it is set aside on appeal[1] or on the application of either party[2], the cause of action will revive, and a plea of merger will fail.

[1] *Petersen v Moloney* (1951) 84 CLR 91, 103–104, para 24.05.
[2] Including the claimant in the case of a default judgment: para 22.05 nn 7–9.

Chapter 21

MERGER IN JUDGMENT: IDENTITY OF CAUSES OF ACTION

21.01 In general a judgment is only a bar to proceedings founded on the same 'cause of action'. However a claimant with alternative remedies or causes of action against the same defendant can only recover on one and must elect. In *United Australia*[1] the plaintiff had alternative remedies for conversion of its cheque and for money had and received. Lord Atkin said[2]:

> '[The plaintiff] was restricted to one of the two remedies ... Having recovered in contract ... [it] cannot ... recover in tort. *Transit in rem judicatam*[3]... [O]n a question of alternative remedies no question of election arises until one or other claim has been brought to judgment. Up to that stage the plaintiff may pursue both remedies together, or pursuing one may amend and pursue the other; but he can take judgment only for the one and his cause of action on both will then be merged in the one'.

These principles were applied in *Mahesan S/O Thambiah v Malaysian Government Officers' Co-operative Housing Society Ltd*[4] where the Privy Council held that a principal could not retain judgment against its bribed agent for damages for fraud and for restitution of the bribe but had to elect. A similar situation arises where a claimant has alternative remedies for damages (or equitable compensation) and an account of profits, and must elect when taking judgment. Where the trial court gave judgment for damages and an account of profits the Privy Council required the plaintiff to elect[5]. A claimant is entitled to make an informed choice, and may require further time or additional discovery[6]. A claimant may have cumulative remedies or causes of action against the same person or different persons[7]. A copyright owner is entitled to damages for infringement and damages for conversion of infringing copies[8]. A local authority has cumulative causes of action against councillors whose wilful breaches of duty caused it financial loss; under the audit provisions of the Local Government Finance Act 1982, and the general law. Hart J said in such a case[9]:

> 'The claims ... are ... in respect of the same essential loss based on the same conduct ... , and the basic principles of compensation applicable to each of the claims is the same. Accordingly ... the claimant is entitled to a judgment based on the auditor's certificates and is also entitled to a judgment, almost certain to be larger, based on the breach of trust claim ... [T]hat ... does not entitle the claimant to recover ... more than the higher of the two sums.'

Where specific performance was refused but the purchaser was awarded damages its insistence that these be paid to a stakeholder pending its appeal was an election to accept damages in lieu of specific performance[10].

1   [1941] AC 1; *Green v Weatherill* [1929] 2 Ch 213, 221 where the plaintiff had alternative remedies for one cause of action; para 21.03 n 2.
2   Ibid at 28.
3   Ibid at 30.
4   [1979] AC 374, 382–383.
5   *Personal Representatives of Tang Man Sit v Capacious Investments Ltd* [1996] AC 514 (*Tang Man Sit*).
6   *Island Records Ltd v Tring International plc* [1996] 1 WLR 1256; *Tang Man Sit* [1996] AC 514, 521; *Warman International Ltd v Dwyer* (1995) 182 CLR 544, 570.
7   *Tang Man Sit* [1996] AC 514, 521–522; para 21.13.
8   *Caxton Publishing Co Ltd v Sutherland Publishing Co* [1939] AC 178.
9   *Westminster CC v Porter* [2003] Ch 436, 451–452.
10 *Meng Leong* [1985] AC 511, 525.

THE ONUS OF PROOF

21.02 The burden of establishing that the causes of action are the same lies on the party who sets up the former judgment[1]. It is *prima facie* discharged by production of the record in the former proceedings. If the former judgment was on a different cause of action (a question of law) the plea fails[2]. If the causes of action may be the same the party setting up the plea must establish identity in fact[3]. If the opposite party claims that the former judgment has been misstated he must plead the equivalent of *nul tiel record*[4].

1   See Chapter 25.
2   *Wadsworth v Bentley* (1853) 23 LJQB 3, 5 per Crompton J: 'the record, when produced, must … shew on its face that the cause of action may be the same as that for which the judgment has been recovered in the former action'; *Guest v Warren* (1854) 9 Exch 379 (recovery for assault and false imprisonment no answer to action for malicious prosecution).
3   *Stafford v Clark* (1824) 2 Bing 377, 381. In *R v Tancock* (1876) 13 Cox CC 217 a jury found that the victims in the indictment for murder and the conviction for manslaughter were the same and Denman J treated the identity of the offences as a question of law.
4   *Wadsworth v Bentley* (1853) 23 LJQB 3.

IDENTITY OF CAUSES OF ACTION

21.03 'Two actions may be brought in respect of the same facts, [if they] give rise to distinct causes of action'[1]. But if the causes of action are substantially the same, the plea of former recovery prevails, despite formal differences, or different remedies[2]. The test has been said to be whether the second action is based on a substantially different cause of action or is an attempt to recover additional damages on the same cause of action[3], but this begs the question.

1   *Brunsden v Humphrey* (1884) 14 QBD 141 CA, 146 (separate causes of action in tort for personal injuries and property damage). In *Rowley v Wilkinson* [1968] NZLR 334 CA where a dentist was asked to extract certain teeth and it was alleged that he had extracted others as well and failed to use due skill, it was held there were two causes of action but this is doubtful. The claims in tort arose out of the same facts and involved the same interest, and since *The Indian Grace* [1993] AC 410 it is clear that there was only one cause of action in contract. The Supreme Court of Canada rejected *Brunsden v Humphrey*

and held that there was one cause of action for both property damage and personal injury arising out of a given 'factual situation'. This enabled a claim for personal injuries to be added to an action for property damage without infringing the rule against the addition of a statute barred cause of action: *Cahoon v Franks* (1967) 63 DLR (2d) 274. In other cases recovery for property damage barred actions for personal injuries: *Cox v Robert Simpson & Co* (1973) 40 DLR (3d) 213 CA Ont; *Malcolm v Carr* (1997) 51 Alta LR (3d) 66 CA.

[2] In *Green v Weatherill* [1929] 2 Ch 213, 221 Maugham J said: 'the cause of action in the two cases is strictly speaking not the same. On the other hand the plea of *res judicata* is not a technical doctrine, but a fundamental doctrine based on the view that there must be an end to litigation'. Judgment for breach of trust against the separate estate of a married woman barred an action seeking judgment for payment into court. In fact they were alternative remedies for one cause of action and the plaintiff had to elect; para 21.01.

[3] *Derrick v Williams* [1939] 2 All ER 559 CA, 566.

21.04 If the same damage is claimed from the same defendant on separate causes of action an unsatisfied judgment on one will not necessarily bar an action on the other but it may be barred by the rule in *Henderson*[1] or as an abuse of process. A claimant with causes of action against a carrier for personal injuries who recovered in tort could not sue in contract. The causes of action, although technically different, are in substance the same. A claimant who obtains consecutive judgments against the same defendant on different causes of action for the same damage must give credit for payments under both judgments. The same damage may be claimed from different defendants but each will be entitled to credit for any payments by the other[2].

[1] (1843) 3 Hare 100; para 7.03.
[2] *United Australia* [1941] AC 1, 20; *Tang Man Sit* [1996] AC 514, 522; *Isaacs & Sons v Salbstein* [1916] 2 KB 139 CA; *B O Morris Ltd v Perrott and Bolton* [1945] 1 All ER 567, 570; *Kohnke v Karger* [1951] 2 KB 670, 676; *Heavaner v Loomes* (1924) 34 CLR 306, 322; *Registrar-General (NSW) v Behn* (1981) 148 CLR 562, 569; *Eastgate Group Ltd v Lindsay Morden Group Inc* [2002] 1 WLR 642 CA, 650–651.

21.05 If the cause of action in the later proceedings is essentially different it will not be barred[1]. The same rule applies to awards[2]. Where there is only one cause of action in substance, and one demand has been split the plea is sustained. Where the residual claim is part of an entire sum, or the same subject matter, recoverable on a single cause of action, the judgment bars an action for the balance[3]. Damages for a cause of action can only be assessed once, and the assessment must compensate for all damage past and future recoverable under that cause of action. A claimant cannot bring a second action to recover damages for supervening and unforeseen consequences of the original wrong[4]. In *Fetter v Beal* the plaintiff having recovered damages 'for an assault and battery in a drunken brawl' sued for further damages when 'part of his skull by reason of the said battery had come out of his head'. The defendant pleaded former recovery and the plaintiff demurred. He argued that the further damage constituted a new cause of action[5]:

> 'Quod Holt negavit. And, per totam curiam, the jury in the former action considered the nature of the wound, and gave damages for all the damages [sic] that it had done to the plaintiff; and, therefore, a recovery in the said action is good here'.

The rule has been modified by s 32A of the Supreme Court Act where there is a chance that the injured person may develop a serious disease or suffer a serious deterioration in his physical or mental condition. The common law merger rule does not apply to fresh or continuing acts of the same character such as repeated defamations, or continuing trespasses or nuisances[6].

1   In *Seddon v Tutop* (1796) 6 Term Rep 607 the plaintiff sued on a promissory note and for goods sold and delivered, and took judgment by default on both causes of action. On the writ of enquiry he only took a verdict on the first and could sue again on the second because there was no final judgment; *Hennell v Fairlamb* (1800) 3 Esp 104 (plaintiff entitled to sue for balance of debt after deducting recovery by set-off. Cross-actions were not then permitted); *Davis v Hedges* (1871) LR 6 QB 687 (purchaser can set off diminution of value from breach of warranty and sue for additional damages); *Hadley v Green* (1832) 2 Cr & J 374; *Few v Backhouse* (1838) 8 Ad & El 789; *Brunsden v Humphrey* (1884) 14 QBD 141 CA where the plaintiff recovered for damage to his cab and then for his personal injuries; *Chamberlain* (1988) 164 CLR 502; para 13.11.

2   An award does not bar an action for claims outside the submission: *Golightly v Jellicoe* (1769) 4 Term Rep 147n; *Ravee v Farmer* (1791) 4 Term Rep 146; *Thorpe v Cooper* (1828) 5 Bing 116 Ex Ch, 129–130; *Gueret v Audouy* (1893) 62 LJQB 633; *E E and Brian Smith (1928) Ltd v Wheatsheaf Mills Ltd* [1939] 2 KB 302. Cf *Dunn v Murray* (1829) 9 B & C 780 (plaintiff who had not attempted to prove a matter in the arbitration was barred). Where serial arbitrations were permitted by a building contract an award did not bar a claim for further defects: *Purser & Co (Hillingdon) Ltd v Jackson* [1977] QB 166, but in other cases an award will be a bar: *Onerati v Phillips Constructions Pty Ltd* (1989) 16 NSWLR 730.

3   *Williams v Lord Bagot* (1825) 3 B & C 772 (plaintiff, with a claim for £7,000, took judgment for £4,000 in the belief that this was all the defendant could pay, and was barred from recovering the balance); *Russell & Sons v Waterford and Limerick Rly Co* (1885) 16 LR Ir 314 (plaintiff, having a claim for damage to 8½ sacks of flour, took judgment for six and was barred from suing for the rest); *Sanders v Hamilton* (1907) 96 LT 679 (judgment for £14 in detinue, when real claim was for £35, recovery of the rest barred); *Furness, Withy & Co Ltd v J and E Hall Ltd* (1909) 25 TLR 233 (item of indemnity claimable in former proceedings); *Derrick v Williams* [1939] 2 All ER 559, 566 per Finlay LJ: '… the essential distinction, … a perfectly obvious one, is between a distinct cause of action and some head of damages'. Once a costs judge has issued a final certificate the receiving party cannot have omitted items included in a further assessment: *Moat Housing* [2008] 1 WLR 1578.

4   *Rothwell v Chemical & Insulating Co Ltd* [2008] AC 281, 291; *Chan v Hui* [2000] HK LRD (Yrbk) 119 CA.

5   (1697) 1 Ld Raym 339, 339–340. In *Holmes v Wilson* (1839) 10 Ad & El 503 the court said: 'the distinction is between an action for damages consequential upon an injury for which the plaintiff has already recovered a judgment, as in *Fetter v Beal*, and an action for a continuing injury'; *Clarke v Yorke* (1882) 52 LJ Ch 32, 34.

6   Para 21.08; *Holmes v Wilson* (1839) 10 Ad & El 503, 511 per Denman CJ: 'the former and the present action are for different trespasses. The former was for erecting the buttresses. This action was for continuing the buttresses so erected. The continued use of the buttresses for the support of the road … was a fresh trespass'; *Clarke v Midland and Great Western Rly Co* [1895] 2 IR 294 (judgment for trespass no bar to action for further trespass).

SPLITTING DEMANDS

21.06 'There is no positive law … against splitting demands which are essentially separable … although the High Court has inherent power to prevent vexation or oppression'[1], but any right to split can only be accepted after careful consideration[2]. In *Williams v Hunt*[3] the court held that it was an abuse to bring a second action when complete relief was available in the first. If the demands are not essentially separable recovery will bar another action. In *Buckland v Johnson* CrowderJ said[4]:

'The plaintiff having a cause of action, in trover or for money had and received, at his election, against two, has brought trover against one, and recovered ... that judgment is for £100 only, and ... the now defendant actually received £148 as the proceeds of the goods converted: and therefore it is contended that the recovery in the former action is no bar as to £48. The circumstance ... of the two amounts being different ... cannot alter the principle ... that the plaintiff having recovered what the jury considered the value of the goods ... cannot now bring money had and received.'

An award of damages by a tribunal of limited jurisdiction bars proceedings in a higher tribunal for additional damages[5]. The claimant brought proceedings for unfair and wrongful dismissal in an employment tribunal, where the jurisdiction was capped at £25,000, purporting to reserve his right to recover further damages in the High Court. The tribunal assessed his damages at £80,000 but awarded the statutory limit. His action in the High Court for the balance was struck out. Mummery LJ said[6]:

'... this was clearly a case of merger of Mr Fraser's cause of action ... in the final judgment of the tribunal ... The claim for the excess is not a separate cause of action. The cause of action ... could not be split into two causes of action, one for damages up to £25,000, and another for the balance.'

[1]   *Brunsden v Humphrey* (1884) 14 QBD 141 CA, 151 per Bowen LJ (it is prohibited in the County Court Acts), and at 147, 148.
[2]   *Seddon v Tutop* (1796) 6 Term Rep 607, 609; para 21.05 n 1.
[3]   [1905] 1 KB 512 CA, 514 (mortgagee's action in Chancery Division for account; second action in Kings Bench Division for principal and interest stayed; para 21.08 n 4).
[4]   (1854) 15 CB 145, 167–168.
[5]   *Fraser v HLMAD Ltd* [2006] ICR 1395 CA, 1403, 1411–1412; para 21.12.
[6]   Ibid at 1403; *Sheriff v Klyne Tugs (Lowestoft) Ltd* [1999] ICR 1170; para 26.16 n 18.

RULES IN CONTRACT

21.07 *The Indian Grace*[1] established a clear rule for contract cases. Where the same facts give rise to more than one breach of the same contract there is only one cause of action. In that case lack of care for the cargo resulted in short delivery and delivery of damaged cargo but there was only one cause of action. Where a plaintiff recovered damages for failure to build in a good and workmanlike manner he could not recover for failure to build with proper materials. There was a single obligation to complete the building in accordance with the contract and only one cause of action[2]. A second action cannot be brought for further defects discovered since judgment in the first[3]. The position is different if there are different contracts. Recovery on a negotiable instrument does not bar an action on a guarantee of the debt for which the negotiable instrument was given[4]. There is no bar where there are breaches at different times[5]. Where an owner repossessed a chattel let under a hire purchase agreement and recovered the instalments already due, this did not bar a claim for the final loss after the chattel was sold[6]. Where a bill of exchange provided for payment of interest on dishonour at a special rate, judgment for the face value without interest did not bar a claim for interest accrued before judgment[7].

[1]   [1993] AC 410.

[2] *Conquer v Boot* [1928] 2 KB 336 approved in *The Indian Grace* [1993] AC 410, 420–421 ('the factual basis ... giving rise to the two breaches is the same'); *Alfred Rowntree & Sons Ltd v Frederick Allen & Sons (Poplar) Ltd* (1935) 41 Com Cas 90, 94 where Goddard J disallowed a second action for the same breach. 'He [the plaintiff] can recover in one action for all damage actual or prospective, and if he does not ask for both he cannot afterwards bring a further action for damages for which he omitted to ask in the first action'; *H E Daniels Ltd v Carmel Exporters and Importers Ltd* [1953] 2 QB 242.

[3] *Honeywood v Munnings* (2006) 67 NSWLR 466 CA.

[4] *Drake v Mitchell* (1803) 3 East 251; *Wegg Prosser v Evans* [1895] 1 QB 108 CA.

[5] *Bristowe v Fairclough* (1840) 1 Man & G 143; paras 7.12, 8.17.

[6] *Overstone Ltd v Shipway* [1962] 1 WLR 117 CA; followed in *Lawlor v Gray* [1984] 3 All ER 345 CA (successive actions on indemnity).

[7] *Florence v Jennings* (1857) 2 CBNS 454; cf *Lordsvale Finance Plc v Bank of Zambia* [1996] QB 752.

RULES IN TORT

21.08 The rules in tort are more complex. The simplest case is where there are successive wrongs. A judgment in defamation does not bar an action for another publication of the same defamatory matter[1], because each publication is a separate tort[2]. The Supreme Court of Canada has held that separate actions cannot be maintained against different persons responsible at different stages for the publication of the same libel in the same edition of a newspaper[3]. The plurality held that proceedings in Ontario were an abuse because there had been 15 actions in Manitoba in which a complete remedy was available[4]. There is considerable force in the dissenting judgment of Kerwin J, which is consistent with *Goldsmith v Sperrings Ltd*[5]. Judgment for damages for pollution did not bar an action for further pollution[6].

[1] *Duke of Brunswick v Pepper* (1848) 2 Car & Kir 683 (different dates and places of publication); *Wadsworth v Bentley* (1853) 23 LJQB 3 (different defamatory matter). Technically there is a separate cause of action in relation to each copy of a newspaper or book delivered to a reader: *Duke of Brunswick v Harmer* (1849) 14 QB 185 but a claimant can plead a single cause of action even where publication occurs over an extended period and the rule is ignored unless the time and place of publication becomes important: *Harris* (2003) 56 NSWLR 276 CA.

[2] *Dingle v Associated Newspapers Ltd* [1961] 2 QB 162 CA, 186; affirmed [1964] AC 371; *Harris* (2003) 56 NSWLR 276 CA.

[3] *Thomson v Lambert* [1938] 2 DLR 545 SC. The publication occurred in 1931.

[4] Ibid at 560 applying *Williams v Hunt* [1905] 1 KB 512 CA. Many of those defendants were joint torteasors but the Supreme Court did not refer to *Brinsmead v Harrison* (1872) LR 7 CP 547, or to any legislation similar to the 1935 Act which displaced the principle that judgment against one joint tortfeasor barred any action against others.

[5] [1977] 1 WLR 478 CA. Those responsible at different stages for the same publication are joint tortfeasors, but different distributors are not joint tortfeasors with each other.

[6] *Freshwater v Bulmer Rayon Co Ltd* [1933] Ch 162 CA, 186; [1933] AC 661, 667.

INDEMNITY

21.09 An employer who paid compensation to a worker and was entitled to be indemnified by a tortfeasor had a separate cause of action for every payment, and a recovery did not bar an action for further payments[1]. The position with a contractual indemnity is the same[2].

¹   *A-G v Arthur Ryan Automobiles Ltd* [1938] 2 KB 16 CA; *South Eastern Sydney AHS v Gadiry* (2002) 54 NSWLR 495 CA; para 8.17.
²   *Lawlor v Gray* [1984] 3 All ER 345 CA.

ACTIONS IN RESPECT OF DIFFERENT INTERESTS

21.10 Where the claimant has different interests judgment in respect of one is not ordinarily a bar to an action in respect of another. Recovery in trespass did not bar an action for conversion[1], recovery for assault and false imprisonment did not bar an action for malicious prosecution[2], recovery for wrongful death did not bar an action in contract for damages to the deceased's person or property which diminished his estate[3]. The best-known example is *Brunsden v Humphrey*[4]. Judgment against a company for rescission and restitution did not bar claims against the promoter and the company for fraud[5]. Parents of a drowned seaman[6] could sue under the Law Reform Act and Lord Campbell's Act although they had already recovered for loss of his kit. A plaintiff having recovered damages for replevin was barred from suing for trespass to the same goods, but not for trespass to the land on which the goods had been seized[7].

¹   *Lacon v Barnard* (1626) Cro Car 35 (former judgment for 'taking and driving' 89 sheep, the second for their conversion).
²   *Guest v Warren* (1854) 9 Exch 379, 383.
³   *Pym v Great Northern Rly Co* (1863) 4 B & S 396, 407 (per Erle CJ: 'the statute ... gives to the personal representative a cause of action beyond that which the deceased would have had if he survived, and based on a different principle'); *Barnett v Lucas* (1872) 6 CL 247 (widow suing in contract as administratrix not barred by recovery under the statute); *Leggott v Great Northern Rly Co* (1876) 1 QBD 599 (same); *Daly v Dublin, Wicklow and Wexford Rly Co* (1892) 30 LR Ir 514 (same). In these cases the legal personal representative sued in different capacities: para 9.22. Cf *Read v Great Eastern Rly Co* (1868) LR 3 QB 555 where the widow's second action for damages suffered by the deceased during his lifetime was barred.
⁴   (1884) 14 QBD 141 CA; para 21.11.
⁵   *Goldrei* [1918] 1 KB 180 CA (fraud not being necessary for rescission); para 7.07.
⁶   *The Oropesa* [1943] P 32 CA.
⁷   *Gibbs v Cruikshank* (1873) LR 8 CP 454.

BRUNSDEN V HUMPHREY[1]

21.11 The plaintiff's cab was damaged in a collision in which he suffered personal injuries. He recovered in the County Court for the damage to his cab and in the High Court for his personal injuries. The majority of the Court of Appeal[2] held that he had separate causes of action because separate rights were infringed. The decision was followed by Lord Wright in *The Oropesa*[3] where 'an entirely different right' was involved in the second action, but it was described by Somervell LJ[4] as 'a somewhat borderline case'. It was referred to with apparent approval in *Wilson v United Counties Bank Ltd*[5] and *Cartledge v E Jopling & Sons Ltd*[6] and treated as settled law in an Indian appeal[7]. Stuart-Smith and Mann LJJ said in *Talbot*[8] that if *Henderson*[9] had been cited in *Brunsden v Humphrey* the decision might have been different but *Henderson* does not bar separate actions on separate causes of action arising out of the same facts. The Supreme Court of Canada[10] declined to follow *Brunsden v Humphrey* and it has been rejected in some States in the United States[11]. It has been followed in Ireland[12] and first doubted in Northern Ireland[13] but then followed[14]. It has been followed in Australia because it is 'too late to question the decision'[15]. Despite the absurdity pointed out by Lord Coleridge CJ of separate causes of action for damage to the plaintiff's trousers and his legs the decision has stood for a very long time. It is relied on every day to bring separate actions for property damage and personal injuries and if it were overruled prior judgments for property damage would bar actions for personal injuries. This is what happened in Canada[16]. The decision, whatever the difficulties, should not be overruled judicially[17]. Only one action may be brought for personal injury[18] and only one for property damage[19].

[1]   (1884) 14 QBD 141 CA; *Macdougall v Knight* (1890) 25 QBD 1 CA, 8.
[2]   Brett MR, Bowen LJ; Lord Coleridge CJ dissenting.
[3]   [1943] P 32 CA, 35.
[4]   *Greenhalgh v Mallard* [1947] 2 All ER 255 CA, 258.
[5]   [1920] AC 102, 131–132.
[6]   [1963] AC 758, 780.
[7]   *Mohammed Khan v Mahbub Ali Mian* [1948] AIR(PC) 78, 84–86. *Brunsden v Humphrey* was treated with some reserve in *Buckland v Palmer* [1984] 1 WLR 1109 CA, 1116; and *Walkin v South Manchester Health Authority* [1995] 1 WLR 1543 CA, 1547.
[8]   [1994] QB 290 CA, 296, 301; paras 12.16–12.17.
[9]   (1843) 3 Hare 100; para 7.03.
[10] *Cahoon v Franks* (1967) 63 DLR (2d) 274; para 21.03 n 1.
[11] *Dearden v Hey* 24 NE 2d 644 (1939) (Supreme Court of Massachusetts).
[12] *Hayes v Callanan* [2002] 1 IR 321.
[13] *Shaw v Sloan* [1982] NI 393 CA, 398.
[14] *Davidson v North Down Quarries Ltd* [1988] NI 214; *Ulster Bank Ltd v Fisher & Fisher* [1999] NI 68.
[15] *Marlborough Harbour Board v Charter Travel Co Ltd* (1989) 18 NSWLR 223 CA, 231 (*Marlborough*); *Jackson v Goldsmith* (1950) 81 CLR 446, 467; *Anshun* (1981) 147 CLR 589, 611.
[16] *Cox v Robert Simpson & Co Ltd* (1973) 40 DLR (3d) 213 CA Ont; *Malcolm v Carr* (1997) Alta LR (3d) 66 CA.
[17] The author once thought otherwise: *Baltic Shipping Co v Merchant* (1994) 36 NSWLR 361 CA, 370.
[18] *Cartledge v E Jobling & Sons Ltd* [1963] AC 758, 780.
[19] *Marlborough* (1989) 18 NSWLR 223 CA, 231.

ACTIONS IN RESPECT OF THE SAME INTEREST

21.12 Where the same interest is involved, a second action on the same facts is barred. A judgment in replevin barred an action for an excessive distress where the goods and seizure were the same[1]. Judgment for the defendant in an action for conversion by sale barred an action for money had and received in respect of the same goods[2]. An award of statutory compensation by a court of summary jurisdiction barred an action to recover additional damages[3]. A plaintiff who recovered the maximum under the Employers' Liability Act 1880 could not claim damages at common law, since the causes of action were the same although the Act excluded the defence of common employment and capped the damages[4]. A statutory cause of action for innocent misrepresentation was substantially the same as a cause of action for negligent misrepresentation based on the same facts[5]. A claim by an unlicensed builder for the price of building work under a contract made unenforceable by statute and a claim in restitution based on the same facts were alternative and inconsistent remedies for what in substance was the same cause of action[6].

In *Serrao v Noel*[7] the Court of Appeal held that a plaintiff who obtained a final injunction for delivery up of share certificates could not bring a second action to recover damages for their detention. There was only one right and one cause of action, and past and prospective damages could have been recovered in the first action[8]. It was followed in New Zealand where consecutive actions were brought for specific performance and damages. In the first[9] the plaintiff, having failed to obtain specific performance on discretionary grounds, had his claim for common law damages summarily dismissed. In the second an action for damages for delay by a purchaser who had enforced specific performance was also summarily dismissed[10]. An action by purchasers for possession, damages for disturbance, and an injunction, barred a later action for specific performance[11]. A successful action against a vendor and its directors for rescission for breach of fiduciary duties owed to the purchaser barred an action for equitable compensation[12]. In *Serrao v Noel*[13] only Baggallay LJ referred to the section in the Judicature Act 1873[14], now s 49(2) of the Supreme Court Act 1981, which provides:

'Every Court ... shall so exercise its jurisdiction in every cause or matter before it as to secure that, as far as possible, all matters in dispute between the parties are completely and finally determined, and all multiplicity of legal proceedings with respect to any of those matters is avoided'.

The equivalent section was relied on in the first of the New Zealand cases. The duty is imposed on the court, but there is also an implied duty on the parties[15].

1   *Phillips v Berryman* (1783) 3 Doug KB 286, 288.
2   *Buckland v Johnson* (1854) 15 CB 145, 162; para 7.08.
3   *Birmingham Corpn v S Allsopp & Sons Ltd* (1919) 119 LT 775. *Wright v London General Omnibus Co* (1877) 2 QBD 271, to the same effect, was criticised in the 1st edn because the defendant was not a party to the first proceeding, and was distinguished in *Patterson v Veitch* (1956) 58 SR NSW 257.
4   *Hills v Co-operative Wholesale Society Ltd* [1940] 2 KB 435 CA; para 21.05.
5   *Effem Foods* (1992) 36 FCR 406, 422 (the first action was under s 52 of the Trade Practices Act 1974 for misleading and deceptive conduct). This part of the decision was not challenged on appeal: (1993) 43 FCR 510, 520; paras 7.06–7.07.
6   *Zavodnyik v Alex Constructions Pty Ltd* (2005) 67 NSWLR 457 CA.
7   (1885) 15 QBD 549 CA; *Van Amstel v Country Roads Board* [1961] VR 780.
8   Ibid at 559; *Green v Weatherill* [1929] 2 Ch 213, 221; para 21.03 n 2.
9   *Dillon v Macdonald* (1902) 21 NZLR 375 CA.
10 *Neylan v Dickens* [1987] 1 NZLR 402 CA.
11 *Rangayya Goundan v Nanjappa Rao* (1901) LR 28 Ind App 221, 226 (cause of action in the first suit the agreement but presumably also its breach).
12 *King v Lintrose Nominees Pty Ltd* (2001) 4 VR 619 CA; para 7.07.
13 (1885) 15 QBD 549, 559.
14 Section 24(7) later s 43 of the Supreme Court of Judicature (Consolidation) Act 1925 which provided 'The High Court ... shall in every cause or matter ... grant ... all such remedies whatsoever as any of the parties ... may appear to be entitled to in respect of any legal or equitable claim properly brought forward by them in the cause or matter, so that, as far as is possible, all matters in controversy between the parties may be completely and finally determined, and all multiplicity of legal proceedings concerning any of those matters avoided'. The sections are directed to the remedies for the cause of action sued on: *The James Westall* [1905] P 47, 51; *United States of America v Motor Trucks Ltd* [1924] AC 196; *Harmer v Armstrong* [1934] Ch 65 CA; *Neeta (Epping) Pty Ltd v Phillips* (1974) 131 CLR 286, 307; *The Conoco Britannia* [1972] 2 QB 543, 554–555. A claimant is not required to join all possible causes of action in the one proceeding; paras 5.12 n 5, 26.18.
15 *Dillon v Macdonald* (1902) 21 NZLR 375 CA, 389.

WHERE REMEDIES CUMULATIVE

21.13   A later claim will not be barred if the causes of action or remedies are cumulative unless the claimant has obtained full satisfaction. The principles were summarised by Lord Nicholls[1]:

> 'Faced with cumulative remedies a plaintiff is not required to choose. He may have both … He may pursue one remedy or the other remedy or both … just as he wishes … He may obtain judgment for both remedies and enforce both judgments. When the remedies are against … different people he may sue both … He may do so concurrently, and obtain judgment against both. Damages to the full value of goods which have been converted may be awarded against two persons for successive conversions of the same goods. Or the plaintiff may sue the two persons successively. He may obtain judgment against one, and take steps to enforce the judgment. This does not preclude him from suing the other. There are limitations on this freedom … In the interests of fairness and finality a plaintiff is required to bring forward his whole case against a defendant in one action.[2]'

Thus a beneficiary's personal remedy against a defaulting trustee and his proprietary tracing remedy are cumulative[3]. Judgment for the defendant in an action for trespass to land where the issue was title did not bar his action for a declaration of title relying on the earlier decision as a *res judicata*[4]. An order by a court of summary jurisdiction for delivery up of goods did not bar an action for damages for their detention[5]. A party may generally enforce an equitable or contractual right to costs although a court has made an order on a less favourable basis[6], but additional costs are not recoverable from the unsuccessful party as a part of the claimant's damages on another cause of action[7]. Prior to the 1982 Act[8] and the decision in *The Indian Endurance*[9] the effect of admiralty judgments *in rem* and *in personam*, was well understood. An action *in rem* was commenced against and served on the ship. If the owners did not appear the action proceeded against the ship which was sold and all claims against her became claims on the fund. If the owners appeared the action proceeded both *in rem* and *in personam*. If the owners did not appear and the plaintiff's judgment was not satisfied he could bring an action *in personam* for the balance. Likewise a plaintiff with an unsatisfied judgment *in personam* could bring an action *in rem*. In other words a cause of action (or remedy) *in personam* did not merge in a judgment *in rem* and *vice versa*, the remedies were cumulative[10].

In *The Indian Endurance*[11] the House of Lords held that actions *in rem* and *in personam* based on the same facts involve the same parties and the same cause of action for the purposes of s 34 of the 1982 Act. Accordingly a foreign judgment *in personam* barred a domestic action *in rem*. This decision has been criticized in England[12] and distinguished or rejected in Singapore[13], New Zealand[14] and Australia[15]. The difficulties would disappear if full effect were given to the former rule that the causes of action were cumulative. On that basis s 34 would only bar second actions *in rem* or *in personam*, and not an action in *rem* after a judgment *in personam* or *vice versa*. Section 34 was intended to extend the domestic rule that a cause of action merged in a judgment[16]. It should not apply where, before the Act, a cause of action in *rem* did not merge in a domestic judgment *in personam* or *vice versa*.

1   *Tang Man Sit* [1996] AC 514, 522.
2   In *Serious Fraud Office v Lexi Holdings plc* [2009] QB 376 CA, 391, Keene LJ cited this
     sentence and referred to s 49(2) of the Supreme Court Act.
3   Ibid at 390–391.
4   *Duedu v Yiboe* [1961] 1 WLR 1040 PC.
5   *Midland Rly Co v Martin & Co* [1893] 2 QB 172.
6   *Gomba* [1993] Ch 171 CA.
7   Para 5.13 n 8.
8   Section 34 provides: 'No proceeding may be brought by a person in England or Wales or
     Northern Ireland on a cause of action in respect of which a judgment has been given in his
     favour in proceedings between the same parties or their privies in a Court in another part
     of the United Kingdom or in a Court of an overseas country, unless that judgment is not
     enforceable or entitled to recognition in England and Wales.'
9   [1998] AC 878.
10   *Nelson v Couch* (1863) 15 CBNS 99; *Yeo and Yeo v Tatem and Dwerryhouse Braginton,
     The Orient* (1871) LR 3 PC 696, 702; *The Cella* (188) 13 PD 82, 85; *The Gemma* [1899]
     P 285 CA, 291–292; *The Johannis Vatis* [1922] P 213; *The Rena K* [1979] QB 377,
     405–406; *The Indian Endurance* [1994] 2 Lloyds Rep 331, 352, 355.
11   [1998] AC 878.
12   Davenport (1998) 114 LQR 169; Teare (1998) LMCLQ 33; Derrington & Turner 'The
     Law and Practice of Admiralty Matters' 207; Derrington (2007) 123 LQR 358.
13   *Kuo v Dauphin Offshore Engineering & Trading Pty Ltd* [1999] 3 SLR 721 CA.
14   *The Irina Zharkikh* [2001] 2 NZLR 801.
15   *Comandate Marine Corpn v Pan Australia Shipping Pty Ltd* (2006) 157 FCR 45.
16   *Barber v Lamb* (1860) 8 CBNS 95; *CarlZeiss (No 2)* [1967] 1 AC 853, 917, 927, 938,
     966.

Chapter 22

MERGER IN JUDGMENT: IDENTITY OF PARTIES

GENERAL RULES

22.01 There can be no bar by former recovery unless the parties in the second action are the same or privies of those in the first[1]. Physical identity must be established by the party setting up the former recovery[2]. Judgment recovered in one capacity does not bar a claim in another[3]. There is identity where the former judgment was recovered by someone united in interest with the later claimant, such as two common informers[4]. Diversity is not established merely because a person is a claimant in one proceeding and counter-claimant[5] or defendant in the other[6].

1 *Isaacs & Sons v Salbstein* [1916] 2 KB 139 CA; Chapter 9.
2 *R v Tancock* (1876) 13 Cox CC 217 (the jury found that the victims in the indictment for murder and the conviction for manslaughter were the same).
3 *Marginson* [1939] 2 KB 426 CA; para 9.22.
4 *Girdlestone* (1879) 4 Ex D 107 CA (plea of former recovery failed because of collusion, but identity not disputed); para 9.13.
5 *Midland Rly Co v Martin & Co* [1893] 2 QB 172.
6 *Hennell v Fairlamb* (1800) 3 Esp 104 (as to so much of the set-off as answered the former claim).

EFFECT OF FORMER JUDGMENT AGAINST ONE OF SEVERAL PERSONS JOINTLY LIABLE

22.02 At common law, judgment against a joint contractor barred proceedings against the others[1]. The position was otherwise where liability was joint and several[2]. The rule for joint liability was abolished by the 1978 Act[3]. At common law the position in tort was the same and judgment against a joint tortfeasor barred proceedings against the others[4]. This was abolished by the 1935 Act[5] which assimilated the position of joint tortfeasors to that of concurrent or consecutive[6] tortfeasors. In such cases, and in the case of persons severally liable in contract, judgment against one does not bar proceedings against the others[7]. Recoveries under any judgment must be taken into account to prevent double recovery[8].

[1]   *King v Hoare* (1844) 13 M & W 494, 504–507; *Kendall v Hamilton* (1879) 4 App Cas 504, 533, 540, 542–544; *Re Hodgson* (1885) 31 Ch D 177 CA; *Hammond v Schofield* [1891] 1 QB 453; *Hoare v Niblett* [1891] 1 QB 781; *McLeod v Power* [1898] 2 Ch 295, 298–299.

[2]   *King v Hoare* (1844) 13 M & W 494, 505. The nature of the liability was determined by the intention of the parties as expressed in the contract: *Parr v Snell* [1923] 1 KB 1; *B O Morris Ltd v Perrott* [1945] 1 All ER 567 CA; *Lombard Australia Ltd v NRMA Insurance Ltd* (1968) 72 SR (NSW) 45 CA.

[3]   Section 3. Similar legislation exists in many Commonwealth jurisdictions, for NZ see *LC Fowler & Sons Ltd v St Stephens College Board of Governors* [1991] 3 NZLR 304, 310–312.

[4]   *Brinsmead v Harrison* (1872) LR 7 CP 547 Ex Ch.

[5]   Section 6, adopted in most Commonwealth jurisdictions.

[6]   *Freshwater v Bulmer Rayon Co Ltd* [1933] Ch 162; [1933] AC 661 (successive pollution by different defendants).

[7]   *Isaacs & Sons v Salbstein* [1916] 2 KB 139 CA, 143; *Bucknell v O'Donnell* (1922) 31 CLR 40.

[8]   Para 21.04 n 2.

22.03   The common law principles on joint liability in tort and contract were based on the maxim: *transit in rem judicatam*[1], merger of the one cause of action against all in a judgment against one[2].

[1]   Para 19.02.

[2]   *King v Hoare* (1844) 13 M & W 494 (per Parke B at 504: 'there is only one cause of action, whether it be against a single person or many', and this 'cause of action is changed into matter of record which is of a higher nature, and the inferior remedy is merged in the higher'); *Kendall v Hamilton* (1879) 4 App Cas 504.

22.04   Where a defendant is liable for the same debt under one contract and liable jointly with others, under another, judgment on the former does not bar an action on the latter[1]. Principal and surety are not jointly liable[2]. The *prima facie* relationship between husband and wife was formerly that of principal and agent and the creditor had to elect[3], but spouses may be jointly liable[4]. Where one person was liable as stakeholder and another as drawer of a cheque for the stake, judgment against one did not bar an action against the other provided there was no double recovery[5].

[1]   *Drake v Mitchell* (1803) 3 East 251; *Wegg Prosser v Evans* [1895] 1 QB 108, CA (judgment on cheque of one joint guarantor no bar to action against both on guarantee).

[2]   *Bermondsey Vestry v Ramsey* (1871) LR 6 CP 247 (judgment against owner for his proportion of paving expenses, recoverable by statute from 'any present or future owner or occupier', no bar to action against occupier, as surety).

[3]   *Beck v Pierce* (1889) 23 QBD 316 CA, 321; *Morel Bros v Earl of Westmorland* [1904] AC 11; *French v Howie* [1906] 2 KB 674 CA; *Moore v Flanagan* [1920] 1 KB 919 CA. Query whether this reflects modern realities.

[4]   *Hoare v Niblett* [1891] 1 QB 781, where joint liability was established and *Morel Bros & Co Ltd v Earl of Westmorland* [1904] AC 11 where it was not.

[5]   *B.O. Morris Ltd v Perrott* [1945] 1 All ER 567 CA; para 21.04 n 2.

PERSONS ALTERNATIVELY LIABLE: ELECTION

22.05   Where one of two persons is liable at the election of a claimant, judgment against one extinguishes the liability of the other: *transit in rem judicatam*[1]. Acceptance of a payment into court by one party alternatively liable, in full satisfaction, operates as a *res judicata* and discharges the other[2]. The principles were stated by the High Court of Australia in *Petersen v Maloney*[3]:

> 'It is a well-settled general principle that, while the commencement of an action against one of two persons alternatively liable does not, the entry of judgment against one of them does constitute a final and irrevocable election'.

In that case a vendor sued both estate agent and purchaser for the deposit and recovered against the agent. He appealed and was met with the argument that he had lost his rights against the purchaser by taking judgment against the agent. The argument failed because the vendor was seeking to set aside the judgment against the agent to obtain judgment against the purchaser[4]. The result does not depend on a true election but on the principle that 'there must not be more than one judgment where there is only one antecedent obligation'[5]. However a creditor who had an agent corporation wound up by the court was not barred from suing the principal[6]. A default judgment against a party alternatively liable is not necessarily a final merger. The court can set the judgment aside on the application of the claimant[7] for mistake[8], but will not act merely because the defendant consents[9].

[1]   *Morel Bros & Co Ltd v Earl of Westmorland* [1904] AC 11; *Moore v Flanagan* [1920] 1 KB 919 CA; *RMKRM v MRMVL* [1926] AC 761; *Banks v Wilson* (1910) 29 NZLR 832.
[2]   *Reardon Smith Line v Cayzer Irvine & Co. Ltd* (1929) 35 Com Cas 270, 280.
[3]   (1951) 84 CLR 91, 102.
[4]   Ibid at 103–104.
[5]   Ibid at 103.
[6]   *Con-Stan Industries of Australia Pty Ltd v Norwich Winterthur Insurance (Australia) Ltd* (1986) 160 CLR 226, 243–244, query.
[7]   *Cannan v Reynolds* (1855) 5 E & B 301; *S Kaprow & Co Ltd v Maclelland & Co Ltd* [1948] 1 KB 618 CA; *Meng Leong* [1985] AC 511, 524; *Macquarie Bank Ltd v Beaconsfield* [1992] 2 VR 461; *Sunray Irrigation Services Pty Ltd v Hortulan Pty Ltd* [1993] 2 VR 40; *Dewar & Sons Ltd v Winder* (1895) 12 TLR 54; *Sanders v Hamilton* (1907) 96 LT 679.
[8]   *Macquarie Bank v Beaconsfield* [1992] 2 VR 461 (judgment for damages to be assessed may have released defendants from guarantee); *Sunray Irrigation Services Pty Ltd v Hortulan Pty Ltd* [1993] 2 VR 40 (plaintiff not aware of undisclosed principal).
[9]   *Hammond v Schofield* [1891] 1 QB 453; *Cross & Co v Matthews and Wallace* (1904) 91 LT 500. In *M. Brennan & Sons Manufacturing Co. Ltd v Thompson* (1915) 33 Ont LR 465 AD, 472 it was suggested that a default judgment against an agent can only be set aside on the application of the plaintiff if the principal consents, but in other cases this has not been required.

22.06 Where an agent contracted for an undisclosed principal, and after discovering the facts the other party sued the principal to judgment, he could not sue the agent, whose liability had been extinguished[1]. Where in proceedings against both principal and agent default judgment was entered against the agent, the action could not proceed against the principal for the only cause of action had merged[2]. Commencement of proceedings against one of the parties liable in the alternative will not ordinarily be a binding election[3]. Where forwarding agents, contrary to instructions, delivered the goods to the consignee, and the principal obtained judgment against it for the price, he could not sue the agents for conversion[4]. In *United Australia*[5] this was said to depend on ratification of the delivery. A claimant is not put to his election where he can sue several persons independently for the same damage. He may take multiple judgments but is not entitled to double satisfaction, and must give credit for any payments[6].

1   *London General Omnibus Co Ltd v Pope* (1922) 38 TLR 270.
2   *Cross & Co v Matthews and Wallace* (1904) 91 LT 500.
3   *Clarkson Booker Ltd v Audjel* [1964] 2 QB 775 CA.
4   *Verschures Creameries Ltd v Hull and Netherlands Steamship Co* [1921] 2 KB 608 CA.
5   [1941] AC 1, 31, 52.
6   Para 21.04.

Chapter 23

AUTREFOIS CONVICT

NEMO DEBET BIS PUNIRI PRO UNO DELICTO[1]

23.01 The plea of *autrefois convict* enforces the doctrine of merger in judgment in the criminal law[2]. An accused who has been convicted[3] of an offence cannot be prosecuted again for that offence. As in civil, so in criminal law – *transit in rem judicatam*: the criminal liability of the prisoner merged in his conviction and his liability to be punished is discharged by the punishment (if any) then imposed[4]. It is often said that the principle behind the plea is that no man ought to be 'placed in jeopardy' or 'harassed' twice for the same offence[5]. But this is not sufficient, because if it were, the plea would be good, even if the former conviction was a nullity for want of jurisdiction, or had been quashed, or if a *nolle prosequi* was entered before sentence was passed[6]. It is the conviction, not the harassment, which creates the bar[7]. While the maxims *nemo debet bis puniri pro uno delicto*, and the previous maxim forbid a second conviction for the same crime, they do not forbid a second prosecution where the same conduct gave rise to separate offences[8]. What has become *res judicata* is the *offence* of which he was convicted. When criminal offences were relatively few and distinct, a single episode or course of conduct might give rise to only one offence. As the criminal law has become more complex, with the proliferation of overlapping statutory offences, a single episode or course of conduct can give rise to many offences and questions of double jeopardy and the pleas in bar have assumed increased significance[9].

[1] This paragraph in the 2nd edn was cited in *Kienapple v R* (1974) 44 DLR (3d) 351 SC 357 by Ritchie J.
[2] *Rogers v R* (1994) 181 CLR 251, 276–277; *Island Maritime* (2006) 226 CLR 328, 343.
[3] There must be a conviction. Where on an indictment containing nine counts the jury agreed on only one, and were discharged without that verdict being taken, the accused could be retried for all offences: *R v Robinson* [1975] QB 508.
[4] *Wemyss v Hopkins* (1875) LR 10 QB 378, 381, *Connelly* [1964] AC 1254, 1320, 1362; *Island Maritime* (2006) 226 CLR 328, 343.
[5] *R v Haughton Inhabitants* (1853) 1 E & B 501, 506; *R v Ollis* [1900] 2 QB 758, 771.
[6] *Richards v R* [1993] AC 217; *Maxwell v R* (1996) 184 CLR 501.
[7] This sentence in the 3rd edn was cited in *Pearce v R* (1998) 194 CLR 610, 627 by Gummow J.
[8] 'The learned Judge did not intend to lay down, and did not lay down, as a general principle of law that a man cannot be placed twice in jeopardy upon the same facts if the offences are different': per Lord Reading CJ in *R v Barron* [1914] 2 KB 570, 575 (an *autrefois*

291

acquit case) referring to *R v King* [1897] 1 QB 214 (an *autrefois convict* case); *R v Tonks* [1916] 1 KB 443, 575; *R v Thomas* [1950] 1 KB 26, 31: 'It is not the law that a person shall not be liable to be punished twice for the same act; it has never been so stated in any case'. In *Connelly* [1964] AC 1254, 1307–1308 Lord Morris said: 'The principle seems clearly to have been recognised that if someone had been either convicted or acquitted of an offence he could not later be charged with the same offence … That, however, did not mean that if two separate offences were committed at the same time a conviction or an acquittal in respect of one would be any bar to a subsequent prosecution in respect of the other. It was the offence or offences that had to be considered. Was there in substance one offence – or had someone committed two or more offences?'

9   *Island Maritime* (2006) 226 CLR 328, 344.

DISTINCTION BETWEEN AUTREFOIS ACQUIT AND AUTREFOIS CONVICT

23.02 The pleas of *autrefois acquit* and *autrefois convict* are based on different principles. *Autrefois acquit* precludes the Crown from reasserting guilt after that has been decided in favour of the accused[1], *autrefois convict* precludes the Crown reasserting guilt after that has formally been determined in its favour by conviction and sentence[2]. *Autrefois acquit* is considered in Chapter 14 which should also be consulted.

1   Chapter 14.
2   *Wemyss v Hopkins* (1875) LR 10 QB 378, 381; *Richards v R* [1993] AC 217; *Maxwell v R* (1996) 184 CLR 501, 509–10; *R v Stone* (2005) 64 NSWLR 413, 428–429; *R v Carroll* (2002) 213 CLR 635, 646.

FINAL ADJUDICATION NECESSARY

23.03 The plea can only be supported by proof of a final adjudication involving both conviction and sentence. Where a plea of guilty to manslaughter was accepted, but a *nolle prosequi* was filed before the accused was sentenced, the plea was not available[1]. A conviction for common assault followed by an order binding over the defendant to keep the peace will support this plea[2]. A conviction which has been quashed will not[3].

1   *Richards v R* [1993] AC 217; *Maxwell v R* (1996) 184 CLR 501, 509–10; *R v Stone* (2005) 64 NSWLR 413, 428–429.
2   *R v Miles* (1890) 24 QBD 423.
3   *R v Marsham* [1912] 2 KB 362; *Bannister v Clarke* [1920] 3 KB 598, 605–607.

HOW FAR OFFENCE CHARGED MUST BE IDENTICAL WITH THAT PREVIOUSLY CHARGED

23.04 In *Connelly*[1] Lord Morris formulated propositions defining the scope of this plea, and that of *autrefois acquit*, which were thought to be part of the ratio[2], but in *R v Beedie*[3] the third and fourth were rejected by Rose LJ. The relevant passages are quoted in para 14.12. This plea in bar is only available where the elements of the offences are identical, or all the elements of one are included in the other. The common law does not prevent an offender being convicted of different offences arising out of the same events. An offender can only be punished for the offence or offences charged and the prosecution will generally frame charges to fully reflect the offender's criminal conduct during the relevant events[4]. Thus an offender could be convicted on the one indictment of maliciously inflicting grievous bodily harm with intent, and breaking and entering a dwelling house and inflicting grievous bodily harm. The offences overlapped but were not identical and the elements of the first were not wholly included in the second or *vice versa*[5].

[1] [1964] AC 1254.
[2] *For example,* successive editions of Archbold until 1997, and the 2nd and 3rd editions of this work.
[3] [1998] QB 356 CA, para 14.12.
[4] Para 14.18; *Pearce v R* (1998) 194 CLR 610, 618.
[5] Ibid at 620.

23.05 The focus is on the elements of the offences[1] and not on the witnesses or their evidence[2]. In *R v Thomas* the accused was convicted of wounding his wife with intent to murder, and after her death was convicted of murder. Humphreys J said[3]:

'... on 2 May the accused was not convicted of [murder] nor of anything which is substantially the same offence or crime as that charged in the [later indictment], nor could he have been since his wife was then alive. It follows that the plea of *autrefois convict* in the strict sense of the term is bound to fail.'

The plea can only answer the offence charged if that was committed before or at the time of the first offence[4]. The true question is 'whether the facts necessary to support a conviction for each offence are the same'[5], but this should not be misunderstood. The court considers the elements of each offence, not the evidence required to secure a conviction[6]. The principle applies to summary prosecutions although, as a matter of procedure, the plea is not available[7]. The Supreme Court of Canada has adopted a different test for *autrefois convict*, known as the rule against multiple convictions[8], which has not been followed elsewhere and, in the author's opinion, is not likely to be[9].

[1] In *R v Thomson Holidays Ltd* [1974] QB 592 a tour operator that distributed a travel brochure containing false statements committed a separate offence each time it was distributed. Accordingly, a plea of *autrefois convict* based on distribution to one group of customers was no answer to prosecutions for communicating it to others.
[2] *Pearce v R* (1998) 194 CLR 610, 615–620, 628.
[3] [1950] 1 KB 26, 29; *R v Morris* (1867) LR 1 CCR 90; *Connelly* [1964] AC 1254, 1318–1319.
[4] *R v Tonks* [1916] 1 KB 443, 450; *R v Thomas* [1950] 1 KB 26.
[5] *Atkinson v United States Government* [1971] AC 197, 211 (attempted armed robbery and aggravated burglary different offences). If a prisoner is charged with murder and convicted of manslaughter another charge of murder on the same facts will be barred, but if he is charged and convicted of manslaughter *R v Tancock* (1876) 13 Cox CC 217 suggests that he may later be indicted for murder. The decision was criticised by Lord Morris in *Connelly* [1964] AC 1254, 1311 and a second prosecution would be barred by the principle that prevents sequential trials for offences of ascending gravity: para 23.06.
[6] *Pearce v R* (1998) 194 CLR 610, 617, 620, 628; *R v Brightwell* [1995] 2 NZLR 435 CA, 438–439.
[7] *Wemyss v Hopkins* (1875) LR 10 QB 378, 381; *Flatman v Light* [1946] KB 414, 419.
[8] *Kienapple v R* (1974) 44 DLR (3d) 351 (5:4 majority). The accused was charged in the one indictment with rape and unlawful sexual intercourse with a girl under 14 to which consent was not a defence. He was convicted on both counts. The majority held that they were alternative charges for the same act, the accused could not be convicted of both, and

his conviction on the second charge was set aside. It is submitted that the majority judgment delivered by Laskin J is flawed, and the dissenting judgment of Ritchie J reflects established common law principles. There is no objection at common law to two or more convictions for separate offences arising out of the same facts provided they are not inconsistent. The convictions in that case were not inconsistent. Although a prosecution on the second charge after a conviction for rape would have been an abuse both charges were in the same indictment. In *R v Prince* (1986) 33 DLR (4th) 724 the Supreme Court reviewed the later Canadian case law and the resulting technicalities.

9   *R v Sessions* [1998] 2 VR 304 CA, 315. In *Pearce v R* (1998) 194 CLR 610 the prisoner was convicted on the same indictment for maliciously inflicting grievous bodily harm with intent and for breaking and entering a dwelling house and inflicting grievous bodily harm. A plea in bar was not available because the second offence contained elements which were not included in the first, and there was no abuse of process because one offence was not wholly included in the other. In *R v Sessions* the court held that the prisoner could not be convicted for both rape (by digital penetration) and recklessly causing serious injury which would punish him twice for the same act. *Pearce* establishes that the prisoner was properly convicted on both charges because the elements of neither charge were wholly included in the other.

LATER CHARGE FOR AGGRAVATED OFFENCE BARRED

23.06 A wider application of the principles which underlie this plea prevents sequential trials for offences of increasing gravity. In *R v Elrington*[1]. Cockburn CJ said:

'… a series of charges shall not be proffered, and whether a party accused of a minor offence is acquitted or convicted, he shall not be charged again on the same facts in a more aggravated form.'

There was a division of opinion in *Connelly*[2] on the application of this principle. All the Law Lords, other than Lord Reid, held that a plea in bar could be available in an *Elrington* case[3], but Lord Devlin and Lord Pearce held[4] that the principle could also apply where a plea in bar was not available and in *R v Beedie*[5] a conviction in breach of this rule where the plea was not available was quashed. This is now the accepted position in Australia[6]. The principle was considered in *R v Arnold* where Hughes LJ, said[7]:

'The *Elrington* principle is a rule against sequential trials. It is in no sense breached if two charges arising out of the same facts are put before the Court on the same occasion.'

1   (1861) 1 B & S 688, 696 (charges of assault, then aggravated assault); approved in *Connelly* [1964] AC 1254, 1315–1317, 1332, 1357–1358, 1363, 1367; *R v Beedie* [1998] QB 356, 362 (regulatory offences, then manslaughter); *R v Dodd* (1991) 56 Aust Crim Rep 451, 457 per Gleeson CJ (conviction for possession of prohibited drug barred charge of possession with intent to supply); *Island Maritime* (2006) 226 CLR 328, 339.
2   [1964] AC 1254.
3   Ibid at 1315, 1332, 1358, 1367.
4   Ibid at 1358, 1367.
5   [1998] QB 356.
6   *R v Carroll* (2002) 213 CLR 635. The earlier view in *R v Dodd* (1991) 56 Aust Crim Rep 451, 457 that the principle is no wider is no longer accepted: *Gilham v R* (2007) 178 Aust Crim Rep 72.
7   [2008] 1 WLR 2881, 2892.

CONVICTION FOR OFFENCE WHOLLY WITHIN LATER CHARGE

23.07   This plea in bar or equivalent applies not only where the elements of each offence are identical, but also where all the elements of one are included in the other[1]. If there are four elements in the first charge and those and others in the second, a conviction on the latter will be the second for the offence with the common elements. If there were six elements in the first charge and four of them in the second, a conviction on the latter will be the second for the offence with the common elements. The problem does not arise, outside Canada, at a trial with overlapping counts. The plea of *autrefois convict* will not be before the jury and verdicts of guilty will be open. Thus a person acquitted of murder may be convicted of manslaughter when both charges were included in the indictment[2]. Where the second prosecution is for an aggravated form[3] of the earlier offence, this and the *Elrington* principle produce the same result. Thus in *Wemyss v Hopkins*[4] a conviction for a statutory offence that 'amounted to an assault' barred a prosecution under another Act for assault. In *Welton v Taneborne*[5] a conviction for driving in a manner dangerous based on a finding of excessive speed barred a prosecution for speeding.

[1]   *Pearce v R* (1998) 194 CLR 610, 620; *Island Maritime* (2006) 226 CLR 328, 339, 342–343, 345.
[2]   *DPP v Nasralla* [1967] 2 AC 238.
[3]   Para 23.06.
[4]   (1875) LR 10 QB 378, 381.
[5]   (1908) 99 LT 668.

SCOPE OF PLEA

23.08   A conviction by an inferior court is a bar to a further prosecution for the same offence in that, or any other court[1]. The plea may be supported by a conviction in a foreign court for the same or substantially the same offence based on the same facts[2]. It is not available where the accused was not in jeopardy abroad, eg where he has been tried in his absence and cannot be extradited[3]. A finding of guilt and the imposition of a penalty by a domestic tribunal will not support the plea[4]. The Supreme Court of Canada held that there was no double jeopardy where a policeman disciplined for assault was later charged with a criminal offence based on the same facts[5], and the Court of Appeal has recently come to the same conclusion where the order of events was reversed[6]. The armed services legislation provides that where a person subject to military law has been tried for an offence by a court-martial, he cannot be tried by a civil court for substantially the same offence, and the reverse also applies[7]. The conviction of a member of the armed forces under military law did not prevent administrative action to dismiss the offender from the service[8].

[1]   *R v Miles* (1890) 24 QBD 423; *R v King* [1897] 1 QB 214; *R v Tonks* [1916] 1 KB 443. For convictions barring proceedings in courts of summary jurisdiction: *R v Brisby* (1849) 18 LJMC 157; *Welton v Taneborne* (1908) 99 LT 668; *R v Marsham* [1912] 2 KB 362.
[2]   *Treacy v DPP* [1971] AC 537, 562; para 14.10.
[3]   *R v Thomas* [1985] QB 604.

23.08 *Autrefois convict*

4   *Lewis v Mogan* [1943] 1 KB 376; *Health Care Complaints Commission v Litchfield* (1997) 41 NSWLR 630 CA (doctor acquitted of criminal offence struck off for the same conduct); *Re Barings plc (No 2), Secretary of State for Trade and Industry v Baker (No. 2)* [1999] 1 WLR 1985 CA.

5   *R v Wigglesworth* (1987) 45 DLR (4th) 235.

6   *R (on the application of Redgrave) v Metropolitan Police* [2003]1 WLR 1136 CA.

7   Army Act 1955 (as amended) ss 133, 134; Air Force Act 1955 (as amended) ss 133, 134; Naval Discipline Act 1957 s 129; Armed Forces Act 1966 (as amended) s 26.

8   *Stuart v Chief of the Army* (1999) 94 FCR 445 (the offence was theft).

WHEN PLEA SHOULD BE RAISED

23.09 The plea of *autrefois convict* is a plea in bar[1] and should be raised on arraignment. The accused has the onus of proof, but only to the civil standard.[2] If there is no case to be tried, the judge can direct the jury to return the appropriate verdict on the plea.[3] Where a meritorious plea is raised for the first time on appeal the court will, if possible, determine it on the merits.[4] The plea cannot be considered with a plea of not guilty.[5]

1   *R v Thomas* [1950] 1 KB 26, 28.

2   *R v Coughlan* (1976) 63 Cr App Rep 33.

3   *R v Tonks* [1916] 1 KB 443, 448.

4   Ibid at 446, 448.

5   *R v Banks* [1911] 2 KB 1095; *R v Kent Newbold* (1940) 62 CLR 398; *R v Stone* (2005) 64 NSWLR 413, 418.

SENTENCING FOR MULTIPLE CONVICTIONS FROM SAME EVENTS

23.10 The principle against double jeopardy is relevant at the sentencing stage when an offender has been convicted of two or more offences arising from the same events. In *Pearce v R* McHugh, Hayne and Callinan JJ said[1]:

> 'To the extent to which the offences of which an offender stands convicted contain common elements, it would be wrong to punish that offender twice for the commission of the elements that are common ... To punish an offender twice if conduct falls in that area of overlap would be to punish offenders according to the accidents of legislative history, rather than ... their just deserts.'

The court distinguished *R v Thomas* where Humphreys J said[2] that 'it is not the law that a person shall not be liable to be punished twice for the same act.' Thomas who had been convicted in his wife's lifetime of wounding her with intent to murder was convicted of murder after her death. The offences had different elements, and the second had not been committed when he was convicted of the first. Pearce had been sentenced for overlapping offences to fully concurrent terms of 12 years with a minimum (non-parole) term of eight years. The High Court held[3] that such an approach could mask error and the judge should have fixed an appropriate sentence for each offence and then considered questions of cumulation, concurrence and totality. Although the overall effect was not disproportionate the individual sentences were flawed because they doubly punished the appellant for the infliction of grievous bodily harm and failed to reflect differences in the conduct being punished.

¹   (1998) 194 CLR 610, 623, and per Gummow J at 629. The offences were maliciously
    inflicting grievous bodily harm with intent, and breaking and entering a dwelling house
    and inflicting grievous bodily harm. The principle was not infringed where the accused was
    sentenced to seven years imprisonment for wounding with intent to cause grievous bodily
    harm and was prosecuted for murder after the victim died when he faced a mandatory
    non-parole period of 20 years: *PNJ v R* (2009) 83 ALJR 384.
²   [1950] 1 KB 26, 31.
³   (1998) 194 CLR 610, 624, 629; *R v Arnold* [2008] 1 WLR 2881, 2892 para [36].

STAY FOR ABUSE OF PROCESS

23.11 This remedy, and the passages in *Connolly*¹ which confirmed its
existence, are considered in paras 14.20–14.23.

¹   [1964] AC 1254.

23.12 The power to stay vexatious or oppressive criminal proceedings
following a conviction was exercised in *R v Beedie*¹. The court referred to the
duty of the prosecution, in the absence of special circumstances, to include in
the indictment all charges founded on the same facts², and the principle that
there must not be sequential trials for offences of increasing gravity³. A
landlord had been convicted of regulatory offences following the death of a
tenant from carbon monoxide poisoning from a defective gas fire. He was
then prosecuted for manslaughter on the same facts. The court held that the
prosecution should have been stayed and quashed the conviction. A plea of
autrefois convict was not available because the elements of the earlier offences
were not within the latter⁴. Where the accused pleaded guilty to charges of
obtaining money by forged instruments, and received light sentences, new
charges relating to different documents and different sums were not an abuse
of process although the relevant documents had been in the possession of the
Crown at the time of the first trial because they were not for the same
criminality⁵.

¹   [1998] QB 356.
²   Ibid at 362, 364 (citing Lord Devlin in *Connelly* at 1353 'it is absolutely necessary that
    issues of fact that are substantially the same should whenever practicable, be tried by the
    same tribunal and at the same time'); para 14.18.
³   Ibid at 366.
⁴   Ibid at 360, 361 (same offence in second indictment), 363 (the same or substantially the
    same charge); *Pearce v R* (1998) 194 CLR 610, 620.
⁵   *R v Williams and Wilson* [1965] NI 52, 61–62.

23.13 The nature of the discretion is considered in para 14.23.

23.14 The recent New South Wales case of *Gilham v R*¹ and the dicta in *R v
Arnold*² are considered in para 14.22.

¹   (2007) 178 Aust Crim Rep 72.
²   [2008] 1 WLR 2881, 2892.

Chapter 24

MERGER IN JUDGMENT: AFFIRMATIVE ANSWERS

24.01 The affirmative answers to a *prima facie* case of *res judicata* estoppel have been considered[1]. Of these, fraud and cross-estoppel can seldom be an answer to a *prima facie* case of former recovery, and public policy and illegality are not relevant.

[1] Chapter 17.

24.02 A claimant cannot be heard to say that he fraudulently secured the judgment pleaded against him[1], but where the claimants are different individuals litigating in the same right, such as common informers, the second can defeat the bar by proof that the first obtained his judgment by fraudulent collusion with the defendant[2]. If the defendant's fraud reduced the claimant's recovery the latter can have the case reopened[3]. The proper remedy is an action to have the judgment set aside for fraud[4] which is not available for foreign judgments. This did not matter before 1982 because a plaintiff with a foreign judgment could sue on his original cause of action. This rule was abolished by the 1982 Act where the foreign judgment is entitled to recognition. A foreign judgment in the EU can only be impeached if fraud is within the public policy exception in Council Regulation 44/2001[5]. If not the only remedy will be a challenge in the country where the judgment was given, if this is possible. Judgments from countries outside the EU may still be challenged for fraud, and a claimant faced with a plea of former recovery based on such a judgment which was procured by the defendant's fraud can plead the fraud in his reply, or in an amendment to the particulars of claim.

[1] *Nemo allegans suam turpitudinem est audiendus* – a familiar maxim of the common law described as founded upon 'moral estoppel': *Gibson v Minet* (1791) 1 Hy Bl 569 HL, 611 per Eyre CB.
[2] *Girdlestone* (1879) 4 Ex D 107 CA.
[3] Para 17.04 n 9.
[4] Para 17.04 n5.
[5] Para 22.05 nn 7–9.

MISTAKE

24.03 A plaintiff sued for specific performance of an agreement for lease for a smaller area than that agreed to. He succeeded, and a lease was executed pursuant to the decree. When the mistake was discovered he brought a second action, and obtained a supplementary decree for the omitted area[1]. A consent judgment may be set aside on the same grounds, including mistake, as a contract[2]. The court can also set aside a default judgment for mistake on the application of the claimant[3].

[1]   *Blinkhorne v Brenchley* (1898) 16 NZLR 498. Query whether the cause of action and the contract had not merged in the original decree: *McGrory v Alderdale Estate Co* [1918] AC 503, 511.
[2]   Para 17.14.
[3]   Paras 17.16, 25.01.

CROSS-ESTOPPEL

24.04 A later judgment cannot create a cross-estoppel[1]. Estoppel may be an affirmative answer where the party entitled to set up the bar waived the right or estopped himself from raising it[2].

[1]   *Showlag v Mansour* [1995] 1 AC 431.
[2]   See paras 17.16 and 25.01. This paragraph in the 2nd edn was cited in *The Indian Grace* [1993] AC 410, 423.

OTHER ANSWERS

24.05 It is an affirmative answer that the former judgment has been reversed[1] or set aside[2]. It is no answer that the claimant is a public official suing on behalf of the Crown[3].

[1]   *Partington v Hawthorne* (1888) 52 JP 807; *M. Brennan & Sons Manufacturing Co. Ltd v Thompson* (1915) 33 Ont LR 465 AD, 470–471.
[2]   Para 22.05; *C Inc plc v L* [2001] 2 Lloyds Rep 459, 480.
[3]   *Chamberlain* (1988) 164 CLR 502; para 13.11.

Chapter 25

MERGER IN JUDGMENT: PLEADING AND PROCEDURE

25.01 The general rules of pleading and procedure have been considered[1]. A party wishing to set up a former recovery must plead it, if possible, at the earliest opportunity[2]. Although in earlier times failure to plead or raise the point at the first opportunity was fatal[3], delay is now only one of the matters considered in the exercise of the discretion to grant leave to amend or otherwise take the point at a later stage[4]. The question may be tried as a preliminary issue. This is preferable to a motion to dismiss the action or strike out a defence as frivolous and vexatious, because the question should be argued in court and not in chambers[5].

[1] Chapter 18.
[2] *Edevain v Cohen* (1889) 43 Ch D 187 CA, 189; para 17.16, 18.03–18.04.
[3] Ibid at 189.
[4] Para 18.09.
[5] *Workington Harbour and Dock Board v Trade Indemnity Co Ltd (No 2)* [1938] 2 All ER 101 HL, 102.

25.02 The plea under the RSC was:

'The plaintiff heretofore, in the Court of --- , sued the defendant in an action for the same cause of action as in the statement of claim alleged, and such proceedings were thereupon had in that action that the plaintiff afterwards by the judgment of the said Court recovered against the defendant £--- for the said cause of action, and the said judgment remains in force'.

25.03 If the claimant disputes the facts in the plea, he should reply no such record, or its equivalent[1]: but if he disputes the identity of the causes of action or the parties, he must raise that issue in his reply[2]. If he challenges the legal sufficiency of the plea[3], or if the defendant challenges the legal sufficiency of the reply[4], the question can be raised on a strike out application, or as a preliminary question of law.

[1] *Florence v Jenings* (1857) 2 CBNS 454.
[2] *Girdlestone* (1879) 4 Ex D 107 CA.
[3] *Gibbs v Cruikshank* (1873) LR 8 CP 454.
[4] *Brinsmead v Harrison* (1872) LR 7 CP 547 Ex Ch.

25.04   An amendment to raise a plea of former recovery should be sought as early as possible, and leave may be refused if sought at a late stage[1]. An amendment will be allowed when the existence of the former judgment becomes known after pleadings have closed[2].

[1]   *Edevain v Cohen* (1889) 43 Ch D 187 CA, 190; *Ketteman v Hansel Properties Ltd* [1987] AC 189; *Aon Risk Services Australia Ltd v Australian National University* (2009) 83 ALJR 951.

[2]   *McLeod v Power* [1898] 2 Ch 295, para 25.05 n 4.

MODE OF RAISING THE QUESTION OF FORMER RECOVERY OTHERWISE THAN BY PLEADING

25.05   A party entitled to plead the former judgment who fails to do so cannot rely upon it as a bar[1] without the necessary amendment. However an unpleaded former judgment may support a plea of payment[2]. Where there was no opportunity, and therefore no duty, to plead the former judgment, the objection must be raised at the earliest opportunity. A party wishing to raise an unpleaded former recovery can do so at the first available occasion before trial where proceedings are conducted without pleadings, or in a court of summary jurisdiction[3], or when the judgment is obtained[4].

[1]   Paras 18.03, 19.01.
[2]   *Barber v Lamb* (1860) 8 CBNS 95; para 20.04.
[3]   *Wemyss v Hopkins* (1875) LR 10 QB 378; *Welton v Taneborne* (1908) 99 LT 668.
[4]   *McLeod v Power* [1898] 2 Ch 295, (the judgment was not obtained until after defence and Byrne J gave effect to the unpleaded objection of former recovery, though he deprived the defendant of costs because he should have amended to plead the former judgment as a 'matter arising pending the action').

PART 3

THE EXTENDED AND ROMAN LAW DOCTRINES

Chapter 26

THE EXTENDED RES JUDICATA DOCTRINE

INTRODUCTION

26.01 Defences of *res judicata* and former recovery are available where the cause of action sued upon has been litigated to judgment[1], and issue estoppels where an issue of fact or law, raised in later proceedings between the same parties, contradicts the determination of an ultimate issue fundamental to an earlier decision[2], subject to the special circumstances exception[3]. Issue estoppels also cover issues which can be inferred were actually decided[4], and other questions fundamental to the earlier decision although, not then, in contention[5]. Finally there is the extended doctrine based on abuse of process. In considering the latter it is important to remember the words of Lowry CJ[6]:

> 'The entire corpus of authority in issue estoppel is based on the theory that it is not an abuse of process to relitigate a point where any of the ... requirements of the doctrine is missing'.

[1] Paras 7.01–7.02, 19.01.
[2] Para 8.23.
[3] Paras 8.31–8.35.
[4] Paras 8.08–8.10.
[5] Paras 8.11–8.12.
[6] *Shaw v Sloan* [1982] NI 393 CA, 397.

REICHEL V MAGRATH

26.02 The doctrine was applied in *Reichel v Magrath*[1] although the plaintiff had the benefit of issue estoppels which were not recognised or acknowledged[2]. The defendant, a clergyman, resigned his parish but changed his mind. The first case[3] established that his resignation had taken effect, and the patrons and the bishop appointed the plaintiff to the vacant parish. The defendant refused to leave and when the plaintiff brought ejectment his plea that he was the rector was struck out as an abuse. Lord Halsbury LC said[4]:

> '... it would be a scandal to the administration of justice if, the same question having been disposed of by one case the litigant were to be permitted by

305

changing the form of the proceedings to set up the same case again ... there must be an inherent jurisdiction in every Court of Justice to prevent such an abuse of its procedure'.

The case law developed along normal lines although in many cases a *res judicata* estoppel was available[5].

1 (1889) 14 App Cas 665.
2 Paras 9.45 nn 2–5, 10.11 nn 3–4.
3 *Reichel v Bishop of Oxford* (1889) 14 App Cas 259.
4 (1889) 14 App Cas 665, 668.
5 *Macdougall v Knight* (1890) 25 QBD 1 CA; *Montgomery v Russell* (1894) 11 TLR 112 CA; *Stephenson v Garnett* [1898] 1 QB 677 CA (an issue estoppel was available although the decision was interlocutory; para 5.31 n 1).

HENDERSON

26.03 The doctrine was cross fertilised with the *Henderson* principle in *Greenhalgh v Mallard*[1]. The extended doctrine has been attributed to *Henderson*[2] but this involved a cause of action estoppel[3]. A partnership between two brothers, Jordan and Bethel, had branches in Newfoundland and Bristol. Their late father had also given £15,000 to Bethel in England in trust for Jordan. Following the death of Jordan in Newfoundland his widow and adult children took proceedings there for an account of the partnership and the estate of the father possessed by Bethel on account of Jordan. Bethel pleaded that Jordan was indebted to him on the balance of the partnership accounts, that the gift from their father formed part of the assets of the partnership, and that the estate of Jordan was indebted to him for a private debt. He failed to appear at the trial and a decree was made *ex parte* for the taking of the accounts. He again failed to appear and the Master found that £15,000 plus interest was due to the widow and adult children, but did not take an account of the partnership because Bethel had not produced the books. The plaintiffs took a decree on further consideration for the balance found by the Master. When they sued Bethel on this decree in England he commenced proceedings in Chancery to enforce the claims he had not pressed in Newfoundland. The judgment of Wigram VC upholding a demurrer to this suit for *res judicata* contained his familiar statement of principle[4]. He added[5]:

> '... the whole of the case made by this Bill might have been adjudicated upon in the suit in Newfoundland, for it was of the very substance of the case there, and prima facie therefore the whole is settled'.

He held that there were no special circumstances to displace the general rule. The decision that an account is final and covers all debit and credit items which could have been brought forward is well established[6].

1 [1947] 2 All ER 255 CA.
2 (1843) 3 Hare 100; 'A closer look at Henderson v Henderson' Handley (2002) 118 LQR 397; paras 7.03, 7.14.
3 *Carl-Zeiss (No 2)* [1967] 1 AC 853, 916, 946, 966; *Arnold* [1991] 2 AC 93, 107; *Johnson* [2002] 2 AC 1, 30–31.
4 Quoted para 7.03.
5 (1843) 3 Hare 100, 116.
6 Paras 7.14–7.15.

HENDERSON AND ABUSE OF PROCESS

26.04 *Henderson* came to attention in *Hoystead*[1] as authority that a decision is *res judicata* on 'any point ... of assumption or admission which was in substance the ratio of and fundamental to the decision'. *Greenhalgh v Mallard*[2] brought the two strands of authority together. The plaintiff failed in an action for conspiracy to injure, ie a conspiracy for an unlawful purpose. He then brought an action on the same facts for conspiracy to injure by unlawful means. Somervell LJ held that a given set of facts gave rise to only one cause of action for conspiracy, and the second action was barred by *res judicata*[3], but he also invoked the *Henderson* principle[4]:

> ' ... res judicata ... is not confined to the issues which the Court is actually asked to decide, but ... covers issues ... which are so clearly part of the subject matter of the litigation, so clearly could have been raised that it would be an abuse of the process of the court to allow a new proceeding to be started in respect of them'.

This decision was followed in *Wright v Bennett*[5] where an action for fraud having failed, the plaintiff brought a second action on the same facts for fraudulent conspiracy. Tucker LJ[6], held that the court should exercise its inherent jurisdiction to prevent the defendants being called on 'in substance and in reality to meet the same old charge'. The other judges agreed, but Cohen LJ rightly held that the action was barred by *res judicata*[7]. In *Asher*[8] the Secretary of State had directed the district auditor to conduct an extraordinary audit of a local authority. He surcharged the councillors who appealed unsuccessfully to the Divisional Court. They then challenged the direction of the Secretary of State in the High Court claiming a declaration that the auditor was not entitled to raise the surcharge. The action was dismissed for abuse of process and Lord Denning MR said[9] that, although the direction could have been challenged in the appeal, the matter was strictly not *res judicata*[10].

[1] [1926] AC 155, 170. *Henderson* was cited in the dissenting judgment of Higgins J: (1921) 29 CLR 537, 561, which was upheld by the Privy Council, but at that stage it had only been cited in England once since 1889 and rarely before that: 67 ER 313.
[2] [1947] 2 All ER 255 CA.
[3] Ibid at 257, 259.
[4] Ibid at 257.
[5] [1948] 1 All ER 227 CA.
[6] Ibid at 230.
[7] Ibid at 230. He was correct.
[8] [1974] Ch 208 CA.
[9] Ibid at 222.
[10] Lawton LJ applied *Henderson* and held that the validity of the direction was *res judicata*: ibid at 228; but the Secretary of State was not a party to the appeal and there could be no *res judicata* estoppel: para 9.05.

YAT TUNG AND THE KILBRANDON PRINCIPLE

26.05 The following year the Privy Council decided *Yat Tung*[1]. In the original proceedings brought by its customer the bank counterclaimed for the balance due under its mortgage and recovered practically the full amount[2]. Its counterclaim assumed the regularity of its sale of the security under the power in the mortgage[3]. The customer then commenced proceedings for a declaration that the sale was fraudulent, or in breach of duty, claiming $900,000 damages. Lord Kilbrandon held that *res judicata* was not available 'since there has not been … any formal repudiation of the pleas raised by the appellant'[4] and the purchaser had not been a party to the earlier proceedings[5]. However he affirmed the finding in the Full Court of Hong Kong that the new claim[6] was an abuse of process because it was '… clearly a matter necessary and proper to be litigated' in the earlier action, but then went further[7]:

> 'But there is a wider sense in which the extended doctrine may be appealed to, so that it becomes an abuse of process to raise in subsequent proceedings matters which could and therefore should have been litigated in earlier proceedings'. [emphasis supplied]

The actual decision was correct but the Kilbrandon principle that would bar proceedings in respect of all matters which could have been litigated in earlier proceedings was far too wide. In any event the judgment on the bank's counterclaim created a cause of action estoppel[8]. The customer's claim for a loss from the 'wrongful' sale[9] properly arose in the mortgage account sought by the bank's counterclaim, and not having been raised, as in *Henderson*, it was barred[10].

[1]   [1975] AC 581.
[2]   Ibid at 586.
[3]   Ibid at 587.
[4]   Ibid at 590.
[5]   The purchaser was a privy claiming under the bank.
[6]   [1975] AC 581, 589.
[7]   Ibid (the Kilbrandon principle).
[8]   Paras 7.14–7.15; 'A closer look at *Henderson v Henderson*' Handley (2002) 118 LQR 397.
[9]   [1975] AC 581, 586, 588.
[10]   The failure of the Board to decide the case on this basis is surprising since *Public Trustee v Kenward* [1967] 1 WLR 1062 was cited; paras 7.14–7.15.

REJECTION OF KILBRANDON PRINCPLE

26.06 The retreat from the Kilbrandon principle began in 1978 with the judgment of Lord Wilberforce in *Brisbane CC v A-G for Queensland*[1]. It was rejected by the High Court of Australia in *Anshun*[2] in 1981, and was criticised in the previous edition[3]. It continued to be applied from time to time in England and it was applied in *Johnson* by the Court of Appeal but rejected by the House of Lords[4]. The facts illustrate the anomalous and unjust results produced by the principle. The plaintiff, a property developer and his company retained the defendants as their solicitors in certain transactions. The company's action for negligence against the solicitors was settled for £1.8 million inclusive of costs. The plaintiff then brought proceedings to recover his personal losses. He had made a deliberate decision, for financial reasons, to defer his personal claims, and the defendants were well aware that a personal action was contemplated when they settled the company's action. The personal action had been pending for four and a half years[5] before the solicitors applied for its summary dismissal as an abuse of process. The Court of Appeal ordered summary dismissal, but this decision was unanimously reversed. Lord Bingham, who gave the principal speech on this issue, rejected the Kilbrandon principle and confined the extended doctrine to cases of recognisable abuse. He said[6]:

> 'The bringing of a claim or the raising of a defence in later proceedings may, without more, amount to abuse if the Court is satisfied ... that the claim or defence should have been raised in the earlier proceedings if it was to be raised at all. I would not accept that it is necessary ... to identify any additional element such as a collateral attack on a previous decision or some dishonesty, but where those elements are present the latter proceedings will be much more obviously abusive, and there will rarely be a finding of abuse unless the later proceeding involves ... unjust harassment of a party. It is, however, wrong to hold that because a matter could have been raised in earlier proceedings it should have been, so as to render the raising of it in later proceedings necessarily abusive. That is to adopt too dogmatic an approach to what should ... be a broad, merits-based judgment which takes account of the public and private interests involved ... one cannot formulate any hard and fast rule to determine whether, on given facts, abuse is to be found or not.'

Johnson has been followed by the Supreme Court of Ireland[7]. The plaintiff brought judicial review proceedings to restrain prosecutions for undue delay which failed. He then brought proceedings to challenge the constitutional validity of the section creating the offences, which were dismissed as abusive since the claim could have been included in the earlier proceedings, but the Supreme Court allowed the plaintiff's appeal.

[1] [1979] AC 411, 425.
[2] (1981) 147 CLR 589.
[3] 3rd edn, para 452.
[4] [2002] 2 AC 1.
[5] Ibid at 20.
[6] Ibid at 31.
[7] *SM v Ireland* [2007] 3 IR 283 SC.

COLLATERAL ATTACK ON CRIMINAL OR CIVIL DECISION

26.07 Thomas LJ, commenting on *Johnson*, said[1]:

> 'It is generally neither necessary nor helpful to refer to the accretion of authority before that decision, [which] clearly sets out the principles the Courts are to apply.'

Although this is true for cases after *Yat Tung* where the Kilbrandon principle was applied, other cases remain relevant. *Hunter* involved civil proceedings for assault against police officers[2]. The principal evidence against Hunter at his criminal trial was his confession, and there was a dispute as to whether, if made, it was voluntary. These issues were litigated during an eight day *voir dire*, the defence alleging police violence. The trial judge admitted the confession. The allegations were raised again before the jury, but the plaintiff was convicted and his appeal failed. The same assaults were relied on in the civil proceedings but a defence of *res judicata* was not available. The action was dismissed as an abuse because in the words of Lord Diplock[3] it was a collateral attack on 'a final decision against the plaintiff ... made by another court of competent jurisdiction in previous proceedings in which the plaintiff had a full opportunity of contesting the decision'[4]. The provisional ruling admitting the confession became final when the plaintiff was convicted[5]. *Hunter* was unanimously reaffirmed in *Arthur Hall* where Lord Steyn said[6]:

> 'It is ... prima facie an abuse to initiate a collateral civil challenge to a criminal conviction. Ordinarily ... [such] a ... challenge ... will be struck out as an abuse of process.'

A recreation instructor convicted of sexual assault on a boy under his supervision was dismissed. A labour arbitrator held, without new evidence, that the presumption raised by the conviction had been rebutted, and directed reinstatement. The proceedings were held to be a collateral attack on the conviction and the decision was quashed on judicial review[7].

---

[1]   *Aldi Stores Ltd v WSP Group plc* [2008] 1 WLR 748 CA, 756–7 (*Aldi*).
[2]   [1982] AC 529.
[3]   Ibid at 541 (Hunter was one of the Birmingham six).
[4]   Ibid. The converse rule that actions for malicious prosecution, malicious arrest and false imprisonment are only maintainable if the earlier proceedings have terminated in favour of the plaintiff is based on the policy reasons that underpin the doctrine of *res judicata*. It is a 'policy which could not allow a criminal prosecution ... terminating [in favour of the plaintiff] to be tried over again on its merits': *Commonwealth Life Assurance v Smith* (1938) 59 CLR 527, 538–539. As Byles J said in *Basébé v Matthews* (1867) LR 2 CP 684, 687: 'If this were not so almost every case would have to be tried over again on its merits'. Conversely as long as a conviction stands no one against whom it is producible is permitted to aver against it: *Bynoe v Bank of England* [1902] 1 KB 467 CA, 470.
[5]   Ibid at 542. The decision has been followed in Ireland, New Zealand and Australia: *Breathnach v A-G* [1989] IR 489; *Reid v New Zealand Trotting Conference* [1984] 1 NZLR 8 CA; *New Zealand Social Credit Political League Inc v O'Brien* [1984] 1 NZLR 84 CA; *Rogers v R* (1994) 181 CLR 251; para 14.31, but note the powerful dissent of McHugh J who held (at 290) that rulings on evidence do not relate to ultimate issues but, following *Hunter*, it was an abuse of process to attempt to relitigate an issue that in substance determined the ultimate issue.
[6]   [2002] 1 AC 615, 679, 685, 706, 727, 730, 752.
[7]   *Toronto v Canadian Union of Public Employees* [2003] 3 SCR 77; *Ontario v Ontario Public Service Employees Union* [2003] 3 SCR 149.

26.08   The principle applies to actions for negligence against lawyers who acted for an accused. Such actions will generally be abusive unless the conviction has been set aside[1], but in *Walpole v Partridge & Wilson*[2] an action against solicitors for failing to appeal from the Crown Court on a question of law was allowed to proceed. There is no presumption that a collateral challenge to a civil decision is abusive[3] because a successful claim against the lawyers does not attack the successful party[4]. Lord Hoffmann gave an example[5] where there would be such an attack. If a defendant failed to justify a serious libel and sued his former lawyers seeking to prove that a properly conducted defence would have established the truth of the libel he would be attacking the reputation of the former claimant in proceedings in which he was not a party. This would be manifestly unfair, and the proceedings would be abusive.

---

[1]   *Arthur Hall* [2002] 1 AC 615, 679, 684, 706, 727; *Folland v Reardon* (2005) 249 DLR (4th) 167 CA Ont; paras 9.34 n 10, 11.02 n 6.
[2]   [1994] QB 106 CA, approved in *Arthur Hall* [2002] 1 AC 615, 703, 706, 727, 742, 752.
[3]   *Arthur Hall* [2002] 1 AC 615, 680, 684, 705, 707.

4   Ibid at 744–745. A judgment in favour of a convicted claimant in civil proceedings against his former lawyers would generate pressure for a pardon, an exercise of the prerogative of mercy, or a rehearing in the Court of Appeal. A judgment in favour of an unsuccessful civil litigant against his former lawyers would generally not trouble the successful party. There are also policy difficulties in awarding damages for being lawfully convicted and sentenced for a crime; paras 9.34 nn 11–12, 11.02 n 7.

5   Ibid at 706–707.

RELEVANT PRE-JOHNSON CASES

26.09 The case management of multiple claims may make inconsistent proceedings abusive[1]. An industrial tribunal faced with some 1,500 equal pay cases decided, with the agreement or acquiescence of all claimants, that 14 test cases would dispose of all of them. When Ashmore attempted to challenge the relevant decision by bringing her case on for trial it was dismissed for abuse of process[2]. There is an analogy between test cases and proceedings on behalf of a class[3], and she could have applied to be added as a party to the relevant test case after judgment to give her standing to appeal[4]. *Barrow v Banksmeadow Agency Ltd*[5] is a decision the other way. The plaintiff had been one of over 3,000 plaintiffs in the successful negligent underwriting claim against the Gooda Walker companies and members' agents. He then brought an action against his members' agent for negligent portfolio selection. An application to have this action dismissed as an abuse of process failed because the case management procedures adopted by the Commercial Court would have prevented the negligent selection claim being determined in the first action. In *Bragg* an insurer who had been at a disadvantage in earlier proceedings[6], was permitted to raise issues which it earlier lost, despite an objection of abuse of process. Defences of fraud in proceedings to enforce foreign judgments have been struck out as an abuse of process where the question of fraud has been litigated in the foreign jurisdiction by the defendant[7] or a party in the same interest[8].

1   Paras 26.09 nn 2 and 5, 26.10 n 6.
2   *Ashmore v British Coal Corpn* [1990] 2 QB 338 CA.
3   Paras 9.17–9.18, 9.20. If this analogy is valid there may have been a *res judicata* estoppel in *Ashmore*.
4   Para 9.20 n 4; cf *George Wimpey UK Ltd v Tewkesbury Borough Council (MA Holdings Ltd intervening)* [2008] 1 WLR 1649 CA.
5   [1996] 1 WLR 257 CA, 263.
6   [1982] 2 Lloyds Rep 132 CA. There was no *res judicata* estoppel (at 134). In the earlier proceedings the defendant could not cross-examine the Lloyds underwriters it had to call on *subpoena*:ibid at 135, 139.
7   *Owens Bank Ltd v Etoille Commerciale SA* [1995] 1 WLR 44 PC.
8   *Spring Gardens* [1991] 1 QB 241 CA.

LATER DEVELOPMENTS

26.10 A decision that a second action is or is not abusive does not, in strictness, involve the exercise of a judicial discretion. 'Either the proceedings are an abuse of the process of the Court or they are not.'[1] Nevertheless that decision requires the assessment and balancing of many factors and an appellate court will exercise restraint[2]. It was not abusive for a claimant who had not joined Part 20 parties as additional defendants in the first action to bring an action against them later[3]. Its decision that they should not be joined was held to be[4] 'sensible and cost effective', and the Part 20 parties had been informed that a second action might be brought. The claimant hoped to obtain satisfaction of its judgment from the excess loss insurers of the original defendant and brought the second action when satisfied there would be no recovery. Thomas LJ said[5]:

> '… there is a real public interest in allowing parties a measure of freedom to choose whom they sue in a complex commercial matter and not to give encouragement to bringing a single set of proceedings against a wide range of defendants or to complicate matters by cross claims … That freedom can and should be restricted by appropriate case management.'[6]

It was not abusive for a claimant to enforce a solicitors' undertaking before commencing complex proceedings for misrepresentation and inducement of breach of contract against them. Proceedings to enforce an undertaking are intended to provide a relatively swift and straightforward remedy[7]. The Court of Appeal has held that delay within the limitation period[8], and lack of diligence in investigating the later claims were irrelevant considerations in determining whether they were abusive[9].

[1]   *Stuart v Goldberg Linde* [2008] 1 WLR 823 CA, 832 (*Stuart*); *Aldi* [2008] 1 WLR 748 CA, 762, 766; cf *Evans v Bartlam* [1937] AC 473, 489.
[2]   *Aldi* [2008] 1 WLR 748 CA, 762; *Stuart* [2008] 1 WLR 823 CA, 846. The distinction is a narrow one: *Stuart* at 846 per Clarke MR.
[3]   *Aldi* [2008] 1 WLR 748 CA.
[4]   Ibid at 762, 766.
[5]   Ibid at 764.
[6]   Ibid at 765: '… for the future, if a similar issue arises in complex commercial multi-party litigation, it must be referred to the Court seised of the proceedings'; *Stuart* [2008] 1 WLR 823 CA, 844 per Sedley LJ (the same); para 26.09 nn 2–5.
[7]   *Stuart* [2008] 1 WLR 823 CA.
[8]   Ibid at 837, 841, 843.
[9]   Ibid at 839, 840.

MERITS OF NEW CLAIM

26.11 In *Johnson* Lord Bingham said that determination of whether later proceedings were abusive required[1] 'a broad merits-based judgment.' In *Stuart* Lloyd LJ said[2] that the merits were not of the later claim as such but 'those relevant to the question whether the claimant could or should have brought his claim as part of the earlier proceedings.' The question did not arise in *Johnson* because the settlement of the company's action evidenced the merits of the personal action. The merits of the later action were not relevant in *Stuart* because the action was not hopeless, and the issues had not been litigated.

[1]   [2002] 2 AC 1, 31.
[2]   [2008] 1 WLR 823, 840.

RELITIGATION AUTHORISED BY STATUTE

26.12 Relitigation may be authorised by statute. The Crown Court made a confiscation order after finding that the matrimonial home formed part of the accused's realisable property rejecting his wife's evidence that she had a beneficial interest. When the Customs and Excise Commissioners applied to the High Court to enforce the order she again asserted her interest. The House of Lords held[1] that it was not an abuse of process to relitigate the issue because she had only been a witness in the criminal proceedings, without the rights of a party, and the legislation contemplated that she would assert her rights as a party in the civil proceedings. The issues in the two courts were related but not the same[2]. Lord Hobhouse said[3]:

> 'it will be a rare case where the litigation of an issue which has not previously been decided between the same parties or their privies will amount to an abuse.'

[1] *Re Norris* [2001] 1 WLR 1388 HL, 1400–1401.
[2] Ibid at 1401.
[3] Ibid at 1402. The appeal was argued after *Johnson* [2002] 2 AC 1 was decided, and although it was not referred to, the decision is consistent with the principles re-established in that case.

ANSHUN[1]

26.13 In 1981 the High Court of Australia decided this important case. The Port of Melbourne Authority hired out a crane under a contract which required the hirer to indemnify it against any claim arising out of its use. A workman injured by the negligent operation of the crane sued the Authority and the hirer. Each sought contribution, but the Authority did not rely on its indemnity. Responsibility was apportioned 90% to the Authority and 10% to the hirer. The Authority then sought to enforce its indemnity. Gibbs CJ, Mason and Aickin JJ found that there was no cause of action or issue estoppel[2] but stayed the action because a judgment enforcing the indemnity would contradict the apportionment[3]. They noted that *Henderson* was the basis of the modern principles and continued[4]:

> 'However in *Yat Tung* … the principle in *Henderson* … was taken too far. Lord Kilbrandon spoke of it becoming 'an abuse of process to raise in subsequent proceedings matters which could and therefore should have been litigated in earlier proceedings' … this statement is not supported by authority.'

They said that the Kilbrandon principle went further than *Greenhalgh v Mallard*[5] or *Brisbane City Council v A-G for Queensland*[6] and continued[7]:

> '… the abuse of process test is not one of great utility. And its utility is no more evident when it is applied to a plaintiff's new proceeding which is said to be estopped because the plaintiff omitted to plead a defence in an earlier action. In this situation we would prefer to say that there will be no estoppel unless it appears that the matter relied upon as a defence in the second action[8] was so relevant to the subject matter of the first action that it would have been unreasonable not to rely on it. Generally speaking it would be unreasonable not to plead a defence if, having regard to the nature of the plaintiff's claim, and its subject matter, it would be expected that the defendant would raise the defence and thereby enable the relevant issues to be determined in the one proceeding.

> In this respect we need to record that there are a variety of circumstances, some referred to in the earlier cases, why a party may justifiably refrain from litigating an issue in one proceeding yet wish to litigate the issue in other proceedings ...'.

Their Honours said it had generally been accepted that a party is estopped from bringing an action seeking a judgment which would conflict with an earlier one[9], and they referred to what Fullagar J[10] said about *Hoystead*[11]:

> ' ... the Commissioner was not merely seeking to raise on the second appeal a point which he ... had omitted to raise on the first appeal. He was seeking to raise a point which could not be decided in his favour consistently with the decision in the first appeal'.

They also referred to the comment of Somervell LJ in *Re Koenigsberg*[12] that in *Hoystead* the Commissioner 'was ... seeking to obtain an order which was on the face of it and in form in direct conflict with the order which had been made previously'. Their Honours continued[13]:

> 'The likelihood that the omission to plead a defence will contribute to the existence of conflicting judgments is obviously an important factor to be taken into account in deciding whether the omission ... can found an estoppel against the assertion of the same matter as a foundation for a cause of action in a second proceeding. By "conflicting" judgments we include judgments which are contradictory, though they may not be pronounced on the same cause of action. It is enough that they appear to declare rights which are inconsistent in respect of the same transaction'.

The indemnity was so closely connected with the claims for contribution that the Authority should have relied on it as a defence to the hirer's claim for contribution and as a cause of action. This would avoid any inquiry into contribution, but if raised later would increase costs and give rise to conflicting judgments. Thus the Authority's claim to enforce its indemnity contravened the extended doctrine[14]. Subsequently in *Tanning Research Laboratories Inc v O'Brien* Brennan and Dawson JJ said[15]:

> 'A plaintiff who has an unadjudicated cause of action which can be enforced only in fresh proceedings [*Duedu v Yiboe* [1961] 1 WLR 1040, 1046] cannot be precluded from taking fresh proceedings merely because he could have and, if you will, should have counterclaimed on that cause of action ... in proceedings in which the opposite party sued him. We do not read ... *Anshun* as holding the contrary, except ... where the relief claimed in the second proceedings is inconsistent with the judgment in the first'.

1   (1981) 147 CLR 589. The Australian case law was reviewed in '*Anshun* today' Handley (1997) 71 ALJR 934.
2   The Authority had causes of action in contract and for contribution and there was a cause of action estoppel in accordance with *Henderson* because its claims to shift the loss to the hirer were based on a common substratum of fact. Cf cases where a claimant has causes of action in contract and tort against the same defendants. The inconsistency between the judgments was a good indication that there was such an estoppel.
3   (1981) 147 CLR 589, 596.
4   Ibid at 601–602.
5   [1947] 2 All ER 255 CA.
6   [1979] AC 411.
7   (1981) 147 CLR 589, 602–603. Cf para 26.05 n 6: 'clearly a matter necessary and proper to be litigated at the same time with all the other issues'.

8   This was a slip. The hirer could not have relied on the extended doctrine in the original proceedings.
9   Ibid at 603.
10   *Brewer* (1953) 88 CLR 1, 15.
11   [1926] AC 155.
12   [1949] Ch 348 CA, 360.
13   (1981) 147 CLR 589, 603–604.
14   A final order for purposes of appeal: *Anshun* (1980) 147 CLR 35. Nothing turns on the distinction between such an order, an order for summary dismissal, or an order entering judgment for the defendant.
15   (1990) 169 CLR 332, 346.

CHAMBERLAIN (NO 2)[1]

26.14 This case illustrates some of the problems with the extended doctrine although hopefully the facts will not recur. The Revenue sued a taxpayer for only 10% of his outstanding tax as a result of the displacement of the decimal point in the writ and statement of claim. Consent judgment was entered for this amount. When the Revenue discovered the mistake it sued for the balance but was met with a defence of *res judicata* or merger. This failed at the trial and on appeal[2] but succeeded in the High Court[3]. The Revenue then brought an action to set aside the consent judgment for unilateral mistake which succeeded[4], but the decision was reversed[5]. The Full Court held that the Revenue could have included that claim in the second action[6] and if the judgment was set aside, a fourth action would be necessary[7]. The Revenue were therefore estopped by the High Court judgment from having the consent judgment set aside[8]. However the High Court had said[9]:

' ... so long as that judgment stands it is not competent for the respondent to bring further proceedings in respect of the same cause of action'.

The Full Court referred to *Caird v Moss*[10] and held that[11] 'the claim now made is inconsistent with the judgment of the High Court', but this was not so. The issue estoppel created by the High Court judgment was limited to the ground on which the Revenue failed[12], which was that the consent judgment barred the second action. There was no issue estoppel against proceedings on any new or altered basis[13]. If the action to set aside the consent judgment succeeded there would be no bar to a claim for the full amount in the original action once the writ and statement of claim were amended. The Revenue had not acted unreasonably by failing to include a claim to set aside the consent judgment in its second action because its argument that *res judicata* was not a defence to an action for assessed tax had succeeded in the lower courts[14]. The Revenue's claim in the third action did not arise out of the same facts as its claim in the second where mistake was not raised.

1   (1991) 28 FCR 21.
2   *Chamberlain (No. 1)* (1987) 13 FCR 94.
3   (1988) 164 CLR 502.
4   (1990) 26 FCR 221. (The author was counsel for the Revenue in the High Court, and at this trial.)
5   (1991) 28 FCR 21.
6   Ibid at 23; cf *Tanning Research Laboratories Inc v O'Brien* (1989) 169 CLR 332, 346.
7   Ibid at 24. This was not so. If the consent judgment in the original action was set aside the Revenue could apply to amend the original writ and statement of claim.

8   Ibid at 24.
9   (1988) 164 CLR 502, 510.
10   (1886) 33 Ch D 22 CA, 36 per Lopes LJ; considered paras 5.24, 7.14.
11   (1991) 28 FCR 21, 26.
12   Paras 2.28, 8.26.
13   Para 8.17.
14   (1987) 13 FCR 94.

THE PARTIES

26.15   Although, as Lord Bingham said in *Johnson*[1], one cannot lay down any hard and fast rules, the following propositions about parties are supported by authority:

(a)   Although most reported cases involved abusive claims, the doctrine applies to abusive defences[2].

(b)   A defendant is in a better position to resist a finding of abuse[3].

(c)   A later action against the original defendant is more likely to be abusive than an action against a different defendant[4], but the doctrine can apply where the claimant or the defendant or both are different[5].

(d)   The doctrine can apply where the first action was compromised[6].

(e)   Contribution proceedings between unsuccessful defendants will not be abusive although they could have been included in the original proceedings[7], but it will be too late to raise any contractual indemnity once contribution has been assessed[8].

(f)   Where a defence of circuity of action[9] was not raised judgment for the claimant should bar the defendant's cause of action because the judgments would be inconsistent[10].

(g)   It is not necessarily abusive for a claimant to sue Pt 20 parties who could have been joined as defendants in the original proceedings[11].

(h)   There is no general rule that bars actions that could have been raised as cross actions in earlier proceedings[12].

(i)   A claimant who elects to bring some claims against a defendant, and defer others until later should, as a general rule, inform the defendant of his intention. A claimant who does not faces an increased risk that later proceedings will be abusive[13], but only if he then knew the facts which entitled him to bring the later claim[14]. A claimant should generally inform the court that he intends to bring other proceedings[15].

(j)   Although the policy which underpins *Henderson* is relevant to successive pre-trial applications for the same relief it is applied less strictly[16].

1   [2002] 2 AC 1, 31.
2   *Reichel v Magrath* (1889) 14 App Cas 665; *Johnson* [2002] 2 AC 1, 31.
3   *Bragg* [1982] 2 Lloyds Rep 132 CA; *McCauley v Vine* [1999] 1 WLR 1977 CA, 1984; *J v Oyston* [1999] 1 WLR 694; *Conlon v Simms* [2008] 1 WLR 484 CA, 517–518, 522–523, 523–524; *Belton v Carlow County Council* [1997] 1 IR 172 SC, 183; cf *KF v White* (2001) 198 DLR (4th) 541 CA Ont.
4   *Bradford & Bingley Building Society v Selden* [1999] 1 WLR 1482 CA, 1491–1492; *Morris v Wentworth-Stanley* [1999] QB 1004 CA, 1017.
5   *Meretz* [2007] Ch 197, 256; *Aldi* [2008] 1 WLR 748 CA, 757–758.
6   *Johnson* [2002] 2 AC 1, 32–33.
7   *Baker v Ian McCall International* [2001] Lloyd's Rep IR 149; *Renaissance Leisure Group Inc v Frazer* (2001) 197 DLR (4th) 336. *Employees Provident Fund Board v Hong Kong and Shanghai Banking Corpn Ltd* [2002] 3 MLJ 512.

8   *Anshun* (1981) 147 CLR 589; para 26.13.
9   *Aktieselskabet Ocean v B Harding & Sons* [1928] 2 KB 371 CA.
10 *Caird v Moss* (1886) 33 ChD 22 CA, 36; paras 5.24, 7.14; *Re Koenigsberg* [1949] Ch 348
    CA, 360.
11 *Aldi* [2008] 1 WLR 748 CA.
12 Para 26.17.
13 *Johnson* [2002] 2 AC 1, 18–19, 61; *Stuart* [2008] 1 WLR 823, 843, 844, 850.
14 *Stuart* [2008] 1 WLR 823, 844, 851.
15 *Aldi* [2008] 1 WLR 748 CA, 765; *Stuart* [2008] 1 WLR 823, 844–845.
16 *Woodhouse v Consignia plc* [2002] 1 WLR 2558 CA, 2575; *Nominal Defendant v
    Manning* (2000) 50 NSWLR 139 CA; *Contra D.A. Christie Pty Ltd v Grant* [1996] 2 VR
    582 CA.

GROUNDS FOR FINDING ABUSE

26.16 The following propositions are also relevant:

(a)   An action or defence by a party who, as claimant or defendant was
      unsuccessful or substantially so in earlier proceedings, in which he had
      a proper opportunity of being heard[1], may be dismissed or struck out as
      an abuse of process[2] where the action or defence is a collateral attack
      on the earlier decision[3], especially if there are aggravating features such
      as ulterior purpose[4], prejudicial delay[5], or the absence of fresh evi-
      dence[6]. Proceedings for fraud brought in 1997 based on facts known to
      the plaintiff in 1995 during the trial of related proceedings between the
      same parties which the plaintiff had not sought to raise by amendment
      were summarily dismissed[7].

(b)   An action or defence by such a party may also be dismissed or struck
      out if they are without merit (frivolous or vexatious) in the light of the
      earlier decision, especially if the parties are the same[8].

(c)   A collateral attack on a civil decision by a party bound by it is not
      necessarily an abuse, but will be where it would be manifestly unfair for
      the issues to be relitigated, or where relitigation would bring the
      administration of justice into disrepute[9]. Lord Hoffmann gave as an
      example the unfairness to a third party if a defendant, who had failed
      to justify a libel, sued his former lawyers and sought to prove that a
      properly conducted defence would have justified the libel[10].

(d)   It may not be abusive for a claimant who was substantially successful to
      seek further compensation through a corporation or another cause of
      action[11].

(e)   A collateral attack by the defendants in damages proceedings on
      findings of abuse of dominant position in competition proceedings in
      Europe affirmed by the European Court was abusive, and the findings
      were binding[12]. On the other hand a collateral attack by a former
      solicitor on findings of fraud affirmed by the Divisional Court when he
      was struck off was not abusive, and the findings were not binding[13].

(f)   It is not abusive for a claimant with an unsatisfied judgment to seek
      further relief[14], or to seek it from other parties[15].

(g)   Further proceedings are not likely to be abusive if the first failed on
      technical or procedural grounds[16].

(h)   The doctrine can apply where a claimant is dissatisfied with the result
      in the first proceedings and seeks further relief or seeks it from a

different defendant. In *Rippon v Chilcotin Pty Ltd*[17] the purchaser of a business sued the vendor for breach of warranties of the accounts annexed to the contract, and misrepresentations to the same effect. He failed on the latter claims because he had relied on the warranties, and only recovered a modest verdict. He then brought an action for misrepresentation against the accountants who prepared the accounts, seeking a different finding on reliance in respect of the same misrepresentations. The action was dismissed as abusive. Another illustration is provided by *Sheriff v Klyne Tugs (Lowestoft) Ltd*[18].

(i) An action by a successful party may also be an abuse, eg an action brought on a judgment of the High Court without good reason[19].

---

[1]   Courts should not attempt to fully define abuse of process: *JH Rayner (Mincing Lane) Ltd v Bank für Gemeinwirtschaft AG* [1983] 1 Lloyd's Rep 462 CA, 468–469; *Johnson* [2002] 2 AC 1, 31.

[2]   It was suggested in *Rayner* [1983] 1 Lloyd's Rep 462 CA, 467 that this 'plea' can only be raised before trial but it should only succeed if it would succeed at trial. Cf *Wall v Radford* [1991] 2 All ER 741 and *Talbot* [1994] QB 290 CA.

[3]   *Reichel v McGrath* (1889) 14 App Cas 665; para 26.02; *Stephenson v Garnett* [1898] 1 QB 677 CA; *Hunter* [1982] AC 529; *Smith v Linskills* [1996] 1 WLR 763 CA (accused suing former solicitor); *Chamberlains v Lai* [2007] 1 NZLR 7 SC; *Kwa v Kuah* [2003] 3 SLR 644; *Tsang v Employees Compensation Assistance Fund Board* [2003] 2 HKLRD 627 CA.

[4]   *Hunter* [1982] AC 529.

[5]   *Smith v Linskills* [1996] 1 WLR 763 CA.

[6]   Ibid.

[7]   *Lim v Lim* (1999) 180 DLR (4th) 87 BCCA.

[8]   *MacDougall v Knight* (1890) 25 QBD 1 CA; *Montgomery v Russell* (1894) 11 TLR 112 CA; *Wall v Radford* [1991] 2 All ER 741; paras 12.05, 12.15; *McLoughlin v Gordons (Stockport) Ltd* [1978] ICR 561 (as an abuse of process case; para 17.30 n 11); *MCC Proceeds* [1998] 4 All ER 675 CA (first action against parent, second against subsidiary, same issue of title). In *Nanang International Sdn Bhd v The China Press Bhd* [1992] 2 MLJ 681, 687 a plaintiff who failed in a libel action brought a second action for the same imputations against other defendants based on different publications and it was stayed. The plaintiff was not entitled to relitigate issues which had already been decided against him. In *Haines v ABC* (1995) 43 NSWLR 404 the plaintiff failed to establish that the publication complained of was capable of conveying the defamatory meaning relied on. His action against another defendant for injurious falsehood and innocent misrepresentation based on the same publication was dismissed as an abuse of process; *Divine Bortey* [1998] ICR 886 CA (action for unfair dismissal failed, action under Race Relations Act abusive).

[9]   *Bairstow* [2004] Ch 1 CA, 16–17.

[10]   *Arthur Hall* [2002] 1 AC 615, 706–707.

[11]   *Johnson* [2002] 2 AC 1, 32.

[12]   *Iberian* [1997] ICR 164, 191. However, the plaintiff, by its active intervention, had become a party to the competiteion proceedings; para 9.12.

[13]   *Coulon v Simms* [2008] 1 WLR 484 CA, reversing Lawrence Collins J [2006] 2 All ER 1024. It is submitted in para 11.08 nn 13 & foll that the striking off decision was *in rem*, and the findings were therefore prima facie evidence *in rem*.

[14]   *Gairy v A-G for Grenada* [2002] 1 AC 167 (unsatisfied judgment against the Crown not enforceable by execution, claim for coercive relief under Constitution not abusive); *Kanawagi v Penang Port Commission* [2001] 5 MLJ 433, 454–455 (declaration by court in 1994 that plaintiff's dismissal void, application in 2000 for consequential relief not barred).

[15]   *Bradford & Bingley Building Society v Seddon* [1999] 1 WLR 1482 CA, 1498.

[16]   *Barakot Ltd v Epiette Ltd* [1998] 1 BCLC 283 CA (second action to recover £1.24 million not abusive when first failed on technical ground).

[17]   (2001) 53 NSWLR 198 CA. The High Court refused special leave (2001) 53 NSWLR 198 CA, 750.

[18] [1999] ICR 1170 CA, 1181. The claimant sued his employer for racial discrimination in an industrial tribunal and settled for £4000. He then sued for damages in the County Court for his post-traumatic stress based on the same facts. Stuart-Smith LJ said: '... the conduct of the master of the employer's vessel lies at the heart of both ... proceedings ... although in the latter the employee assumes the additional burden of proving negligence ... the employee could have brought ... his whole claim for compensation in the tribunal ... The principle of public policy is that claims that ... could have been litigated in one tribunal shall not be allowed to be litigated in another.' The decision would now be supported on the ground of abuse of process or merger since the damages in each case would be the same; para 21.06.

[19] Paras 2.47–2.48, 2.52.

CROSS ACTIONS

26.17 In sale of goods and similar cases judgment for the supplier for the price of the goods etc does not bar an action by the buyer etc for breach of warranty that could have been set up in the action for the price[1]. The Federal Court of Australia has held that matters based on the same facts which could have been included in an earlier cross-claim were barred. The court said[2]:

'... where as here a defendant's claim is intimately connected with that of the plaintiff, in the sense that each arises substantially out of the same matters of fact, there is every reason to require that both be litigated at the same time; thereby minimising costs and avoiding the possibility of inconsistent judgments'.

There is Canadian authority that unpleaded claims that would have supported defences of equitable set off in earlier proceedings are barred[3] but the existence of any general rule to this effect must be doubted. An equitable set off is a cause of action that impeaches the claimant's title to his cause of action and as such is an equitable defence[4]. It may be a cross action for breach of warranty[5]. The analogy of the sale of goods and similar cases should apply and unpleaded equitable set offs should not be barred except in proceedings for an account where there would be a cause of action estoppel[6]. However a judgment for possession in favour of a mortgagee, without judgment for the mortgage debt, will not bar an action against the mortgagee, for selling at an undervalue, or for breach of a contract for further advances[7].

[1] *Davis v Hedges* (1871) LR 6 QB 687. The purchaser may reasonably wish to delay his action for breach of warranty because (at 690) 'it may take some time to ascertain to what amount the value of the article or work is diminished by the plaintiff's default' and in any event an action must be brought to recover any consequential loss: ibid at 691; para 8.16.

[2] *Bryant v Commonwealth Bank of Australia* (1995) 57 FCR 287, 298. Since the plaintiff had previously raised cross-claims based on substantially the same facts the case was within *Greenhalgh v Mallard* [1947] 2 All ER 255 CA and *Wright v Bennett* [1948] 1 All ER 227 CA. The bank sued in the earlier proceedings for its mortgage debt, and the new cross claims were barred by a cause of action estoppel: paras 7.14–7.15.

[3] 420093 BC Ltd v Bank of Montreal (1995) 128 DLR (4th) 488 Alta CA (abuse of process for company privy of its surety directors to raise claims which sureties could have pleaded as equitable set offs).

[4] *Bank of Boston Connecticut v European Grain & Shipping Ltd* [1989.] AC 1056, 1101 & foll.

[5] Ibid.

[6] Paras 7.14–7.15.

[7] *Murphy v Abi-Saab* (1995) 37 NSWLR 280 CA.

SUPREME COURT ACT S 49(2)

26.18   Reference has already been made to this section[1] which provides:

> 'Every court ... shall so exercise its jurisdiction in every cause or matter before it as to secure that, as far as possible, all matters in dispute between the parties are completely and finally determined, and all multiplicity of legal proceedings with respect to any of those matters is avoided'.

The section does not require a party to include in the one proceeding all causes of action arising from the same facts. As its terms indicate, it is limited to 'matters in dispute' in the proceedings and the grant of all appropriate remedies for them. Jessel MR said that the effect of its predecessor in the Judicature Act 1873[2] was:

> '... that whenever a subject of controversy arises in an action which can conveniently be determined between the parties ... the court should, if possible, determine it ... to prevent further and needless litigation'.

[1]   Paras 21.12 nn 13–15, 21.13 n 2.
[2]   *Re Tharp, Tharp v Macdonald* (1878) 3 PD 76 CA, 81, 88.

TESTS FOR ABUSE

26.19   Attempts have been made to formulate a test of abuse for cases other than those where the new claim is abusive because it is without merit. Somervell LJ referred[1] to 'issues ... which are so clearly part of the subject matter of the litigation, so clearly could have been raised that it would be an abuse of the process of the court to allow a new proceeding to be started in respect of them'. The Full Court of Hong Kong in a passage approved by Lord Kilbrandon[2], asked whether the new claim 'was ... so clearly a matter necessary and proper to be litigated at the same time with all the other issues' in the earlier proceedings. The High Court of Australia in *Anshun*[3] asked whether the new issue was so relevant in the first action that it was unreasonable not to rely on it. Wigram VC referred in *Henderson*[4] to 'points which properly belonged to the subject matter of litigation in earlier proceedings'. Somervell LJ ('part of the subject matter of the litigation') and the Full Court of Hong Kong ('necessary and proper') echoed this approach. The test in *Anshun* was an attempt to identify the underlying principle, based on the requirement in *Henderson* that the point should 'properly belong' to the earlier litigation.[5]

[1]   *Greenhalgh v Mallard* [1947] 2 All ER 255 CA, 257.
[2]   *Yat Tung* [1975] AC 581, 589.
[3]   (1981) 147 CLR 589.
[4]   [1982] AC 529, 536.
[5]   Para 7.03.

OBJECTIVE AND SUBJECTIVE CONSIDERATIONS

26.20   The relevance of the omitted claims to the original proceedings, whether the new proceedings are a collateral challenge to the original decision, the risk of conflicting judgments, and any finding that the defendant is being 'unjustly harassed' will be determined objectively. Subjective considerations may be relevant such as the need to conserve resources in time and money[1], and the reasonableness of the claimant's choices[2]. Decisions by claimants to first seek summary enforcement of a solicitors' undertaking and proceed later to enforce other causes of action were reasonable[3]. A claimant who attempted to enforce its judgment against the defendant's insurers rather than join Part 20 parties as additional defendants did not act abusively when it sued them later. It made that choice in its own interests, but it was 'a sensible and cost effective way of proceeding', and 'there were good reasons why [it] acted as it did.'[4] A passenger, the widow of one of the drivers in a two car collision, who decided to await the outcome of proceedings under the Fatal Accidents Act and on behalf of her husband's estate before bringing her own action was not being abusive because 'it was not unreasonable for the plaintiff ... to await the outcome.'[5]

[1] *Johnson* [2002] 2 AC 1, 18.
[2] A claimant who fails to obtain a *quia timet* injunction is not bound to accept damages under Lord Cairns Act but may await the accrual of actual damage: *Meretz* [2002] Ch 197, 261; para 26.17 n 1.
[3] *Ulster Bank Ltd v Fisher* [1999] N1 68; *Stuart* [2008] 1 WLR 823 CA, 837, 841, 843.
[4] *Aldi* [2008] 1 WLR 748 CA, 762–763, 765.
[5] *McNally v Williams* [2001] NI 106.

CONCLUSION

26.21 A claimant is not required to pursue all available remedies against all possible defendants in the one proceeding. Provided he acts reasonably he may choose between available alternatives subject to the *res judicata* doctrine, and the need to avoid inconsistent judgments, so long as any later proceedings are not without merit, frivolous or vexatious, in the light of an earlier decision.

Chapter 27

RES JUDICATA IN ROMAN LAW ETC

27.01 The English doctrine of *res judicata* has been influenced by the civil law through the former Ecclesiastical Courts and the High Court of Admiralty which applied canon and civil law; through knowledge of the civil law acquired at the universities; through borrowings; and from Scots decisions in the House of Lords and Scots Law Lords. Our law[1], that of other civilised states[2], and public international law[3], are, in the main, consistent with the principles developed by the Roman jurists. It is therefore instructive to compare the two systems.

[1] *Barrs v Jackson* (1842) 1 Y & C Ch Cas 585, 588–589 per Knight-Bruce VC: 'with the rules of the civil law, rightly understood, ... the law of England generally agrees'; *Nelson v Couch* (1863) 15 CBNS 99, 108 per Willes J, who said the English rules were 'entirely consistent ... with the rules of the civil law'.

[2] In *Sheoparsan Singh v Ramnandan Singh* (1916) LR 43 Ind App 91, 98 the Privy Council said 'their Lordships desired to emphasise that the rule of *res judicata*, while founded on ancient precedent, is dictated by a wisdom which was for all time ... Though the rule of the Code might be traced to an English source, it embodies a doctrine in no way opposed to the spirit of the law as expounded by the Hindu commentators. Vijnanesvara and Nilakantha included the plea of a former judgment among those allowed by law, each citing for that purpose the text of Katyayana, who describes the plea thus: "if a person though defeated at law, sue again, he should be answered, – You were defeated formerly. This is called the plea of former judgment" '.

[3] *South West Africa Case* [1966] ICJR 4, 240–241 per Koretsky J and 332–333 per Jessup J: 'the rule of *res judicata* ... a clear example of a general principle of law recognised by civilised nations. It rests upon the maxim *interest reipublicae ut sit finis litium* ... the essentials for the application of the *res judicata* principle [are] identity of parties, identity of causes and identity of object in the subsequent proceedings'.

THE EXCEPTIO REI JUDICATAE

27.02 The fundamental principles of Roman law, collected in the last book of the Digest[1], include the maxim *res judicata pro veritate accipitur*[2] frequently cited in English judgments[3], which closely corresponds with the 'uncontrollable verity' which Coke accorded to the proceedings of courts of record[4]. Every *res judicata* was treated by the civilians as incontrovertible on the merits provided it was brought to the notice of the tribunal[5].

1   The collection of extracts from the commentaries of the most authoritative of the Roman jurists, commonly called 'the Digest'. The mode of citation in the following notes is that now usually adopted: 'D' stands for 'Digest'; the first figure after the 'D' indicates the number of the Book; the second, that of the Title, or Chapter; the third, that of the Section; and the fourth (where there is a fourth), that of the clause, or paragraph, or 'fragment'. When the clause is an introductory one, without a number, the abbreviation 'pr' (for 'principium') is used.
2   D 50 17 (*Regulae Diversae*, Reg 207, cited from Ulpian).
3   *Barrs v Jackson* (1842) 1 Y & C Ch Cas 585. This passage and the maxim were referred to in *Rogers v R* (1994) 181 CLR 252, 273.
4   2 Co Litt 260a.
5   Just Inst iv. 13. 5 '*si judicio tecum actum fuerit sive in rem sive in personam, nihilominus ob id actio durat, et ideo ipso jure postea de eadem re adversus te agi potest: sed debes per exceptionem rei judicatae adjurari*'. If the defendant, intentionally or negligently, failed to inform the Praetor that he wanted to raise a question of *res judicata* by an *exceptio*, that question was not submitted to the judex in the issue he was directed to try, but, if that question was raised, the issue required the judex to decide it ('*si ea res non judicata sit*' being added to the ordinary 'formula').

27.03   The justification of the doctrine was said in the Digest to be the interest of the community in being protected against the multiplication of suits and the scandal of conflicting decisions[1], and, the effect of a judicial decision in absorbing the cause of action[2]. The former is the basis of the English doctrine of *res judicata* estoppel[3], the latter of our rules relating to 'former recovery' and 'merger in judgment'[4].

1   D 44 2. 6 (from Paulus *ad Edictum*, lib. lxx): '*ne aliter modus litium multiplicatus summam atque inexplicabilem faciat difficultatem, maxime si diversa pronuncientur*'. This accorded with Greek law and custom: see Soph Ajax, 1239–1249 where Agamemnon upbraids Teucer for daring to question the decision of the majority of the judges, and enlarges on the confusion of law, order, finality, and decency which would result if a defeated party could canvass the correctness of a *res judicata*. This passage in the text was cited in *Rogers v R* (1994) 181 CLR 252, 280.
2   In English law a cause of action merges in a judgment given on it; but the civilians considered that there were two mergers. The claim was absorbed in the action on commencement ('*res in judicium deducta*'), and the latter merged in the *res judicata*.
3   Paras 1.03–1.04.
4   Para 1.04.

27.04   The *exceptio rei judicatae* approximates the English rule. 'The *exceptio*', says Ulpian, 'is an effective bar to any proceeding in which the same question ... which has already been decided is put in controversy again between the same parties'[1]. The Roman rule did not distinguish between the effect of a *res judicata* as a bar to contradiction, and as a bar to repetition, but was a general prohibition against reopening the *res judicata*, in any form, and for any purpose.

1   D 44 2. 7. 4, citing from Ulpian *ad Edictum*, lib. xv, a passage adopted from Julian's *Digest*, lib. iii: '*generaliter, ut Julianus definit, exceptio rei judicatae obstat, quotiens inter easdem personas eadem quaestio revocatur, vel alio genere judicii*'. Cf D 44 2. 3, where the same rule is stated in slightly different language.

ROMAN AND ENGLISH LAW ON IDENTITY OF SUBJECT MATTER

27.05   Our law requires the subject matter of both actions to be the same[1]. Roman law required proof that both related to *idem corpus*, and *eadem* *quantitas*[2] as at the same point of time[3], but the discovery of *nova instrumenta* which had been within the means of knowledge of a party during the former proceedings did not negative identity, or make the subject matter *alia res*[4].

[1] Chapters 7 and 21.
[2] D 44 2. 13, citing Paulus *ad Edictum*, lib. lxx ('*cum quaeritur, haec exceptio noceat, necne, inspiciendum est, an idem corpus sit*'), and D 44 2. 13, from Ulpian *ad Edictum*, lib. lxxv ("*quantitas eadem*"). In D 44 2. 7, a number of illustrations are given. Thus, it is said that the *exceptio* applies to any one of the properties, or to any part of the land, building, ship, or goods, or to any fraction of the sum, the subject of the previous decision, but questions as to whether the subject (in a physical sense) of the former adjudication extends to the income, or produce, or *fructus* of that subject (eg the produce of a tree, or of a *praegnans ancilla*) do not admit of an unqualified answer, and must be determined, in each case, by reference to the particular facts.
[3] D 44 2. 17: '*si rem meam a te petiero, tu autem ideo fueris absolutus quod probaveris sine dolo malo te desiisse possidere, deinde postea coeperis possidere, et ego a te petam, non nocebit mihi exceptio reijudicatae*'. Other examples are given in D 44 2.11.1–6, and D 44 2.18, 19.
[4] D 44 2.27 (citing Neratius, lib. vii, *Membranarum*): '*nec jam interest ... si quis, postea quam contra eum judicatum esset, nova instrumenta causae suae reperisset.*'

27.06 In English law a plea of *res judicata* cannot succeed unless the question of law, or issue of fact, in controversy is the same as that determined by the former judgment[1]. In Roman law no *exceptio rei judicatae* was effective unless the subject matter of the *res judicata*, and of the subsequent action, was *eadem quaestio*[2], or, *idem jus*[3], or unless the foundations of the former judgment and the subsequent proceedings was *eadem causa petendi*[4]. This was the 'ground of complaint', not 'form of action or remedy'; for as in English law[5], the civilians insist that, if both proceedings related to the same question of right or title, it made no difference that the former proceeding was *alio genere judicii*[6], or *diverso genere actionis*[7].

[1] Chapters 7 and 21.
[2] Para 27.04 n 1.
[3] D 44 2. 13 (from Ulpian *ad Edictum*, lib. lxxv).
[4] D 44 2. 14. pr.
[5] Paras 7.05 & foll, 21.01 & foll.
[6] D 44 2. 7. 4, cited para 27.04 n 1.
[7] D 44 2. 5 (from Ulpian *ad Edictum*, lib. lxxiv): '*cum quis actione mutata experitur, etsi diverso genere actionis quam instituit videtur de eadem re agere*'. An instance is then given – an *actio mandati*, followed by an *actio negotiorum gestorum*.

IDENTITY OF PARTIES

27.07 Each system requires the parties (or their privies) in both proceedings to be the same[1]. Identity must be physical and jural, so that two persons may have the same character, or *persona*, while the same person litigating in two capacities may constitute two *personae*. Paulus states that where judgment is obtained against the heir for the *dolus* of the deceased, there is no objection for *res judicata* to an action against him based on his own fraud[2].

[1] D 44 2. 3 ('*inter eosdem*'), and D 44 2. 7. 4 ('*inter easdem personas*'). For privies, see D 44 2. 11. 7–10, and D 44 2. 28. As to the English rules: paras 9.22 and 22.01.
[2] D 44 2. 22 (from Paulus *ad Edictum*, lib. xxxi): '*etsi actio sit cum haerede de dolo defuncti, deinde de dolo haeredis agatur, exceptio rei judicatae non nocebit, quia de alia reagitur*'.

27.08 Roman law distinguished between actions *in rem* and *in personam*[1], but the distinction was not as important as in English law[2]. Proceedings *in rem*, where the 'actor' represented the community are referred to in many places in the Digest, such as the *popularis actio*, corresponding to the Scottish action of declarator[3], and actions for sacrilege (*actio sepulchri violati*), for obstructing the administration of justice, for falsification of public records (*actio de albo corrupto*), and for certain public nuisances[4].

[1]   Just Inst iv. 13. 5, n 8 ('*sive in rem sive in personam*'). In an ordinary action *in personam* the praetor's direction to the judex was: '*si paret Numerium Negidium Aulo Agerio dare facere, praestare … opportere, condemna; si non paret, absolvito*'. In an action *in rem* the formula ran: '*siparet hominem ex jure Quiritium Auli Agerii esse, condemna; si non paret, absolvito*'.
[2]   Chapter 10.
[3]   Para 10.13.
[4]   D 9 3 ('*De his quae effuderint vel dejecerint*').

REFERENCES IN ENGLISH AUTHORITIES TO ROMAN LAW

27.09 The references though not numerous, are not unimportant. A judgment delivered by Knight-Bruce VC[1], a great master of the civil law, is prefaced by the citation of Ulpian's *res judicata pro veritate acciputur*[2], and a statement that 'with the rules of the civil law, rightly understood, the law of England generally agrees'[3], which he illustrates from the Digest[4]. This judgment has often been cited[5]; although it was reversed on the facts by Lord Lyndhurst LC[6].

[1]   *Barrs v Jackson* (1842) 1 Y & C Ch Cas 585.
[2]   D 50 17 (*Diversae Regulae*), Reg 207.
[3]   Ibid at 588–589.
[4]   Ibid at 589 where he cites D 44 2. 6. 6, 7, 12, 13, 14, 27, and the passage from Vinnius in para 27.11.
[5]   For example, *Nelson v Couch* (1863) 15 CBNS 99, 119.
[6]   *Barrs v Jackson* (1845) 1 Ph 582.

27.10 The general statement of Ulpian from Julian[1] has been cited by Lord Macnaghten[2], and Lord Shaw[3].

[1]   Para 27.04 n 1.
[2]   *Badar Bee* [1909] AC 615, 623.
[3]   *Bradshaw v M'Mullan* [1920] 2 IR 412 HL, 423. The passage is miscited in the reporter's note as D 44 7. 4, instead of D 44 2. 7. 4.

27.11 Vinnius, the Dutch commentator, in his annotated edition of Justinian's Institutes, summed up the *exceptio rei judicatae*, as follows: '*exceptio rei judicatae non aliter petenti obstat quam si eadem quaestio inter eosdem revocetur; itaque ita demum nocet si omnia sint eadem, idem corpus, eadem quantitas, idem jus, eadem causa petendi, eadem conditio personarum*'[1]. This[2] has been quoted by Knight-Bruce VC, Lord Campbell LC[3], and Kay J[4].

[1]   In a note to '*per exceptionem rei judicatae*' in Just. Inst. iv. 13. 5, para 27.02 n 5.
[2]   '*Eadem quaestio inter easdem personas*' is taken from D 44 2. 7. 4; '*idem corpus*', from D 44 2. 12; '*eadem quantitas, idem jus*', from D 44 2. 13; and '*eadem causa petendi, et eadem conditio personarum*', from D 44 2. 14.

3   *Hunter v Stewart* (1861) 4 De GF & J 168, 176.
4   *Caird v Moss* (1886) 33 Ch D 22, 28.

MODERN ROMAN-DUTCH LAW IN SOUTH AFRICA

27.12 Some consideration of the modern Roman-Dutch law of South Africa will be instructive. An influential decision, frequently followed, was that of Greenberg J in *Boshoff v Union Government* who said[1]:

> 'The civil [law] authorities laid down two requirements for this plea, namely that the proceedings on which reliance is placed must be between the same parties and that the same question ... must arise. I need not refer to any other authority ... than ... *Bertram v Wood*[2] ... where the then Chief Justice quotes a passage from Vinnius (4.13.5) ... that this exception only applies if there is the same question between the same persons. In Roman-Dutch law the requisites have been split into three ... but ... it is merely a further subdivision of the two ... mentioned in Vinnius. According to Voet[3] (44.2.3) ... the exception can only be employed when the action which has been terminated is again set in motion by the same parties, about the same thing, and based on the same cause of action. ... Voet cannot be using the words "cause of action" ... in the narrow pleading sense ... The requisites have been referred to in ... *Mitford's Executors v Ebdens Executors*[4] ... where the Court [said]: "it will be necessary to enquire whether that judgement was given in an action (1) with respect to the same subject matter (2) based on the same ground, and (3) between the same parties." The wording is different to the rule laid down in Voet but I do not think in the present case anything arises out of that difference.'

The plaintiff claimed damages for the unlawful termination of his lease and eviction. The defendant raised a plea of *res judicata* based on a default judgment for ejectment following its cancellation of the lease. Greenberg J held that although the causes of action were different the averment of cancellation was an essential ingredient of the Government's cause of action in the earlier case, so that a decision on that question was essential, and the defence of *res judicata* succeeded.

1   [1932] TPD 345, 348–349.
2   (1893) 10 SC 180.
3   Another Dutch jurist.
4   [1917] AD 682.

27.13 In *ABSA Bank* the Appellate Division approved[1] the decision in *Boshoff* on the availability of issue estoppel[2] under Roman-Dutch law, although Greenberg J had referred to the first edition of this work[3]. It confirmed earlier decisions that it was not the form of action, but the identity of the question, which determined the availability of the plea[4], held that the underlying principle of *res judicata* was the same as in English law[5], and concluded[6]:

> '... there can be no objection to considering the manner in which application of issue estoppel has developed in English law. In fact, since Spencer Bower's exposition ... was used as a guideline ... in *Boshoff* ... it would be unwise not to follow up further guidelines in subsequent English decisions.'

1   [1995] (1) SA 653, [1995] SALR Translations 52, 62.

² Ibid at 59.
³ Ibid at 60.
⁴ Ibid at 61.
⁵ Ibid at 61.
⁶ Ibid at 63.

RES JUDICATA IN THE EUROPEAN COURT

27.14 Article 21 of the Brussels Convention and Article 27 of Council Regulation 44/2001 apply where proceedings on the same cause of action are pending between the same parties in the courts of different Member States. To prevent conflicting decisions it provides that the court first seised has exclusive jurisdiction. The European Court has held that the identity of the causes of action and the parties are 'independent questions', that is independent of the national laws of the two countries[1]. Since the great majority of the judges are from civil law countries these questions are likely to be decided in accordance with general principles derived from Roman law.

[1] *Drouot* [1999] QB 497 ECJ, Advocate General paras 24–25, the Court para 16; *The Tatry* [1999] QB 515 ECJ, the Court para 30.

Index

Index

Index